Navigating Trust in Sustainability Reporting and Assurance

Saleh F.A. Khatib
Faculty of Business, Sohar University, Sohar, Oman

Alhamzah F. Abbas
Faculty of Management, Universiti Teknologi Malaysia, Johor Bahru, Malaysia

IGI Global
Scientific Publishing
Publishing Tomorrow's Research Today

Published in the United States of America by
IGI Global Scientific Publishing
701 East Chocolate Avenue
Hershey, PA, 17033, USA
Tel: 717-533-8845
Fax: 717-533-8661
Website: https://www.igi-global.com E-mail: cust@igi-global.com

Library of Congress Cataloging-in-Publication Data

Names: Khatib, Saleh, 1991- editor. | Abbas, Alhamzah, 1990- editor.
Title: Navigating trust in sustainability reporting and assurance / [edited by] Saleh Khatib, Alhamzah Abbas.
Description: Hershey, PA : IGI Global Scientific Publishing, [2025] | Includes bibliographical references and index. | Summary: "This multidisciplinary book provides a comprehensive exploration of sustainability assurance and its critical role in fostering transparency, accountability, and trust in corporate sustainability efforts"-- Provided by publisher.
Identifiers: LCCN 2024058297 (print) | LCCN 2024058298 (ebook) | ISBN 9798337301174 (hardcover) | ISBN 9798337301181 (paperback) | ISBN 9798337301198 (ebook)
Subjects: LCSH: Sustainable development reporting. | Trust.
Classification: LCC HD60.3 .T78 2025 (print) | LCC HD60.3 (ebook) | DDC 658.4/083--dc23/eng/20250206
LC record available at https://lccn.loc.gov/2024058297
LC ebook record available at https://lccn.loc.gov/2024058298

British Cataloguing in Publication Data
A Cataloguing in Publication record for this book is available from the British Library.

Editorial Advisory Board

Table of Contents

Detailed Table of Contents

This chapter explores the integration of mathematical education with Education for Sustainable Development (ESD) to enhance corporate employees' understanding and application of Environmental, Social, and Governance (ESG) metrics. It highlights how mathematical literacy and data literacy improve employees' ability to analyze ESG data, promoting decision-making transparency and report credibility. The study employs a theory-driven analytical framework supported by case studies from companies such as Shell, Walmart, and IKEA to demonstrate the practical impact of mathematics in ESG reporting. The chapter also examines the role of mathematical modeling, such as lifecycle assessments and carbon footprint calculations, in quantifying environmental impacts. By combining theoretical insights with real-world applications, it underscores the transformative potential of targeted mathematical education in advancing corporate sustainability practices.

This study seeks to explore the influence of perceived environmental corporate social responsibility on sustainable innovation within the hotel industry, with particular emphasis on the mediating role of green intrinsic motivation. A total of 396 responses collected from full-time employees at five-star hotels in Egypt were analyzed using Partial Least Squares Structural Equation Modeling (PLS-SEM) with WarpPLS statistical software version 7.0. The findings indicate that perceived environmental corporate social responsibility has a positive impact on both sustainable innovation and green intrinsic motivation. Furthermore, green intrinsic motivation not only

The study also identified key challenges, including the lack of sustainability reporting standards specific to Islamic finance and the need to strengthen the capacity of Islamic financial institution practitioners regarding sustainability assurance. The implications of this study include practical guidance for Islamic financial institutions in formulating effective and sharia-based sustainability policies.

Mega-events like the FIFA World Cup, Olympics, international expos, and marathons, although glorified for their cultural, social, and economic significance, present considerable environmental concerns. The surge of players and spectators, along with significant infrastructure development and operating requirements, frequently leads to resource exhaustion, waste production, and environmental stress. Acknowledging the need to ease these effects, organisers have progressively implemented sustainable procedures to diminish environmental deterioration. This study examines the execution of sustainable practices at large-scale events and assesses their efficacy in promoting environmental responsibility and establishing enduring legacies. This study emphasises that despite existing hurdles, the progress achieved in incorporating sustainability provides significant insights for future initiatives. Proactive planning, stakeholder engagement, and ongoing innovation are recognised as essential facilitators of success.

Preface

In an era where transparency and accountability have become the cornerstones of business success, sustainability assurance has emerged as a crucial mechanism for demonstrating a company's dedication to environmental and social responsibilities. The demand for reliable, credible sustainability reporting is growing rapidly, fueled by increasing pressure from consumers, investors, and regulatory bodies. Organizations are expected not only to disclose their sustainability initiatives but also to validate their claims through rigorous assurance processes.

Sustainability assurance is a process that verifies the accuracy and credibility of a company's environmental, social, and governance (ESG) reporting. By ensuring that corporate sustainability claims are reliable, this process fosters transparency and accountability, ultimately building trust with stakeholders. Typically conducted by third-party auditors, sustainability assurance evaluates whether a company's ESG practices align with established standards such as the Global Reporting Initiative (GRI) and the Sustainability Accounting Standards Board (SASB). Its primary goal is to promote ethical business practices and enable informed decision-making by stakeholders.

This book provides a comprehensive exploration of sustainability assurance, delving into its critical role in fostering transparency, accountability, and trust in corporate sustainability efforts. It bridges the gap between theoretical discussions and practical applications, offering a nuanced understanding of how assurance practices influence corporate transparency and contribute to ethical business operations. Our work enhances current research by examining the institutional determinants and outcomes of sustainability assurance, the regulatory frameworks that shape assurance practices, and the broader economic impacts of verified ESG reporting.

Additionally, this book introduces readers to the complex ecosystem of assurance providers and methodologies, providing insights into best practices and the challenges faced by professionals in the field. Through real-world case studies, expert interviews, and practical tools, it extends beyond existing literature to offer actionable guidance for academics and professionals alike. Furthermore, we explore emerging trends, including technological advancements in sustainability assurance, and anticipate the evolving expectations of stakeholders. This forward-looking perspective seeks to provide a roadmap for continuous improvement and innovation in sustainability practices.

Designed for a diverse audience, this book will benefit academics and practitioners in business, management, and finance—particularly those engaged with corporate sustainability, environmental governance, and responsible business practices. Business professionals, including corporate social responsibility officers, environmental consultants, and sustainability managers, will find valuable insights into how sustainability assurance can enhance transparency and accountability in corporate operations. Academics and students specializing in sustainable finance, environmental management, corporate governance, and business ethics will gain a deeper understanding of the theoretical frameworks and empirical applications of sustainability assurance. Policymakers and regulatory professionals will also find this book useful in understanding how assurance mechanisms can enhance corporate compliance and stakeholder trust.

Finally, this book will appeal to investors, stakeholders, and the general public who seek to assess the credibility of sustainability reports and understand how businesses align their operations with ESG principles. By taking an interdisciplinary approach—integrating perspectives from environmental science, corporate governance, and ethics—this book serves as a vital resource for those interested in advancing sustainability assurance in both academic and professional contexts.

We hope this book will contribute to meaningful discussions, inspire future research, and support the development of more robust and transparent sustainability assurance practices.

Chapter 1
Introduction to Sustainability Assurance

Alhamzah F. Abbas
https://orcid.org/0000-0002-7508-9340
Faculty of Management, Universiti Teknologi Malaysia, Johor Bahru, Malaysia

Saleh F.A. Khatib
https://orcid.org/0000-0001-7652-4191
Faculty of Business, Sohar University, Sohar, Oman

ABSTRACT

Sustainability assurance has emerged as a critical tool for enhancing trust and transparency in corporate sustainability reporting. This chapter delves into the processes, frameworks, and challenges of sustainability assurance, highlighting its role in validating environmental, social, and governance (ESG) claims. By examining standards such as ISAE 3000 and AA1000AS, the chapter highlights how assurance mechanisms enhance credibility and reduce risks, such as greenwashing. However, adoption remains inconsistent globally, reflecting differences in regulatory frameworks, stakeholder engagement, and provider independence. Finally, the chapter examines competition with non-accounting providers of assurance services. This creates a solid foundation for trustworthy ESG data, paving the path for sustainable business practices in an increasingly scrutinized world by aligning corporate accountability with stakeholder expectations. The analysis ends with insights that can improve the quality of assurance and help tackle barriers to its widespread adoption.

DOI: 10.4018/979-8-3373-0117-4.ch001

1. DEFINITION AND OVERVIEW OF SUSTAINABILITY ASSURANCE

Sustainability assurance is the process through which an independent team determines the credibility and reliability of an organization's sustainability reports, claims, or initiatives (Hazaea et al., 2022). This assurance process assesses the accuracy and completeness of information on an organization's sustainability performance (Environmental, social, and governance - ESG metrics). Sustainability assurance enhances the credibility of corporate sustainability reporting by providing independent assessment and is often a requirement from external stakeholders and regulators requiring increased transparency in corporate responsibility behaviors. Also known as sustainability assurance, the process through which an independent third party reviews and verifies a company's sustainability disclosures, to confirm that the information contained in the reports is accurate, trustworthy, and in line with established reporting standards. In principle, such a process is intended to enhance the credibility of sustainability reporting, thereby increasing stakeholders' trust in the organization's engagement with ESG matters (Manetti & Becatti, 2009).

The demand for sustainability assurance has become more pronounced in the past decade as companies have come under scrutiny from stakeholders like investors, customers, and regulators to provide information that is transparent and verifiable. Sustainability assurance usually covers an evaluation of both qualitative and quantitative data provided in a company's sustainability report. International Standard on Assurance Engagements (ISAE) 3000 and Account Ability's AA1000 Assurance Standard are among the commonly used assurance standards nowadays, outlining a robust process for achieving comprehensive and reliable assurance (O'Dwyer & Owen, 2005).

The level of assurance that can be provided varies from limited to reasonable assurance. Limited assurance, often applied to sustainability reporting, involves a lower level of scrutiny and focuses on specific metrics or sections of the report, whereas reasonable assurance provides a more in-depth and comprehensive review, similar to a financial audit (Simnett et al., 2009). Sustainability assurance brings credibility and nationalization to corporate sustainability practices. It also mitigates greenwashing risks, as it subjects sustainability claims to external scrutiny. This provides a level of assurance for stakeholders so that informed decisions can be made regarding a company's actual environmental and social performance (Zadek, et al., 2004).

Sustainability assurance activities can be dated to the 1930s, though they have received significant focus in the last four decades (Fuhrmann et al., 2017; Jia et al., 2020; Maroun, 2020). Growing awareness of the destructive effects of global economic growth, climate change, and wealth inequality has prompted a more critical look at the role of the firm in social advancement. In response, large corporations increasingly pursue (Jia et al., 2020; Maroun, 2020) and report on sustainability initiatives. CSR reports are used by corporations to communicate their efforts with sustainability. Demand for sustainability assurance is growing rapidly, yet high-quality assurance remains a significant challenge for both providers and the firms reporting. The lack of sufficient framework is one of the most significant barriers that undermine not only the credibility and reliability of assurance but also the functioning of sustainability reports (Traxler et al., 2020). Infrastructure/assets fail to integrate missing components with information systems or fail to balance cost/benefit, weak legal channels, weak enforcement mechanisms in place, and lack of standardization in scientific guidelines/social norms. In contrast, while clear rules and regulations govern financial assurance, there is a higher complexity resulting in contentiousness in the production of assurance statements that are both reliable and high-quality for sustainability reports (Boiral et al., 2019; Cho et al., 2014).

Moreover, most firms do not know enough about which assurance services to choose. In many parts of the world, sustainability assurance is still mostly voluntary, with a competitive market allowing several assurance providers (Farooq & De Villiers, 2019). These providers are commonly characterized as accounting firms and non-accounting firms such as consultancies (Edgley et al., 2015; Farooq & De Villiers, 2019). Consultancies turn to environmentalists, biologists, and ethicists for specialized knowledge on sustainability (Edgley et al., 2015; Farooq & De Villiers, 2019; Yan et al., 2022), whereas accounting firms (i.e., the very Big Four) tout their specialized expertise in assurance. This divergence has fueled a continuing debate over the ability of each type of provider to provide assurance services and how this should be defined. Additionally, the assurance process itself can become complicated with the quality and credibility of the assurance statements being allocated to the matters of client pressure (managerial capture) and revenue-generating objectives of the assurance practitioners (professional capture) (Farooq & De Villiers, 2019).

Sustainability assurance is the independent examination of sustainability processes and reports at the level of an enterprise to improve credibility and reliability and the decision-making usefulness of information for stakeholders (Harindahyani & Agustia, 2023). The assurance process is usually divided into five steps: selection, identification, screening and validation, and evaluation, as described in Yan et al. (2022). Popular assurance standards include ISAE 3000, AA1000, and SA8000 (Odintsova, 2024). Assurance levels can be categorized as reasonable, limited, hybrid, or not specified (Harindahyani & Agustia, 2023). Despite its importance, adoption of sustainability assurance remains limited (Marx & Dyk, 2011). Challenges include the absence of stakeholder engagement and concerns about assurance provider independence (Yan et al., 2022). As sustainability reporting evolves, there is a growing trend towards integrated reporting, combining financial and sustainability information, with recommendations for independent assurance of such reports (Marx & Dyk, 2011).

However, the field faces challenges such as managerial and professional capture, particularly in settings with weak regulatory frameworks (Lemma et al., 2024). Institutional investors, regardless of their investment horizon, play a significant role in promoting sustainability assurance adoption, which can improve analyst precision and reduce capital costs (García-Sánchez et al., 2022). The practice is embedded within the established auditing field and encompasses various elements, including a tripartite arrangement, subject matter, suitable criteria, evidence, and a written report (Farooq et al., 2023). Many organizations are undertaking sustainability assurance, but it is hindered by a lack of sustainability-related stakeholder involvement and independence of assurance providers (Yan et al., 2022; Farooq et al., 2023)—making it a critical area to standardize and create better regulatory frameworks. Sustainability assurance response helps organizations leverage credibility with their stakeholders, understand their risks better, and improve internal processes related to sustainability. For example, stakeholders have become more insistent on the verification of non-financial data because of its impact on long-term value and the company's reputation. Furthermore, sustainability assurance is valuable for identifying areas for performance improvement and fostering a culture of transparency and accountability within organizations (O'Dwyer, Owen, & Unerman, 2011).

2. IMPORTANCE OF SUSTAINABILITY IN BUSINESS AND SOCIETY

Corporate Social Responsibility (CSR) extends beyond being merely a cost, constraint, or charitable action. It serves as "a source of opportunity, innovation, and competitive advantage" (Porter & Kramer, 2006). However, its effective execution can be shaped by various factors, such as the company's size, level of diversification, investment in research and development, and prevailing market conditions (McWilliams & Siegel, 2001). Academic research frequently aims to track and reflect societal discussions regarding the social responsibilities of businesses. CSR often encompasses three main domains: commercial responsibility, ethical responsibility, and social responsibility (Singh & Del Bosque, 2008). Commercial responsibility involves a company's commitment to delivering high-quality products or services and being honest and fair in its marketing practices while promoting these offerings to customers (Singh & Del Bosque, 2008). Ethical responsibility pertains to fulfilling obligations toward stakeholders such as shareholders, suppliers, and distributors. It includes protecting human rights and upholding norms that may not necessarily be codified in law. For some socially responsible corporations, ethical principles in business dealings may take precedence overachieving superior economic performance (Singh & Del Bosque, 2008). The third domain, social responsibility, emphasizes philanthropic actions. This can include allocating resources to environmental protection or addressing social challenges that benefit society's most vulnerable groups. Social responsibility often promotes stewardship principles, such as corporate donations to charities or support for religious, cultural, sports, and heritage activities, all aimed at enhancing societal well-being (Camilleri, 2017).

The concept of "sustainable development" has been defined in various ways, but the most widely recognized definition originates from the 1987 Brundtland Report, also known as Our Common Future. This report made a pivotal connection between human progress and environmental responsibility, emphasizing the importance of preserving resources for future generations (Camilleri, 2014). While the sustainable development agenda initially required substantial empirical research three decades ago, the current focus has shifted towards actionable policies and tangible measures. Governments and businesses are increasingly adopting a proactive approach to addressing social and environmental challenges. Porter and Kramer (2011) suggested that governments could establish performance standards for large corporations while allowing businesses to determine how best to achieve these objectives.

Today, there is a growing consensus around core principles and regulatory frameworks. Key standards include the Global Reporting Initiative's Sustainability Reporting Guidelines, the UN Global Compact, the Sustainable Development Goals, the World Resources Institute's Greenhouse Gas Protocol, and the UN Principles for Responsible Investment. The shift toward sustainable and responsible business practices represents a gradual yet critical process, requiring momentum to influence public opinion, policymaking, and corporate behavior. Notably, many of the world's largest corporations are actively refining their codes of conduct, implementing certifiable standards, and engaging in sustainability initiatives. These efforts are reflected in their corporate programs, industry-wide collaborations, green policies, triple-bottom-line reporting, and educational materials, such as documentaries focused on sustainability (Camilleri, 2017).

Nevertheless, many of the global challenges are still present today — be they climate change, water depletion, biodiversity loss, bribery and corruption or income inequality, among others. The importance of sustainability in business and society has become undeniable, especially as companies increasingly recognize their role in addressing global challenges like climate change, resource depletion, and social inequities. Sustainable practices benefit both companies and society by reducing negative environmental impacts, enhancing social equity, and creating long-term value. Sustainability has become increasingly important in business and society, encompassing environmental, social, and economic aspects (Sahin & Çankaya, 2019). Companies are adopting sustainability as a business strategy, with over

50% of U.S. Business Roundtable members embracing it (Hill & Seabrook, 2013). Sustainability reporting was developed such that it has gathered from voluntary social and environmental reports to sustainability reports containing non-financial information (Sahin & Çankaya, 2019). This evolution indicates that companies are being increasingly acknowledged as part of society, not just their economy (Bansal, 2023). Corporate sustainability encompasses economic, environmental, social, and managerial issues, with sustainability reports tracking their developments (Sahin & Çankaya, 2019). Business, as an important social institution, influences society either positively or negatively depending on their decision and actions, hence sustainability has become a critical consideration for long-term strategy for any business (Bansal, 2023).

Recent research shows just how important sustainability is becoming to both business and society. According to the study, micro and small enterprises in Slovakia acknowledge the need to start dealing with sustainability, with minimization of waste presented as the priority (Demjanovičová & Varmus, 2021). Family businesses are a large number of all firms in Western societies, and they increasingly tread the path of sustainability via a different type of governance structure and behaviors (Clauss et al., 2022). The relationship between Corporate Social Responsibility (CSR) and sustainability is a topic of interest, with the United States contributing the most to the publications (Meseguer-Sánchez et al., 2021). The persistence of sustainable practices in family firms is affected by religious, reputational, and chief executive officer-related variables, while eco-innovation is an important strategic choice for responding to the demands of the markets (Curado & Mota, 2021). Together, these studies highlight the fundamental importance of sustainability as a guiding principle for business models, social foundations, and societal norms in different sectors and types of organizations.

3. CONTEXT AND IMPORTANCE OF SUSTAINABILITY ASSURANCE

Sustainability assurance has emerged as a global practice to enhance accountability in sustainability reporting (Junior et al., 2014). While sustainability reporting has increased, Sustainability assurance adoption has stagnated (Junior et al., 2014). Sustainability assurance is entirely voluntary and thus, engagement scope and goals vary (Farooq & Villiers, 2017). Assurance providers may rely on ISAE3000 for accountants, and AA1000AS for non-accountants (Farooq & Villiers, 2017). More than 60% of reports worldwide are assured by non-Big 4 firms (Mock et al., 2007). Country and industry-specific practices show that the European Union is more prepared in terms of assured reports (Mock et al., 2007). In South Africa, despite recommendations for integrated reporting and independent assurance, only a limited number of companies obtain SA (Marx & Dyk, 2011). The market for SA services is influenced by various drivers and inhibitors at both macro and micro levels (Farooq & Villiers, 2017), highlighting the need for further research to understand and improve SA practices worldwide.

Research indicates that firm size, ESG performance, and industry affiliation drive the demand for SRA (Vander Bauwhede & Van Cauwenberge, 2022). Mandatory SRA has been found to positively impact firm value by strengthening legitimacy and reducing information asymmetry (Jeriji & Nasfi, 2022). However, the communication of assurance topics requires careful consideration, as overly explicit references may negatively affect credibility perceptions (Baier et al., 2021). Institutional investors, regardless of their investment horizon, play a crucial role in promoting SRA adoption, which can improve analyst precision and reduce capital costs (García-Sánchez et al., 2021). While SRA generally enhances the reliability of sustainability information for stakeholders, there is a need for standardized assurance processes to optimize its benefits for the capital market and sustainable development goals (García-Sánchez et al., 2021).

4. THE ROLE OF TRUST IN SUSTAINABILITY ASSURANCE

Trust is paramount in sustainability assurance and reporting. External assurance mechanisms are emerging as important tools to restore trust and legitimacy in the sustainability disclosures of companies (Pizzi et al., 2024). The quality of sustainability assurance can be measured by the depth of the assurance process and the breadth of the assurance statement, with sustainability performance and assurance provider type influencing these aspects (Hummel et al., 2019). The sustainability domain has extended authority from standard-setting organizations to certifying and accrediting parties leading not only to greater complexity of private regulatory systems but also to a rethinking of the meaning of independence (Loconto, 2017). Trust is a foundation for social sustainability as it can take on many meanings depending on the lens from security to customer relationship management and can be seen as an interaction phenomenon (Zieni et al., 2017). These findings emphasize the need for trust and assurance to improve the credibility and effectiveness of sustainability statements and governance.

5. REGULATORY FRAMEWORKS AND STANDARDS FOR ASSURANCE

Over the last few years, the boom of the regulatory frameworks, and the customer's demand (transparency, risk management, accountability) made the standards and procedures for assurance evolve and it is obvious that they do so rapidly. Corporate scandals, technological shifts, as well as changes in regulatory requirements for financial as well as non-financial reporting have led to this evolution. Below is a summary of literature to date, and of relevant standards and frameworks in this domain.

As sustainability assurance practices have evolved alongside developments in laws and regulations, different standards have appeared. The most commonly cited normative frameworks in this field are the Global Reporting Initiative (GRI), Assurance Standard AA1000AS, and ISAE3000 (International Standard on Assurance Engagement) (Gillet-Monjarret, 2018). In France, the regulatory framework for SA is defined by the Grenelle 2 law (Law No. 2010-788) of July 12, 2010, which positioned France as a leader in societal transparency. Under this law, independent third-party assurance became mandatory for companies listed on regulated markets starting from the financial year ending December 31, 2011, and for certain unlisted companies (with more than 500 employees and a net turnover exceeding €100 million) from December 31, 2016 (Decree No. 2012-557 of April 24, 2012).

This independent third-party organization (ITO) must be authorized by COFRAC, the French accreditation body. COFRAC-accredited providers issue both a certificate of attendance, verifying the inclusion of the 42 indicators outlined in Article 225 of the Grenelle 2 Law (as detailed in Article R.225-105-1 of the Commercial Code), and a reasoned opinion on the reliability of the disclosed information. The attendance certificate ensures the presence of mandatory indicators, while the reasoned opinion assesses the accuracy and sincerity of the information, which may include qualifications or reservations as necessary. Additionally, the provider's report must detail the procedures undertaken to complete the assurance process.

For professional accountants performing SA missions, the National Company of Statutory Auditors (CNCC) introduced a professional practice standard, NEP 9090, on December 27, 2013. This standard defines the assurance provider's responsibilities and distinguishes between two types of engagements: reasonable assurance (providing high but not absolute certainty) and limited assurance (providing moderate or lower certainty). The CNCC also developed a "technical opinion" to provide independent ITOs with tools for effectively implementing sustainability assurance in line with the international standard ISAE 3000.

In 2014, the European Parliament and Council adopted Directive 2014/95/EU (October 22, 2014), which mandates the disclosure of non-financial information. Member States were required to incorporate this directive into their national laws by 2017. France implemented this directive through Ordinance No. 2017-1180 (July 19, 2017) and Decree No. 2017-1265 (August 9, 2017). Starting from financial years beginning on or after September 1, 2017, companies falling under this directive must include a "declaration of non-financial performance" in their management reports.

Unlike previous requirements, this declaration is not a standardized list of CSR information applicable to all companies. Instead, it must provide a tailored presentation of the company's business model, significant risks related to major non-financial issues, policies and procedures addressing those risks, their outcomes, and relevant key performance indicators. The directive applies to large companies with over 500 employees and either a net turnover exceeding €100 million or a total balance sheet surpassing this threshold for unlisted companies. Organizations may choose international, European, or national frameworks, such as the GRI guidelines or the ISO 26000 standard, to guide their reporting.

The directive also stipulates that statutory auditors ensure the required information is disclosed in the management report. Member States can mandate an independent assurance service provider to verify this information. In France, statutory auditors or the Board of Providers must confirm that the non-financial performance declaration, as required by Article L.225-102.1, is included in the report (Article L.823-10 of the French Commercial Code). However, statutory auditors are not responsible for verifying the accuracy or compliance of the disclosed information. Instead, an independent third-party organization (ITO) must be appointed to review entities meeting the above thresholds. The ITO is tasked with producing a report containing a reasoned opinion on the declaration's compliance and the fairness of the information, based on Article R.225-105. The report must also detail the ITO's due diligence procedures. The introduction of sustainability assurance regulations has imposed regulatory pressure on companies (Islam & Dellaportas, 2011; Gillet-Monjarret, 2018; Gillet-Monjarret, 2022) and established standards for ITO involvement. This raises questions about how such regulations have influenced the practice of sustainability assurance.

5.1 Overview of Regulatory Frameworks for Assurance

The development of assurance standards has played a crucial role in shaping the sustainability assurance process and improving its quality (Simnett, 2012). While differences exist among these standards, their integration is often seen as an effective approach to conducting external assurance of sustainability information (Thostrup Jagd, 2014). Standards such as GRI, ISO 26000, AA1000AS, and ISAE3000 are complementary rather than competitive. Their combination allows for leveraging the strengths of each to enhance the oversight and reliability of assurance reports, as there is no fundamental methodological conflict between them (Gillet-Monjarret, 2022).

The expectations of users of societal information are diverse, reflecting varying perspectives on CSR. Combining standards can address these varied demands and better align with user needs (Thostrup Jagd, 2014). However, as Martinez-Ferrero and García-Sánchez (2016) note, the choice of standards often depends on the type of provider conducting the assurance. For instance, accounting firms tend to use ISAE 3000, while lay consultants are more likely to adopt AA1000AS. Although frameworks like GRI and ISO 26000 assist companies and assurance providers, including accounting firms and specialist consultants, in implementing sustainability assurance, they lack guidance on execution details and methods for measuring the quality of results (Sethi et al., 2017). Furthermore, Hickman and Cote (2019) highlight the potential for "managerial capture," where managerial influence may distort the assurance process. This issue is exacerbated by the absence of unified reporting standards and a clear consensus on the overarching objectives of CSR reports and their assurance.

This has influenced the uptake of sustainability assurance practices which is an isomorphic process (Boiral & Gendron, 2011). There are several standards—ISAE 3000, AA1000, and their combination which present a framed approach to sustainability assurance and contribute to institutionalizing new practice (Iansen-Rogers & Oelschlaegel, 2005). As highlighted by Perego and Kolk (2012), these pressures are particularly strong in the initial period of adoption and largely driven by the powerful role of professional accounting and auditing organizations.

The recent passing of laws including Grenelle 2 has been accompanied by more visible changes like assurance reports, which demonstrate the coercive capacity of regulatory pressures in steering companies towards adopting more sustainability assurance practices. The law cannot determine the exact content of a report, rather it represents a move towards greater standardization in sustainability assurance, which will diminish fears regarding the inconsistency of report content and improve comparisons and legitimacy (Gillet-Monjarret & Riviere-Giordano, 2017). They inform that through assurance it is also possible to influence stakeholders' expectations which contributes to enhancing perceptions of sustainability reports legitimacy (Maroun, 2019). These findings suggest that abilities such as reliability, completeness, and clarity qualities are increasingly being considered by sustainability assurance reports over time, as they were not as prevalent in the initial years of sustainability assurance reporting. To improve the reliability of sustainability information and to provide trust, clarity, and accuracy of sustainability information has been developed assurance (GilletMonjarret 2022). In terms of value-adding, assurance adds value to the reported information and hence makes it more useful for the stakeholders (Maroun, 2019).

Regulatory frameworks for assurance are designed to establish guidelines and enforce compliance within industries, especially in finance, healthcare, environmental management, and IT. Several international organizations, including the International Organization for Standardization (ISO) itself and the International Federation of Accountants (IFAC), develop and govern various Enterprise Assurance frameworks to maintain global standards in assurance practices. There is a growing recognition in the recent literature that sound regulatory frameworks must allow for flexibility to suit industry-specific needs and emerging risks like cybersecurity risk and environmental damage (IFAC, 2023). In particular, the US, UK, and EU member countries have taken steps to ensure that their standards converge with international frameworks, such as the ISAs issued by the IESBA, so that there is a relatively uniform approach across borders (Vanstraelen, 2022).

5.2 Key Standards for Assurance

Although many entities are providing information about sustainability performance and risks, and some of them are ranking the performance, sustainability rating agencies (SRA) have become the major actors in this field (Bessire & Onnée, 2010; Chelli & Gendron, 2013; Escrig-Olmedo et al., 2019; Kotsantonis et al., 2016). SRAs have flourished alongside the exponential growth of sustainable and responsible investments (SRIs), a sector that included USD 12 trillion in assets within the United States in 2018—more than one-quarter of all managed assets in the country (Connaker & Madsbjerg, 2019; The Forum for Sustainable and Responsible Investment, 2018). SRIs rely fundamentally on the availability of reliable and comparable information regarding ESG performance and corporate sustainability risks (Diouf & Boiral, 2017; Escrig-Olmedo et al., 2019).

Although sustainability reports aim to address the growing demand for such information, their content is often inconsistent, poorly standardized, and difficult to compare across companies (Boiral & Henri, 2017). Furthermore, the reliability of sustainability disclosures has been widely criticized in academic literature. Studies frequently highlight issues such as a lack of transparency, the concealment of information that might harm a company's reputation, tendencies toward greenwashing, and the use of sustainability reports primarily as public relations tools (e.g., Haller, Van Staden, & Landis, 2018; Marquis et al., 2016).

Although external assurance of sustainability reports is expected to improve the credibility of information, whether it has such an effect remains a controversial issue (Boiral, Heras-Saizarbitoria, & Brotherton, 2019; Bollas-Araya & Polo-Garrido, 2018). It is not easy to interpret corporate sustainability information because of its complexity, diversity, and non-transparency. This increasingly includes specialized organizations that make use of and comparison of companies' sustainability performance possible. Sustainability rating agencies (SRAs), by offering rankings on corporate sustainability, act as intermediaries between companies that disseminate this information and stakeholders, particularly sustainable and responsible investment (SRI) practitioners, who rely on it (Rahdari & Rostamy, 2015).

The growing influence of sustainability issues on corporate reputation and market value has prompted SRAs to develop various products to address investor needs and risk aversion. These include ESG risk assessments, alert services, controversy monitoring, tracking non-compliance with international human rights standards, and monitoring violations of fundamental ethical principles. Some SRAs, such as RepRisk, have specialized in ESG risk analysis and prevention, positioning themselves as leaders in global business intelligence for due diligence on ESG and responsible business conduct risks (RepRisk, 2019). Others have expanded their offerings through acquisitions; for example, MSCI acquired RiskMetrics in 2010 to enhance its decision-making tools. As MSCI Chairman and CEO Henry Fernandez stated, this merger aimed to leverage complementary product capabilities, broaden the client base, and realize synergies in costs and revenue (MSCI, 2010).

Despite the variety of SRAs and their services, sustainability risk analyses generally focus on evaluating ESG risks linked to companies, industries, or regions (LeBlanc & Kislevitz, 2016). These assessments typically follow two main approaches (Dawkins, 2018; Mercer, 2019): negative screening, which excludes unethical or harmful companies or activities and creates "blacklists," and positive screening, which ranks "best-in-class" organizations based on their ESG scores. Although SRAs address critical needs in assessing and managing sustainability risks, their activities have drawn criticism in the literature (Capelle-Blancard & Petit, 2017; Doyle, 2018). Studies have frequently pointed out the opacity and ambiguity of their evaluation methods (SustainAbility, 2018).

Competitive dynamics and unwillingness to disclose methodologies that lead to the lack of transparency of SRAs are often cited as reasons for SRAs' lack of transparency. But that raises alarming questions about the trustworthiness of the rankings they produce. Several studies have raised the reliability of such (L-Rank) rankings (e.g., Chatterji, Durand, Levine, & Touboul, 2016; Mooij, 2017), highlighting that, while being based on the same data, results in terms of SRA ranks differ strongly between different L-Rank configurations. The traditional rankings are criticized for their superficial rationality, as they poorly account for the complexity of sustainability issues (Boiral & Henri, 2017; Capelle-Blancard & Petit, 2017). These criticisms reflect wider concerns regarding the blurring of definitions around sustainability and the difficulty of robust performance measurement in this area (Escrig-Olmedo, Muñoz-Torres, et al., 2017; Rajak & Vinodh, 2015).

The notion of rational myths has been used to study different situations, such as misalignment between hierarchy and practices, accounting as a symbol, and the dichotomy between the supposed robustness of standards (for example, ISO) and their real use by employees (Boiral, 2007, 2012). These myths reveal the gap between the organization's quest for legitimacy (by suggesting that they are embracing rational systems and methods)—and the typically symbolic or ceremonial internal practices that only mechanically conform to institutional pressures (Boiral et al., 2020). For SRAs, it is crucial to project sustainability risk ratings as rational, reliable, and measurable – any threat to this ideal will undermine their legitimacy and imperialism. If this relative rationality is challenged, it could bring into question the – already frail (Dawkins, 2018) – the credibility of the SRAs undermining the standing of sustainable and responsible investments (SRI) that depend on them and amount to considerable financial assets.

The study of the sociology of quantification and the power of numbers highlights the increasing dependence on quantitative data to describe multifaceted, complex, hard-to-count phenomena (Kennedy & Hill, 2018). Quantitative data can be greatly trusted, and such data also lends legitimacy to the actions taken by public and private organizations, conjuring an illusion of control and objectivity that can be misleading. Kennedy and Hill (2018, p. 830) note that "regimes of datafication…change ideas of objectivity, value and dispassionate rational analysis" meaning that "where numbers, metrics, and statistics dominate, renewed belief in objectivity/rationality can be witnessed." SRAs, by quantifying sustainability risks, thereby embody and enable this process of objectification and rationalization about sensitive social issues that raise many institutional demands and pressures for control.

But whether and how this rationality is truly internalized within the internal workings of the SRAs remains to be explored. So far, the internal workings of SRAs have been the understudied component (Boiral et al., 2020), and no research has yet examined what practitioners conducting sustainability risk ratings believe about the rationality and consistency of their rating process. It will be important through field studies that involve these practitioners to understand better how these practices fit the rationality representations that SRAs offer.

International Standards on Assurance Engagements ISAE 3000 — ISAE 3000 from IFAC is an international standard for non-audit engagements. It issues guidance on assurance of non-financial information, e.g. sustainability reports and corporate social responsibility (CSR) indicators. This standard is becoming more and more common among organizations that report on environmental, social, and governance (ESG) factors in enhancing the robustness and reliability of the disclosed information (O'Dwyer & Unerman, 2023). ISO 27001 and ISO 27005 for Information Security: As cyber security becomes increasingly important; ISO 27001 and ISO 27005 have also become significant standards for information security management and risk assessment. Context and significance These standards outline a systematic approach for organizations to control sensitive information, protect data privacy, and protect against cyber risks, which are vital for trust in digital assurance practice (Ahmad & Solms, 2023). In the financial services sector, IFRS 17 is an important milestone towards consistency in the measurement and presentation of insurance contracts. IFRS 17 effective 2023 is expected to provide better transparency - a true picture of financial performance as well as the risk being exposed to all stakeholders in the insurance and banking sectors. Meanwhile, this standard is the most critical one to improve the comparability of insurers worldwide (Zeff & Nobes, 2023).

5.3 Challenges and Criticisms in Sustainability Assurance

The assurance standards are evolving rapidly, but there are critical challenges that emerge when standards are not adaptable to different organizations. The use of blockchain for audit trails and artificial intelligence for data analytics is changing the nature of interoperability between the digital and physical worlds, needing frequent updates to traditional counters. The researchers argued that standards should strike a balance between being rigorous and adaptable which provides tones for auditors and assurance professionals to comply but rely heavily on professional judgment in challenging circumstances (Teoh & Francis, 2023). In addition, without a common standard, the assurance practices performed can differ by jurisdiction, with Canada allowing for significant variation. Although international standards aim to harmonize these practices, local laws and culture often come into play in the transposing of the frameworks on the ground, this contributes to differences in the quality and scope of the assurance (Knechel & Salterio, 2022).

Due to the complex and fragmented nature of non-financial reporting and its challenges, the development of sustainability assurance is hindered (Sonnerfeldt & Pontoppidan, 2020). For example, there are no established standards for reporting or verification, leading to the need for criteria to assess the sustainability claims (Wallage, 2000). Although the primary goal of sustainability audits is to improve the credibility and reliability of sustainability reports, it is subject to criticism and have contextual challenges (Hazaea et al., 2022). The assurance process can be viewed as a five-step process, consisting of provider selection, identification, screening, validation, and evaluation (Yan et al., 2022). However, barriers including lack of stakeholder engagement and independence of assurance providers are obstacles to the adoption and realization of sustainability assurance (Yan et al., 2022). However, the road ahead is not without its difficulties, and sustainability assurance is still a tool needed to support the actions of non-financial reporting in favor of sustainability in businesses (Sonnerfeldt & Pontoppidan, 2020).

6. KEY PLAYERS AND PROVIDERS OF ASSURANCE SERVICES

This lack of regulation allows public accounting firms, referred to as accounting assurance providers (AAPs), to share the market with a diverse group of non-accounting sustainability assurance providers (NAAPs), such as environmental and management consultancies and non-governmental organizations (Perego & Kolk, 2012). Overall, the number of companies providing some assurance of their sustainability reports has steadily increased since 2005 (KPMG, 2005–2017). As these surveys suggest, leading global audit firms have been the most popular choice for services related to sustainability assurance engagements, with their involvement rising from 58% in 2005 to 64% subsequently (KPMG, 2015), further entrenching their status as a leading brand. However, NAAPs are still major players with their own established brands in the sustainability assurance market (Verdantix, 2013).

Developments in financial statement auditing and criticisms in that field motivate the need to better understand the new activities, such as sustainability assurance, that are arising in the assurance landscape. This appears increasingly relevant in light of the growing importance of non-financial disclosures about corporate accountability and the development of integrated reporting (Humphrey, O'Dwyer, & Unerman, 2017). However, previous studies have mainly been based on the analysis of sustainability assurance reports, providing a shallow understanding of the practice (and variations among providers) (Low & Boo, 2012). One reason for the very limited research differentiating between sustainability assurance providers is that research has often focused on sustainability assurance provider characteristics (e.g., brand or industry specialization (Martínez-Ferrero & García-Sanchez, 2018). Adopting Abbott's (2014) framework on systems of professions, the study treats the differentiation of providers as a jurisdictional contest in which expert knowledge and assurance activities become affiliated with providers' occupational types and client groups. Based on in-depth interviews with sustainability assurance practitioners of AAP and NAAP firms in the UK, the analysis offers insights into practitioners' use of standards, differentiation strategies, and approaches to sustainability assurance engagements.

Differences are stark in what standards and guidelines are employed, how materiality is determined and stakeholders defined, the scope of assurance engagement, the composition of the team, and what depth of expertise is enabled. Furthermore, the study shows that, divided by the category of provider, they are not homogenous (Channuntapipat et al., 2020). These results contribute more detailed insights on jurisdictional relations between provider types to existing research on the wide variation with sustainability assurance (e.g., Channuntapipat, Samsonova–Taddei & Turley, 2019). Third, it responds to earlier proposals about internal conflict among sustainability assurance practices, revealing how conflict was mollified through even greater recourse to technical artifacts, such as internal standards and methodologies.

Previous studies show that there is a difference between users of sustainability reports regarding the perceived value of and quality of sustainability assurance (Perego & Kolk, 2012; Pflugrath et al., 2011). Such discrepancies may arise, in part, from the distinctions between the types of providers- accounting assurance providers (AAP) and non-accounting assurance providers (NAAP). This perception of independence enhances the perceived assurance quality of AAPs. Unlike NP, NAAPs are appreciated for the actionable recommendations and insights derived from the assurance process (Perego & Kolk, 2012). These differences could emerge at least in part due to differences between types of providers accounting assurance providers (AAPs) vs. non-accounting assurance providers (NAAPs). The independent nature of AAPs further contributes to a higher quality of assurance perception. The assurance process yields actionable recommendations and insights which creates value for NAAPs (Perego & Kolk, 2012).

Research also indicates that AAPs prioritize rigorous data verification and the defensibility of their assurance opinions (O'Dwyer et al., 2011), whereas NAAPs focus on providing feedback to improve client practices and fostering stakeholder engagement in the reporting process (Manetti & Toccafondi, 2012). Despite these insights, most empirical evidence on SA practices has come from content analysis of assurance statements, with limited studies like O'Dwyer (2011) exploring practitioner perspectives, primarily within Big4 accounting firms. The professional and commercial logics influencing the development and execution of SA services (Carter & Spence, 2014). It explores how competition among professional groups drives differentiation strategies based on distinct knowledge, expertise, and interpretations of the assurance process and its outputs. Using a conceptual framework grounded in Abbott's work on professions, the study investigates SA as a jurisdictional contest, where providers compete for market niches, thus contributing to the diversity of practices. The next section outlines the theoretical foundation of this analysis.

The market for sustainability assurance services is evolving, with various providers competing for this emerging opportunity (Wong et al., 2016). Key players include accounting firms, particularly the Big 4, and non-accounting consultants specializing in sustainability or general advisory services (Farooq & Villiers, 2017; Wong et al., 2016). Firm characteristics are related to the choice of assurance provider (Wong et al., 2016) including size, profitability, and liquidity. The presence of international standards or the professional background of the provider does not affect the assurance process and quality significantly (Vaz Ogando et al., 2018). On the other hand, the availability of non-financial information assurance is determined by the board committees and financial auditors (García-Sánchez et al., 2021). The range of engagement scopes and objectives in the market is underpinned by macro and micro-level motivators (Farooq & Villiers; 2017). While the nature of sustainability information and the regulatory context poses challenges, this area also opens new opportunities for the accounting profession (Wong et al., 2016; Vaz Ogando et al., 2018).

7. GLOBAL TRENDS AND FUTURE OF SUSTAINABILITY ASSURANCE

Sustainability assurance is a novel topic, and the number of studies has increased sharply during the last few years. China has been the most studied market from a geographic standpoint, in particular, the role and importance of sustainability assurance in institutions. However, studies across other markets are still scarce. More research is needed in both developed and developing countries which have been less well represented in the literature. Guidara et al. (2021) highlighted the need for research in emerging economies characterized by more severe auditing problems. Studies within you and Arab countries, where research is scarce, could provide further perspective. Finally, contrasting analytical studies on the overlooked Chinese and American contexts would enhance the literature.

Further examination could be done on environmental and carbon assurance, especially in economically advanced countries. Comparative analysis of different legal jurisdictions may better explain the impact of specific institutional and legal environments within which sustainability assurance operates (Al-Shaer & Zaman, 2018). The above-mentioned study is the only one ever to investigate auditing's role in promoting sustainability in the private sector, presenting an evident gap for further studies. Research may also investigate the potential for auditing to contribute toward the promotion of sustainability in non-profit organizations or waqf institutions (Sulaiman & Alhaji Zakari, 2019). Thus far, the numbers of empirical studies that employed questionnaires and interviews are limited, demonstrating the need for some research using those methodologies (Ghani et al., 2018; Roopa & Rani, 2012) Surveys, only as one example, would give good data on the social, cultural, economic and philosophical aspects of sustainability assurance. Interviews were conducted by Al-Shaer and Zaman (2018) to gain an understanding of the role of auditing in organizations. Future research can make a stronger contribution to this literature by addressing methodological threats, and in particular endogeneity problems.

Theoretical frameworks could also expand understanding of the relationship between auditing and sustainability, demonstrating the critical role of sustainability audits for stakeholders. Future studies might explore this relationship using robust theoretical approaches. The implication of environmental transformations during the COVID-19 crisis is yet another promising avenue of exploration, especially related to the role of sustainability assurance in times of crisis. The review also pointed out a dearth of research on the interaction of internal and external auditing in fostering sustainability. Future studies may examine their interactive roles and the attributes of audit committee members in terms of gender preferences and how they impact sustainability practices (Wang et al., 2020). Moreover, the demand for assurance and the risk faced by auditors about litigation have spurred in the wake of the COVID-19 pandemic, indicating spillover effects on auditor work, fees, and quality of assurance. It would be useful to explore how these phenomena play out in a post-pandemic world.

Theoretical lenses may even widen the framing of the audit-sustainability relationship and reiterate the necessary nature of sustainability auditing to the interest-holders. Future studies could also attempt to test this relationship with established theories. Suggesting a new avenue for more future research, one possible area for investigation is to study the changes in environmental considerations and the new role of sustainability assurance that follows the post-COVID-19 era. Future studies can also examine interactive acts as members of a group audit committee, with members' characteristics and gender preferences simultaneously influencing sustainability practices (Wang et al., 2020).

Since the need to monitor sustainability activities has increased significantly, assurance activities could become an important tool that requires the development of standards that meet all stakeholder needs. Researchers might also delve deeper into this space through conversations with regulators, audit institutions, and stakeholders. Exploring contextual and processual aspects can help studies to disaggregate determinants like auditor tenure, auditor qualifications, market competition, audit rotation, and their effects on sustainability activities and disclosures (Ruiz-Barbadillo & Martínez-Ferrero, 2020; Tahinakis & Samarinas, 2017). Finally, the existing works overlook the impacts of experienced environmental crises like COVID-19 on sustainability assurance systems and how well they can adapt to new economic behavior (Castka et al., 2020; Johnsson et al., 2020; Khatib & Nour, 2021). This line of inquiry could shed light on the adaptation of assurance practices in shifting global circumstances.

The sustainability trends highlight that the adoption of sustainability reporting in the world is proceeding in a catching-up or even booming manner whereas assurance catches up neglected (Alsahali & Malagueño, 2021; Junior et al., 2013) The practice has become a global phenomenon, taking place in both developed and emerging economies (Junior et al., 2013). The market share of engineering firms is growing, although the industry is dominated by accounting firms (Alsahali & Malagueño, 2021). There is growing consensus that the International Standard for Assurance Engagements 3000 will be utilized by non-accounting assurers (Alsahali & Malagueño, 2021). Since 2014, sustainability assurance has attracted considerable attention from the research community, with Spain, the USA, the United Kingdom, and Australia being the most productive countries (Oware & Moulya, 2022). However, the US lags behind other countries in assuring corporate responsibility reports (Miller et al., 2017). Future research opportunities include exploring determinants of assurance and its impact on the accounting industry (Miller et al., 2017). Looking forward, regulatory bodies are likely to focus on enhancing the applicability of assurance standards to non-financial information, especially in the context of ESG reporting. Research indicates that stakeholders are increasingly valuing non-financial assurance, pressuring organizations to provide verified information that reflects their social and environmental impact (O'Dwyer & Unerman, 2023).

In conclusion, regulatory frameworks and standards for assurance are crucial for establishing trust and accountability in various industries. As these frameworks continue to adapt to emerging trends, they will play an essential role in shaping transparent, reliable assurance practices that meet stakeholder expectations.

REFERENCES

Ahmad, M., & Solms, R. V. (2023). Information Security Assurance and the Impact of ISO 27001 in Cyber Risk Management. *Journal of Information Security and Applications*, 72, 102919.

Al-Shaer, H., & Zaman, M. (2018). Credibility of sustainability reports: The contribution of audit committees. *Business Strategy and the Environment*, 27(7), 973–986. DOI: 10.1002/bse.2046

Alsahali, K. F., & Malagueño, R. (2022). *An empirical study of sustainability reporting assurance: current trends and new insights. Journal of accounting & organizational change, 18*(5), 617-642.

Baier, C., Göttsche, M., Hellmann, A., & Schiemann, F. (2022). Too good to be true: Influencing credibility perceptions with signaling reference explicitness and assurance depth. *Journal of Business Ethics*, 178(3), 695–714. DOI: 10.1007/s10551-020-04719-7

Bansal, R. (2023). *Corporate Social Responsibility and Business Sustainability.* Issue 2 Indian JL & Legal Rsch., 5, 1.

Bessire, D., & Onnée, S. (2010). Assessing corporate social performance: Strategies of legitimation and conflicting ideologies. *Critical Perspectives on Accounting*, 21(6), 445–467. DOI: 10.1016/j.cpa.2010.01.015

Boiral, O. (2007). *Corporate greening through ISO 14001: a rational myth?. organization science, 18*(1), 127-146.

Boiral, O. (2012). ISO certificates as organizational degrees? Beyond the rational myths of the certification process. *Organization Studies*, 33(5-6), 633–654. DOI: 10.1177/0170840612443622

Boiral, O., & Henri, J. F. (2017). Is sustainability performance comparable? A study of GRI reports of mining organizations. *Business & Society*, 56(2), 283–317. DOI: 10.1177/0007650315576134

Boiral, O., Heras-Saizarbitoria, I., & Brotherton, M. C. (2019). Assessing and improving the quality of sustainability reports: The auditors' perspective. *Journal of Business Ethics*, 155(3), 703–721. DOI: 10.1007/s10551-017-3516-4

Boiral, O., Heras-Saizarbitoria, I., & Brotherton, M. C. (2020). Professionalizing the assurance of sustainability reports: The auditors' perspective. *Accounting, Auditing & Accountability Journal*, 33(2), 309–334. DOI: 10.1108/AAAJ-03-2019-3918

Boiral, O., Talbot, D., & Brotherton, M. C. (2020). Measuring sustainability risks: A rational myth? *Business Strategy and the Environment*, 29(6), 2557–2571. DOI: 10.1002/bse.2520

Brendan LeBlanc, CPA, C. I. A., & Kislevitz, J. (2016). Integrating sustainability into enterprise risk management. *The CPA Journal*, 86(6), 12.

Camilleri, M. (2014). Advancing the sustainable tourism agenda through strategic CSR perspectives. *Tourism Planning & Development*, 11(1), 42–56. DOI: 10.1080/21568316.2013.839470

Capelle-Blancard, G., & Petit, A. (2017). The weighting of CSR dimensions: One size does not fit all. *Business & Society*, 56(6), 919–943. DOI: 10.1177/0007650315620118

Carter, C., & Spence, C. (2014). Being a successful professional: An exploration of who makes partner in the Big 4. *Contemporary Accounting Research*, 31(4), 949–981. DOI: 10.1111/1911-3846.12059

Castka, P., Searcy, C., & Fischer, S. (2020). Technology-enhanced auditing in voluntary sustainability standards: The impact of COVID-19. *Sustainability (Basel)*, 12(11), 4740. DOI: 10.3390/su12114740

Channuntapipat, C., Samsonova-Taddei, A., & Turley, S. (2019). Exploring diversity in sustainability assurance practice: Evidence from assurance providers in the UK. *Accounting, Auditing & Accountability Journal*, 32(2), 556–580. DOI: 10.1108/AAAJ-05-2017-2940

Channuntapipat, C., Samsonova-Taddei, A., & Turley, S. (2020). Variation in sustainability assurance practice: An analysis of accounting versus non-accounting providers. *The British Accounting Review*, 52(2), 100843. DOI: 10.1016/j.bar.2019.100843

Chatterji, A. K., Durand, R., Levine, D. I., & Touboul, S. (2016). Do ratings of firms converge? Implications for managers, investors and strategy researchers. *Strategic Management Journal*, 37(8), 1597–1614. DOI: 10.1002/smj.2407

Chelli, M., & Gendron, Y. (2013). Sustainability ratings and the disciplinary power of the ideology of numbers. *Journal of Business Ethics*, 112(2), 187–203. DOI: 10.1007/s10551-012-1252-3

Cho, H., C., Michelon, G., M. Patten, D., & W. Roberts, R. (2014). CSR report assurance in the USA: An empirical investigation of determinants and effects. Sustainability Accounting. *Management and Policy Journal*, 5(2), 130–148.

Clauß, T., Kraus, S., & Jones, P. (2022). Sustainability in family business: Mechanisms, technologies and business models for achieving economic prosperity, environmental quality and social equity. *Technological Forecasting and Social Change*, 176, 121450. DOI: 10.1016/j.techfore.2021.121450

Connaker, A., & Madsbjerg, S. (2019). The state of socially responsible investing. *Harvard Business Review*, 17.

Curado, C., & Mota, A. (2021). A systematic literature review on sustainability in family firms. *Sustainability (Basel)*, 13(7), 3824. DOI: 10.3390/su13073824

Dawkins, C. E. (2018). Elevating the role of divestment in socially responsi- ble investing. *Journal of Business Ethics*, 153(2), 465–478. DOI: 10.1007/s10551-016-3356-7

Demjanovičová, M., & Varmus, M. (2021). Changing the perception of business values in the perspective of environmental sustainability. *Sustainability (Basel)*, 13(9), 5226. DOI: 10.3390/su13095226

Diouf, D., & Boiral, O. (2017). The quality of sustainability reports and impression management: A stakeholder perspective. *Accounting, Auditing & Accountability Journal*, 30(3), 643–667. DOI: 10.1108/AAAJ-04-2015-2044

Doyle, T. M. (2018). Ratings that don't rate: the subjective world of ESG ratings agencies. American Council for Capital Formation, 65-71.

Edgley, C., Jones, M. J., & Atkins, J. (2015). The adoption of the materiality concept in social and environmental reporting assurance: A field study approach. *The British Accounting Review*, 47(1), 1–18. DOI: 10.1016/j.bar.2014.11.001

Escrig-Olmedo, E., Fernández-Izquierdo, M. Á., Ferrero-Ferrero, I., Rivera-Lirio, J. M., & Muñoz-Torres, M. J. (2019). Rating the raters: Evaluating how ESG rating agencies integrate sustainability principles. *Sustainability (Basel)*, 11(3), 915. DOI: 10.3390/su11030915

Escrig-Olmedo, E., Muñoz-Torres, M. J., Fernández-Izquierdo, M. Á., & Rivera-Lirio, J. M. (2017). Measuring corporate environmental performance: A methodology for sustainable development. *Business Strategy and the Environment*, 26(2), 142–162. DOI: 10.1002/bse.1904

Farooq, M. B., Azantouti, A. S. A., & Zaman, R. (2023). Non-financial information assurance: a review of the literature and directions for future research. Sustainability accounting, management and policy journal, (ahead-of-print).

Farooq, M. B., & De Villiers, C. (2017). The market for sustainability assurance services: A comprehensive literature review and future avenues for research. *Pacific Accounting Review*, 29(1), 79–106. DOI: 10.1108/PAR-10-2016-0093

Farooq, M. B., & De Villiers, C. (2019). How sustainability assurance engagement scopes are determined, and its impact on capture and credibility enhancement. *Accounting, Auditing & Accountability Journal*, 33(2), 417–445. DOI: 10.1108/AAAJ-11-2018-3727

The Forum for Sustainable and Responsible Investment. (2018). Sustain- able investing assets reach $12 trillion as reported by the US SIF Foundation's biennial Report on US Sustainable, Responsible and Impact Investing Trends [Press release]. Retrieved from https://www. ussif.org/files/US%20SIF%20Trends%20Report%20 2018% 20Release.pdf

Fuhrmann, S., Ott, C., Looks, E., & Guenther, T. W. (2017). The contents of assurance statements for sustainability reports and information asymmetry. *Accounting and Business Research*, 47(4), 369–400. DOI: 10.1080/00014788.2016.1263550

García-Sánchez, I. M., Aibar-Guzmán, B., & Aibar-Guzmán, C. (2022). What sustainability assurance services do institutional investors demand and what value do they give them? Sustainability Accounting. *Management and Policy Journal*, 13(1), 152–194.

García-Sánchez, I. M., Raimo, N., Amor-Esteban, V., & Vitolla, F. (2023). Board committees and non-financial information assurance services. *The Journal of Management and Governance*, 27(1), 1–42. DOI: 10.1007/s10997-021-09613-6

Ghani, E. K., Jamal, J., Puspitasari, E., & Gunardi, A. (2018). Factors influencing integrated reporting practices among Malaysian public listed real property companies: A sustainable development effort. *International Journal of Managerial and Financial Accounting*, 10(2), 144–162. DOI: 10.1504/IJMFA.2018.091662

Guidara, A., Ammari, A. E., & Khlif, H. (2022). Strength of auditing and reporting standards, ethical behavior of firms and sustainability: A cross-country investigation. *EuroMed Journal of Business*, 17(1), 105–116. DOI: 10.1108/EMJB-10-2020-0107

Haller, A., Van Staden, C. J., & Landis, C. (2018). Value added as part of sustainability reporting: Reporting on distributional fairness or obfuscation? *Journal of Business Ethics*, 152(3), 763–781. DOI: 10.1007/s10551-016-3338-9

Harindahyani, S., & Agustia, D. (2023). The assurance providers' role in improving the independent assurance statement quality on sustainability reporting. *Accounting Research Journal*, 36(1), 37–54. DOI: 10.1108/ARJ-01-2021-0024

Hazaea, S. A., Zhu, J., Khatib, S. F., Bazhair, A. H., & Elamer, A. A. (2022). Sustainability assurance practices: A systematic review and future research agenda. *Environmental Science and Pollution Research International*, 29(4), 4843–4864. DOI: 10.1007/s11356-021-17359-9 PMID: 34787810

Hill, D. C., & Seabrook, K. A. (2013). Safety& Sustainability: Understanding the Business Value. *Professional Safety*, 58(06), 81–92.

Hummel, K., Schlick, C., & Fifka, M. (2019). The role of sustainability performance and accounting assurors in sustainability assurance engagements. *Journal of Business Ethics*, 154(3), 733–757. DOI: 10.1007/s10551-016-3410-5

Humphrey, C., O'Dwyer, B., & Unerman, J. (2017). Re-theorizing the configuration of organizational fields: The IIRC and the pursuit of 'Enlightened' corporate reporting. *Accounting and Business Research*, 47(1), 30–63. DOI: 10.1080/00014788.2016.1198683

IFAC. (2023). *International Standards on Assurance Engagements (ISAE) 3000: Assurance on Non-Financial Information*. IFAC Official Website.

Jeriji, M., & Nasfi, A. (2023). The value relevance of mandatory sustainability reporting assurance. *South African Journal of Accounting Research, 37*(2), 122-138.

Jia, F., Yin, S., Chen, L., & Chen, X. (2020). The circular economy in the textile and apparel industry: A systematic literature review. *Journal of Cleaner Production*, 259, 120728. DOI: 10.1016/j.jclepro.2020.120728

Junior, R. M., Best, P. J., & Cotter, J. (2014). Sustainability reporting and assurance: A historical analysis on a world-wide phenomenon. *Journal of Business Ethics*, 120(1), 1–11. DOI: 10.1007/s10551-013-1637-y

Kennedy, H., & Hill, R. L. (2018). The feeling of numbers: Emotions in everyday engagements with data and their visualisation. *Sociology*, 52(4), 830–848. DOI: 10.1177/0038038516674675

Khatib, S. F., & Nour, A. (2021). The impact of corporate governance on firm performance during the COVID-19 pandemic: Evidence from Malaysia. *Journal of Asian Finance, Economics and Business, 8*(2), 0943-0952.

Knechel, W. R., & Salterio, S. E. (2022). *Auditing: Assurance and Risk*. Routledge.

Kotsantonis, S., Pinney, C., & Serafeim, G. (2016). ESG integration in investment management: Myths and realities. *The Bank of America Journal of Applied Corporate Finance*, 28(2), 10–16. DOI: 10.1111/jacf.12169

KPMG. (2005). *KPMG international survey of corporate responsibility reporting 2005.*

KPMG. (2008). *KPMG international survey of corporate responsibility reporting 2008.*

KPMG. (2011). *KPMG international survey of corporate responsibility reporting 2011.*

KPMG. (2013). *The KPMG survey of corporate responsibility reporting 2013.*

KPMG. (2015). *The KPMG survey of corporate responsibility reporting 2015.*

KPMG. (2017). *The road ahead: The KPMG survey of corporate responsibility reporting 2017.*

Lemma, T. T., Negash, M., Lulseged, A., & Maroun, W. (2024). Sustainability assurance and corporate environmental accountability. *Business Strategy and the Environment*, 33(4), 3167–3183. DOI: 10.1002/bse.3643

Loconto, A. M. (2017). Models of assurance: Diversity and standardization of modes of intermediation. *The Annals of the American Academy of Political and Social Science*, 670(1), 112–132. DOI: 10.1177/0002716217692517

Low, K. Y., & Boo, E. F. (2012). Do contrasting statements improve users' understanding of different assurance levels conveyed in assurance reports? *International Journal of Auditing*, 16(1), 19–34. DOI: 10.1111/j.1099-1123.2011.00439.x

Manetti, G., & Becatti, L. (2009). Assurance services for sustainability reports: Standards and empirical evidence. *Journal of Business Ethics*, 87(S1), 289–298. DOI: 10.1007/s10551-008-9809-x

Manetti, G., & Toccafondi, S. (2012). The role of stakeholders in sustainability reporting assurance. *Journal of Business Ethics*, 107(3), 363–377. DOI: 10.1007/s10551-011-1044-1

Maroun, W. (2020). A conceptual model for understanding corporate social responsibility assurance practice. *Journal of Business Ethics*, 161(1), 187–209. DOI: 10.1007/s10551-018-3909-z

Marquis, C., Toffel, M. W., & Zhou, Y. (2016). Scrutiny, norms, and selective disclosure: A global study of greenwashing. *Organization Science*, 27(2), 483–504. DOI: 10.1287/orsc.2015.1039

Martínez-Ferrero, J., & García-Sánchez, I. M. (2018). The level of sustainability assurance: The effects of brand reputation and industry specialisation of assurance providers. *Journal of Business Ethics*, 150(4), 971–990. DOI: 10.1007/s10551-016-3159-x

Marx, B., & van Dyk, V. (2011). Sustainability reporting and assurance: An analysis of assurance practices in South Africa. *Meditari Accountancy Research*, 19(1/2), 39–55. DOI: 10.1108/10222521111178628

Mercer. (2019). *The ABC of ESG.* Canada: https://www.mercer.ca/content/ dam/ mercer/attachments/north-america/canada/ca-2019-the-abc-of- esg-environmental-social-governance.pdf

Meseguer-Sánchez, V., Gálvez-Sánchez, F. J., López-Martínez, G., & Molina-Moreno, V. (2021). Corporate social responsibility and sustainability. A bibliometric analysis of their interrelations. *Sustainability (Basel)*, 13(4), 1636. DOI: 10.3390/su13041636

Miller, K. C., Fink, L., & Proctor, T. Y. (2017). Current trends and future expectations in external assurance for integrated corporate sustainability reporting. *J. Legal Ethical & Regul. Isses*, 20, 1.

Mock, T. J., Strohm, C., & Swartz, K. M. (2007). An examination of worldwide assured sustainability reporting. *Australian Accounting Review*, 17(41), 67–77. DOI: 10.1111/j.1835-2561.2007.tb00455.x

Mooij, S. (2017). *The ESG rating and ranking industry; Vice or virtue in the adoption of responsible investment?* https://dx.doi.org/10.2139/ssrn.2960869

MSCI. (2010). MSCI Inc. to Acquire RiskMetrics Group, Inc. [Press release]. http://ir.msci.com/static-files/15e6a432-4c0a-424a-ae5c-e79490273e90

O'Dwyer, B. (2011). The case of sustainability assurance: Constructing a new assurance service. *Contemporary Accounting Research*, 28(4), 1230–1266. DOI: 10.1111/j.1911-3846.2011.01108.x

O'Dwyer, B., Owen, D., & Unerman, J. (2011). Seeking legitimacy for new assurance forms: The case of assurance on sustainability reporting. *Accounting, Organizations and Society*, 36(1), 31–52. DOI: 10.1016/j.aos.2011.01.002

O'Dwyer, B., & Owen, D. L. (2005). Assurance statement practice in environmental, social and sustainability reporting: A critical evaluation. *The British Accounting Review*, 37(2), 205–229. DOI: 10.1016/j.bar.2005.01.005

O'Dwyer, B., & Unerman, J. (2023). The Role of Assurance in Sustainability and ESG Reporting. *Accounting, Auditing & Accountability Journal*, 36(4), 861–888.

Odintsova, T. (2024). Updating the Informational and Control Practices in the Sustainability Agenda. *Economics and Culture*, 21(1), 133–148. DOI: 10.2478/jec-2024-0010

Oware, K. M., & Moulya, V. H. (2023). The outlook of sustainability assurance in global trends: A bibliometric review and research agenda. *South Asian Journal of Marketing*, 4(2), 110–127. DOI: 10.1108/SAJM-06-2022-0039

Perego, P., & Kolk, A. (2012). Multinationals' accountability on sustainability: The evolution of third-party assurance of sustainability reports. *Journal of Business Ethics*, 110(2), 173–190. DOI: 10.1007/s10551-012-1420-5

Pflugrath, G., Roebuck, P., & Simnett, R. (2011). Impact of assurance and assurer's professional affiliation on financial analysts' assessment of credibility of corporate social responsibility information. *Auditing*, 30(3), 239–254. DOI: 10.2308/ajpt-10047

Pizzi, S., Venturelli, A., & Caputo, F. (2024). Restoring trust in sustainability reporting: The enabling role of the external assurance. *Current Opinion in Environmental Sustainability*, 68, 101437. DOI: 10.1016/j.cosust.2024.101437

Porter, M. E., & Kramer, M. R. (2006). *Strategy & society. The link between competitive advantage and corporate.*

Rahdari, A. H., & Rostamy, A. A. A. (2015). Designing a general set of sustainability indicators at the corporate level. *Journal of Cleaner Production*, 108, 757–771. DOI: 10.1016/j.jclepro.2015.05.108

Rajak, S., & Vinodh, S. (2015). Application of fuzzy logic for social sustainability performance evaluation: A case study of an Indian automotive component manufacturing organization. *Journal of Cleaner Production*, 108, 1184–1192. DOI: 10.1016/j.jclepro.2015.05.070

RepRisk. (2019). *About Us*. https://www.reprisk.com/about-reprisk

Rimmel, G. (2020). Sustainability audit and assurance. In *Accounting for Sustainability* (pp. 180–192). Routledge. DOI: 10.4324/9781003037200-17

Roopa, S., & Rani, M. S. (2012). Questionnaire designing for a survey. *The Journal of Indian Orthodontic Society*, 46(4, suppl1), 273–277. DOI: 10.1177/0974909820120509S

Ruiz-Barbadillo, E., & Martínez-Ferrero, J. (2020). Empirical analysis of the effect of the joint provision of audit and sustainability assurance services on assurance quality. *Journal of Cleaner Production*, 266, 121943. DOI: 10.1016/j.jclepro.2020.121943

Şahin, Z., & Çankaya, F. (2020). The importance of sustainability and sustainability reporting. New Approaches to CSR. *Sustainability and Accountability*, I, 45–59.

Seguí-Mas, E., Bollas-Araya, H. M., & Polo-Garrido, F. (2018). Assurance on corporate governance reports in Spain: Towards an enhanced accountability or a new form of public relations? *Administrative Sciences*, 8(3), 32. DOI: 10.3390/admsci8030032

Simnett, R., Vanstraelen, A., & Chua, W. F. (2009). Assurance on sustainability reports: An international comparison. *The Accounting Review*, 84(3), 937–967. DOI: 10.2308/accr.2009.84.3.937

Singh, J., de los Salmones Sanchez, M. D. M. G., & del Bosque, I. R. (2008). Understanding corporate social responsibility and product perceptions in consumer markets: A cross-cultural evaluation. *Journal of Business Ethics*, 80(3), 597–611. DOI: 10.1007/s10551-007-9457-6

Sonnerfeldt, A. L. L., & Pontoppidan, C. A. (2020). The challenges of assurance on non-financial reporting. *Accounting, Economics, and Law : A Convivium*, 10(2), 20180050. DOI: 10.1515/ael-2018-0050

Sulaiman, M., & Alhaji Zakari, M. (2019). Financial sustainability of state waqf institutions (SWIs) in Malaysia. *Journal of Islamic Accounting and Business Research*, 10(2), 236–258. DOI: 10.1108/JIABR-05-2016-0054

SustainAbility (2018). Rate the raters 2018: Ratings revisited. London: New York, San Francisco. https://sustainability.com/wp-content/ uploads/2017/12/SA-RateTheRaters_Ratings-Revisited_March18.pdf

Tahinakis, P. D., & Samarinas, M. P. (2017). Attributes of audit quality and weak fiscal sustainability countries. International Journal of Banking. *Accounting and Finance*, 8(1), 20–51.

Teoh, S. H., & Francis, J. R. (2023). Assurance and Professional Judgment in the Digital Age. *Auditing*, 42(2), 27–54.

Traxler, A. A., Schrack, D., & Greiling, D. (2020). Sustainability reporting and management control–A systematic exploratory literature review. *Journal of Cleaner Production*, 276, 122725. DOI: 10.1016/j.jclepro.2020.122725

Tur-Porcar, A., Roig-Tierno, N., & Llorca Mestre, A. (2018). Factors affecting entrepreneurship and business sustainability. *Sustainability (Basel)*, 10(2), 452. DOI: 10.3390/su10020452

Van Mourik, C., & Walton, P. J. (Eds.). (2014). *The Routledge companion to accounting, reporting and regulation*. Routledge.

Vander Bauwhede, H., & Van Cauwenberge, P. (2022). Determinants and value relevance of voluntary assurance of sustainability reports in a mandatory reporting context: Evidence from Europe. *Sustainability (Basel)*, 14(15), 9795. DOI: 10.3390/su14159795

Vanstraelen, A. (2022). Harmonization of Assurance Standards: Challenges and Opportunities. *European Accounting Review*, 31(3), 453–478.

Vaz Ogando, N., Ruiz Blanco, S., & Fernandez-Feijoo, B. (2018). A provider's approach to the assurance market of sustainability reports in Spain. *Administrative Sciences*, 8(3), 28. DOI: 10.3390/admsci8030028

Verdantix. (2013). *Global sustainability leaders survey: Brands.*

Wallage, P. (2000). Assurance on sustainability reporting: An auditor's view. *Auditing*, 19(s-1), 53–65. DOI: 10.2308/aud.2000.19.s-1.53

Wong, J., Wong, N., Li, W. Y., & Chen, L. (2016). Sustainability assurance: An emerging market for the accounting profession. *Pacific Accounting Review*, 28(3), 238–259. DOI: 10.1108/PAR-11-2014-0038

Yan, M., Jia, F., Chen, L., & Yan, F. (2022). Assurance process for sustainability reporting: Towards a conceptual framework. *Journal of Cleaner Production*, 377, 134156. DOI: 10.1016/j.jclepro.2022.134156

Zadek, S., Raynard, P., Forstater, M., & Oelschlaegel, J. (2004). The future of sustainability assurance. *ACCA Research Report.*

Zeff, S. A., & Nobes, C. W. (2023). *International Financial Reporting: A Comparative Approach*. Wiley.

Zieni, B., Chitchyan, R., & Heckel, R. (2017). *Trust as a sustainability requirement. CEUR-WS. org. Abbott, A. (2014). The system of professions: An essay on the division of expert labor*. University of Chicago press.

Chapter 2
Collaborative Expertise in Sustainability Reporting and Assurance:
Harnessing Multidisciplinary Synergies for Enhanced Outcomes

Akansha Sharma
https://orcid.org/0009-0002-5372-1269
Independent Researcher, India

Amresh Kumar Ray
https://orcid.org/0009-0004-8571-4068
Forvis Mazars, India

ABSTRACT

The objective of this chapter is to explore the interconnected roles of sustainability reporting and assurance, emphasizing how collaborative expertise enhances the effectiveness of both processes. Sustainability reporting serves as a platform for organizations to communicate their Environmental, Social, and Governance (ESG) performance, challenges, and commitments to stakeholders, fostering transparency and accountability. However, the credibility of these reports hinges on the accuracy and integrity of the disclosed information, which is reinforced through sustainability assurance—an independent evaluation that validates the reliability and completeness of ESG disclosures. This chapter aims to highlight the critical role of multidisciplinary expertise in strengthening both reporting and assurance.

DOI: 10.4018/979-8-3373-0117-4.ch002

1. INTRODUCTION

With the increasing importance of sustainability in corporate strategy and long-term business resilience, the demand for reporting and assurance for the consistent and credible data is increasing in the business world. The stakeholders, including investors, shareholders, regulators, customers and communities are highly relying on the sustainability reports for understanding and knowing about the company's commitments, strategies and performance on the ESG disclosures (Kay, Brindisi, & Martin, 2020). In this, Sustainability reporting serves as the primary channel through which organisations and businesses are transparently communicating their activities, goals and achievements Further, to ensure the credibility of the disclosures, assurance is being seen as an important aspect in the disclosure requirements.

Sustainability and its reporting have evolved a lot in the past one decade. With the introduction of new regulations, standards and compliances, the disclosure requirements have become complex and have interlinked various environmental and societal challenges such as climate change, biodiversity loss, water pollution, greenhouse emissions, labour rights, corporate governance, diversity, supply chain management, etc. This complexity helps in ensuring that the risk of greenwashing by companies in their disclosures is reduced and the confidence of stakeholders in their business is increased. (PwC, 2023).

With the disclosure requirements become both complex and diverse, it is important that the issues are tackled by experts who have in depth knowledge of the topic, with multi-dimensional issues, comes the needs for multidimension experts who not only have technical knowledge of the topic but also can provide strategic insights and in depth understanding of what is the best the company can do to stay both financial and ethically strong in the field. Thus, comes the need for collaboration.

By Multidisciplinary collaborations we mean bringing together the knowledge and skills from various domains to bring out the best in the company. This includes domains such as strategy, environmental science, human resources, information technology, chartered accountants, legal team etc. The richer the blend of expertise involved in the reporting of information, the better is the depth and quality of reporting as well as assurance as the aggregate of multiple disciplines can effectively tackle the various challenges involved in the complex ESG related issues by generating insights, uncovering risks and fostering creative solutions, making the disclosure more robust as well as relevant to stakeholders from various sectors and thus enhancing the validity and scope of the reported information, strategies formed and targets declared. (Saruchera, 2025).

The convergence of sustainability reporting, assurance and the collaboration of experts too has been explored in the sections below along with how integration helps resolve the growing complexities in the ESG Domain.

It has been observed through real world examples that the organisations that combine experts from multiple domains are not only meeting compliance requirements but are also unlocking strategic value, making resilient business models and creating long-term success plans. A few such examples include big names such as Coca-Cola, Microsoft and Unilever whose efforts and practices of integrating multidisciplinary approach in their sustainability journey have made them leaders in not just their field of business but also cheerleaders in sustainability action. Such real-world examples have been discussed in the sections that follow for an in-depth understanding and practical approach to out subject of study. These examples will enlighten the reader with the integrative approach necessary to tackle sustainability and ESG in the current scenario.

2. WHAT IS SUSTAINABILITY REPORTING?

Sustainability reporting refers to the disclosure of non-financial information by the businesses which help stakeholders such as investors, customers, communities etc know the company's actions, performance and future goals and initiatives towards the ESG topics (Dienes, Sassen, & Fischer, 2016).

The principle of sustainability reporting lies in the transparent communication of initiatives, challenges and risks to a broad range of stakeholders in one single report which is published yearly showing companies' progress and growth in terms of non-financial data which enchases trust, transparency and credibility while creating a stand in the market and acts a differentiator. It also discloses how the company plans to work in the future years showcasing the stakeholders its plans for stability resilience and business continuity and thus creating a sense of long-term success and value creation (Shrivastava & Berger, 2010).

Sustainability reporting is usually carried out on a yearly basis, and the time and months of reporting may vary for each company depending on their geographic region, alignment with financial reporting or internal discussions by the company heads and executive management.

Companies many choose to report data in multiple sustainability frameworks available or in one depending on the company's expertise, availability of resources and requirements of the investors, regulatory bodies and stakeholder.

The companies usually declare the non-financial information/sustainability data on their websites, or directly sharing the same to the concerned stakeholders and where necessary submit it to the government bodies such as Securities and Exchange Board of India (SEBI) in India, Securities and Exchange Commission (SEC) in USA and Securities and Exchange Surveillance Commission (SESC) in Japan etc.

A. Time frames

The various time frames when sustainability reports are published include-

- **Callender year (CY):** This usually consists of data from January to December
- **Financial Year (FY):** The financial year may vary from region to region and may also vary based on the company's financial data disclosures. Examples are as follows:

In India and Japan financial year is considered from April to March and thus Indian and Japanese companies declare their non-financial information also for the same time. Whereas, in Australia Financia year is considered from 1 July to 30 June and thus their sustainability reports when aligned with financial data is usually published in the mentioned time (WatchWire, 2025).

As an exception, some companies may choose to keep the reporting of their non-financial information separate from the financial and thus the standalone document may choose a different time for disclosure.

B. Sustainability Frameworks

There are various globally recognized frameworks available for the disclosure of sustainability data or for sustainability reporting. These standards are established to provide a clear, universally acceptable, widely known and uniform system of reporting which can easily be used by stakeholders to compare information shared by various companies and make decisions accordingly. Although the scope, structure and manner of reporting of all these structures may vary but the goal remains the same, providing clear, comparable, consistent and transparent data to the stakeholders. A few of the widely used frameworks have been discussed below-

- **Global Reporting Initiative (GRI)**

GRI Reporting standard focuses on providing data on economy, environment and society and focuses on broader sustainability matters rather than just quantitative metrics and gives a modular structure where companies can choose to declare information on the topics which are material to them and their stakeholders rather than providing disclosure on every ESG Topic. This is attained through material assessment of the company's priority impacts, risk and opportunities (Global Reporting Initiative, n.d.).

- **Task force on climate related financial disclosure (TCFD)**

TCFD focuses on companies' climate related financial disclosures and helps companies identify how climate change can pose as a risk and opportunity for the long-term success of their business. It consists of four main criteria on which the reporting is carried out: Governance, Strategy, Risk Management, Metrics and Targets. A key feature of this reporting is the scenario analysis of risk and opportunity and further integration of the data into its overall strategy and business continuity plan (Task Force on Climate-related Financial Disclosures, n.d.).

- **Business responsibility and Sustainability Reporting (BRSR)**

This framework has been introduced in India by SEBI to improve the ESG disclosures in the country and make companies accountable for their actions in a comparable and transparent manner. This framework is formed keeping in mind the best practices followed globally but matching the requirements of the Indian market. It makes companies disclosure their metrics, targets, goals and policies related to ESG in an organised manner (Securities and Exchange Board of India, 2021).

- **Corporate Sustainability Reporting Directive (CSRD)**

CSRD is a European Union regulation, which has recently been introduced after removing the Non-Financial Reporting Directive (NFRD). This works on European Sustainability Reporting Standard (ESRS) and aims at making companies disclose their impact on environment and society. A key feature of this reporting is double materiality assessment which involves the disclosure of companies risks and opportunities in terms of impact and financial impact of the company (KPMG, 2024).

- **Sustainability Accounting and Standard Board (SASB)**

SASB is an industry specific standard, which includes eleven sectors and seventy-seven industries, which have the ESG Disclosures most relevant to that industry. This is a very investor friendly framework, and it is easily comparable because each company from a specific industry making disclosures as per SASB will be declaring information on the same set of ESG topics set out by industry experts as per SASB (Deloitte, n.d.).

C. Disclosure Type

The disclosure requirements of most standards are very similar; the following are a few disclosure requirements which companies need to report to when considering disclosing a sustainability report (Stedman & Paul, 2024).

- **General Disclosure:** Company name, revenue, CSR details etc. are a few pieces of information that are usually included in this section of the report.
- **Environmental:** GHG emissions, water stewardship, air emissions, waste management and circular economy, biodiversity loss, climate change adaptation and mitigation etc. are included in this section. (Kouloukoui et al., 2019)
- **Social:** Diversity, equity and inclusion, turnover rate, health and safety management, child labour, forced labour, minimum wage, community engagement initiatives, respect for human rights, paternity leaves etc. are some of the disclosures in this section of reporting. (Al Amosh & Mansor, 2018)
- **Governance:** Disclosures on the governance structure, independence, skills and expertise of the management and supervisory board, role of the board of directors in sustainability of the company, company policies such as the code of conduct, whistleblowing system, training provided to the employees, management of suppliers, relationship with customers etc. are some of the disclosures made in this section of reporting. (Stedman & Paul, 2024)

3. WHAT IS SUSTAINABILITY ASSURANCE?

Sustainability assurance is an independent, systematic process that evaluates and verifies the accuracy, reliability, and completeness of an organization's sustainability disclosures. These disclosures typically encompass ESG performance including metric, targets, activities and initiatives for impacts, risk and opportunities which are communicated through sustainability reports, integrated annual reports, standalone ESG reports or other channels such as website pages etc. (Palgrave Macmillan, Cham, 2018) By providing objective validation of reported data, sustainability assurance increases stakeholder confidence, mitigates the risks of misrepresentation, and ensures alignment with established reporting frameworks and standards. Unlike financial assurance, which focuses on financial data, sustainability assurance deals with non-financial metrics such as greenhouse gas (GHG) emissions, water usage, community engagement, turnover rate, diversity, supplier management, and ethical labour practices. The process often involves collaboration with independent third-party assurance providers, who apply internationally recognized standards such as:

- **ISAE 3000:** A standard for non-financial assurance engagements. (Manetti & Becatti, 2008)
- **AA1000AS:** A principles-based assurance standard emphasizing inclusivity, materiality, and responsiveness. (Manetti & Becatti, 2008)
- **ISO Standards:** Including ISO 14064 for GHG verification and ISO 26000 for social responsibility.

The increasing importance of sustainability assurance lies in its role as a key mechanism for validating ESG claims and ensuring transparency, particularly considering rising scrutiny from stakeholders and regulatory bodies. As organizations are held accountable for their environmental and social impacts, assurance has become crucial for building trust and credibility (Hayatun N. Burhan & Rahmanti, 2022).

Assurance can be of three types, depending on the degree of confidence of the auditor in the declared information:

A. Limited Assurance

Limited assurance is the lowest level of confidence an auditor provides after reviewing the disclosures of a company. The auditor usually checks only 30-40 per cent of the evidence when they provide this confidence level in a report. (Hodge, Subramaniam, & Stewart, 2009)

B. Moderate Assurance

When the auditor performs comprehensive data assessment and checks and samples a good number of documents, it is called moderate assurance. This assurance is higher than limited but lower than reasonable. (Hodge, Subramaniam, & Stewart, 2009)

C. Reasonable Assurance

Reasonable assurance is the highest level of confidence an auditor can provide to the data set declared by a firm. It involves detailed testing and processing of documentation in detail. (Hodge, Subramaniam, & Stewart, 2009)

A company or business may choose to go for any level of assurance depending on the time, requirements, need and financial ability of the firm and it will help them in creating trust among the stakeholder regarding the information stated in their sustainability report as it will give confidence to the reader that the information is fairly presented and does not involve green washing or is incorrectly representing information on progress, quantitative measures and other details of the company which can influence their decision on working, investing, or being involved with the company in general. This is a very crucial step as an assurance letter from an external auditor increases the value of the report and makes it stand out in the world of sustainability. (Hodge, Subramaniam, & Stewart, 2009)

It is important to note that a lot of regulatory bodies in various standards and countries are making assurance a mandatory requirement of the ESG data.

An interesting example of the same can be found in India, where under the BRSR framework mandates certain set of companies to get reasonable assurance on a few critical disclosure requirements such as water management, waste generation and disposal, Scope 1 and 2, diversity of employees whereas can go for limited assurance for the other non- critical indicators such as total number of employees, turnover rate, number of board members, trading houses etc. These critical indicators which are most relevant to the country have already been declared by SEBI and companies must adhere to this practice when declaring their ESG or sustainability information using BRSR framework. This ensures that the company is making sure to take high level confidence on some of the most important ESG disclosures, while maintaining and managing the finances and not having to spend hefty amounts on reasonable assurance of the whole report. (Yadav, 2024)

Similarly, under CSRD the companies operating in the EU are mandated to take at least limited assurance of their data when declaring information using the ESRS Standard. EU plans to implement reasonable assurance in the coming years and make the data available in the public domain more reliable and trustworthy. (Accountancy Europe, 2024)

4. WHY IS ASSURANCE IMPORTANT IN SUSTAINABILITY?

Sustainability assurance plays a vital role in enhancing the credibility, reliability, and transparency of an organization's sustainability reporting. With stakeholder scrutiny expanding and regulatory frameworks becoming more robust assurance acts a cornerstone for validating non-financial performance, mitigate risk and foster trust among the stakeholders (Gillet-Monjarret & Rivière-Giordano, 2017).

Below is a list of reasons as to why assurance is indispensable in sustainability:

- **Increasing credibility and trust**

Independent verification of an organisations sustainability data and claims is called assurance. It demonstrates transparency and accountability in the commitments made by the reporting body. Third-party assurance helps in gaining stakeholder confidence, in the current time when green washing accusations can lead to severe reputational damage to the firm. It further helps to establish consumer trust by ensuring transparency of environmental and social claims in association with the product and services. (Springer, Cham, 2017)

- **Compliance with respect to reporting and legal obligations**

Global regulatory frameworks such as GRI, CSRD, BRSR and SASB have either made it mandatory or encourage organisation that along with reporting clear, comparable and accurate data, assurance is taken on the disclosed data, hence, assurance helps ensure compliance with these regulations, further reducing reputational risk due to incorrect data.

- **Mitigating Risk**

Assurance identifies and highlights any data inaccuracies, operational efficiencies and regulatory non- compliances in the system enables organisations to address the same, at the same time ensuring minimized exposure to legal, financial and reputational risks.

For example, Coca-Cola during its assurance process uncovered shortcomings in data collection in their plants w.r.t water consumption. Thus, the company decided to implement a robust monitoring system, which significantly reduced future water related risk for them (Coca-Cola Company, 2023).

- **Meeting Investor Expectations**

Investors are highly demanding and rely on ESG data in the current scenarios and to increase trust, build trust and meet expectations, it is important to provide verified data. Thus, assurance can influence investment decision. (Hawn, Chatterji, & Mitchell, 2017)

- **Enabling Internal Improvements**

The verification process involved in assurance enables companies to identify operational inefficiencies, gaps in data collection tools and processes and insights for strategic and operational improvements, fostering culture of continuous improvement and enhancement, thus integrating sustainability objectives in corporate efficiency (Bjarnason, Runeson, Borg, et al., 2014).

- **Enhancing Stakeholder Engagement**

Engagement with stakeholders such as regulators, investors, consumers, NGOs, employees etc. is enhanced when reliable data sets are provided to them, thus assurance can facilitate dialogue transparency and ensure that stakeholder expectations are being met by the organisation's actions (Mathur, Price, & Austin, 2008).

- **Protecting against Greenwashing**

Misleading claims and incorrect data presentation of ESG related data is known as greenwashing, and claims of greenwashing can damage an organisations reputation, and assurance here communicates that the data is indeed correct and is strong evidence for accurate and consistent data (Jones & Tremblay, 2024).

- **Facilitating Strategic Decision- Making**

Verified data helps companies set realistic, evidence-based goals and decisions and thus facilitate in informed strategic decision making (Steinmeier & Stich, 2017).

- **Upgrading Global Competitiveness**

The world market is becoming competitive day by day and verified sustainability data sets apart organisations from others as they foster higher levels of trust with investors, customers and other stakeholders, thus enhancing competitiveness (World Economic Forum, 2025).

5. INTEROPERABILITY OF SUSTAINABILITY ASSURANCE AND REPORTING

The linkage between sustainability reporting and assurance plays a vital role to enhance transparency and credibility of ESG data disclosures, where reporting is serving as a mechanism through which the organisation chooses to communicate its performance and goals to the relevant stakeholders and independent verification by third party ensuring that the presented data is indeed reliable, thus validating the completeness and accuracy of that data.

With the increase in regulatory compliances for disclosing sustainability data, there is a greater need for transparency which is not only accurate but also reliable, comprehensive and aligned with the global best practices.

The intersection between the two creates a mechanism for organization to demonstrate accountability and with the increasing stakeholder pressure for maintaining stakeholder trust it is important that their sustainability process remains transparent and thus the interplay between reporting and assurance becomes important and is vital in the era of disclosing sustainability information (Leal, Guédria, & Panetto, 2019).

6. ROLE OF MULTIDISCIPLINARY EXPERTISE IN INTEGRATING ASSURANCE AND REPORTING

The role of multidisciplinary expertise arises and becomes essential to ensure that the ESG data disclosures are both accurate and comprehensive. As we already know that sustainability reporting requires data from various segments of the business as well as various sources which includes both internal and external systems such as the plants, corporate office, supply chain partners, agencies etc., thus exploring the fact that the data collection is so multidimensional in nature, it becomes crucial that diverse fields collaborate to interpret, present and verify the data in this report (Institute of Internal Auditors, 2022).

These experts play a crucial role in:

- **Ensuring Accurate Data Verification**

The fact that the sustainability report is the sole communication means for the company to present its non-financial performance data to its stakeholders, it is very important and critical to ensure the accuracy of this data presented and thus multidisciplinary experts ensure that the data is correct and verified at different levels in the organisation.

For example:

Data scientists and analysts work on validating, collecting and processing data related to quantitative metrics such as Greenhouse gas emission, waste and water management.

Environmental experts assess the impact of operations on the natural resources such as biodiversity loss, Environment impact assessment of the product and its processes etc.

Social governance professionals make sure that data related to human rights, Community engagement, employee engagement, labour rights is accurately reported and validated.

Legal experts play a major role in ensuring that the policies and procedures are in place as per regulatory requirements and all the compliances are being followed and reported properly and transparently.

Thus, engagement with experts in multiple fields makes the organisation confident that the data being presented and verified is both accurate and reliable for a transparent communication to the stakeholders.

- **Improving the quality of ESG Disclosures**

The collaboration of reporting and consulting results in high quality Sustainability/ESG Data disclosures. With the multi-disciplinary teams contributing their knowledge and skills to ensure comprehensiveness and alignment with best practices available globally. The collaboration makes sure that the disclosures are reflecting the complexity and importance of sustainability issues with the organisation and providing a crystal-clear picture of the organisations ESG Performance. Further, the involvement as discussed by experts from various fields helps in identifying any potential risk, opportunity, gap or inaccuracies in the data sets, providing an opportunity for improvement in the further years and the company progresses towards meeting its sustainability targets and goals.

7. IMPORTANCE OF COLLABORATIVE EXPERTISE IN ASSURANCE

Assurance is a complex process and it being involved in sustainability makes it even more complex as it's a new concept for the world to grasp. Further, it consists of various factors under E, S and G, each of which require specialized knowledge and expertise to handle and meet the demands of the regulatory bodies and alignment with the frameworks. Each sustainability data point such as climate change, water usage, waste management, air pollution, human rights, diversity, corporate governance, policies etc. requires a certain degree of understanding and thus a company should not rely on a single skill set but bring together a team of people from various backgrounds for the best outcomes.

A. Addressing the complexity of ESG Issues

Sustainability is a complex challenge with various dimensions that require the insights and expertise from various specialists.

For example, Nestle has focused and worked extensively on its biodiversity initiatives, for this they did an interesting collaboration between agronomists, ecologists and local Non- Governmental Organizations (NGO) which led to an interesting set of thoughts and ideas which provided them with a comprehensive understanding of the impacts of the cocoa farming and practices involved. This gave them an overview of which sectors the company can work on to do better in terms of biodiversity impacts and create a positive and actual impact on both the environment and society involved. This collaboration has resulted in better supplier management, leading to a reduction in deforestation and improvement in the supply chain making it more sustainable and greener. This has demonstrated the power of collaboration and multiple expertise in the field of sustainability as a whole (Nestlé, n.d.).

B. Enhancing the accuracy of data verification

Verification of data is one of the most important components of sustainability reporting and data collection. This ensures that the data which we present is accurate, consistent and reliable (Bureau Veritas, n.d.).

For example, in the case of GHG Accounting, data scientists and environmentalists work together to ensure all the emissions are accounted for in a correct and proper manner, only then will the company be able to set reliable targets for the future, reduce their emissions is a progressive manner and work on their sustainability goals along-side meeting regional and global targets.

For example, companies who have been reported to be working with data scientists and experts such as agricultural, land use, food and technology to validate supplier level emissions data, have reduced scope 3 emissions to as high as 25%, which was possible only when the company was fully aware of the most accurate emissions data. This led to a better position of the firm in market and among stakeholders and also moving forward it will also help the company save financially and economically be more viable in terms of its supplier engagement (He, Gao, & Wang, 2022).

8. PROFESSIONAL CONTRIBUTION TO SUSTAINABILITY

Professionals play a major role in sustainability accounting, reporting and assurance. They are major contributors to the development of various frameworks and are the building bricks to the development of the concept of sustainability and ESG. Further, they are the main reason how companies are able to understand, find and interpret the risk, opportunities and challenges related to a single entity, nation and even globally. Since on the global levels discussion and relevance are created by various experts from different fields of work, it is important that in reporting and assurance also the same manner of work is being followed and implemented to communicate the organisations ESG activities, performances and plans. Thus, already said and explained in this chapter, it is important to have diverse sets of minds and ideas when exploring sustainability for a company (Salgado, Abbott, & Wilson, 2017). Below are explored the roles and contributions of various professional groups in sustainability build up-

A. Environmental Scientists and Climate Experts

Environmental and climate scientists can play an important role in assuring, verifying and validating the environmental aspects of sustainability related disclosures. Their skills and knowledge are one of the most important aspects in dealing with sustainability as a whole and their expertise ensures that the reported data is scientifically accurate and reliable. They verify and ensure that the sustainability practices and goals are in line with global best practices and environmental goals set by various organizations working towards climate mitigation and adaptation such as Paris Agreement, UN Sustainable Development Goals etc.

- **Contribution in Assurance**

a. Verification of GHG Emissions Related Data:

Environment scientists and climate experts make sure that the data across various business segments is collected and assured in a clear and transparent manner, further witch correct and accurate data, they through their thorough understanding on the topic make sure that the company works on mitigation and adaptation and that the finances are being used in the correct manner.

b. Verification of Water Management Data:

Water management is one of the main environmental issues for each company, as per regulations as well as with the company's own impact, because every product or services will in some way or the other require the usage and consumption of water. Thus, proper consumption, management and utilisation of water becomes very important. Environmental experts and their understanding of water management can help a company stay safe from regulations, save financially by correct usage, align with the requirements and expectations of the stakeholders, and also make sure that there is no stoppage of work due to incorrect water management both in terms of business management and local community management.

c. Impact of Biodiversity:

Biodiversity effects of a company's operations are best assessed but the people who have knowledge of a particular geography, the various plants, animals and other species which exist in their area of interest. This can only be done by experts who have studied and have sound technical and other expertise on the topic; thus biodiversity experts are crucial when understanding the effect of same from the company and on the company from biodiversity.

- **Contribution in Reporting**

a. Carbon Neutrality goals and climate related disclosures:

With the clarity and understanding of climate change, environmental and climate experts can help companies in setting realistic and achievable targets and thus prevent companies from looking like they are trying to greenwash and also make progress in the consecutive years on the topics they have agreed to work upon.

b. Reporting on risk related to biodiversity, water, pollution etc.:

They can assist in preparing specific data points under various sustainability frameworks which require the interpretation and understanding of experts to be reported, as it is very important that the meaning of indicators are well understood before reporting them publicly as it would be your only mode of communication to the stakeholders regarding the company's performance and progress.

c. Alignment with Frameworks:

The experts can make sure the understanding pf data points, discussion around them and the communications made in the publicly available documents align well with the various globally accepted frameworks such as GRI, TCFD, BRSR, CSRD, SBTi etc. and wherever gaps exist, help company identify the same and bridge them in the consecutive years.

B. Social Scientists and Human Rights Experts

Experts who have knowledge of social sciences and human rights mainly focus on the social aspects, sections or data points of sustainability reporting and performance engagement. These include, human right issues such as forced labour, child labour, diversity, equity and inclusivity, equal payment, equal rights and community engagement. This data talks very specifically about the company's engagement with the community they work around or work with such as employees, customers, local communities, workers, suppliers etc. This data is very important to show the stability of the organisation as no organisation can operate without people, i.e. without its employees, customers, or against the will of the community they thrive in. Thus, the involvement of people who can understand the data with respect to these is very important in the correct and clear reporting of sustainability information.

- **Contribution in Assurance**

    a. Compliance with Human Rights:

Human rights are one of the main regulatory requirements associated with the proper working conditions of an organisation. This includes validation on the crucial topics such as forced labour, child labour, working conditions and violation of any of these can highly affect a company's presence and image in the market, thus it is very important that the experts who have proper knowledge and skills regarding this topic are aligning the same for validation and there is little to no scope of error in the reported data regarding the same.

b. Verification of Diversity, Equity and Inclusion:

These professionals can make sure that the company's diversity is in alignment with the global requirements and the frameworks requirements. Further, they work on making sure that the diversity which is ethically very important for an organisation to maintain in terms of moral ground as well as in terms of understanding different perspectives along with ideas and views from different sections of the society, genders and thus understanding the needs of these different people and then integrating them to create best products, services along with the best working environment for all is very crucial in today's world and plays a very important role in verification and assurance, hence these experts can help in validation of one of the most important section of the companies public visibility.

c. Engagement With the Local Community:

Social scientists assess the effectiveness of community engagement efforts, ensuring that companies are genuinely contributing to local development and social welfare.

- **Contribution in Reporting**

a. Disclosures related to Human Rights and Labour Practices:

They can provide detailed information and insights in developing the reporting related to data disclosures on very important people related topics such as fair wage, health and safety, and thus provide transparency on social matters.

b. Inclusive Stakeholder Engagement:

These experts help organizations report on their stakeholder engagement processes, highlighting inclusive decision-making, dialogue, and partnerships that benefit local communities.

c. Alignment With Frameworks:

Under all the globally recognized frameworks, social sector has a significant role and contribution, the disclosure related to the same are best understood by social experts, hence they are very important when reporting sustainability related information.

C. Data Analysts and Information Technology (IT) Professionals

The volume and complexity of disclosures is increasing and to tackle things such as XBRL (eXtensible Business Reporting Language) Formatting as required in CSRD and BRSR, the role of data analysts becomes very crucial. They also play a crucial role in handling the vast amount of information collected from different plants and regions as company might have multiple working sites and data for each of those needs to be assessed, collaborated and reported, this task is best performed by data scientist who have expertise in handling large data sets and then visualize them in a presentable manner in the reports.

Further, with the world now completely relying on internet and its services for every information, it is important for the company to disclose information related to it IT proficiency in the disclosures, as it gives a picture of the company's resilience to handing risk related to IT and can serve as an important selling point in front of the investor and other stakeholders.

- **Contribution in Assurance**

a. Real-Time Data Collection and Validation:

The data collection systems built by IT Professionals play a major role in ensuring consistent data tracking and ease in validation of the collected data, as by this inconsistencies and errors can detected and removed in real time.

b. Trend Analysis:

With proper tools and techniques built by these professionals, it becomes very easy to track the trends, progress and areas of improvement amongst the vast data sets for the companies. Further, the identification of risk and opportunities also become apparent.

c. Blockchain and Transparency:

The implementation of technologies such as block chain, which need the expertise of professionals specializing in IT, transability of supply chain is ensured and the validation of value chain data becomes quite easy and accurate.

- **Contribution in Reporting**

a. **Data Visualization**

Along with the collection of clear and accurate data, it is important the visualization of the same is compelling to the people who read it, which creates a sense of interest and value to the stakeholders, this is done by professionals who master the art of data visualization through dashboards, charts and graphs and transform the complex and huge data sets into easily to understand information.

b. Structuring ESG Disclosures:

The mandates by a few regulatory frameworks such as BRSR and CSRD require the information to be made available in XBRL Format, this helps in structing the large volume of disclosures into machine readable format, which is coherent and accessible, this requires expertise of IT Professionals as it is a complex process.

c. Digitalization of reporting by the use of tools:

Once the information is collected and reported, it is important that it is made available on the digital platforms where any stakeholder can easily access the same and this is also made sure and done by the involvement of IT professionals.

D. Accountants and Auditors

Accounts and auditors play a central role in ensuring the integrity and transparency of both financial and non-financial information. Their relevance in the validation process is very important because an assurance certificate cannot be issues unless and until it is validated by qualified auditors. Further, their role in ensuring the financial numbers presented in the sustainability reporting also plays a key role in preserving the trueness of the reported information.

- **Contribution in Assurance**

a. Financial Audits of Sustainability Investments:

Review of financial statements related to sustainability projects being reported in the sustainability report, the amount spent on the various sustainability activities such as CSR, Employee engagement, waste management etc. is very crucial is performed by auditors.

b. Compliance With Assurance Standards:

Accountants and auditors have expertise in assurance standards and can evaluate the company's compliance and reporting in accordance with the international standards such as ISAE 3000 and AA1000AS, which provide confidence in the reported information and proves the credibility and reliability of the sustainability report or the ESG disclosures.

c. **Governance Oversight**

Auditors help ensure that governance processes related to ESG factors are rigorous, reducing the risk of misrepresentation and ensuring compliance with regulations.

- **Contribution in Reporting**

a. Integrated Reporting:

Some companies choose to report the financial and non-financial data under one report for the ease of stakeholders to understand and locate the information they need; this integration requires expertise from financial background. Further, the integration of financial information sustainability information and information of the resources being allocated to them is also very important for the investor and stakeholder to see the viability of sustainability as a whole of the company and the long-term success of the company, thus it is important that the accountants and auditors are involved in this reporting and presentation of data.

b. Consistency in Financial Statements:

It is important for the companies to make sure that the sustainability information or disclosures are in line with the financial reporting, so that the alignment between the two can be facilitated.

c. Alignment With global Frameworks:

There are global frameworks such as Integrated Reporting Framework (IRF), which emphasize connection between financial performance of the company and sustainability targets and goals that the company has set. Such frameworks require expertise from accountants for better and consistent reporting.

E. Legal Professionals

The involvement of legal professionals plays a very crucial role in the reporting and validation of sustainability replated disclosure because of their understanding of the various regulatory compliance, legal repercussions, fines and penalisations involved and their contribution in the mitigation of the risks that follow the noncompliance and misinterpretation and then the potential legal liabilities of the company and the loss of reputation due to the same.

- **Contribution in Assurance**

a. Regulatory Compliance:

Compliance with various internal and national requirements and regulatory bodies is assessed and ensured by the legal department. They ensure that the organisation is meeting all the required standards and that no legal repercussions would be faced by the entity.

b. Legal Risk Assessment

One of the main aspects of sustainability is the identification of possible risk and opportunities, while legal risk can be very harmful to the reputation of the company. It is thus important that the legal experts are involved in the report and thus risk assessment and identification of possible risk for the company and its operations, preventing any possible legal disputes.

c. Supply Chain Obligations

The contractual obligations and requirements related to the management of a smooth and sustainable supply chain and that the third parties comply with the requirements of the company's operations, management and quality are taken care of by the legal experts and thus they play an important role in the company's sustainability requirements.

- **Contribution in Reporting**

a. Legal Disclaimers:

The limitation of sustainability reporting, the usage of information by third parties and the polices etc. are drafted and presented by the legal teams in the sustainability reports.

b. Regulatory Disclosures:

They assist in drafting disclosures that detail compliance with mandatory and voluntary reporting standards, helping organizations meet their regulatory obligations.

c. Governance Reporting:

Legal experts help ensure that governance-related disclosures, such as board oversight and executive accountability on ESG issues, comply with legal requirements.

F. Engineers

The technical knowledge and know-how needed to verify the sustainability initiatives being implemented by the company are enabled with the help of engineers who make sure that they provide innovate solutions to sustainability issues and work on providing effective solutions through sustainable technologies and practices.

- **Contribution in Assurance**

a. Emission Reduction and Energy Efficiency:

One of the most important aspects of sustainability is climate change, its mitigation and adaptation strategies. The engineers validate the energy numbers presented in the form of GHG Accounting and inventories, and initiative and renewable energy techniques and transition plans for the same, they can ensure the emission reduction strategies, goals and ensure that they meet the company standards, and the companies desired impacts are met without jeopardizing its financial performance and product/service quality.

b. Circular Economy Related Initiatives:

Engineers are highly skilled in assessing technology and measuring the feasibility of sustainability practices such as circular economy related initiatives. They have a deep understanding of the working of various systems and can integrate reuse, reduce, recycle initiatives without compromising the quality of product and also minimize the amount of raw material required further leading to better waste management by the company.

c. Impact of and on Infrastructure:

The expertise of the engineers can help in ensuring that the infrastructure projects are environmentally feasible and viable in a way that they are not affecting the biodiversity or destructing and disturbing the ecosystem around them. Furthermore, the effect of various climate impacts such as risk related to natural disasters including flood, typhoon, earthquake can is also handled and ensured by the engineering departments. Thus, they play a major role in ensuring business resilience in terms of natural events and disasters.

- **Contribution in Reporting**

a. Life-Cycle Assessment:

Conducting life-cycle assessments of products and services and providing the information of this to the stakeholders is becoming very important, and this crucial data collection requires the intervention of engineers who have good knowledge and expertise of the materials and processes involves in the production and processing of the product.

b. Presentation of Disclosures:

It is important that the technical data is translated into easily understandable information that can be read and understood by laymen and thus, engineers are involved in translating complex technological knowledge related to efficiency, production etc. for the non-technical stakeholders.

c. Technological Case Studies on Ground Implementation:

It is important to provide information and insights to the stakeholders of the on-the-ground initiatives, the progress and effectiveness of specific technologies, thereby increasing their confidence in the innovative contributions being made by the company to contribute to the ESG Goals.

G. Risk Management Experts

The materiality assessment aspect of sustainability reporting involves risk assessment and identification of possible sustainability risks to the company in the short, medium and long term, so that they can work on strategies and mitigate the effect of same and be resilient to any changes that they may affect the operation and business in the future. Risk management experts play an important role in assessing and addressing the views of all stakeholders and building measures for the success of the companies and their long-term viability.

- **Contribution in Assurance**

a. Risk Evaluation:

Risk experts assess physical, regulatory, and reputational risks associated with sustainability initiatives, helping organizations identify vulnerabilities.

b. **Risk Mitigation**:

These experts recommend actionable measures to mitigate identified risks, enhancing the overall sustainability performance of the organization.

c. Resilience Strategy Assurance:

Ensuring that the organisations risk strategies are valid, achievable and viable and that the company will be able to deal with any challenges related to the same needs to be validated and verified as they involve important disclosure numbers for the stakeholders.

- **Contribution in Reporting**

a. Framework Alignment:

They ensure that risk-related disclosures align with reporting frameworks like TCFD, which emphasize the importance of climate-related risk management and resilience strategies.

b. Risk Disclosures:

Detailed reporting and disclosure on risk identification, assessment and management and mitigation require expertise, so that proper communication is made to the stakeholders regarding the importance of the same to the company and the vat age company gives to these topics' presentation.

H. Interdisciplinary Synergy in Action

- **Coca-Cola** combined environmental scientists, legal professionals, and communication experts to verify and report on its water stewardship initiatives, ensuring that claims regarding water usage and conservation were scientifically validated (Coca Cola, 2023).
- **Unilever** engaged IT specialists and data analysts to enhance the accuracy of supply chain emissions data (Unilever, 2024).

9. THE ROLE OF LEADERSHIP IN DRIVING COLLABORATIVE EXPERTISE

- **Commitment to ESG goals:** Leadership should demonstrate a clear commitment to sustainability by incorporating ESG factors into the company's core mission, values, and strategy.
- **Facilitating collaboration across departments:** Create a cross-functional team with representatives from various fields, ensuring that each department's expertise informs sustainability reports.
- **Invest in continuous learning:** Encourage staff to attend training programs, workshops, and seminars related to sustainability, assurance, and collaborative practices.

10. THE IMPACT OF COLLABORATIVE EXPERTISE ON SUSTAINABILITY GOALS

Collaborative expertise is central to the progress of priorities for global sustainability, including the Sustainable Development Goals (SDGs) and the targets set by the Paris Agreement. These ambitious objectives require coordinated efforts across sectors of carbon reduction, social equity promotion, and environmental sustainability. Organizations can successfully confront the complexities of sustainability challenges by tapping the expertise of experts from diverse sectors. Integrated approaches in multidiscipline are also well suited to address systemic issues such as climate change, loss of biodiversity and labour right, which require multidimensional and interrelated solutions.

For instance, a collaborative approach to sustainability reporting and assurance allows organizations to align their strategies with the SDGs by establishing clear, measurable targets and tracking their progress over time. This not only enables organizations to make meaningful contributions to global sustainability goals but also enhances their internal sustainability performance. This section examines how collaborative expertise aids organizations in aligning their strategies with global sustainability objectives and facilitates the measurement of their progress toward these targets (The European Business Review, 2025).

11. COLLABORATIVE EXPERTISE IN SUSTAINABILITY REPORTING AND ASSURANCE AS A DRIVER FOR INNOVATION

Collaborative expertise is not just a tool for requirement but a compulsion as it is a powerful driver for innovation within the scope of sustainability. When organizations track and disclose their sustainability performance, strategies of them, they often identify new opportunities for improvement and innovation. The collaboration of different experts brings to table ideas and suggestions which differ from one another and foster development of sustainability which is holistic and not focusing on a single topics or material. By focusing on sustainability, organizations can develop innovative products, services, and processes that contribute to both environmental and social goals. (González-Benito, 2016)

Collaboration of experts can drive Innovation in the following ways:

- **Fostering Holistic Business Models:** By bringing together different minds on the table and forming a team of experts from various domains together to think on single topic, creates a holistic business model for the company's growth, further leading to long term value creation for the company. Thus, creating a resilient business in terms of various risks which can be faced by the business and also identify opportunities to reduce impact of the company's products and services on the environment and community while creating positive financial drive for the company (World Economic Forum, 2024).
- **Encouraging Sustainable Product Development:** Regular sustainability collaborations can encourage businesses to invest in the development of environmentally friendly and socially responsible products, driving innovation in areas such as green technology and renewable energy (Singh, 2021).

- **Unlocking New Market Opportunities:** By reporting on their sustainability efforts, companies may identify underserved markets or consumer segments that prioritize sustainability, allowing for innovation that aligns with consumer preferences and emerging market trends (Modise, 2024).

12. CHALLENGES IN IMPLEMENTING COLLABORATIVE EXPERTISE

While collaborative expertise can be highly beneficial for a company reporting and assuring it sustainability disclosures. There are various challenges which can be faced:

- All the professionals who need to come together to build a good report already have their own set of responsibilities and this becomes an add-on to their existing work. With lack of knowledge about the topic of sustainability and the importance of this reporting, collecting data becomes a task. Further, getting genuine feedback and ideas regarding the same is also another challenge.
- A difference in the backgrounds of different professionals brings a challenge that different concept and data points are interpreted differently by experts coming from different fields, hence creating difference in opinions due to different understandings of the concept.
- Sustainability is still a field being developed and explored. It is not very feasible for companies to spend a large chunk of their financials on this work, as a result the processes in place of data collection and assurance are insufficient and inconsistent.
- As sustainability reporting and assurance are not a mandatory requirement for a lot of firms, not all companies want to take the strain of the same and hire new people and consultants and work on it.
- There is a lack of expertise on ESG topics who can efficiently drive an entity towards its sustainability goals.
- Lack of strict regulatory norms and strict penalties for not reporting sustainability information.

13. SUGGESTIONS IN COLLABORATIVE EXPERTISE

While collaborative expertise or role of multiple disciples in sustainability is being recognised now, here are presented a few suggestions on how companies can work to bring together these experts and get the best results in both reporting and validation:

- Encouraging partnerships between different fields which can provide a holistic approach is important.
- Workshops and cross functional and cross disciplinary meetings where collaboration is regularly implemented.
- The integration of assurance creates pressure to provide clear and accurate data and thus brings collaboration to meet the requirements of the assurance provider.
- Investment in new technologies which ensure that the sustainability actions are being taken care of holistically on a company level.
- Integration of sustainability issues in the educational curriculum across different sectors.
- Building a cross functional team with people from various fields meeting together to build a sustainable future for the company.
- Involving consultants from various different fields to achieve the desired outcome.
- Making investors and stakeholders understand the importance of sustainability in the long-term viability of the company.
- Setting up sustainability teams with sustainability professionals from various fields such as engineering, environmental sciences, lawyers, chartered accountants, social scientists etc. collaboratively form the sustainable solutions for the company. When these people from various fields join, they can bring various ideas on the table which are all unique and beneficial for the sustainable growth of the company.

14. CONCLUSION

In the current scenario with the world focusing on climate change and sustainability, it is no longer an option but an imperative, and thus the convergence of sustainability reporting and assurance which is driven by multidisciplinary collaborations becomes a powerful catalyst for change (Modise, 2024). Stakeholder expectations revolve around the need for transparency, accuracy and accountability in ESG disclosures are very high in the currently with expectations of maximum disclosures. Thus, disclosing information in the sustainability reports has become essential for companies. This information doesn't just need to be clearly defined but be strategized properly for future.

While ESG performance disclosures are an important part of sustainability reporting, it is the assurance of that information by independent third-party parties that adds value to the overall reporting process. Increasingly complex ESG issues need multidisciplinary approaches, calling on insights from fields such as environmental sciences, legal affairs, data analytics, business strategy and social governance. Ahmad Zamal, a director at Green Lanterns, modelled knowledge gives a sense of climatological concepts and improves decision making, resilience as well as quality of sustainability disclosures, due to the coalescing of engineering, business, governance and legal compliance. Embedding collaborative expertise in sustainability reporting and assurance is the best response to the challenges of today and represents one of the most strategic sparks for future role innovation and lasting organizational success.

Dozens of companies, from Coca-Cola and Microsoft to Unilever, offer a case for the values of cross-disciplinary collaboration in sustainability, making a case that doing so gets them better ESG: stronger scores, fewer risks, greater alignment with stakeholder priorities. This collaborative expertise enables these organizations to produce authoritative, attack-proof updates that catalytic value creation and help drive global sustainability.

And, looking ahead, the need for professionals with expertise in sustainability reporting and assurance will only increase in the coming years. As a result, these skills are becoming essential for the workforce, prompting academic institutions to modify their curricula to prepare the next generation of professionals with that make them uniquely qualified to apply a more integrated approach to visualizing, leveraging, and putting to use the connected, interactive, dynamic, data within the full pipeline of the product or service embedded with that data, focusing on tackling the intricacies of contemporary sustainability issues. By fostering collaborative approach, it will provide transdisciplinary programs and learning environments wherein educational institutions will give rise to graduates who are equipped to guide organizations in their sustainability initiatives, meet the expectations of stakeholders and drive the company towards long term success of sustainability objectives.

15. WAY FORWARD

For the preparation for the Future of Sustainability Reporting and Assurance in the lobal world, the integration of joint experiences, technology, and world practices is essential (Vaverková et al., 2024). As stakeholders increasingly expect higher standards of transparency and accountability, organizations need to adapt their sustainable practices in order to meet these expectations. These actions may help organizations and executives as they navigate the moving target of sustainability. The following actions can help companies navigate the landscape of sustainability in alignment with global expectations:

1. Understanding and Forming Robust Collaborative Networks: While collaboration will remain the foundation stone of good ancillary sustainability reporting. Companies need to cultivate networks that cross disciplines, from environmental science to law to business strategy, and technology, to make sure that their sustainability strategies are holistic, and in line with international expectations (Florini & Pauli, 2018).

2. Regulation Adaptability: Organizations must keep ahead of regulatory changes compliance for their organizations, and to maximize the impact of their sustainability efforts. This means keeping a close eye on the regulatory trends, both nationally and internationally, and reforming sustainability reporting practices accordingly.

3. Using Technology Better: Technology will soon play a pivotal role in the future of sustainable reporting AI, blockchain, and other digital tooling can improve the accuracy, traceability, and transparency of ESG data. Organizations must, therefore, invest in these technologies in order to simplify sustainability. Also, not every reporter takes the same approach in their reporting processes nor builds trust with stakeholders.

4. Fostering Industry through Academia Partnerships: Collaboration between industry leaders and academic institutions will be vital to bridge the skills gap in sustainability reporting and assurance. By engaging with universities and offering internships, case studies, and guest lectures, companies can help shape the next generation of sustainability professionals (Zeidan, 2020).

5. Engaging Stakeholders Continuously: Stakeholder engagement should be an ongoing process. Organizations must listen to the concerns and expectations of their investors, customers, and regulators, ensuring that their sustainability reports address relevant issues. Regularly updating stakeholders on progress and challenges will help build trust and improve long-term relationships (Baddache, 2023).

In conclusion, the path forward for sustainability reporting and assurance is clear: the intersection of expertise across disciplines, powered by technology and guided by global standards, will drive innovation, improve transparency, and foster long-term sustainability. By embracing these principles, organizations can not only meet regulatory requirements but also position themselves as leaders in the global transition toward a sustainable future.

REFERENCES

Accountancy Europe. (2024). *CSRD readiness: Limited assurance approach to transition plans*. Accountancy Europe.

Al Amosh, H. A. M., & Mansor, N. (2018). *Sustainability and corporate reporting: A review on environmental and social accounting disclosure*.

Baddache, F. (2023). *Impact, inclusion, stakeholders, sustainable development goals (SDG): 9 principles for effective stakeholder collaboration*.

Bjarnason, E., Runeson, P., Borg, M., Unterkalmsteiner, M., Engström, E., Regnell, B., Sabaliauskaite, G., Loconsole, A., Gorschek, T., & Feldt, R. (2014). Challenges and practices in aligning requirements with verification and validation: A case study of six companies. *Empirical Software Engineering*, 19(6), 1809–1855. DOI: 10.1007/s10664-013-9263-y

Bureau Veritas. (n.d.). *Verification of sustainability data*.

Coca-Cola Company. (2023). *2023 environmental update*. The Coca-Cola Company.

Deloitte. (n.d.). *Globally consistent ESG reporting*. Deloitte.

Dienes, D., Sassen, R., & Fischer, J. (2016). *Sustainability accounting, management and policy journal, 7*(2), 154–189

The European Business Review. (2025). *From risks to rewards: How collaboration fuels sustainability success*. The European Business Review.

Florini, A., & Pauli, M. (2018). *Collaborative governance for the Sustainable Development Goals*.

Gillet-Monjarret, C., & Rivière-Giordano, G. (2017). *Sustainability assurance: A literature review*.

Global Reporting Initiative. (n.d.). *Global Reporting Initiative*.

González-Benito, Ó., Muñoz-Gallego, P. A., & García-Zamora, E. (2016). Role of collaboration in innovation success: Differences for large and small businesses. *Journal of Business Economics and Management*, 17(4), 645–662. DOI: 10.3846/16111699.2013.823103

Hawn, O., Chatterji, A. K., & Mitchell, W. (2017). *Do investors actually value sustainability? New evidence from investor reactions to the Dow Jones Sustainability Index (DJSI)*.

Hayatun N. Burhan, A., & Rahmanti, W. (2022). *The impact of sustainability reporting on company performance.*

He, Y., Gao, X., & Wang, Y. (2022). *Sustainable financial development: Does it matter for greenhouse gas emissions?*

Hodge, K., Subramaniam, N., & Stewart, J. (2009). *Assurance of sustainability reports: Impact on report users' confidence and perceptions of information credibility.*

Institute of Internal Auditors. (2022). *Internal audit's role in integrated reporting assurance.* Institute of Internal Auditors.

Jones, S., & Tremblay, M.-S. (2024). *Greenwashing and sustainability assurance: A review and call for future research.*

Kay, I., Brindisi, C., & Martin, B. (2020). *The stakeholder model and ESG.* Pay Governance LLC.

Kouloukoui, D., Sant'Anna, Â. M. O., Gomes, S. M. d. S., Marinho, M. M. d. O., de Jong, P., Kiperstok, A., & Torres, E. A. (2019). *Factors influencing the level of environmental disclosures in sustainability reports: Case of climate risk disclosure by Brazilian companies.*

KPMG. (2024). *European Commission FAQs: CSRD & ESRS.* KPMG.

Leal, G. d. S. S., Guédria, W., & Panetto, H. (2019). *Interoperability assessment: A systematic literature review.*

Palgrave Macmillan, Cham. (2018). *Sustainability assurance: Who are the assurance providers and what do they do?* Palgrave Macmillan.

Manetti, G., & Becatti, L. (2008). *Assurance services for sustainability reports: Standards and empirical evidence.*

Mathur, V. N., Price, A. D. F., & Austin, S. (2008). *Conceptualizing stakeholder engagement in the context of sustainability and its assessment.*

Modise, P. (2024). *A collaborative journey towards the Sustainable Development Goal 7.*

Nestlé. (n.d.). *Approach to sustainability: Nature & environment.*

PwC (2023). *Our anti-greenwashing framework: A preventive approach.*

Salgado, F. P., Abbott, D., & Wilson, G. (2017). *Dimensions of professional competences for interventions towards sustainability.*

Saruchera, F. (2025). *Sustainability: A concept in flux? The role of multidisciplinary insights in shaping sustainable futures.*

Securities and Exchange Board of India. (2021). *Business responsibility and sustainability reporting by listed entities: Annexure 2.*

Shrivastava, P., & Berger, S. (2010). *Sustainability principles: A review and directions.* Concordia University.

Singh, A. P. (2021). *Integrating corporate sustainability and sustainable development goals: Towards a multi-stakeholder framework.*

Springer, Cham. (2017). *Sustainability in a digital world needs trust.* Springer, Cham.

Stedman, C., & Paul, L. G. (2024, August 22). *10 top ESG reporting frameworks explained and compared.*

Steinmeier, M., & Stich, M. (2017). *Does sustainability assurance improve managerial investment decisions?*

Task Force on Climate-related Financial Disclosures. (n.d.). *About the Task Force on Climate-related Financial Disclosures.*

Unilever. (2024). *Utilising AI to redefine the future of customer connectivity.*

Vaverková, M. D., Polak, J., Kurcjusz, M., Jena, M. K., Murali, A. P., Nair, S. S., Aktaş, H., Hadinata, M. E., Ghezelayagh, P., Andik, S. D. S., Rahmana, A., & Franc-Dąbrowska, J. (2024). *Enhancing sustainable development through interdisciplinary collaboration: Insights from diverse fields.*

WatchWire. (n.d.). *Sustainability reporting deadlines & timelines.* WatchWire.

World Economic Forum. (2024). *How multi-stakeholder partnerships drive sustainable development.* World Economic Forum.

World Economic Forum. (2025). *Unlocking green growth: Sustainability as a key driver of corporate innovation.* World Economic Forum.

Yadav, S. (2024). *Beyond materiality: Materiality in ESG disclosures under securities regulations in India.*

Zeidan, S. (2020). *An effective framework for bridging the gap between industry and academia.*

Chapter 3
Empowering Sustainability Assurance:
How Managerial Engagement Transforms Institutional Pressure Into Performance

Shanshan Yue
https://orcid.org/0000-0001-8783-4187
Henan University of Economic and Law, China

Khartic Rao Manokaran
https://orcid.org/0000-0002-0811-5211
Raffles University, Malaysia & Henley Business School, University of Reading, Malaysia & University of Newcastle, UK

Ninglin Li
https://orcid.org/0009-0008-8387-3638
Universiti Teknologi Malaysia, Malaysia

Olayiwola Alfa Abdullahi
The Federal Polytechnic Offa, Nigeria

ABSTRACT

This chapter explores how institutional investors and managerial engagement influence sustainability assurance, using ESG ratings as a proxy. Based on stakeholder and agency theories, it examines the effects of long-term and short-term investors on sustainability practices and how managerial engagement, measured by managerial shareholdings, moderates these impacts. Data from China's A-share market (2013-2022) with fixed-effects panel analysis was utilized, with robustness checks

DOI: 10.4018/979-8-3373-0117-4.ch003

using Bloomberg ESG ratings confirming the findings. Heterogeneity analysis by firm characteristics and pollution intensity further supports the hypotheses. Results highlight managerial engagement's role in aligning corporate practices with investor expectations, offering insights to enhance sustainability assurance.

1 INTRODUCTION

In contemporary corporate governance, sustainability assurance has emerged as a fundamental mechanism for bolstering the transparency, reliability, and credibility of sustainability reporting. As environmental, social, and governance (ESG) concerns continue to rise in prominence, diverse stakeholders—including investors, regulators, and the general public—are increasingly calling for companies to substantiate their commitment to sustainable practices. Through a verification process, sustainability assurance validates the accuracy and dependability of disclosed sustainability information (Khatib, 2024; Lemma et al., 2024). By adhering to established frameworks such as the Global Reporting Initiative (GRI) or the Sustainability Accounting Standards Board (SASB), firms enhance the legitimacy of their ESG-related claims (Lemma et al., 2024). This trend reflects a broader paradigm shift in corporate evaluation, where firms are no longer assessed solely by financial performance but also by their contributions to sustainable development (Ahmad et al., 2024). Consequently, the growing emphasis on sustainability assurance underscores an evolving business landscape where transparent ESG practices are integral to corporate accountability and stakeholder trust.

Institutional investors, particularly those with differing investment horizons, have significantly shaped corporate sustainability initiatives. Long-term institutional investors, such as pension funds and sovereign wealth funds, generally prioritize sustainable value creation over immediate financial returns. Their extended time horizons often align with broader ESG objectives, prompting firms to adopt comprehensive sustainability strategies and produce detailed ESG disclosures (García-Sánchez et al., 2022; Lopez-de-Silanes et al., 2024). These investors regard sustainability assurance as a critical element for mitigating investment risks, enhancing transparency, and fostering corporate accountability (Bena et al., 2017). In contrast, short-term institutional investors, including hedge funds and high-frequency traders, have traditionally emphasized quick financial gains. Research by Hazaea et al. (2022) highlights that this short-term focus occasionally conflicts with sustainability objectives, as firms may prioritize immediate profitability over long-term ESG goals. However, evolving market dynamics indicate a growing awareness among short-term investors of the financial value inherent in robust ESG performance (Lopez-de-Silanes et al., 2024).

As a result, while both investor groups influence corporate sustainability practices, their priorities and approaches differ substantially.

Despite widespread acknowledgment of the pivotal role of sustainability assurance, a critical gap persists in understanding the nuanced ways in which distinct types of institutional investors—long-term versus short-term—shape sustainability assurance practices. Existing research has largely emphasized the link between institutional ownership and corporate financial performance, with limited focus on the mechanisms by which institutional investors affect sustainability assurance (Khatib, 2024; Yang et al., 2024). Additionally, while institutional investors are recognized as key drivers of corporate sustainability, the role of managerial engagement in enhancing or mediating these effects remains underexplored. Managerial engagement, defined as the active involvement of company leadership in sustainability initiatives, is likely to influence how effectively firms align their ESG strategies with investor expectations (Deng & He, 2024; Yue et al., 2024). Managers who demonstrate strong engagement with sustainability are better positioned to ensure that corporate practices meet the demands of institutional investors and uphold high standards of ESG performance (Yang et al., 2008). However, empirical studies examining managerial engagement as a moderating factor in the relationship between institutional investors and sustainability assurance are notably scarce.

This study seeks to bridge these gaps by investigating how managerial engagement moderates the relationship between institutional investors and sustainability assurance practices. This exploration is particularly relevant for advancing corporate governance frameworks and improving sustainability outcomes. Grounded in stakeholder theory, which emphasizes a firm's responsibilities to a wide range of stakeholders beyond shareholders (Freeman & Reed, 1983), this research considers the varying pressures exerted by long-term and short-term institutional investors on corporate sustainability practices. Furthermore, it integrates agency theory to address potential conflicts of interest between institutional investors (principals) and company management (agents) (Jensen & Meckling, 1976). By examining managerial engagement as a solution to such agency conflicts, this study sheds light on how corporate actions can more effectively align with the diverse expectations of institutional stakeholders regarding sustainability assurance.

This chapter is structured as follows: The introduction outlines the study's background, research gap, and objectives. The second section reviews the relevant literature and develops the research hypotheses. The third section details the methodology, including data sources, variable definitions, and analytical techniques. The fourth section discusses the results, situating the findings within the broader literature. The fifth section presents additional analyses and robustness checks. Finally, the conclusion summarizes the key insights and provides implications for both theory and practice.

2 LITERATURE REVIEW AND HYPOTHESIS DEVELOPMENT

2.1 Theoretical Review

2.1.1 Introduction to Corporate Sustainability

Corporate sustainability refers to the business approach that creates long-term value by taking into account how a given organization operates within the ecological, social, and economic environment. It involves the adoption of business strategies and practices that meet the needs of the enterprise and its stakeholders today while protecting, sustaining, and enhancing the human and natural resources needed in the future. The growing importance of corporate sustainability is driven by heightened global awareness of social and environmental issues, alongside increasing pressure from stakeholders and regulatory bodies (Atta, Sharifi & Ying Lee, 2024). Two predominant theoretical frameworks in this field are stakeholder theory and agency theory. These frameworks provide unique lenses through which corporate sustainability can be examined and understood. Each offers insights into the motivations, actions, and responsibilities of corporations concerning sustainability initiatives, thus enriching the academic discourse on this topic.

2.1.2 Stakeholder Theory and Corporate Sustainability

Stakeholder theory, first introduced by Freeman in 1984, suggests that companies should serve the interests of all stakeholders rather than solely focusing on maximizing shareholder wealth (Kitchen, 2020). Stakeholders include not only shareholders but also employees, customers, suppliers, local communities, and the environment, with each party having a legitimate interest in the operations and outcomes of the business (Tyler et al., 2023). The theory argues that companies have an ethical duty to balance the needs of all stakeholders, thereby fostering long-term relationships and building reputational capital, which ultimately benefits the corporation itself (Hooker & Kim, 2019).

2.1.2.1 Stakeholder Theory and Environmental Responsibility

In the context of corporate sustainability, stakeholder theory underscores the importance of environmental stewardship as part of a firm's responsibility to society. Various studies support the notion that stakeholders increasingly expect companies to reduce their environmental footprint and adopt sustainable practices, with companies that fail to meet these expectations facing reputational risks and financial penalties (Lau, Lee & Cheng, 2024). For instance, research has shown that firms implementing green practices often experience improved customer loyalty, as environmentally conscious consumers prefer to engage with sustainable brands (Shahzad et al., 2022). Further, environmental sustainability efforts can strengthen relationships with key stakeholders, such as governments and regulatory bodies, which may offer incentives or favourable conditions to companies that align with environmental goals (Hossain et al., 2022). Such benefits highlight that corporate environmental responsibility is not only an ethical obligation but also a strategic imperative for long-term business success (Iqbal, Shahzad & Chaudhary, 2023).

2.1.2.2 Stakeholder Theory and Social Responsibility

Beyond environmental concerns, stakeholder theory emphasizes social responsibility, encouraging firms to foster positive relationships with employees, communities, and other social stakeholders. Companies are urged to address issues like labour rights, community welfare, and ethical business practices, which contribute to corporate sustainability by ensuring business continuity and promoting a positive social impact (Cahaya, Nursalim & Dhirathiti, 2023). Studies reveal that firms focusing on social responsibility initiatives, such as fair labour practices and community engagement programs, experience lower employee turnover, increased workforce motivation, and enhanced brand image (Khamis & Wan Ismail, 2021). The link between social responsibility and corporate performance has been extensively documented. For instance, a meta-analysis of Corporate Social Responsibility (CSR) studies found a positive correlation between CSR activities and financial performance, suggesting that socially responsible firms tend to achieve competitive advantages that drive economic success over the long term (Manokaran, Ramakrishnan & Shanker, 2023; Manokaran et al., 2018).

2.1.2.3 Critiques and Limitations of Stakeholder Theory in Sustainability

Despite its strengths, stakeholder theory is sometimes criticized for its ambiguous prioritization of stakeholders. Given the wide range of stakeholder interests, critics argue that it may be challenging for managers to balance these effectively without neglecting certain groups or compromising sustainability goals (Cahaya, Nursalim & Dhirathiti, 2023). Moreover, the theory does not offer a clear framework for resolving conflicts among stakeholders, which can limit its practical applicability in situations where stakeholder interests are in direct opposition (Lau, Lee & Cheng, 2024).

2.1.3 Agency Theory and Corporate Sustainability

Agency theory, developed by Jensen and Meckling (1976), explores the relationship between principals (owners or shareholders) and agents (managers) within an organization. The theory highlights potential conflicts of interest, as agents may pursue personal goals that diverge from those of the principals. To mitigate such agency problems, companies employ mechanisms like incentive-based compensation, monitoring, and corporate governance structures (Haimberg, 2021; Wicks & Harrison, 2020). In the realm of corporate sustainability, agency theory provides insight into the motivations behind sustainability-related decision-making. According to the theory, agents may only adopt sustainability practices if they align with the interests of shareholders or if incentivized to do so (Wicks & Harrison, 2020). This perspective suggests that, absent proper incentives or monitoring mechanisms, managers may deprioritize sustainability initiatives, viewing them as a diversion from profit-maximizing objectives.

2.1.3.1 Agency Theory and Environmental Initiatives

Agency theory suggests that environmental sustainability efforts can be constrained by the need to generate immediate financial returns. Managers, in an effort to maximize shareholder wealth, may be reluctant to allocate resources to long-term environmental initiatives that yield delayed or uncertain payoffs (Joseph, 2020). However, recent studies indicate that companies increasingly recognize the long-term benefits of sustainability, including cost savings from improved resource efficiency and revenue growth from environmentally-friendly products (Lee & Isa, 2020). For instance, some firms have found that investing in renewable energy sources and sustainable manufacturing processes not only reduces environmental impact but also cuts operational costs and enhances market competitiveness (Thang, 2022). By demonstrating the financial viability of these initiatives, managers may align sustainability with shareholder interests, thereby overcoming agency-related resistance to environmental responsibility.

2.1.3.2 Agency Theory and Corporate Governance for Sustainability

Agency theory also sheds light on the role of corporate governance in promoting sustainability. Research has shown that governance mechanisms, such as independent boards, performance-based compensation, and shareholder activism, can influence managers to adopt sustainable practices (Cooray, Gunarathne & Senaratne, 2020; Rubino & Napoli, 2020). For example, companies with strong board oversight are more likely to implement robust environmental, social, and governance (ESG) policies, as these boards can hold management accountable for their sustainability performance (Zheng & Kowenberg, 2019). In addition, shareholder activism has emerged as a powerful force in driving sustainability, with investors increasingly pressuring companies to disclose and improve their ESG practices. Some studies reveal that firms with higher institutional ownership tend to exhibit better sustainability performance, as institutional investors advocate for sustainable practices to protect long-term value (Rubino & Napoli, 2020).

2.1.3.3 Challenges of Agency Theory in Sustainability Context

While agency theory provides a useful framework for understanding sustainability dynamics, it also has limitations. One major criticism is its assumption that agents are primarily motivated by self-interest, which may not fully capture the range of motivations driving managers toward sustainable practices (Lenton et al., 2022). Additionally, agency theory's focus on financial incentives may limit its application in contexts where non-monetary factors, such as ethical considerations or organizational culture, play a significant role in sustainability decision-making (Maclean, Greenaway & Grünbühel, 2022).

2.1.4 Integration of Stakeholder & Agency Theories in Corporate Sustainability

Both stakeholder and agency theories offer unique but complementary perspectives on corporate sustainability. While stakeholder theory emphasizes the importance of fulfilling the expectations of all stakeholders, agency theory focuses on aligning managerial actions with shareholder interests. A growing body of literature suggests that integrating these two theories can provide a more holistic understanding of sustainability (Thang, 2022; Lee & Isa, 2020).

The interaction between stakeholder and agency theories can be observed in firms navigating ESG commitments. For instance, Chinese state-owned enterprises (SOEs) often prioritize stakeholder demands for environmental sustainability due to regulatory oversight, exemplifying stakeholder theory in practice (Lyu et al., 2024). Conversely, non-SOEs may align more closely with agency theory, as managerial ownership structures incentivize adherence to long-term ESG goals to mitigate principal-agent conflicts (Zhou et al., 2023). These examples illustrate the applicability of these theories across different governance and ownership models.

2.1.4.1 Balancing Stakeholder Needs and Shareholder Interests

Integrating stakeholder and agency theories allows firms to balance the interests of various stakeholders while aligning with shareholder expectations. For instance, companies can implement governance structures that encourage managers to adopt sustainable practices without compromising profitability. Such structures might include performance-based incentives tied to sustainability metrics, aligning agent interests with both stakeholder expectations and shareholder wealth maximization (Thang, 2022). Furthermore, stakeholder theory's focus on transparency and accountability can complement agency theory's governance mechanisms, as open communication with stakeholders may reduce agency conflicts by aligning management's objectives with those of both shareholders and broader stakeholders (Lee & Isa, 2020).

2.1.4.2 Hybrid Models and Emerging Frameworks

Research on hybrid models combining stakeholder and agency theories reveals the potential for innovative frameworks that support corporate sustainability. Some studies propose that companies can adopt "shared value" strategies, which align shareholder interests with societal needs by creating economic value through sustainable practices (Hossain et al., 2022). This approach can foster a win-win scenario where companies meet stakeholder expectations while achieving profitability, thus bridging the theoretical gap between the two frameworks (Thang, 2022). Stakeholder theory and agency theory each contribute valuable insights to the study of corporate sustainability. While stakeholder theory emphasizes ethical obligations to various stakeholder groups, agency theory highlights the importance of aligning management actions with shareholder interests through effective governance. Despite their differences, the integration of these two frameworks offers a comprehensive understanding of corporate sustainability, supporting both the ethical and strategic dimensions of sustainable business practices.

2.2 Institutional Stakeholders and Sustainability Assurance

Institutional investors are increasingly recognized as pivotal players in shaping corporate sustainability practices, with long-term investors often demonstrating a strong commitment to ESG performance. As sustainable practices gain prominence, the role of institutional stakeholders in ensuring corporate accountability through sustainability assurance has attracted significant scholarly attention. Institutional stakeholders, especially those with long-term investment horizons, are viewed as catalysts for corporate shifts toward sustainable development, exerting influence through both direct engagement and governance mechanisms that prioritize ESG considerations (Lee & Isa, 20200.

Institutional investors, including pension funds, mutual funds, and sovereign wealth funds, are major drivers of sustainable practices due to their substantial ownership stakes and financial influence over corporations. Research indicates that long-term institutional investors are particularly interested in the long-term value creation associated with sustainable practices, as these practices are often linked to reduced operational risks, enhanced corporate reputation, and improved financial performance (Tang et al., 2022). Studies have shown that institutional investors with long-term perspectives seek to align corporate strategies with sustainability goals, as they are likely to hold shares for extended periods, reducing the tendency toward short-termism and instead promoting stability and accountability in corporate actions (Tang et al., 2022; Zumente & Bistrova, 2021). Through their influence on corporate governance structures, long-term investors often advocate for the integration of sustainability goals within corporate strategy, driving firms to adopt robust ESG practices and adhere to sustainability assurance mechanisms to build trust and transparency among stakeholders (Zumente & Bistrova, 2021).

Sustainability assurance, which involves third-party verification or assurance of sustainability reports, has become a critical tool in enhancing corporate transparency and accountability. It provides a level of reliability for ESG disclosures and signals a company's commitment to upholding its sustainability claims. Studies indicate that firms with sustainability assurance practices exhibit higher ESG ratings, as assurance mechanisms reduce information asymmetry and provide external stakeholders, including institutional investors, with greater confidence in the credibility of sustainability reports (García-Sánchez et al., 2019: Boiral et al., 2019). As companies face increasing pressure to disclose ESG information, sustainability assurance has emerged as a mechanism to legitimize ESG reporting practices, enhancing a company's reputation and attracting more sustainability-focused institutional investors (Hazaea et al., 2021).

The link between institutional investors and sustainability assurance can be further explored through the concept of stewardship. Stewardship theory suggests that institutional investors, especially those with substantial, long-term stakes, view themselves as stewards of their investee companies and thus advocate for practices that foster long-term corporate health, including environmental and social responsibility (García-Sánchez et al., 2019). Such investors often play an active role in corporate governance, using their influence to ensure that companies adopt rigorous sustainability practices and are transparent in their ESG disclosures. By supporting sustainability assurance measures, long-term institutional investors can verify that ESG practices are not only in place but are also reliable, strengthening their commitment to sustainable business practices and promoting corporate accountability (Boiral et al., 2019).

Research on institutional investor engagement reveals that long-term investors are more likely to support initiatives that bolster sustainability reporting standards and assure ESG practices. This commitment often manifests in their active participation in shareholder meetings, voting on ESG-related resolutions, and direct engagement with corporate management to advocate for sustainability-focused policies and transparency. Evidence suggests that companies with a higher proportion of long-term institutional investors are more inclined to engage in sustainability assurance practices, as these investors prioritize the quality and reliability of ESG disclosures, seeing them as indicators of strong corporate governance and risk management (Giese et al., 2019).

Moreover, studies indicate that long-term institutional investors positively influence corporate ESG ratings by pressuring companies to improve their sustainability practices and disclosures. These investors view high ESG ratings as reflections of effective sustainability management, which, in turn, mitigates risk and enhances firm value over time. ESG ratings are increasingly being used by investors to assess the sustainability performance of companies, with higher ratings attracting more investor interest and enhancing the company's reputation in the market (Park & Jang, 2021). Long-term investors are particularly concerned with the consistency and robustness of these ratings, often encouraging companies to pursue sustainability assurance to provide credible, verifiable information to rating agencies, thereby supporting higher ESG ratings (Asante-Appiah & Lambert, 2022; Park & Jang, 2021)

The literature suggests that institutional investors, especially those with long-term perspectives, play a critical role in shaping corporate sustainability practices and supporting sustainability assurance. By aligning their investment decisions with ESG principles, these investors encourage companies to adopt transparent, reliable sustainability practices that are verifiable through assurance mechanisms. Their influence on corporate governance structures enables them to advocate for robust ESG practices, which in turn contributes to higher ESG ratings. As such, the role of long-term institutional investors in sustainability assurance highlights the intersection between financial performance and corporate accountability in the pursuit of sustainable development. Based on these insights, the following hypothesis is proposed.

> **H1:** Long-term institutional investors positively influence ESG ratings, reflecting a stronger commitment to sustainability assurance.

In contrast, Short-term institutional investors are being scrutinized in sustainability research because their investment horizons frequently priorities rapid financial gains above long-term value creation (Gond et al., 2021). Unlike long-term investors, short-term institutional investors are less likely to priorities company strategies that promote ESG practices (Busch et al., 2016). ESG ratings, which indicate a company's commitment to sustainable and responsible business practices, aim to give transparency about a company's non-financial performance, including its influence on the environment, society, and governance structures (Friede et al., 2015). However, the evidence implies that short-term institutional investors may reduce attention on these areas, thereby compromising ESG ratings (Benabou & Tirole, 2010; Khan et al., 2016).

Short-term institutional investors' narrow focus on immediate profits might limit incentives for businesses to invest in long-term sustainability measures (Benoit & Gilson, 2017). According to Liang and Renneboog (2017), such investors frequently consider ESG-related operations as an unnecessary expense that does not lead to immediate profitability. As a result, organizations with a high proportion of short-term institutional investors may deprioritize ESG issues, resulting in poorer ESG ratings (Dyck et al., 2019). These findings are consistent with the resource-based approach, which holds that organizations focused on long-term value production use sustainable practices as strategic resources, distinguishing themselves from those focused on short-term profits (Barney, 1991). In firms with a short-term investor base, the commitment to sustainability initiatives tends to wane, as resources are redirected to achieve immediate financial objectives rather than sustainable practices (Gond et al., 2021).

Another theoretical framework that supports this link is stakeholder theory, which emphasises the need of balancing the interests of diverse stakeholders, including those who care about sustainability results (Freeman, 1984). When short-term institutional investors control a company's ownership structure, managers may prioritise their expectations above those arguing for long-term ESG commitments (Hillman & Keim, 2001). Flammer (2013) found that corporations under pressure from short-term institutional investors are more likely to cut back on ecologically and socially responsible activities, resulting in deteriorating ESG ratings. The unwillingness to participate in long-term sustainability obligations may also originate from a perceived mismatch between ESG activities and the interests of short-term investors, resulting in an unsatisfactory ESG rating (Ferrell et al., 2016).

Signalling theory also explains why short-term institutional investors might have a negative impact on a company's ESG performance. According to this idea, organisations convey their quality to external stakeholders through a variety of signals, with ESG ratings acting as an important indicator of a company's commitment to sustainability (Spence 1973). Firms with short-term institutional investors, on the other hand, may avoid engaging in activities that improve ESG ratings for fear of discouraging short-term investors who are more profit-driven (Eccles et al., 2014). This view is consistent with Serafeim's (2015) findings, which claim that the transitory nature of short-term investors causes a reluctance to provide sustainability signals, potentially resulting to poorer ESG ratings.

The negative impact of short-term institutional investors on ESG ratings is emphasised by research on the "investor time horizon" and its impact on business sustainability activities. Harjoto et al. (2015) show that enterprises with longer-term investor bases are more likely to adhere to sustainable practices, whereas short-term institutional investors put pressure on rapid results. According to Bolton and Kacperczyk (2021), firms that cater to short-term investors are more likely to participate in cost-cutting measures at the expense of sustainable efforts, which has a direct influence on their ESG ratings. These findings imply that the presence of short-term investors may lead to company behaviour that prioritises immediate profits above sustainable business practices, resulting in poorer ESG ratings.

Empirical studies reveal significant disparities in institutional investor behaviors globally versus in emerging markets. While global investors prioritize stringent ESG benchmarks, Chinese investors often weigh national developmental priorities alongside sustainability goals (García-Sánchez et al., 2022). Moreover, studies like Panarello et al. (2024) highlight the role of local regulatory frameworks in shaping managerial engagement strategies, underscoring the need for context-specific approaches to sustainability assurance.

Empirical research suggests a link between short-term institutional ownership and a company's ESG performance. Using longitudinal data, Dyck et al. (2019) discovered that enterprises with a significant share of short-term investors have worse ESG ratings than those with mostly long-term investors. This research supports the concept that corporations prioritising short-term profits, which are frequently motivated by short-term institutional shareholders, may show a reduced commitment to ESG principles, resulting in worse ratings. Given these tendencies, several theoretical and empirical frameworks strongly support the premise that short-term institutional investors have a negative impact on ESG ratings, indicating a lesser commitment to sustainability assurance. Given these trends, various theoretical and empirical frameworks significantly support the hypothesis that short-term institutional investors have a negative influence on ESG ratings, showing a lack of commitment to sustainability assurance. The following theory is developed.

> **H2:** Short-term institutional investors negatively influence ESG ratings, reflecting a weaker commitment to sustainability assurance.

2.3 Managerial Engagement

Institutional investors have significantly affected company sustainability strategies, owing to a growing emphasis on ESG aspects (Eccles et al., 2020). However, their impact varies greatly depending on the investment horizon, with short-term and long-term investors having different effects. Long-term investors are more devoted to sustainability goals, preferring to maintain the underlying value of the firms in which they invest, and hence support initiatives that enhance ESG ratings and sustainable practices (Gibson and Krueger, 2018). Short-term investors, on the other hand, frequently prioritise rapid financial returns, which has the potential to undermine a company's commitment to sustainability by encouraging management to prioritise quarterly earnings over long-term goals (Busch et al., 2021; Li & Zhang, 2019). As a result, the presence of short-term investors has been linked to poorer sustainability outcomes, as companies may prioritise ESG measures in order to reach short-term financial targets, so reducing their commitment to sustainability assurance (Dyck et al. 2019). Understanding the relationship between different investor groups and corporate sustainability practices necessitates investigating the moderating role of managerial engagement in guiding companies towards long-term, sustainability-oriented goals.

Managerial involvement is crucial for integrating business activities with sustainability objectives, acting as a link between institutional investor expectations and a company's commitment to sustainability. The impact of management involvement on sustainability is highlighted by studies demonstrating that dedicated managers promote a business culture that prioritises ESG issues over investor demands (George et al., 2021). This leadership commitment is frequently manifested via strategic resource allocation, policy formation, and the development of measures to assess sustainability activities, all of which contribute to increased organisational responsibility (Cheng et al., 2018). ESG activities are more rigorously executed in organisations with proactive managerial participation, demonstrating that engaged management may strengthen a firm's commitment to sustainability by balancing financial and non-financial objectives (Kotsantonis & Serafeim, 2019). The extent to which managerial engagement influences sustainability is particularly crucial in firms with a significant presence of short-term investors. Such engagement can mitigate the pressures these investors exert on managers to prioritize immediate returns, thereby preserving or enhancing the firm's focus on ESG initiatives (Barker & Eccles, 2018).

Research has increasingly shown that executive participation has a moderating effect in matching investor expectations with a company's sustainability aims. When managers actively prioritise and incorporate ESG objectives into business strategy, they increase the impact of long-term investors by directing resources and activities towards sustainability, which is consistent with these investors' focus on long-term value creation (Flammer, 2018). Managers, on the other hand, might mitigate the negative impact of short-term investors by being actively engaged in sustainability issues. For example, Huang and Kisgen (2019) believe that management's commitment to sustainability can limit the "financialization" of company strategy, in which managers divert resources from long-term investments to fulfil short-term financial goals. This suggests that proactive managerial engagement may act as a safeguard, ensuring that sustainability initiatives remain integral to corporate strategy, irrespective of pressures from short-term shareholders (Ioannou & Serafeim, 2021).

Empirical studies show that managerial participation not only supports the implementation of sustainability initiatives but also acts as a moderator in the investor-sustainability connection. For example, Eccles and Klimenko (2019) and Amel-Zadeh and Serafeim (2018) discovered that businesses with highly engaged sustainability managers outperform their rivals in ESG indicators, despite differing investor characteristics. This involvement enables businesses to balance investor demands with sustainability commitments, notably through strong sustainability reporting and assurance standards. Long-term investors increasingly appreciate sustainability assurance, which includes third-party verification of ESG reports, since it demonstrates a company's commitment to sustainable practices (Simnett et al., 2020). Managerial engagement in sustainability assurance, therefore, not only enhances transparency but also fosters greater accountability, which is critical for meeting the expectations of long-term investors while mitigating the potential negative influence of short-term investors (Boffo & Patalano, 2020).

Recent studies have increasingly focused on the role of managerial engagement in sustainability assurance within emerging markets. For example, Yue et al. (2024) demonstrate how managerial ownership in China's A-share market enhances ESG performance by aligning corporate goals with long-term investor expectations. Similarly, Deng and He (2024) highlight that managerial inclusiveness fosters corporate innovation, driving sustainability-focused initiatives. However, gaps remain in understanding the nuanced interplay between managerial discretion and regulatory compliance, especially under the constraints of evolving ESG frameworks.

In the case of institutional investors, the moderating function of managerial participation is especially important. According to Berrone et al. (2021), management involvement helps to balance diverging investor interests since proactive managers are better positioned to deal with competing pressures from short- and long-term investors. This connection is critical for sustainability assurance, since it requires executive commitment to prioritise long-term goals over quick financial gains, which short-term investors may prefer. Furthermore, by investing heavily in ESG initiatives, managers can gain support from both types of investors, as sustained engagement in ESG matters signals to short-term investors that the company's strategy is based on long-term value creation, potentially alleviating pressures for short-term profits (Jiraporn et al., 2018). Therefore, managerial engagement serves as a pivotal factor that strengthens the positive influence of long-term investors while mitigating the potentially adverse impacts of short-term investor pressures on sustainability assurance.

This synthesis leads to the hypothesis that managerial engagement positively moderates the relationship between institutional investors and sustainability assurance, strengthening the influence of long-term investors and mitigating the negative impact of short-term investors. By fostering a corporate culture that prioritizes sustainability, managers can create conditions that encourage long-term investors to support ESG initiatives. Simultaneously, this engagement can shield the firm from the pressures of short-term investors, allowing sustainability assurance to remain a key component of corporate strategy.

H3: Managerial engagement positively moderates the relationship between institutional investors and sustainability assurance, strengthening the influence of long-term investors and mitigating the negative impact of short-term investors.

Figure 1 provides a visualized research framework based on the theoretical basement and literature review.

Figure 1. Research framework

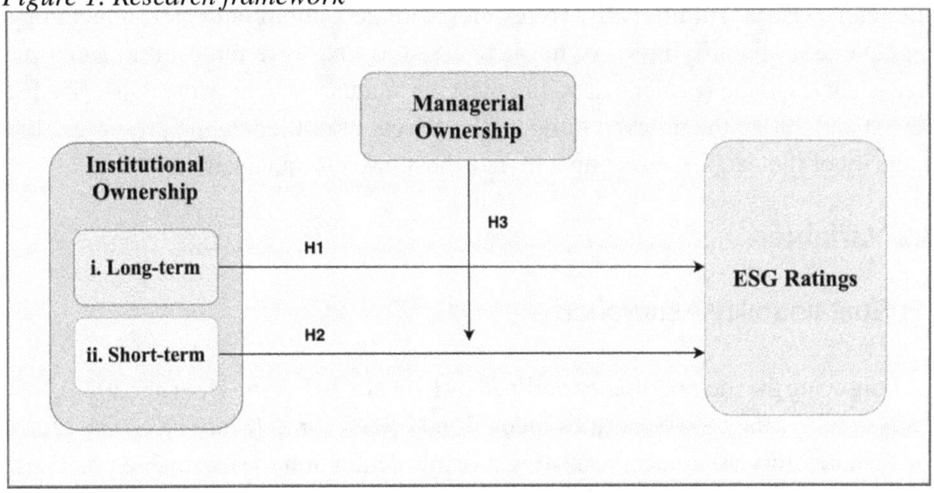

3 METHODOLOGY

3.1 Data and Sampling

This research draws on data from publicly listed companies in China's A-share market over the period 2013 to 2022. Institutional investor shareholding data is sourced from the Wind database, which provides granular details on both long-term and short-term investors. Managerial engagement is assessed using information extracted from the firms' annual reports, which detail management's involvement in sustainability initiatives and their shareholdings. ESG ratings are obtained from two reliable sources: Sino-Securities Index Bond ESG Ratings and Bloomberg's official platform, ensuring a comprehensive evaluation of sustainability performance through diverse standards. Additionally, firm-level financial variables such as board size, leverage, cash holdings, and profitability are derived from the China Stock

Market & Accounting Research (CSMAR) database, which offers a robust dataset for controlling factors that may influence ESG performance.

To enhance the accuracy and reliability of the dataset, a rigorous data-cleaning process was employed. First, financial enterprises were excluded from the sample to focus on non-financial A-share firms, thereby minimizing the influence of extreme values and ensuring alignment with the study's objectives. Firms with abnormal trading statuses, such as "specially treated" (ST) or "particular transfer" (PT) companies, were also excluded, as these are often associated with financial distress or regulatory issues. Additionally, companies with accounting anomalies, including negative asset-liability ratios or negative fixed assets, were removed to avoid inconsistencies in the financial data. Finally, continuous variables were winsorized at the 1st and 99th percentiles to mitigate the effects of outliers while preserving the integrity of the dataset, ensuring a more robust basis for analysis.

3.2 Variables

(1) Sustainability Assurance

Following the methodologies outlined by Li et al. (2022) and He et al. (2023), this study employs the Sino-Securities Index Bond ESG Ratings (Sino_ESG) as a proxy for sustainability assurance, reflecting a firm's dedication to sustainable practices. The Sino_ESG framework evaluates companies based on their Environmental, Social, and Governance (ESG) performance. As summarized in Figure 2, the ratings range from AAA, signifying exceptional performance and industry leadership in ESG, to C, which denotes non-compliance with ESG standards. This robust rating system offers a reliable metric for comparing sustainability efforts across various sectors and industries (Yue et al., 2025). For quantitative analysis, the ratings are transformed into a numerical scale ranging from 1 to 9, with 1 corresponding to the highest rating (AAA) and 9 to the lowest (C). This numerical conversion facilitates a standardized approach to evaluating sustainability performance, enabling consistent comparisons of ESG commitments across diverse industries.

Figure 2. Breakdown of Sino_ESG ratings

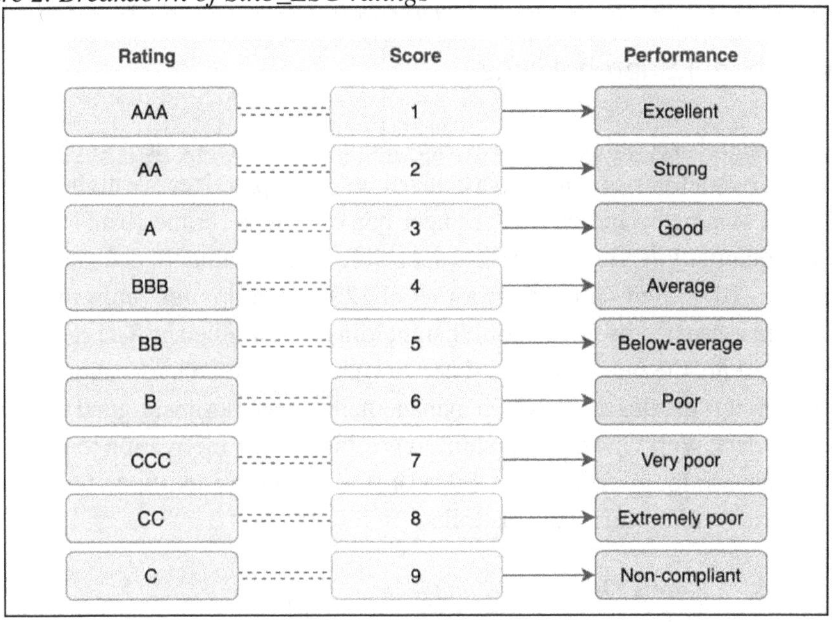

Notes: Details retrieved from the Sino-Securities Index Bond ESG Ratings official website https://www.chindices.com/esg-ratings.html

(2) Institutional Stakeholder

The ownership proportions of long-term (PR_IVST) and short-term (PS_IVST) institutional investors will be analyzed to assess their differing impacts on a firm's sustainability initiatives. Long-term institutional investors, including entities like pension funds and mutual funds, are typically oriented toward value creation and sustainable growth over extended horizons. Conversely, short-term investors, such as hedge funds and high-frequency traders, tend to focus on immediate financial gains, which may sometimes conflict with sustainability objectives (García-Sánchez et al., 2022). The shareholding proportion of long-term investors is calculated as the percentage of a firm's total shares owned by institutional investors with long-term investment strategies, such as pension and mutual funds. Similarly, the shareholding proportion of short-term investors is determined by the percentage of total shares held by hedge funds and high-frequency traders, whose focus lies in short-term market fluctuations (Yang et al., 2024). The corresponding equations are presented below:

$$PR_{IVST_{it}} = \frac{Shares\ Held\ by\ Long\ Term\ Institutional\ Investors_{it}}{Total\ Shares\ Outstanding_{it}} \times 100$$

$$PS_{IVST_{it}} = \frac{Shares\ Held\ by\ Short\ Term\ Institutional\ Investors_{it}}{Total\ Shares\ Outstanding_{it}} \times 100$$

(3) Managerial Shareholdings

Managerial shareholdings serve as a key indicator of management's commitment to a firm's overall performance, particularly its ESG practices. A higher level of managerial ownership indicates a stronger personal stake in the firm's long-term success, potentially leading to more responsible and sustainable decision-making (Bian et al., 2023; Ongsakul, Jiraporn, et al., 2021). In this research, managerial engagement is proxied by managerial shareholdings, as outlined by Yue et al. (2024), which represents the percentage of shares owned by the firm's management. This measure reflects the degree to which management's interests are aligned with those of shareholders, with higher ownership suggesting greater motivation to pursue actions that support long-term sustainability objectives. The proportion of managerial shareholdings will be calculated as follows:

$$Mngmhldn_{it} = \frac{Shares\ Owned\ by\ Management_{it}}{Total\ Shares\ Outstanding_{it}} \times 100$$

(4) Control Variables

To control for firm-specific factors that may influence ESG ratings, several variables are included in the analysis. Board size (BSize) represents the total number of directors on a company's board, with larger boards often linked to improved governance and more effective oversight (Hussain et al., 2020). Dividends (Div) serve as an indicator of a firm's payout policy, which can signal financial stability and a commitment to shareholder interests (García-Sánchez et al., 2020). Cash holdings (Cash), calculated as the ratio of cash and cash equivalents to total assets, reflect a firm's liquidity and capacity to invest in sustainability-related initiatives (Ongsakul, Jiraporn, et al., 2021). Leverage (Lev), defined as the debt-to-assets ratio, captures the firm's financial structure, influencing both risk-taking behavior and long-term sustainability strategies (Li et al., 2022). CEO duality (Dual) is a binary variable indicating whether the CEO also holds the position of board chair, which may impact governance efficiency and strategic decision-making. Tangibility (Tang) measures the proportion of fixed assets, shaping a firm's capital structure and resource allocation. Finally, profitability measures such as Return on Assets (ROA) and Earnings per Share (EPS) are incorporated to account for a firm's financial performance, which can affect its ability to allocate resources toward sustainability efforts (Khatib et al., 2023; Yang et al., 2024). All the variables are summarized as Table 1.

Table 1. Summary of variables

Variable	Proxy	Calculation/Measurement
Sustainability Assurance	Sino ESG	ESG ratings from Sino ESG database
Institutional Stakeholder	PR_IVST	Proportion of shares held by long-term institutional investors
	PS_IVST	Proportion of shares held by short-term institutional investors
Managerial Engagement	Mngmhldn	Percentage of managerial shareholdings in the firm
Control Variables	BSize	Number of directors on the board
	Div	Dividend per share, or total dividends divided by shares
	Cash	Cash and cash equivalents divided by total assets
	Lev	Total debt divided by total assets
	Dual	Binary variable: 1 if CEO is also the board chair, 2 otherwise
	Tang	Fixed assets divided by total assets
	ROA	Net income divided by total assets
	EPS	Net income divided by number of outstanding shares

3.3 Model Specification

Following the methodology of Hausman (1978) and Khatib et al. (2023), a Hausman test was conducted to determine whether a fixed effects (FE) or random effects (RE) model would be more suitable for analyzing the data. This test is crucial for addressing unobserved heterogeneity among firms over time, ensuring a more precise evaluation of the relationships under investigation. The primary focus is on assessing the moderating role of managerial engagement in the relationship between institutional investors and ESG ratings. Specifically, the analysis examines whether managerial shareholdings enhance the positive impact of long-term investors while mitigating the negative effects of short-term investors. The results of the Hausman test yielded a chi-squared statistic of 232.14 with a p-value of 0.000***. At a significance level of $p < 0.01$, we reject the null hypothesis, which posits that the difference in coefficients between the fixed effects and random effects models is not systematic. This outcome indicates that the fixed effects model is more appropriate for this study, as it effectively captures time-invariant, unobserved firm-specific characteristics that are likely correlated with the independent variables. As such, the FE model provides a robust framework for analyzing how managerial engagement moderates the influence of institutional investors on ESG ratings while accounting for firm-specific attributes that might otherwise be overlooked. The model specification is presented as follows:

For long-term institutional investors,

$$ESG_{it} = \alpha_i + \beta_1 PR_I VST_{it} + \beta_3 Mngmhldn_{it}$$

$$+\beta_4\left(PR_{IVST_{it}} \times Mngmhldn_{it}\right) + \sum_{k=1}^{k}\gamma_k X_{kit} + \lambda_t + \epsilon_{it}$$

For short-term institutional investors,

$$ESG_{it} = \alpha_i + \beta_2 PS_I VST_{it} + \beta_3 Mngmhldn_{it}$$

$$+\beta_5\left(PS\_IVST_{it} \times Mngmhldn_{it}\right) + \sum_{k=1}^{k}\gamma_k X_{kit} + \lambda_t + \epsilon_{it}$$

Where, $ESG_{i,t}$ represents the ESG rating of firm i at time t, α_i denotes the firm fixed effects, capturing time-invariant characteristics specific to each firm, $PR\_IVST_{i,t}$ and $PS\_IVST_{i,t}$ represent long-term (pressure-resistant) and short-term (pressure-sensitive) institutional investors respectively, $Mngmhldn_{i,t}$ indicates managerial engagement (measured by managerial shareholdings), ($PR\_IVST_{i,t} \times Mngmhldn_{i,t}$) and ($PS\_IVST_{i,t} \times Mngmhldn_{i,t}$) are the interaction terms between institutional investor types and managerial engagement, capturing the moderating effect, $\sum_{k=1}^{k}\gamma_k X_{kit}$ represents a vector of control variables (such as board size, leverage, cash holdings, etc.), λ_t represents time fixed effects, controlling for time-specific shocks, ϵ_{it} is the error term.

4 DISCUSSION OF RESULTS

4.1 Descriptive Analysis

Table 2 presents the descriptive statistics for the key variables in this study. Sino ESG, used as a proxy for sustainability assurance, has a mean score of 4.1, reflecting a moderate level of ESG ratings among firms, with values ranging from 1 to 8, indicating substantial variability. PR_IVST (long-term investors) has an average value of 0.013, while PS_IVST (short-term investors) averages 0.016, suggesting a slightly higher presence of short-term investors within the sample. Managerial Engagement (Mngmhldn), represented by managerial shareholdings, has a mean of 14.98 with a relatively high standard deviation, highlighting variations in management's commitment to their firms. Control variables, such as Dual, reveal that most CEOs in the sample also serve as board chairs. These observations underscore the diversity in corporate governance practices and sustainability profiles across the firms analyzed. The correlation matrix in Table 3 provides further insights. Sino ESG ratings exhibit a positive correlation with both long-term investors (PR_IVST,

0.092) and managerial engagement (Mngmhldn, 0.098), suggesting that these factors are associated with improved sustainability performance. Conversely, short-term investors (PS_IVST) show a negative correlation with Sino ESG (-0.088), implying that a stronger presence of short-term investors may be linked to a reduced focus on sustainability goals. These initial findings provide a foundation for the subsequent analysis.

Table 2. Descriptive statistics

Variable	Obs	Mean	Std. Dev.	Min	Max
Sino ESG	34227	4.1	1.011	1	8
PR IVST	35473	.013	.029	0	1
PS IVST	35473	.016	.037	0	.537
Mngmhldn	32729	14.984	20.126	0	99.701
BSize	36078	8.357	1.482	5	11
Div	29452	.613	47.278	0	8111.924
Cash	44792	.718	.809	.013	3.108
Lev	28004	.435	.198	.063	.791
Dual	35078	1.691	.462	1	2
Tang	45649	.191	.144	.002	.506
ROA	33718	.033	.066	-.298	.127
EPS	33714	.441	1.166	-10.71	49.93

Table 3. Correlations matrix

Variables	(1)	(2)	(3)	(4)	(5)	(6)	(7)	(8)	(9)	(10)	(11)	(12)
(1) Sino_ ESG	1.000											
(2) PR_ IVST	0.092	1.000										
(3) PS_ IVST	- 0.088	0.240	1.000									
(4) Mngmhldn	0.098	0.020	0.156	1.000								
(5) BSize	0.058	0.032	- 0.041	- 0.201	1.000							
(6) Div	- 0.001	- 0.002	0.024	- 0.004	0.010	1.000						

continued on following page

Table 3. Continued

Variables	(1)	(2)	(3)	(4)	(5)	(6)	(7)	(8)	(9)	(10)	(11)	(12)
(7) Cash	0.118	0.054	0.108	0.220	-0.087	0.016	1.000					
(8) Lev	-0.070	-0.019	-0.073	-0.270	0.130	-0.012	-0.643	1.000				
(9) Dual	0.010	-0.013	-0.083	-0.246	0.193	0.004	-0.103	0.105	1.000			
(10) Tang	-0.089	-0.071	-0.061	-0.142	0.084	0.009	-0.204	0.029	0.073	1.000		
(11) ROA	0.242	0.110	0.202	0.175	0.017	-0.009	0.256	-0.321	-0.036	-0.036	1.000	
(12) EPS	0.176	0.155	0.190	0.119	-0.007	-0.003	0.166	-0.126	-0.041	-0.077	0.515	1.000

4.2 Baseline Regression

Table 4 presents the regression results evaluating the influence of institutional stakeholders on Sino ESG ratings. Column (1) shows that long-term investors (PR_IVST) have a significant positive effect on ESG ratings (2.625, $p < 0.01$), indicating that firms with a higher proportion of long-term investors are more likely to achieve better ESG performance. Column (2) highlights the negative and significant impact of short-term investors (PS_IVST) on ESG ratings (-0.953, $p < 0.01$), suggesting that a stronger presence of short-term investors correlates with reduced sustainability efforts. Among control variables, board size (BSize), cash holdings (Cash), CEO duality (Dual), tangibility (Tang), ROA, and EPS exhibit positive and significant effects ($p < 0.01$), emphasizing their role in enhancing ESG performance. In contrast, dividends (Div) and leverage (Lev) are not statistically significant in either model. Both models include year and industry fixed effects, with R^2 values of 0.110 and 0.106, respectively.

The positive impact of long-term investors reflects their role in driving corporate sustainability through sustained value creation. These investors encourage transparent governance practices aligned with long-term goals, insulating firms from short-term pressures and reinforcing their commitment to stakeholder needs (Freeman & Reed, 1983; Valentinov, 2023). This aligns with stakeholder theory, which underscores the importance of addressing diverse stakeholder interests to achieve sustainability objectives. Conversely, the negative effect of short-term investors illustrates the challenges posed by their focus on immediate returns, often at the expense of long-term ESG initiatives (Cescon, 2002). This diversion of resources undermines sustainability performance, as noted by Florencio et al. (2024) and Yang et al. (2024).

Control variables such as board size and cash holdings emphasize the importance of governance structures and financial resources in supporting sustainability efforts. Together, these findings highlight the need for robust governance to balance investor expectations and promote consistent ESG performance.

Table 4. Impact of institutional stakeholder on Sino_ESG ratings

Variables	Column (1)	Column (2)
	Sino_ESG	Sino_ESG
PR_IVST	2.625***	
	(10.808)	
PS_IVST		-0.953***
		(-4.732)
BSize	0.024***	0.026***
	(5.511)	(5.747)
Div	0.000	-0.000
	(0.013)	(-0.185)
Cash	0.047***	0.050***
	(4.273)	(4.478)
Lev	0.059	0.074
	(1.235)	(1.541)
Dual	0.067***	0.067***
	(4.778)	(4.742)
Tang	0.234***	0.219***
	(4.090)	(3.816)
ROA	3.457***	3.459***
	(16.181)	(15.804)
EPS	0.062***	0.067***
	(9.592)	(10.339)
_cons	3.506***	3.509***
	(69.845)	(69.759)
Year_Fixed	Yes	Yes
Industry_Fixed	Yes	Yes
N	23024	23024
R^2	0.110	0.106
Adj. R^2	0.106	0.103

Notes: The t-values are given in brackets. *** $p<0.01$, ** $p<0.05$, * $p<0.1$.

4.3 Moderating Effect of Managerial Engagement

Table 5 explores the moderating role of managerial engagement in the relationship between institutional investors and Sino ESG ratings. Column (1) evaluates the influence of long-term investors (PR_IVST) and their interaction with managerial engagement (PR_Mgh), while Column (2) focuses on short-term investors (PS_IVST) and their interaction with managerial engagement (PS_Mgh). In Column (1), PR_IVST has a positive and significant coefficient (3.709, $p < 0.01$), confirming that higher proportions of long-term investors are associated with improved ESG ratings. The interaction term PR_Mgh is also positive and significant (0.069, $p < 0.01$), indicating that managerial engagement enhances the positive impact of long-term investors on sustainability performance. This suggests that engaged management strengthens the influence of long-term investors, fostering better sustainability outcomes. In Column (2), PS_IVST has a negative and significant effect (-1.106, $p < 0.01$), demonstrating that short-term investors negatively influence ESG ratings. However, the interaction term PS_Mgh is positive and marginally significant (0.015, $p < 0.1$), suggesting that managerial engagement can partially mitigate the adverse effects of short-term investors on ESG performance.

These findings provide strong support for H3, which posits that managerial engagement positively moderates the relationship between institutional investors and sustainability assurance. Managerial engagement amplifies the positive effects of long-term investors and partially offsets the negative impacts of short-term investors. Engaged management aligns strategic priorities with those of long-term investors, fostering a shared commitment to sustainability (Yue et al., 2025). As noted by Kim et al. (2019), this alignment supports long-term value creation over immediate financial returns. Similarly, Khatib et al. (2023) and Yue et al. (2024) emphasize that higher managerial shareholdings incentivize management to prioritize ESG initiatives, aligning corporate actions with long-term stakeholder interests. Conversely, short-term investors prioritize immediate financial gains, often at odds with long-term sustainability goals. However, the marginally significant interaction between PS_IVST and managerial engagement suggests that engaged management can serve as a balancing mechanism, maintaining some level of sustainability focus despite short-term pressures (Ain et al., 2021; Cahyono et al., 2023). These findings underscore the critical role of managerial engagement as a moderating force. By bridging the competing priorities of short- and long-term investors, engaged management reinforces stakeholder theory's emphasis on balancing diverse interests to achieve sustainable corporate outcomes. Managerial engagement thus emerges as a key driver of resilience and sustainability in the face of conflicting investor demands.

Table 5. Moderating role of managerial engagement

Variables	Column (1)	Column (2)
	Sino_ESG	Sino_ESG
PR_IVST	3.709***	
	(11.948)	
PR_Mgh	0.069***	
	(5.814)	
PS_IVST		-1.106***
		(-3.782)
PS_Mgh		0.015*
		(1.666)
Mngmhldn	0.003***	0.002***
	(7.422)	(5.433)
BSize	0.025***	0.027***
	(5.630)	(5.930)
Div	0.000	-0.000
	(0.012)	(-0.225)
Cash	0.048***	0.050***
	(4.330)	(4.459)
Lev	0.061	0.072
	(1.238)	(1.467)
Dual	0.075***	0.075***
	(5.235)	(5.181)
Tang	0.284***	0.265***
	(4.873)	(4.540)
ROA	3.175***	3.168***
	(14.347)	(13.990)
EPS	0.082***	0.089***
	(10.538)	(11.419)
_cons	3.434***	3.450***
	(64.679)	(64.721)
Year_Fixed	Yes	Yes
Industry_Fixed	Yes	Yes
N	22353	22353
R^2	0.114	0.109
Adj. R^2	0.110	0.105

Notes: The t-values are given in brackets. *** p<0.01, ** p<0.05, * p<0.1.

5 ADDITIONAL ANALYSIS

5.1 Robustness Checks

Table 6 presents regression results using Bloomberg ESG ratings (Blmg_ESG) as an alternative measure of corporate sustainability to assess the robustness of the findings. Column (1) evaluates the influence of long-term investors (PR_IVST) and their interaction with managerial engagement (PR_Mgh), while Column (2) examines short-term investors (PS_IVST) and their interaction with managerial engagement (PS_Mgh). In Column (1), the coefficient for PR_IVST is positive but not statistically significant (3.822), indicating that long-term investors do not have a strong direct influence on ESG performance when measured using Bloomberg ESG ratings. Similarly, the interaction term PR_Mgh is also insignificant, suggesting that managerial engagement does not significantly amplify the effect of long-term investors in this context. Conversely, Column (2) shows that PS_IVST has a significant negative impact on Bloomberg ESG ratings (-1.987, $p < 0.01$), consistent with the idea that short-term investors prioritize immediate returns, often at the expense of sustainability goals. However, the interaction term PS_Mgh is positive and significant (0.571, $p < 0.01$), indicating that managerial engagement can partially mitigate the negative effects of short-term investors on ESG ratings. These findings provide partial support for H3, particularly in mitigating the influence of short-term investors.

The results suggest that the role of managerial engagement may depend on the ESG rating standard employed. Long-term investors and managerial engagement have limited influence on Bloomberg ESG ratings, likely because such international standards often reflect sustainability expectations aligned with advanced economies. As Truong (2024) explains, Bloomberg ESG ratings emphasize global benchmarks and advanced sustainability practices, which may not fully capture the nuances of managerial influences in emerging markets. In contrast, local standards like Sino_ESG, which consider the regulatory and economic priorities of developing economies, provide a more contextually relevant assessment of corporate sustainability (He et al., 2023). This divergence highlights the challenges faced by developing countries in meeting stringent international sustainability benchmarks. While international standards serve as aspirational goals, they often require resources and governance capabilities that are more achievable in advanced markets. For emerging economies like China, locally relevant ESG practices offer a practical pathway to align with global standards gradually. Companies must strategically balance local developmental priorities with the expectations of global stakeholders, enabling sustainable progress while addressing the growing demand for uniform ESG benchmarks (Ahmad et al., 2024).

Table 6. Impact of institutional stakeholders on Bloomberg_ESG ratings (alternative variable)

Bloomberg ESG Ratings	Column (1)	Column (2)
	Blmg_ESG	Blmg_ESG
PR_IVST	3.822	
	(1.257)	
PR_Mgh	0.071	
	(0.547)	
PS_IVST		-1.987***
		(-5.247)
PS_Mgh		0.571***
		(4.626)
Mngmhldn	-0.027***	-0.039***
	(-4.222)	(-5.906)
BSize	0.418***	0.416***
	(8.157)	(8.137)
Div	-0.000	0.000
	(-0.084)	(0.327)
Cash	0.009	0.007
	(0.063)	(0.047)
Lev	6.848***	7.032***
	(11.683)	(11.996)
Dual	-0.189	-0.248
	(-1.045)	(-1.375)
Tang	-0.878	-0.819
	(-1.282)	(-1.198)
ROA	11.117***	13.839***
	(4.417)	(5.386)
EPS	0.563***	0.584***
	(7.858)	(8.199)
_cons	22.521***	22.737***
	(33.626)	(34.068)
Year_Fixed	Yes	Yes
Industry_Fixed	Yes	Yes
N	8512	8512

continued on following page

Table 6. Continued

Bloomberg ESG Ratings	Column (1)	Column (2)
R^2	0.508	0.510
Adj. R^2	0.503	0.505

Notes: The t-values are given in brackets. *** p<0.01, ** p<0.05, * p<0.1.

5.2 Heterogeneity Test -Firm Characteristics

Table 7 examines the moderating role of managerial engagement on Sino ESG ratings across different ownership structures, focusing on State-Owned Enterprises (SOEs) and non-SOEs. Columns (1) and (2) analyze SOEs, while Columns (3) and (4) focus on non-SOEs. For SOEs, PR_IVST exhibits a positive and significant effect on ESG ratings (1.832, $p < 0.01$), indicating that long-term investors contribute positively to sustainability performance. In non-SOEs, the effect of PR_IVST is even larger and significant (6.614, $p < 0.01$), suggesting that long-term investors have a stronger influence in privately owned firms due to greater governance flexibility. Regarding short-term investors (PS_IVST), results differ by ownership. In SOEs, PS_IVST has no significant effect, suggesting that short-term investors have limited influence on state-owned firms' sustainability performance. For non-SOEs, PS_IVST has a negative coefficient but is not statistically significant, indicating a weak and inconsistent effect.

Managerial engagement plays a critical moderating role in both ownership types. In SOEs, the interaction between PS_IVST and managerial engagement (PS_Mgh) is positive and significant (0.077, $p < 0.01$), demonstrating that engaged management can mitigate the negative effects of short-term investors. Similarly, in non-SOEs, PS_Mgh shows a positive and significant effect (0.362, $p < 0.1$), reinforcing the importance of managerial engagement in addressing short-term investor pressures, especially in private firms. These findings underscore significant differences in how SOEs and non-SOEs respond to institutional investor influences. Long-term investors have a stronger positive impact in non-SOEs, where market-driven demands for sustainability are more pronounced (Bai et al., 2024). Non-SOEs, less constrained by state directives, are better positioned to align strategies with long-term investor priorities, supporting sustainable value creation (Florencio et al., 2024; Freeman & Reed, 1983). Conversely, SOEs exhibit resilience to short-term investor pressures due to structural protections and accountability to government stakeholders focused on broader social objectives (Genin et al., 2021; Zhou et al., 2017). Managerial engagement is pivotal, especially in SOEs, where decision-making authority enables management to counteract short-term investor pressures and align with sustainability goals (Wang & Yung, 2011; Yue et al., 2024). This strategic alignment highlights managerial engagement as a key mechanism for balancing stakeholder demands across ownership structures, reinforcing stakeholder theory's emphasis on governance adaptability (Gao et al., 2022). These findings suggest firms must strategically leverage managerial engagement to achieve sustainable corporate outcomes in increasingly ESG-focused environments.

Table 7. Moderating role of managerial engagement within different firm characteristics

Firm Characteristics	SOEs=1		SOEs=0	
	Sino_ESG	Sino_ESG	Sino_ESG	Sino_ESG
PR_IVST	1.832***		6.614***	
	(4.116)		(4.522)	
PR_Mgh	0.039		0.304	
	(0.828)		(1.296)	
PS_IVST		-0.165		-2.254
		(-0.312)		(-1.508)
PS_Mgh		0.077***		0.362*
		(2.789)		(1.768)
Mngmhldn	-0.001	-0.003**	-0.007	0.003
	(-0.542)	(-2.235)	(-1.209)	(0.477)
BSize	0.037***	0.038***	0.004	0.002
	(5.021)	(5.161)	(0.164)	(0.065)
Div	0.000	0.000	0.288***	0.298***
	(0.084)	(0.034)	(3.737)	(3.815)
Cash	0.026	0.026	0.071	0.079
	(1.243)	(1.225)	(1.156)	(1.261)
Lev	0.013	0.014	0.252	0.272
	(0.162)	(0.172)	(1.054)	(1.125)
Dual	0.161***	0.157***	-0.053	-0.062
	(5.215)	(5.075)	(-0.719)	(-0.830)
Tang	0.155*	0.136	0.801***	0.826***
	(1.677)	(1.475)	(2.863)	(2.913)
ROA	1.448***	1.379***	3.085**	2.849**
	(3.449)	(3.236)	(2.321)	(2.076)
EPS	0.171***	0.178***	0.285***	0.311***

continued on following page

Table 7. Continued

Firm Characteristics	SOEs=1		SOEs=0	
	(10.275)	(10.705)	(3.415)	(3.674)
_cons	3.362***	3.385***	3.181***	3.243***
	(33.753)	(33.996)	(11.630)	(11.722)
Year_Fixed	Yes	Yes	Yes	Yes
Industry_Fixed	Yes	Yes	Yes	Yes
N	8724	8724	1103	1103
R^2	0.155	0.155	0.281	0.264
Adj. R^2	0.147	0.146	0.236	0.218

Notes: The t-values are given in brackets. *** p<0.01, ** p<0.05, * p<0.1.

6 ETHICAL & REGULATORY CHALLENGES

The chapter highlights significant findings on sustainability assurance, institutional investors, and managerial engagement, yet it implicitly reveals a landscape of ethical and regulatory challenges. A critical examination on these findings indicates that these challenges are multi-dimensional, reflecting both the inherent conflicts in stakeholder interests and the evolving complexity of regulatory environments. One ethical challenge lies in balancing the priorities of short-term and long-term institutional investors. As the manuscript indicates, short-term investors often pressure firms to prioritize immediate financial gains, potentially at the expense of environmental, social, and governance goals (Dyck et al., 2019). This misalignment can lead to ethical dilemmas for managers, who may need to sacrifice long-term sustainability initiatives to satisfy short-term demands, undermining their fiduciary responsibility to broader stakeholder interests, including future generations (Freeman & Reed, 1983). Furthermore, firms operating in high-polluting industries face heightened scrutiny, yet the manuscript suggests that managerial engagement can be inconsistent in mitigating adverse impacts (Lyu et al., 2024). This raises ethical questions about selective prioritization of sustainability practices based on industry visibility, potentially neglecting less visible but equally critical ESG dimensions.

Regulatory challenges are equally pronounced. As the manuscript acknowledges the reliance on ESG ratings for sustainability assurance, discrepancies in rating methodologies such as the divergence between Sino_ESG and Bloomberg ESG standards highlight the absence of universally accepted benchmarks (He et al., 2023). This inconsistency creates opportunities for regulatory arbitrage, where firms may selectively adhere to less stringent local standards to project compliance, thereby eroding the credibility of sustainability disclosures. Additionally, this study's focus on emerging markets reveals gaps in regulatory enforcement, where developing economies may lack the institutional capacity to impose rigorous sustainability mandates, exacerbating the risk of greenwashing (Tang et al., 2022).

The interplay between managerial engagement and investor influence underscores the ethical hazard of agency problems. While engaged managers can amplify sustainability efforts, their discretion in resource allocation could lead to selective reporting or manipulation of ESG metrics to appease influential stakeholders without achieving substantive sustainability improvements (Jensen & Meckling, 1976). This raises concerns about the authenticity and accountability of reported ESG practices, especially when third-party assurance mechanisms remain underdeveloped or unevenly enforced (Lemma et al., 2024) In summary, this chapter implicitly highlights critical ethical and regulatory challenges rooted in conflicting stakeholder priorities, inconsistent ESG standards, and varying regulatory enforcement. Addressing these challenges requires not only harmonized global frameworks but also strengthened mechanisms for accountability and transparency, ensuring that sustainability assurance delivers genuine, long-term societal value.

7 CONCLUSION AND IMPLICATION

This study examines the influence of institutional investors and managerial engagement on Sino ESG ratings across industries with varying pollution intensities. The results highlight the contrasting roles of long-term and short-term investors in driving corporate sustainability. Long-term investors (PR_IVST) have a significant positive impact on ESG ratings, indicating their ability to support sustainability initiatives and encourage firms to align with long-term goals. Conversely, short-term investors (PS_IVST) negatively influence ESG ratings, reflecting their preference for immediate financial returns over sustainability efforts. The moderating role of managerial engagement shows that engaged management amplifies the positive effects of long-term investors but has limited success in mitigating the negative effects of short-term investors. Heterogeneity analysis reveals that long-term investors have a stronger positive influence in high-polluting industries, while short-term investors exert a more pronounced negative impact in such sectors. These findings underscore the importance of managerial engagement and investor types in shaping sustainability efforts across industry contexts.

The study contributes to stakeholder theory by illustrating the roles of diverse stakeholders, particularly long-term investors, in driving corporate ESG commitments, especially in environmentally sensitive industries. It also reinforces agency theory, showing how managerial engagement aligns firm actions with sustainability goals.

Practically, the findings emphasize the importance of fostering relationships with long-term investors and implementing governance policies that align managerial incentives with sustainability objectives. High-polluting industries, in particular, should prioritize strategies that counterbalance short-term pressures by reinforcing governance and transparency. However, the study's focus on managerial engagement leaves scope for future research on other drivers, such as board diversity or corporate culture. Additionally, expanding the analysis to incorporate regional variations and alternative sustainability metrics could enhance the applicability of these findings to broader contexts, aiding firms in balancing investor interests while meeting global sustainability expectations.

8 SCOPE FOR FUTURE RESEARCH

The chapter presents a solid foundation for understanding the dynamics of sustainability assurance, institutional investor behaviour, and managerial engagement. However, it opens multiple avenues for future research that can address unexplored areas and refine the existing body of knowledge. These opportunities are both methodological and thematic, emphasizing critical gaps that require further exploration. Future research could delve into how governance structures can be reformed to address the ethical dilemmas highlighted in the manuscript, particularly the conflicting pressures from short-term and long-term institutional investors. Studies could explore mechanisms to institutionalize ethical decision-making within managerial frameworks, balancing profitability with sustainability and fairness to all stakeholders (Freeman & Reed, 1983). The chapter also underscores the divergence between local (Sino_ESG) and global (Bloomberg ESG) standards, revealing a critical gap in the harmonization of sustainability metrics. Future studies could investigate the feasibility and impact of establishing universally accepted ESG rating systems, including how these frameworks might accommodate regional variations without compromising their integrity (He et al., 2023).

Emerging technologies such as blockchain and artificial intelligence could revolutionize sustainability assurance by enhancing transparency and reducing information asymmetry. Research could explore how these technologies can be integrated into ESG reporting and assurance processes to ensure real-time validation of sustainability claims, mitigating risks of greenwashing (Lemma et al., 2024). The findings indicate variations in the influence of institutional investors and managerial engagement across sectors and regions. Comparative studies focusing on industries with differing environmental impacts or contrasting regulatory landscapes could provide deeper insights into the contextual factors driving ESG performance (Lyu et al., 2024).

While the chapter examines immediate ESG ratings, future research could track the long-term impact of sustainability initiatives on corporate financial performance, resilience, and stakeholder trust. Longitudinal studies could also investigate the role of consistent managerial engagement in sustaining ESG improvements over time (Tang et al., 2022). Another promising area is the behavioural dynamics of institutional investors, exploring how cultural, economic, or psychological factors influence their ESG priorities. This could include studies on how investor education and advocacy campaigns shape the demand for rigorous sustainability assurance (García-Sánchez et al., 2019). Future research should also examine the effectiveness of regulatory mechanisms in fostering robust sustainability assurance practices. This includes evaluating the role of penalties, incentives, and international cooperation in aligning corporate behaviour with sustainability goals in diverse regulatory environments (Tang et al., 2022). By addressing these areas, future research can provide a more nuanced understanding of sustainability assurance, helping to align corporate practices with the growing global emphasis on environmental, social, and governance accountability.

REFERENCES

Adebayo, A. (2023). Synthesizing State-Owned Enterprises and Public Entrepreneurship. *International Journal of Interdisciplinary Organizational Studies*, 18(2), 37–64. DOI: 10.18848/2324-7649/CGP/v18i02/37-64

Ahmad, H., Yaqub, M., & Lee, S. H. (2024). Environmental-, social-, and governance-related factors for business investment and sustainability: A scientometric review of global trends. *Environment, Development and Sustainability*, 26(2), 2965–2987. DOI: 10.1007/s10668-023-02921-x PMID: 36714213

Ain, Q. U., Yuan, X., & Javaid, H. M. (2021). The impact of board gender diversity and foreign institutional investors on firm innovation: Evidence from China. *European Journal of Innovation Management*, 25(3), 813–837. DOI: 10.1108/EJIM-10-2020-0439

Akhter, W., & Hassan, A. (2024). Does corporate social responsibility mediate the relationship between corporate governance and firm performance? Empirical evidence from BRICS countries. *Corporate Social Responsibility and Environmental Management*, 31(1), 566–578. DOI: 10.1002/csr.2586

AlMalki, H. A., & Durugbo, C. M. (2023). Systematic review of institutional innovation literature: Towards a multi-level management model. *Management Review Quarterly*, 73(2), 731–785. DOI: 10.1007/s11301-022-00259-8

Alves, S. (2021). CEO duality, earnings quality and board independence. *Journal of Financial Reporting and Accounting*, 21(2), 217–231. DOI: 10.1108/JFRA-07-2020-0191

Amel-Zadeh, A., & Serafeim, G. (2018). Why and how investors use ESG information: Evidence from a global survey. *Financial Analysts Journal*, 74(3), 87–103. DOI: 10.2469/faj.v74.n3.2

Asante-Appiah, B., & Lambert, T. A. (2022). The role of the external auditor in managing environmental, social, and governance (ESG) reputation risk. *Review of Accounting Studies*, 28(4), 2589–2641. DOI: 10.1007/s11142-022-09706-z

Atta, N., Sharifi, A., & Ying Lee, C. (2024). The relationship between the rule of law and environmental sustainability: Empirical evidence from the analysis of global indices. *International Journal of Sustainable Development and World Ecology*, 31(8), 1–17. DOI: 10.1080/13504509.2024.2371159

Bai, G. V., Frank, D., & Prabhu, K. S. (2024). Does ESG disclosure enhance firm performance during COVID-19? Evidence from Nifty 500 firms. *Investment Management and Financial Innovations*, 21(3), 74–83. DOI: 10.21511/imfi.21(3).2024.07

Barker, R., & Eccles, R. G. (2018). Should corporations have a purpose? *Harvard Business Review*, 96(3), 1–7.

Barney, J. (1991). Firm resources and sustained competitive advantage. *Journal of Management*, 17(1), 99–120. DOI: 10.1177/014920639101700108

Bena, J., Ferreira, M. A., Matos, P., & Pires, P. (2017). Are foreign investors locusts? The long-term effects of foreign institutional ownership. *Journal of Financial Economics*, 126(1), 122–146. DOI: 10.1016/j.jfineco.2017.07.005

Benabou, R., & Tirole, J. (2010). Individual and corporate social responsibility. *Economica*, 77(305), 1–19. DOI: 10.1111/j.1468-0335.2009.00843.x

Benoit, D. F., & Gilson, C. (2017). Institutional investors, corporate governance, and firm performance. *Corporate Governance*, 25(3), 206–217.

Berrone, P., Cruz, C., Gomez-Mejia, L. R., & Larraza-Kintana, M. (2021). Socioemotional wealth and corporate responses to institutional pressures: Do family-controlled firms pollute less? *Administrative Science Quarterly*, 55(1), 82–113. DOI: 10.2189/asqu.2010.55.1.82

Bian, H., Kuo, J.-M., Pan, H., & Zhang, Z. (2023). The role of managerial ownership in dividend tunneling: Evidence from China. *Corporate Governance*, 31(2), 307–333. DOI: 10.1111/corg.12478

Boffo, R., & Patalano, R. (2020). ESG investing: Practices, progress and challenges. *OECD Paris Working Papers on Finance, Insurance, and Private Pensions.*

Boiral, O., Heras-Saizarbitoria, I., Brotherton, M., & Bernard, J. (2019). Ethical Issues in the Assurance of Sustainability Reports: Perspectives from Assurance Providers. *Journal of Business Ethics*, 159(4), 1–15. DOI: 10.1007/s10551-018-3840-3

Bolton, P., & Kacperczyk, M. (2021). Do investors care about carbon risk? *Journal of Financial Economics*, 142(2), 517–549. DOI: 10.1016/j.jfineco.2021.05.008

Busch, T., Bauer, R., & Orlitzky, M. (2016). Sustainable development and financial markets: Old paths and new avenues. *Business & Society*, 55(3), 303–329. DOI: 10.1177/0007650315570701

Busch, T., Bauer, R., & Orlitzky, M. (2021). Sustainable development and financial markets: Old paths and new avenues. *Business & Society*, 60(1), 7–48.

Cahaya, F. R., Nursalim, N., & Dhirathiti, N. (2023). Expectations on Labour-Related CSR Reporting: Voices from Labour Unions in Indonesia and Thailand. *Social and Environmental Accountability Journal*, 43(3), 235–258. DOI: 10.1080/0969160X.2023.2167847

Cahyono, S., Harymawan, I., & Kamarudin, K. A. (2023). The impacts of tenure diversity on boardroom and corporate carbon emission performance: Exploring from the moderating role of corporate innovation. *Corporate Social Responsibility and Environmental Management*, 30(5), 2507–2535. DOI: 10.1002/csr.2500

Cescon, F. (2002). Short-term perceptions, corporate governance and the management of R & D in Italian companies. *The Journal of Management and Governance*, 6(3), 255–270. DOI: 10.1023/A:1019631730439

Chebbi, K. (2024). Examining the interplay of sustainable development, corporate governance, and stock Price crash risk: Insights from ESG practices. *Sustainable Development (Bradford)*, 32(1), 1291–1309. DOI: 10.1002/sd.2733

Chen, S., Farooq, U., Aldawsari, S. H., Waked, S. S., & Badawi, M. (2024). Impact of environmental, social, and governance performance on cash holdings in BRICS: Mediating role of cost of capital. *Corporate Social Responsibility and Environmental Management*, n/a(n/a). DOI: 10.1002/csr.3012

Cheng, B., Ioannou, I., & Serafeim, G. (2018). Corporate social responsibility and access to finance. *Strategic Management Journal*, 35(1), 1–23. DOI: 10.1002/smj.2131

Chung, C. Y., & Song, J. M. (2024). Institutional investors by nationality and long-term investor value appropriation. *Research in International Business and Finance*, 67, 102153. DOI: 10.1016/j.ribaf.2023.102153

Cooray, T., Gunarathne, A. D., & Senaratne, S. (2020). Does Corporate Governance Affect the Quality of Integrated Reporting? *Sustainability (Basel)*, 12(10), 4262. DOI: 10.3390/su12104262

Deng, S., & He, J. (2024). Managerial inclusiveness and corporate innovation in China. *Accounting and Finance*, 64(1), 381–410. DOI: 10.1111/acfi.13149

Dyck, A., Lins, K. V., Roth, L., & Wagner, H. F. (2019). Do institutional investors drive corporate social responsibility? International evidence. *Journal of Financial Economics*, 131(3), 693–714. DOI: 10.1016/j.jfineco.2018.08.013

Eccles, R. G., Ioannou, I., & Serafeim, G. (2014). The impact of corporate sustainability on organizational processes and performance. *Management Science*, 60(11), 2835–2857. DOI: 10.1287/mnsc.2014.1984

Eccles, R. G., & Klimenko, S. (2019). The investor revolution. *Harvard Business Review*, 97(3), 106–116.

Eccles, R. G., Lee, L., & Stroehle, J. C. (2020). The social origins of ESG: Analyzing the ESG rating industry through a multiple lens approach. *Organization & Environment*, 33(4), 566–591.

Ferrell, A., Liang, H., & Renneboog, L. (2016). Socially responsible firms. *Journal of Financial Economics*, 122(3), 585–606. DOI: 10.1016/j.jfineco.2015.12.003

Flammer, C. (2013). Corporate social responsibility and shareholder reaction: The environmental awareness of investors. *Academy of Management Journal*, 56(3), 758–781. DOI: 10.5465/amj.2011.0744

Flammer, C. (2018). Green bonds: Effectiveness and implications for public policy. *Environmental and Energy Policy and the Economy*, 1(1), 1–31.

Freeman, R. E. (1984). *Strategic management: A stakeholder approach.* Pitman.

Freeman, R. E., & Reed, D. L. (1983). Stockholders and Stakeholders: A New Perspective on Corporate Governance. *California Management Review*, 25(3), 88–106. DOI: 10.2307/41165018

Friede, G., Busch, T., & Bassen, A. (2015). ESG and financial performance: Aggregated evidence from more than 2000 empirical studies. *Journal of Sustainable Finance & Investment*, 5(4), 210–233. DOI: 10.1080/20430795.2015.1118917

García-Meca, E., & Pucheta-Martínez, M. C. (2018). How Institutional Investors on Boards Impact on Stakeholder Engagement and Corporate Social Responsibility Reporting. *Corporate Social Responsibility and Environmental Management*, 25(3), 237–249. DOI: 10.1002/csr.1451

García-Sánchez, I.-M., Aibar-Guzmán, B., Raimo, N., & Vitolla, F. (2024). Embracing tomorrow: Global insights on corporate commitment to the 2030 Agenda. *Measuring Business Excellence*, ahead-of-print(ahead-of-print). DOI: 10.1108/MBE-04-2024-0044

García-Sánchez, I.-M., Aibar-Guzmán, C., & Aibar-Guzmán, B. (2020). The effect of institutional ownership and ownership dispersion on eco-innovation. *Technological Forecasting and Social Change*, 158, 120173. DOI: 10.1016/j.techfore.2020.120173

García-Sánchez, I.-M., Aibar-Guzmán, C., Núñez-Torrado, M., & Aibar-Guzmán, B. (2022). Are institutional investors "in love" with the sustainable development goals? Understanding the idyll in the case of governments and pension funds. *Sustainable Development (Bradford)*, 30(5), 1099–1116. DOI: 10.1002/sd.2305

George, G., Haas, M. R., & Pentland, A. (2021). Big data and management. *Academy of Management Journal*, 57(2), 321–326. DOI: 10.5465/amj.2014.4002

Gibson, R., & Krueger, P. (2018). The sustainability footprint of institutional investors. *Journal of Business Ethics*, 149(1), 53–72. DOI: 10.1023/B:BUSI.0000004367.60776.b3

Giese, G., Lee, L., Melas, D., Nagy, Z. I., & Nishikawa, L. (2019). Foundations of ESG Investing: How ESG Affects Equity Valuation, Risk, and Performance. *Journal of Portfolio Management*, 45(5), 69–83. DOI: 10.3905/jpm.2019.45.5.069

Gond, J. P., Patriotta, G., & Schultz, F. (2021). How do companies embed corporate social responsibility across organizational functions? *The Academy of Management Annals*, 15(1), 229–287.

Haimberg, Y. (2021). *Can an Agency Role-Reversal Lead to an Organizational Collapse? A Study Proposal.*

Harjoto, M. A., Jo, H., & Kim, Y. (2015). Corporate governance and CSR nexus. *Journal of Business Ethics*, 132(3), 453–469.

Hausman, J. A. (1978). Specification tests in econometrics. *Econometrica*, 46(6), 1251–1271. DOI: 10.2307/1913827

Hazaea, S. A., Zhu, J., Khatib, S. F. A., Bazhair, A. H., & Elamer, A. A. (2022). Sustainability assurance practices: A systematic review and future research agenda. *Environmental Science and Pollution Research International*, 29(4), 4843–4864. DOI: 10.1007/s11356-021-17359-9 PMID: 34787810

He, Y., Zhao, X., & Zheng, H. (2023). How does the environmental protection tax law affect firm ESG? Evidence from the Chinese stock markets. *Energy Economics*, 127, 107067. DOI: 10.1016/j.eneco.2023.107067

Hillman, A. J., & Keim, G. D. (2001). Shareholder value, stakeholder management, and social issues: What's the bottom line? *Strategic Management Journal*, 22(2), 125–139. DOI: 10.1002/1097-0266(200101)22:2<125::AID-SMJ150>3.0.CO;2-H

Hooker, J., & Kim, T. W. (2019). Ethical Implications of the Fourth Industrial Revolution for Business and Society. *Business & Society*, •••, 360.

Hossain, M. I., Ong, T. S., Teh, B. H., Said, R. M., & Siow, M. L. (2022). Nexus of Stakeholder Integration, Green Investment, Green Technology Adoption and Environmental Sustainability Practices: Evidence from Bangladesh Textile SMEs. *Pertanika Journal of Social Science & Humanities*, 30(1). Advance online publication. DOI: 10.47836/pjssh.30.1.14

Huang, R., & Kisgen, D. J. (2019). Corporate governance, managerial ownership, and the impact of institutional investors on ESG ratings. *Journal of Financial Intermediation*, 40, 36–57.

Ioannou, I., & Serafeim, G. (2021). Corporate sustainability: A strategy? *California Management Review*, 64(1), 1–23.

Iqbal, R., Shahzad, K., & Chaudhary, R. (2023). Green human resource management practices as a strategic choice for enhancing employees' environmental outcomes: An affective events theory perspective. *International Journal of Manpower.*

Jiraporn, P., Jiraporn, N., Boeprasert, A., & Chang, K. (2018). Does corporate social responsibility (CSR) improve credit ratings? Evidence from geographic identification. *Journal of Banking & Finance*, 79, 115–135.

Joseph, J. (2020). Exploring the Agency-Structure Dynamics in State–Society Relations in Contemporary China: The Case of Securitization of the Environmental Sector. *China Report (New Delhi, India)*, 56(2), 182–203. DOI: 10.1177/0009445520916873

Khamis, N. I., & Wan Ismail, W. K. (2021). The impact of corporate social responsibility on corporate image in the construction industry: A case of SMEs in Egypt. *Journal of Sustainable Finance & Investment*, 12(1), 128–146. DOI: 10.1080/20430795.2021.1930992

Khan, M., Serafeim, G., & Yoon, A. (2016). Corporate sustainability: First evidence on materiality. *The Accounting Review*, 91(6), 1697–1724. DOI: 10.2308/accr-51383

Kitchen, J. (2020). A stakeholder theory perspective on business models: value creation for sustainability: Freudenreich, B., Lüdeke-Freund, F. and Schaltegger, S. (2019). *Journal of Business Ethics*. In press: DOI: . *Social and Environmental Accountability Journal*, 40(1), 98.DOI: 10.1007/s10551-019-04112-z

Kotsantonis, S., & Serafeim, G. (2019). Four things no one will tell you about ESG data. *The Bank of America Journal of Applied Corporate Finance*, 31(2), 50–58. DOI: 10.1111/jacf.12346

Lau, A. K. W., Lee, P. K. C., & Cheng, T. C. E. (2024). The relationships between ethical codes of conduct, ethical supplier risks, and financial performance: A buyer-supplier perspective. *Production Planning and Control*, •••, 1–20. DOI: 10.1080/09537287.2024.2359547

Lee, S. P., & Isa, M. M. (2020). Environmental, Social and Governance (ESG) Practices and Performance in Shariah Firms: Agency or Stakeholder Theory? *Asian Academy of Management Journal of Accounting and Finance*, 16(1), 1–34. DOI: 10.21315/aamjaf2020.16.1.1

Lenton, T.M., Benson, S., Smith, T., Ewer, T., Lanel, V., Petykowski, E., Powell, T., Abrams, J.F., Blomsma, F., & Sharpe, S. (2022). Operationalising positive tipping points towards global sustainability. *Global Sustainability*, 5.

Li, W., & Zhang, R. (2019). Corporate social responsibility, institutional investors, and firm value: Evidence from China. *Sustainability*, 11(12), 1–19.

Liang, H., & Renneboog, L. (2017). On the foundations of corporate social responsibility. *The Journal of Finance*, 72(2), 853–910. DOI: 10.1111/jofi.12487

Liu, Z., Jubb, C., & Abhayawansa, S. (2024). Choice of financial audit firm and ESG assurance firm: The role of board of director characteristics. *The British Accounting Review*, 101505, 101505. Advance online publication. DOI: 10.1016/j.bar.2024.101505

Lopez-de-Silanes, F., McCahery, J. A., & Pudschedl, P. C. (2024). Institutional Investors and ESG Preferences. *Corporate Governance: An International Review*, n/a(n/a). DOI: 10.1111/corg.12583

Luo, Y., Wang, Y., Hong, C., He, P., & Zheng, X. (2023). The shattered "Iron Rice Bowl": Effects of Chinese state-owned enterprise reform on depressive symptoms in later life. *Social Psychiatry and Psychiatric Epidemiology*, 58(8), 1193–1200. DOI: 10.1007/s00127-023-02437-9 PMID: 36973356

Lyu, F., Zhang, Z., Fu, G., Liu, Z., & Treepongkaruna, S. (2024). Multiple shareholding institutional investors and green governance of heavy-polluting industries. *Business Strategy and the Environment*, 33(4), 3569–3587. DOI: 10.1002/bse.3667

Maclean, K., Greenaway, A., & Grünbühel, C. M. (2022). Developing methods of knowledge co-production across varying contexts to shape Sustainability Science theory and practice. *Sustainability Science*, 17(2), 325–332. DOI: 10.1007/s11625-022-01103-4 PMID: 35194465

Mahran, K., & Elamer, A. A. (2024). Shaping ESG commitment through organizational psychological capital: The role of CEO power. *Business Strategy and the Environment*, n/a(n/a). DOI: 10.1002/bse.4007

Manokaran, K. R., Ramakrishnan, S., & Shanker, H. S. (2023). Sectoral Analysis of Malaysian Companies' CSR Initiatives for Organizational Risk Management. *International Journal of Academic Research in Business & Social Sciences*, 13(9). Advance online publication. DOI: 10.6007/IJARBSS/v13-i9/18583

Manokaran, K. R., Ramakrishnan, S. A., Hishan, S. S., & Soehod, K. (2018). The Impact Of Corporate Social Responsibility On Financial Performance: Evidence from Insurance firms. *Management Science Letters*, 8, 913–932. DOI: 10.5267/j.msl.2018.6.016

Panarello, D., Gatto, A., Sadik-Zada, E. R., & Aldieri, L. (2024). Energy sustainability, vulnerability and resilience. *Discover Sustainability*, 5(1), 326. DOI: 10.1007/s43621-024-00534-6

Park, S.R., & Jang, J.Y. (2021). The Impact of ESG Management on Investment Decision: Institutional Investors' Perceptions of Country-Specific ESG Criteria. *International Journal of Financial Studies*.

Rubino, F. E., & Napoli, F. (2020). What Impact Does Corporate Governance Have on Corporate Environmental Performances? An Empirical Study of Italian Listed Firms. *Sustainability (Basel)*, 12(14), 5742. DOI: 10.3390/su12145742

Shahzad, M., Qu, Y., Ur Rehman, S., Ding, X., & Razzaq, A. (2022). Impact of stakeholders' pressure on green management practices of manufacturing organizations under the mediation of organizational motives. *Journal of Environmental Planning and Management*, 66(10), 2171–2194. DOI: 10.1080/09640568.2022.2062567

Simnett, R., Vanstraelen, A., & Chua, W. F. (2020). Assurance on sustainability reports: Revisiting the influence of auditor and firm characteristics. *Accounting, Organizations and Society*, 47, 16–26.

Spence, M. (1973). Job market signaling. *The Quarterly Journal of Economics*, 87(3), 355–374. DOI: 10.2307/1882010

Tang, H. (2022). The Effect of ESG Performance on Corporate Innovation in China: The Mediating Role of Financial Constraints and Agency Cost. *Sustainability (Basel)*, 14(7), 3769. DOI: 10.3390/su14073769

Tang, Y. M., Chau, K. Y., Fatima, A., & Waqas, M. (2022). Industry 4.0 technology and circular economy practices: Business management strategies for environmental sustainability. *Environmental Science and Pollution Research International*, 29(33), 49752–49769. DOI: 10.1007/s11356-022-19081-6 PMID: 35218493

Tao, M., Lin, B., & Poletti, S. (2024). From policy to practice: How China's emissions trading scheme shapes ESG greenwashing at the firm level? *Journal of Environmental Management*, 370, 122681. DOI: 10.1016/j.jenvman.2024.122681 PMID: 39366221

Truong, T. H. D. (2024). Environmental, social and governance performance and firm value: Does ownership concentration matter? *Management Decision*, ahead-of-print(ahead-of-print). DOI: 10.1108/MD-10-2023-1993

Tyler, B. B., Lahneman, B., Cerrato, D., Cruz, A. D., Beukel, K., Spielmann, N., & Minciullo, M. (2023). Environmental practice adoption in SMEs: The effects of firm proactive orientation and regulatory pressure. *Journal of Small Business Management*, 62(5), 2211–2246. DOI: 10.1080/00472778.2023.2218435

Valentinov, V. (2023). Stakeholder Theory: Toward a Classical Institutional Economics Perspective. *Journal of Business Ethics*, 188(1), 75–88. DOI: 10.1007/s10551-022-05304-w

Velte, P. (2024). Climate board governance and carbon assurance – European evidence. *Journal of Global Responsibility*, ahead-of-print(ahead-of-print). DOI: 10.1108/JGR-02-2024-0034

Venturelli, A., & Pizzi, S. (2024). SDG reporting in social and environmental accounting research. In *The Routledge Handbook of Accounting for the Sustainable Development Goals*. Routledge. DOI: 10.4324/9781003404118-27

Wang, L., & Yung, K. (2011). Do State Enterprises Manage Earnings More than Privately Owned Firms? The Case of China. *Journal of Business Finance & Accounting*, 38(7–8), 794–812. DOI: 10.1111/j.1468-5957.2011.02254.x

Wicks, A.C., & Harrison, J.S. (2020). *Towards a More Productive Dialogue Between Stakeholder Theory and Strategic Management.*

Yang, C., Lai, H., & Leing Tan, B. (2008). Managerial Ownership Structure and Earnings Management. *Journal of Financial Reporting and Accounting*, 6(1), 35–53. DOI: 10.1108/19852510880000634

Yang, C., Zhu, C., & Albitar, K. (2024). ESG ratings and green innovation: A U-shaped journey towards sustainable development. *Business Strategy and the Environment*, n/a(n/a). DOI: 10.1002/bse.3692

Yang, Z., Su, D., Xu, S., & Han, X. (2024). Institutional investors and corporate green innovation: Evidence from China. *Pacific Economic Review*, 29(2), 230–266. DOI: 10.1111/1468-0106.12440

Yue, S., Bajuri, N. H., Khatib, S. F. A., & Lee, Y. (2024). New quality productivity and environmental innovation: The hostile moderating roles of managerial empowerment and board centralization. *Journal of Environmental Management*, 370, 122423. DOI: 10.1016/j.jenvman.2024.122423 PMID: 39243639

Yue, S., Bajuri, N. H. B., Khatib, S. F. A., & Alshareef, M. N. (2025). Ownership with a green twist: The role of top managers in driving environmental innovation. *China Finance Review International, ahead-of-print*(ahead-of-print). DOI: 10.1108/CFRI-03-2024-0121

Yue, S., Bajuri, N. H. B., Ye, G., & Ullah, F. (2025). Green Awakening: The Rising Influence of Minority Shareholders and ESG in Shaping China's Sustainable Future. *Sustainable Futures : An Applied Journal of Technology, Environment and Society*, 100441, 100441. Advance online publication. DOI: 10.1016/j.sftr.2025.100441

Yue, S., Norkhairul, B. H., Khatib, S. F. A., & Lee, Y. (2024). Financing creativity: How state-owned and foreign ownership shape innovation engagement in China. *Kybernetes*, ahead-of-print(ahead-of-print). DOI: 10.1108/K-03-2024-0797

Zhang, J., Li, Y., Xu, H., & Ding, Y. (2023). Can ESG ratings mitigate managerial myopia? Evidence from Chinese listed companies. *International Review of Financial Analysis*, 90, 102878. DOI: 10.1016/j.irfa.2023.102878

Zheng, C., & Kouwenberg, R. (2019). A Bibliometric Review of Global Research on Corporate Governance and Board Attributes. *Sustainability (Basel)*, 11(12), 3428. DOI: 10.3390/su11123428

Zhou, K. Z., Gao, G. Y., & Zhao, H. (2017). State Ownership and Firm Innovation in China: An Integrated View of Institutional and Efficiency Logics. *Administrative Science Quarterly*, 62(2), 375–404. DOI: 10.1177/0001839216674457

Zhou, P., Song, F. M., & Huang, X. (2023). Environmental regulations and firms' green innovations: Transforming pressure into incentives. *International Review of Financial Analysis*, 86, 102504. DOI: 10.1016/j.irfa.2023.102504

Zrnic, A., Pekanov, D., & Borozan, D. (2024). Assessing the Sustainability Reporting Transparency and Engagement of European Energy Companies. *Energies*, 17(19), 19. Advance online publication. DOI: 10.3390/en17194934

Chapter 4
Enhancing ESG Reporting With Mathematical Thinking and Emerging Technologies

Dantong Li
https://orcid.org/0009-0008-5011-6059
Universiti Teknologi Malaysia, Malaysia

Qiang Zhang
https://orcid.org/0009-0006-5041-6794
Universiti Teknologi Malaysia, Malaysia

Sharifah Binti Osman
https://orcid.org/0000-0003-2896-9377
Universiti Teknologi Malaysia, Malaysia

Yijing Du
https://orcid.org/0009-0005-7171-1082
Universiti Teknologi Malaysia, Malaysia

Najua Syuhada Binti Ahmad Alhassora
Universiti Teknologi Malaysia, Malaysia

Ninglin Li
https://orcid.org/0009-0008-8387-3638
Universiti Teknologi Malaysia, Malaysia

ABSTRACT

As corporate accountability demands grow, transparent sustainability reporting is essential for stakeholder trust. This chapter explores how mathematical thinking, integrated with artificial intelligence (AI) and blockchain, transforms environmental, social, and governance (ESG) reporting. Statistical models, optimization algorithms, and uncertainty analysis enhance data validation, resource management, and decision-making. AI and blockchain enable automation, data integrity, and traceability, addressing ESG challenges. Practical applications in energy, manufacturing, and logistics demonstrate how these methods optimize efficiency, reduce

DOI: 10.4018/979-8-3373-0117-4.ch004

carbon footprints, and align ESG goals with profitability. The chapter addresses privacy, scalability, and standardization challenges, emphasizing global collaboration, policy support, and mathematical literacy. By integrating human oversight with AI and blockchain, organizations can set new benchmarks in transparency, accountability, and sustainability.

1 INTRODUCTION

In the modern corporate environment, trust and transparency are important factors in the credibility of sustainability reports. Stakeholders, including investors, regulators, and consumers, demand clear and accurate descriptions of companies' environmental, social, and governance (ESG) initiatives (Kulkarni et al.2023; Birindelli et al., 2022). However, the complexity and data-driven nature of sustainability reporting often requires advanced methods to ensure that the information presented is reliable and verifiable. This chapter explores the role of mathematical thinking, methods, and tools in addressing these challenges, particularly by improving the accuracy, transparency, and credibility of ESG data (Kaya & Tuncer, 2021; Zhang et al., 2023).

Mathematical methods such as statistical analysis, predictive modeling, and optimization algorithms provide a powerful framework for improving the accuracy of sustainability reporting (Lilhore et al., 2022). These tools not only help companies verify ESG data, but also enable them to predict sustainability outcomes and optimize resource allocation (Lee & Brahmasrene, 2020). Furthermore, by integrating advanced technologies such as artificial intelligence (AI) and blockchain, data verification can be automated and an immutable record of ESG activities created, significantly improving transparency and accountability (Hasan et al., 2024; Pathirana et al., 2022).

The combination of mathematics and technology has played an important role in improving the transparency and credibility of ESG data. Mathematics provides companies with a logical, abstract and precise framework, making the analysis and verification of complex data more systematic. At the same time, technology enhances this process through automation and transparency. For example, blockchain technology ensures the credibility of data sources through its tamper-proof distributed ledger function, while artificial intelligence (AI) can efficiently process large-scale data sets, identify patterns and anomalies, and thus improve the overall quality and efficiency of ESG reporting (Pathirana et al., 2022). This synergy enables companies to manage and optimize data more reliably throughout the entire process from data collection to verification.

The Technology-Organization-Environment (TOE) framework provides a robust theoretical foundation for enterprises seeking to adopt mathematical and technological tools to enhance sustainability practices. This framework emphasizes three critical dimensions—technological capabilities, organizational characteristics, and the external environment—that collectively shape the adoption of new technologies (Awa et al., 2017).The technological dimension highlights factors such as the ease of use, reliability, and compatibility of tools with existing systems, exemplified by blockchain and AI's role in ESG data processing.Organizational dimension focuses on internal dynamics, including resource allocation, employee training, and senior management support, which accelerate the adoption of advanced tools through strategic leadership and technical upskilling. And the environmental dimension encompasses external pressures, such as industry competition, regulatory requirements, and market demand for transparency, which compel companies to adopt more sophisticated tools to meet rising ESG expectations.

By addressing these dimensions, the TOE framework provides a systematic perspective for understanding the drivers and barriers to adopting technologies that improve ESG data processing. For example, the growing global demand for ESG transparency highlights the need for advanced tools that can ensure data standardization and credibility across industries and regions.The TOE framework serves as a structured lens to examine how companies adopt ESG tools and practices. It underscores the interplay between technological, organizational, and environmental factors, offering valuable insights into how businesses navigate the complexities of sustainability reporting. This perspective is particularly critical in light of evolving trends, as businesses adapt their strategies to align with new regulatory demands, technological advancements, and heightened stakeholder expectations.To illustrate this interplay, Table 1 outlines the dimensions of the TOE framework, their key elements, and the practical challenges they address in ESG reporting. This table demonstrates how the framework enables a systematic understanding of the adoption of advanced tools like blockchain and AI, emphasizing their role in enhancing data accuracy, standardization, and transparency.

Table 1. TOE Framework for ESG Reporting Adoption

Dimension	Key Elements	Practical Challenges in ESG Reporting
Technology (T)	- Usability and reliability of tools - Compatibility with existing systems - Data accuracy through blockchain and AI	-Lackofunifiedglobal ESGdatastandards - Difficulty in processing and verifying unstructured ESG data
Organization (O)	- Resource allocation - Skills and training for employees - Support from senior management	- High costs of implementing AI and blockchain solutions -Insufficient organizational expertise in advanced ESG tools
Environment (E)	- Industry competition - Regulatory pressures (e.g., CSRD, ISSB standards) - Market demand for transparency	-Regional differences in ESG regulations - Complex compliance requirements for multinational organizations

Building on the TOE framework, the analysis of emerging trends provides a practical lens to examine the evolving ESG landscape. Table 2 offers a comparative overview of ESG reporting trends from 2023 to 2024, providing a comprehensive understanding of key shifts in regulations, technology adoption, and stakeholder priorities. This comparison highlights how businesses are adapting their strategies to align with new demands for transparency, technological integration, and accountability in sustainability reporting.By combining the TOE framework with an analysis of these trends, organizations can better navigate the complexities of sustainability reporting, ensuring that their practices remain robust and aligned with evolving global expectations.

Table 2. Comparison of ESG Reporting Trends: 2023 vs. 2024

Aspect	2023 Trends	2024 Trends
Regulatory Oversight	Increase in ESG regulations such as CSRD and ISSB standards.	New ESG regulations, including CSRD and ISSB, focus on transparency and comparability of ESG data.
Data Quality	Demand for better ESG data to meet investor expectations.	Improved ESG measurement and reporting practices driven by higher investor demand.
Climate Risk Focus	Companies report on climate risks and decarbonization progress, including GHG emissions.	Climate risk reporting remains a priority with more focus on disclosing emissions reduction strategies.
Integration into Strategy	ESG factors are integrated into long-term business plans to identify risks and opportunities.	Businesses align ESG data with broader strategic goals to optimize stakeholder satisfaction.
Greenwashing Scrutiny	Increased lawsuits due to greenwashing practices.	Stricter enforcement and regulations to address misleading environmental claims.

continued on following page

Table 2. Continued

Aspect	2023 Trends	2024 Trends
Supply Chain Transparency	Focus on detailed supply chain disclosures to meet stakeholder and regulatory expectations.	Managing entire supply chain ESG impacts, including Scope 3 emissions, becomes the norm.
Social Issues	Greater attention to diversity, equity, and inclusion (DEI) programs and social reporting.	Continued focus on DEI initiatives with expanded reporting on broader social impacts.
Global Standardization	Adoption of frameworks to ensure ESG report consistency and reliability.	Enhanced efforts toward globally harmonized ESG reporting standards.
Technology Investments	Adoption of digital tools to improve ESG data collection and reporting.	Increased investment in AI and digital platforms for better ESG data management and reporting.
Consumer Behavior	Focus on ESG disclosures to influence investor confidence and corporate responsibility.	Emphasis on disclosing environmental product performance to impact consumer purchase decisions.
Accountant Role	Limited involvement of accountants in ESG reporting.	Greater role for CPAs in ESG assurance and data accuracy validation.

While these evolving trends showcase remarkable progress, Kaya and Tuncer (2021) highlight several persistent challenges that businesses must address. ESG data continues to lack global unified standards in definitions and indicators, making cross-company and cross-industry comparisons difficult. Additionally, regional differences in ESG regulations and the complexity of processing unstructured ESG data further complicate compliance efforts. To overcome these challenges, the combination of mathematics and technology offers innovative solutions. For example, blockchain technology enables companies to record and share standardized ESG data globally, achieving consistency and transparency. Simultaneously, AI technology facilitates the analysis and verification of unstructured data, enhancing accuracy, comparability, and compliance across regions. By leveraging these tools, companies can not only meet regulatory demands but also improve the overall credibility of their sustainability reports.

This chapter will further explore the practical applications of mathematical methods and emerging technologies in enhancing the transparency and reliability of ESG reporting, providing actionable insights for both academics and practitioners. The chapter's primary objective is to provide a detailed examination of the role that mathematical methods play in ensuring the reliability and transparency of sustainability reports. Specifically, it seeks to:

1. Highlight the synergy between mathematical thinking and emerging technologies in structuring and analyzing sustainability reports.

2. Explore mathematical models for ESG data verification, emphasizing statistical tools and predictive analytics.
3. Illustrate the application of optimization algorithms for sustainable resource allocation and efficiency improvement.
4. Provide real-world case studies demonstrating the effectiveness of mathematical and technological approaches in enhancing ESG data credibility.
5. Investigate future directions in ESG reporting, focusing on the transformative potential of AI and blockchain and addressing associated challenges.

Figure 1 conceptual framework of this chapter

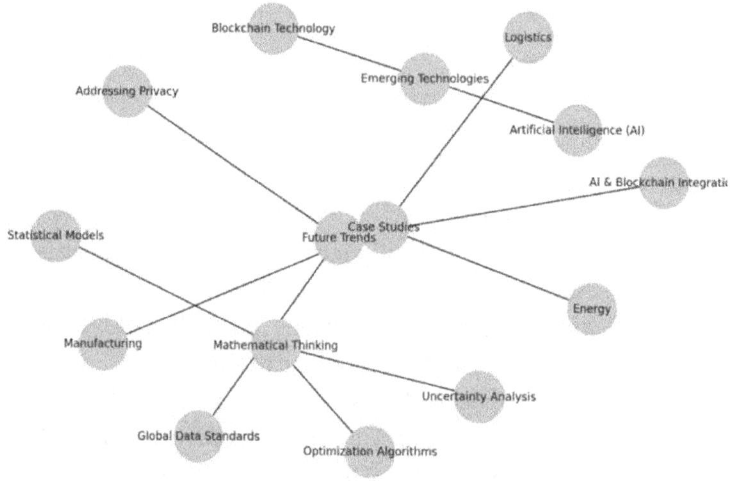

Figure 1 is a simplified conceptual framework diagram. It focuses on the core components of the chapter: Mathematical Thinking, Emerging Technologies, Case Studies, and Future Trends, with their key elements. This visual representation provides a clear and concise overview of the chapter's purpose.

2 THE POTENTIAL OF INTEGRATING MATHEMATICAL THINKING WITH AI AND BLOCKCHAIN

2.1 AI's Support for Mathematical Thinking

Mathematical thinking refers to the cognitive processes and strategies individuals use to understand and solve mathematical problems, encompassing abilities such as posing questions, interpreting mathematical statements, and navigating the limits of mathematical concepts (Lepore, 2024). It is a developmental process influenced by both genetics and experiences, fostering logical reasoning and the ability to engage with mathematical symbols and language . Importantly, mathematical thinking is not only a key goal of education but also a fundamental means of learning and developing critical thinking skills, which are indispensable for addressing real-world challenges (Romero et al.2024; Kallia et al.2021). The importance of foundational numeracy and literacy skills is emphasized, as these are prerequisites for engaging with more advanced quantitative reasoning tasks.

In the realm of sustainability, mathematical thinking is particularly significant. It supports the modeling of sustainability on local, regional, and global scales, enabling the assessment of environmental risks, the impacts of human activities, and the formulation of predictive models to guide science and policy. Furthermore, mathematical thinking facilitates the optimization of processes in industries such as supply chain management, where it improves efficiency, reduces costs, and enhances sustainability by addressing manufacturing costs, inventory management, and logistics design (Lee et al., 2020). This capability underscores the importance of integrating mathematical thinking into decision-making processes, especially as we strive to meet sustainable development goals without compromising the needs of future generations .

An emerging development in this context is the integration of Artificial Intelligence (AI) with mathematical thinking, which has become a transformative force in data-driven decision-making processes. At its core, AI employs mathematical principles such as linear algebra, probability, and calculus to design and optimize models capable of handling vast and complex datasets. For example, linear algebra forms the foundation for neural networks, where matrix operations enable weight adjustments and transformations. Similarly, probability and statistics are vital for evaluating models, predicting trends, and managing uncertainties in data (Pathirana et al., 2022).

A critical application of AI in the ESG domain is its ability to automate data processing and validation. By employing machine learning algorithms, AI can analyze historical data to detect anomalies, ensuring the alignment of ESG reports with observed patterns. For instance, regression models integrated with AI help predict carbon emission trends while validating them against actual data. Such integration enhances the credibility and accuracy of sustainability reporting (Kulkarni et al., 2023). Additionally, AI's capability to process unstructured data, such as social media and news articles, through natural language processing (NLP) exemplifies its support for mathematical abstraction. By converting qualitative information into quantifiable metrics, AI simplifies complex issues and generates actionable insights (Rodriguez and Cruz, 2023).

2.2 Blockchain's Support for Mathematical Thinking

Blockchain technology is a revolutionary framework that has gained significant attention for its ability to create a decentralized and immutable ledger. This technology is underpinned by mathematical algorithms that are essential for ensuring data security, transparency, and trustworthiness. The foundation of blockchain is built upon cryptographic principles, such as hash functions and public-key cryptography, which provide robust mechanisms for data integrity and transaction validation (Zhang et al., 2023). These mathematical underpinnings exemplify the logical rigor and precision characteristic of mathematical thinking.

One of the pivotal contributions of blockchain to ESG reporting is its ability to provide data traceability and validation. By recording each transaction with timestamps and source tags, blockchain creates an immutable audit trail, ensuring data authenticity throughout its lifecycle. This capability addresses common concerns about data integrity and enhances the reliability of sustainability reporting (Kaya and Tuncer, 2021). Furthermore, smart contracts—self-executing programs based on predefined rules—utilize mathematical logic to automate the verification of ESG data. This reduces reliance on manual checks and fosters trust among stakeholders by standardizing processes (Bai et al., 2021). Blockchain also addresses challenges in ESG data standardization. By embedding predefined formats and validation rules into its framework, it minimizes discrepancies caused by varying reporting protocols across industries. Such standardization ensures consistency and comparability of ESG metrics, facilitating better decision-making for organizations and stakeholders alike.

Blockchain serves as a critical enabler of sustainability goals, providing innovative solutions across domains such as carbon credit trading, energy management, and supply chain optimization. Mulligan et al. (2024) underscores that blockchain's decentralized structure and ability to secure data integrity make it invaluable in ensuring the accountability and transparency of ESG reporting. For example, blockchain-enabled solutions like permissioned ledgers can integrate seamlessly with existing regulatory frameworks, ensuring compliance with evolving standards such as the Corporate Sustainability Reporting Directive (CSRD) and International Sustainability Standards Board (ISSB) guidelines. Moreover, blockchain supports real-time data verification in voluntary carbon markets, enhancing the credibility of carbon offset initiatives.

The R&D team at EGS has proposed three key concepts for building applications using blockchain technology. Smart contracts, which are fully digital and typically micro-computers stored within the blockchain, are enabled by EGS to become "intelligent," featuring transparency, information management services, accuracy, speed, and security. EGS specializes in emerging blockchain technologies like Ethereum and Hyperledger, with the capability to build smart contract systems that have the potential to disrupt industries such as insurance, real estate, healthcare, and finance. Consensus mechanisms, including Proof of Work (PoW) and Proof of Stake (PoS), are algorithmic methods developed by EGS to achieve consensus on the validity of transactions.

Mulligan et al. (2024) recommend systems based on PoS algorithms due to their advantages, such as reduced energy consumption, lower hardware costs, protection against malicious actors, decentralized structure without cartel formation, and enhanced security. Lastly, permissioned blockchains designed by EGS utilize PoS, accelerating transaction settlement processes while maintaining a controlled network environment.Blockchain solutions also demonstrate potential in addressing the complexities of sustainability metrics, aligning technological capabilities with global sustainability frameworks like the UN's Sustainable Development Goals (SDGs). These systems not only ensure data security and integrity but also promote cross-border collaboration for sustainability initiatives, reinforcing blockchain's role as a transformative tool for achieving net-zero goals.

Figure 2. The core benefits of blockchain technology

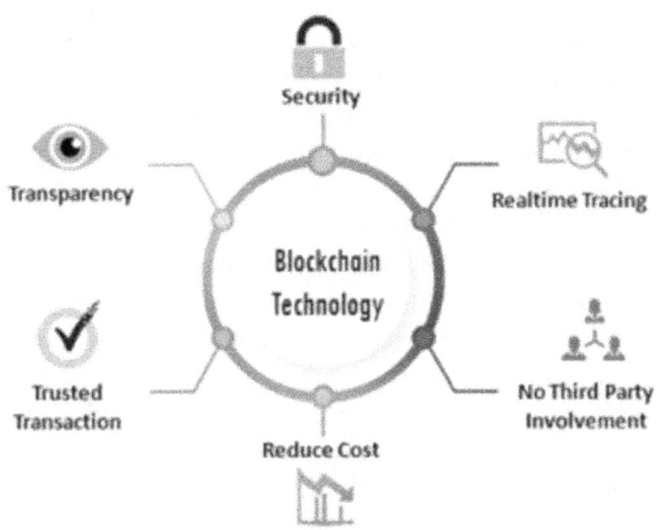

Figure 2 visually represents the core benefits of blockchain technology, including its focus on Security, Transparency, Realtime Tracing, the facilitation of Trusted Transactions, the elimination of the need for Third Party Involvement, and its potential to Reduce Cost. These features collectively contribute to the transformative impact of blockchain across various sectors, enhancing efficiency and trust in data management and transactions.

2.3 The Synergy Between AI and Blockchain

The integration of AI and blockchain creates transformative opportunities for enhancing mathematical thinking across diverse domains, particularly in sustainability and governance. AI leverages blockchain-verified datasets to extract actionable insights, enabling advanced modeling and predictive analytics. Conversely, blockchain ensures the provenance, integrity, and immutability of training data, providing a robust foundation for reliable and transparent AI models. Together, these technologies establish a powerful synergy that not only elevates analytical precision but also fosters trust in data-driven decision-making processes, addressing critical challenges in areas like ESG reporting, supply chain management, and carbon markets (Kulkarni et al., 2023; Perera et al., 2024).

Blockchain's decentralized ledger system ensures traceability and data security through immutable records, supported by smart contracts to automate data verification and standardization. This infrastructure reduces manual processes, aligns with emerging regulatory frameworks, and strengthens the foundation for responsible AI applications (Bai et al., 2021; Mulligan et al., 2024). On the other hand, AI enhances blockchain's utility by analyzing verified datasets to identify patterns, predict trends, and optimize processes. For instance, AI-driven analytics can streamline carbon credit trading or uncover inefficiencies in global supply chains, contributing to better decision-making aligned with ESG goals. Additionally, the integration of AI and blockchain within edge computing frameworks, such as multi-access edge computing (MEC), further reduces latency and enhances real-time decision-making in sustainability and beyond .

This synergy exemplifies the evolution of mathematical thinking in the digital age. Blockchain employs cryptographic principles such as hash functions and consensus mechanisms, while AI utilizes mathematical models like neural networks and probabilistic algorithms. By integrating these technologies, organizations can address complex challenges with greater precision and efficiency, driving progress toward sustainable development and innovation across industries. This convergence not only advances sustainability goals but also sets a precedent for future digital solutions that integrate security, transparency, and analytical robustness.

3 MATHEMATICAL MODELS AND METHODS IN SUSTAINABILITY ASSURANCE

Mathematical models and methods are foundational for ensuring the reliability and credibility of sustainability reports. By integrating advanced analytical techniques with emerging technologies such as blockchain and AI, companies can enhance the accuracy, transparency, and utility of ESG data. These methods provide novel solutions for data validation, resource optimization, and risk management, ultimately fostering greater trust among stakeholders.

3.1 Mathematical Models for Data Validation and Analysis

Mathematical models are indispensable for the validation and analysis of ESG data, ensuring the reliability and credibility of sustainability reports. Statistical analysis, a fundamental mathematical approach, plays a crucial role in this process. Techniques such as regression analysis are employed to identify trends and patterns, particularly in areas like carbon emissions and energy consumption. For instance, regression models can predict future carbon emissions based on historical data, allowing organizations to anticipate environmental impacts and verify their alignment with reported metrics. This predictive capability is vital for strategic planning and compliance with sustainability standards.

Moreover, hypothesis testing is another statistical method that assesses the validity of sustainability claims. By comparing reported data against industry benchmarks or expected norms, companies can ensure that their ESG data is not only accurate but also consistent with industry standards. Recent advancements in AI and data analytics have further enhanced the robustness of hypothesis testing, enabling real-time validation of ESG metrics across multiple datasets. Emerging tools also integrate spatial and temporal analyses to identify discrepancies in geographically distributed data sources. These innovations significantly improve the credibility and transparency of sustainability reports.The integration of mathematical models with emerging technologies like blockchain and AI further amplifies the accuracy, transparency, and utility of ESG data. Blockchain provides an immutable ledger for data validation, while AI uncovers hidden patterns within datasets, allowing for deeper insights and proactive decision-making. These combined models have become essential for addressing complex sustainability challenges.

3.2 AI-Supported Mathematical Thinking

AI enhances traditional mathematical models by providing advanced tools for processing and analyzing large datasets. Specific mathematical techniques used in AI include gradient descent for optimizing models, matrix operations in neural networks, and distribution functions for probabilistic predictions. For instance, gradient descent algorithms are crucial in machine learning for finding the optimal solution to minimize error in predictive models, such as those predicting climate change trends.AI's ability to process unstructured data, such as textual ESG reports or satellite imagery, sets it apart from traditional methods. Natural Language Processing (NLP) techniques, supported by mathematical frameworks like linear algebra and probability, enable AI to extract meaningful information from non-numerical data. For example, NLP can analyze corporate ESG disclosures to identify inconsistencies or trends that may not be evident through numerical analysis alone. This capability is critical in handling the increasing volume of unstructured ESG data.Compared to traditional statistical methods, AI-supported models exhibit superior efficiency and adaptability. They can process vast amounts of data in real time, identify complex relationships, and adjust predictions based on new inputs. For example, an AI-driven regression model can update climate trend forecasts dynamically as new environmental data becomes available, ensuring greater accuracy and relevance. Additionally, AI's ability to integrate with optimization algorithms enhances its capacity for solving multi-variable ESG challenges, such as balancing economic performance with environmental sustainability.

3.3 Blockchain-Supported Mathematical Thinking

Blockchain technology relies heavily on mathematical principles to ensure data security, transparency, and consistency. At its core are cryptographic techniques, such as hash functions and elliptic curve cryptography, which form the backbone of blockchain's secure and immutable ledger. Hash functions, for instance, generate unique digital fingerprints for each data entry, ensuring that any alteration is immediately detectable.Smart contracts, a key feature of blockchain, operate on mathematical logic. These self-executing contracts enforce rules and conditions automatically, eliminating the need for intermediaries. For example, smart contracts can validate ESG data submissions by cross-referencing them with predefined thresholds or benchmarks, ensuring compliance and consistency in reporting. Distributed ledger technology, underpinned by consensus algorithms like Proof of Stake (PoS) and Proof of Work (PoW), ensures that all participants in the blockchain network agree on the authenticity of data entries.Mathematical models also play a role in optimizing blockchain's storage and retrieval mechanisms. Techniques such as compression algorithms and distributed indexing improve the efficiency of blockchain systems, enabling them to handle large volumes of ESG data without compromising performance. Additionally, embedding mathematical models within blockchain can facilitate real-time data consistency checks, ensuring that reported metrics align with verified sources.

3.4 Synergy Between AI and Blockchain in ESG Data Validation

The integration of AI and blockchain creates a powerful synergy for ESG data validation. Blockchain provides a secure and traceable foundation for data, while AI offers advanced analytics and predictive capabilities. Together, they enhance the transparency, accuracy, and utility of ESG reports.For instance, AI can analyze blockchain-verified datasets to uncover patterns and anomalies, ensuring that ESG metrics are both accurate and actionable. Predictive models powered by AI can forecast future sustainability outcomes based on historical blockchain data, offering stakeholders valuable insights into potential risks and opportunities. Conversely, blockchain ensures the integrity of the data used to train AI models, reducing biases and enhancing the reliability of predictions.By combining the strengths of both technologies, organizations can address the challenges of ESG data validation comprehensively. This approach not only strengthens the credibility of sustainability reports but also fosters greater trust among stakeholders, positioning companies as leaders in responsible and transparent practices.

4 OPTIMIZATION ALGORITHMS FOR RESOURCE MANAGEMENT

Optimization algorithms are pivotal for sustainable resource management as they provide systematic approaches to address complex resource allocation challenges. Techniques such as linear programming and multi-objective optimization enable companies to allocate resources like energy, water, and raw materials in a sustainable manner while meeting operational demands. These algorithms help minimize waste, reduce environmental footprints, and maximize operational efficiency, contributing significantly to sustainability goals.

Linear programming, for example, is widely used to solve optimization problems where resource constraints are present. It allows businesses to allocate limited resources efficiently, such as optimizing energy usage in manufacturing processes to lower operational costs and emissions. Similarly, multi-objective optimization balances competing objectives, such as reducing greenhouse gas emissions while maintaining production levels or achieving cost efficiency without compromising sustainability goals.

Recent advancements have integrated dynamic optimization techniques, enabling real-time resource allocation in response to changing conditions. For instance, real-time optimization models have been successfully applied in the energy sector to balance electricity supply and demand during peak usage periods. These models reduce energy wastage and enhance grid reliability by prioritizing renewable energy sources like solar and wind.In logistics and supply chain management, optimization models have proven instrumental in reducing transportation inefficiencies. By analyzing routes and schedules, companies can minimize fuel consumption, cut delivery times, and lower overall emissions. This not only improves environmental performance but also reduces costs, providing a win-win solution for businesses and the planet.

Chen et al.(2023) emphasized that these methods allow companies to align environmental responsibility with economic performance, proving that sustainability and profitability can coexist. Additionally, with the integration of AI and IoT technologies, optimization algorithms now have the capability to incorporate real-time data from sensors and other sources, further enhancing their accuracy and adaptability.For example, a multinational company implemented a genetic algorithm to optimize its supply chain network, reducing transportation emissions by 20% while maintaining on-time delivery rates. Similarly, in water resource management, optimization algorithms have been used to allocate water resources during drought conditions, ensuring equitable distribution while protecting critical ecosystems.

By balancing environmental responsibility with economic efficiency, optimization algorithms not only address immediate sustainability challenges but also lay the foundation for long-term resilience and sustainable growth. Their flexibility and scalability make them indispensable tools for organizations striving to meet the growing demands of a sustainable future.

4.1 Uncertainty and Risk Management

In the realm of long-term environmental projections, uncertainty is a persistent challenge due to the intricate interplay of variables such as climate change, resource availability, regulatory changes, and economic fluctuations. Effectively managing these uncertainties necessitates the use of advanced mathematical models and analytical tools, enabling organizations to identify risks, quantify their potential impacts, and design proactive strategies for mitigation.

Mathematical tools such as probability distributions are crucial for understanding the likelihood of various outcomes. These tools allow organizations to model uncertainties in areas such as fluctuating energy prices, potential supply chain disruptions, or future carbon emissions. By preparing for a spectrum of possible scenarios, organizations can better mitigate risks and develop resilience against unexpected challenges. Monte Carlo simulations, for example, are extensively used to model complex, probabilistic scenarios, providing a statistical basis for evaluating both best-case and worst-case outcomes.

Sensitivity analysis plays an equally vital role in managing uncertainty by identifying the most influential factors in sustainability strategies. By quantifying how variations in key inputs—such as energy costs, resource availability, or market demand—affect overall results, sensitivity analysis enables businesses to focus on areas that yield the greatest impact. For instance, it is often employed to optimize renewable energy projects, where fluctuating wind or solar output can affect grid reliability and project profitability.

Scenario planning complements these mathematical tools by offering a structured approach to evaluating potential future conditions. This involves creating multiple scenarios based on varying assumptions, such as more stringent environmental policies, technological advancements, or economic shifts. Scenario planning provides organizations with strategic flexibility, allowing them to adapt to evolving circumstances while maintaining focus on long-term sustainability goals.Advances in AI and machine learning have significantly augmented traditional risk management methods. AI models excel in analyzing large datasets, uncovering patterns, and enabling real-time adjustments. Predictive analytics, powered by AI, can anticipate risks such as extreme weather events that may disrupt supply chains. By proactively addressing these risks, businesses can safeguard operations and enhance efficiency. Additionally, AI algorithms improve the reliability of ESG reporting by identifying anomalies and ensuring data consistency across diverse sources.

Incorporating uncertainty modeling into financial planning further strengthens an organization's ability to manage risks. Tools such as Value at Risk (VaR) and Conditional Value at Risk (CVaR) enable companies to estimate the financial implications of environmental risks, such as fluctuating carbon pricing or water shortages. These insights help organizations allocate resources effectively and avoid unexpected costs, aligning financial stability with sustainability objectives.Effective uncertainty and risk management is not just about technical precision; it is also about transparency and accountability. Organizations that openly address risks and demonstrate preparedness can build trust among stakeholders, including investors, regulators, and consumers. This transparency reinforces the organization's reputation as a responsible and forward-thinking entity, fostering stronger relationships with its stakeholders.

By leveraging mathematical models, AI, and scenario-based planning, companies can navigate the complexities of environmental uncertainty with greater confidence. This strategic approach ensures that sustainability initiatives remain robust and adaptable, aligning with both immediate needs and long-term objectives. The integration of these advanced tools not only enhances operational resilience but also positions organizations to thrive in an era of heightened environmental awareness and accountability.

4.2 Blockchain for ESG Data Validation

Blockchain technology complements mathematical models by providing an immutable ledger for recording ESG data. This decentralized system ensures that every data entry is time-stamped, source-authenticated, and securely stored. The transparency and traceability of blockchain enable companies to address long-standing issues of data inconsistencies and reporting inaccuracies in ESG metrics. By establishing a tamper-proof record, blockchain enhances the credibility and reliability of sustainability reporting.For instance, a manufacturing company used blockchain to record carbon emissions data across multiple operational sites, reducing discrepancies in reporting cycles and enhancing data transparency (Pathirana et al., 2022). Table 3 illustrates how blockchain improves the accuracy and comparability of ESG data.

Table 3. Example of Blockchain-Recorded ESG Data

Site	Reported Emissions (tons CO_2e)	Blockchain-Recorded Emissions (tons CO_2e)	Discrepancy
Site A	1,200	1,210	-10
Site B	1,500	1,500	0
Site C	2,000	1,980	+20

Blockchain's transparency allowed stakeholders to verify data consistency and reliability, reducing ambiguities in ESG reporting. Its tamper-proof nature further enhanced the credibility of the company's ESG claims, fostering trust among investors, regulators, and consumers.The application of blockchain technology in ESG reporting is transformative, as it significantly improves data accuracy and reduces the risk of manipulation. Each transaction or entry in the blockchain is verified by a network of nodes, ensuring that all recorded data is consistent and free from unauthorized modifications. This validation process aligns with the growing demand for transparency in corporate sustainability initiatives, where stakeholders require verifiable evidence of environmental, social, and governance performance

Figure 3 provides a detailed representation of the layered architecture of blockchain technology specifically applied to ESG data management. The diagram emphasizes the step-by-step process of handling ESG data, from its initial collection to its secure storage, validation, and eventual utilization by various stakeholders.

The process begins with **data input** collected from IoT sensors and systems, which record critical information such as metrics, geolocation, application data, and logs. This raw data is sent to the system via APIs, where it undergoes hashing to create unique digital signatures. The hashed information is then securely stored on the blockchain, ensuring that the data remains tamper-proof and immutable.

The **blockchain infrastructure** lies at the core of the system, depicted as a sequential chain of blocks representing the secured storage of ESG data. Each block contains hashed information, ensuring that any modifications or updates are traceable. The system allows updates to be captured while preserving all previous versions in the form of a comprehensive audit trail. This functionality is encapsulated in the "Edit" and "Audit" features of the diagram.The diagram further showcases the blockchain's ability to validate data through advanced mechanisms such as **Proof of ESG Cloud**, where the integrity and accuracy of the data are verified in real time. Other critical blockchain features include:

- **Merkle Proof**, which enables quick validation of data integrity.
- **SPV Check**, a lightweight mechanism allowing third parties to verify specific transactions without accessing the full blockchain.
- **Private/Public Auditability**, providing flexibility for organizations to choose between privacy-preserving audits or public transparency.

On the right-hand side of the diagram, blockchain's **automation and collaborative capabilities** are depicted. Smart contracts enable automated processes such as compliance checks or carbon credit trading. Additionally, the system supports seamless integration with chain partners, including regulators, investors, and other stakeholders, ensuring smooth collaboration within the ESG ecosystem.

This layered architecture, as illustrated in Figure 3, highlights the transformative potential of blockchain in ESG data management. By leveraging technologies such as IoT integration, tamper-proof data storage, real-time validation, and automation, organizations can achieve unparalleled transparency, reliability, and compliance in their sustainability reporting efforts. The diagram not only underscores the robustness of blockchain technology but also provides a practical framework for implementing advanced ESG data management systems.

Figure 3. Layered Blockchain Architecture for ESG Data Management

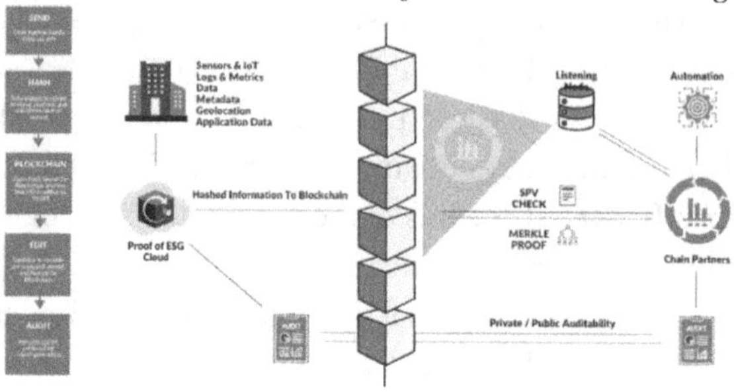

In addition to its validation capabilities, blockchain facilitates the standardization of ESG data across industries. By embedding predefined reporting protocols and structures into its framework, blockchain ensures that companies adhere to consistent metrics and formats. This standardization addresses discrepancies that often arise due to varying reporting methodologies, enabling better comparability across organizations and sectors. The ability to harmonize ESG data reporting is particularly crucial for multinational companies operating in diverse regulatory environments. **Figure 4 below showcases a blockchain-based interface for ESG reporting, providing real-world examples of its practical application. This interface allows companies to record, store, and export data in formats such as Excel and PDF while enabling real-time tracking of key metrics like greenhouse gas emissions and electricity usage. The user-friendly visualization underscores blockchain's operational simplicity and its role in reducing discrepancies, enhancing the accuracy and transparency of ESG reporting.**

Figure 4. Blockchain-Based ESG Reporting Interface

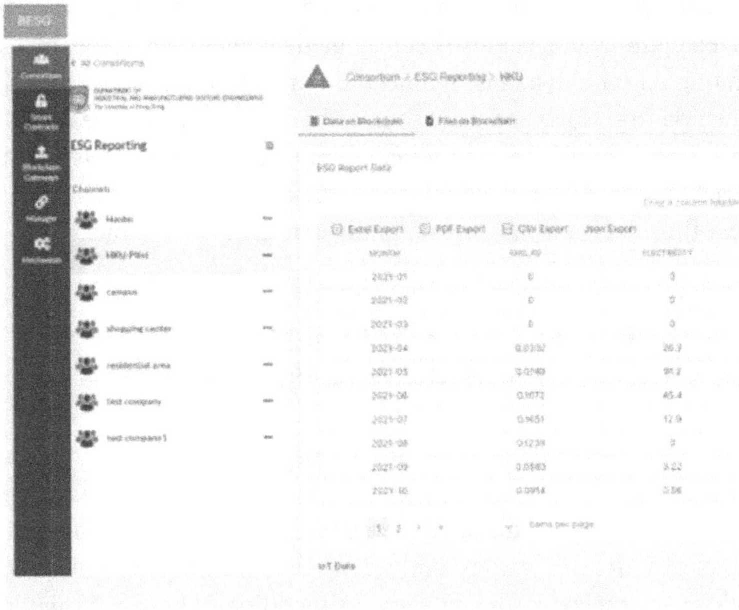

Furthermore, blockchain technology enhances stakeholder engagement by providing real-time access to verified ESG data. Investors, regulators, and consumers can access up-to-date information directly from the blockchain, fostering a higher level of trust and accountability. This real-time accessibility also reduces the administrative burden on companies, as automated verification processes eliminate the need for extensive manual audits. Blockchain-based smart contracts further streamline this process by automating compliance checks, ensuring that sustainability targets are met without additional oversight.

4.3 AI-Driven Optimization for Sustainability

AI augments mathematical models by analyzing vast datasets to uncover patterns, predict trends, and optimize resource utilization. For instance, a global logistics company integrated AI predictive modeling with mathematical optimization algorithms to reduce carbon emissions across its supply chain. By analyzing historical transportation data, the AI model forecasted energy consumption under various scenarios and suggested optimal routes and schedules. This initiative resulted in a 15% reduction in energy consumption and a 10% decrease in greenhouse gas emissions .

AI-driven optimization has also been applied in renewable energy management. By integrating AI with dynamic optimization models, companies can balance energy production from solar and wind sources based on real-time weather data. This ensures consistent supply while minimizing reliance on fossil fuels. Furthermore, AI-enhanced models enable continuous monitoring and adaptive responses, supporting real-time decision-making in rapidly changing environments.

5 CASE STUDIES: APPLYING MATHEMATICS TO ENHANCE TRUST IN SUSTAINABILITY REPORTING

Mathematical methodologies are indispensable in addressing challenges in sustainability assurance. By leveraging advanced tools such as statistical analysis, optimization techniques, and predictive modeling, companies can validate ESG data, optimize resource utilization, and forecast sustainability outcomes with greater accuracy. This section explores how these methodologies have been applied across industries such as energy, manufacturing, and logistics, showcasing their ability to enhance transparency and credibility in corporate sustainability efforts.

5.1 Case Studies

Case Study 1: Validation of Carbon Emission Data Using Integrated Systems

In the context of growing demands for accurate carbon emission disclosures, organizations are leveraging advanced technologies such as statistical models, AI, and blockchain to validate and manage their emissions data. **Figure 5**, titled "Sustainable Framework for Greenhouse Gas Emission Management and Carbon Trading," visually represents a holistic approach to managing greenhouse gas (GHG) emissions through manure collection, storage, utilization, and carbon trading. This circular framework integrates advanced data collection and validation techniques to ensure accurate accounting and reporting of emissions.

Methodology and Implementation

Figure 5 illustrates a multi-stage process for carbon emission management:

1. Manure Collection: The process begins with the systematic collection of manure from agricultural facilities, depicted in the image with arrows linking farms and manure management systems.
2. Manure Management Devices (MMDs): Key GHGs such as **CO_2**, **N_2O**, **CH_4**, and **NH_3** are monitored through IoT-enabled MMDs, which collect and transmit real-time data for analysis.
3. Manure Storage and Utilization: The stored manure is either treated to reduce emissions or redirected for renewable energy production, such as biogas projects, enhancing sustainability.
4. Carbon Emission Accounting and Trading: The image highlights how precise accounting facilitates carbon trading, where GHG reductions are converted into tradeable credits, providing economic incentives for sustainable practices.

Statistical and AI-driven models are applied to analyze the captured data:

- Regression Models: These link emissions data to variables like livestock count, feed types, and manure treatment methods, identifying critical factors contributing to emissions.
- Time-Series Models: These models uncover seasonal trends and anomalies, helping predict future emissions and optimize resource allocation.

Blockchain ensures the integrity and immutability of the collected data. By securely storing emissions metrics, blockchain provides a transparent audit trail, facilitating compliance and boosting stakeholder confidence.

Outcomes and Impact

The integration of IoT sensors, statistical models, AI, and blockchain has transformed carbon emission management, enabling organizations to:

- Optimize Manure Utilization: Emissions are redirected into renewable energy projects, such as biogas, reducing environmental footprints.
- Facilitate Carbon Trading: Accurate GHG data supports the monetization of carbon savings, creating financial incentives for sustainable practices.
- Enhance Data-Driven Decision-Making: Organizations gain actionable insights to optimize storage, usage processes, and emissions reduction strategies.

This comprehensive approach, as illustrated in **Figure 5**, underscores the critical role of integrating advanced technologies in achieving accurate carbon accounting and fostering long-term sustainability goals.

Figure 5. Sustainable Framework for Greenhouse Gas Emission Management and Carbon Trading

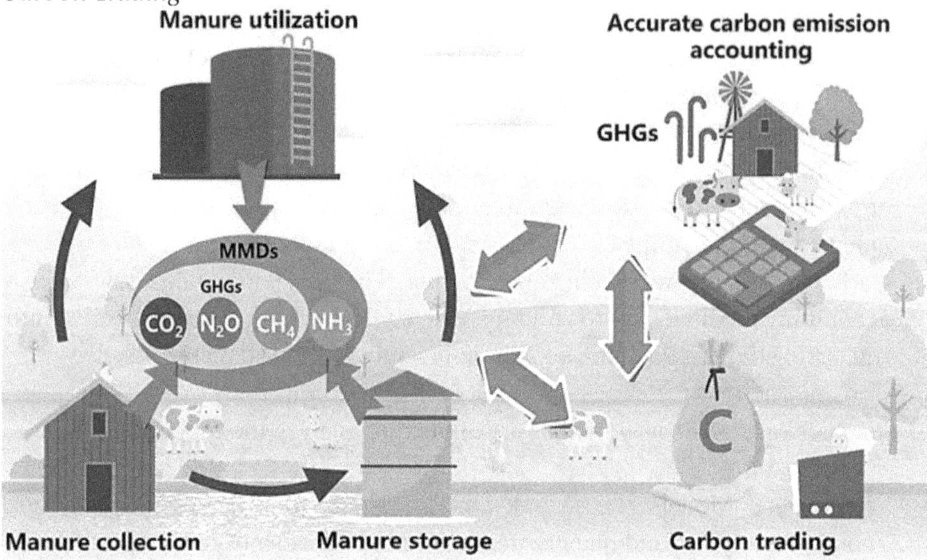

Case Study 2: Optimization of Water and Energy Usage in Renewable Wastewater Treatment

Efficient resource management is critical to achieving sustainability, particularly in industries such as wastewater treatment, where energy-intensive processes often pose environmental challenges. **Figure 6**, titled "Integration of Renewable Energy in 100% Sustainable Wastewater Treatment Plants," is adapted from the research of Campana et al.(2021). It illustrates a closed-loop system integrating renewable energy sources, advanced storage mechanisms, and resource optimization technologies.

Methodology and Implementation

Figure 6 provides a comprehensive framework for optimizing water and energy usage within a wastewater treatment plant powered entirely by renewable energy. The diagram highlights the interplay of various components:

1. Renewable Energy Sources: The system incorporates **solar PV systems** and **wind turbines**, which supply clean energy directly to the plant. These renewable sources form the backbone of the energy input, reducing reliance on traditional fossil fuels.

2. Energy Storage and Management: To address energy intermittency, the plant employs a combination of **battery systems** for short-term storage and **hydrogen storage (H_2)** powered by electrolyzers and fuel cells. This dual-storage mechanism ensures uninterrupted operations, even during periods of low solar or wind energy production.
3. Electricity Network Integration: The treatment plant connects to the broader electricity network, enabling surplus energy to be fed back into the grid and optimizing resource allocation.
4. Circular Wastewater System: Wastewater produced by industries and municipalities is processed in a closed-loop system. This ensures efficient recycling, treatment, and discharge into **water bodies**, while minimizing waste and environmental impact.
5. AI and Optimization Algorithms: Advanced AI-driven optimization techniques, including linear programming and multi-objective optimization, are applied to manage water and energy usage. These algorithms analyze real-time data from IoT sensors placed across the system, ensuring dynamic and efficient resource allocation.

Outcomes and Impact

The integration of renewable energy and optimization techniques, as shown in Figure 6, has led to:

- Energy Efficiency: A reduction in energy consumption by 20% through real-time optimization of renewable energy use and storage systems.
- Water Resource Conservation: Enhanced water recycling and reduced wastage, achieving up to a 15% improvement in water reuse efficiency.
- Economic and Environmental Benefits: Reduced operational costs and a significant decrease in greenhouse gas emissions, aligning with sustainability objectives.

Broader Implications

The deployment of such systems, enhanced by AI and supported by blockchain technology for secure and transparent data management, offers a scalable model for industries worldwide. Blockchain ensures the integrity of operational data, allowing stakeholders to validate energy savings and emissions reductions confidently. By integrating mathematical models, renewable energy systems, and advanced technologies, this framework exemplifies the role of resource optimization in advancing sustainability goals while maintaining high productivity.

Figure 6. Integration of Renewable Energy in 100% Sustainable Wastewater Treatment Plants

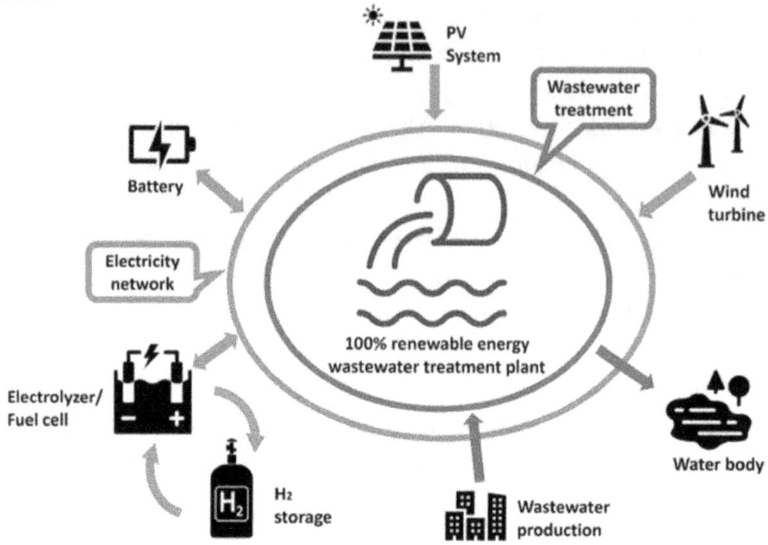

Case Study 3: Predictive Modeling for Sustainability Outcomes in Manufacturing

Predictive modeling plays a critical role in addressing sustainability challenges by leveraging advanced technologies such as machine learning (ML) and deep learning (DL). Figure 7, titled "Integrated Framework for Predictive Quality in Manufacturing Using Machine and Deep Learning," illustrates a comprehensive system that combines manufacturing processes, data analytics, and AI-driven modeling to achieve predictive insights for improved sustainability outcomes.

Methodology and Implementation

Figure 7 demonstrates a structured approach consisting of three interconnected components:

1. Manufacturing Process (Left Panel): The process begins with the design, simulation, and production stages, guided by expert systems. Key elements include:
    - Simulation and Design: Tools like CAD and simulation models enable optimized product development.
    - Production: Real-time data is collected from manufacturing processes.

- Expert Systems: Feedback mechanisms ensure process consistency and quality.

2. Data Basis (Middle Panel): This layer is the foundation of predictive modeling, integrating diverse data sources:
   - Design Factors: Product design inputs affecting quality and performance.
   - Sensors and Parameters: IoT-enabled sensors monitor real-time production parameters such as temperature, pressure, and energy usage.
   - Product Quality Metrics: Quality metrics are continuously updated to build reliable datasets for further analysis.

The collected data is centralized in a database for subsequent AI-driven processing.

3. Machine and Deep Learning (Right Panel): The final stage utilizes ML and DL models for data analysis and prediction:
   - Model Training and Testing: Historical data is used to train algorithms like neural networks, identifying key patterns and anomalies.
   - Model Deployment and Prediction: The models process real-time data to predict future outcomes, such as product quality, resource consumption, and operational efficiency.

Outcomes and Impact

The integration of predictive modeling tools outlined in Figure 7 delivers significant benefits for sustainability and operational efficiency:

- Sustainability Metrics Optimization: ML and DL algorithms analyze resource consumption patterns, enabling companies to minimize waste and reduce energy use by up to 15%.
- Improved Product Quality: Real-time feedback ensures that products meet sustainability and performance standards, fostering customer satisfaction.
- Proactive Risk Mitigation: Predictive models identify potential risks, such as equipment failures or production bottlenecks, allowing for timely interventions.
- AI-Blockchain Synergy: Blockchain technology can be integrated into this system to ensure the traceability and transparency of production and quality data, reinforcing stakeholder confidence.

Broader Implications

This case study highlights the transformative role of AI-driven predictive modeling in advancing sustainability goals. By linking mathematical thinking with cutting-edge technologies, companies can achieve a balance between operational efficiency and environmental responsibility. The framework presented in Figure 7, drawn from the research of Tercan and Meisen (2022), serves as a scalable model for industries aiming to integrate sustainability into their core operations.

Figure 7. Integrated Framework for Predictive Quality in Manufacturing Using Machine and Deep Learning

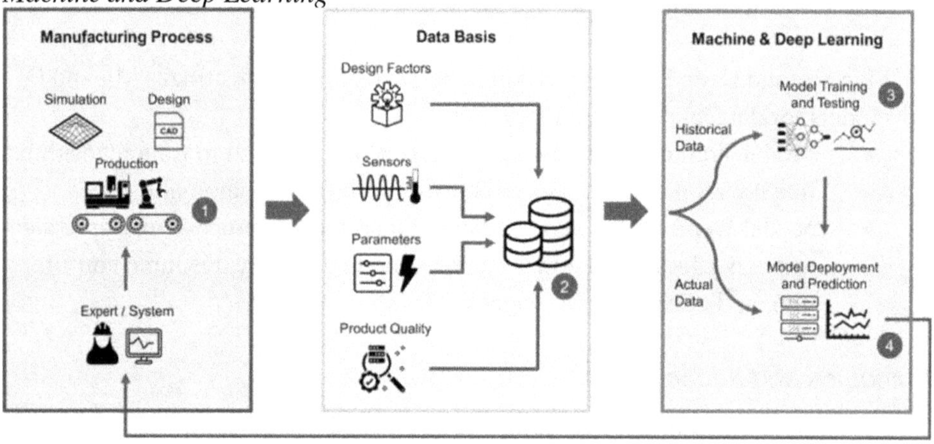

Case Study 4: Financial Sector in Green Investment Assessment

The financial sector is playing an increasingly critical role in mobilizing green finance to promote sustainability. **Figure 8,** titled **"Integrated Framework for Mobilization of Green Finance,"** outlines six essential pillars that collectively support the development and governance of green financial systems. This structured representation emphasizes the interplay of diverse elements essential for fostering sustainable investment practices and ensuring financial stability.

Figure 8. Integrated Framework for Mobilization of Green Finance

Methodology and Implementation

Figure 8 illustrates the core components of green finance mobilization, which include:

Capacity Building and Governance

Establishing robust governance frameworks is fundamental to ensuring the transparency and effectiveness of green finance initiatives. These frameworks guide the development and implementation of policies that promote sustainable investments while fostering accountability among stakeholders. Capacity building plays a complementary role by equipping stakeholders, including policymakers, financial institutions, and investors, with the skills and knowledge required to evaluate, plan, and execute green finance strategies effectively. This dual approach ensures that governance and expertise are aligned to maximize the impact of green finance initiatives.

Risk Identification and Assessment

Identifying and assessing risks associated with green investments is critical for sustainable financial planning. Advanced mathematical models, such as Monte Carlo simulations, provide comprehensive evaluations by incorporating variables like market volatility, policy shifts, and environmental risks. These tools enable financial institutions to simulate multiple scenarios, identify potential vulnerabilities, and develop strategies to mitigate risks. By leveraging such quantitative methods, stakeholders can make informed decisions that balance environmental sustainability with financial security.

Financial Stability

Maintaining financial stability while advancing green finance initiatives is a key priority for the financial sector. Mathematical optimization techniques and AI-driven predictive models offer valuable insights into the economic implications of sustainable investments. These tools assess profitability, environmental impact, and resource allocation, ensuring that green investments contribute to long-term economic growth without compromising sustainability objectives. Financial stability is further supported by mechanisms that monitor and adapt to market dynamics, ensuring a balanced approach to risk and reward.

Microprudential Supervision and Regulations

Effective regulatory frameworks are essential for aligning financial institutions with Environmental, Social, and Governance (ESG) goals. Microprudential supervision ensures that financial institutions adhere to standards designed to promote sustainable practices. Blockchain technology plays a transformative role by providing an immutable ledger for ESG data and green bond transactions, enhancing compliance and transparency. This combination of regulatory oversight and technological innovation fosters trust among stakeholders and promotes adherence to sustainability objectives.

Fostering Inclusive Green Finance

Inclusive green finance ensures that financial resources are accessible to all, including small and medium enterprises (SMEs) and underrepresented communities. This approach facilitates broader participation in sustainability initiatives, empowering diverse stakeholders to contribute to green economic development. By fostering inclusivity, green finance initiatives not only address environmental challenges but also promote social equity and economic growth, creating a more sustainable and inclusive financial ecosystem.

Sustainable Islamic Finance

Sustainable Islamic finance integrates Sharia-compliant principles with green financial instruments to promote ethical and sustainable development. Instruments like sukuk (Islamic bonds) are designed to support projects that align with both religious and environmental values. These instruments leverage mathematical models to evaluate environmental benefits and financial returns, ensuring that investments meet sustainability goals while adhering to Islamic ethical standards. This unique approach bridges the gap between traditional finance and sustainability, offering a model that is both principled and impactful.

Outcomes and Impact

The application of advanced technologies and mathematical models in the green financial sector has led to several transformative outcomes:

- Enhanced Transparency and Accountability: Blockchain-enabled systems provide stakeholders with real-time, immutable records of green bond transactions, fostering trust in green financial instruments (Almadadha, 2024).
- Optimized Investment Portfolios: Knowledge Discovery from Data (KDD) methods integrated with blockchain platforms uncover patterns and optimize green investment strategies, leading to maximized returns and environmental benefits.
- Balanced Trade-offs: Multi-objective optimization techniques allow financial institutions to navigate trade-offs between profitability and sustainability, ensuring long-term viability.

Broader Implications

The integration of mathematical models, AI, and blockchain technologies in green finance mobilization underscores a paradigm shift in the financial sector. These tools enable firms to align their investment strategies with global ESG goals while maintaining financial stability. The framework depicted in Figure 8 offers a scalable model for global markets to adopt sustainable finance practices, paving the way for transparency, accountability, and innovation in green investment.

Case Study 5: Cross-Industry Collaboration in Logistics and Energy

Figure 9, titled **"Integrated Logistics and Energy Management System"**, illustrates the multi-layered complexities of international trade, transportation chains, and physical flows. This framework highlights the interplay between logistics and energy sectors, emphasizing the importance of data-driven optimization and cross-industry collaboration in achieving ESG objectives.

Figure 9 Integrated Logistics and Energy Management System

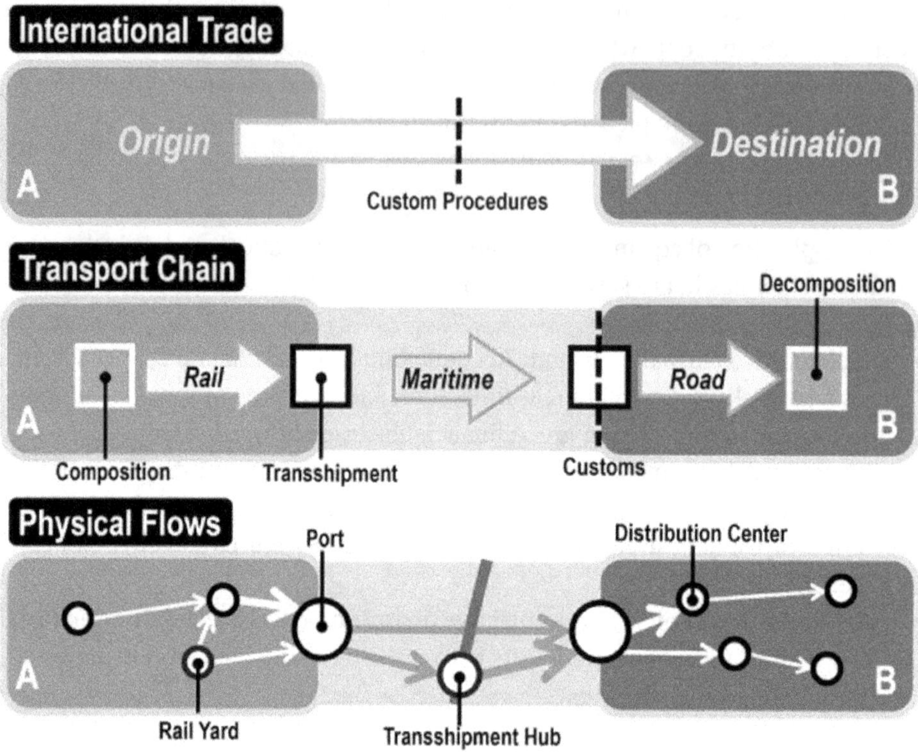

Methodology and Implementation

The figure presents three key layers of the system:

1. **International Trade Layer:** At this level, goods are transported from Origin (A) to Destination (B). The flow is represented by a single streamlined arrow, symbolizing the overarching goal of seamless and efficient global trade. Optimizing this layer involves strategic planning of routes, customs compliance, and minimizing delays.
2. **Transport Chain Layer:** This layer decomposes the movement of goods into transport modalities, including rail, maritime, and road logistics. Each mode of transport is interconnected and relies on the efficient handoff of goods across nodes. The incorporation of real-time energy grid data into these logistics chains allows for dynamic energy allocation and optimization. For instance, rail and road vehicles transitioning to renewable energy sources reduce the overall carbon footprint.

3. **Physical Flows Layer:** This layer visualizes the granular movement of goods using circular nodes and directional arrows. It illustrates the networked nature of physical logistics, showing how goods diverge, converge, and flow across multiple pathways. Using machine learning models combined with genetic algorithms, the system predicts optimal paths and allocates resources such as fuel and energy to minimize inefficiencies.

Advanced Technologies in Use

- **Mathematical Models:** Linear programming and multi-objective optimization models are employed to optimize energy consumption across the transport chain. These methods enable precise calculation of fuel requirements and emissions reductions for each transport leg.
- **AI Integration:** Machine learning algorithms analyze real-time traffic, weather conditions, and energy data to predict delays and recommend route adjustments dynamically. AI also ensures that renewable energy sources are prioritized in the transport process.
- **Blockchain Technology:** A blockchain ledger records every step in the logistics chain, ensuring transparency and traceability. This approach builds stakeholder confidence by providing verifiable data on energy usage and ESG compliance.

Outcomes and Impact

The integration of data-driven logistics and energy management systems yields measurable improvements:

- Energy Efficiency: By optimizing transport routes and shifting to renewable energy, companies achieve up to a 25% reduction in fuel consumption.
- Reduced Carbon Emissions: Transitioning to rail and maritime transport powered by renewable energy cuts emissions by 30%, contributing to global sustainability goals.
- Enhanced Stakeholder Trust: Blockchain-backed traceability ensures compliance with ESG standards, fostering trust among regulators, customers, and investors.

Broader Implications

This case study underscores the importance of cross-industry collaboration in addressing sustainability challenges. By aligning the logistics and energy sectors through advanced technologies, companies can achieve operational excellence while meeting ESG objectives. The visual representation in Figure 9 provides a clear and actionable roadmap for integrating mathematical thinking, AI, and blockchain into logistics and energy systems, enabling sustainable growth across industries.

5.2 The Role of Mathematical Tools in Stakeholder Engagement and Trust-Building

Mathematical tools are not only essential for internal ESG data validation but also play a pivotal role in building stakeholder confidence. By translating complex data into accessible and transparent formats, these tools foster greater trust and collaboration between companies and their stakeholders.Mathematical graphs, charts, and dashboards provide clear and intuitive visual representations of ESG data, making it accessible to a wide range of stakeholders, including those without technical expertise. For example, emission trends, resource consumption patterns, and forecasted impacts can be visualized using bar charts, line graphs, or interactive dashboards. These tools not only enhance understanding but also empower stakeholders to make informed decisions based on the presented data. Heatmaps, for instance, are particularly effective in highlighting areas of concern, such as regions with high emissions or excessive resource usage.Interactive dashboards are another transformative tool. They allow stakeholders to interact with real-time data, adjusting parameters to explore various sustainability scenarios. For instance, a dashboard might enable investors to view carbon emissions reductions under different energy mix strategies, fostering deeper engagement and accountability. By simplifying complex ESG metrics, visualization tools bridge the gap between technical analyses and stakeholder comprehension, promoting transparency and inclusivity.

Mathematical rigor is foundational to fostering trust in sustainability reporting. Precise, consistent, and verifiable data demonstrates a company's commitment to transparency, aligning its ESG reports with stakeholder expectations. For instance, accurate calculations of carbon footprints, supported by clear methodologies, assure stakeholders of the validity of sustainability claims. Mathematical tools such as regression analysis and optimization algorithms further reinforce this trust by providing evidence-based insights.Transparency in data communication is equally critical. By using mathematical techniques to cross-verify data from multiple sources, companies ensure that reported metrics are accurate and free of inconsistencies. Blockchain integration enhances this transparency by creating immutable records of ESG data, ensuring that stakeholders can trace data back to its origin. This level of precision and accountability fosters a strong narrative of corporate integrity, encouraging stakeholders to place greater confidence in the organization's sustainability efforts.

Beyond ensuring technical accuracy, mathematical tools serve as a bridge for fostering collaboration between companies and their stakeholders. By providing a common analytical framework, these tools enable stakeholders to align their priorities with corporate sustainability goals. For example, multi-objective optimization models can balance competing interests, such as reducing environmental impacts while maintaining profitability, fostering mutual understanding and alignment. Collaboration is further strengthened by the actionable insights generated through predictive analytics. These insights enable stakeholders to engage in proactive discussions about potential challenges and opportunities. For instance, a mathematical model might predict resource shortages under certain scenarios, prompting collaborative efforts to develop contingency plans. Such interactions not only build trust but also strengthen partnerships, ensuring that all parties are working towards shared sustainability objectives.

Recent advancements in AI and machine learning have amplified the capabilities of mathematical tools in stakeholder engagement. Predictive models powered by AI can provide stakeholders with insights into the long-term impacts of sustainability initiatives. For example, stakeholders can visualize how specific investments in renewable energy or water conservation projects will affect ESG performance over a decade. These forward-looking analyses enable more strategic and informed decision-making.Moreover, machine learning algorithms enhance real-time adaptability. Stakeholders can be alerted to deviations from projected ESG targets through automated notifications, enabling timely interventions. This responsiveness not only strengthens accountability but also builds a dynamic and collaborative relationship between companies and their stakeholders.

Mathematical tools are instrumental in building trust and fostering collaboration in sustainability efforts. Through data visualization, transparent communication, and collaborative frameworks, these tools bridge the gap between technical complexity and stakeholder engagement. By leveraging advancements in AI and machine learning, companies can further enhance their ability to engage stakeholders and maintain trust, ensuring the success of their sustainability initiatives in an increasingly scrutinized global landscape.

Figure 10 highlights the pivotal role of AI and Machine Learning (ML) in creating interconnected and optimized supply networks across various sectors. The diagram illustrates how AI and ML algorithms serve as the backbone of modern supply chain management, enhancing sustainability and operational efficiency. Across sectors such as factories, cities and offices, agriculture, forestry, transportation, energy supply, and power stations, these technologies analyze operational data, predict inefficiencies, and optimize processes. For example, predictive maintenance in industrial facilities minimizes downtime, while AI-driven precision farming optimizes crop yields and resource utilization. Similarly, AI-powered logistics streamline transportation by optimizing routes and reducing emissions, while real-time analytics ensure stable energy generation and distribution in power networks.

At the core of this system, AI and ML algorithms facilitate seamless **interface development**, enabling effective communication between data sources and stakeholders. These algorithms continuously improve through real-time and historical data **training**, while customized **development** ensures adaptability for sector-specific needs. This integrated framework demonstrates the interconnected nature of industries within a supply network, with AI and ML as the driving technologies. By fostering collaboration, transparency, and data-driven decision-making, these advancements align ESG objectives with industry performance, propelling global sustainability goals.

Figure 10. AI-Driven Supply Network Integration for Sustainability

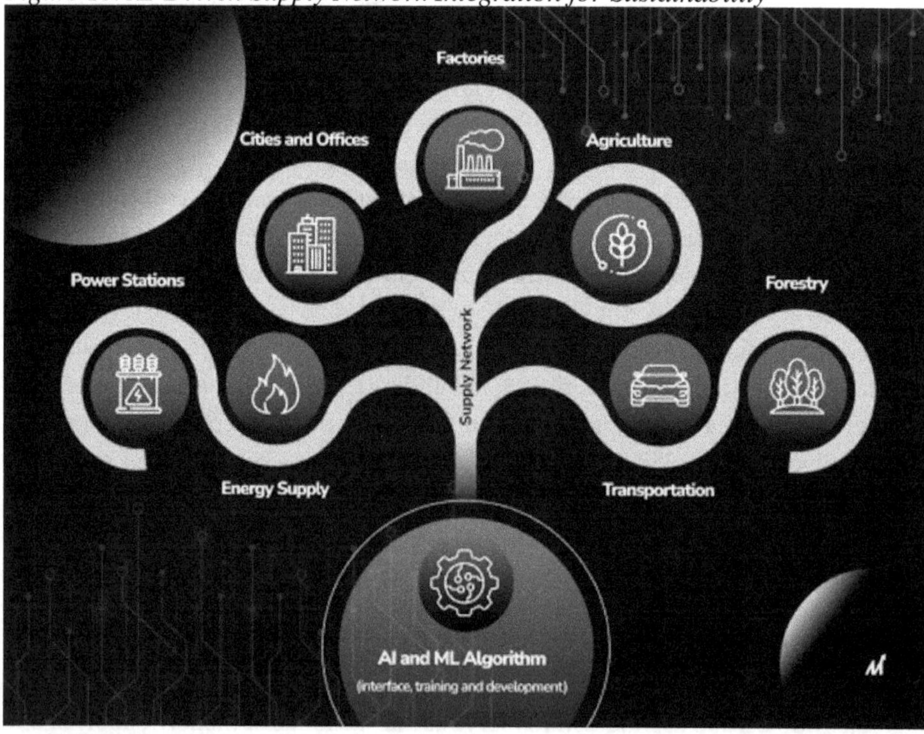

6 EMERGING TRENDS: STRENGTHENING FUTURE DIRECTIONS IN AI AND BLOCKCHAIN FOR ESG REPORTING

The integration of artificial intelligence (AI) and blockchain technologies into sustainability assurance is revolutionizing ESG reporting. These technologies hold immense potential for automating data processes, improving transparency, and standardizing ESG metrics across industries. As the demand for accountability in corporate sustainability grows, AI and blockchain offer innovative solutions to address existing challenges while setting the stage for future advancements.

6.1 AI's Role in Automating ESG Reporting

AI is transforming ESG reporting by introducing tools that enable real-time risk analysis, predictive modeling, and sustainability forecasting. Machine learning algorithms are capable of processing large ESG datasets to identify patterns and anomalies, enabling organizations to detect potential compliance issues before they escalate. By streamlining data processing and analysis, AI reduces human error and significantly enhances the efficiency of reporting.

One of the most impactful applications of AI is its ability to create dynamic ESG reports. These reports adjust in real time as data inputs evolve, ensuring that stakeholders have access to the most current and actionable insights. For example, AI can continuously monitor energy consumption patterns and predict the impact of operational changes on carbon emissions. This level of responsiveness not only improves the accuracy of reports but also allows companies to align their actions with sustainability goals more effectively.

Natural language processing (NLP) capabilities further expand AI's utility in ESG reporting. NLP enables the extraction of relevant information from unstructured data sources, such as regulatory updates, social media content, and corporate disclosures. By analyzing text data, AI can assess public sentiment, identify reputational risks, and provide insights into how well an organization's ESG goals align with stakeholder expectations. Industries such as energy and manufacturing already leverage predictive analytics powered by AI to forecast resource utilization and emissions, supporting long-term planning and operational alignment with sustainability objectives.

6.2 Blockchain as a Tool for Standardizing ESG Reporting

Blockchain addresses one of the fundamental challenges in ESG reporting: the lack of standardization and trust in data sources. As a decentralized, immutable ledger, blockchain ensures the authenticity and traceability of ESG metrics. Each transaction recorded on a blockchain network is time-stamped and source-authenticated, creating a verifiable history of activities such as energy use, waste generation, and supply chain transactions.

One of blockchain's most significant contributions is its ability to drive cross-industry standardization in ESG data reporting. By embedding predefined data formats and validation protocols, blockchain ensures consistency across reports from different companies and sectors. For example, in the food production industry, blockchain can track the lifecycle of raw materials from farm to table, providing transparency that bolsters consumer trust. Similarly, in logistics, blockchain verifies the sustainability claims of transportation providers, ensuring compliance with environmental regulations.

Moreover, blockchain's smart contracts facilitate automated compliance checks, reducing the need for manual interventions. These self-executing contracts can validate ESG data submissions against regulatory standards or internal benchmarks, streamlining the reporting process while enhancing accuracy. Such automation is particularly valuable for multinational corporations operating across diverse regulatory landscapes.

6.3 Future Applications Across Industries

6.3.1 Supply Chain Transparency

Blockchain and AI combined offer unparalleled transparency in supply chain operations, a critical factor in meeting ESG objectives. Blockchain's ability to create a tamper-proof and traceable record of transactions ensures that the origins and movement of raw materials can be verified. For example, in the retail sector, blockchain can document the provenance of raw materials, ensuring ethical sourcing and reducing the risk of fraud. AI enhances this process by analyzing large volumes of supply chain data to identify inefficiencies, suggest process improvements, and predict potential disruptions.This integration is particularly beneficial for logistics operations, where reducing carbon emissions and optimizing delivery routes are paramount. AI-powered algorithms can forecast demand fluctuations and optimize fleet management, while blockchain ensures that every stage of the transportation process is transparent and compliant with sustainability standards. Together, these technologies enable organizations to achieve greater accountability, operational efficiency, and environmental impact reduction.

6.3.2 Energy and Resource Optimization

In the energy sector, AI and blockchain are being utilized to address the dual challenges of optimizing resource allocation and reducing carbon footprints. AI algorithms, such as predictive analytics and machine learning models, forecast energy demand based on historical usage patterns and external factors like weather conditions. These forecasts allow for better planning and utilization of renewable energy resources, reducing reliance on fossil fuels.Blockchain complements these efforts by securely tracking renewable energy credits (RECs), ensuring that transactions are transparent and verifiable. This approach helps eliminate double counting of RECs and builds trust among stakeholders, including regulators and consumers. Additionally, blockchain enables peer-to-peer energy trading, where excess energy from renewable sources can be sold directly to other users, further enhancing resource efficiency and fostering a decentralized energy market.

6.3.3 Healthcare and Pharmaceuticals

The healthcare and pharmaceutical industries are beginning to explore the potential of blockchain and AI to align operations with ESG goals. Blockchain can track the environmental impact of pharmaceutical production and distribution, providing detailed records of raw material sourcing, energy consumption, and waste management. This level of traceability not only ensures compliance with environmental regulations but also strengthens trust with stakeholders.AI, on the other hand, analyzes healthcare data to identify correlations between environmental factors and patient health outcomes. For example, AI can predict the impact of air quality on respiratory conditions, enabling healthcare providers to proactively address environmental health risks. Additionally, optimization algorithms supported by AI can streamline waste management in healthcare facilities, reducing both environmental impact and operational costs. Together, these technologies help the healthcare sector achieve sustainability while maintaining high standards of care and efficiency.

6.4 Challenges and Considerations

6.4.1 Data Privacy, Safety, Regulation, and Ethics

6.4.1.1 AI Safety

AI safety refers to the process of leveraging artificial intelligence (AI) to enhance an organization's security posture. This involves using AI systems to automate threat detection, prevention, and remediation, effectively addressing cybersecurity challenges such as data breaches and network attacks. AI safety tools often utilize machine learning (ML) and deep learning to analyze vast datasets, including network traffic, application usage, and user behaviors. By identifying patterns and establishing security baselines, these tools can flag anomalies that indicate potential threats in real time.

The Advantages of AI in Cybersecurity:

- Enhanced Threat Detection: AI algorithms analyze large datasets in real time, improving the speed and accuracy of detecting potential cyber threats, including advanced and previously undetectable attack vectors.
- Faster Incident Response: Automated threat response capabilities enable organizations to quickly investigate and neutralize security incidents, reducing potential damage.
- Operational Efficiency: By automating routine security tasks, AI allows security teams to focus on strategic initiatives while minimizing human error.
- Proactive Defense: Predictive analytics powered by AI help organizations anticipate and prepare for emerging threats.
- Cost Savings: AI can significantly reduce the cost of responding to data breaches. Organizations with extensive AI-enabled cybersecurity systems save an average of $1.76 million per incident.

Despite its advantages, AI poses new challenges, particularly in data security and ethical deployment. AI systems are only as reliable as their training data, and compromised datasets can lead to inaccurate predictions or reinforce biases. Moreover, threat actors are increasingly leveraging AI to automate attacks, such as sophisticated phishing campaigns and adversarial attacks, underscoring the need for robust AI governance and security measures.

6.4.1.2 Blockchain to Address Deepfakes and Data Ethics

Blockchain technology, combined with decentralized cloud storage, offers robust solutions to address deepfakes and data ethics challenges. AI advancements have amplified risks such as deepfakes—highly realistic but fabricated media—and data manipulation, raising concerns about trust and credibility. These threats demand a reliable framework for data integrity and ethical AI deployment.

Key Advantages of Blockchain in Data Integrity:

- Decentralized Data Storage: Blockchain eliminates single points of failure by distributing data across global nodes, reducing vulnerabilities to cyberattacks.
- Immutability: Data stored on the blockchain cannot be tampered with, ensuring the integrity of records and providing a verifiable audit trail.

- Provenance and Traceability: Blockchain tracks the lifecycle of data, distinguishing between AI-generated deepfake content and original, unaltered media.

Blockchain addresses critical issues in AI ethics by ensuring transparency, reducing biases, and protecting data integrity. For instance, decentralized cloud storage and blockchain networks can continuously verify data integrity, preventing unauthorized access and building trust in AI-generated information. These systems also support data lineage, providing clear visibility into how data has been collected, processed, and used.

Deepfake detection and data ethics frameworks are crucial to mitigate the risks associated with AI. Blockchain can serve as a foundational technology for trustworthy AI systems, helping organizations navigate the challenges of maintaining data security while fostering innovation.

6.4.1.3 Ethics in AI-Blockchain Integration

The integration of AI and blockchain presents transformative opportunities but also raises ethical considerations that demand immediate attention. As these technologies redefine industries, the balance between innovation and responsible development becomes critical.

Benefits of AI-Blockchain Integration:

- Efficiency: AI automates tasks, such as data analysis and decision-making, while blockchain ensures secure and immutable record-keeping.
- Enhanced Security: AI-driven threat detection complements blockchain's decentralized architecture, creating resilient systems that safeguard sensitive information.
- Transparency and Decentralization: AI enhances decision-making in decentralized blockchain systems by distributing authority and mitigating risks associated with central points of failure.

Ethical Challenges and Solutions:

- Bias and Fairness: AI systems inherit biases from their training data, which can lead to discriminatory outcomes in blockchain environments. Transparent algorithms and equitable data practices are essential to address these issues.
- Accountability: The complexity of AI-driven blockchain systems requires clear delineation of responsibility. Auditing “black-box” AI algorithms and enforcing transparency are critical for ensuring trust.

- Privacy vs. Transparency: Blockchain's inherent transparency must be balanced with privacy concerns, particularly when handling sensitive information. AI-enhanced encryption and access controls can provide a solution.

Responsible AI-Blockchain Practices:

- Establishing ethical frameworks and industry-wide guidelines to govern the use of AI in blockchain.
- Promoting human oversight in critical decision-making processes, particularly for ethical and financial implications.
- Encouraging collaborative governance models that involve stakeholders, regulators, and technology providers.

AI and blockchain, when combined, hold immense potential to reshape industries, but their implementation must be guided by ethical principles to prevent misuse and ensure equitable benefits. Organizations must proactively address these challenges, fostering innovation while safeguarding societal values.

6.4.2 High Implementation Costs

The upfront investment required to deploy AI and blockchain solutions can be prohibitive, especially for small and medium-sized enterprises (SMEs). The costs of acquiring the necessary infrastructure, hiring skilled personnel, and maintaining these systems can deter widespread adoption. Governments and industry consortia may play a critical role in overcoming this barrier by offering subsidies, grants, or tax incentives to encourage the integration of these technologies. Additionally, collaborative initiatives among companies to share blockchain networks or AI platforms can reduce individual costs and facilitate broader adoption.

6.4.3 Cross-Industry Collaboration

The lack of standardized ESG data reporting frameworks across industries presents another significant challenge. Effective adoption of AI and blockchain technologies requires cooperation among industries, governments, and technology providers to establish global standards for data formats, validation protocols, and reporting practices. However, conflicting priorities and resistance to change often hinder such collaborations. Overcoming this barrier will require concerted efforts to build consensus on ESG data standards. Organizations such as the International Sustainability Standards Board (ISSB) and the Task Force on Climate-Related Financial Disclosures (TCFD) can serve as catalysts for harmonizing reporting practices.

Blockchain technology can further facilitate standardization by embedding predefined reporting protocols into its architecture, ensuring uniformity across industries.

The convergence of AI and blockchain technologies is poised to revolutionize ESG reporting by enabling greater transparency, standardization, and efficiency. These technologies address many of the current challenges in sustainability assurance by automating processes, ensuring data integrity, and providing real-time insights. However, to fully realize their potential, organizations must address challenges such as data privacy concerns, high implementation costs, and the need for cross-industry collaboration.Looking ahead, AI and blockchain are likely to become indispensable tools in ESG reporting, setting new benchmarks for accountability and innovation in corporate sustainability. By addressing these challenges proactively and leveraging the strengths of these technologies, organizations can drive meaningful progress toward a more transparent, efficient, and sustainable future.

7 CONCLUSION AND IMPLICATIONS OF THE STUDY

This chapter demonstrates how integrating mathematical methods with advanced technologies like AI and blockchain can transform ESG reporting, offering unprecedented levels of credibility, transparency, and utility. By applying statistical analysis, optimization algorithms, and uncertainty modeling, organizations can improve data validation, optimize resources, and foster stakeholder trust. These methods provide a robust foundation for addressing complex sustainability challenges, aligning operational goals with global ESG standards.

Lepore (2024) emphasized, “Limitations in AI's training data and algorithms can lead to errors, reinforcing the need for human oversight in teaching and learning quantitative concepts.” This underscores the importance of mathematical literacy and a strong foundation in mathematical thinking as prerequisites for effectively implementing algorithms and technological tools. Despite these advancements, the adoption of these tools faces significant hurdles, including high implementation costs, data privacy concerns, and a lack of standardized reporting frameworks. Overcoming these challenges requires collaborative efforts across industries, governments, and technology providers to establish global standards and innovative funding mechanisms.

Looking forward, the future of ESG reporting lies in further refining these methodologies for predictive sustainability analysis, real-time risk management, and enhanced stakeholder engagement. Mathematical literacy among professionals, coupled with the seamless integration of AI and blockchain, will be crucial in realizing these advancements. Developing mathematical thinking is fundamental not only for algorithm design but also for understanding and applying complex technologies ethically and accurately. As Karaali (2023) noted, the limitations of AI and blockchain underscore the need for human oversight in applying these tools ethically and accurately. By embracing this balanced approach, organizations can drive meaningful progress toward a transparent, efficient, and sustainable future.

The integration of AI and blockchain with mathematical thinking offers significant practical benefits for ESG reporting. Companies can leverage these tools to enhance decision-making efficiency, ensuring alignment with ESG goals through data-driven insights and predictive analytics. This integration fosters corporate accountability by promoting transparency in ESG disclosures, which aids compliance with regulatory standards and improves investor confidence. Additionally, the adoption of these technologies allows organizations to optimize resource use, reduce carbon footprints, and manage risks more effectively, aligning profitability with sustainability objectives. These advancements collectively empower businesses to meet stakeholder expectations while achieving operational excellence.

The study underscores the urgent need for international collaboration to establish standardized ESG reporting metrics and protocols, especially for blockchain and AI tools. Uniform standards can reduce inconsistencies, facilitate global comparability, and promote greater trust in sustainability reports. Governments and regulatory bodies play a critical role in this process by incentivizing the adoption of these technologies through supportive policies, grants, and subsidies. Such measures not only accelerate technological adoption but also ensure that smaller organizations can overcome financial barriers, fostering inclusivity in the pursuit of global sustainability goals.

Future research should focus on sector-specific applications of AI and blockchain, tailoring these technologies to industries such as healthcare, logistics, and agriculture for enhanced ESG optimization. The integration of IoT with AI and blockchain presents an exciting avenue for real-time ESG reporting, enabling dynamic data collection and analysis. Exploring the synergy between AI and blockchain can lead to frameworks that enhance data accuracy and scalability, addressing existing challenges in ESG practices. Additionally, the role of human oversight in mitigating biases and ensuring ethical AI applications warrants further investigation. Longitudinal impact studies are essential to evaluate the long-term effects of these technologies on organizational sustainability performance and stakeholder trust, providing a comprehensive understanding of their transformative potential.

By integrating these practical, policy, and educational implications with the proposed research directions, this chapter provides a compelling roadmap for leveraging mathematical thinking and emerging technologies to redefine ESG reporting. It sets a benchmark for innovation, accountability, and global impact, fostering meaningful progress toward a sustainable future.

REFERENCES

Almadadha, R. (2024). Blockchain technology in financial accounting: Enhancing transparency, security, and ESG reporting. *Blockchains*, 2(3), 312–333. DOI: 10.3390/blockchains2030015

Awa, H. O., Ojiabo, O. U., & Orokor, L. E. (2017). Integrated technology-organization-environment (TOE) taxonomies for technology adoption. *Journal of Enterprise Information Management*, 30(6), 893–921. DOI: 10.1108/JEIM-03-2016-0079

Bai, C., Sarkis, J., & Dou, Y. (2021). Blockchain technology for enhancing sustainable supply chains. *International Journal of Production Research*, 59(5), 1450–1465. DOI: 10.1080/00207543.2020.1871594

Birindelli, G., Dell'Atti, S., & Patrizia Iannuzzi, A. (2022). ESG ratings and corporate sustainability: Evidence from European banks. *Journal of Cleaner Production*, 364, 132526. DOI: 10.1016/j.jclepro.2022.132526

Campana, P. E., Mainardis, M., Moretti, A., & Cottes, M. (2021). Corrigendum to "100% renewable wastewater treatment plants: Techno-economic assessment using a modelling and optimization approach.". *Energy Conversion and Management*, 244, 114531. DOI: 10.1016/j.enconman.2021.114214

Chen, S., Song, Y., & Gao, P. (2023). Environmental, social, and governance (ESG) performance and financial outcomes: Analyzing the impact of ESG on financial performance. *Journal of Environmental Management*, 345, 118829. DOI: 10.1016/j.jenvman.2023.118829

Hasan, H. R., Musamih, A., Salah, K., Jayaraman, R., Omar, M., Arshad, J., & Boscovic, D. (2024). Smart agriculture assurance: IoT and blockchain for trusted sustainable produce. *Computers and Electronics in Agriculture*, 224, 109184. DOI: 10.1016/j.compag.2024.109184

Kallia, M., van Borkulo, S. P., Drijvers, P., Barendsen, E., & Tolboom, J. (2021). Characterising computational thinking in mathematics education: A literature-informed Delphi study. *Research in Mathematics Education*, 23(2), 159–187. DOI: 10.1080/14794802.2020.1852104

Karaali, G. (2023). Artificial intelligence, basic skills, and quantitative literacy. *Numeracy*, 16(1), 9. DOI: 10.5038/1936-4660.16.1.1438

Kaya, H. D., & Tuncer, G. (2021). Sustainability reporting practices of global companies: Trends and challenges. *Sustainable Development*, 29(4), 664–680. DOI: 10.1002/sd.2174

Kulkarni, A. V., Joseph, S., & Patil, K. (2023). *Role of artificial intelligence in sustainability reporting by leveraging ESG theory into action*. https://www.researchgate.net/publication/371434141

Lee, C. C., & Brahmasrene, T. (2020). Emerging trends in integrating artificial intelligence into sustainability reporting. *Environmental Research Letters*, 15(2), 024011. DOI: 10.1088/1748-9326/ab719f

Lee, C. C., & Brahmasrene, T. (2020). Emerging trends in integrating artificial intelligence into sustainability reporting. *Environmental Research Letters*, 15(2), 024011. DOI: 10.1088/1748-9326/ab719f

Lepore, M. (2024). A holistic framework to model students' cognitive processes in mathematics education through fuzzy cognitive maps. *Heliyon*, 10(16). Advance online publication. DOI: 10.1016/j.heliyon.2024.e35863

Lilhore, U. K., Poongodi, M., Kaur, A., Simaiya, S., Algarni, A. D., Elmannai, H., & Hamdi, M. (2022). Hybrid model for detection of cervical cancer using causal analysis and machine learning techniques. *Computational and Mathematical Methods in Medicine*, 2022(1), 4688327. DOI: 10.1155/2022/4688327

Mulligan, C., Morsfield, S., & Cheikosman, E. (2024). Blockchain for sustainability: A systematic literature review for policy impact. *Telecommunications Policy*, 48(102676). Advance online publication. DOI: 10.1016/j.telpol.2023.102676

Pathirana, S. M., Zhang, J., & Cheung, R. (2022). Blockchain and artificial intelligence for ESG verification: A comprehensive review. *Journal of Environmental Management*, 320, 115803. DOI: 10.1016/j.jenvman.2022.115803

Rodriguez, S., & Cruz, R. (2023). Integrating AI and blockchain for improved ESG reporting: A case study approach. *Sustainable Business Review*, 8(2), 45–62. DOI: 10.1016/sbr20234562

Romero Ariza, M., Quesada Armenteros, A., & Estepa Castro, A. (2024). Promoting critical thinking through mathematics and science teacher education: The case of argumentation and graphs interpretation about climate change. *European Journal of Teacher Education*, 47(1), 41–59. DOI: 10.1080/02619768.2021.1961736

Tercan, H., & Meisen, T. (2022). Machine learning and deep learning-based predictive quality in manufacturing: A systematic review. *Journal of Intelligent Manufacturing*, 33(7), 1879–1905. DOI: 10.1007/s10845-022-01963-8

Zhang, Y., Tian, H., & Lee, S. (2023). Transparency and innovation in ESG disclosures: The role of technology in shaping stakeholder trust. *Business Strategy and the Environment*, 32(1), 45–58. DOI: 10.1002/bse.3502

Chapter 5
Enhancing the Credibility of Banks' Sustainability Reporting in Mercosur Countries

Walter Daniel Ovelar-Fernández
Autonomous University of Asunción, Paraguay

Maria del Mar Gálvez-Rodríguez
https://orcid.org/0000-0002-3708-6229
Universidad de Almería, Spain

Maria García-Gonzáles
Universidad de Almería, Spain

Maria del Carmen Caba-Pérez
https://orcid.org/0000-0002-8452-5909
Universidad de Almería, Spain

ABSTRACT

This paper examines Sustainability Report Assurance (SRA) in the banking sector of Mercosur countries, focusing on its role in improving the quality of Sustainable Development Goals (SDG) disclosures and trends in SRA practices. Findings show that banks with assured sustainability reports do not significantly outperform non-assured banks in disclosure quality. Both rely primarily on qualitative information, with non-assured banks emphasizing completed actions over plans and providing greater visibility into stakeholder engagement. SRA trends reveal that Mercosur banks commonly use Big Four accounting firms and maintain consistency in as-

DOI: 10.4018/979-8-3373-0117-4.ch005

surance adoption and provider selection. However, the assurance level is typically limited, which reduces its impact on report quality. Improvements are necessary for SRA to transition from symbolic to substantive reporting, enabling it to better enhance transparency and credibility in SDG reporting within the banking sector.

INTRODUCTION

In emerging economies, sustainability reporting remains a voluntary and unregulated practice (Lemma et al., 2024; Yan et al., 2022). Sustainability Report Assurance (SRA) plays a crucial role in bolstering stakeholders' confidence in corporate disclosures related to ethical conduct and sustainability performance. Consequently, the use of SRA has grown significantly over the past decade (Alsahali & Malagueño, 2022; Karagiannis et al., 2022; Khatib, 2024; Maroun, 2020; Sari, 2024). Assurance practices refer to the systematic processes, procedures, and mechanisms organizations use to verify the reliability, integrity, and credibility of their reported information, encompassing financial statements, non-financial disclosures, and sustainability reports (Farooq & De Villiers, 2019; Sari, 2024).

Despite its potential, there are ongoing concerns about the ability of SRA to enhance the reliability and credibility of disclosed information, particularly regarding the quality of information included in sustainability reports (Alsahali & Malagueño, 2022). Additionally, most studies on sustainability reporting and SRA focus on countries such as China, the United States, India, and European nations (Li et al., 2024; De Silva et al., 2024). This concentration leaves a significant gap in understanding the impact of assurance practices on sustainability reporting in emerging regions like Africa and Latin America (KPMG, 2022). Furthermore, the assurance on a sustainability report varies depending on industries (Lemma et al., 2024). Hence there is a call for more research that explores SRA focusing on specific industry practices (Sari, 2024).

The banking industry is pivotal in advancing sustainability initiatives, including the Sustainable Development Goals (SDGs). Banks contribute to economic welfare while supporting environmental quality, social cohesion, and long-term prosperity through investment and financing activities (Kumar, 2022; Li et al., 2024). For example, banks can encourage socially and environmentally responsible investments and require their clients—such as corporations, public administrations, and households—to meet socio-environmental criteria as a condition for economic support (Chatzitheodorou et al., 2021; Gunawan et al., 2022).

Despite their potential role in promoting a sustainable economy, studies analyzing banks' accountability in sustainability initiatives, such as actions aligned with the SDGs, remain limited. Even fewer studies explore assurance practices related to SDG reporting. Existing research tends to focus on the number of SDGs pursued by banks rather than on the quality of disclosures associated with such reporting practices (Avrampou et al., 2019; Cosma et al., 2020; Sardianou et al., 2021; Aguado-Correa et al., 2023). This gap is particularly pronounced in emerging regions such as Africa, Latin America, and the Middle East (Lui & Zainuldin, 2024; Gálvez-Rodríguez et al., 2024; Sahi et al., 2022; Sebastião et al., 2024). Additionally, there is a pressing need for a deeper understanding of SRA's role in enhancing reporting quality (Khan et al., 2021; Michelon et al., 2015; Quick & Inwinkl, 2020), particularly in addressing gaps in emerging economies (Lemma et al., 2024).

In this context, focusing on the banking sector in Latin American countries within the Southern Common Market (MERCOSUR), this paper aims to achieve two main objectives. First, it seeks to analyze the role of sustainability report assurance in enhancing disclosure quality regarding SDG reporting. Second, it examines patterns of assurance practices within banks. To achieve these objectives, the paper poses the following research questions:

RQ1: Does assurance of SDG reporting by banks in Mercosur countries influence disclosure quality? Specifically:

- **RQ1.1:** What and how much information is disclosed?
- **RQ1.2:** What is the managerial orientation of the reporting?
- **RQ1.3:** What are stakeholders toward whom banks direct their reporting practices?

RQ2: What are the trends in SRA practices within the Mercosur banking sector? Specifically:

- **RQ2.1:** What is the most common type of assurance provider?
- **RQ2.2:** Is there a consistent approach to adopting assurance practices and selecting assurance providers?
- **RQ2.3:** What are the most common levels of assurance?

This study offers both academic and practical insights. Academically, it advances the understanding of SDG reporting disclosure quality in the banking sector, particularly in emerging economies (Aguado-Correa et al., 2023; Lui & Zainuldin, 2024; Sahi et al., 2022; Sebastião et al., 2024). It addresses the research gap on the extent to which assurance practices enhance disclosure quality (Alsahali & Malagueño, 2022; Lemma et al., 2024; García-Sánchez, 2021), particularly in integrating quantitative and monetary information (Mio, 2010; Michelon et al., 2019). Additionally, it responds to the need for a deeper understanding of assurance activities (Aliyu, 2024; Alsahali & Malagueño, 2022; Farooq et al., 2023; Sari, 2024). Practically, the findings will improve understanding of assurance practices and highlight areas requiring enhancement to foster credibility in the banking sector. Recommendations will promote best practices for transparent accountability in banks' sustainability actions, ultimately enhancing stakeholder trust and confidence in banks' genuine commitment to societal and environmental welfare.

LITERATURE REVIEW

Theoretical Framework

Legitimacy theory is one of the most widely used approaches to understand sustainability disclosure (Chowdhury et al., 2020; Li et al., 2024) and assurance practices (Aliyu, 2024), alongside stakeholder theory, agency theory, and institutional theory. According to Suchman (1995:574), legitimacy is defined as "a generalized perception or assumption that the actions of an entity are desirable, proper, or appropriate within some socially constructed system of norms, values, beliefs, and definitions". Under this approach, companies use information disclosure, such as sustainability reporting, to reveal details about their environmental and social performance, thereby legitimizing their operations (Deegan & Rankin, 1996; Guthrie et al., 2006; Aluchna et al., 2023). Similarly, legitimacy theory provides a framework for understanding how businesses use external assurance to meet stakeholders' expectations of appropriate behavior (Alsahali & Malagueño, 2022; Saraswati et al., 2023). Assurance processes, as social constructs, build trust by fostering a favorable perception among audiences about a company's "good practices." Hence, through sustainability reporting assurance, companies can enhance their legitimacy (Aliyu, 2024).

Within the legitimacy framework, corporate sustainability strategies are categorized as either substantive or symbolic (Ashforth & Gibbs, 1990; Deegan, 2019). These strategies differ primarily in the degree of execution and goal alignment (Iatridis & Kesidou, 2018). Symbolic disclosure emphasizes appearance over substance, focusing on presentation rather than genuine change (Silva, 2021). This approach often aims to favorably shape stakeholder perceptions, leading stakeholders to mistakenly believe the organization is committed to social standards. In contrast, substantive management involves tangible, meaningful changes to business operations, ensuring alignment with social standards through genuine improvements (Michelon et al., 2015). Truong et al. (2021) argue that while substantive actions demand significant resources and organizational transformation to improve environmental outcomes, symbolic actions are less resource intensive.

From the symbolic and substantive perspective, prior research suggests that sustainability reporting and SRA often lean toward symbolic rather than substantive strategies, raising concerns about businesses' true commitment to societal progress and environmental protection. For instance, Michelon et al. (2015) found that UK companies' sustainability reporting practices predominantly align with symbolic approaches. In this vein, García-Meca & Martínez-Ferrero (2021) showed that companies engage in SDG reporting as a symbolic act to address legitimacy issues and to respond to stakeholder pressure.

In the banking sector, existing literature highlights the importance of adopting substantive strategies for sustainability, although knowledge about sustainability reporting and SRA practices remains limited. Furrer et al. (2012) emphasize the varying levels of commitment and effectiveness among banks in addressing climate change, underscoring the potential for substantive action but also the risks of symbolic compliance. Maas et al. (2016) argue that substantive strategies, which involve significant management changes and operational improvements, help banks attract external stakeholders (Branco & Rodrigues, 2008). Conversely, symbolic strategies in banks focus on activities like reputation building (Perez-Batres et al., 2012), ceremonial compliance (Khan et al., 2020), and greenwashing (Wu et al., 2020).

Hence there is a need for more understanding to determine whether sustainability reporting and SRA in the banking sector are symbolic acts or truly reflect substantive commitments.

Assessing the Quality Disclosure in Reporting Practices

The literature highlights that adequate corporate reporting practices provides several positive consequences to organizations related to investment and innovation, financing costs, operations, financial risk, performance, and overall organizations' value (Li et al., 2024). Amongst the sustainability initiatives to report we can highlight those actions that contribute to achieve the SDGs (Majeed et al., 2024). These are a set of 17 interconnected goals to be achieved by 2030 that can be grouped into three dimensions: Economic growth, social inclusion, and environmental protection. SDGs 8, 9, 10, 12 and 17 are related to the economic dimension, SDGs 1, 2, 3, 4, 5, 7, 11 and 16 are associated with the social dimension, and finally, SDGs 6, 13, 14 and 15 are linked to the environmental dimension (United Nations General Assembly, 2015).

An adequate corporate reporting practice is linked to the quality of the information shared to organizations' stakeholders. Although there is no clear consensus on the definition of "disclosure quality" (Yekini, 2023; Baalouch et al., 2019), the most commonly used dimensions for measuring disclosure quality in reporting practices are: the quantity of relevant information shared which refers by the breadth of information the company provided —what is disclosed— (Menassa, 2010; Michelon et al., 2015); the accuracy of the disclosures which refers to the accuracy by the qualitative, quantitative, and monetary details shared —How is disclosed? — (Mio,

2010; Michelon et al., 2015); and the management's perspective by whether the information was forward-looking or backward-looking —How is the managerial orientation? — (Michelon et al., 2015; García-Meca; Martínez-Ferrero, 2021; Silva, 2021).

Another critical dimension is the inclusion of stakeholders in reporting practices —who are the stakeholders toward whom banks direct their sustainability efforts? —since sustainability reports must identify the relevant stakeholders and describe their involvement in the organization's sustainability initiatives (Ardiana, 2023; García-Sánchez, 2021). However, the literature has paid little attention to this aspect, and existing studies reveal that companies tend not to provide detailed information on stakeholder participation. Additionally, they often fail to disclose how companies address the concerns of various stakeholder groups (Moratis & Brandt, 2017). This trend needs to change, as society increasingly demands detailed evidence of whether companies truly consider stakeholder concerns, issues, and goals in their actions (Kaur & Lodhia, 2014).

Focusing on the quality dimensions mentioned above, existing research has primarily examined what information is disclosed in sustainability reports indicating the need for a better amount of information (eg: Lui & Zainuldin, 2024). Specific to SDG disclosure, Sarduinou et al. (2021), using a sample of 37 European banks, found that most European banks focus on promoting SDGs closely aligned with their core business. Similarly, Aguado-Correa et al. (2023) analyzed the SDG disclosures of 12 Spanish banks and noted that these banks concentrated on SDGs where their activities had the greatest impact, particularly SDGs 8, 13, and 4. In contrast, research on SDG reporting in less-developed countries is limited. Ijaz et al. (2020) observed that Pakistani banks lag in implementing and adequately reporting on SDGs, focusing mainly on SDGs 8, 3, and 4. Chagas et al. (2022), analyzing reports from 11 of Brazil's largest banks, highlighted the poor quality of these disclosures.

In conclusion, further research is needed to expand the understanding of the quality of information disclosure by banks in emerging countries, particularly those in Latin America. Such research should explore the extent to which banks provide not only qualitative narratives but also incorporate quantitative and monetary data to demonstrate their commitment to the 2030 Agenda. Additionally, studies should examine managerial approaches and identify the stakeholders toward whom banks direct their SDG-related sustainability practices.

Sustainability Report Assurance

Assurance on sustainability reporting has increased in popularity over recent years (Aliyu, 2024; KPMG, 2020; Mnif et al., 2019) as it ensures the reliability and trustworthiness of sustainability reports (Khatib, 2024; Isack, & Aschauer, 2024).

However, more research is needed to understand the trends in assurance practices and even more in emerging countries (Lemma et al., 2024).

Assurance practices over sustainability reporting can vary considerably in terms such as the assurance provider type, the consistency of companies in adopting assurance, level of assurance and the standards used in the assurance engagement (Aliyu, 2024; Alsahali & Malagueño, 2022; Farooq et al., 2023). Regarding the type of assurance provider, it can be categorized into a) independent third-party assurance providers, which include both accounting and non-accounting assurers, as well as b) other types. Within the category of independent third-party assurance, accounting assurers can be further divided into Big Four firms and other accounting companies. Non-accounting assurers include engineering and consulting firms. The "other types" category encompasses certification and consultation firms (Alsahali & Malagueño, 2022). Previous studies indicate that Big Four firms dominate the assurance market (Lemma et al., 2024). However, the number of sustainability reports assured by engineering firms has significantly increased in recent years (Farooq et al., 2023; Larrinaga et al., 2020; Perego & Kolk, 2012; Sierra et al., 2013; Yan et al., 2022; Zorio et al., 2013).

The consistency of companies in adopting assurance refers to whether businesses regularly utilize assurance for their reports and whether they change assurance providers over time (Alsahali & Malagueño, 2022). Likewise, there are two levels of assurance as defined by the IAASB in the ISAE 3000 standard issued in 2005 (Smith et al., 2011): reasonable assurance and limited assurance. The level of assurance reflects the degree of certainty that the assurance provider has regarding the report being free from material error. Reasonable assurance requires more thorough investigation and substantial evidence compared to limited assurance. While the distinction between what constitutes reasonable versus limited assurance is somewhat ambiguous (Farooq & de Villiers, 2019), reasonable assurance generally involves deeper scrutiny and more extensive evidence gathering. Limited assurance, in contrast, focuses on identifying significant issues without exhaustive testing. According to Maroun (2020), these two types can be further categorized as substantive assurance and symbolic assurance, respectively. In this sense, reasonable assurance aligns with substantive assurance because it adds value and enhances the credibility of disclosures. On the other hand, limited assurance is often viewed as symbolic, serving primarily to manage societal expectations rather than providing in-depth verification (Maroun, 2019).

Moreover, there are concerns about the positive impact of SRA on disclosure quality due to the regulatory framework, technological advancements, and socio-economic factors affecting assurance practices (Dasinapa & Ermawati, 2024). Regarding the regulatory framework, there are recent regulatory developments, such as the Corporate Sustainability Reporting Directive - Directive (EU) 2022/2464, which demands more robust and standardized sustainability disclosures, as well as independent assurance to verify the accuracy and reliability of such disclosures. However, these initiatives have a lack of clear guidance on reporting requirements and the delivery of assurance engagements (Aliyu, 2024 and Sari, 2024). Hence there is a call for policies that focused on aspects of assurance procedures, such as defining the scope of assurance, ensuring its consistency, and determining the nature of external stakeholder engagement (Aliyu, 2024).

Delving further reporting regulatory framework in emerging economies, previous research indicates that sustainability reporting remains voluntary and unregulated in these countries (Sebastião et al., 2024). In this regard, Lemma et al (2024) highlights that South Africa's regulatory framework is “weak”, which allows dominant players to shape sustainability assurance norms and practices to serve their interests rather than enhancing environmental accountability. Likewise, the assurance on a sustainability report varies depending on industries with those from “pollution intensive” being the sectors most use this practice (Lemma et al., 2024). Similarly, in Latin American countries such as the four Mercosur nations—Argentina, Brazil, Paraguay, and Uruguay—SRA is voluntary, with no national legislation or regulatory enforcement by governing bodies. Although Argentina has some provincial laws on the subject, these only cover the voluntary aspects of sustainability reporting and assurance (Palacios et al., 2022 Suárez-Rico et al., 2022). This lack of regulatory oversight may partially explain why SRA adoption in Latin America lags the global average of 47%. In this sense the financial services sector performs even worse, with an assurance rate of just 27%, significantly below the regional average (KPMG, 2023).

With respect to other challenges related to the adoption of digital technologies such as artificial intelligence, blockchain, Internet of Things and big data, previous studies show that these technologies offer great opportunities for assurance providers. In particular these technologies help to improve assurance quality, enhance risk assessment, and uncover insights that may have been overlooked using traditional assurance methods. However, these advancements also pose ethical implications such as data privacy, cybersecurity, and algorithmic interpretation. Hence, a deeper exploration into precision, reliability and limitations of the data generated by these technologies in sustainability reporting and SRA are needed. Consequently, there is a call for a robust data governance framework that ensures authenticity of data generated and minimizes the risks of using these technologies for greenwashing purposes, albeit this will imply additional compliance costs on assurance companies (Dasinapa & Ermawati, 2024; De Silva et al., 2024).

Finally, regarding the socio-economic forces on the assurance practice, previous research has identified a lack of financial resources, expertise, and capacity to implement comprehensive assurance frameworks. This imbalance in resources further exacerbates the difficulty of achieving widespread adoption of assurance practices across diverse organizational contexts (Sari, 2024).

In conclusion, further research is essential to address variations in assurance practices—such as provider types, consistency in adoption, and levels of assurance—along with regional disparities, regulatory gaps, and ethical challenges, to enable assurance to drive transparent and accountable sustainability reporting globally.

METHODOLOGY

Sample

To conduct the research first was considered the population of banks recognized by the respective central banks of the four MERCOSUR signatory countries (Argentina, Brazil, Paraguay, and Uruguay) which are was composed of 269 banks. The final sample of banks was selected based on those whose reports are available on their official website and content information regarding SDGs, in particular the last report available was related to the year 2022. The final sample consisted of 38 banks, 14% of the original sample. Likewise, we can observe that the type of report used to disseminate information regarding their commitment to the 2030 Agenda mainly provides a sustainability report based on GRI standards. To a lesser extent, the accountability of the integration of SDGs in banking management is published in the integrated report format. On the other hand, we found in total that 19 of these banks had assured their sustainability report (see Table 1).

Table 1. Population and sample

	MERCOSUR	Central Bank of Argentina	Central Bank of Brazil	Central Bank of Paraguay	Central Bank of Uruguay
Banks	269	80	161	18a	10
Banks with SDG reporting	38	10	20	4	4
Assurance	19	4	14	0	1
Non-Assurance	19	6	6	4	3

a: Includes the Development Financial Agency (DFA), a second-tier state bank in Paraguay
Source Authors' own compilation

Method

A comparative analysis was conducted to identify differences in the quality of disclosure regarding banks' practices aligned with the SDGs, depending on whether the reports were externally assured or not. Specifically, a deductive content analysis was applied, with data coded into predefined categories based on the literature review in Section 2. The analysis focused on the following dimensions: a) What and how much is disclosed: This examines whether sustainability reports include practices aligned with any of the 17 SDGs and whether the information is presented qualitatively, quantitatively, or monetarily; b) Managerial orientation: This assesses whether the reports highlight future-oriented practices or focus on past actions, detailing specific steps already undertaken; c) Stakeholder identification: This evaluates whether the reports specify the beneficiaries of the banks' SDG-related sustainability practices (see Table 2 for coding procedure examples). To provide a more comprehensive understanding of disclosure practices, additional factors were considered, such as the length of the banks' sustainability reports, measured by the number of pages, and the total number of sustainability reports available.

Table 2. Examples of coding quality disclosure

What and how much is disclosed?		
Qualitative	Quantitative	Monetary
SDG 16. *The implementation of the Positive Impact Commitments is led by the Marketing and Sustainability Management. The governance structure that accompanies this implementation is the Executive Committee, with whom a meeting schedule is maintained throughout the year.*	SDG 12. *33% allocated to native forest conservation projects in Misiones in collaboration with the Forest Bank. We managed to save 122,162 square meters of the Atlantic Forest from the Las Araucarias I and II Project, located in Misiones, Argentina, offsetting 6,648 tnCO2eq of our 2021 operational carbon footprint.*	SDG13. *We play a fundamental role in supporting the transition to a low-carbon economy and helping to accelerate climate change solutions in our core business activities. Our Climate Commitments include mobilizing $100.000 million in climate-related financing by 2025, and we aim to be a net-zero emissions bank by 2050.*
How is the managerial orientation?		
Future: forward-looking disclosure		Past: back-looking disclosure

continued on following page

Table 2. Continued

<table>
<tr><td>SDG5.
Achieve 26% of women in leadership positions by 12/31/2023, in order to reflect the profile of the BB employee base.</td><td>SDGs 16 and 17. *With the purpose of contributing to the development of a long-term public agenda, we ally with entities that work on strengthening democracy and its institutions through dialogue among different groups (politicians, businesspeople, academics, think tanks, and others) to find shared visions and generate basic agreements.*</td></tr>
<tr><td colspan="2">**What are stakeholders toward with whom banks direct their reporting practices?**</td></tr>
<tr><td colspan="2">SDG 1, 2
"clients, government, community, investors, providers, strategic partners among others"</td></tr>
</table>

To determine whether notable differences exist in disclosure quality, managerial orientation, stakeholder identification, depending on whether the reports were externally assured or not, the Mann-Whitney U test was employed for each item in the study. This test, a non-parametric alternative to the t-test, is particularly suitable for analyzing two independent groups when the sample size is small and normality and homoscedasticity cannot be assumed (Sheskin, 2011). This approach has been utilized in similar studies on disclosure quality in the banking sector (Menassa, 2010).

To analyze trends in SRA practices within the MERCOSUR banking sector and in alignment with the literature review in Section 2, the three parameters were examined. In particular, a) assurance provider type: differentiating between services provided by independent third party assurance, including accounting firms and non-accounting firms- and others; b) consistency: evaluating whether banks consistently adopt assurance practices and maintain consistency in their choice of assurance provider and; c) level of assurance: assessing whether reports indicate reasonable assurance, which involves thorough scrutiny, or limited assurance, which entails less detailed evaluation. For the analysis, a dichotomous scoring system was employed. Following Krippendorff (2018), a single researcher conducted the analysis after an initial assessment by the entire research team, mitigating risks related to inter-coder reliability.

RESULTS

Results Comparative Analysis

Results on What and How Much Information is Disclosed.

Table 3 presents the results for RQ1.1, which focuses on the comparative analysis of the quantitative, qualitative, and monetary levels of SDG disclosure across their social, economic, and environmental dimensions. Overall, MERCOSUR banks, whether their sustainability reports are assured or non-assured, primarily disclose their actions aligned with the SDGs in a qualitative manner. Limited attention is given to providing quantitative or monetary information to demonstrate how these banks implement their sustainability practices. Furthermore, both groups tend to report more extensively on SDGs related to the economic and social dimensions, with less emphasis on those aligned with the environmental dimension. Interestingly, non-assured reports exhibit higher levels of disclosure compared to assured reports, with significant differences observed in SDG 7 (Affordable and Clean Energy) and SDG 6 (Clean Water and Sanitation). These findings align with previous studies in African countries, where narrative reporting predominates (Lemma et al., 2024), and support prior research indicating the limited impact of assurance services on the quality of sustainability reporting, particularly in contexts like Bangladesh and the United Kingdom (Akhert et al., 2023; Michelon et al., 2015).

Delving deeper into qualitative disclosures, non-assured reports show the highest reporting rates across all three main dimensions. Within the social dimension, sustainability practices most frequently reported are aligned with SDG 4 (Quality Education) and SDG 5 (Gender Equality). For the economic dimension, SDG 10 (Reduced Inequalities) reaches 68.42%, the highest qualitative reporting rate, followed by SDG 8 (Decent Work and Economic Growth). In contrast, qualitative disclosure under assurance reporting is lower than that of non-assured reports. For instance, reporting on SDG 1 (No Poverty) decreases from 47.37% in non-assured reports to 26.32% in assured reports. However, the most reported SDGs under assurance—SDG 8, SDG 10, and SDG 13 (Climate Action)—remain consistent, albeit at reduced rates (36.84%–47.37%).

With respect to quantitative disclosures, non-assured reports show relatively low percentages, with most SDGs hovering around 5.26%. Notable exceptions include SDG 8 (Decent Work and Economic Growth), which reaches 10.53%, while SDG 6 (Clean Water and Sanitation) records 0%. For assured reports, quantitative disclosures are generally consistent with those in non-assured reports, ranging between 5.26% and 10.53%. For example, reporting on SDG 5 (Gender Equality) increases from 5.26% in non-assured reports to 10.53% in assured ones.

Monetary disclosures, the least prevalent type, are similarly sparse in both non-assured and assured reports. In non-assured reports, most SDGs report monetary data at a default level of 5.26%. Higher reporting is observed for SDG 1 (No Poverty) and SDG 13 (Climate Action) at 11% and 10.53%, respectively, while some SDGs (e.g., SDG 3, SDG 14, and SDG 15) show no monetary reporting. In assured reports, monetary disclosures are slightly more consistent, with 10.53% reported for multiple SDGs (e.g., SDG 13). Nevertheless, monetary disclosures remain less common compared to qualitative and quantitative data.

Lastly, significant differences were identified in the length of reports and the years of reporting available. MERCOSUR banks with assured sustainability reports tend to produce longer reports. However, these reports appear to be less focused on accountability for sustainability practices aligned with the SDGs. Additionally, these banks demonstrate greater consistency in maintaining visibility on their sustainability practices over the years.

In conclusion, the analysis reveals that MERCOSUR banks predominantly rely on qualitative disclosures when reporting their SDG-aligned practices, with limited inclusion of quantitative and monetary details, regardless of assurance status. Banks with non-assured reports tend to provide higher levels of disclosure related to SDG actions. In contrast, banks with assured reports often produce longer reports that include content unrelated to SDGs and offer greater accessibility by making reports from the past four years available. Nevertheless, in both cases, a more balanced focus across all SDG dimensions, particularly environmental aspects, remains necessary.

Table 3. Comparative quality disclosures result for SDGs classified by non-assurance and assurance

SDGs	NON ASSURANCE			ASSURANCE		
	Qualitative	Quantitative	Monetary	Qualitative	Quantitative	Monetary
TOTAL	**48.55**	**3.64**	**4.84**	**30.18**	**5.66**	**7.50**
SDG - SOCIAL DIMENSION	45.39	3.29	5.32	30.27	4.60	5.92
SDG 1 - No poverty	47.37	5.26	11.00	26.32	5.26	10.53
SDG 2 - Zero hunger	26.32	5.26	0.00	31.58	0.00	10.53
SDG 3 - Good health and well-being	42.11	0.00	0.00	26.32	5.26	0.00
SDG 4 - Quality Education	63.16	0.00	5.26	42.11	5.26	0.00
SDG 5 - Gender equality	57.89	5.26	5.26	42.11	10.53	5.26
SDG 7 - Affordable and clean energy	42.10**	5.26	5.26	10.53**	5.26	10.53
SDG 11 - Sustainable cities and economies	31.58	0.00	10.53	15.79	0.00	5.26

continued on following page

Table 3. Continued

SDGs	NON ASSURANCE			ASSURANCE		
	Qualitative	Quantitative	Monetary	Qualitative	Quantitative	Monetary
SDG 16 - Peace. justice and strong institutions	52.63	5.26	5.26	47.37	5.26	5.26
SDG - ECONOMIC DIMENSION	62.11	6.32	5.26	43.16	8.42	7.37
SDG 8 - Decent work and economic growth	63.16	10.53	5.26	47.37	10.53	10.53
SDG 9 - Industry. innovation and infrastructure	63.16	5.26	5.26	42.11	10.53	5.26
SDG 10 - Reduced inequalities	68.42	5.26	5.26	42.11	10.53	10.53
SDG 12 - Responsible consumption and production	63.16	5.26	5.26	47.37	5.26	5.26
SDG 17 - Partnership for the goals	52.63	5.26	5.26	36.84	5.26	5.26
SGD – ENVIRONMENTAL DIMENSION	38.16	1.32	3.95	17.11	3.95	9.21
SDG 6 - Clean water and sanitation	31.58**	0.00	5.26	5.26**	5.26	10.53
SDG 13 - Climate action	63.16	5.26	10.53	36.84	10.53	10.53
SDG 14 - Life below water	31.58	0.00	0.00	10.53	0.00	5.26
SDG 15 - Life on land	26.32	0.00	0.00	15.79	0.00	10.53
	Assurance	Non-assurance				
Extension of pages	154***	111***				
Number of sustainability reporting available	4***	3***				

* Significance at level 10%; ** significance at level 5%*** significance at level 1%

Results on the Managerial Orientation of the Reporting

Table 4 analyzes the managerial orientation in SDG reporting, distinguishing between future-oriented (forward-looking) and past-oriented (backward-looking) disclosures across non-assurance and assurance frameworks (RQ1.2). The data reveal significant differences, indicating that MERCOSUR banks without assured reports primarily focus on past actions, detailing specific activities undertaken to meet SDG commitments. In contrast, banks with assurance practices adopt a mixed approach, emphasizing both future-oriented initiatives and specific past actions.

In total, 59.52% of non-assurance cases predominantly focus on historical results and outcomes, with no instances of future-oriented reporting. Conversely, 8.55% of MERCOSUR banks with assured reports include future-oriented data, while 38.07% also provide past-oriented disclosures.

Regarding the social dimension, significant differences were observed in SDG 1 (No Poverty), SDG 4 (Education), SDG 5 (Gender Equality), and SDG 7 (Affordable and Clean Energy). Non-assurance banks provide significantly more past-oriented information for SDG 1 and SDG 4, with 68.4% of reports compared to 36% for assured reports. Similarly, over half of non-assurance reports detail past activities related to SDG 7, whereas less than 22% of assured reports do so. However, for SDG 5, assurance reports are more inclined to include future-oriented information on gender equality initiatives compared to non-assurance reports.

With respect to the economic dimension, differences were noted in SDG 8 (Decent Work) and SDG 10 (Reduced Inequalities). Around 15% of assurance reports highlight future goals and activities to promote decent work, while none of the non-assurance reports provide such information. Additionally, nearly 80% of non-assurance reports focus on past activities, compared to less than 50% of assurance reports.

In the environmental dimension, significant difference was identified for SDG 13 (Climate Action). Most non-assurance banks report on actions already undertaken to combat climate change, whereas less than half of assurance reports provide similar past-oriented information. In addition, while no non-assurance banks report future goals or activities related to SDG 13, some assurance reports (15%) include future-oriented plans instead of offering comprehensive details on past actions.

In conclusion, the analysis highlights significant differences in managerial orientation between non-assurance and assurance SDG reporting among MERCOSUR banks. Non-assurance reports focus heavily on past-oriented disclosures, detailing completed actions, while assurance reports adopt a mixed approach, incorporating both past achievements and future goals.

Table 4. Managerial orientation

SDGs	NON-ASSURANCE		ASSURANCE	
	Future	Past	Future	Past
TOTAL	**0.00**	**59.52**	**8.55**	**38.07**
SDG - SOCIAL DIMENSION	0.0	54.6	5.9	34.2
SDG 1 - No poverty	0.0	68.4*	0.0	36.8*
SDG 2 - Zero hunger	0.0	31.6	5.3	36.8
SDG 3 - Good health and well-being	0.0	42.1	0.0	31.6
SDG 4 - Quality Education	0.0	68.4*	10.5	36.8*
SDG 5 - Gender equality	0.0*	68.4	15.8*	42.1
SDG 7 - Affordable and clean energy	0.0	52.6**	5.3	21.1**
SDG 11 - Sustainable cities and economies	0.0	42.1	0.0	21.1

continued on following page

Table 4. Continued

SDGs	NON-ASSURANCE		ASSURANCE	
	Future	**Past**	**Future**	**Past**
SDG 16 - Peace, justice and strong institutions	0.0	63.2	10.5	47.4
SDG - ECONOMIC DIMENSION	0.0	72.6	10.5	48.4
SDG 8 - Decent work and economic growth	0.0**	73.7	15.8**	52.6
SDG 9 - Industry, innovation and infrastructure	0.0	73.7	10.5	47.4
SDG 10 - Reduced inequalities	0.0	78.9**	15.8	47.4**
SDG 12 - Responsible consumption and production	0.0	73.7	5.3	52.6
SDG 17 - Partnership for the goals	0.0	63.2	5.3	42.1
SGD – ENVIRONMENTAL DIMENSION	0.0	51.3	9.2	31.6
SDG 6 - Clean water and sanitation	0.0	68.4	15.8	42.1
SDG 13 - Climate action	0.0*	78.9**	15.8*	47.4**
SDG 14 - Life below water	0.0	31.6	0.0	15.8
SDG 15 - Life on land	0.0	26.3	5.3	21.1

**Significance at level 5%

Results on Stakeholders Toward Whom Banks Direct Their Reporting Practices

Table 5 examines whether MERCOSUR banks identify stakeholders in their sustainability initiatives across both assurance and non-assurance reports. Overall, the identification of stakeholders to whom banks direct their reporting practices is low. This aligns with previous studies highlighting that a key shortcoming of sustainability reports is the limited inclusion and engagement of stakeholders (García-Sánchez, 2021; Ardiana, 2023). Assurance reports demonstrate less transparency (19.1%) in stakeholder identification compared to non-assurance reports (35.9%). This trend is consistent across all three dimensions. In both cases, MERCOSUR banks more frequently report stakeholders accountable to actions related to the economic dimension, nearly doubling those reported for the social dimension. Stakeholders associated with actions tied to the environmental dimension are minimally recognized.

Focusing on the statistical differences observed within the social dimension, SDG 1 (No Poverty) and SDG 4 (Quality Education) stand out. Approximately 40% of non-assurance reports by MERCOSUR banks specify the stakeholders targeted by SDG 1-related actions, compared to around 16% for assurance reports. Similarly, over 50% of non-assurance reports identify the stakeholders impacted by actions supporting SDG 4, whereas only 10% of assurance reports do so.

In the economic dimension, MERCOSUR banks exhibit a strong commitment to identifying stakeholders affected by their actions to support SDG 8 (Decent Work and Economic Growth). Non-assurance reports achieve a 100% mention rate for stakeholder identification in this area. In contrast, slightly more than 31% of assurance reports explicitly detail the stakeholders impacted by the banks' actions.

Table 5. Sustainability reporting linked to stakeholders

SDGs	Non-assurance	Assurance
TOTAL	35.9	19.1
SDG - SOCIAL DIMENSION	37.5	15.1
SDG 1 - No poverty	36.8*	15.8*
SDG 2 - Zero hunger	10.5	26.3
SDG 3 - Good health and well-being	21.1	10.5
SDG 4 - Quality Education	57.9*	10.5*
SDG 5 - Gender equality	57.9	5.3
SDG 7 - Affordable and clean energy	21.1	15.8
SDG 11 - Sustainable cities and economies	42.1	31.6
SDG 16 - Peace, justice and strong institutions	52.6	5.3
SDG - ECONOMIC DIMENSION	61.1	26.3
SDG 8 - Decent work and economic growth	100.0*	31.6*
SDG 9 - Industry, innovation and infrastructure	52.6	31.6
SDG 10 - Reduced inequalities	52.6	26.3
SDG 12 - Responsible consumption and production	52.6	21.1
SDG 17 - Partnership for the goals	47.4	21.1
SGD – ENVIRONMENTAL DIMENSION	9.2	15.8
SDG 6 - Clean water and sanitation	10.5	21.1
SDG 13 - Climate action	26.3	21.1
SDG 14 - Life below water	0.0	10.5
SDG 15 - Life on land	0.0	10.5

* Significance at level 10%

Results About Trends in SRA

This section explores how businesses approach assurance in sustainability reporting (RQ2), focusing on the type of assurance provider, consistency in the adoption of assurance practices and choice of assurance provider, and the level of assurance.

Regarding the type of assurance provider (see Figure 1), the majority of banks (93.55%) opt for independent third-party assurance, indicating a preference for legitimacy and expertise. The "Big Four" accounting firms dominate this category and in the following order PwC (48.39%), KPMG (24.19%), Deloitte (12.90%) and Ernst & Young (8.06%). These findings align with previous studies that highlight the global trend of using Big Four firms for SRA (Alsahali & Malagueño, 2022). The preference for these firms is likely due to their solid reputations and global networks, which give them a competitive edge over non-accounting firms (Martínez-Ferrero & García-Sánchez, 2017). Moreover, no banks use engineering or consulting firms for SRA, which could indicate a lack of recognized expertise or trust in this area. Additionally, there is an emerging interest in certifications (6.45%). This later result is in line with previous research noting the increasing use of certification firms (Alsahali & Malagueño, 2022). Regarding expert opinion, this service is not used by MERCOSUR banks.

Figure 1. Type of SRA provider

Figure 2 illustrates the consistency with which banks adopt assurance practices and select assurance providers. According to the findings, more than half of MERCOSUR banks (68.42%) consistently choose the same assurance provider. This result is like the 63% found in the global study by Alsahali & Malagueño (2022), which included both listed and non-listed firms across multinational and small enterprises. This consistency may be due to factors such as cost, experience, or service quality. However, a significant minority of banks occasionally switch providers, and no banks have opted for non-accounting providers. This confirms that engineering or consulting firms are not present in the assurance market. Furthermore, only 5.26% of firms switched to basic certification, possibly due to financial constraints or shifts in banks' reporting preferences.

Figure 2. Consistence of SRA provider

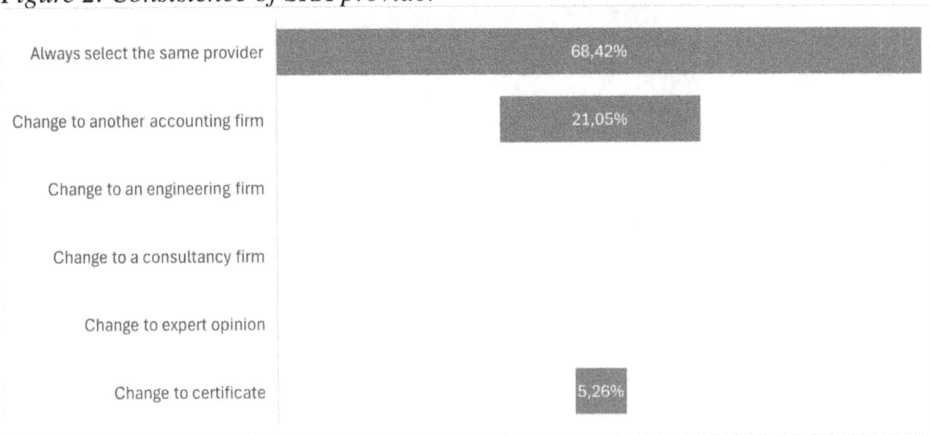

The level of assurance (Figure 3), which can be classified as limited/moderate or reasonable/high, reflects the assurance provider's confidence that the report is free of errors (IAASB, 2013). Data indicates no banks choose reasonable assurance, which is more stringent and costly. Instead, all MERCOSUR banks select limited assurance (100%), providing a modest level of confidence in the information reported. This suggests that banks prioritize symbolic reporting over substantive reporting (Michelon et al., 2015) These findings are consistent with previous studies indicating that the scope and depth of sustainability report assurance are limited (Lemma et al., 2024; Alsahali & Malagueño, 2022)

Figure 3. Level of assurance

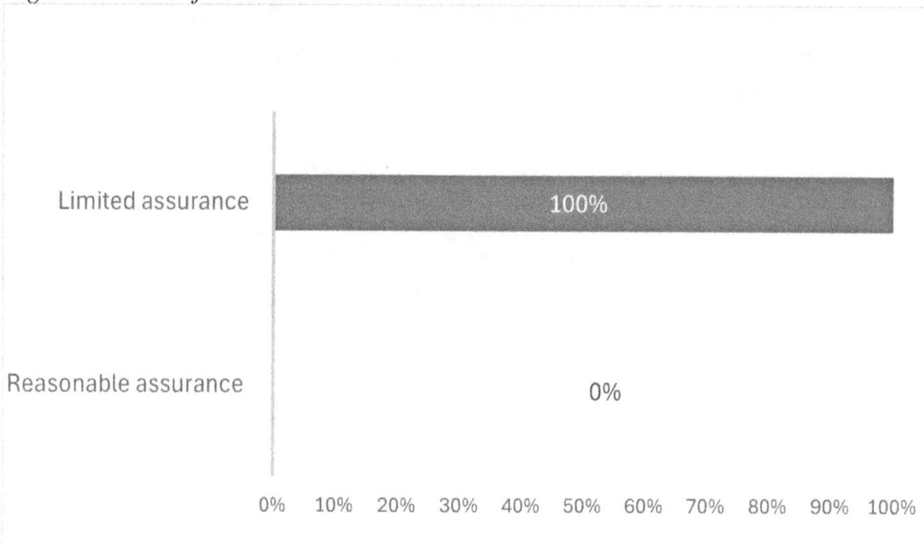

In conclusion, current trends in SRA of MERCOSUR banks reflect a dominance of accounting firms, consistency in using assurance in their report over the years, and with the same provider, using a limited level of assurance.

CONCLUSION AND FUTURE RESEARCH

Banks play a critical role in societal progress and environmental protection. However, there is an urgent call for greater accuracy and credibility in their sustainability reports. In emerging economies, such as those in Latin America, where sustainability reporting regulations are lacking, sustainability assurance is gaining prominence. This is due to its expected role as a key mechanism to assure stakeholders that banks are substantively, rather than symbolically, committed to sustainability initiatives, including their contributions to the Sustainable Development Goals (SDGs).

This study examines sustainability report assurance (SRA) in the banking sector of MERCOSUR countries with two main objectives: first, to evaluate its role in improving the quality of SDG disclosures—considering what and how the information is disclosed, the managerial orientation, and the level of stakeholders' identification in the banks' sustainability reports—and second, to analyze trends in SRA practices.

The findings reveal that, in general, a greater amount of information shared on sustainability practices is needed. This aligns with prior studies in emerging markets, which emphasize the need for enhanced sustainability disclosure (Lui &

Zainuldin, 2024). Moreover, consistent with research in developed countries, banks predominantly disclose information on SDGs tied to their economic contributions to national growth (Aguado-Correa et al., 2023; Avrampou et al., 2019; Chagas et al., 2022). This result could be because the banking sector is not a "polluting sector," and industries with negative environmental impacts are often more motivated to showcase their engagement in protecting the planet and people (Li et al., 2024).

Moreover, SRA has not significantly improved the quality of SDG disclosures. In fact, non-assurance reports often provide more detailed information on banks' SDG commitments compared to assured reports. When considering how information is presented, sustainability disclosures are predominantly qualitative, with limited quantitative data and even less monetary information for stakeholders to assess the financial efforts directed toward supporting SDGs. While previous studies in non-banking sectors call for SRA to improve disclosure quality (Lemma et al., 2024; Michelon et al., 2015), this study highlights the need for the banking sector to enhance quantitative and monetary disclosures related to SDGs.

In terms of managerial orientation, significant differences exist between non-assurance and assurance reports. Non-assurance reports largely focus on past actions, detailing specific activities undertaken to meet SDG commitments. In contrast, assurance reports adopt a mixed approach, presenting information on both future-oriented initiatives and past actions. Hence, this result suggests that, specific to the MERCOSUR banking industry, assurance practices do not adequately encourage banks to report on results or demonstrate alignment between organizational strategies and SDGs. This lack of detailed information on objectives and outcomes aligns with results obtained in similar studies focused on developed countries like the UK (Michelon et al., 2015) and in industries with higher environmental sensitivity (Garcia-Meca & Martínez-Ferrero, 2021).

Another key shortcoming of SRA lies in its limited attention to stakeholders in reporting practices. MERCOSUR banks generally fail to identify the stakeholders targeted by their sustainability initiatives in their reports. This mirrors findings from studies on Fortune Global 500 companies, which also show a low level of stakeholder engagement in sustainability reporting (Ardiana, 2023). Thus, this study underscores growing concerns that SRA does not sufficiently prioritize stakeholder roles in the reporting process (Lemma et al., 2024; Aliyu, 2024).

Regarding the trends in SRA practices among MERCOSUR banks, the findings highlight that only half of the banks analyzed opt to assure their sustainability reports. This may stem from the tendency for assurance practices to be more prevalent among firms operating in "pollution-intensive" industries (Lemma et al., 2024). Additionally, the results indicate a strong preference for independent third-party assurance, with the Big Four accounting firms (PwC, KPMG, Deloitte, and Ernst & Young) dominating over non-accounting providers, such as consulting or engineering firms.

MERCOSUR banks demonstrate consistency in maintaining assurance practices over the years, typically sticking with the same Big Four firm. When banks switch providers, they usually select another Big Four firm, mirroring trends observed in non-financial organizations across different sizes and contexts (Alsahali & Malagueño, 2022). In terms of the level of assurance, MERCOSUR banks exclusively opt for limited assurance rather than the more rigorous reasonable assurance. This choice may reflect a focus on protecting the assurance provider rather than prioritizing stakeholder accountability, a trend also observed in other emerging countries (Lemma et al., 2024; Khabit et al., 2024) and developed economies (Aliyu, 2024). Consequently, the findings suggest that SRA practices in MERCOSUR banks lean toward symbolic rather than substantive reporting.

In summary, this study offers both academic and practical contributions. At the academic level, it addresses the gap in comparative analyses of SRA across countries (Sari, 2024; Sahi et al., 2022), providing valuable insights into assurance practices in Latin America, a region often overlooked in reporting literature (Sebastião et al., 2024). The findings also highlight the need for continued research into the dynamics of sustainability assurance (Khatib, 2024), leveraging the symbolic and substantive perspectives of legitimacy theory to better understand banks' decision-making on reporting policies.

As for the practical implications, the results underscore the need for a paradigm shift in how banks and assurance firms approach sustainability reporting. Banks should demonstrate a greater commitment to sustainability initiatives, particularly those supporting the Sustainable Development Goals (SDGs). This requires aligning their strategies with sustainability priorities and using reporting as a substantive expression of their dedication to societal progress and environmental protection. Additionally, banks must invest in expertise and capacity to adopt comprehensive assurance frameworks that enhance the credibility of their reports.

For assurance firms, the lack of clear guidelines on reporting requirements and assurance engagement delivery (Aliyu, 2024; Sari, 2024) demands greater responsibility. Assurance providers must recognize their critical role in improving reporting practices. Failing to do so risks diminishing their perceived value. They should aim to deliver assurance at a reasonable level, with a clear focus on the needs of stakeholders.

Finally, public authorities in Latin America should prioritize regulatory frameworks that encourage substantive sustainability practices among banks. Policies and initiatives aimed at strengthening assurance procedures are needed to address existing regulatory gaps and ethical challenges. This will ensure that assurance drives transparent and accountable sustainability reporting within MERCOSUR countries.

This study is not without limitations, which points to avenues for future research. First, it focuses solely on the banking sector in MERCOSUR countries, limiting the generalizability of its findings to other economic sectors or regions. Future studies could conduct comparative analyses of the impact of SRA on the quality of sustainability disclosures in banks from Latin America and other emerging economies, such as those in Africa. Second, the methodology is primarily descriptive and quantitative. Further qualitative research could explore the barriers faced by banks and assurance firms in Latin American countries. Additionally, future studies could examine how organizational factors, such as digital capabilities and organizational size, influence the quality of disclosures, the selection of assurance providers, and decisions to switch providers.

REFERENCES

Aguado-Correa, F., de la Vega-Jiménez, J. J., López-Jiménez, J. M., Padilla-Garrido, N., & Rabadán-Martín, I. (2023). Evaluation of non-financial information and its contribution to advancing the sustainable development goals within the Spanish banking sector. *European Research on Management and Business Economics*, 29(1), 100211.

Akhter, F., Hossain, M. R., Elrehail, H., Rehman, S. U., & Almansour, B. (2023). Environmental disclosures and corporate attributes, from the lens of legitimacy theory: A longitudinal analysis on a developing country. *European Journal of Management and Business Economics*, 32(3), 342–369.

Aliyu, S. (2024). Issues in sustainability reporting assurance: Evidence from interviews. *Sustainability Accounting. Management and Policy Journal*, 15(3), 628–653. DOI: 10.1108/SAMPJ-07-2023-0457

Alsahali, K. F., & Malagueño, R. (2022). An empirical study of sustainability reporting assurance: current trends and new insights. *Journal of accounting & organizational change*, 18(5), 617-642. DOI: 10.1108/JAOC-05-2020-0060

Aluchna, M., Roszkowska-Menkes, M., Jastrzębska, E., & Bohdanowicz, L. (2023). Sustainability reporting as a social construct: The systematic literature review within socio-political view. *Social Responsibility Journal*, 19(8), 1535–1554. DOI: 10.1108/SRJ-06-2022-0231

Ardiana, P. (2023). Stakeholder engagement in sustainability reporting by Fortune Global 500 companies: A call for embeddedness. *Meditari Accountancy Research*, 31(2), 344–365. DOI: 10.1108/MEDAR-12-2019-0666

Avrampou, A., Skouloudis, A., Iliopoulos, G., & Khan, N. (2019). Advancing the sustainable development goals: Evidence from leading European banks. *Sustainable Development*, 27(4), 743–757. DOI: 10.1002/sd.1938

Baalouch, F., Ayadi, S., & Hussainey, K. (2019). A study of the determinants of environmental disclosure quality: Evidence from French listed companies. *The Journal of Management and Governance*, 23(4), 939–971. DOI: 10.1007/s10997-019-09474-0

Branco, M. C., & Rodrigues, L. L. (2008). Social responsibility disclosure: A study of proxies for the public visibility of Portuguese banks. *The British Accounting Review*, 40(2), 161–181.

Chagas, E. J. M. D., Albuquerque, J. D. L., Maia Filho, L. F. A., & Ceolin, A. C. (2022). Sustainable development, disclosure to stakeholders and the Sustainable Development Goals: Evidence from Brazilian banks' non-financial reports. *Sustainable Development*, 30(6), 1975–1986.

Chatzitheodorou, K., Tsalis, T. A., Tsagarakis, K. P., Evangelos, G., & Ioannis, N. (2021). A new practical methodology for the banking sector to assess corporate sustainability risks with an application in the energy sector. *Sustainable Production and Consumption*, 27, 1473–1487. DOI: 10.1016/j.spc.2021.03.005

Chauvey, J. N., Giordano-Spring, S., Cho, C. H., & Patten, D. M. (2015). The normativity and legitimacy of CSR disclosure: Evidence from France. *Journal of Business Ethics*, 130(4), 789–803.

Chowdhury, M. A. A., Dey, M., & Abedin, M. T. (2020). Firms' attributes and environmental disclosure: Evidence from listed firms in Bangladesh. *Asian Journal of Accounting Perspectives*, 13(2), 57–77. DOI: 10.22452/AJAP.vol13no2.4

Cosma, S., Venturelli, A., Schwizer, P., & Boscia, V. (2020). Sustainable development and European banks: A non-financial disclosure analysis. *Sustainability*, 12(15), 6146.

Dasinapa, M. B., & Ermawati, Y. (2024). Insights into Emerging Trends Shaping the Future of Audit and Assurance. *Advances in Managerial Auditing Research*, 2(2), 75–86. DOI: 10.60079/amar.v2i2.292

De Silva, P., Gunarathne, N., & Kumar, S. (2024). *Exploring the impact of digital knowledge, integration and performance on sustainable accounting, reporting and assurance*. Meditari Accountancy Research. https://doi.org/10.1108/MEDAR-02-2024-2383

Deegan, C., & Rankin, M. (1996). Explaining Corporate Annual Report Disclosures: A Legitimacy Theory Perspective. *Accounting, Auditing & Accountability Journal*, 9(2), 18–38.

Deegan, C. M. (2019). Legitimacy theory: Despite its enduring popularity and contribution, time is right for a necessary makeover. *Accounting, Auditing & Accountability Journal*, 32(8), 2307–2329. DOI: 10.1108/AAAJ-08-2018-3638

Farooq, M. B., Azantouti, A. S. A., & Zaman, R. (2024). Non-financial information assurance: A review of the literature and directions for future research. *Sustainability Accounting. Management and Policy Journal*, 15(1), 48–84. DOI: 10.1108/SAMPJ-03-2023-0166

Furrer, B., Hamprecht, J., & Hoffmann, V. H. (2012). Much ado about nothing? How banks respond to climate change. *Business & Society*, 51(1), 62–88.

Gálvez-Rodríguez, M. D. M., Ovelar-Fernández, W. D., & Caba-Pérez, C. (2024). Information Disclosure on the Integration of SDGs into Banking Management: The MERCOSUR Countries Case. In *Environmentally Sustainable Production: Research for Sustainable Development* (pp. 37–56). Springer Nature Switzerland.

Gao, F., Dong, Y., Ni, C., & Fu, R. (2016). Determinants and economic consequences of non-financial disclosure quality. *European Accounting Review*, 25(2), 287–317.

García-Meca, E., & Martínez-Ferrero, J. (2021). Is SDG reporting substantial or symbolic? An examination of controversial and environmentally sensitive industries. *Journal of Cleaner Production*, 298, 126781.

García-Sánchez, I. M. (2021). Corporate social reporting and assurance: The state of the art: Información social corporativa y aseguramiento: El estado de la cuestión. *Revista de Contabilidad-Spanish Accounting Review*, 24(2), 241–269.

Gunawan, J., Permatasari, P., & Sharma, U. (2022). Exploring sustainability and green banking disclosures: A study of banking sector. *Environment, Development and Sustainability*, 24(9), 11153–11194. DOI: 10.1007/s10668-021-01901-3

Guthrie, J., Cuganesan, B., & Ward, B. (2006). Legitimacy Theory and Corporate Social Disclosure. *Accounting, Auditing & Accountability Journal*, 19(1), 1–29.

Helfaya, A., Whittington, M., & Alawattage, C. (2019). Exploring the quality of corporate environmental reporting. *Accounting, Auditing & Accountability Journal*, 32(1), 63–193.

Iatridis, K., & Kesidou, E. (2018). What drives substantive versus symbolic implementation of ISO 14001 in a time of economic crisis? Insights from Greek manufacturing companies. *Journal of Business Ethics*, 148(4), 859–877.

Ijaz, A., Siddiqui, S. H., & Rasheed, R. (2020). SDGs implementation and future recommendations: A case of banking sector in Pakistan. *Pakistan Journal of Social Sciences*, 40(4), 1687–1699.

International Auditing and Assurance Standards Board (IAASB). (2013). ISAE 3000 (revised), assurance engagements other than audits or reviews of historical financial information. *International Auditing and Assurance Standards Board*. www.iaasb.org/publications-resources/international-standard-assurance-engagements-isae-3000-revised-2

Isack, M., & Aschauer, E. (2024). The Role of CSR Report Assurance and ESG Rating in Bank Manager's Judgement on ESG Lending Decisions. *International Journal of Auditing*. Advance online publication. DOI: 10.1111/ijau.12369

Karaman, A. S., Orazalin, N., Uyar, A., & Shahbaz, M. (2021). CSR achievement, reporting, and assurance in the energy sector: Does economic development matter? *Energy Policy*, 149, 112007. DOI: 10.1016/j.enpol.2020.112007

Kaur, A., & Lodhia, S. K. (2014). The state of disclosures on stakeholder engagement in sustainability reporting in Australian local councils. *Pacific Accounting Review*, 26(1/2), 54–74. DOI: 10.1108/PAR-07-2013-0064

Khan, H. Z., Bose, S., Mollik, A. T., & Harun, H. (2021). "Green washing" or "authentic effort"? An empirical investigation of the quality of sustainability reporting by banks. *Accounting, Auditing & Accountability Journal*, 34(2), 338–369. https://doi.org/10.1108/AAAJ-01-2018-3330

Khatib, S. F. A. (2024). Sustainability Assurance and Corporate Environmental Accountability. *Social and Environmental Accountability Journal*, 44(2), 176–177. DOI: 10.1080/0969160X.2024.2336721

Khatib Khatri, I., & Kjærland, F. (2023). Sustainability reporting practices and environmental performance amongst nordic listed firms. *Journal of Cleaner Production*, 418, 138172. DOI: 10.1016/j.jclepro.2023.138172

KPMG. (2020). The time has come the KPMG survey of sustainability reporting 2020. *KPMG's Global Center of Excellence for Climate Change and Sustainability.* https://assets.kpmg/content/dam/kpmg/xx/pdf/2020/11/the-time-has-come.pdf

KPMG. (2022). Sustainability Report Big shifts, small steps. *KPMG's Global Center of Excellence for Climate Change and Sustainability.*https://assets.kpmg.com/content/dam/kpmg/xx/pdf/2023/04/big-shifts-small-steps.pdf

KPMG. (2023). *Guía práctica de ESG: Medio ambiente, sociedad y gobernanza.* https://assets.kpmg.com/content/dam/kpmg/co/sac/pdf/2023/03/bc-ESG-esp.pdf

Krippendorff, K. (2018). *Content analysis: An introduction to its methodology*. Sage publications.

Larrinaga, C., Rossi, A., Luque-Vilchez, M., & Núñez-Nickel, M. (2020). Institutionalization of the contents of sustainability assurance services: A comparison between Italy and United States. *Journal of Business Ethics*, 163, 67–83.

Lemma, T. T., Negash, M., Lulseged, A., & Maroun, W. (2024). Sustainability assurance and corporate environmental accountability. *Business Strategy and the Environment*, 33(4), 3167–3183. DOI: 10.1002/bse.3643

Li, L., Saat, M. M., Khatib, S. F. A., Chu, P., & Sulimany, H. G. H. (2024). Navigating the impact: A comprehensive analysis of ESG disclosure consequences through systematic review. *Business Strategy & Development*, 7(2), e382. DOI: 10.1002/bsd2.382

Lodhia, S., Kaur, A., & Kuruppu, S. C. (2022). The disclosure of sustainable development goals (SDGs) by the top 50 Australian companies: Substantive or symbolic legitimation? *Meditari Accountancy Research*, 31(6), 1578–1605.

Lui, T. K., & Zainuldin, M. H. (2024). From boardroom to sustainability reporting: stakeholder-RBV insights into ESG disclosures among Malaysian banks. *The Bottom Line (New York, N.Y.)*. Advance online publication. DOI: 10.1108/BL-04-2024-0046

Maas, K., Schaltegger, S., & Crutzen, N. (2016). Integrating corporate sustainability assessment, management accounting, control, and reporting. *Journal of Cleaner Production*, 136, 237–248. DOI: 10.1016/j.jclepro.2016.05.008

Mahdi Sahi, A., Mahdi Sahi, A., Abbas, A. F., & Khatib, FA, S. (2022). Financial reporting quality of financial institutions: Literature review. *Cogent Business & Management*, 9(1), 2135210. DOI: 10.1080/23311975.2022.2135210

Majeed, A. H., Abbas, A. F., Kadhim, K. G., & Kzar, M. F. (2024). Poverty reduction and the sustainable development goals: A bibliometric study focused on the Global South. *Development in Practice*, 1–25. DOI: 10.1080/09614524.2024.2428801

Makarenko, I., Sukhonos, V., Zhuravlyova, I., Legenchuk, S., & Szołno, O. (2020). Sustainability reporting assessment for quality and compliance: The case of Ukrainian banks' management reports. *Banks and Bank Systems*, 15(2), 117–129. DOI: 10.21511/bbs.15(2).2020.11

Maroun, W. (2019). Does external assurance contribute to higher quality integrated reports? *Journal of Accounting and Public Policy*, 38(4), 106670.

Maroun, W. (2020). A conceptual model for understanding corporate social responsibility assurance practice. *Journal of Business Ethics*, 161(1), 187–209.

Martínez-Ferrero, J., & García-Sánchez, I. (2017). Coercive, normative and mimetic isomorphism as determinants of the voluntary assurance of sustainability reports. *International Business Review*, 26(1), 102–118.

Menassa, E. (2010). Corporate social responsibility: An exploratory study of the quality and extent of social disclosures by Lebanese commercial banks. *Journal of applied accounting research, 11*(1), 4-23.

Michelon, G., Patten, D. M., & Romi, A. M. (2019). Creating legitimacy for sustainability assurance practices: Evidence from sustainability restatements. *European Accounting Review*, 28(2), 395–422.

Michelon, G., Pilonato, S., & Ricceri, F. (2015). CSR reporting practices and the quality of disclosure: An empirical analysis. *Critical Perspectives on Accounting*, 33, 59–78. DOI: 10.1016/j.cpa.2014.10.003

Mio, C. (2010). Corporate social reporting in Italian multiutility companies: An empirical analysis. *Corporate Social Responsibility and Environmental Management*, 17(5), 247–271. DOI: 10.1002/csr.213

Mnif Sellami, Y., Dammak Ben Hlima, N., & Jarboui, A. (2019). An empirical investigation of determinants of sustainability report assurance in France. *Journal of Financial Reporting and Accounting*, 17(2), 320–342.

Moratis, L., & Brandt, S. (2017). Corporate stakeholder responsiveness? Exploring the state and quality of GRIbased stakeholder engagement disclosure of European firms. *Corporate Social Responsibility and Environmental Management*, 24(4), 312–325. DOI: 10.1002/ csr.1408

Perego, P., & Kolk, A. (2012). Multinationals' Accountability on Sustainability: The Evolution of Third-party Assurance of Sustainability Reports. *Journal of Business Ethics*, 110(2), 173–190. DOI: 10.1007/s10551-012-1420-5

Perez-Batres, L. A., Miller, V. V., Pisani, M. J., Henriques, I., & Renau-Sepulveda, J. A. (2012). Why do firms engage in national sustainability programs and transparent sustainability reporting? Evidence from Mexico's clean industry program. *Management International Review*, 52, 107–136. DOI: 10.1007/s10551-012-1419-y

Quick, R., & Inwinkl, P. (2020). Assurance on CSR reports: Impact on the credibility perceptions of non-financial information by bank directors. *Meditari Accountancy Research*, 28(5), 833–862.

Reporting: Towards a conceptual framework. *Journal of Cleaner Production*, 377, 134156. DOI: 10.1016/j.jclepro.2022.134156

Saraswati, E., Rachmawati, Y., & Anjani, A. (2023). Quality of Banking Sustainability Reports: Symbolic or Substantive? *European Journal of Applied Sciences, Vol*, 11(6), 157–171.

Sardianou, E., Stauropoulou, A., Evangelinos, K., & Nikolaou, I. (2021). A materiality analysis framework to assess sustainable development goals of banking sector through sustainability reports. *Sustainable Production and Consumption*, 27, 1775–1793. DOI: 10.1016/j.spc.2021.04.020

Sari, R. (2024). Assurance Practices for Ethical and Sustainable Business Practices. *Advances in Managerial Auditing Research*, 2(2), 97–108. DOI: 10.60079/amar.v2i2.342

Sebastião, A. M., Tavares, M. C., & Azevedo, G. (2024). Evolution and Challenges of Sustainability Reporting in the Banking Sector: A Systematic Literature Review. *Administrative Sciences*, 14(12), 333. DOI: 10.3390/admsci14120333

Sethi, S. P., Martell, T. F., & Demir, M. (2017). An evaluation of the quality of corporate social responsibility reports by some of the world's largest financial institutions. *Journal of Business Ethics*, 140, 787–805.

Sheskin, D. J. (2011). *Handbook of Parametric and Nonparametric Statistical Procedures* (5th ed.). Chapman and Hall/CRC.

Sierra, L., Zorio, A., & García-Benau, M. A. (2013). Sustainable Development and Assurance of Corporate Social Responsibility Reports Published by Ibex-35 Companies. *Corporate Social Responsibility and Environmental Management, 20*(6), 359-370. .1303DOI: 10.1002/csr

Silva, S. (2021). Corporate contributions to the Sustainable Development Goals: An empirical analysis informed by legitimacy theory. *Journal of Cleaner Production*, 292, 125962.

Smith, J., Haniffa, R., & Fairbrass, J. (2011). A conceptual framework for investigating 'capture' in corporate sustainability reporting assurance. *Journal of Business Ethics*, 99(3), 425–439.

Suchman, M. (1995). Managing legitimacy: Strategic and institutional approaches. *Academy of Management Review*, 20(3), 571–610.

Truong, Y., Mazloomi, H., & Berrone, P. (2021). Understanding the impact of symbolic and substantive environmental actions on organizational reputation. *Industrial Marketing Management*, 92, 307–320.

Wu, Y., Zhang, K., & Xie, J. (2020). Bad greenwashing, good greenwashing: Corporate social responsibility and information transparency. *Management Science*, 66(7), 3095–3112. DOI: 10.1287/mnsc.2019.3340

Yan, M., Jia, F., Chen, L. & Yan, F. (2022). *Assurance process for sustainability*

Yekini, K., Omoteso, K., & Adegbite, E. (2021). CSR communication research: A theoretical-cummethodological perspective from semiotics. *Business & Society*, 60(4), 876–908.

Zorio, A., García-Benau, M. A., & Sierra, L. (2013). Sustainability development and the quality of assurance reports: Empirical evidence. *Business Strategy and the Environment*, 22(7), 484–500. https://doi.org/10.1002/bse.1764

ADDITIONAL READING

Baldissera, A. (2023). Sustainability reporting in banks: History of studies and a conceptual framework for thinking about the future by learning from the past. *Corporate Social Responsibility and Environmental Management*. Advance online publication. DOI: 10.1002/csr.2491

European Commission. (2019). *JRC Technical Report, Interlinkages and policy coherence for the Sustainable Development Goals implementation*, 4. http://publications.jrc.ec.europa.eu/repository/bitstream/JRC115163/sdg_interlinkages_jrc115163_final_on_line.pdf

Garcia-Sanchez, I.-M., Rodriguez-Ariza, L., Aibar-Guzman, B. A., & Aibar-Guzman, C. (2020). Do institutional investors drive corporate transparency regarding business contribution to the sustainable development goals? *Business Strategy and the Environment*. Advance online publication. DOI: 10.1002/bse.2485

Global Reporting Initiative & AG Sustentable. (2020). *Divulgación ASG y de sostenibilidad en mercados de capitales. Una mirada a América Latina*. https://www.globalreporting.org/media/gnelv4de/informe_divulgacion_gri.pdf

Hamad, S., Lai, F. W., Shad, M. K., Khatib, S. F., & Ali, S. E. A. (2023). Assessing the implementation of sustainable development goals: Does integrated reporting matter? *Sustainability Accounting. Management and Policy Journal*, 14(1), 49–74. DOI: 10.1108/SAMPJ-01-2022-0029

Hassan, A., Elamer, A. A., Fletcher, M., & Sobhan, N. (2020). Voluntary assurance of sustainability reporting: Evidence from an emerging economy. *Accounting Research Journal*, 33(2), 391–410.

Hassan, A. N. O., Győri, Z., & Abdelrahman, R. E. K. (2022). Sustainable Development Goals Disclosure Practices through Integrated Reporting: An Empirical analysis on European Financial Institutions. *Edukacja Ekonomistów I Menedżerów*, 62(4). .DOI: 10.33119/EEIM.2021.62.1

Khan, H. Z., Bose, S., Mollik, A. T., & Harun, H. (2021). "Green washing" or "authentic effort"? An empirical investigation of the quality of sustainability reporting by banks. *Accounting, Auditing & Accountability Journal*, 34(2), 338. DOI: 10.1108/AAAJ-01-2018-3330

Mock, T. J., Strohm, C., & Swartz, K. M. (2007). An examination of worldwide assured sustainability reporting. *Australian Accounting Review*, 17(41), 67–77.

United Nations. (2022). *The Sustainable Development Goals: Report 2022*. Department of Economic and Social Affairs, United Nations. https://home.kpmg/xx/en/home/insights/2020/11/the-time-hascome-survey-of-sustainability-reporting.html.

KEY TERMS AND DEFINITIONS

Banking Sector: Financial institutions that provide banking services to private and public organizations, as well as individual customers.

Quality Disclosure: The extent to which firms disclose information that meets stakeholders' needs, encompassing various dimensions such as relevance, accuracy, and the inclusion of qualitative, quantitative, and monetary details. It also considers managerial orientation and the identification of stakeholders toward whom organizations direct their sustainability practices.

MERCOSUR: Latin American countries that are members of the Southern Common Market. The States Parties to MERCOSUR, signatories of the Treaty of Asuncion, are Argentina, Brazil, Paraguay, and Uruguay.

SDG Disclosure: The accessibility of information regarding an organization's actions and commitments to the Sustainable Development Goals (SDGs).

Sustainable Development Goals (SDGs): Objectives adopted by the United Nations in 2015 as a universal call to action to end poverty, protect the planet, and ensure that by 2030, all people can enjoy peace and prosperity.

Sustainable Development Goal Dimensions: The SDGs are grouped into three dimensions of sustainable development: economic growth, social inclusion, and environmental protection.

SDGs Related to the Economic Dimension: This group includes SDGs 8, 9, 10, 12, and 17.

SDGs Related to the Social Dimension: This group includes SDGs 1, 2, 3, 4, 5, 7, 11, and 16.

SDGs Related to the Environmental Dimension: This group includes SDGs 6, 13, 14, and 15.

Sustainability Report Assurance (SRA): An independent and external evaluation of a company's reporting, conducted to enhance the credibility of its sustainability reports.

Chapter 6
Ethical Considerations in Sustainability Reporting and Assurance

Vikas Ramesh Adhegaonkar
https://orcid.org/0009-0007-8867-0947
Sri Balaji Vidyapeeth University, India

Chinmoy Goswami
https://orcid.org/0009-0007-9012-7820
Sri Balaji Vidyapeeth University, India

Abhijeet Thakur
https://orcid.org/0000-0003-1493-8983
Sri Balaji Vidyapeeth University, India

ABSTRACT

This chapter discusses why ethics are essential in sustainability reporting assurance. It shows that clear, accurate ESG (Environmental, Social, and Governance) reports build trust and help prevent "greenwashing," which is when companies give false information about their environmental efforts. Ethical reporting goes beyond just following the law; it helps companies create long-term relationships with stakeholders and improves their reputation. The chapter also discusses the difficulties companies face in being ethical, especially in regions with fewer regulations, and highlights the value of third-party verification to build credibility. Ethical reporting can lead to loyal customers, attract investors, and help tackle big global issues like climate change. With new laws on the horizon, companies that report ethically will build trust and continuously improve, creating a stronger, more sustainable future.

DOI: 10.4018/979-8-3373-0117-4.ch006

1. INTRODUCTION

Sustainability reporting is becoming one of the critical practices that companies are adopting in its reporting. This is because ever-growing demand by society the company should fulfil its environment, social and governance responsibilities which are commonly known as ESG. These reports present a broad picture of how companies handle their ESG responsibilities. But when these reports are made available to the stakeholders the question comes of reliability, accuracy, and alignment of report with actual business practices. Organisations which are committed to ethics are more likely to initiate those activities which address ESG related issues. These efforts of the organisations are reflected in the form of ESG reporting. It is not enough for sustainability reporting to just meet legal requirements or make stakeholders happy. This is a way to build trust through openness and fulfilling ethical responsibility. When people act ethically in this way, they make sure that everyone is honest about sustainability issues and there is no need for greenwashing. Greenwashing is when people present wrong information about their environmental efforts. These kinds of actions not only hurt a company's image, but also make the stakeholders are less likely to trust them. Ethics in reporting on sustainability are more than just following the law. Ethical reporting can help the companies build long lasting relationship with the stakeholders and show its commitment for sustainability. Today governments are also concerned about ESG issues and expect organisations should do something more than what law requires. This chapter discusses how ethics play a big part in sustainable reporting and assurance. It also discusses why ethics are important to businesses, the problems they face and how to ensure organisation's honest efforts at every stage of reporting. It also gives practical advice on the important issue of ethics in deciding the future of business sustainability and gives case studies of what worked and what didn't in terms of sustainability assurance.

1.1. The Importance of Ethics in Sustainability Reporting

Why Ethics Matter

Ethics are the foundation of sustainability reporting, shaping how businesses communicate their environmental, social, and governance (ESG) practices to their stakeholders. In today's business world, being ethical is not just a suggestion; it's an expectation. When companies report on their sustainability efforts, ethics ensure that the information provided is honest, clear, and not misleading (Wang & Sarkis, 2017). Without ethical principles, sustainability reports can become tools for greenwashing—where companies falsely portray themselves as more environmentally or socially responsible than they really are. This challenges trust and damages the purpose of these reports.

Organisations are legally responsible for providing accurate, reliable, and transparent information to its stakeholders. Hence ethics play an important role in its overall reporting and in case of sustainability reporting its not only legal obligation but fundamental commitment to its stakeholders. Stakeholders, such as consumers, investors and regulators depend on these reports to understand a company's real sustainability efforts and its performance (Robert, Michael, & Sydney, 2014). These genuine efforts by these organisations help to build trust with their stakeholders who expect transparency and accountability. But if companies manipulate their reporting, then it results in loss of trust with stakeholders or facing serious consequences like legal trouble (Torreli, Balluchi, & Lazzini, 2020). Ethics in sustainability reporting are also essential to prevent greenwashing. Greenwashing occurs when companies mislead the public about their environmental or social efforts to seem more sustainable than they truly are (Delmas & Burbano, 2011). This dishonest behaviour not only misguides stakeholders but also creates a broader sense of scepticism about corporate sustainability efforts. Greenwashing creates doubts in the consumers' minds and takes attention away from companies which are making sincere efforts for sustainable development. In long term ethical reporting is crucial to distinguish between companies that are genuinely making a positive impact and those who are busy in greenwashing (Bowen & Aragon-Correa, 2014).

Another important reason why ethics matter is that society is becoming more environmental sensitive and expressing their concern of environmental damage. Also, governments are creating rules and regulations to ensure the businesses are serious in its overall reporting. For example, European Union's Non-Financial Reporting Directive requires companies to disclose information about how they handle social, environmental, and governance issues (Antonini & Conde, 2024). Ethical reporting helps companies comply with these regulations and promotes a culture of accountability with their stakeholders which goes beyond what law requires. Additionally, ethical sustainability reporting contributes to long-term business success. Research shows that companies that practice ethics, including in their sustainability reporting, tend to have stronger reputations, better financial performance, and higher customer loyalty (Eccles, Ioannou, & George, 2014). When companies are honest and open about their sustainability efforts, they create a positive cycle in which consumers and investors are more likely to support them, which in turn leads to more success. Ethical reporting can also help companies identify areas where they can improve and genuinely work toward more sustainable practices. On the other hand, unethical reporting may offer short-term benefits, such as a better public image, but these gains are often temporary. When the truth comes out, the long-term consequences of misleading stakeholders can be severe (Dahlsrud, 2008). When companies are serious about sustainability reporting then its impact not only touch to the external stakeholders, but it also positively influences internal stakeholders too. Internal stakeholders, such as employees, are also affected by a company's ethical climate. Businesses can easily create responsible and accountable corporate culture with following high ethical standards. This can lead to higher employee satisfaction and loyalty because employees are more likely to stay with a company when employees' values align with the company's values. Also, when companies critically assess themselves on various parameters through sustainability reporting it encourages everyone to continuously improve the system and make required changes wherever necessary (Bag, Srivastava, Gupta, Sivarajah, & Wilmot, 2024). Finally, ethical behaviour in sustainability reporting is essential to addressing global challenges such as climate change, poverty, and inequality. Companies play a significant role in shaping the future of the planet and these small actions will have a positive impact on the society in the long run. Ethical reporting ensures that businesses are transparent about their contributions to solving these global challenges and are held accountable for their actions. As sustainability reporting becomes more common, it is essential that companies follow high ethical standards, so their reports reflect real efforts to create a more sustainable world (Kolk, 2008).

1.2. Building Trust Through Transparency

Companies can build trust between organizations and their stakeholders through openness and transparency. Companies openly share information about their practices, performance, and sustainability efforts which is demonstration of accountability and a commitment to ethical standards. This openness builds strong relationships with stakeholders and creates greater loyalty, support, and success.

When companies provide necessary information to stakeholders it helps to foster trust to make informed decisions. The disclosure of a company's sustainability practices and performance enables stakeholders to assess the organization's commitment to sustainable development. (Carol, 2014) conducted research that shows that increased transparency in sustainability reporting helps to enhance the company's sustainability claims and nurture relationship with stakeholders. Likewsie, transparent practices help the organizations to address stakeholder concerns and manage risks effectively. Companies following ethical practices like to openly discuss issues like supply chain challenges or environmental impacts and that help these companies proactively address stakeholder concerns before they escalate into problems. For example, a study conducted by (Deegan, 2002) discusses the importance of transparent reporting practices which enables the companies to communicate their strategies and challenges to stakeholders and that helps to reduce scepticism of stakeholder's. Transparency depends on good communication. Companies who openly and honestly discuss their environmental initiatives are probably going to inspire the confidence of their employees. According to (Hummel & Schilck, 2016), stakeholders build trust and favourably view the organization's legitimacy if sustainable practices are properly communicated. Such a goal to offer easily available knowledge would show the dedication of a company to sustainability and help to build faith among its employees. Another advantage of transparency in the market could be competitive one. Companies that are open about their sustainability practices often attract consumers who respect ethical and sustainable business practices. Research by (Eccles, Ioannou, & George, 2014) indicates that companies with strong sustainability practices and transparency bring better financial performance with customer loyalty. This highlights the notion that transparent practices of the company can help to differentiate itself among several market competitors.

Independent third-party verification also serves to maintain the credibility of sustainability reports. The use of independent auditors by companies when verifying claims about sustainability adds a layer of credibility to the report. Independent assurance, according to (O'Dwyer & Owen, 2005), is a confidence-building element: It makes stakeholders believe that the information reported is accurate and reliable. This goes beyond building trust because it also reduces the risk of greenwashing, which is known to occur in companies where they exaggerate their efforts at sustainability. While transparency in itself is what helps to build trust, the promise of it needs to be coupled with accountability. A company that shares its sustainability efforts will also have to account for its own activities. If organizations do not comply with their sustainability goals or misrepresent their practices, they will lose the credibility that they have established. (Abhayawansa, Adams, & Neesham, 2021) also argue that there can be extreme damage to the reputation if there is no accountability, as this further leads to a decrease in stakeholder trust. It throws light on the fact that while transparency is a requirement, the information presented must be accurate and truthful to the efforts.

Hence, transparency becomes an essential element in boosting trust between organizations and other stakeholders. Beyond the sustainability practices' revelations, organizations can portray accountability, respond to stakeholder questions, and enhance their relation by being transparent. For instance, as studies have shown, (Carol, 2014), (Deegan, 2002), (Hummel & Schilck, 2016), (Eccles, Ioannou, & George, 2014) and (O'Dwyer & Owen, 2005) show that transparency boosts loyalty and support stakeholder provide to an organization. Transparency, however, needs to be commensurate with accountability, which constitutes the *sine qua non* of trust. Organizations are likely to prosper today and in the foreseeable future where stakeholders demand transparency and truthfulness regarding sustainability reporting.

1.3. Risks of Greenwashing

Greenwashing is a burgeoning element of corporate responsibility in sustainability, where companies indulge in providing a false impression about the environmental responsibility they have. Misleading promotion of a business's products, policies, or practices as more environmentally friendly than they are known to be is what is referred to as greenwashing. Risks of greenwashing range from potential harm to the reputation to financial loss. In this section discussion is provided on those dangers and review some contemporary examples that demonstrate the severe repercussions for organizations that engage in such practices.

What is Greenwashing?

Greenwashing refers to the provision of misleading information that overstates or gives false claims of environmental benefit from a firm's practice, products, or policies. Many organizations recognise the importance of sustainability; however, not all firms are devoted to sustainable change. Instead, some just want to look "green" to win the green consumer and investor. Such an act deceives stakeholders and betrays moves towards sustainability (Delmas & Burbano, 2011).

The prominent example of greenwashing is the one where a company markets a product as "natural" or "eco-friendly" but does not provide any additional proof or certification. Most of these slogans have nothing to do with any form of change in the process of its manufacture and only add to a misleading story of the company's initiatives on sustainability (Chen & Chag, 2013).

I. Reputation Damage

Reputation Damage: One of the most immediate and damaging risks of greenwashing is reputational harm. In an informationally rich environment, consumers and stakeholders are empowered, as never before, to analyse claims promoted by a corporation. When companies are caught greenwashing, not only reputational but financial fall-out is swift and usually devastating, and a brand's reputation damage is long-term.

Reputation Damage Case: Volkswagen. Then, in 2015, it was found that Volkswagen had been cheating on emission tests. The vehicles were marketed as "clean diesel," but in reality, the cars would emit nitrogen oxides at levels up to 40 times higher than allowed. This scandal, now dubbed "Diesel gate," not only ruined consumer trust for Volkswagen but completely marred its reputation worldwide (Rhodes, 2016). The firm was fined billions of dollars and suffered a permanent loss of customer confidence.

Another recent example comes from H&M, which is a big fashion retailer. In its new brand collection called "Conscious," H&M was accused of greenwashing because it promoted material usage that was friendly to the environment. According to (Bick, Halsey, & Eknega, 2018), reports from regulators and watchdogs pointed out that there was no substantial evidence to support such claims, hence misleading the consumers who ended up damaging the reputation of the brand to environmentally conscious consumers.

II. Financial Consequences

While greenwashing damages the reputation of a company, it also has some severe financial implications. In most cases, the financial costs are directly related to consumers' lost trust in the brand, financial or legal penalties, and the long-term degradation of brand value.

For example, the Volkswagen greenwashing scandal involved fines, vehicle recalls, and settlements worth over $30 billion (Rhodes, 2016). That apart from the intangible loss related to customer loyalty and market share. Consumers who remained loyal to the Volkswagen brand began to see it as a company that prioritized profit over ethics. The result was a stop in sales and a drop in the company's stock price.

Another example is BP. This corporation lost millions of dollars following the failed attempt to portray itself as an environmentally friendly company. Advertising as a carbon-reducing company, the BP corporation faced massive challenges when it faced examination over its activities in 2010, by an oil spill from Deepwater Horizon. The world witnessed how the greenwash image of the company derailed, and it was lined up to pay a massive sum of $18.7 billion, one of the costliest corporate settlements in history (Laufer, 2003). This is the kind of financial experience that can be derived from firms that do not live up genuinely to their sustainability promise.

III. Regulatory and Legal Risks

Increased legal risk regarding greenwash due to the developing environmental regulation. The majority of world governments and regulatory bodies are enforcing stricter laws and guidelines against companies that mislead the general public about their environmental practices. The stricter the regulations become, so are the legal penalties and fines against the companies that indulge in greenwashing.

For instance, the European Union has recently introduced the Corporate Sustainability Reporting Directive (CSRD), which will oblige corporations to meet higher standards of environmental disclosure. The threat of fines in addition to an already heavy risk of greenwashing besides a failure to live up to standards or accusation of misrepresentation of stakeholders.

In the United States, the Federal Trade Commission (FTC) has also stepped up its enforcement against deceptive environmental claims. FTC's "Green Guides" are there to assist marketers avoid false or misleading claims about environmental benefits of their products. Companies violating the guidelines face legal action. For example, Keurig Green Mountain was legally sued for misleading advertisement for coffee pods being recyclable when they are not commonly accepted in recycling facilities. The action led to a settlement but highlighted the rising legal risks that firms face if they fail to properly disclose sustainability information.

IV. Long-Term Implications for Sustainability Objectives

Greenwashing undermines the global call for sustainability through misleading consumers and the weakening of efforts from companies that truly are working towards sustainability. When consumers cannot believe the sustainability practices by businesses, they tend to disbelieve any and all sustainability initiatives. In this case, consumers stop making sustainable choices as they think that all businesses are simply greenwashing (Bowen & Aragon-Correa, 2014).

Moreover, greenwashing diverts resources and attention away from real solutions to environmental and social challenges. There are companies who are showing themselves as an environmentally friendly company but offer very little help for solving issues like climate change and other. That not only damages the environment but also slows down the progressive steps toward serious corporate responsibility

2. ETHICAL CHALLENGES IN SUSTAINABILITY ASSURANCE

When the auditors have a relationship with the firms then auditors can be biased to give favourable assessments to business sustainability practices due to their conflicts of interest. Today auditing firms offer both sustainability consultancy and assurance services. As a result, auditing firm helps in designing a company's sustainability strategy is also responsible for auditing its performance hence auditing firm might compromise auditing ethics. This dual role played by an auditing firm creates a to conflict of interest and raise doubts on assurance process. That ultimately caused a reduction in the stakeholder confidence in the reliability and objectivity of the sustainability reports.

2.1 Conflicts of Interest

I. Causes of Conflicts of Interest

The same firms providing both assurance and consulting services is major source of conflicts of interest. In this context, because firms depend on income from both sorts of services, they may not be able to avoid issuing favourable reports to ensure future business opportunities. This therefore creates an ethical dilemma for those auditors to favour financial interests over the accuracy of the sustainability report (Al-Shaer, 2020).

Also, in a competitive marketplace, there can be pressure on the firms to retain clients. In the event that the auditors issue a negative report, such a move would severely impact the reputation of the company, forcing the client to obtain assurance services elsewhere. In this sense, there is a possibility that auditors may tend to avoid negative comments to preserve business relationships (Olivier, Iñaki, Heras, Marie, & Bernard, 2019).

Another issue is the "self-review" threat, where auditors end up reviewing their own consulting work. This occurs when the same firm is responsible for both designing and assessing the company's sustainability practices. Auditors may be less likely to highlight shortcomings in the company's performance that will raise the question about the consultancy services provided by the firm (Hazaea, Zhu, & Khatib, 2022).

II. Ethical Dilemmas

The main ethical dilemma faced by auditors in the sustainability assurance is the conflict between quality of report and client retention. However, auditors have a professional duty to provide accurate and impartial assessments of sustainability practices of the client. But this becomes difficult when they are financially dependent on the company, they are auditing. As auditors issue favourable reports to maintain client relationships then the integrity of the sustainability report is compromised (Oncioiu, et al., 2020).

Greenwashing is another problem in the biased reporting —when companies falsely present themselves as more sustainable than they are. These false claims of sustainability practices mislead stakeholders. Companies and auditors face ethical questions about the long-term impacts of such behaviour on public trust and environmental sustainability (Moodaley & Telukdarie, 2023).

III. Mitigating Conflicts of Interest

There are several methods to mitigate conflicts of interest in sustainability assurance. One of the most effective solutions is to separate consulting and assurance services. When the auditing firm fully separates itself from providing sustainability consultancy and assurance services to the same client, it ensures the integrity of these reports. Hence these independent auditing firms can follow the auditing ethics, as they do not have any direct financial interest in the outcome of the assurance process (Free, Jones, & Tremblay, 2024).

Another approach is to strengthen regulatory frameworks that govern sustainability assurance. For example, an auditing firm must mandatorily disclose any conflicts of interest with the client. This can help to create transparency and allow stakeholders to better assess the reliability of the audit. By making conflicts of interest public, auditors are encouraged to maintain higher standards of objectivity (Do & Vo, 2023).

Additionally, companies can use third-party assurance services from independent auditors. These auditors should not have any sort of relationship with the company. Independent audits are less likely to be influenced by conflicts of interest and provide a more accurate and impartial assessment of sustainability performance (Perego & Kolk, 2012).

Moreover, improving professional standards and ethical training for auditors can help mitigate the risks of bias. An ethical culture can make the auditors more responsive to transparency and accuracy rather than relationships with clients. Ethical training can reinforce the importance of being independent even when clients apply pressure to them in order to prevent biased practice (Simnett, Vanstraelen, & Chua, 2009).

2.2 Accuracy and Completeness in Sustainability Reporting

In sustainability reporting, accuracy and completeness of the report has a lot of significance which helps to build credibility and trust among stakeholders. The data collection process to measure sustainable practices presents significant challenges as it must be collected from various departments and in various formats. The performance metrics of sustainability have been evolving which is creating complexity (Adams & Evans, 2004) and diversity of data sources (Bebbington, Larrinaga, & Moneva, 2008). This subsection of the chapter explores these challenges and analyses the ethical responsibilities of organizations to provide full and accurate sustainability performance data.

Challenges of Data Collection

I. Diversity of Data Sources

Sustainability data is collected from various departments to cover its environmental, social, and economic effects. As the data must be collected from a wide range of departments data collection is process becomes complicated. For instance, environmental data come from emissions monitoring, energy usage logs, and waste disposal records, while social data may be sourced from employee surveys, community engagement activities, and supplier audits (Bebbington, Unerman, & Eds, 2014). This complexity in the data necessitates robust systems which will aggregate the data and standardize it for multipurpose uses.

II. Inconsistent Metrics and Standards

One of the challenges in sustainability reporting is that there are non-standardized metrics and frameworks (Boiral, 2013). There are some guidelines published by various organizations, such as the Global Reporting Initiative. However, these differences are notable at the inter-industry and inter-regional levels This makes it hard to ensure that the reported data is both comparable and meaningful. Companies face difficulties in identifying the most appropriate indicators and benchmarks to represent their distinct sustainability impacts. Hence it is not easy for companies to communicate their sustainability efforts without standard guidelines. This becomes even more challenging for the stakeholders to understand the information provided by the data (Morioka & Carvalho, 2016).

III. Data Quality and Reliability

In sustainability reporting, ensuring the data quality and its reliability is a persistent issue. The reason is while collecting the data, inaccurate data received due to the measurement errors, estimation uncertainties, and biases in data collection (Simnett, Vanstraelen, & Chua, 2009). Apart from that, sustainability reporting often involves subjective judgements for the selection of sustainability parameters. For example, the selection of parameters involves carbon emissions or water uses as key parameter, now it is based on the subjective judgement of manager for parameter selection (Adams, 2004). These subjective elements can introduce variability and compromise the integrity of reported data.

IV. Technological and Resource Constraints

Many organizations are faced with technology and resource constraints, which currently bar them from obtaining the full data of sustainability (Lozano, 2013). More specific companies are found to face more hindrances since they lack a proper structure or experience to exploit sophisticated data collection methods (Eccles, Ioannou, & George, 2014). Hence, such ventures are likely to publish partial or archaic data. Even such limited data may even erode credibility in their sustainability claims. While reports depend on minimal information, stakeholders are likely to question its accuracy and reliability. As such, these limitations may hinder the success of sustainability reporting among firms. Therefore, it is essential to overcome these constraints as the first step toward improving the quality of sustainability reporting.

V. Ethical Responsibilities in Reporting
   a) Transparency and Honesty

Organizations have a moral duty to make certain transparency and honesty in sustainability reporting. This duty includes disclosing each nice and bad factors of performance, avoiding selective reporting that would misinform stakeholders (Rob, Dave, & Keith, 1987). Transparent reporting fosters duty and enables stakeholders to make knowledgeable selections based on a holistic view of sustainability overall performance (Deegan, 2002).

b) Comprehensive Disclosure

Corporate disclosure is an ethical reporting method giving a complete and honest account of an organisation's sustainability practices. It provides a clear and balanced picture of the organisation's efforts to act responsibly towards the environment and society. By providing all relevant information including positive and negative to its stakeholder's organisation can build transparency and holds the company accountable for its environmental and social impact (O'Dwyer & Owen, 2005). European union has adopted Corporate Sustainability Reporting Directive (CSRD) which insist to report companies on their initiative on environmental and social impact. The key aim of this is to promote sustainable practices among large and listed small and medium size companies. These companies have to report on their strategies, target sets and initiative in the area of social, environmental and governance issues. Companies have to report on various parameters from climate change to water conservation efforts to gender equality to addressing various governance issues.

Case Study

To illustrate these challenges, consider the following case study:

Case Study: JKLT Turbine Ltd.'s Path to Sustainability

In the rolling hills of wind farms across the globe, JKLT Turbine Ltd stood as a beacon of clean energy. Its wind turbines dotted landscapes, quietly powering homes and businesses while giving more relief from carbon footprints. To the outside world, JKLT had become everything right about sustainability-it produced green energy itself. In its own backyard, however, the storm was brewing as the company claimed its bright victories. By 2022, JKLT had become a behemoth in the renewables space, having had turbines generating 15% clean electricity consumed in some parts. Marketing material was full of statistics on reductions in carbon emissions worldwide. The company became tagged as indestructible in caring for health and the environment. However, not far below the gloss, cracks were starting to form. An independent review of JKLT's internal operations revealed some very disturbing news. While the company's turbines were making a hole in carbon emissions around the world, the manufacturing process was another story altogether. One of its largest factories was sited in a drought-prone region and was guzzling water at unsustainable rates, depleting the local groundwater reserves. The manufacturing was an energy-intensive activity relying on coal-powered grids that pumped out more carbon than the company admitted. JKLT was confronting a cruel reality: whereas the product was green, the production process couldn't have been more away from it. Knowing they had to do something fast in light of the public scrutiny of the company and the responsibility towards the environment, JKLT's leadership called out for a total revamping of their factories. Solar panels were fitted on these factories to produce energy from renewable resources rather than fuel. They went bold with a plan to reduce water usage by 40% through innovative recycling systems and carbon neutrality by 2030. In 2023, JKLT released its new sustainability report. This one said nothing but the whole story, unembellished and not about glorifying the good-old days. Here, they got honest with their failures. This one was an honest recount of successes and areas of difficulty, pointing direction to go forward. This time, stakeholders applauded JKLT not only because of the green products but also saluted the company for transparency and real change. Not only was it a reduction in carbon emissions; instead, everything emanating from its functioning aligned with their principles.

Discussion Questions:

- How do these challenges reflect the complexities companies face when their products are green but their operations are not?
- Were these measures sufficient, or could the company have taken more aggressive steps?
- Why is it important for companies to disclose both successes and shortcomings in their sustainability reports? How might this affect stakeholder trust?
- What strategies could the company implement to ensure this goal is met? What potential obstacles might they face along the way?
- How can companies balance profitability with sustainability, especially when faced with operational inefficiencies?

2.3 Challenges in Emerging Markets

In emerging markets, firms face ethical dilemmas during the reporting of sustainability. This is because sustainability regulations are often poorly defined. Sustainability regulations either do not exist or these regulations are not strictly monitored. Multinationals operating in these regions face challenges in their reporting due to the local business practices and international standards during the reporting of sustainability.

The issue here lies in a conflict between the local economic interests of the country and the pressure for compliance with global sustainability expectations. Many emerging markets have concentrated on fast economic growth that compromises environmental degradation and weaknesses in social governance. MNCs are compelled to lower their sustainability standards to be able to compete with local companies which are not as strongly held accountable by the rigid reporting requirements imposed by the international organizations like the GRI (Kolk, 2008).

An excellent example is in extractive industries, where companies in states with weak governance structures are found indulging in environmentally harmful operations that would acceptable in developed countries. For instance, multinational mining firms have faced criticism in the Democratic Republic of the Congo for contributing towards environmental degradation and violation of human rights (Hilson & Maconachie, 2017).

These needs have been addressed by MNCs through capacities-building initiatives for better local sustainability reporting practices. For example, Unilever provided training to local distributors and auditors in developing nations on how to adhere to the environmental sustainability standards. Such initiatives not only enhance ethical behaviour but also leads to improvement in sustainability reports' transparency and reliability (Zimon, Arianpoor, & Salehi, 2022).

Additionally, capacity building of the local auditors is highly essential to increase a sustainability assurance process. This will be possible if MNCs train the local auditors on the sustainability standards. In that case, there would be more accurate and transparent assessments by the local auditors, and consequently, there would be a possibility of reduced greenwashing and unethical practices (P. & A., 2012). Such investments can lead to an even more ethical reporting environment, even in regions with limited regulatory monitoring.

3. MAINTAINING INTEGRITY IN THE REPORTING PROCESS

3.1 Developing Ethical Reporting Practices

Ethical reporting practices are critical to maintaining the credibility and integrity of the sustainability disclosures. Stakeholders, including conscious consumers, employees, investors and regulators are increasingly calling upon companies to consistently provide a clear and fair efforts of their environmental, social, and governance (ESG) activities. This subsection identifies some of the best practices of ethical reporting and underscores the need for full disclosure of data.

One of the salient principles of ethical sustainability reporting is full data disclosure. This essentially means that data regarding a firm's sustainability performance must be adequate enough to get the idea of carbon emissions, water usage, labor practices, and other sustainability practices. Transparency in data collection and reporting ensures that stakeholders receive an accurate picture of a company's ESG efforts. Full disclosure should include quantitative data like emission levels but also qualitative information such as community engagement initiatives and even employee well-being programs. Without full transparency companies are likely to lose the stakeholder trust as stakeholders feel that some key information is being hidden or manipulated to exhibit a better impression (Adams & Whelan, 2009). Indeed, partial or selective disclosure causes reputational damage and even financial sanctions, but, more importantly, raises stakeholders' attention to the extent of a company's ESG performance (Michelon, Pilonato, & Ricceri, 2015).

The other important practice is reporting on both successes and failures of sustainability efforts. Ethical reporting is less about getting rid of celebrations of success but more of shortcomings and faults. Companies that emphasize the great benefits of their contributions toward sustainability but fail to include or mute the negative impacts are practicing selective reporting and hence are likely to face accusations of greenwashing (Cho, Michelon, Patten, & Roberts, 2015). Prudent stakeholders and regulators are aware of such tactics and may question companies that appear to be taking easy ways out. Thus, ethical reporting demands that the companies should take responsibility for their failure and state how they shall rectify it. This is not about making a show of public relations but building trust along with serious implementation of sustainability practice (Boiral, 2013).

The other important point is that third party auditors too play a vital role to ensure ethical reporting. It is an external audit that provides a completely independent assessment of a company's performance towards sustainability as well as helping to verify the accuracy and completeness of the reported data (Perego & Kolk, 2012). A company appoints independent auditors when preparing its sustainability report to maintain the credibility of their sustainability report and to minimize the risk of greenwashing. Audits establish whether the information collected is valid but also ensure that the reporting procedures of the firm are in consonance with the international standards of reporting, for example, that are upheld by the Global Reporting Initiative (GRI) and the Sustainability Accounting Standards Board (SASB). Independent assurance is significant in ensuring stakeholder confidence that sustainability disclosures are reliable as it is essential in ethical reporting (Reimsbach, Hahn, & Gürtürk, 2018).

Also, stakeholder engagement plays a crucial role in maintaining ethical reporting standards. Companies that engage stakeholders during the reporting processes usually tend to produce balanced and comprehensive reports (Torreli, Balluchi, & Lazzini, 2020). Stakeholder engagement may also take the form of soliciting comments from investors, employees, local communities, and environmental groups, hence incorporating diverse perspectives into sustainability reporting. This can be a way to inclusiveness, not just an enhancement of the quality of the report but also a way of ensuring that they touch on the most relevant issues to the stakeholders. Such an engagement encourages transparency and accountability as companies have a higher likelihood of reporting on the issues closest to the hearts of those affected by their operations.

Finally, continuous improvement is a vital aspect of ethical reporting. Sustainability is an evolving field and, therefore, so are its reporting practices. Thus, reporting frameworks require changes by the management of a company as new challenges and standards emerge. Ethical reporting means that reporting frameworks should keep changing with the changes in business practices, regulatory requirements, and expectations of different stakeholders (Lock & Seele, 2016). Companies expressing their commitment to continuous improvement in their sustainability efforts are more likely to build trust over time and maintain a strong ethical reputation with stakeholders.

3.2 Ensuring Independence in Assurance

Any auditor should have independence while providing assurance. Independence is the most critical element in sustainability assurance, enhancing the credibility and reliability of sustainability reports. Independence is the cornerstone that allows auditors to provide unbiased objective assurance on a company's environmental, social, and governance (ESG) reporting. A key principle is that auditors must remain free from conflicts of interest to ensure the integrity of report. This part discusses the most significant guidelines to ensure independence and integrity in the sustainability assurance process.

The first crucial guideline that ensures the independence of the auditor is the third-party auditors' selection. The third-party auditors have to be chosen strictly by the companies, and they have to choose individuals who have no prior experience with the firm's financial audit or consulting services. This separation prevents the potential conflict of interest that could arise from long-standing relationships between the auditor and the firm being audited (Wallage, 2000). A further suggestion is to rotate audit partners every two years or so as some regulatory standards demand to minimize the risks associated with over-familiarity and complacency of the auditor toward the audit firm (Boiral, 2013).

In addition, transparency and clarity of the terms of engagement increase auditor independence. Clearly articulated scope of audit and unrestricted access to data for the audit ensure a very comprehensive and independent review. For effective differentiation of services, consulting services must clearly distinguish with auditing services to avoid ethical (Bebbington, Unerman, & Eds, 2014).

Professional standards are no doubt highly relevant to auditor independence. Frameworks, including ISAE 3000 and AA1000, provide clear guidelines on the process for conducting non-financial audits and stipulate against what benchmarks the auditors have to assess sustainability information (Dando & Swift, 2003). These standards insist on objectivity, impartiality, and rigor in an audit process that give much more confidence to stakeholders concerning the credibility of assurance. Ultimately, external auditors should work together with internal auditors to create a robust system of checks and balances. Internal audit teams can play a complementary role by assessing risk and ensuring compliance, but they must not substitute the independence that external auditors bring to the table (Gao & Zhang, 2019).

In general, independence of the auditor in the sustainability assurance process can be ensured through tight selection criteria, adherence to professional standards, clear engagement terms, and regular rotation of audit teams. These practices collectively enhance the transparency, reliability, and trustworthiness of sustainability reports and thus meet the ethical obligation toward stakeholders.

3.3 The Role of Auditors in Upholding Ethics

The auditor plays a significant role in keeping ethical standards and ensuring the data accuracy as well as the transparency of the processes involved. The most fundamental duty of the auditor is making sure that the reported data for sustainability metrics presents an accurate reflection of the environmental, social, and governance performance of the organization. The auditor has the responsibility of verifying any inconsistencies or misstatements that could mislead stakeholders to protect the information's reliability (Boiral, 2013).

Transparency is a cornerstone of ethical reporting. In this respect, auditors have a responsibility in ensuring that all relevant information regarding the sustainability efforts are disclosed without any prejudice. This involves not only recognising positive aspects of sustainability achievement but also acknowledging the areas where the efforts are short, which help to build trust between the company and its stakeholders in general.

In addition, auditors are tasked with the responsibility of data integrity and other ethical standards of auditing including ISAE 3000 and AA1000 Assurance Standard. Such standards call for principles of objectivity, impartiality, and professional scepticism toward the organizations to be audited (Reimsbach, Hahn, & Gürtürk, 2018). These standards guide auditors in conducting independent reviews, preventing potential conflicts of interest that could arise from close ties with the organizations they audit. Furthermore, the auditors should not be susceptible to biases or undue influences, and therefore, the assessment ought to be unbiased as well.

Auditors also play the role of gatekeepers in ensuring that the sustainability report is within the legal and regulatory framework. It means comparing how the firm is performing in comparison to sustainability standards and frameworks, such as GRI (Simnett, Vanstraelen, & Chua, 2009). Auditors have thus emerged as critical conduits through which continuous improvement can be realized by making suggestions on how the sustainability practices and reporting tool can be improved (Jeffrey, Cohen, & Simnett, 2015).

4. THE FUTURE OF ETHICS IN SUSTAINABILITY REPORTING AND ASSURANCE

4.1 The Role of Technology

The emergence of artificial intelligence and blockchain had put forth a new approach to the current model of sustainability reporting, thereby targeting accuracy and transparency in it. Artificial intelligence is yet one of the key sources through which sustainability data is garnered, as well as analysed for companies to efficiently process the voluminous amounts of information. The many pattern and anomaly issues in emissions data that can be identified by machine learning algorithms mean that companies can set more precise sustainability targets and strategies. Analytics powered by artificial intelligence also allow monitoring in real-time, so organizations can take proactive steps to carry out operations to their best and achieve a level of sustainability (Sullivan et al., 2022).

Blockchain technology provides a decentralized framework that has been established to log transactions made in reference to sustainability initiatives. This means its immutable nature ensures that once data is recorded, its alteration without consensus is impossible; this capability gives strength to claims of sustainability. This can be quite useful for tracking the product lifecycle from the extraction of raw materials to end-of-life disposal (Hsu et al., 2021). Companies can provide verifiable data on ethical sourcing using blockchain, thereby reducing greenwashing risk (Torreli, Balluchi, & Lazzini, 2020).

In addition to data integrity, the application of technology in sustainability reporting enhances stakeholder engagement. The corporation will be able to share information regarding the sustainability efforts it is undertaking to its stakeholders in real time, which means immediate responses by the stakeholders regarding the sustainability efforts (Bai & Sarkis, 2010). Two-way communication may help organizations understand the concerns of the stakeholders much better, thus forming better sustainability strategies that meet the expectations of the stakeholders. For instance, social media networks can facilitate direct interaction between an organization and its customers, hence creating the sense of accountability and responsiveness in that organization (Delai & Takahashi, 2018).

Though several merits of technology exist in the concept of sustainability reporting, concern with ethics cannot be turned a blind eye. As companies embrace the adoption of AI and data analytics, the issues at the core level become their privacy concerns and data protection (Friedman, 2020). Organizations must ensure that their data collection methodologies respect the right to the stakeholders' privacy along with the lawful compliance. However, there is also the danger of algorithmic bias-through which false conclusions might be produced when the data used to train AI systems are not representative or not well trained (Dastin, 2018). The success of dealing with these ethical concerns will be highly paramount for organizations interested in responsible leverage of technology in their sustainability reporting practices.

This demands an effort to become better. The involvement of technology in sustainability reporting demands dedication to continue bettering. The firms ought to put resources into training staff on the proper use of the systems alongside promoting cultures embracing innovation and ethics (Jeanine, et al., 2024). Businesses should keep technologically updated regarding the life of the fast pace digital life and get an application in reporting. Ultimately, the role of technology in sustainability reporting goes beyond mere efficiency and it is about building a framework of trust and accountability. By utilizing AI and blockchain effectively, organizations can enhance the credibility of their sustainability claims, providing stakeholders with the assurance that the reported data is accurate, complete, and aligned with actual business practices.

4.2 Evolving Stakeholder Expectations

This dramatic change in the expectations of the stakeholders about sustainability reporting compels firms to adopt responsible practices. Operating in a worldwide integrated world, organizations are very demanding that such stakeholders like investors, customers, employees, and regulators are looking forward to greater accountability from the organizations for their ESG practices. The increase in awareness of climate change, social iniquities, and issues related to governance demand this shift, making the corporation behave in the expectable manner at the end.

The key users in this shift are investors, who find themselves increasingly preferring the consideration of ESG factors when investing. A number of studies have found that a relationship exists between strong sustainability practice and good financial performance. This will make companies acting within the principles of ESG more attractive to investment (Eccles et al., 2014). Organizations must then enhance transparency through a more effective presentation of sustainability reports to improve attractiveness of capital as well as maintain investor trust (Khan, Serafeim, & & Yoon, 2016).

Consumer behaviour is also changing dramatically. Since consumers become increasingly conscious about issues on the environmental and social landscape, they tend to be attracted to brands that have genuine commitments towards sustainability. Studies show that consumers are willing to pay a premium for products in companies that are transparent regarding their sustainability practices. With growing demand for ethical products, organizations have to ensure that information coming out in their sustainability reports is not only truthful but also reflects strong and sustained efforts to better societal and environmental output. Organizations engaging in greenwashing—that is, exaggeration or obscuration regarding sustainability efforts—risk losing customer loyalty and the menace of massive reputational and brand loss (Free, Jones, & Tremblay, 2024).

Stakeholder engagement now becomes an integral part of successful sustainability reporting. Responding to their stakeholders (investors, customers, employees, and local communities) produces well-balanced and fair reports which properly reflect the sustainability practices of such a business (Chen & Chag, 2013). Stakeholder engagement into the report will provide different insights from various stakeholders thus making it easy for the organizations to identify and correct potential flaws. This participatory approach not only raises the quality of the sustainability reports but also makes stakeholders enjoy the trust-building process, as they believe their voices are important in the decision-making process.

In addition, companies are realizing the importance of integrating sustainability into their corporate strategy. Sustainability is no longer considered a peripheral issue but is rather a core part of a business operation because it also creates long-run value. Such integration requires ethical reporting practice integration with strategic objectives that an organization has set. Every likelihood is there that a successful synchronization of such sustainability initiatives with the business goals will allow companies to better meet stakeholder expectations, achieving sustainable growth ultimately (Porter & Kramer, 2011).

The methodology followed in measuring and reporting on sustainability performance also relates to the need for increased transparency in sustainability reporting. Stakeholders expect organisations to disclose both their successes and challenges met with the setbacks. Reporting transparently creates an understanding of the complexity of issues in sustainability on the stakeholders' side, thus making the organizational efforts credible in order to overcome such problems (Martin & Schouten, 2020). Companies speaking candidly about their sustainability journey, the mistakes, and what they have learned are very likely to build a real relationship with stakeholders. In summary, the evolving expectations of stakeholders are reshaping the landscape of sustainability reporting. Companies must respond to these changes by adopting ethical, transparent reporting practices that reflect their genuine commitment to sustainability. Engaging stakeholders, aligning sustainability with corporate strategy, and providing comprehensive, honest disclosures are essential strategies for organizations aiming to build trust and credibility in their sustainability initiatives

4.3 Building a Culture of Integrity

Fostering a culture of integrity within organizations is paramount for ensuring the long-term credibility and trustworthiness of sustainability practices. An ethical organizational culture encourages employees at all levels to prioritize sustainability and accountability, aligning their actions with the company's values and objectives (Schwartz, 2017). To cultivate such a culture, organizations must employ multiple strategies, including comprehensive training programs, strong leadership commitment, and mechanisms for recognizing and rewarding ethical behaviour.

I. Training and Education

Training and education play a critical role in building a culture of integrity. Organizations should provide employees with comprehensive training on ethical practices related to sustainability reporting (Sult, Wobst, & Lueg, 2023). This training should cover not only the technical aspects of sustainability metrics but also the ethical implications of reporting practices. By educating employees about the importance of transparency, accuracy, and honesty in sustainability reporting, organizations empower them to make informed decisions that align with ethical standards. Continuous education programs should also be implemented to keep employees updated on emerging trends, regulatory changes, and best practices in sustainability reporting.

II. Leadership Commitment

Leadership commitment is essential for instilling an ethical culture within organizations. When leaders demonstrate a strong commitment to sustainability and ethical practices, it sets a positive example for employees to follow (Free, Jones, & Tremblay, 2024). Leaders should actively engage with employees, communicate the organization's sustainability goals, and emphasize the importance of ethical reporting in achieving these objectives (Abeysekera, 2022). Regular communication from leadership about the organization's sustainability achievements, challenges, and strategies reinforces the message that ethical behavior is a core value of the organization.

III. Incentivizing Ethical Behaviour

Moreover, incentivizing ethical behavior is crucial for fostering a culture of integrity. Organizations can implement reward systems that recognize employees who demonstrate a commitment to ethical reporting and sustainability practices (Alexander, 2020). These incentives can take various forms, including recognition programs, performance bonuses, or opportunities for professional development. By acknowledging and rewarding ethical behavior, organizations reinforce the message that integrity is valued and expected, encouraging employees to prioritize ethical considerations in their work.

IV. Reporting Mechanisms

Establishing clear channels for reporting ethical concerns is another critical component of building a culture of integrity. Organizations should create mechanisms that allow employees to report ethical violations or concerns without fear of retaliation (Kaptein, 2011). This may involve anonymous reporting systems, whistleblower protections, or regular forums for open dialogue about ethical issues. By fostering a safe environment for employees to voice their concerns, organizations can address potential ethical breaches proactively, enhancing trust within the organization.

V. Continuous Improvement

Moreover, organizations should cultivate a culture of continuous improvement in their sustainability practices. Encouraging employees to provide feedback on sustainability initiatives and reporting practices can lead to valuable insights and improvements (Jeanine, et al., 2024). Regularly reviewing and updating sustainability policies, based on employee input and changing circumstances, ensures that the organization remains responsive to emerging challenges and stakeholder expectations. This iterative approach fosters a sense of ownership among employees, motivating them to actively engage in the organization's sustainability efforts.

VI. Integration of Ethics into Decision-Making

In addition to internal strategies, organizations should integrate ethics into their decision-making processes. This requires establishing frameworks that guide employees in making choices that align with the organization's ethical standards (Khan, Serafeim, & & Yoon, 2016). Decision-making models that prioritize ethical considerations alongside financial and operational goals can help embed integrity into the organizational culture. Regularly evaluating the impact of decisions on sustainability outcomes can also provide valuable insights into the effectiveness of the organization's ethical framework.

CONCLUSION

This chapter has underscored the vital role of ethics in sustainability reporting and assurance. It is established that ethical behaviour is the very base for credible sustainability practices, providing trust and accountability between a company and its stakeholders. Discussion points out the importance of transparency. It is necessary to communicate openly as well as clearly with others regarding building a relationship that will last. We also explored some of the high-risk areas of greenwashing specifically, where firms falsely claim their environmental efforts-precisely to discredit the whole industry. We talked through some ethical issues relating to assurance about sustainable activities-including conflict of interest as well as imperatives for accuracy and completeness of such assurance. Additionally, we touched upon particular challenges organisations must work with in emerging markets, where regulatory framework might be more lenient. Emphasis also lay in independent third-party verification for credulity purposes and reducing misleading claims. Generally, upholding high marks for ethical sustainability reporting should not be only a matter of compliance but rather embracing the right ethically bounded sense of sustainability as an engagement tool with stakeholders.

Companies using an ethical approach in sustainability reporting are on the way to long-term benefits. Ethical reporting enhances the reputation of a company because stakeholders, whether they are customers, investors or employees, always tend to patronize firms they can trust. This results in customer loyalty; that is, the recipe for sustainable business success. Ultimately, ethical practices about reporting enhance financial performance since the form of communication may attract more investment and make it easier to access capital. By giving the right report of their ESG initiatives, companies can identify areas of improvement and the drive to innovate in more sustainable business practices. More than that, maintaining integrity in reporting on sustainability also helps organizations avoid the pitfall of greenwashing, hence reducing risks of law and finance against misleading claims. While the regulatory environment will be that much tighter, with the European Union's Corporate Sustainability Reporting Directive but one example, the best placed would-be ethical reporting companies. After all, ethical reporting builds accountability and continuous improvement-the marks of resolving big global problems like climate change and social inequality.

Transparency, honesty, and independence are some of the values that should set the tone for a sustainable future of reporting. When businesses undertake changes in their understanding of responsibility toward society and the environment, ethics-practice appurtenance must underlie a strategy. Important-value companies will not only enhance their reputation but also shape a more sustainable and equitable world. Committing to ethical reporting and assurance can ensure building organizational trust and a culture of integrity within organizations, further strengthening the good manners of organizations in their respective industries and beyond.

REFERENCES

Abeysek.era, I. (2022). A framework for sustainability reporting. *Sustainability Accounting, Management and Policy Journal*, 1386-1409.

Abhayawansa, S., Adams, C., & Neesham, C. (2021). Accountability And Governance In Pursuit Of Sustainable Development Goals: Conceptualising How Governments Create Value. *Accounting, Auditing & Accountability Journal*, 34(4), 923–945. DOI: 10.1108/AAAJ-07-2020-4667

Adams, C., & Evans, R. (2004). Accountability, Completeness, Credibility and the Audit Expectation Gap. *Journal of Corporate Citizenship*, 2004(14), 97–115. DOI: 10.9774/GLEAF.4700.2004.su.00010

Adams, & Whelan. (2009). Conceptualising future change in corporate sustainability reporting. *Accounting, Auditing & Accountability Journal*, 118-143.

Al-Shaer, H. (2020). Sustainability reporting quality and post-audit financial reporting quality: Empirical evidence from the UK. *Business Strategy and the Environment*, 2355-2373.

Alexander, S. (2020). A Study On Effectiveness Of Reward System On Employee Motivation In BPO Sector. *IJRAR*, 523-530.

Antonini, C., & Conde, J. (2024). Environmental Management Control Systems and Environmental Innovation: Unintended Consequences of the EU Non-financial Reporting Directive. *Management Accounting Research*, 65, 2015–2045. DOI: 10.1016/j.mar.2024.100903

Bag, S., Srivastava, G., Gupta, S., Sivarajah, U., & Wilmot, N. (2024). The effect of corporate ethical responsibility on social and environmental performance: An empirical study. *Industrial Marketing Management*, 117, 356–370. DOI: 10.1016/j.indmarman.2024.01.016

Bai, C., & Sarkis, J. (2010). Green supplier development: Analytical evaluation using. *Journal of Cleaner Production*, 18(12), 1200–1210. DOI: 10.1016/j.jclepro.2010.01.016

Bebbington, J., Larrinaga, C., & Moneva, J. (2008). Corporate Social Reporting and Reputation Risk Management. *Accounting, Auditing & Accountability Journal*, 21(3), 337–361. DOI: 10.1108/09513570810863932

Bebbington, U. J., & Eds, O. (2014). *Sustainability Accounting and Accountability*. Routledge.

Bick, R., Halsey, E., & Eknega, C. (2018). The Global Environmental Injustice of Fast Fashion. *Environmental Health : A Global Access Science Source*, 17(1), 1–4. DOI: 10.1186/s12940-018-0433-7 PMID: 30591057

Boiral, O. (2013). Sustainability Reports as Simulacra? A Counter-account of A and A+ GRI Reports. *Accounting, Auditing & Accountability Journal*, 26(7), 1036–1071. DOI: 10.1108/AAAJ-04-2012-00998

Bowen, F., & Aragon-Correa, J. A. (2014). Greenwashing in corporate environmentalism research and practice:The importance of what we say and do. *Organization & Environment*, 27(2), 107–112. DOI: 10.1177/1086026614537078

Carol, A. (2014). The Ethical, Social and Environmental Reporting-performance Portrayal Gap. *Accounting, Auditing & Accountability Journal*, 731–757.

Chen, Y., & Chag, S. (2013). Greenwash and Green Trust: The Mediation Effects of Green Consumer Confusion and Green Perceived Risk. *Journal of Business Ethics*, 114(3), 489–500. DOI: 10.1007/s10551-012-1360-0

Cho, M., Michelon, G., Patten, D. M., & Roberts, R. W. (2015). CSR disclosure: The more things change…? *Accounting, Auditing & Accountability Journal*, 28(1), 14–35. DOI: 10.1108/AAAJ-12-2013-1549

Dahlsrud, A. (2008). How corporate social responsibility is defined: An analysis of 37 definitions. *Corporate Social Responsibility and Environmental Management*, 15(1), 1–13. DOI: 10.1002/csr.132

Dando, N., & Swift, T. (2003). Transparency and assurance: Minding the credibility gap. *Journal of Business Ethics*, 44(2), 195–200. DOI: 10.1023/A:1023351816790

Deegan, C. (2002). Introduction: The Legitimising Effect of Social and Environmental Disclosures – A Theoretical Foundation. *Accounting, Auditing & Accountability Journal*, 15(3), 282–311. DOI: 10.1108/09513570210435852

Delmas, A., & Burbano, V. (2011). The Drivers of Greenwashing. *California Management Review*, 54(1), 64–87. DOI: 10.1525/cmr.2011.54.1.64

Do, T., & Vo, X. (2023). Is Mandatory Sustainability Disclosure Associated With Default Risk? Evidence From Emerging Markets. *Finance Research Letters*, 55, 1038–1056. DOI: 10.1016/j.frl.2023.103818

Eccles, R., Ioannou, I., & George, S. (2014). The Impact of Corporate Sustainability on Organizational Processes and Performance. *Management Science*, 60(11), 2835–2857. DOI: 10.1287/mnsc.2014.1984

Eccles, R., & Serafeim, G. (2013). A tale of two stories: Sustainability and the quarterly earnings call. *The Bank of America Journal of Applied Corporate Finance*, 25(3), 8–19. DOI: 10.1111/jacf.12023

Free, C., Jones, S., & Tremblay, S. (2024). Greenwashing and sustainability assurance: A review and call for future research. *Journal of Accounting Literature*, 256–291. DOI: 10.1108/JAL-11-2023-0201

Gao, S., & Zhang, J. (2019). Internal audit involvement in sustainability assurance. *Journal of Corporate Governance*, 434-449.

Hazaea, Z., Zhu, J., Khatib, S. F. A., Bazhair, A. H., & Elamer, A. A. (2022). Sustainability Assurance Practices: A Systematic Review and Future Research Agenda. *Environmental Science and Pollution Research International*, 29(4), 4843–4864. DOI: 10.1007/s11356-021-17359-9 PMID: 34787810

Hilson, G., & Maconachie, R. (2017). Formalizing Artisanal and Small-Scale Mining: Insights, Contestations and Clarifications. *Area*, 49(4), 443–451. DOI: 10.1111/area.12328

Hummel, C., & Schilck, C. (2016). The Relationship between Sustainability Performance and Sustainability Disclosure-Reconciling Voluntary Disclosure Theory and Legitimacy. *Theory.Journal of Accounting and Public Policy*, 35(5), 455–476. DOI: 10.1016/j.jaccpubpol.2016.06.001

Jeanine, K.-K., Benedikt, M., Nevena, S., & Nannan, X., lHarald, K., & Juho, H. (2024). Challenges In The Adoption Of Sustainability Information Systems: A Study On Green IS In Organizations. *International Journal of Information Management*, 1027–1054.

Jeffrey, R., Cohen, J., & Simnett, R. (2015). CSR and Assurance Services: A Research Agenda. *Auditing*, 59–74.

Kaptein, M. (2011). Developing and testing a measure for the ethical culture of organizations: The Ethical Culture Index. *Journal of Business Ethics*, 617–634.

Khan, M., Serafeim, G., & Yoon, A. (2016). Corporate sustainability: First evidence on materiality. *The Accounting Review*, 169–196.

Kolk, A. (2008). Sustainability, Accountability, and Corporate Governance: Exploring Multinationals' Reporting Practices. *Business Strategy and the Environment*, 17(1), 1–15. DOI: 10.1002/bse.511

Laufer, W. (2003). Social Accountability and Corporate Greenwashing. *Jouranl of Business Ethics*, 253-261.

Lock, I., & Seele, P. (2016). Deliberative Lobbying? Toward a Noncontradiction of Corporate Political Activities and Corporate Social Responsibility? *Journal of Management Inquiry*, 25(4), 415–430. DOI: 10.1177/1056492616640379

Lozano, R., Lukman, R., Lozano, F. J., Huisingh, D., & Lambrechts, W. (2013). Declarations for Sustainability in Higher Education: Becoming Better Leaders, through Addressing the University System. *Journal of Cleaner Production*, 48, 10–19. DOI: 10.1016/j.jclepro.2011.10.006

Michelon, G., Pilonato, S., & Ricceri, F. (2015). CSR Reporting Practices And The Quality Of Disclosure: An Empirical Analysis. *Critical Perspectives on Accounting*, 33, 59–78. DOI: 10.1016/j.cpa.2014.10.003

Moodaley, W., & Telukdarie, A. (2023). Greenwashing, Sustainability Reporting, and Artificial Intelligence: A Systematic Literature Review. *Sustainability (Basel)*, 15(2), 1481–1502. DOI: 10.3390/su15021481

Morioka, S. N., & de Carvalho, M. M. (2016). A Systematic Literature Review Towards A Conceptual Framework For Integrating Sustainability Performance Into Business. *Journal of Cleaner Production*, 136, 134–146. DOI: 10.1016/j.jclepro.2016.01.104

O'Dwyer, B., & Owen, D. (2005). Assurance Statement Practice In Environmental, Social And Sustainability Reporting: A Critical Evaluation. *The British Accounting Review*, 37(2), 205–229. DOI: 10.1016/j.bar.2005.01.005

Olivier, B., Iñaki, H., & Heras, S., Marie, & Bernard, J. (2019). Ethical Issues in the Assurance of Sustainability Reports: Perspectives from Assurance Providers. *Journal of Business Ethics*, 1111–1125.

Oncioiu, I. D-M, P., AE, A., A, ., F, R., M, P., & Marin-Pantelescu. (2020). The Role of Environmental, Social, and Governance Disclosure in Financial Transparency. *Sustainability*.

P., P., & A., K. (2012). Multinationals' Accountability on Sustainability: The Evolution of Third-party Assurance of Sustainability Reports. *Journal of Business Ethics*, 173-190.

Perego, P., & Kolk, A. (2012). Multinationals' Accountability on Sustainability: The Evolution of Third-party Assurance of Sustainability Reports. *Journal of Business Ethics*, 110(2), 173–190. DOI: 10.1007/s10551-012-1420-5

Reimsbach, Hahn, & Gürtürk, A. (. (2018). Integrated reporting and assurance of sustainability information: An experimental study on professional investors' information processing., 27(3), 559-581. *European Accounting Review*, 559–581. DOI: 10.1080/09638180.2016.1273787

Rhodes, C. (2016). Democratic Business Ethics: Volkswagen's Emissions Scandal and the Disruption of Corporate Sovereignty. *Jouranl of Busienss Ethics*, 1501-1518.

Rob, G., Dave, O., & Keith, M. (1987). *Corporate Social Reporting: Accounting and Accountability*. Prentice Hall.

Robert, E., Michael, K., & Sydney, R. (2014). *The Integrated Reporting Movement: Meaning, Momentum, Motives, and Materiality*. Wiley.

Simnett, R., Vanstraelen, A., & Chua, W. F. (2009). Assurance on Sustainability Reports:An International Comparison. *The Accounting Review*, 84(3), 937–967. DOI: 10.2308/accr.2009.84.3.937

Sult, A., Wobst, J., & Lueg, R. (2023). The role of training in implementing corporate sustainability: A systematic literature review. *Corporate Social Responsibility and Environmental Management*, •••, 1–30.

Tobias, H., Jonatan, P. L. P., & Frank, F. (2015). Tensions in Corporate Sustainability: Towards an Integrative Framework. *Journal of Business Ethics*, 297–316.

Torreli, R., Balluchi, F., & Lazzini, A. (2020). Greenwashing and Environmental Communication: Effects on Stakeholders' Perceptions. *Business Strategy and the Environment*, 29(2), 407–421. DOI: 10.1002/bse.2373

Wallage, P. (2000). Assurance on Sustainability Reporting: An Auditor's View. *Auditing*, 19(s-1), 53–65. DOI: 10.2308/aud.2000.19.s-1.53

Wang, Z., & Sarkis, J. (2017). Corporate Social Responsibility Governance, Outcomes, and Financial Performance. *Journal of Cleaner Production*, 162, 1607–1616. DOI: 10.1016/j.jclepro.2017.06.142

Zimon, G., Arianpoor, A., & Salehi, M. (2022). Zimon G, Arianpoor A, Salehi M. Sustainability Reporting and Corporate Reputation: The Moderating Effect of CEO Opportunistic Behavior. Sustainability. 2022; 14(3):1257. *Sustainability*, 1257–1275. DOI: 10.3390/su14031257

Chapter 7
Harnessing AI and Blockchain in Sustainability Assurance:
Trends Shaping the Future of Verification

K. Balaji
https://orcid.org/0000-0002-3065-3294
Christ University, Bengaluru, India

ABSTRACT

The integration of artificial intelligence (AI) and blockchain technology is revolutionizing sustainability assurance, setting new benchmarks for transparency, accuracy, and accountability. This article explores current trends and innovative applications of AI and blockchain in verifying corporate sustainability efforts, from automated data analysis to secure, decentralized record-keeping. By leveraging AI for real-time monitoring and data insights, organizations can better track environmental and social impacts, while blockchain ensures data integrity and traceability across supply chains. These advancements enhance stakeholder trust and support regulatory compliance, addressing increasing demands for robust sustainability verification in global markets. Furthermore, the paper discusses challenges such as data privacy and implementation costs, offering insights into the potential long-term impact of these technologies on corporate governance. By examining recent case studies and market trends, this article outlines a future where technology-driven assurance processes.

DOI: 10.4018/979-8-3373-0117-4.ch007

I. INTRODUCTION

As organizations worldwide intensify their focus on sustainability, there is a growing demand for robust systems that can verify and authenticate corporate claims regarding environmental and social performance. This is where sustainability assurance, a structured process for verifying the accuracy and completeness of sustainability reports, plays a vital role. Traditional methods, however, face limitations in terms of scalability, speed, and accuracy. Emerging technologies like artificial intelligence (AI) and blockchain are reshaping this field by providing innovative solutions for monitoring, tracking, and validating sustainability-related data. AI, with its capabilities in data analytics and pattern recognition, enables organizations to assess their sustainability metrics in real time, reducing the potential for human error and subjective biases. Meanwhile, blockchain technology offers a secure and transparent platform for storing and sharing verified data, providing traceability throughout complex supply chains.

By integrating these technologies into sustainability assurance practices, companies can enhance stakeholder trust and demonstrate accountability in ways that were previously challenging or resource-intensive. However, the shift towards digital verification tools is not without its challenges. Issues such as data security, privacy, and implementation costs present obstacles that need to be carefully managed. The purpose of this article is to investigate how AI and blockchain are currently being harnessed to meet the evolving demands of sustainability assurance, highlight the benefits and challenges of their application, and provide actionable recommendations for both corporate and academic settings. In doing so, this study contributes to a deeper understanding of technology's potential in building a more transparent, accountable, and sustainable future.

1.1. Global Blockchain AI Market in Sustainability

The Global Blockchain AI Market is projected to experience significant growth across various industries from 2022 to 2030, as indicated by the upward trend in market share across all verticals. This steady rise reflects the increasing adoption of blockchain and AI technologies as they become essential for enhancing security, transparency, and efficiency. These technologies are gaining traction as industries leverage AI for predictive insights and blockchain for secure, tamper-proof data storage. This synergy offers compelling solutions for sectors that prioritize data integrity and automation, making blockchain AI an attractive investment.

Among the different sectors, BFSI (Banking, Financial Services, and Insurance) and Healthcare & Life Sciences are particularly notable. Both these sectors show substantial market share from 2022, likely due to the critical need for data security and compliance in finance and healthcare. In finance, blockchain AI aids in fraud detection, risk management, and faster, more secure transactions. Similarly, in healthcare, these technologies enable secure patient data management, facilitate interoperability between healthcare providers, and enhance clinical research capabilities, all of which contribute to better patient outcomes and regulatory compliance. These sectors' early adoption and sustained growth underscore blockchain AI's role in sectors where data sensitivity is paramount. Figure 1 below shows the global market size of AI and Block Chain in sustainability.

Figure 1. Global market size of AI and blockchain in sustainability

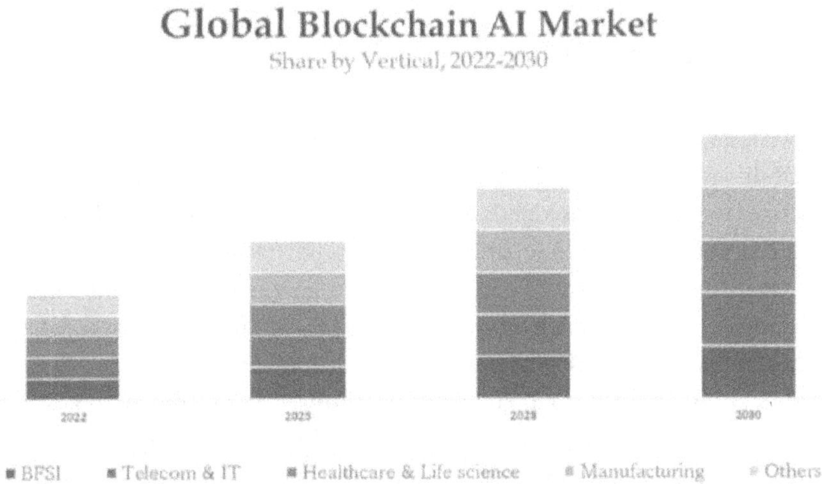

The above Figure 1 shows that the Telecom & IT and Manufacturing sectors are also projected to see remarkable growth by 2030. Telecom and IT benefit from blockchain AI in managing large volumes of data, enhancing cybersecurity, and automating customer interactions. The manufacturing industry, on the other hand, leverages blockchain AI to improve supply chain transparency, optimize production processes, and ensure quality control. Blockchain's ability to provide a secure, immutable record of transactions and AI's predictive capabilities enable manufacturers to improve efficiency and traceability, especially in complex, globalized supply chains.

By 2030, the "Others" category shows a notable increase, suggesting that emerging industries are also starting to recognize and adopt blockchain AI solutions. This growth indicates that the technology's applications are broadening beyond traditional sectors, potentially including areas like energy, retail, and education. The widening application scope speaks to blockchain AI's versatility, as it becomes relevant to new use cases that benefit from the enhanced security, automation, and real-time insights these technologies offer.

Objectives of the Study

The primary objective of this study is to explore how AI and blockchain can optimize sustainability assurance processes and to assess the potential impacts of these technologies on corporate transparency and governance. Additional objectives include identifying current trends, challenges, and practical applications, as well as providing actionable recommendations for effective technology integration.

II. REVIEW OF LITERATURE

Abdulla, A., et al. (2020) explored the integration of early digital tools in sustainability reporting, emphasizing the importance of transparency in environmental practices to meet stakeholder demands. Their findings highlighted the need for corporate systems that could reliably manage and disclose environmental data, noting that manual methods were insufficient for comprehensive sustainability reporting. These insights helped shape the expectations of transparency and data reliability that later underpinned sustainability assurance processes. By the 1990s, corporate accountability and environmental sustainability were prominent topics in research. Balaji, K. (2024) introduced the triple bottom line concept, arguing that businesses should measure success beyond financial metrics to include social and environmental impact. Although not specifically focused on AI or blockchain, Elkington's framework laid a theoretical foundation for sustainability assurance practices, as it emphasized the need for verifiable, accurate reporting of environmental and social outcomes (Bellagarda, J. S., et.al, 2022). This multi-dimensional approach to corporate performance created a demand for technologies that could facilitate comprehensive data tracking and reporting.

At the same time, researchers began to recognize the challenges of data complexity and volume in sustainability reporting. Dohale, V., et.al, (2022) examined the early use of data processing systems in environmental impact assessments and noted that, while effective, they were limited by data integrity issues. A study pointed out that without advanced technology to ensure accuracy, these assessments could not fully address stakeholder concerns regarding transparency. Dora, M., et.al, (2022) study on Unlocking the Potential of BI-Enhancing Banking Transactions Through AI&ML Tools underscored the need for technologies capable of handling large datasets and verifying data authenticity—a need later fulfilled by AI and blockchain. In the early 2000s, academic interest grew in digital systems for enhancing corporate accountability. Balaji, K. (2024) b discussed the role of technology in monitoring and verifying sustainability commitments, recognizing that automated systems could improve data accuracy and reliability. Balaji, K. (2025) c. Neuromarketing and Sustainable Finance: Real-World Case Studies of Green Investment Promotions. proposed that, with advancements, digital tools could potentially transform sustainability reporting by allowing real-time data tracking and verification. This perspective aligns closely with the functionalities provided by modern AI-driven tools and blockchain technology.

Around this time, Hoang, T. D., et.al, (2022) emphasized the strategic advantage of sustainable practices and how digital verification tools could support corporate responsibility. They argued that integrating sustainability into core business strategies not only mitigated environmental risks but also created competitive advantage. Hong, Z., et.al, (2024) study on Exploring the Drivers and Effects on Supply Chain Resilience and Performance in an Emerging Market Using Artificial Intelligence research underscored the growing recognition of sustainability as integral to business success and the need for assurance mechanisms that could reliably support it. The mid-2000s saw further examination of automated systems and digital databases in corporate governance and reporting. Indrasari, M., et.al, (2024) investigated the benefits and limitations of early digital platforms in sustainability assurance, concluding that while beneficial, these systems needed to evolve to handle more complex reporting requirements. This study highlights an early awareness of the gaps in technology that would later be filled by blockchain's immutability and AI's data processing capabilities.

By 2008, blockchain and AI were beginning to gain attention, albeit not directly linked to sustainability assurance at this time. Nevertheless, some researchers speculated on their potential applications. For instance, Jabeur, S. B., et.al, (2022) introduced the concept of blockchain for transparency in organizational transactions, foreshadowing its eventual adoption for verification purposes. They discussed how a decentralized ledger could enhance trust and transparency, though its application in sustainability was still speculative. Jagatheesaperumal, S. K., et.al, (2021) study on Artificial Intelligence for Enhanced Anti-Money Laundering and Asset Recovery: A New Frontier in Financial Crime Prevention analysis laid foundational principles for blockchain's eventual role in transparent, traceable data handling. Similarly, K. Balaji (2024) discussed the potential of emerging data analytics and AI technologies to transform corporate operations by providing data-driven insights into organizational performance. Though not directly focused on sustainability, the study suggested that AI could streamline data processing and support informed decision-making. This research pre-empted AI's potential for real-time monitoring and impact assessment in sustainability contexts.

From 2010 to 2013, academic literature began to explore the integration of digital systems specifically for sustainability and transparency. Kazeem, K. O., et.al, (2023) investigated the role of technology in promoting sustainable business practices, emphasizing the need for robust data verification systems. They argued that as sustainability became a central concern for stakeholders, the demand for accurate and verifiable data increased, making a case for technologies that could automate and authenticate reporting. These insights presaged blockchain's and AI's applications in maintaining data integrity within sustainability assurance frameworks. Simultaneously, Nuseir, M., et.al, (2020) explored corporate sustainability reporting and the need for assurance mechanisms that could adapt to increasing volumes of data and complexity. The authors pointed out that manual verification processes could not keep up with the data demands of modern sustainability initiatives and proposed the development of automated systems for greater accuracy and scalability. Their analysis laid the groundwork for AI's eventual role in sustainability assurance by highlighting the benefits of automation and real-time data analysis.

Finally, Obaideen, K., et.al, (2022) focused on the transparency and accountability challenges in sustainability reporting, noting that conventional assurance methods were prone to human error and inconsistencies. They called for systems that could enhance accountability through objective, data-driven verification processes. Ohalete, N. C., et.al, (2023) The Nexus of Smart Contracts and Digital Twins Transforming Green Finance study indirectly highlighted the potential benefits of AI's predictive analytics and blockchain's data integrity features. The growing integration of artificial intelligence (AI) and blockchain in sustainability assurance over the past decade has sparked extensive research on their potential to enhance data transparency, accuracy, and reliability.

With advancements in digital technology, several scholars have explored AI's capabilities in data processing and analytics to improve sustainability reporting. One of the pioneering studies by Rane, N., et.al, (2023) examined the role of machine learning algorithms in environmental data analysis, suggesting that AI could streamline real-time tracking of corporate sustainability metrics, reducing manual data entry errors and enhancing reporting accuracy. Similarly, Sharma, S., et.al, (2024) investigated AI's predictive capabilities, noting that machine learning models help companies forecast environmental impacts based on historical data trends, providing a proactive approach to managing sustainability (Srivastava, A., et.al, (2024)). Blockchain's potential for enhancing transparency and traceability has also been widely discussed. Taghikhah, F., et.al, (2022) examined blockchain's application in supply chain sustainability, demonstrating how decentralized ledgers allow for secure, tamper-proof recording of transactional data, thereby addressing common transparency issues in traditional supply chains and emphasized blockchain's potential to trace raw materials, providing an auditable trail that assures stakeholders of the ethical sourcing of products. Similarly, they explored blockchain's role in waste management systems, arguing that decentralized verification could ensure more reliable tracking of waste disposal and recycling processes, thus supporting circular economy goals.

In recent years, researchers have delved into the convergence of AI and blockchain in sustainability assurance, noting how these technologies complement each other's strengths. For instance, a study on AI's analytical capabilities combined with blockchain's immutable record-keeping, proposing a hybrid model for improved verification accuracy. He also argued that while AI models analyse complex sustainability metrics, blockchain ensures that these results are securely stored and accessible to relevant stakeholders. Similarly, there is a model that integrates AI-driven monitoring systems with blockchain, enhancing trust and transparency in sustainability disclosures by ensuring real-time data accuracy and immutability.

Several studies have highlighted the applications of AI and blockchain in specific sustainability domains, such as carbon emissions monitoring and waste management. The study also explored AI's role in carbon accounting, demonstrating how machine learning algorithms could accurately track and predict emissions data. A more recent study by Nuseir, M., et.al, (2020) examined blockchain's potential in certifying carbon credits, arguing that decentralized ledgers enable verifiable carbon offset tracking, reducing the risk of double-counting in carbon markets.

In summary, the literature highlights the transformative potential of AI and blockchain in enhancing sustainability assurance by improving data transparency, accuracy, and traceability. Researchers have demonstrated AI's ability to streamline data analysis and predictive modelling for environmental metrics, while blockchain provides secure, decentralized records that enhance traceability. However, challenges such as scalability, data privacy, and regulatory ambiguity remain, requiring innovative solutions and interdisciplinary collaborations. This synthesis underscores the need for further research into hybrid AI-blockchain models and calls for policy frameworks that support responsible technology integration. By addressing these challenges, AI and blockchain can fulfil their potential to revolutionize sustainability assurance and contribute to a transparent, accountable global economy.

III. METHOD

The study adopts a qualitative research approach, reviewing recent literature on AI and blockchain applications in sustainability assurance, analysing case studies, and conducting interviews with industry professionals. By synthesizing information from these sources, the study aims to provide a comprehensive view of the current landscape and identify best practices for integrating technology into sustainability assurance.

3.1. The Convergence of AI and Blockchain

Artificial intelligence (AI) and blockchain are two of the most transformative technologies of our time. Individually, they have the potential to revolutionize a multitude of industries and transform economic and social interactions and relationships. When combined, they unlock a new frontier of possibilities that can empower a new generation of applications that benefit both from the vast productivity gains unlocked by AI and the security and transparency enabled by blockchain technology. The Figure 2 below shows the Convergence of AI and Blockchain in sustainability reporting

Figure 2. Convergence of AI and blockchain in sustainability reporting

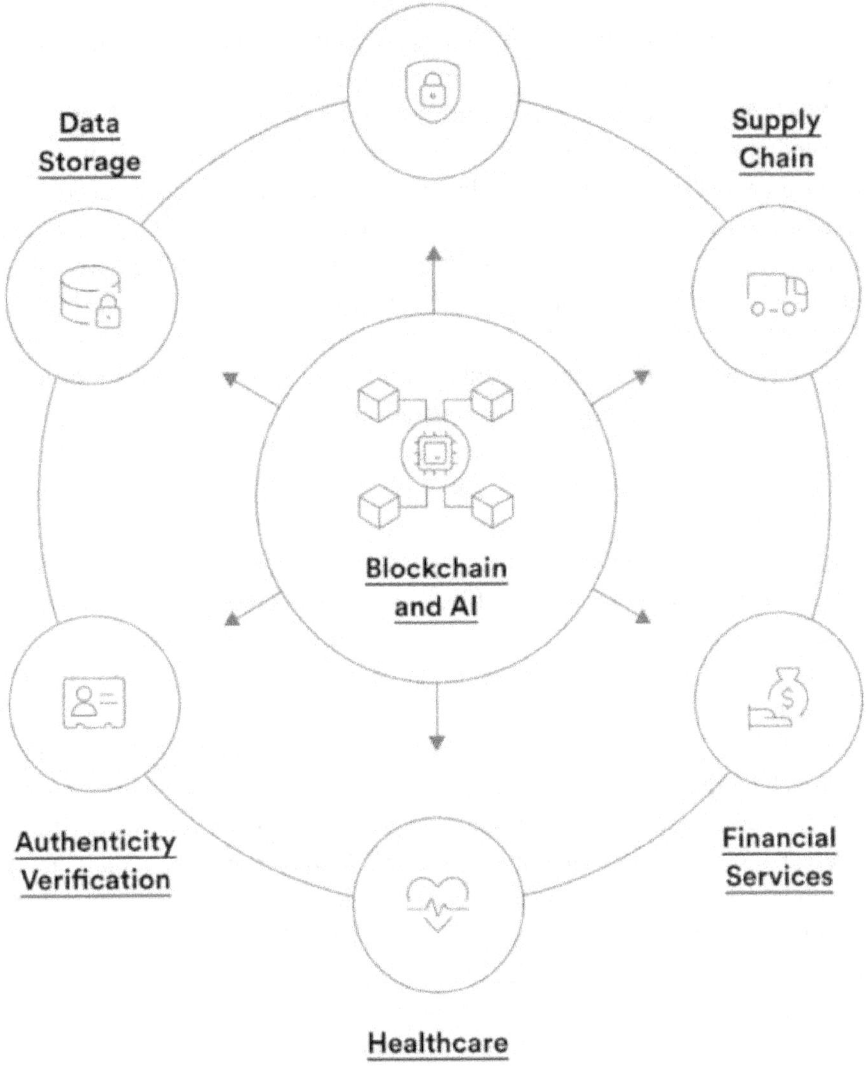

According to a report by Spherical Insights (Figure 2), the intersection of blockchain and AI is projected to grow into a billion-dollar industry within the next decade. Despite this potential, the integration of these two technologies has so far remained relatively underexplored, leaving room for further investigation as the two segments progress toward broader mainstream adoption.

In this post, we outline the concept of AI in blockchain, explore the potential convergence of these two technologies, and discuss the benefits that can come as a result of their combination.

3.2. AI and Blockchain Use Cases

In this section, we'll explore an array of potential use cases that highlight the potential impact of AI and blockchain integrations.

Security: Decentralized infrastructure and blockchain technology can act as encryption-backed guardrails for AI systems. In such a model, AI systems can be deployed with built-in safeguards that reduce their ability to be misused or utilized for adversarial behaviours. Developers of AI can encode specific parameters within which AI can access various key systems, and private keys can enforce these conditions with the help of tamper-proof decentralized infrastructure like blockchains, smart contracts, and oracles.

Decentralized, blockchain-based systems have been designed from the ground up to combat manipulation by various adversaries, and these security measures could extend to the use of adversarial AI agents. Unlike centralized systems, where a single point of failure can put the entire system at risk, decentralized infrastructure is spread across multiple nodes and multiple independent private keys, making it more difficult for a single adversary to compromise the entire system. The utility of AI models and the security of blockchains can help reduce attack vectors and bolster the security of AI applications, enabling organizations to leverage the full potential of AI while maintaining a high standard of security enforced by cryptographic guarantees.

Supply Chain: A smart contract is a computer program hosted and executed on a blockchain that consists of code specifying predetermined conditions that, when met, trigger outcomes. The self-executing nature of smart contracts offers some inherent advantages when it comes to leveraging the power of artificial intelligence. AI models incorporated into smart contracts could utilize specific predetermined conditions to execute tasks: Detecting the need for additional inventory and executing the order with an external supplier, for example. The combination of blockchain and AI could also improve transparency and reduce the potential impact of fraud through the digitization of paper-based processes, and by enabling the real-time tracking of goods from production to delivery. By combining AI-driven predictive analytics with blockchains, companies can gain better insights into demand patterns, optimize inventory management, and make data-driven decisions to minimize costs. This use case can also offer benefits in other fields, such as disaster relief. AI-driven analytics combined with blockchain-based supply chain tracking could help humanitarian organizations optimize resource allocation during natural disasters. By providing real-time data on the availability and location of essential supplies, emergency relief efforts can be optimized so that supplies are allocated to their ideal destination.

Authenticity Verification: The capabilities of deep learning models, such as DALL-E, Stable Diffusion, and Midjourney, have highlighted the profound potential of generating images and different forms of media purely based on natural language text prompts (or using other forms of media). While these models highlight the transformative potential of AI to increase productivity and supercharge the scope of human creativity, they could also be used in an adversarial manner to manipulate public opinion by spreading misinformation and propaganda or creating deep fakes and other misleading synthetic media.

Underpinned by cryptography and encryption, blockchain technology can help validate the authenticity of images, video files, text documents, or other types of media by being able to cryptographically verify where a piece of content originates from and whether it has been tampered with or altered in any way. This type of cryptographic watermarking technology can also be used for tamper-proof timestamping to help verify the authenticity of "who knew what when." In a future where it becomes imperative to be able to differentiate between AI- and human-generated content for maintaining stability in society, cryptographic validation and timestamping could facilitate the creation of decentralized platforms for content curation, verification, and distribution. Such platforms could empower content creators and users to establish trust regarding the information that is being propagated by ensuring that the media they spread is unaltered, authentic, and underpinned by a transparent and verifiable history. Moreover, blockchain tokens—specifically non-fungible tokens (NFTs)—could present a solution to combat the challenges associated with verifying the authenticity and provenance of digital content. NFTs, which are unique digital assets, can be used to represent ownership and verify the origins of various forms of media, including images, videos, text, music, and others.

By assigning an NFT to a piece of content, creators can establish a digital fingerprint that ensures the content's traceability on-chain. When a piece of content is minted as an NFT, its origin, ownership history, and any subsequent modifications become transparent and easily verifiable. Such technologies becoming standardized could foster more accountability with online content, where publishers are better incentivized to maintain the authenticity of their work while ordinary people can more confidently discern between genuine content and content that's been tampered with.

Data Analytics: One of the most useful benefits of blockchain technology is its ability to provide unparalleled data provenance. Storing data in a highly secure and decentralized blockchain-based network may be one of the best ways to ensure data integrity over the long term. This naturally makes blockchain networks a good breeding ground for large-scale data analytics.

As blockchain technology increasingly underpins key aspects of human economic and social activity, large-scale analytics using sophisticated machine learning models could harness the vast sets of data generated on-chain. By doing so, these models could identify overarching trends and offer actionable intelligence through predictive analytics, enabling both businesses and individuals to make informed decisions about the opportunities that emerge from the on-chain economy. In addition, AI models could help optimize calculations for algorithms that are used in the consensus process in blockchain systems, for example, Bitcoin mining, helping decrease latency and compute requirements for blockchain nodes.

Financial Services: Decentralized finance (DeFi) enables anyone with an Internet connection to access transparent financial services that involve peer-to-peer transactions and immutable smart contracts. The growth of the DeFi ecosystem has been momentous, and AI models could take advantage of the increasing variety and complexity of financial services offered by this ecosystem by using DeFi as an economic layer to execute actions and tasks based on predetermined instructions.

A large language model securely connected to the Internet could perform routine tasks involving payments or economic exchange by utilizing the on-chain financial stack of the Web3 industry. Due to the inherent composability of blockchain applications, AI models could carry out complex interconnected loops of financial transactions without having to rely on intermediaries and an opaque, paper-based financial system. In addition, AI-powered automated investment strategies in DeFi applications can offer entirely new financial services underpinned by secure, transparent, and decentralized infrastructure. Due to the decision-making capabilities of AI and blockchain's effectiveness in recording real-time economic activity, a combination of the two technologies could also enable automated compliance and fraud-detection processes powered by machine learning algorithms.

Healthcare: Certain implementations of blockchain technology can be ideal for storing sensitive data, which can then be utilized by advanced AI models to analyse health data and identify recurring patterns, and make accurate diagnoses based on medical scans and records. In addition, novel encryption techniques, such as homomorphic encryption, could enable running computations on this data without compromising data privacy. AI and blockchain technology can enhance data management, privacy, and security in healthcare by facilitating the secure storage and sharing of patient records, medical research data, and other sensitive information. This could allow healthcare and longevity researchers to collaborate more effectively from different physical locations while upholding the highest standards of data security. By leveraging blockchain technology as a foundation for data storage, AI-driven diagnostic tools and custom treatment plans could be developed with increased data privacy, leading to a more efficient and personalized healthcare system.

Transparency: A challenge presented by current deep learning models is the lack of transparency in their decision-making processes. Due to the immense complexity of these models, which sometimes involve hundreds of billions of parameters, even experts can struggle to explain why a particular model generates a specific output when prompted with a specific input. While this opacity can often be a property of the underlying deep-learning architectures, and creating AI models that can explain or indicate their own decision-making is ultimately up to AI researchers, the inherent transparency of blockchain networks can help address some of the issues associated with this lack of transparency. By facilitating a transparent record of data, blockchains can enable AI models to provide a clear framework for their operations. This allows for the analysis of audit trails on the decision-making patterns of algorithms, and the use of an immutable data ledger to reveal what data the models are relying on, ultimately helping to contribute to greater integrity.

Decentralized Data Storage: Many AI models rely on exceedingly large data sets. While data is only one component, this training data can significantly influence the capabilities of the AI system. Decentralized storage solutions enabled by blockchain-based systems, such as Filecoin, IPFS, and Arweave, could help preserve training data integrity and ensure accurate provenance in the future. Additionally, as mentioned earlier, innovative encryption techniques could enable deep learning models to be trained on encrypted datasets while safeguarding privacy and confidentiality. Integrating blockchain-based storage solutions into the deep learning stack could enhance the security and reliability of AI systems while simultaneously promoting transparency and trust in their decision-making.

Smart Contract Development: With the emergence of AI-assisted development tools, such as GitHub Copilot, the productivity of smart contract developers can be increased by orders of magnitude. Smart contract applications could be further augmented with AI-powered APIs, which provide analytics of real-world sensors, sentiment analysis, or generative models, to bring forth an entirely new generation of Web3 applications. Smart contracts could be driven by natural language instead of programming languages such as Solidity. In such a setup, users' program smart contracts using natural language, which is then "interpreted" by individual validators that convert the prompt into its machine-readable code equivalent. The validators then come to consensus on the correct smart contract output which is then executed by the blockchain network.

3.3. Tools and Technologies in AI and Blockchain Supporting Sustainability Assurance Frameworks

The intersection of artificial intelligence (AI) and blockchain in sustainability assurance has introduced several tools and technologies designed to enhance transparency, accountability, and data reliability in sustainability reporting and assurance frameworks. The overview of some key tools and technologies in AI and blockchain that are supporting these frameworks:

AI-Driven Data Analytics and Machine Learning Algorithms: The integration of artificial intelligence (AI) into sustainability assurance frameworks is transforming how organizations collect, analyse, and report sustainability data. AI-driven data analytics and machine learning algorithms facilitate the processing of vast amounts of information, yielding actionable insights that empower companies to make informed decisions regarding their sustainability efforts. For instance, predictive analytics models can forecast environmental impacts, allowing businesses to anticipate emissions, resource usage, and waste generation trends. Natural Language Processing (NLP) further enhances this capability by analysing textual data from sustainability reports, social media, and news articles to gauge public sentiment and identify emerging trends in corporate environmental impact. Additionally, computer vision technology can be employed in remote sensing applications to monitor deforestation, pollution, and changes in land use, thus providing accurate, real-time data that supports transparent and accountable sustainability reporting. AI-based emission tracking systems, such as IBM's Environmental Intelligence Suite, enable organizations to monitor and manage their carbon footprints more effectively, ensuring compliance with sustainability standards and regulatory requirements.

Blockchain-Based Traceability and Decentralized Ledgers: Blockchain technology plays a crucial role in enhancing the transparency and reliability of sustainability assurance frameworks. By providing a decentralized and tamper-proof ledger, blockchain enables organizations to record and verify sustainability-related data across their supply chains. One of the most significant applications of blockchain in this context is the use of smart contracts, which automate compliance checks and verification processes. This reduces the need for human intervention and minimizes the risk of errors or fraud. Platforms like VeChain leverage distributed ledger technology to trace raw materials throughout the supply chain, ensuring that products are sourced ethically and sustainably. Furthermore, tokenized carbon credits created on blockchain platforms, such as Climate Trade, facilitate transparent trading in carbon markets, reducing opportunities for fraud and enhancing trust in carbon offset transactions. Blockchain's decentralized nature also aids in waste management efforts by providing secure records for waste handling and recycling, promoting circular economy practices and enhancing accountability.

Integrated AI-Blockchain Platforms for Sustainability Assurance: The combination of AI and blockchain into integrated platforms presents a robust solution for sustainability assurance, allowing organizations to leverage the strengths of both technologies. These hybrid verification models enable real-time monitoring and trustworthy verification of sustainability metrics across various industries. For instance, IBM's blockchain solution for supply chains integrates AI analytics to provide comprehensive tracking of sustainability data at multiple stages of production. This approach ensures compliance with sustainability standards and allows organizations to respond swiftly to any discrepancies.

IoT Sensors and Remote Monitoring with AI and Blockchain Integration: IoT (Internet of Things) sensors, when combined with AI and blockchain technologies, enable continuous data collection and monitoring of environmental parameters across various facilities and ecosystems. These sensors collect critical information regarding emissions, pollutants, and resource usage, providing organizations with real-time insights into their sustainability practices. AI processes the data generated by these sensors, allowing companies to derive actionable insights for improving operational efficiencies and reducing environmental impact. Blockchain technology secures this data, ensuring its integrity and immutability for transparent reporting. For example, energy management systems powered by IoT and AI can monitor energy consumption, while blockchain verifies this data, creating a reliable record that assures stakeholders of the organization's compliance with sustainability targets. Additionally, remote sensing technologies equipped with AI and blockchain capabilities can track natural resource usage, monitor pollution levels, and assess ecological footprints, creating a comprehensive overview of a company's environmental impact.

Sustainability Reporting and Compliance Platforms: AI and blockchain technologies significantly enhance the processes of sustainability reporting and compliance. AI-driven platforms, such as Enablon and Sustainalytics, streamline sustainability reporting by automating data collection and analysis, allowing organizations to generate comprehensive reports with greater efficiency. These platforms also integrate blockchain technology to ensure that sustainability reports are tamper-proof and verifiable, enhancing their credibility among stakeholders. The capability for data integration and auditability provided by blockchain allows companies to present transparent sustainability claims backed by reliable records. Furthermore, blockchain-based solutions like Circularise promote compliance with circular economic principles by verifying the recyclability of materials, ensuring that companies adhere to sustainable production standards. This combination of AI and blockchain not only improves reporting accuracy but also fosters greater trust in sustainability initiatives.

Renewable Energy Certification and Marketplace Platforms: The integration of AI and blockchain technologies facilitates efficient management and trading of renewable energy certifications and credits. Blockchain platforms provide transparent marketplaces for trading renewable energy certificates (RECs), enabling organizations to offset their energy footprints effectively. For example, Power Ledger utilizes blockchain to enable peer-to-peer trading of renewable energy credits, while its AI features monitor energy production and consumption patterns in real time. Digital

Renewable Energy Certificates offered by companies like Energy Web provide verifiable trading environments that enhance transparency and compliance with regulatory standards. AI further supports these platforms by analysing energy usage patterns and predicting future consumption, enabling organizations to optimize their renewable energy strategies. This synergy not only promotes greater accountability but also encourages organizations to adopt more sustainable energy practices.

Carbon Credit Tracking and Offset Marketplaces: The collaboration between AI and blockchain technologies is instrumental in establishing transparent and efficient carbon credit tracking and offset marketplaces. Digital carbon marketplaces, such as Carbonplace and CarbonX, leverage blockchain to create secure and verifiable environments for trading carbon credits. These platforms ensure that carbon offset transactions are recorded immutably, reducing the potential for fraud and enhancing stakeholder trust. AI plays a critical role in this process by providing accurate tracking of carbon emissions and offsets, enabling companies to assess their compliance with sustainability targets effectively. Furthermore, AI-driven analytics can predict future carbon footprint trends based on historical data, allowing organizations to develop proactive strategies for emission reductions. With the inclusion of IoT-enabled monitoring systems, companies can track real-time emissions data from their facilities, optimizing their sustainability efforts while ensuring accurate reporting and compliance with environmental standards. In conclusion, the integration of AI and blockchain technologies is revolutionizing sustainability assurance frameworks, offering innovative tools and methodologies that enhance transparency, reliability, and efficiency in sustainability practices. By leveraging these technologies, organizations can not only improve their sustainability reporting and compliance but also foster greater trust among stakeholders and contribute to a more sustainable future.

3.4. Case Studies of Successful Applications by Companies Across the World with AI and Blockchain in Sustainability Assurance

IBM (Established 1911): IBM, a leading technology and consulting company, has a long-standing commitment to innovation, particularly in leveraging advanced technologies like AI and blockchain to enhance sustainability. The IBM Environmental Intelligence Suite exemplifies the company's dedication to addressing environmental challenges and improving sustainability assurance processes. In 2021, IBM launched its Environmental Intelligence Suite, which integrates AI-driven analytics with blockchain technology to provide organizations with actionable insights into their environmental impacts. The suite enables companies to monitor emissions, energy consumption, and supply chain sustainability in real time. Through this platform, organizations can gain visibility into their sustainability metrics, allowing them to make data-driven decisions that positively impact their environmental footprint.

IBM's collaboration with agricultural organizations highlights the practical applications of this technology. By implementing a blockchain solution for tracking food products, IBM facilitates transparency in the supply chain, ensuring that sustainability standards are met. The blockchain system verifies the origins of agricultural products, allowing stakeholders to confirm compliance with sustainable practices. The value generated by IBM's sustainability initiatives is multifaceted. Organizations utilizing the Environmental Intelligence Suite report significant reductions in operational costs due to improved efficiency in resource management. Additionally, by enhancing compliance reporting processes, companies can mitigate risks associated with regulatory penalties. IBM's solutions foster trust among consumers, as businesses can substantiate their sustainability claims through transparent and verifiable data. IBM's innovative use of AI and blockchain technologies underscores the potential for technology to drive sustainable practices across industries. By enhancing visibility and accountability in sustainability assurance processes, IBM positions itself as a leader in promoting responsible business practices.

Unilever (Established 1929): Unilever, a global leader in consumer goods, has demonstrated a strong commitment to sustainability through its Sustainable Living Plan, launched in 2010. The plan aims to reduce the company's environmental impact while increasing its positive social effects. Unilever's innovative use of AI and blockchain technologies is central to achieving these objectives. In its efforts to enhance supply chain transparency, Unilever has implemented a blockchain solution to track the sourcing of palm oil, a critical raw material. By establishing a transparent and traceable supply chain, Unilever ensures that its palm oil is sourced sustainably, thereby minimizing deforestation and promoting ethical labor practices. Blockchain technology enables all stakeholders to verify the sustainability claims associated with their products, fostering consumer trust. Unilever has also harnessed AI to optimize production processes and forecast demand more accurately. By analysing vast datasets, the company can identify trends and patterns that inform strategic decision-making. This integration of AI in supply chain management not only reduces waste but also improves the overall efficiency of operations.

The sustainability initiatives at Unilever have yielded significant value. By employing blockchain technology, the company enhances the credibility of its sustainability claims, fostering trust among consumers and stakeholders. Additionally, AI-driven analytics help Unilever reduce operational costs and improve sustainability metrics, reinforcing its commitment to responsible sourcing. Unilever's proactive approach to integrating AI and blockchain into its sustainability practices illustrates the potential for these technologies to drive positive changes in the consumer goods industry. The company's initiatives not only enhance transparency but also contribute to a more sustainable future.

VeChain (Established 2015): VeChain is a blockchain platform that focuses on enhancing supply chain transparency and sustainability. Established in 2015, the company has dedicated itself to providing solutions that allow businesses to track and verify the sustainability of their products. VeChain collaborates with various industries, including food and beverage, luxury goods, and logistics. One of VeChain's notable projects involves its partnership with the China Chain-Store & Franchise Association (CCFA) to establish a blockchain-based food safety platform. This platform enables consumers to trace the origins of food products, ensuring that they meet safety and sustainability standards. By integrating IoT devices with blockchain technology, VeChain provides real-time data on product conditions during transportation, enhancing the accountability of supply chains.

The use of AI further amplifies VeChain's capabilities by analysing large volumes of data related to supply chain performance. This data-driven approach helps businesses identify inefficiencies and optimize their operations to meet sustainability goals. The value generated from VeChain's initiatives is evident in the increased consumer trust and engagement. Companies using VeChain's blockchain solutions have reported improved brand loyalty, as consumers are more inclined to support businesses that demonstrate a commitment to sustainability. Additionally, the transparency offered by the blockchain platform helps organizations comply with regulations and avoid penalties, leading to enhanced operational efficiency and cost savings. VeChain's innovative application of AI and blockchain technologies demonstrates the potential for these tools to transform sustainability assurance practices across various industries. By providing transparency and accountability in supply chains, VeChain fosters a culture of sustainability that benefits both businesses and consumers.

Microsoft (Established 1975): Microsoft, a global technology leader, has made significant strides in integrating AI and blockchain technologies into its sustainability initiatives. The company's commitment to achieving carbon neutrality by 2030 drives its innovative approach to sustainability, leveraging advanced technologies to enhance its environmental performance. In 2021, Microsoft collaborated with various organizations to launch the "Carbon Trust" initiative, which utilizes blockchain technology to track carbon credits. This initiative enables companies to buy and sell verified carbon credits transparently, ensuring that sustainability claims are credible. By employing AI to assess and validate carbon offsets, Microsoft enhances the reliability of carbon credit trading.

Additionally, Microsoft has developed tools that utilize AI to analyse data related to energy consumption and emissions across its operations. These tools empower businesses to optimize resource utilization and reduce their environmental impact, aligning with sustainability objectives. The value generated from Microsoft's sustainability efforts is substantial. The integration of AI in monitoring and reporting processes allows the company to optimize resource utilization, leading to reduced operational costs. The blockchain platform enhances trust among stakeholders, providing verifiable data regarding carbon credits. Microsoft's initiatives not only bolster its reputation as a responsible corporate citizen but also set a standard for other organizations seeking to enhance their sustainability assurance practices. Microsoft's proactive use of AI and blockchain technologies in its sustainability efforts highlights the potential for technology to drive meaningful change in environmental practices. By enhancing transparency and accountability, Microsoft positions itself as a leader in promoting sustainable business operations.

Walmart (Established 1962): Walmart, one of the largest retail corporations globally, has made significant investments in sustainability assurance through the application of AI and blockchain technologies. The company's commitment to sustainable sourcing and operational efficiency has led to innovative initiatives aimed at enhancing transparency in its supply chain. In 2018, Walmart launched a blockchain initiative to improve food safety and traceability in its supply chain. By utilizing blockchain technology, Walmart can track the journey of food products from farm to store, ensuring they meet safety and sustainability standards. This capability allows the company to identify the source of contamination rapidly, reducing the time required to address food safety issues.

Walmart also employs AI analytics to optimize inventory management and reduce waste. By analysing consumer demand patterns, Walmart can make informed decisions regarding inventory levels, leading to improved efficiency and sustainability in its operations. The value generated by Walmart's sustainability initiatives is significant. By enhancing transparency in its supply chain, Walmart fosters consumer trust and loyalty. The integration of AI has resulted in cost savings and improved operational efficiency, contributing to the company's overall sustainability goals. Walmart's leadership in sustainability assurance not only strengthens its brand reputation but also sets a benchmark for other retailers in the industry. Walmart's innovative use of AI and blockchain technologies in its sustainability practices underscores the potential for technology to drive positive change in the retail sector. By enhancing transparency and accountability in its supply chain, Walmart is well-positioned to meet the demands of environmentally conscious consumers.

Coca-Cola (Established 1886): Coca-Cola has made significant strides toward sustainability through innovative initiatives that leverage AI and blockchain technologies. The company's commitment to responsible sourcing and environmental stewardship is exemplified by its "World Without Waste" initiative, launched in 2018. Coca-Cola has partnered with the blockchain platform Everledger to enhance the traceability of its supply chain, particularly in the sourcing of sugar. This initiative allows the company to verify the sustainability of its sugar supply, ensuring compliance with environmental and social standards. The integration of blockchain technology enhances transparency, enabling consumers to trace the origins of their beverages.

Additionally, Coca-Cola utilizes AI analytics to optimize packaging and reduce waste. By analysing data related to consumer behaviour and production processes, the company can make informed decisions that align with its sustainability goals. The value generated by Coca-Cola's sustainability initiatives is evident in enhanced consumer trust and brand loyalty. By leveraging blockchain technology, the company can substantiate its sustainability claims, fostering confidence among stakeholders. The use of AI in optimizing operations leads to cost savings and improved efficiency, reinforcing Coca-Cola's commitment to responsible business practices. Coca-Cola's innovative use of AI and blockchain technologies demonstrates the potential for these tools to drive sustainability in the beverage industry. By enhancing transparency and accountability in its supply chain, Coca-Cola sets a standard for other companies in the sector.

Tesla (Established 2003): Tesla, a leader in electric vehicles and renewable energy solutions, is committed to sustainability through innovative technologies. The company's initiatives focus on reducing carbon emissions and promoting sustainable energy practices. Tesla has implemented AI technologies to optimize battery performance and enhance energy efficiency in its vehicles. The integration of AI enables real-time monitoring and predictive analytics, allowing Tesla to improve its electric vehicle technology continuously. Additionally, Tesla's advancements in solar energy solutions promote the use of renewable resources, furthering its sustainability goals. Tesla has also explored the use of blockchain for tracking carbon credits associated with its electric vehicle production. By ensuring transparency in carbon offset practices, Tesla enhances the credibility of its sustainability claims.

The value generated from Tesla's sustainability initiatives is substantial. The company's commitment to electric vehicles positions it as a leader in the automotive industry, attracting environmentally conscious consumers. The use of AI in optimizing energy consumption and battery performance leads to cost savings and improved operational efficiency. Tesla's innovative integration of AI and blockchain technologies underscores the potential for these tools to drive sustainability in the automotive sector. By enhancing transparency and accountability in its practices, Tesla is well-positioned to lead the transition to a more sustainable future.

Procter & Gamble (Established 1837): Procter & Gamble (P&G) has established itself as a leader in sustainability through its commitment to responsible sourcing and environmental stewardship. The company's initiatives leverage AI and blockchain technologies to enhance its sustainability assurance processes. P&G has implemented a blockchain-based platform to improve the traceability of its supply chain, particularly in the sourcing of palm oil. By ensuring that its palm oil is sourced sustainably, P&G minimizes its environmental impact and promotes ethical practices within its supply chain. The integration of blockchain technology enhances transparency, enabling consumers to verify the sustainability of P&G's products.

AI is utilized within P&G to analyse data related to product performance and consumer behaviour. This data-driven approach enables the company to optimize its operations and reduce waste, aligning with its sustainability objectives. The value generated from P&G's sustainability initiatives is evident in increased consumer trust and engagement. By leveraging blockchain technology, the company enhances the credibility of its sustainability claims, fostering confidence among stakeholders. Additionally, AI-driven analytics lead to improved efficiency and cost savings, reinforcing P&G's commitment to responsible sourcing. P&G's innovative use of AI and blockchain technologies demonstrates the potential for these tools to drive sustainability in the consumer goods industry. By enhancing transparency and accountability in its practices, P&G sets a standard for responsible business operations.

3.5. Cases of Companies in Real-World Implementations Combining AI and Blockchain for Sustainability Assurance, Such as Renewable Energy Tracking or Eco-Friendly Agriculture

The real-world cases where companies have successfully integrated AI and blockchain to ensure sustainability, focusing on renewable energy tracking, eco-friendly agriculture, and ethical supply chain management.

Power Ledger: Real-Time Renewable Energy Tracking: Power Ledger, an Australian technology company, has pioneered a platform that leverages AI and blockchain to enable real-time tracking of renewable energy generation and consumption. Using blockchain, Power Ledger records each energy transaction between producers and consumers, creating a decentralized energy marketplace where users can buy and sell renewable energy directly. AI algorithms analyse energy consumption patterns, optimize energy flow, and manage peak demands, helping to reduce reliance on non-renewable sources. This AI-powered analysis enables accurate demand forecasts, enhancing the efficiency and reliability of the energy grid. Power Ledger's model has been implemented in Australia, Japan, and the United States, providing communities and businesses with a transparent, efficient system for supporting renewable energy adoption and reducing carbon footprints.

TE-FOOD and Provenance: Blockchain-Verified Sustainable Agriculture: TE-FOOD, a supply chain tracking company, partnered with Provenance to provide traceability solutions for the agriculture industry, using blockchain and AI to verify sustainable and eco-friendly farming practices. TE-FOOD's blockchain records every stage of the agricultural supply chain, from farm to retail, ensuring that data such as harvest conditions, transport, and processing methods are immutable and transparent. AI algorithms within the system monitor environmental data, such as pesticide levels and water usage, allowing for verification of compliance with sustainable farming standards. For example, TE-FOOD's technology has been used in Southeast Asia to verify the sustainable sourcing of products like rice and vegetables, giving consumers confidence in eco-friendly farming practices and empowering farmers to adopt more sustainable approaches.

Iberdrola and FlexiDAO: Verifiable Renewable Energy Certificates: Iberdrola, a global energy company, collaborated with FlexiDAO to implement a blockchain-based system for verifying renewable energy certificates (RECs) in real time. This system tracks every kilowatt-hour of green energy from production to consumption, allowing Iberdrola's corporate clients to ensure that their energy sources are genuinely renewable. Blockchain ensures that RECs cannot be duplicated or tampered with, while AI-powered analytics optimize energy usage patterns, forecast demand, and detect anomalies. By using these certificates, Iberdrola's customers can confidently showcase their commitment to renewable energy, as the system provides verifiable evidence of renewable energy consumption, which is increasingly important for regulatory compliance and investor relations.

Unilever and GreenToken: Sustainable Palm Oil Sourcing: Unilever collaborated with GreenToken to verify sustainable palm oil sourcing using blockchain and AI, providing transparent information on each supply chain transaction. Blockchain records allow Unilever to trace palm oil from its source to the final product, ensuring the product's origin meets sustainability standards. AI algorithms further analyze supplier data to detect irregularities, flagging any non-compliant sources or practices. Consumers can scan QR codes to access detailed information about the product's journey, from cultivation to final packaging. This verification process has been instrumental in reducing deforestation and promoting eco-friendly agricultural practices in palm oil production, positioning Unilever as a leader in sustainable sourcing.

Ripe.io: Blockchain-Enabled Eco-Friendly Agriculture Verification: Ripe.io, a U.S.-based agritech company, uses blockchain and AI to bring transparency to food production and promote eco-friendly agriculture. By employing blockchain, Ripe.io tracks and verifies each step of the produce journey, from growth conditions on the farm to transport and retail. AI applications analyse environmental factors such as soil health, water usage, and pest control practices, ensuring these metrics align with sustainable agriculture standards. This verification helps farmers implement eco-friendly practices while giving consumers transparency regarding their food's origin and environmental impact. Ripe.io's technology is particularly valuable in the organic and sustainably sourced produce market, where transparency and trust are paramount for consumers.

Siemens and LO3 Energy: Community-Level Renewable Energy Verification: Siemens, in partnership with LO3 Energy, has implemented a blockchain-based platform that enables community-level verification of renewable energy sources. This initiative provides local residents and businesses access to a transparent energy market where they can track and verify the origin of their electricity in real-time. Blockchain ensures all transactions within the community's energy network are transparent and tamper-proof, while AI algorithms help forecast energy demand and optimize the allocation of resources. This setup has been implemented in several pilot projects in the U.S. and Germany, empowering communities to actively support renewable energy while reducing dependency on traditional power grids.

These companies exemplify how AI and blockchain can create verifiable and transparent systems for sustainability assurance, addressing the challenges of greenwashing, inefficiencies, and trust deficits across industries from agriculture to energy. By leveraging real-time data and immutable records, these solutions help promote sustainable practices, meet regulatory standards, and drive consumer confidence in sustainability claims.

IV. SOLUTIONS AND RECOMMENDATIONS

To address challenges such as data security and implementation costs, companies should consider incremental adoption strategies, starting with pilot programs to test AI and blockchain integration. Additionally, partnerships with technology providers and increased employee training on digital tools are recommended to facilitate smoother transitions. Regulatory frameworks should also be enhanced to support and guide companies in adopting these technologies responsibly.

V. FUTURE RESEARCH DIRECTIONS

Future research could investigate the long-term impacts of AI and blockchain on sustainability assurance and explore region-specific regulatory requirements and challenges. Comparative studies on the effectiveness of different AI and blockchain applications across industries would also provide valuable insights.

VI. IMPLICATIONS OF THE STUDY ON ACADEMIA AND INDUSTRY

For academia, this study provides a foundation for exploring new research areas in sustainability assurance technology and encourages interdisciplinary studies involving technology, business ethics, and environmental science. In industry, the findings underscore the need for companies to adopt cutting-edge technologies to meet stakeholder expectations, providing practical insights for businesses striving to enhance their sustainability reporting and assurance practices.

VII. CONCLUSION

AI and blockchain represent promising solutions for enhancing the transparency, accuracy, and accountability of sustainability assurance processes. As companies and regulators increasingly demand reliable sustainability reporting, these technologies provide the tools needed to meet these expectations efficiently. By addressing existing challenges and adopting a proactive approach to technology integration, organizations can better align with sustainability goals and contribute to a more transparent global economy. This study highlights the significant potential of AI and blockchain in sustainability assurance, urging further exploration and adoption of these technologies across industries.

REFERENCES

Abdulla, A., Wang, B., Qian, F., Kee, T., Blasiak, A., Ong, Y. H., Hooi, L., Parekh, F., Soriano, R., Olinger, G. G., Keppo, J., Hardesty, C. L., Chow, E. K., Do, D., & Ding, X. (2020). Project IDentif. AI: Harnessing artificial intelligence to rapidly optimize combination therapy development for infectious disease intervention. *Advanced Therapeutics*, 3(7), 2000034. DOI: 10.1002/adtp.202000034 PMID: 32838027

Balaji, K. (2024). Harnessing AI for Financial Innovations: Pioneering the Future of Financial Services. In Jermsittiparsert, K., Phongkraphan, N., & Lekhavichit, N. (Eds.), *Modern Management Science Practices in the Age of AI* (91–122). IGI Global., DOI: 10.4018/979-8-3693-6720-9.ch004

Balaji, K. (2024). The Nexus of Smart Contracts and Digital Twins Transforming Green Finance With Automated Transactions in Investment Agreements: Leveraging Smart Contracts for Green Investment Agreements and Automated Transactions. In Jafar, S., Rodriguez, R., Kannan, H., Akhtar, S., & Plugmann, P. (Eds.), *Harnessing Blockchain-Digital Twin Fusion for Sustainable Investments* (287–315). IGI Global., DOI: 10.4018/979-8-3693-1878-2.ch012

Balaji, K. (2024) Artificial Intelligence for Enhanced Anti-Money Laundering and Asset Recovery: A New Frontier in Financial Crime Prevention. In *2024 Second International Conference on Intelligent Cyber Physical Systems and Internet of Things (ICoICI)*. Coimbatore, India. 1010-1016, DOI: 10.1109/ICoICI62503.2024.10696100

Balaji, K. (2025). AI as a Game Changer: How Digital Entrepreneurs Are Redefining Business Practices. In Tunio, M. (Ed.), *Improving Entrepreneurial Processes Through Advanced AI* (21–48). IGI Global., DOI: 10.4018/979-8-3693-1495-1.ch002

Bellagarda, J. S., & Abu-Mahfouz, A. M. (2022). An updated survey on the convergence of distributed ledger technology and artificial intelligence: Current state, major challenges and future direction. *IEEE Access : Practical Innovations, Open Solutions*, 10, 50774–50793. DOI: 10.1109/ACCESS.2022.3173297

. Dohale, V., Akarte, M., Gunasekaran, A., & Verma, P. (2022). Exploring the role of artificial intelligence in building production resilience: Learnings from the COVID-19 pandemic. *International Journal of Production Research*, 62(15), 5472-5488. .2022.2127961DOI: 10.1080/00207543

Dora, M., Kumar, A., Mangla, S. K., Pant, A., & Kamal, M. M. (2022). Critical success factors influencing artificial intelligence adoption in food supply chains. *International Journal of Production Research*, 60(14), 4621–4640. DOI: 10.1080/00207543.2021.1959665

Hoang, T. D., Ky, N. M., Thuong, N. T. N., Nhan, H. Q., & Ngan, N. V. C. (2022). Artificial intelligence in pollution control and management: Status and future prospects. In Ong, H. L., Doong, R., Naguib, R., Lim, C. P., & Nagar, A. K. (Eds.), *Artificial intelligence and environmental sustainability: Challenges and solutions in the era of Industry 4.0* (23–43). Springer., DOI: 10.1007/978-981-19-1434-8_2

Hong, Z., & Xiao, K. (2024). Digital economy structuring for sustainable development: The role of blockchain and artificial intelligence in improving supply chain and reducing negative environmental impacts. *Scientific Reports*, 14(1), 3912. Advance online publication. DOI: 10.1038/s41598-024-53760-3 PMID: 38365912

Indrasari, M., Syamsudin, N., & Tampubolon, L. R. R. U. (2024). Enhancing SME product brand equity in the digital age as strategic approaches in the era of artificial intelligence. *International Journal of Business, Law, and Education*, 5(1), 1139–1152. DOI: 10.56442/ijble.v5i1.512

Jabeur, S. B., Ballouk, H., Mefteh-Wali, S., & Omri, A. (2022). Forecasting the macrolevel determinants of entrepreneurial opportunities using artificial intelligence models. *Technological Forecasting and Social Change*, 175. *Article*, 121353, 121353. DOI: 10.1016/j.techfore.2021

Jagatheesaperumal, S. K., Rahouti, M., Ahmad, K., Al-Fuqaha, A., & Guizani, M. (2021). The duo of artificial intelligence and big data for industry 4.0: Applications, techniques, challenges, and future research directions. *IEEE Internet of Things Journal*, 9(15), 12861–12885. DOI: 10.1109/JIOT.2021.3139827

Kazeem, K. O., Olawumi, T. O., & Osunsanmi, T. (2023). Roles of artificial intelligence and machine learning in enhancing construction processes and sustainable communities. *Buildings (Basel, Switzerland)*, 13(8), 2061. Advance online publication. DOI: 10.3390/buildings13082061

Nuseir, M., Basheer, M. F., & Aljumah, A. (2020). Antecedents of entrepreneurial intentions in smart city of Neom Saudi Arabia: Does the entrepreneurial education on artificial intelligence matter? *Cogent Business & Management*, 7(1). *Article*, 1825041, 1825041. DOI: 10.1080/23311975.2020

Obaideen, K., Abdelkareem, M. A., Wilberforce, T., Elsaid, K., Sayed, E. T., Maghrabie, H. M., & Olabi, A. G. (2022). Biogas role in achievement of the sustainable development goals: Evaluation, challenges, and guidelines. *Journal of the Taiwan Institute of Chemical Engineers*, 131, 104207. Advance online publication. DOI: 10.1016/j.jtice.2022.104207

Ohalete, N. C., Aderibigbe, A. O., Ani, E. C., Ohenhen, P. E., Daraojimba, D. O., & Odulaja, B. A.Nzubechukwu Chukwudum OhaleteAdebayo Olusegun Aderibig-beEmmanuel Chigozie AniPeter Efosa OhenhenDonald Obinna DaraojimbaBukola A. Odulaja. (2023). AI-driven solutions in renewable energy: A review of data science applications in solar and wind energy optimization. *World Journal of Advanced Research and Reviews*, 20(3), 401–417. DOI: 10.30574/wjarr.2023.20.3.2433

Rane, N., Choudhary, S., & Rane, J. (2023). Sustainable tourism development using leading-edge artificial intelligence (AI), blockchain, internet of things (IoT), augmented reality (AR) and virtual reality (VR) technologies. *SSRN*. DOI: 10.2139/ssrn.4642605

Sharma, S., Singh, G., Sharma, C. S., & Kapoor, S. (2024). Artificial intelligence in Indian higher education institutions: A quantitative study on adoption and perceptions. *International Journal of System Assurance Engineering and Management*. Advance online publication. DOI: 10.1007/s13198-023-02193-8

Srivastava, A., & Maity, R. (2023). Assessing the potential of AI–ML in urban climate change adaptation and sustainable development. *Sustainability (Basel)*, 15(23), 16461. Advance online publication. DOI: 10.3390/su152316461

Taghikhah, F., Erfani, E., Bakhshayeshi, I., Tayari, S., Karatopouzis, A., & Hanna, B. (2022). Artificial intelligence and sustainability: Solutions to social and environmental challenges. In Asadnia, M., Razmjou, A., & Beheshti, A. (Eds.), *Artificial intelligence and data science in environmental sensing* (93–108). Academic Press. DOI: 10.1016/B978-0-323-90508-4.00006-X

KEY TERMS AND DEFINITIONS

1. **AI-Driven Data Analytics - Uses AI to analyze sustainability data:** generating actionable insights for forecasting and decision-making.
2. **Machine Learning Algorithms - Automate the analysis of large datasets:** identifying trends and predicting environmental impacts for improved sustainability.
3. **Natural Language Processing (NLP) - Analyzes text from reports:** media, and public sources to gauge sustainability-related sentiment and trends.
4. **Computer Vision Technology - Employs AI in remote sensing to monitor land use:** pollution, and deforestation for real-time environmental tracking.
5. **Emission Tracking Systems - Uses AI to track and manage emissions data:** enabling organizations to meet regulatory and sustainability goals.
6. **Blockchain-Based Traceability - Provides decentralized:** tamper-proof tracking of products through supply chains to verify sustainable sourcing.

7. **Decentralized Ledgers - Records sustainability data in a secure:** unalterable format, enhancing transparency across the supply chain.

Chapter 8
Impact of Investor Sentiments on Stock Returns in India:
An ESG Perspective

Avi Anand
https://orcid.org/0009-0002-4423-6405
Christ University, India

Amit Kumar
Christ University, India

ABSTRACT

This book chapter aims to explain how the investor sentiments in India impacts the returns of ESG stocks, further investigating how the stocks return gets affected positively or negatively by the behavior of investors after examining the ESG reports of a company. This study also provides a comparative analysis about the performance of ESG stocks over Non ESG stocks in the Indian Market. This includes understanding about the increased focus on ESG metrics which leads to superior stock performance, lower risk, or enhanced investor confidence compared to non-ESG investments. Hence, it provides us with a holistic picture of Indian market through an ESG perspective.

DOI: 10.4018/979-8-3373-0117-4.ch008

1. INTRODUCTION

Integrating environmental, social and governance metrics into investment has gained attraction among the investors and asset management institutions in India. ESG factors have significantly shaped the investment strategies among the investors. Indian businesses are driven to demonstrate their dedication to sustainability and ethical business practices in order to draw these investors and obtain foreign finance. The investors are more attracted towards the companies which are working towards environmentally friendly practices, raising awareness regarding climate change and reducing carbon emission. The investors also find how a company efficiently manages the resources which cause less pollution to the environment along with maximizing waste management practices. Investors pay close attention to how a company minimizes harm to the ecosystem and takes care of wildlife while protecting nature. Investors want to know how companies handle social issues within their operations and throughout their supply chains, which includes their fair wages, providing a safe working environment and having policies against discrimination. They keep a check on how a company manages a supportive and inclusive workspace, which also maintains a healthy work-life balance. Investors appreciate companies that actively engage with stakeholders, respond to community needs, and aim to create value that goes beyond just making money. Investors value companies with a well-structured, diverse, and independent board because they can better represent the interests of shareholders and provide good strategic guidance. They also evaluate whether executive incentives encourage sustainable performance and responsible behaviour. The companies should have strong shareholders' rights and transparent practice to gain trust and accountability of the investors, highlighting certain ESG considerations that are prominent amongst the investors.

The big question is whether investors are bothered about this sustainability-related information privilege. The history of financial crises and stock market crashes has proven the dominant role of investor sentiment on asset pricing and stock markets' efficiency, raising doubt on the standard finance models where rational investors equate capital market prices to the present value of expected future cash flows. Investor sentiments have been widely researched in connection with the stock market, equity market, cryptocurrency market and the green industry stock prices. Traditional stock market theories have explained market dynamics, but they did not consider viewing it from the outlook of investor sentiment. Moreover, they failed to explain the different behaviours of the investors in the stock market that influenced stock returns. Investors' sentiment is an important element of the stock market because it contributes to regular fluctuations in the stock price which creates ambiguity about future returns on investments. There have been various changes in the Indian financial market, especially in the basic structure, for example, shifting from a savings-oriented economy to an investment-oriented economy.(H & Rishad, 2020). Nowadays, the investors are more inclined towards investing among the ESG stocks.

Investor Sentiments basically impacts on the trade volume, market price and return on investment of a particular security. An investor analyses the ESG reports of a company by considering all the key aspects and accordingly takes a decision. ESG information influences investment allocation decisions in an emerging economy. It was concluded that the link between a firm's financial performance and ESG is still inconclusive.

1.1 Aims and Objectives

This research aims to develop an understanding in how investor sentiment impacts the stock returns of ESG companies in the Indian stock market. There has been a global interest for investing in the ESG stocks that are affected by the general behaviour of an investor. This study seeks to find the effect on the ESG stocks which are impacted in a positive or negative way by the sentiments of an Indian investor. The question that arises is how the ESG disclosure of the company changes the mood or emotion of an investor in taking risks and trading of a security.

The objective of this study is to analyze how variations in investor sentiment impact the returns of ESG stocks in the Indian market. This includes understanding whether increased focus on ESG metrics leads to superior stock performance, lower risk, or enhanced investor confidence compared to non-ESG investments. It also aims to find whether ESG stocks truly outperform non-ESG stocks in India in terms of returns or risk. This aims to do a comparative analysis between ESG vs. Non-ESG stocks which attracts the investors in order to gain more return in investment

This study holds a relevance for investors, companies and policymakers by offering an overall picture about the ESG metrics affecting stock performance and investors' confidence in the evolving Indian market.

2. LITERATURE REVIEW

Investor sentiment is the group psyche or psychology of market participants that has been proven to affect asset pricing, trading volume, and volatility. H. P. and Rishad (2020) discussed how irrational investor behavior determines the stock market volatility in India. The study used some of the most advanced econometric techniques such as GARCH framework and Granger causality tests to prove how changes in sentiment contribute significantly to market instability.

For example, euphoria in upswing cycles results in the overpriced value of assets, whereas bearish sentiments in downward cycles results in sharp liquidations. When retail investors are a large number like in the case of countries such as India, sentiment-driven behavior is likely to be exacerbated. Retail investors do not have similar behaviours as the institutions, and it is more likely to follow short-term market news, emotional triggers, and speculation-based fads and this makes the market extremely sensitive.

The study further continues to detail the implications for policymakers and market participants: On the one hand, policymakers must view it as an important regulatory input in stabilizing the market. On the other, investors should take into consideration its elements to reduce biases in their decisions.

2.1 Behavioural Finance Framework

Conventional finance theories, like the Efficient Market Hypothesis (EMH), assume that asset prices incorporate all information available and, therefore, assume rational behavior on the part of investors. The real-world market dynamics frequently contradict this assumption, so behavioral finance emerged as a new framework. Behavioral finance studies psychological biases, emotions, and social influences affecting investor behavior. Some biases are:

Herding Behavior: Investors fail to understand fundamentals, hence blindly follow market trends, forming price bubbles or crashes. Overconfidence: Overestimation of ability to predict movement thus calls for more risk taking. Loss Aversion: Fear of losses is greater than the desire for equivalent gains and causes irrational behavior during market downturns.

These biases are particularly relevant in ESG investing. Investors, for instance, might over-invest in a high-ESG stock during the environmental awareness time, thereby inflating valuations. Overconfidence may also lead to underestimation of risks because they feel safe with ESG investments, hence a balance is needed.

2.2 ESG Performance and Financial Outcomes

The increasing significance of ESG metrics reflects the trend of sustainability in investment decision-making. Yin, Li, and Su (2023) considered the effect of ESG performance on returns on stocks by focusing on Chinese firms between 2011 and 2020. Applying a fixed-effects panel model, they revealed that higher ESG-scoring firms attract long-term investors, thereby increasing financial stability and reducing stock volatility.

The authors pointed to several transmission mechanisms whereby the ESG practices have financial implications:

Improved Investor Trust: ESG transparency reduces information asymmetry, which allows them to make better decisions. A: Lower risk premiums High scores on the ESG indicators have implications for lowering several components of perceived riskiness over these investments.

During Crisis: ESG-focused firms show resilience and stability during recession due to their sustainability and ethical governance. Although conducted in China, such a study is relevant in India where pressures of regulations and investor preferences drive its adoption of ESGs. Implications of the result suggest an improvement in enhancing ESG information disclosure mechanisms for building investor confidence in emerging markets.

2.3 Global Empirical Evidence on ESG Investing

Several international studies have validated the financial advantages of ESG investing. In this regard, Cheng et al. (2014) showed that companies with high ESG practices involve lower capital costs and efficient operations. This study provides evidence that sustainability initiatives align not only with ethical factors but also contribute to profits.

Friede, Busch, and Bassen (2015) conducted a meta-analysis on over 2,000 studies on ESG performance and financial outcomes. Results showed that 90 percent of the studies found a nonnegative relationship, with most indicating positive correlation. This further supports the notion that ESG integration is both a moral and financial advantage. Fatemi, Glaum, and Kaiser (2018) state that ESG practice gives reputation advantages. According to their research, companies that have high ESG scores are more attractive to loyal investors when the economy is in decline because such investors perceive alignment between ESG firms and long-term societal and environmental goals.

2.4 Investor Sentiment and ESG Integration

The interaction between sentiment and ESG metrics is an emerging field of research. Some studies suggest that investor sentiment can act as a multiplier on the effect of ESG initiatives. ESG-focused companies, for instance, during bull runs are generally hailed as safer and in accordance with the global sustainability trend, causing the stock prices to surge. Instead, they may perform better than non-ESG stocks when investor sentiment is negative, owing to their perception as more stable and ethically appealing.

These studies analyzing the dynamic interplay of these factors have revealed the feedback mechanism between sentiment and ESG performance. Strong ESG disclosures augment investor sentiment, increasing stock returns. This feedback loop is particularly important when considering investor preferences, which could be evolving fast in emerging markets such as India.

2.5 Relevance to Indian Market

Unique market features in India present an excellent context for studying the play between investor sentiment and ESG performance: a significant retail participation in the Indian stock market where retail investors dictate the markets and retail investors are more susceptible to following sentiment while also more likely to fall prey to behavioral biases in their decision making, thus exaggerating the impact of sentiment on outcomes in the market. Mandatory CSR spending has given a regulatory push in increasing the awareness of CSR on the part of the corporate and the investors alike, while SEBI has enforced ESG reporting. ESG reporting is increasingly aimed at standardizing and integrating ESG practices within investing.

Volatile Market Conditions: Indian markets are sensitive to the global economic changes and domestic policy change. This market remains behavioral wherein sentiment-driven behaviors often sink deeper than fundamental analysis.

2.6 The Challenges With Gathering Sentiment With ESG Matters are as Follows

Unequal competition: The variable methods of rating, for instance, among various rating agencies, hinder comparisons between companies, thus delaying timely decision-making by the investors.

Lack of stability belief toward ESG stocks: If speculative buying or speculative selling sentiment-based behaviours affect the price, this erodes the impact of the long-term focus on returns that many investors assign to these ESG stocks, such perceptions hamper the development of ESG stocks.

These would require a better teamwork approach toward formulating a standard on ESG reporting frameworks, educating investors on the financial benefits of sustainability, and developing tools for real-time sentiment analysis.

It brings to light potentially new areas of research in ESG, and sentiment driven by recent technological and methodological advances:

Artificial Intelligence and Machine Learning: These techniques are used to analyze unstructured data from social media or news articles, revealing investor sentiment in close to real-time.

Sector-Specific ESG analysis: Knowledge of how ESG performance is gained across a sector would allow for greater insight as to its financial impact. An example may be environmental issues which could be more impactful in energy-intensive sectors, versus social aspects which would be dominant in labor-intensive sectors.

Cross-market comparisons: Comparative studies introduce how cultural, regulatory, and economic differences will influence the relationship between ESG and investment practices from developed to emerging markets.

One of the major issues covered in recent financial literature is relating ESG scores with stock returns. There are repeated findings showing that those stocks having high ESG ratings give higher realized returns as compared to those having low ESG ratings. The empirical evidence relating to the U.S. stock market further supports this phenomenon and puts the proposition forth that the positive returns from ESG stocks might not necessarily be the result of the risk-return paradigm, but because investors are seeking sustainability. One such explanation is the demand-driven discount rate channel, whereby investor preferences for ESG characteristics increase stock valuations, which in turn lowers the discount rates. This is supported by models from Fama and French (2007) and Pastor et al. (2020), which relate ESG demand to financial outcomes. Contrary to this, the risk channel theory, which argues that ESG stocks decrease financial risks such as reputational damage, is not supported by strong empirical evidence.

Seminal works, such as Kempf and Osthoff (2007) and El Ghoul et al. (2011), offer consistent evidence that ESG portfolios exhibit positive realized returns but explain the puzzle mainly through changes in investor demand rather than cash-flow improvement. This paper highlights the change in the understanding of the investment dynamics driven by ESG.

ESG factors increasingly underline stock return; however, most of the literature is within the framework of socially responsible investing. Much research has classified companies that follow ESG better-performing on risk management and enjoying greater investor confidence. This argument has been analyzed through portfolio performance, the interactions of their stock prices, and constructing an ESG index (La Rorre, 2019).

Mixed results are reported in the literature on portfolio performance. Some, such as Gloßner (2018), argue that ignoring ESG risks can negatively affect long-term performance, while others find little effects depending on horizons. Similarly, the impact of ESG on stock prices is still debated. The research shows that ESG ratings do have an impact on valuations, but the effect is heterogeneous across industries and depends on market-specific factors.

One of the common issues in the ESG scoring methodologies has been the lack of uniformity of metrics and evaluation frameworks which leads to discrepancies. Now, on one hand this is a red flag if it is standardized.

In summary, it appears that ESG factors have an association with positive effects on the returns of some companies' shares, though in no way general or direct. Further research should be done to explain these dynamics and regional and sector-specific nuances.

2.7 Exploring the Nexus Between ESG Ratings and Stock Returns

Insights from Indian Markets "Environmental, Social, and Governance (ESG) as factors in investment decisions are gaining ground globally and in India. ESG investing aligns financial goals with sustainability goals. The study of ESG ratings reveals the importance of metrics in measuring the commitment of companies toward the adoption of sustainability metrics of environmental stewardship, ethical governance, and social responsibility. Numerous studies were found which indicate an inconclusive relationship between ESG performance and financial returns. While the better ESG scores are sometimes related to profitability and against risks resilience, other studies have identified inconsistencies in the methodology of these ratings and greenwashing (Dhuri, 2024).

ESG mutual funds have emerged as a strong instrument in India for responsible investing while its financial performance is widely debated. Studies indicate the key focus on governance. Environmental and social metrics show relatively less importance. Preferences of sectors are technology and finance. It reflects the broader market trends. The regulatory framework in India, like Business Responsibility and Sustainability Reporting in SEBI, faces challenges at its ESG ecosystem-the lack of standardization as well as low investor knowledge.

Thus, while ESG investments open avenues for alignment with sustainability objectives, their financial implications necessitate balanced assessments of traditional metrics and scores of ESG to strengthen decision-making.

2.8 The Role of ESG Factors in Shaping Financial Performance and Investor Sentiment in India

Academic and practical interest in the link between ESG factors and financial performance has been noted in India. ESG investing combines sustainability with profitability for corporate enterprise and, more importantly, puts a strong emphasis on accountability and ethical governance. A panel study of firms quoted on NSE 100 ESG Index shows that performance based on ESG enhances profitability measured by ROA and the firm's valuation as gauged through Tobin's Q ratio. Companies with better ESG scores have strong operational practices, which help manage and engage with stakeholders, thereby improving long-term shareholder value (Stotz, O. 2021).

2.9 ESG Considerations Into the Workings of the Company in India

Indian companies are slowly inducting the ESG considerations into the workings of the company, largely because of the extant regulatory frameworks, such as mandatory CSR expenditure under the Companies Act (2013). ESG practices are, however, quite heterogeneous in terms of their ability to generate stock returns. For instance, some companies are better financially due to sustainability efforts, but the ESG disclosure is quite abstract from the performance of equities. The reasons are because metrics are not standardized, limited disclosure practices exist, and sectoral impacts are uneven.

The study emphasizes the importance of comprehensive ESG frameworks and transparency in building investor confidence. As ESG integration continues to evolve, understanding how investor sentiment interacts with ESG-driven financial strategies for sustainable market growth in India is vital (Dalal, 2019).

2.10 The Emerging Landscape of ESG Investing in India: Impact on Stock Returns and Investor Sentiment

ESG, or Environmental, Social, and Governance investing, has become a major phenomenon in India, similar to trends worldwide about sustainable financial practices. With the onset of COVID-19, ESG-based mutual funds have risen with high numbers, as investors increasingly look beyond the financials and pay attention to sustainability, governance, and social responsibility alongside the returns. Currently, India offers over 23 ESG funds, moving forward towards responsible investing.

There are diversified landscapes relating to the performance of these mutual funds regarding ESG. Funds have historically outperformed benchmarks, therefore providing very good risk-adjusted return, as for instance, the historical performance of Quant ESG Equity Fund, but mixed because of higher expenses and poor management, on the other hand, regarding the SBI Magnum Equity ESG Fund. Sharpe Ratio, Treynor Ratio, and Jensen Alpha must be paid specific attention to and are highly emphasized return and risk considerations.

However, the investment in ESG in India faces several challenges, such as investor awareness and inconsistent reporting frameworks. Despite all these challenges, the better long-term performance of ESG funds over traditional investments presents a huge opportunity for sustainable financial growth. This emerging trend also underscores the increasing role of investor sentiment in shaping the trajectory of ESG investments in India (Rabindra Bharti, 2023).

2.11 Investor Sentiment and Stock Returns in India

An ESG perspective sentiment trends along with their implications on returns to stock have emerged as latest buzzwords in the financial literature on sustainable investment focusing more than anything else, it would appear, on the theme of ESG. Facts do indeed seem to indicate the promising nature of ESG for assessing financial performance within an ethical and sustainable context. Indian markets, as an emerging economy, pose unique problems that include volatility at a high level, regulatory complexities, and limited transparency for the relationship between sentiment of investors, ESG scores, and stock returns.

Researches show that higher ESG scores are generally linked with more efficient risk management and stable potential returns globally, but evidence from India is not as uniform. Undoubtedly, ESG practices have volatility reduction but the predictability in terms of return remains unknown as there is inadequate data and a lack of awareness among investors. Institutional investors and public opinion have focused their attention on ESG issues. Hence, a movement has taken place towards sustainable portfolios.

Despite the hurdles, ESG-focused strategies are increasingly shaping the investment scenario in India. This pattern highlights the necessity of enhanced ESG reporting standards along with real-time data availability and investor education to fully leverage the potential of the ESG elements in aligning the performance of stockholding with sustainable development goals (Meher, 2020).

2.12 Investor Sentiment Role in Determining the Returns of Stocks

Investor sentiment plays a very significant role in determining the returns of stocks, more particularly when it is about an emerging Indian market. This effect is quite massive when seen from an ESG perspective, and for the investors all over the world, it has become much more important now.

Investment sentiment in India often depends on a mix of factors such as the economic policy, what is happening in the global markets, or corporate news.

This attitude finds further meaning in ESG. Good ESG practices by companies increase the confidence of investors, therefore their stocks perform better since such actions are in tune with the values of a new class of socially responsible investors. Stocks, however, crash at an alarming rate when the company fails to meet the expectations of ESG or reports emerge on certain negative issues. These firms in India, that maintain themselves as sustainable ones, defend the credibility and position themselves for a brighter opportunity in the long term where investors trust them, indicate how sentiment and ESG correlate and how ethics and environmental concerns are becoming an even stronger component for financial markets. And most of all, this reflects that it's not just numbers; there is a lot more that makes financial decisions (Kunzimina, 2023).

2.13 Convergence of Investor Sentiment with ESG in India

Convergence of investor sentiment with Environmental, Social and Governance, or ESG criteria has elicited immense attention towards stock market dynamics in India. Since ESG factors remain on an upward curve globally, it is being realized gradually how ESG affects the investor's behavior and India's market outcome.

The sentiment among investors, as shaped by macroeconomic conditions, political events, and market trends, has a direct effect on stock price volatility. Adding ESG to the picture complicates the dynamic, though. Companies that have strong ESG will find more positive investor attention and stability in stock performance, at least. Poor ESG performance or controversy will damage investor confidence, sending stocks into a tailspin.

The Indian market, which is very fast-developing and evolving regulatory, offers fertile ground to study this relationship. ESG-aligned companies in India are perceived as being lower risk and more future-ready compared to global sustainability goals and investor expectations. These perceptions tend to be associated with higher premium stock valuations and better resilience in the case of market downturns. Further research goes on to indicate that ESG disclosure and transparency play the critical role in forming sentiments in positive directions that compel investment flows and then impact market performance.

Building the green future becomes more and more popular worldwide; the interaction between investors' incentive and stock profits in India from an ESG (Environmental, Social and Governance) angle has become very prominent. It has been brought up the investors' behaviors, which stem from their values, social norms, and market trends, which were referred to as the main reasons why they chose the investments that are in line with ESG standards. Sustainability of environmental, social, and governance related practices has strongly influenced market sentiments and investment decisions.

2.14 Significance of the Insight into the Investors' Moods in India

In India, countries interpreting more of the tensor of ESG factors for investment have undergone significant transformations and now, they align financial objectives with ethical issues. Research shows companies with a proven ESG record usually gain investor support. The result is that the company will have a good performance in the stock market with a reduction in risk during the recession. Alternatively, a company with bad ESG practices might turn around and pull the stock down a slope. Such factor attaches ESG to being a risk absorbent as well as a value-added factor in the Indian stock market.

The set of biases that move along the lines of over-cut and bias through herd means makes the situation even more complex in the sentiment-ESG investment relationship. On the one hand, investors may give a small scale of importance to ESG or they may overestimate the issue of ESG. These biases probationers include the cognitive psychological part of psychology with a loss of avoidance and peer effect that is linked to choices in ESG domain.

The adoption of ESG standards by the companies strengthens transparency and accountability along with fueling the long-term needs of investors. Through the implementation of behavioral or ESG speed bumps, the Indian market can create a sustainable growth-oriented board, and responsible investing will be balanced.

The link between the characteristics of ESG along with investors' sentiments and stock returns in India is being explored more lately, particularly in the periods of market instability. Research shows that ESG compliance affects the behaviors of investors and the perceptions of the market despite it being controversial to what its role is in stock returns during crises. Yet, a number of studies claim that eco-friendly companies are highlighted as those who are closer to clients. Their sustainability and transparency commitments, investors' regular preferences to security, are considered a guarantee of their compliance with the requirements. Along with the best input/output parts you will need also to work with the other data to emphasize the input/output sequences, so it will not be a simple task.

Nevertheless, the data from the COVID-19 crisis presented a more complex picture. Indian companies consistently rated for ESG compliance from 2016–2019, compared to their performance in the year 2020 which was a crisis period, were studied and provided unexpected results. Although it was often said that good ESG performance would have protected companies from the downturn during the outbreak, there was almost no difference in stock returns performance of high and low ESG firms. Instead, a key relationship between dividend yield and market performance emerges during the same time. Based on the dividends of high ESG companies during the period, priority was given to the profits overall (Upadhyaya et al, 2023).

The term “ESG irrelevance” is the most common one to be used here, from the philosophical aspect of this phenomenon that ESG compliance is not enough to shield companies from the market through any kind of crisis. Even though it is clear from ESG alignment what the organization's responsibility is and how this can attract ethical investors, ethical behavior in these times might not be enough to be liked by them. For example, covid-19 firms are subject to the short-term stock return to which the mechanism is linked to the lack of fuzzing students while the Purdue Owl can't be blamed for the mistakes non-native students make.

This paper reviews the significance of the insight into the investors' moods (based on information received from both financial and ESG factors), in India. It pinpoints the necessity for further exploration of the interconnection between ESG practices and stock performance under different market conditions. The aforementioned approach is considered so companies and investors can have better operational capacity to maneuver the cobweb of sustainability investments without committing ethical violations and at the same time profitably (Bodhanwala et al, 2023).

2.15 Firms with Good ESG Practices That Help Manage Risk

According to studies, companies that totally follow ESG exhibit lower volatility and a stable payment return, so it has been generally agreed long term about the interest of investors in such activities. For example, firms with good ESG practices that help manage risk while giving some internal benefit to society due to the economic and environmental benefits of these practices. Nevertheless, there is ambiguity regarding the nature of such ESG activities in the Indian context due to the inconsistency in metrics and limited engagement of stakeholders in these activities. Indeed, the empirical findings lend evidence to support the notion regarding corporate governance, social responsibility, and environmental stewardship influencing performance. For example, various initiatives of Reliance Industries in energy conservation, promotion of waste management, and biodiversity conservation are an example of better contribution toward socioeconomic and financial performance due to the ESG framework:

With the rise of ESG investment in India, integration of non-financial criteria into investment decisions will be crucial for achieving transparency and sustainability as well as long-term return in keeping with investor sentiment, market expansion, and sustainability objectives.

Environmental, Social, and Governance (ESG) factors are slowly but surely becoming popular terms in company sustainability and financial performance research. They have come a long way from Corporate Social Responsibility (CSR); thus, principles evolved under ESG are more fitting in the context of environment and governance matters. The literature concerns itself with all those variables of finance as affected by ESG variables: risk, cost of capital, and cash flow. For example, on an aggregation basis, ESG engagement usually leads to lower risk and reduced capital costs, although there are different results based on measurement differences on the ESG regarding metrics measuring firm performance (Xie et al., 2019).

These methodologies largely apply panel regression; there is very much less application of advanced techniques like big-data analytics and machine-learning methods. The effect of industrial and geopolitical on these either completely altruistic or strategic-oriented CSR activities, for example, altruistic define cost-benefit of society while strategic one aligned with financial goals. Besides, disclosures have also enhanced transparency in most cases and confidence in stakeholders, increasing ultimately the value of a firm.

Although given substantial information, however, some still stand in gaps in understanding the long-term causation between the two: ESG initiatives and firm performance. Limitations include that of the database-of- single reference such as Scopus with possible selection bias. Future studies could take into account different data sources and advanced analysis along with contexts such as global realities and national ESG rating. Such studies might take us closer to realizing how much ESG contributes to firms' environmental and financial sustainability improvements while at the same time (Saini et al, 2023).

2.16 Value of Investors and Their Investment Decisions With Respect to ESG Stocks

The elements of sustainable investment are environmental, social, as well as governance (ESG) factors that have endured the traditional notion of investment, aiming to maximize the business shareholder wealth. Now, not only should one consider the maximization of wealth but also the well-being of society and nature (Rose, 2021). Investments in ESG cross $40 trillion across the globe with emerging economies still at the very early stages with respect to funds focusing on ESG. In India, for instance, by the year 2021, the assets under management in India in ESG increased from Rs. 2630 crore in 2019 to more than Rs. 12,300 crore (Business Standard, 2021).

Thus, individual values are considered to be important determinants for individual investment attitudes toward ESG stocks: egoistic values prioritize self-interest and economic gain, in contrast with altruistic values, which look at the betterment of society or the environment (Gatersleben et al., 2012). Some studies, for example, testify to the fact that most individuals prefer investing in ESG stocks during crises as they tend to survive crises better and yield more sustainable returns in the long run (Beloskar & Rao, 2022). More significantly, values provide a critical segue, into behavioral intentions, to bridge cultural and group differences (Han & Yoon, 2015).

The relationship of the ESG metrics to the financial performance has been widely researched, though not yet been conclusive (Revelli & Viviani, 2015). The present research, therefore, proposes the bold attempt to examine the relationship between egoistic as well as altruistic values concerning ESG-investment unlike any other, since such research believes that such investigation would matter in respect to the behavior of investors in India. India is that economy which aspires to grow through sustainable development while industrialization accelerates (Raut et al, 2023).

Nicely structured empirical evidence would remain extremely helpful in regard to ESG performance versus stock returns. The debate still goes on and actually includes both positive (Edmans, 2011; Lins et al., 2017; Albuquerque et al., 2019) as well as negative (Chava, 2014; Bolton and Kacperczyk, 2022) effects. One of the problems pointed out by Pastor et al. (2022) is expected versus realized stock returns, showing that noisy ESG measures indeed dull these relationships.

Disparity among scores from various ESG ratings creates yet another source of noise. The average pairwise correlation over agents is a mind-blowingly low 0.36 (Berg et al., 2022). These differences create a common regression hurdle, or, in other words, cause attenuation bias with respect to the relationship by biasing coefficients toward zero. Only quite recently did studies by Christensen et al. (2021) and Avramov et al. (2022) look at the disequilibrium in ESG ratings and firm level risk premiums but fell short of correcting for measurement noise.

This research is based upon a classic errors-in-variables model in that it involves a 2SLS regression in which one agency's ESG rating is instrumented by ratings from other agencies, thereby diminishing the component of noise and increasing measurement precision. The adjusted coefficients circulate a median change of 2.1 times, indicating that ESG performance will show a more robust relationship with financial outcomes. Increased rows of complementary ESG ratings have proven more robust for model performance as compared to averaging over scores or principal component analysis methodologies. The standard will be most expressive when one benefits from the use of cross-ME ESG ratings to reduce the measurement noise and to strengthen empirical analyses (Florian Berg et al, 2022).

In Tackling the Problem of Noise (2022), aspects regarding environmental, social and governance (ESG) issues are highlighted as the most valued towards making investment decisions and its consequential effects on returns of the stocks. It brings out one of the core problems: the issue of the difference in ESG rating used by various organizations sometimes referred to as "noise in ESG". This rating discrepancy creates a fog within investors which makes it difficult for them to make well-informed decisions in regard to the ESG investment philosophy.

Research to this end indicates that there exists a considerable tradeoff between ESG ratings across authoritative rating agencies due to differences in rating approaches, metrics employed, and rated agencies' bias. A more contradictory aspect of the same situation is that it can also mislead investors who believe such ratings to be reliable sources for judging the sustainability performance of corporations. The article emphasizes that it is not only stock valuation but also the so-called noise in the ESG ratings that distorts the market perception and the volume of investments made.

Main part of the findings is the extent of heterogeneity of the estimated ESG factors within the returns of the stock. The stocks with high scoring ESG on the probable scale tend to get the attention of investors whose aim is to create a sustainable portfolio in the markets; however, this can be limited by the array of inconsistency that ratings come along with. The paper also looks deeper into the focus of such noise on the ultimate performance of the companies financially (Liu et al, 2024).

3. IMPORTANCE OF ESG IN TODAY'S SCENARIO

3.1 ESG Investing: Worldwide and Indian View

This is another major movement, which is quite obvious given the current global and environmental trends – such international markets are emerging with greater appetite for operational best practices, social equality and effective governance It is not only Western countries, which may be referred to as mature countries, where this has developed; this trend is also developing in the rapidly emerging Indian continent where it is witnessing such admiration. Regulatory measures are emphasizing and facilitating the growth of ESG investing in India. The BRSR framework issued by the Securities and Exchange Board of India mandates publicly traded entities to fulfill their ESG reporting obligations. In India, institutional investors, in particular, are utilizing ESG rating scores in their investment portfolios.

This phenomenon can also be traced to the rise in ESG Mutual Funds as well which is on an uptrend; these provide investing avenues which speak of the conscience behavior of investment avenues for the changing mindset of the investor. However, there is evidence in the literature that the association between the ESG ratings system and the financial performance is rather intricate and, more often than not, empirically has been unresolved.

3.2 ESG Scores: Meaning and Significance

The Environmental, Social and Governance ESG raters evaluate corporations based on environmental, social and corporate governance factors. ESG ratings present value for investors in relation to sustainability.

Environmental Metrics

Environmental metrics determine the company's impact on natural resources, actions taken to avert climate change, use of energy, and waste disposal procedures. As an illustration, renewable energy users or carbon reduction companies can be measured to have performed better on the environmental metrics. This is very applicable in the Indian context where environmental degradation and resources scarcity are major issues.

3.3 Social Metrics

Social assessments evaluate the interaction of a business with its workforce, its clientele, and its communities. Diversity in the workplace, labor practices, community engagement, and safety of the measure figures include among others. Those businesses that harmonize the workplace and followers of the employees' focus score better socially.

3.4 Governance Metrics

Governance has to do with the management of a firm, shareholders' rights, transparency, and legal compliance as well as ethical adherence. Good governance guarantees accountability while limiting the chances for corruption or other unaccounted for actions. Governance is probably the most stresses area of all in all these reports particularly in India where scam after scam has eroded investor confidence.

3.5 Association between ESG and financial objectives

Despite the increasing focus placed on ESG metrics, the association between performance with respect to ESG and financial returns is inconclusive. Some of these studies show that companies with higher ESG ratings systematically outperform their competitors for reasons such as better risk management, greater trust of stakeholders and cheaper sources of funds. But many other studies stress the flawed nature of the scoring calculation methodologies employed, the albatross of the greenwashing effect that disavows the credibility of the construct as a whole.

3.6 Negative Correlations

Usually, there is evidence that ESG engagement correlates positively with less risk and lower cost of capital. It is predicted that companies that implement high ESG practices will be subject to negative impacts of changes to law or regulation, market volatility, and reputation, to a lesser degree.

Similar studies in India are hopeful regarding ESG mutual funds which are at a nascent stage and can provide reasonable returns consistent with the morals of the investors. The sectors that are able to best respond to ESG concepts include the technology and finance sectors, which go on to get more funding.

Variability of focus and thrust in measurement as well as evaluations which are subjectively grounded lead to inconsistent results. For instance, rating agencies' ESG rating for the same company will differ, as the reason of evaluation differs.

Overstating one's ESG successes, more popularly known as greenwashing, raises issues of legitimacy of ESG disclosures and refines influences of investors.

Some others argue that ESG investments may take leverage in the long term which would be placing off the investor that is more aggressive on short term return.

3.7 Sectoral Focus and Regulations

Indian market is characterized by typical sectoral appetites and regulatory regimes of ESG practice.

Sectoral Focus

Due to respective properties of dealing with sustainable metrics and developing remedies towards adverse environmental and social climate, the sectors of technology and finance lead the space of ESG investing in India.

Energy and manufacturing sectors, which are heavily polluters, are under greater pressure but they too offer prospects of ESG related change.

3.8 Legal Framework

In a good way, the BRSR framework of SEBI has assisted listed companies in enhancing ESG accountability and engaging in more transparent practices. But many challenges still exist including absence of standardization in ESG reports and low awareness levels among retail investors.

4. UNDERSTANDING ESG IN THE INDIAN CONTEXT

The Indian market, as depicted through the indices such as NIFTY 50 and BSE Sensex, remains pretty responsive to the global trends; however specific socio-economic issues that crop up in India become the ESG priorities; environment, particularly climate change and pollution, labor practices integrated with the social requirements for community development and governance transformation. The Indian companies also increasingly incorporate ESG frames into their business practices as well since long-term success is determined by the ability to combine profitability and sustainability.

SEBI makes the listed companies give ESG metrics through BRSR. It brings in regulatory push and makes disclosure quite transparent and pushes the investor to factor in all these ESG criteria while it makes decisions.

4.1 The Integration of ESG in the Indian Stock Market and its Impact on Returns

ESG investing has revolutionized the finance landscape of the world by integrating non-financial elements into investment decisions. However, for an emerging economy like India, though well reported for the case of developed markets, an increasing focus on regulations, awareness among investors, and corporate sense of responsibility toward sustainability have driven the trend. This paper looks into the integration of ESGs in relation to returns on stocks in India and nuances associated with such a change.

4.2 Indians Increasing Demand for ESG Investments

It goes a little like this: Lately, some institutional investors, mutual funds and foreign capital have invested in India, ESG instruments. Indeed, the data show that with more and more money streaming into FIIs with solid ESG practice. That is the idea - companies with strong ESG tend to have lower probabilities of regulatory fines and reputational risk are less exposed to long-run financial instability.

These include renewable energy companies and pharmaceutical companies, where ESG stipulations are fully reflected in their practices. NTPC and Tata Power appear among the favorite stocks of these concern investors who seek companies that can kick in the clean energy transition.

4.3 ESG and Indian Stock Market Returns

ESG performance, similar to the rest of the world, is negatively correlated with Indian stock returns. On average, companies that display an ESG-compliant nature tend to be more stable and showcase higher risk-adjusted returns over longer horizons, even though this trend may sometimes be nuanced and sector-dependent.

It goes hand-in-glove with investor confidence that in turn is related to the cost of capital and, by extension, with better valuations. Research studies on this topic have revealed the following: ESG-oriented Indian companies, such as major industries in renewable energy and IT, outperformed their peers in Indian stock indices. These are both sectors that coincide well with global sustainability goals, hence attractive to impact-driven investors.

Sector Specific Trends

Not all industries will be well paid back by ESG implementation. The heavy industries such as mining and manufacturing are those that have yet to rid themselves of the hassle of being compliant with environmental standards. Losers, in many ways, are firms that show clear intent to improve performance on ESG metrics. For instance, green technology using firms performed better in stock performance.

Resilience in Crisis

Companies with a strong ESG framework have been able to survive the economic shocks triggered by the COVID-19 pandemic. In this regard, companies which focus on employee welfare, community support, and environmental safety are perceived as more trustworthy. This has helped them maintain investor confidence.

Market Perceptions and Premiums

ESG compliance in India increasingly commands a market premium. Companies ranked high on ESG indices like the NIFTY ESG Index command better valuations. The premium reflects that ESG-aligned companies are forward-looking and well-prepared to face challenges of regulation and environment.

5. TESTING ESG INTEGRATION IN INDIA AND ITS ISSUES

Though the Indian stock market may have several benefits of ESG integration, it may face certain issues:

Inconsistent Data and Metrics

Standard ESG data is nonexistent, which is another major challenge. For example, it is arguably why different rating methods resulted in ratings from agencies that leave investors more confused than committed. Companies face challenges concerning the lack of clear frameworks for disclosing respective ESG information.

Cost of Compliance

Most Indian firms, especially the SMEs are expensive to engage in ESG practices. They are running very thin margins; thus, it becomes difficult to invest in sustainability.

Awareness Gap

ESG investing is a relatively new concept in India. Retail investors are the majority in the market who have no knowledge about ESG principles. Thus, it also generates relatively low demand for ESG-compliant financial products.

Short-termism: This is common among many Indian investors and contrary to the long view ESG strategies are based on. If defined correctly, companies will not be willing to invest in the ESG initiatives.

Growth Opportunities

A lot of space remains in the Indian market for growth through ESG:

Political and legislative support:

Some of the policies that give space to the company to work for the ESG goals are as follows: National Action Plan on Climate Change, Renewable Energy Mission. The incentives for the green bonds and tax advantages create added incentives to invest in ESG Corporate Programs.

Like Indian conglomerates who set standards for ESG performance that would be followed by other firms-the Tata Group, Mahindra, and Infosys come to mind first-success stories point toward these financial and reputational gains because of their adoption of sustainability measures. ESG Funds ESG-themed mutual funds have now become the new buzzword in India. Fund houses educating investors on the merits of sustainable investments and wherein demand for ESG-compliant stocks goes up.

Technology innovations help the companies to really feel the ESGs in an effective and efficient manner. Better monitoring tools minimize the damage caused by environmental factors, while the digital platform enhances governance and further increases the level of transparency. The ESG factors are now integrated into the strategies of global investors, and India is all set to be a destination for sustainable investments. Integration will gain pace through the changing regulatory environment as well as investor awareness. Renewable energy, financial services, and technology are going to lead the way. Traditional industries will feel the heat of change. This, however, can overcome even data standardization, investor education, and cost hurdles of widespread ESG adoption. All stakeholders-the regulators, corporations, and investors-must collaborate to build a harmonious ecosystem that favors the adoption of ESG principles.

6. COMPARATIVE ANALYSIS ESG VS NON – ESG STOCKS

It's one of the world's fastest-growing markets; the Indian finance market, especially with a radical shift towards incorporating sustainability into their investments. Now, ESG investments emerge as a much more convincing story than the well-tested, non-ESG investments. The analysis will attempt to understand how the ESG versus non-ESG investment stock returns in India compare and what is behind this performance and robustness while also exploring their longer-term sustainability.

1. ESG Stocking

The ESG stock indicates the companies which are perpetually striving to bring their businesses under environmentally friendly and social responsibility-oriented ideas. It has been rightly seen that TCS, Infosys, and NTPC have come out as sound examples in terms of strong ESGs. The above-mentioned three are presently striving to lower their environment, create social equality, and help a healthy governance mechanism.

2. Non-ESG Stocking:

Non-ESG stocks refer to those whose business operation is more dependent on the basis of financial performance rather than their major focus on sustainability and ethics. Generally, such firms come in the industries of coal mining, tobacco, and traditional energy production, for instance Coal India or ITC.

7. COMPARATIVE PERFORMANCE ANALYSIS

7.1 Returns and Volatility of Stocks

ESG Stocks:

Indian ESG stocks have empirically been proven to offer more stable risk-adjusted returns over the longer-term. From the historical evidence of the companies of NIFTY 100 ESG Index, it could easily be deduced that any kind of market volatility was of extremely low volatility particularly pertaining to the COVID-19 pandemic period. It mainly sums up to the faith the investor has in their sustainability efforts and the good governance practice.

Non-ESG Stocks:

The stock of non-ESG companies often tends to be more volatile. It becomes highly sensitive to regulatory risks and changes in global policies within those sectors that are more politically sensitive, whether that is fossil fuels or any such industry that has been scarred by environmental controversy. Thus, while growth is up, such stocks may generate more short-term returns; ESG stocks will not crack up so easily when things are bad.

7.2 Short-term vs Long-Term Returns

ESG Stocks

ESG-linked investments have been more in tune with the long-term approach. That follows the worldwide trend which is rising day by day towards sustainable finance along with the interest of institutional investors and foreign investment. A classic example is seen in the case of India's clean energy industry, which has gradually increased with time since the government launched initiatives for promoting renewable energy. Such trends can easily be seen in companies such as Tata Power who adopted ESG.

Non-ESG Stocks

In the short-term horizon, while the non-ESG equities seem to be doing well, especially in the boom era of high industrial and energy consumption, it is at the cost of the ever-increasing reputational, regulatory, and operational risks that will bleed into profitability in the longer horizon.

7.3 Crises Resilience

ESG Stocks:

ESG stocks perform pretty well during economic or environmental downturns because they are risk sensitive, employee friendly, and community conscious. For example, in the case of a pandemic, the Infosys stock appreciated due to human-centric policies of the workforce, thereby increasing investor's confidence and hence maintaining performance on the stock.

Non-ESG stocks

These impacts generally occur in non-ESG equities, mainly those in dangerous industries, allowing market shocks. Sometimes there may be huge drops in the value due to regulatory issues and operational disruption and consumer trust. during a crisis.

8. RELATIVE PERFORMANCE INFLUENCERS

8.1 Regulatory and Policy Favor

ESG investments are increasingly on the preference list of the Indian regulatory framework. Policies, such as the SEBI mandated BRSR, which enhances transparency, attract the investor to the ESG-compliant firms. To the contrary, non-ESG firms face climbing compliance costs and restrictions.

8.2 Investor Preferences

With the ever-growing pattern of ESG-based mutual funds and global investors seeking sustainable portfolios, there has been greater demand for ESG stocks while non-ESG stock has been on the back foot since diversion of capital from the industries perceived to threaten long-run value to society is in place.

8.3 Risk Exposures

ESG stocks do not have any risks of environmental fines, governance scandals, or social unrest. In fact, the usual reputational and operational risks often bother the minds of investors over non-ESG stocks that have, for instance, the mining or tobacco business.

8.4 Financial Performance Measures

Although ESG stocks focus on return with sustainability, non-ESG focuses on immediate returns on finances in the risk of less stability in the long run. ESG companies usually recycle in the form of green technology or employee welfare; thus, it creates an intangible asset that can enhance long-term shareholder value.

9. SECTORAL ANALYSIS

9.1 Renewable Energy Compared with Fossil Fuels

Government incentives and international demand for clean energy have also backed Indian renewable energy companies such as Suzlon and ReNew Power in sustaining their rising valuations. On the other hand, fossil fuel companies are said to be falling as investor appetite declines with greater global efforts at decarbonizing such companies as Coal India.

9.2 Technology and IT

Table 1. Indian IT majors

Company	ESG Classification	5-Year Stock price change percent	Current Price ( )	Market Cap (crores)
Tata Consultancy Services (TCS)	ESG	79.83%	4,038.84	14,86,129.00
Infosys	ESG	165.50%	1,917.30	8,02,696.00
NTPC	ESG	165.56%	320.00	3,15,481.00
Tata Power	ESG	545%	367.00	1,19,490.00
Coal India	Non-ESG	83%	372.20	2,34,523.00
ITC	Non-ESG	90.72%	450.00	5,62,401.00
Oil and Natural Gas Corporation (ONGC)	Non-ESG	111.40%	268.18	3,41,240.00
Vedanta	Non-ESG	176%	438.90	1,74,560.00

The several Indian IT majors like Infosys and TCS are ESG leaders due to good governance and socially responsible moves. Such companies have regularly outperformed the traditional non-ESG sectors as a result of high international demands and investor confidence.

9.3 Traditional Manufacturing and Mining

In inbuilt environmental impacts, the conventional heavyweights like steel and mining will find it tough to deliver on ESG compliances. At the same time, even while JSW Steel puts up all its vigorous green efforts, its ESG peer remains laggard in attracting a premium sustainable investment.

10. STATISTICAL ANALYSIS

10.1 Interpretation

1. Growth Over 5 Years

ESG Stocks

Tata Power has indeed been a superstar, rocketing an impressive 545% in just five years! NTPC and Infosys did extremely well, growing by nearly 165%. TCS, though not explosive, still showed tremendous growth at nearly 80%. On average, ESG stocks have grown about 240%, which is impressive. Read on for some exciting stats on that too.

Non-ESG Stocks:

In that, Vedanta has stood tall at 176%, followed by ONGC at 111%, ITC at 90%, and Coal India at 83% growth. So, the average here for non-ESG stocks worked out to be somewhere around 115%.

Takeaway: As a whole, ESG stocks have grown much stronger. Tata Power leads here. That is proof that in the long run, sustainable investments are becoming increasingly rewarding.

2. Latest Stock Prices

ESG Stocks:

TCS is the costliest at 4,038 and reflects the number of premium investors ready to pay for its stability and performance. Other ESG stocks like Infosys, NTPC, and Tata Power are between 320 and 1,917.

Non-ESG Stocks

Vedanta and ITC are expensive at 439 and 450, while Coal India and ONGC are inexpensive at 372 and 268.

Takeaway: ESG stocks are generally priced at a premium level as an indicator of investors' trust in these shares for their sustainability and good governance.

3. Market Value (Market Cap)

ESG Stocks:

The top two in this space are TCS and Infosys, with respective market values of 14.8 lakh crores and 8 lakh crores. Tata Power is significantly smaller at 1.2 lakh crores.

Non-ESG Stocks:

Of the non-ESG companies, ITC and ONGC are 5.6 lakh crores and 3.4 lakh crores in terms of market value; Vedanta and Coal India are smaller yet significant by comparison.

Conclusion: The giant ESG companies like TCS and Infosys are way ahead in terms of market value to portray the strong confidence that investors have in them.

4. Stability and Risks

ESG stocks are less volatile in nature due to the presence of well-managed companies having a long-term focus, good governance, and sustainable practices.

Risks are there with non-ESG stocks-things such as environmental fines or regulatory issues. These make their prices unpredictable, even though they sometime deliver quick gains.

Takeaway: ESG stocks feel like a safer bet for long-term stability, while non-ESG stocks are riskier and more sensitive to market shocks.

5. Highlights by Sector

ESG: Tata Power has seen tremendous growth of 545%. It reflects the high demand for renewable energy. TCS and Infosys are also performing well as they have developed a brand for sustainability and responsibility.

Non-ESG: Though companies such as Vedanta and ITC are facing really tough challenges like very strict regulations, they have still delivered robust growth but at a higher risk.

The fact is that long-term growth shows ESG stocks to be way outperforming the non-ESG stocks. It simply proves that there are more and more investors interested in companies that truly care about sustainability and good practices. Although the return on non-ESG stocks is still good, it carries more risks that include regulations and environmental controversies. At times, investors seem to lean towards ESG companies because they feel that they are safe, stable, and better aligned to future trends.

10.2 India ESG and Non-ESG Stocks Comparison- Challenges

1. Non-consistency of data: One of the major issues is that the ESG metrics for companies are not standard, and it is really difficult to underreport and have lesser comparisons for non-ESG businesses.
2. Market Maturity Since the ESG investing concept is still at an early stage in India than developed international markets, there is relatively limited access to history data to compare long-term trends. Non-ESG stocks form market capitalization, which may change the overall performance metric of the index.
3. Cost of ESG adoption small companies will face the challenge of cost in implementing ESG practices, and thus their competitiveness will be compromised with larger ESG compliant companies.

    1: Future Prospect 1. ESG investments are growing as pressures from increased regulation and awareness from the investing population, the ESG market of India shall take significant growth. Green finance containing green bonds and mutual fund investment following ESG will dominate mainstream growth.

    2. Transition for Non-ESG Companies Earning pressure on non-ESG firms will increase over time, which will push them toward sustainability. Most cement and steel industries have recently been exploring greener technology for further better results in the marketplace.
    3. Technological Function These trends will ultimately provide space to bridge the difference of ESGs and non-ESG performances with more technological integration. Green tech inventions, alongside AI-driven tools, might ensure that the previous generations can upgrade to some form of new sustainable models of businesses.

11. IMPLICATIONS

From the research findings, the implications are for investors, companies, and policy makers. These are:

1. Investor Impact

This research integrates ESG metrics in investment decisions to reduce risks and fulfill long-term financial goals. Investors are motivated to closely scrutinize ESG disclosures and not become victims of greenwashing. Financial literacy combined with access to quality ESG data will empower retail investors into making better decisions.

2. For Businesses

Businesses have to realize that investors require more sustainability and the opportunity of ESG practices toward high performance financial outcomes. Business openness to and soundness in ESG frameworks will attract long-term investments and reduce the operational risks by having a more potent and strong relationship with its stakeholder. Green technology investment and ethical practice have to be heavily invested to ensure staying competitive in the market, as governed by ESG practices.

3. For Policymakers

The findings suggest that the standard ESG reporting guidelines should be formulated by the regulatory authority and disclosure policies should be followed with strict action. Policymakers should ensure the environment, which would enhance ESG practices, also provide tax incentives for the green projects and subsidies to sustainable projects, can help the cause. Public awareness drive also helps to create awareness among investors about ESG investment advantages.

4. For Researchers

Future studies may further explore the sector-specific effect and interaction between ESG metrics and investor sentiment. Methodologically, machine learning and big data analytics are going to be used for measuring investor sentiment in real-time and therefore will measure its consequence for stock performance. On a cross-country comparative note, it will give an international generalizability of the findings. ESG integration does carry with it transformational potential, which influences both the investor mood and Indian stock performance. Despite all this, the merits of ESG investments-from financial stability to ethical accountability-make for an excellent case for widespread acceptance. The Indian market, due to its socio-economic terrain, offers an excellent ground to evolve ESG practices and make the growth sustainable by aligning financial objectives with global sustainability goals. By surmounting existing barriers and tapping into emerging opportunities, stakeholders can come together to build a resilient and equitable investment ecosystem.

11.1 Future Scope of ESG Investment in India

The future prospects of ESG, or Environmental, Social, and Governance, for stock investment in India are vaguely bright. The increase is not only because of growing awareness but also thanks to the favorable policies that are being supported by global trends. Sustainability has now become an issue that is central for businesses and governments not only in Europe and Africa but also in Asia. India is also on the same path, which makes an ESG investment in Indian companies a way of sustainability.

The main reason is that the government is on the right path of green energy and sustainability but there are other factors such as the green building movement. The solar companies that have spearheaded have got investment because of the government's National Solar Mission along with the renewable energy targets. The companies that embrace sustainable practices such as Tata Power and NTPC will be the early adopters of the green energy sources that are in demand.

Institutional and foreign investors are also interested in ESG-compliant companies. In view of the global sustainability thematic funds that are targeting the Indian ESG market, companies with ESG tendencies would be prime candidates for foreign investment. The data that shows the advances in regulation like "SEBI" making BRSR obligatory, which results in the good oversight of the overall situation covering the environment and governance, are the further arguments for this statement. There is also the social aspect to the younger generation of investors that are open to purchasing ESG products. People are not only interested in how much they will earn but even more in a significant positive effect. ESG-driven mutual funds and portfolios have the upper hand, being that they can achieve the same growth potential.

It was predicted by Google that all of the innovative ESG centered companies will be hugely profitable in long terms. Companies that are ESG-focused would gain a high advantage in comparison to their non-ESG counterparts, thereby bringing about financial improvement, environmental preservation, corporate governance, social inclusion, the economy as a whole, and customer satisfaction. Moreover, the investment can ensure a combination of stability with the growth of the returns number. In recent years, ESG investments have been seen to not only benefit the environment but also the economic sector of the country whilst providing more money for the people. The substantial influence of large companies is huge in today's world (companies that share the view of ESG strategies).

12. CONCLUSION

The paper explores the intricate relationship of investor sentiment and returns on stock in the Indian context of ESG metrics. The results give very convincing evidence that consideration of ESG is not a global phenomenon but rather an important driver of financial decision-making in emerging markets. The increasing ESG frameworks, which the companies portray with implied effects on the investor sentiment and return in stock, indicate that in investment strategies, the focus is increasingly shifting towards altering the overall dynamics within that stock market. The Indian sensibility flows hand in glove with sensibility.

How much investor psychology-sometimes overly optimistic, sometimes scared, or risk-averse-bend ESG measures to relate how they might perform is calculated by this study. ESG Stocks are very resilient to any sort of economic slowdown or crisis mainly because the nature of governance appears stable, has an ethical flavor of governance, and takes a very sustainable approach toward business practices. This is highly relevant to the Indian context, for companies with a high ESG score have managed to consistently attract long-term investors into the company, creating in the process financial stability without volatility. In other words, a comparative analysis of ESG and non-ESG stocks is used for explaining the financial benefits through investment in ESGs.

Even if non-ESG shares will fetch the short-term higher returns, regulatory and reputation issues together with market turmoil have more likely created risks to that particular share. This makes the ESG stocks be supporting long-term thinking in as much as it will prove to be a fresh substitute for the Indians that give a chance to learn who gives them support nowadays increasingly. This is because such issues relate to the form of practice needed for his long-lasting and ethical requirements. But, on the contrary, the study has also thrown many challenges that have in the end limited the potential investments of ESG into maximum. Some of the significant problems include the non-homogenized reporting framework of ESG, data incomparability, and greenwashing. This problem results in uncertainty for the investors, so it impacts the ESG metrics credibility. The other major challenge is that the compliance of ESG for SMEs is very costly.

REFERENCES

Bodhanwala, S., & Bodhanwala, R. (2023). Environmental, social and governance performance: Influence on market value in the COVID-19 crisis. *Management Decision*, 61(10), 2442–2466. DOI: 10.1108/MD-08-2022-1084

Dalal, K. K., Thaker, N., & IUP. (2019). ESG and corporate financial performance: A panel study of Indian companies. *The IUP Journal of Corporate Governance, XVIII*(1). Retrieved from https://www.researchgate.net/publication/371177996

Dhuri, M., Sinha, R., Shukla, S., & CRISIL. (2024). ESG ratings in India: Assessing their reliability for investment decisions. *European Economic Letters, 10*(1), 27–31. Retrieved from http://eelet.org.uk

Groww. (n.d.). *Explore stocks*. Retrieved January 5, 2025, from https://groww.in/stocks/user/explore

H.P., H., & Rishad, A. (2020). An empirical examination of investor sentiment and stock market volatility: Evidence from India. *Financial Innovation, 6*(1), Article 26. DOI: 10.1186/s40854-020-00198-x

Kuzmina, J., Maditinos, D., Norena-Chavez, D., Grima, S., & Kadłubek, M. (2023). ESG integration as a risk management tool within the financial decision-making process. In *Contemporary Studies in Economic and Financial Analysis* (pp. 105–113). DOI: 10.1108/S1569-37592023000111A007

La Torre, M., Mango, F., Cafaro, A., & Leo, S. (2020). Does the ESG index affect stock return? Evidence from the Eurostoxx50. *Sustainability (Basel)*, 12(16), 6387. DOI: 10.3390/su12166387

Liu, M., Ling, Y., & Lee, C. (2024). Does ESG performance and investor attention affect stock volatility? An empirical study based on panel data and mixed-frequency data. *Applied Economics*, 1–15. Advance online publication. DOI: 10.1080/00036846.2024.2423068

Meher, B. K., Hawaldar, I. T., Mohapatra, L., Spulbar, C., & Birau, R. (2020). The effects of environment, society, and governance scores on investment returns and stock market volatility. *International Journal of Energy Economics and Policy*, 10(4), 234–239. DOI: 10.32479/ijeep.9311

Performance Review Of ESG Investing In India. (2023). Rabindra Bharati University. *Journal of Economics*, XXVII(10), 121–122.

Raut, R. K., Shastri, N., Mishra, A. K., & Tiwari, A. K. (2023). Investor's values and investment decision towards ESG stocks. *Review of Accounting and Finance*, 22(4), 449–465. DOI: 10.1108/RAF-12-2022-0353

Saini, M., Aggarwal, V., Dhingra, B., Kumar, P., & Yadav, M. (2023). ESG and financial variables: A systematic review. *International Journal of Law and Management*, 65(6), 663–682. DOI: 10.1108/IJLMA-02-2023-0033

Singhania, M., & Saini, N. (2022). Systems approach to environment, social and governance (ESG): Case of Reliance Industries. *Sustainable Operations and Computers*, 3, 103–117. DOI: 10.1016/j.susoc.2021.11.003

Stotz, O. (2021). Expected and realized returns on stocks with high- and low-ESG exposure. *Journal of Asset Management*, 22(2), 133–150. DOI: 10.1057/s41260-020-00203-z

Upadhyaya, C., Khan, S., & Sandanshive, V., Awasthi, G. (2023). A study of the impact of behavioral factors on ESG investment. *Journal of Contemporary Issues in Business and Government*, 29(1), 546–548. DOI: 10.47750/cibg.2023.29.01.039

Yin, X., Li, J., & Su, C. (2023). How does ESG performance affect stock returns? Empirical evidence from listed companies in China. *Heliyon*, 9(5), e16320. DOI: 10.1016/j.heliyon.2023.e16320 PMID: 37305472

Chapter 9
Integrate Mathematical Understanding to Sustainability Assurance:
A New Way to Enhance Firm ESG Metrics

Qiang Zhang
https://orcid.org/0009-0006-5041-6794
Universiti Teknologi Malaysia, Malaysia

DanTong Li
https://orcid.org/0009-0008-5011-6059
Universiti Teknologi Malaysia, Malaysia

Mohamad Ikram Zakaria
https://orcid.org/0000-0002-2171-8279
Universiti Teknologi Malaysia, Malaysia

NingLin Li
https://orcid.org/0009-0008-8387-3638
Universiti Teknologi Malaysia, Malaysia

Norulhuda Binti Ismail
Universiti Teknologi Malaysia, Malaysia

YiJing Du
https://orcid.org/0009-0005-7171-1082
Universiti Teknologi Malaysia, Malaysia

ABSTRACT

This chapter explores the integration of mathematical education with Education for Sustainable Development (ESD) to enhance corporate employees' understanding and application of Environmental, Social, and Governance (ESG) metrics. It highlights how mathematical literacy and data literacy improve employees' ability to analyze ESG data, promoting decision-making transparency and report credibility. The study employs a theory-driven analytical framework supported by case studies from companies such as Shell, Walmart, and IKEA to demonstrate the practical impact of

DOI: 10.4018/979-8-3373-0117-4.ch009

mathematics in ESG reporting. The chapter also examines the role of mathematical modeling, such as lifecycle assessments and carbon footprint calculations, in quantifying environmental impacts. By combining theoretical insights with real-world applications, it underscores the transformative potential of targeted mathematical education in advancing corporate sustainability practices.

1. INTRODUCTION

Environmental, Social, and Governance (ESG) metrics, as critical indicators of a company's non-financial performance, are widely used to evaluate corporate performance in environmental protection, social responsibility, and governance structures (Choi, 2022; Widyawati, 2020). ESG metrics are essential not only for assessing corporate sustainability but also as a cornerstone of Socially Responsible Investment (SRI), aiding investors in gauging a company's long-term potential and understanding its commitment to social responsibilities (Cruz & Matos, 2023; Widyawati, 2020). Transparent disclosure of ESG data enables companies to establish a responsible brand image among the public and investors, attracting sustainability-focused stakeholders (Lui, 2019; Sciarelli et al., 2021). According to a 2023 report by PwC, global ESG-related assets under management are projected to reach $33.9 trillion by 2026, representing over 21% of total managed assets. However, the disconnect between ESG investment growth and the lack of standardized, transparent reporting practices raises a critical question: Can companies effectively meet stakeholder expectations without improving data literacy and analytical capabilities among employees? This evaluation system has rapidly developed in global markets, becoming a significant standard for assessing corporate contributions to society and the environment (Keeley et al., 2022; Mashayekhi et al., 2024). High-quality integrated reporting can improve transparency in companies' disclosure of SDGs and enhance stakeholder trust (Hamad et al., 2023).

The urgency of addressing these challenges is heightened by growing regulatory pressures and public expectations. As ESG metrics become integral to corporate strategies, the lack of standardized training and analytical tools for managing complex ESG data presents a significant barrier to achieving transparency and trust. This research is particularly timely as corporations increasingly seek innovative solutions to enhance their workforce's data literacy and decision-making capabilities. By integrating mathematical education with ESG training, this study provides a practical pathway to improve employees' analytical skills, ensuring more reliable ESG disclosures and stronger alignment with global sustainability goals.

Education has been identified as a cornerstone for achieving sustainable development, as emphasized in the United Nations' Sustainable Development Goals (SDGs). Specifically, **Goal 4 (Quality Education)** aims to ensure inclusive and equitable quality education while promoting lifelong learning opportunities for all. This research aligns closely with this objective by addressing the intersection of education and sustainability, particularly through improving mathematical and data literacy in corporate environments. By equipping employees with the analytical skills necessary to interpret complex ESG metrics, this study contributes to advancing corporate practices that reflect the values of Goal 4, fostering a broader societal impact.

The importance of education as a sustainable development priority is underscored in the SDGs framework, as illustrated in **Figure 1** below.

Figure 1. United Nations sustainable development goals (SDGs)

(UNDESA, 2015)

Modern corporations face increasing ESG compliance pressures alongside financial objectives. With heightened demands from global regulators and investors for corporate social responsibility, non-compliance with ESG standards often results in reputational damage and diminished market competitiveness (Choi, 2022; Cruz & Matos, 2023; Zumente & Bistrova, 2021). Corporations must not only answer to investors but also address consumer expectations and regulatory pressures, making compliance critical for corporate survival (Boiral & Heras-Saizarbitoria, 2019; Radovilsky et al., 2018). For resource-intensive and pollution-heavy industries, failing to improve ESG compliance may lead to heightened risks such as legal disputes and reputational crises (Lui, 2019; Mashayekhi et al., 2024; Solaimani, 2024).

Currently, most corporate ESG training focuses on theoretical knowledge and lacks depth in data analysis and practical application skills. Such training approaches often fail to equip employees with the necessary data interpretation capabilities, leaving them without the analytical tools required to address complex ESG data, thereby limiting corporate ESG execution (Choi, 2022; Cruz & Matos, 2023; Widyawati, 2020). Environmental management training can significantly improve employees' ability to handle complex data such as carbon emissions disclosures, thereby improving corporate performance (Khatib et al., 2023). In an increasingly data-driven business environment, the disconnect between traditional theoretical training and practical application hinders employees from translating knowledge into effective ESG decision-making tools (Sciarelli et al., 2021).

The absence of systematic training in data analysis skills poses challenges for employees in interpreting complex ESG reports. This limitation impacts corporate transparency and the credibility of disclosures, reducing the effectiveness of traditional training in enhancing data interpretation and decision-making quality (Choi, 2022; Zumente & Bistrova, 2021). Existing training does not meet the demand for improved data literacy, affecting employees' ability to identify and process data, particularly in managing compliance risks and disclosures, thus constraining overall corporate sustainability performance (Cruz & Matos, 2023; Lui, 2019; Solaimani, 2024).

Mathematical education plays a significant role in enhancing employees' data interpretation, logical analysis, and critical thinking skills. By improving mathematical literacy, companies can cultivate stronger data analysis and data literacy skills among employees, thereby enhancing the accuracy and reliability of ESG data (Keeley et al., 2022; Widyawati, 2020; Zumente & Bistrova, 2021). Mathematical literacy aids employees in identifying patterns and trends within complex ESG data, improving practical application and providing more reliable support for ESG decision-making (Mashayekhi et al., 2024; Radovilsky et al., 2018).

Integrating mathematical education with ESG training is an effective way to enhance employees' analytical capabilities and improve reporting transparency. In a data-driven corporate environment, mathematical literacy not only helps employees interpret complex ESG data but also strengthens corporate reputation, fostering greater trust in corporate ESG performance among stakeholders (Boiral & Heras-Saizarbitoria, 2019; Cruz & Matos, 2023). This interdisciplinary training approach equips employees with advanced ESG data analysis skills, further enhancing the transparency and credibility of corporate reports (Keeley et al., 2022; Radovilsky et al., 2018).

Combining mathematical education with Education for Sustainable Development (ESD) fosters a systematic perspective on sustainability within corporations. This combination not only develops employees' logical analysis skills but also deepens their understanding of corporate environmental and social responsibilities, encouraging greater focus on sustainability goals. By strengthening mathematical literacy and ESD education, companies can more effectively achieve long-term sustainability and environmental responsibility objectives (Cruz & Matos, 2023; Radovilsky et al., 2018; Widyawati, 2020).

The main purpose of this research is to explore the answer of "*How can mathematical education enhance employees' understanding of ESG, thereby promoting corporate sustainability?*" By focusing on improving mathematical and data literacy, this study aims to bridge the gap between theoretical training and practical applications, ensuring employees can handle complex ESG data. This research specifically seeks to develop measurable improvements in employee proficiency in analyzing ESG data, thereby enhancing reporting transparency, decision-making accuracy, and corporate sustainability practices. In an era where ESG accountability defines corporate success, can organizations truly thrive without equipping their workforce with the analytical tools to navigate complex sustainability challenges? This study not only addresses this question but also offers actionable insights to drive progress in corporate ESG practices.

2. LITERATURE REVIEW

2.1 The Role of Mathematical and Data Literacy in Corporate Environments

Mathematical literacy in corporate settings is defined as employees' ability to utilize mathematical logic, model identification, and data processing skills to interpret complex data (Choi, 2022; Radovilsky et al., 2018; Widyawati, 2020; Zhang, 2024). As noted by Zhou & Yang (2022), mathematical data analysis literacy encompasses not only the ability to understand and apply mathematical concepts but also the capacity to reflect on and adapt mathematical models to dynamic real-world scenarios, ensuring analytical rigor in corporate decision-making. This capability is central to enabling data-driven decision-making in businesses, encompassing not only traditional computational skills but also the understanding and application of mathematical models to support real-world data analysis needs. Jablonka (2003) emphasizes that the essence of mathematical literacy lies in applying mathematical logic and models effectively. This is particularly crucial for analyzing ESG metrics, as it determines whether employees can accurately interpret complex ESG data to identify risks and opportunities. Beyond being a tool for data analysis, mathematical literacy is a vital skill for employees to adapt flexibly and swiftly in an ever-changing corporate environment.

In modern corporations, mathematical literacy helps employees construct effective frameworks for interpreting ESG data. This skill not only supports efficient data comprehension but also facilitates viable solutions to complex ESG issues. However, promoting mathematical literacy in corporate environments faces several challenges: training often emphasizes basic skill acquisition over practical application of models and logic, and employees' mathematical backgrounds can vary significantly, leading to inconsistent proficiency levels in practice (Cho, 2015; Jablonka, 2003). Addressing these challenges requires corporations to invest more resources in mathematical literacy training to help employees make accurate decisions in dynamic ESG contexts (Nielsen, 2023; Widyawati, 2020).

Mathematical literacy plays a crucial role in ESG report analysis, enabling employees to understand underlying trends and risks while enhancing the scientific rigor and transparency of reports. This, in turn, allows stakeholders to better comprehend a company's ESG performance (Boiral & Heras-Saizarbitoria, 2019; Cruz & Matos, 2023; Radovilsky et al., 2018). Despite its significance, mathematical literacy faces practical limitations in application. Employees' varying levels of mathematical proficiency can lead to misinterpretations of complex data, while those lacking hands-on experience may struggle to navigate intricate ESG metrics. These challenges underscore the need for standardized mathematical education to improve ESG data literacy.

Data literacy encompasses skills in data collection, processing, analysis, and visualization, enabling employees to discern data patterns more effectively and apply insights to decision-making (Lui, 2019; Zumente & Bistrova, 2021). Advanced data literacy enhances data sensitivity, empowers employees to present data sources effectively, and boosts report credibility (Nielsen, 2023; Spiegeleer et al., 2020). However, literature highlights the widespread lack of sufficient data literacy training in corporations, leaving many employees ill-equipped to interpret and manage complex data. This shortfall not only diminishes the value of data in decision-making but also undermines the transparency of ESG reports (Bele et al., 2023; Hahn et al., 2015).

The role of data literacy in ESG reporting lies in employees' ability to process and present ESG-related data effectively. Employees must possess the capability to filter and interpret complex sustainability data to accurately communicate corporate performance in ESG metrics (Cruz & Matos, 2023; Sciarelli et al., 2021; Solaimani, 2024). With increasing demands for data transparency and compliance, advanced data literacy becomes indispensable. However, the inherent complexity of ESG data has left many corporations unable to provide systematic data literacy training, resulting in employees' limited ability to interpret carbon emission data, social impact metrics, and other ESG indicators clearly. Addressing this requires corporations to design training programs tailored to the unique characteristics of ESG data, ensuring employees can accurately filter, process, and present ESG information (Arvidsson & Dumay, 2022a; Manteaw, 2008).

Data literacy not only enhances report transparency but also fosters a sense of accountability among employees, ensuring credibility in presenting data sources (Manteaw, 2008; Pandey et al., 2011). In ESG reporting, transparency and accountability are inseparable, as advanced data literacy ensures consistency and completeness in reports. However, many corporations' data literacy training programs fail to address the accurate presentation and interpretation of ESG data sources, raising doubts about report credibility among stakeholders. Therefore, efforts to improve data literacy should prioritize fostering transparency and accountability to enhance the overall credibility of ESG reports (Nielsen, 2023).

While prior research underscores the importance of mathematical and data literacy in interpreting complex ESG data and improving reporting transparency (Boiral & Heras-Saizarbitoria, 2019; Cruz & Matos, 2023; Radovilsky et al., 2018), significant gaps remain. Most studies focus on theoretical frameworks or isolated applications, without offering integrated, interdisciplinary approaches to systematically enhance employees' analytical capabilities. Moreover, the application of mathematical education to address ESG reporting challenges remains underexplored, leaving a critical gap in the development of practical, scalable training solutions tailored to corporate needs.

2.2 Application of Mathematical Modeling in ESG Reporting

Lifecycle Assessment (LCA) is a model used to evaluate the environmental impact of a product or service throughout its entire lifecycle, encompassing production, usage, transportation, and disposal stages (Pandey et al., 2011). As highlighted by Odey et al. (2021), LCA serves as a critical framework in ESG reporting by enabling businesses to systematically identify and quantify environmental trade-offs, thereby improving transparency and accountability in sustainability practices. By quantifying carbon emissions, water usage, and other ecological impacts, LCA provides a systematic analytical tool for businesses. However, its practical application faces challenges related to data complexity and consistency, which can affect the accuracy and operational feasibility of the model in certain scenarios (Khasreen et al., 2009; Kitamura et al., 2020).

In ESG reporting, the LCA model is widely used to assess the environmental footprint of products, thereby enhancing the transparency and scientific rigor of corporate environmental performance (Kitamura et al., 2020; Mashayekhi et al.,

2024). Nonetheless, its application is hindered by issues such as inconsistencies among data sources and difficulties in data collection, limiting its ability to achieve the desired level of transparency for some companies. To address these challenges, businesses need to implement systematic data management and technical support to ensure that LCA models accurately reflect environmental impacts (Hahn et al., 2015; Khasreen et al., 2009).

Through the application of LCA, companies can scientifically quantify environmental impacts, providing precise and transparent data to support ESG reporting. This approach not only enhances the scientific validity of ESG reports but also increases stakeholder trust in corporate environmental responsibility. However, the effectiveness of LCA depends on the extent to which companies manage data collection, standardization, and consistency. Improving these aspects can help businesses better realize the potential of LCA in ESG reporting (Kitamura et al., 2020; Popescu et al., 2023).

Carbon footprint calculation is another essential method, used to quantify greenhouse gas emissions generated by corporate activities, including both direct and indirect emissions (Pandey et al., 2011; Popescu et al., 2023). It helps companies clearly demonstrate their environmental impacts across Scope 1, 2, and 3 emissions. However, challenges arise in its practical application, particularly in collecting data for Scope 3 indirect emissions. Despite these difficulties, carbon footprint calculation is vital for enhancing the transparency and credibility of corporate ESG reports (Kitamura et al., 2020; Spiegeleer et al., 2020).

The role of carbon footprint calculation in quantifying environmental impacts is significant, especially in improving ESG report transparency by clearly identifying and presenting sources and quantities of emissions (Pandey et al., 2011; Radovilsky et al., 2018). Many companies, however, struggle to accurately quantify indirect emissions, a challenge that is especially pronounced in emission-intensive industries. To overcome these challenges, companies need to establish reliable systems for data collection and management, enabling more effective application of carbon footprint calculations (Cruz & Matos, 2023).

Carbon footprint calculation contributes significantly to improving ESG report transparency, fostering better stakeholder understanding and trust in corporate environmental performance. However, without adequate data management systems, businesses may struggle to fully realize the transparency and scientific rigor of this method (Pandey et al., 2011; Zumente & Bistrova, 2021). Therefore, companies must invest in robust data collection and management processes to ensure the integrity of their ESG reports (Kitamura et al., 2020).

Despite the widespread use, existing mathematical models like LCA and carbon footprint calculations face limitations in data standardization and operational feasibility (Kitamura et al., 2020; Pandey et al., 2011). Additionally, research seldom examines how employees' mathematical and data literacy levels impact the accuracy and effectiveness of these models in ESG reporting. Addressing this gap requires developing training programs that integrate mathematical modeling with hands-on practices, ensuring employees can effectively navigate the complexities of ESG data.

2.3 Theories of Education for Sustainable Development

Education for Sustainable Development is an interdisciplinary educational approach aimed at fostering employees' understanding and commitment to environmental, social, and economic responsibilities (Lui, 2019). As noted by Fekih Zguir et al. (2021), ESD emphasizes a holistic integration of sustainability values into organizational practices, promoting critical thinking and problem-solving skills essential for addressing complex ESG challenges. It serves as the cornerstone of sustainability education and an effective method for enhancing corporate employees' sense of environmental responsibility (Ferrer-Estévez & Chalmeta, 2021). However, a key challenge for businesses lies in aligning ESD theory with the practical needs of employees' daily tasks to ensure its applicability and effectiveness (Lambini et al., 2021; Ssossé et al., 2021).

In corporate settings, ESD utilizes contextual case studies and cross-departmental collaboration to strengthen employees' environmental and social responsibility (Ferrer-Estévez & Chalmeta, 2021; Lambini et al., 2021). Despite its benefits, these approaches face operational challenges, such as the significant resources required to design ESD programs tailored to specific industries and job roles, which may not be feasible for many small and medium-sized enterprises (Radovilsky et al., 2018).

ESD promotes the internalization of environmental and social responsibility through task-oriented learning, making it particularly suitable for dynamic corporate environments (Boiral & Heras-Saizarbitoria, 2019; Lambini et al., 2021; Sciarelli et al., 2021). However, task-oriented learning methods may be less effective without the support of real-world business scenarios. Thus, businesses must ensure that ESD training is closely linked to actual work contexts to maximize its impact.

By integrating theory with practical application, ESD enables employees to better fulfill ESG responsibilities in their daily work. This approach not only enhances employees' understanding of ESG goals but also facilitates the achievement of corporate sustainability objectives in practice (Bele et al., 2023; Ssossé et al., 2021). Nevertheless, many corporate ESD programs overly emphasize theory while lacking practical components, limiting their effectiveness in raising ESG awareness. Companies should adopt more case-based teaching and simulated practice to enhance training outcomes.

Fostering environmental and social responsibility awareness through ESD not only improves employees' understanding of ESG principles but also enhances the credibility and transparency of corporate ESG reports. By including ESD practices as examples in ESG reports, businesses can further strengthen stakeholders' trust in their environmental accountability. However, companies must prioritize the sustainability of ESD training to ensure the long-term credibility of the ESG performance demonstrated in their reports (Manteaw, 2008; Nielsen, 2023).

Existing studies have demonstrated the potential of ESD in enhancing employees' understanding of sustainability and their commitment to ESG principles (Bele et al., 2023; Ssossé et al., 2021). However, many ESD programs remain overly theoretical, with limited integration of practical applications such as mathematical and data literacy training. This gap highlights the need for an interdisciplinary approach that bridges ESD theory with real-world corporate practices, enabling employees to apply sustainability concepts in data-driven decision-making processes.

3. METHODOLOGY

3.1 Theory-Driven Analytical Approach

This study adopts a theory-driven analytical approach, building upon established frameworks in mathematical literacy, data literacy, mathematical modeling, and Education for Sustainable Development (ESD) to systematically explore the role of mathematical education in enhancing employees' understanding and application of ESG metrics. Tsang (2014) defines theory-driven analysis as deducing general statements or propositions from observations, emphasizing its suitability for complex, multidimensional research fields. Through the expansion of theoretical frameworks, this approach reveals the deeper relationships underlying data contexts (Tsang, 2014). In this study, methodology provides a comprehensive conceptual framework to deconstruct and analyze the multifaceted roles of mathematical literacy in ESG applications.

The theory-driven approach is highly applicable to ESG research, particularly given the complexity of ESG data interpretation. It enables the theoretical generalization of educational methods' functions and limitations in complex contexts (Tsang, 2014). Christie et al. (2000) highlight that in regional development and management studies, theory-driven analysis offers multidimensional perspectives that guide the interpretation of management processes. This is particularly effective in multidimensional ESG scenarios, ensuring that educational theories extend beyond theoretical domains and are validated through multifaceted empirical analysis (Christie et al., 2000).

This approach relies on a framework supported by mathematical and data literacy, centered on critical thinking and data analysis capabilities, ensuring robust theoretical support for the findings. The integration of mathematical and data literacy forms the core framework for developing employees' data interpretation skills, aligning with corporate demands for handling ESG data in data-driven work environments (Christie et al., 2000; Tsang, 2014). Additionally, Orlikowski & Baroudi (1991) emphasize that theory-driven methods enhance the analytical capabilities of information literacy through structured tools, further highlighting their relevance in education and ESG data application fields.

Mathematical modeling, such as Lifecycle Assessment (LCA), serves as an integral part of the theory-driven analysis. LCA provides a robust method for quantifying corporate environmental impacts, contributing to the scientific rigor of ESG analysis. Furthermore, ESD's role in promoting environmental responsibility education among employees provides theoretical grounding for this study. This analytical framework effectively integrates theory and practice, enabling corporations to establish cohesive methodologies for scientifically measuring ESG metrics and delivering environmental responsibility education (Orlikowski & Baroudi, 1991; Tsang, 2014).

The theory-driven analytical approach bridges theory and practice. By facilitating deep theoretical generalizations and defining "boundary conditions," this method systematically links mathematical education with ESG applications, supporting the translation of education into practical use (Tsang, 2014). Within this analytical structure, the approach elucidates the conceptual connections between complex educational methods and practical applications, reinforcing the integration of ESG data literacy in educational settings (Christie et al., 2000).

3.2 Case Summaries as Theoretical Support

In theory-driven analysis, case summaries provide diverse perspectives to strengthen the practical relevance of theoretical analysis. Tsang (2014) asserts that case summaries are flexible and applicable for demonstrating the generalizability of theories while retaining their adaptability to specific contexts. This study uses case summaries to enhance analytical depth and effectively demonstrate the application of mathematical education in ESG practices across different industries.

The rationale for choosing case summaries over in-depth case studies lies in their diversity and broad applicability. Compared to detailed analyses, case summaries showcase the theoretical applicability across varied contexts, minimizing the limitations of single-case studies and extending the scope to a wider range of ESG applications. Orlikowski & Baroudi (1991) highlight that case summaries efficiently validate theoretical applicability across diverse contexts, making them suitable for comprehensive ESG analysis needs.

Cross-industry case selection validates the generalizability and reliability of the theories in various scenarios. Tsang (2014) notes that cross-industry cases enhance the broad applicability and versatility of theories. In ESG practices, cases from large corporations provide a rich validation background for theoretical analysis (Tsang, 2014).

Representative cases are crucial for theory validation. In this study, mature ESG practices from companies like Shell, Walmart, Coca-Cola, and IKEA offer highly representative examples of how mathematical education and data literacy contribute to ESG data processing and interpretation within corporations. By validating these theories through real-world practices, theoretical analysis extends beyond abstract frameworks, fostering a close connection with practical applications (Christie et al., 2000).

Case summaries not only provide practical references for theoretical analysis but also render the theoretical concepts of mathematical education in ESG applications more actionable, further validating the connection between theory and practice. Eisenhardt (1989) emphasizes that case studies can translate theories into concrete, actionable examples, enabling research to better align theory with practice through verification and application (Eisenhardt, 1989).

4. THEORETICAL INSIGHTS AND ANALYTICAL FRAMEWORK FOR ESG EDUCATION

4.1 Mathematical Literacy

Mathematical literacy in corporate environments encompasses a range of abilities, including numerical logic, pattern recognition, and data processing. These capabilities go beyond basic computational skills, enabling employees to interpret complex data and apply logical reasoning (Jablonka, 2003; Widyawati, 2020). In the context of ESG data, mathematical literacy is particularly crucial as it enhances employees' analytical and critical thinking skills, helping them identify patterns and trends within data and make scientifically grounded decisions in data-driven processes (Choi, 2022; Nielsen, 2023). This skill set is essential for supporting corporate sustainability decision-making, especially when dealing with large volumes of complex ESG data (Radovilsky et al., 2018; Zumente & Bistrova, 2021).

The importance of mathematical literacy also lies in its ability to provide employees with a comprehensive framework for understanding and critically evaluating data. Such a framework is particularly vital for addressing ESG-related needs, including risk assessment and ensuring data transparency (Cruz & Matos, 2023). For example, employees equipped with logical reasoning and data interpretation skills can better understand the long-term trends of environmental impact data, enabling them to make strategic decisions aligned with corporate objectives (Keeley et al., 2022). Thus, fostering mathematical literacy not only strengthens employees' data processing capabilities but also significantly enhances their data literacy in ESG practices, enabling them to tackle complex environmental and social challenges with a systematic and forward-looking approach.

To provide a clearer understanding of the role of mathematical literacy in ESG data management, Table 1 summarizes the research topics, key findings, application examples, and impacts on ESG reporting from existing literature. These studies offer both theoretical and empirical support, highlighting the critical importance of mathematical literacy in data-driven decision-making and corporate sustainability strategies.

Table 1. Summary of key literature on mathematical literacy and ESG practices

Author and Year	Research Topic	Key Findings	Application Example	Impact on ESG Reporting
Pandey et al. (2011)	Carbon Footprint Calculation Methods	Provides a systematic framework for quantifying greenhouse gas emissions.	Shell	Enhances carbon management and improves reporting credibility.
Keeley et al. (2022)	ESG Metrics and Social Equity	Highlights the role of ESG metrics in supporting sustainable investments and emphasizes social equity considerations.	IKEA	Improves transparency and builds stakeholder trust.
Radovilsky et al. (2018)	Skills Requirements in Data Analytics	Emphasizes the need for mathematical and statistical literacy to meet the evolving requirements of business analytics and data science.	Walmart	Strengthens data processing and enhances report clarity.

Mathematical literacy is more than a computational skill, it serves as a core competency for data-driven decision-making. In corporate ESG practices, mathematical literacy helps employees identify risks and trends in complex environmental data, analyze underlying patterns, and lay the groundwork for long-term strategic planning (Radovilsky et al., 2018). Research highlights that when combined with data literacy, mathematical literacy enables employees to better collect, process, and present data, particularly in enhancing transparency and the accuracy of reports. This is crucial for ensuring the credibility and trustworthiness of ESG reports (Sciarelli et al., 2021; Spiegeleer et al., 2020).

When dealing with critical metrics such as carbon emissions and resource consumption, mathematical literacy empowers employees to use data models to identify long-term trends and make data-supported recommendations. For instance, mathematical models like Lifecycle Assessment (LCA) play a vital role in quantifying environmental impacts, supporting carbon footprint management, and improving the transparency of corporate reporting. This highlights the value of mathematical literacy in ESG reporting (Kitamura et al., 2020; Pandey et al., 2011). Consequently, mathematical literacy not only helps employees understand their corporate ESG responsibilities but also provides scientific support for sustainable practices.

Mathematical literacy is indispensable for interpreting ESG data, particularly in analyzing complex environmental indicators like carbon emissions and resource usage. Employees with strong mathematical literacy can identify long-term trends and potential risks in ESG data, allowing them to pinpoint factors influencing corporate environmental performance. Additionally, mathematical logic and pattern recognition enable them to convert data into actionable insights, supporting sustainability decision-making (Keeley et al., 2022; Solaimani, 2024). For example, through mathematical modeling, employees can gain a better understanding of corporate resource consumption patterns and formulate forward-looking environmental strategies (Mashayekhi et al., 2024).

In particular, mathematical literacy allows employees to effectively filter and process complex carbon emissions data, identifying key sources and long-term impacts. This precision in data analysis not only enhances the transparency of environmental reports but also demonstrates the company's ESG efforts to stakeholders, boosting its image of social responsibility (Arvidsson & Dumay, 2022). Thus, mathematical literacy plays a pivotal role in ESG data analysis and interpretation, improving employees' technical skills and enabling them to provide more scientific and credible data in stakeholder-facing reports.

Shell's use of carbon footprint algorithms to quantify greenhouse gas emissions exemplifies the importance of mathematical literacy in helping employees understand and manage complex data (Radovilsky et al., 2018). Through the Carbon Disclosure Project (CDP), Shell also promotes data transparency, integrating carbon emission data into corporate decision-making and enhancing employee capabilities in carbon management (Tang & Luo, 2011). This systematic approach to collecting and managing carbon emission data not only demonstrates Shell's commitment to environmental protection but also provides a reliable data foundation for its long-term environmental strategies.

Shell further strengthens its employees' mathematical and data literacy through targeted training programs, enabling them to interpret carbon footprint data more effectively. This training equips employees to identify and understand key trends in carbon emission data, providing reliable support for corporate environmental policies

(Pandey et al., 2011). Through carbon footprint calculations, Shell's employees can conduct precise quantitative analyses of emissions and offer data-backed recommendations for environmental strategies. This data-driven approach to decision-making has proven valuable in Shell's environmental management, significantly enhancing the scientific rigor and transparency of its ESG reports and reinforcing its market reputation for responsibility (Keeley et al., 2022).

In summary, Shell's application of carbon footprint algorithms and employee training demonstrates how mathematical literacy facilitates effective data interpretation and application in corporate environments, particularly in ESG data management. This capability is not only a critical tool for advancing corporate environmental strategies but also an essential support for employees to make scientific judgments when dealing with complex data. Shell's case highlights that improving mathematical literacy empowers employees with higher levels of expertise and reliability in carbon management and ESG reporting, which is vital for enhancing corporate market competitiveness and social responsibility.

4.2 Data Literacy

Data literacy refers to employees' comprehensive abilities in data collection, processing, analysis, and visualization, covering everything from basic data management to complex data interpretation (Bergman et al., 2018). Employees with strong data literacy can efficiently gather and organize data, identify key patterns in complex corporate environments, and improve decision-making quality through data-driven insights. In the context of ESG reporting, data literacy enables employees to present data with transparency, providing stakeholders with clear and accurate data representations that significantly enhance the credibility and social responsibility of reports (Hahn et al., 2015).

The critical impact of data literacy on ESG reporting cannot be overlooked. First, data literacy enhances employees' sensitivity to data sources, enabling them to better understand the generation, transmission, and analysis of data during processing. This is crucial for assessing the accuracy and reliability of data, especially when handling multi-source ESG data (Bele et al., 2023). Additionally, employees with strong data literacy can uncover deeper meanings within data, helping companies reveal genuine environmental impacts and anticipate potential risks in their ESG reports.

Data literacy directly supports the analysis of ESG metrics. Specifically, employees with data literacy can identify key trends and variables within environmental, social, and governance data, granting companies greater agility and accuracy in complex sustainability decision-making. To further illustrate the significance of data literacy in enhancing ESG practices, Table 2 provides a summary of key literature highlighting the role of data organization, transparency, and alignment with sustainability goals. These studies underline the critical impact of data literacy on improving the quality and reliability of ESG reporting.

Table 2. Summary of key literature on data literacy and ESG practices

Author and Year	Research Topic	Key Findings	Application Example	Impact on ESG Reporting
Bergman et al. (2018)	Data Literacy and Sustainable Development Goals	Highlights the importance of data organization and interpretation in supporting sustainable development goals.	UNESCO Chair Programs	Enhances data-driven decision-making for achieving SDGs.
Hahn et al. (2015)	Transparency in Carbon Disclosure	Emphasizes how transparent data management improves trust in corporate reporting and public perception.	Voluntary Carbon Disclosure Initiatives	Strengthens credibility and social responsibility of reports.
Bele et al. (2023)	ESG Investments and SDGs	Demonstrates the dependency between ESG investments and SDG alignment in corporate strategies.	EU ESG Investments	Ensures consistency in ESG reporting for achieving sustainability.
Manteaw (2008)	Corporate Social Responsibility and Education	Discusses the role of corporate social responsibility in fostering educational programs for sustainable development.	CSR Initiatives by Global Corporations	Improves workforce education and understanding of sustainability.

From Table 2, it is evident that data literacy plays a pivotal role in ensuring the reliability and transparency of ESG reports. For example, Bergman et al. (2018) emphasize the value of structured data interpretation in achieving SDGs, while Hahn et al. (2015) highlight the importance of transparency in building stakeholder trust. These insights collectively reinforce the necessity of fostering data literacy within organizations to enhance ESG reporting and align with broader sustainability objectives.

For example, data literacy enables employees to handle carbon emission data more precisely and identify potential long-term environmental trends (Manteaw, 2008). This capability is vital for ESG reporting, as it ensures transparency and authenticity in demonstrating sustainability performance, thereby enhancing corporate social responsibility and public trust (Nielsen, 2023). Furthermore, data literacy enhances the transparency of ESG reports, allowing employees to present clear and verifiable ESG data to stakeholders (Bergman et al., 2018). In the face of compliance and regulatory pressures, data literacy equips employees with the skills to filter, organize, and present ESG data, ensuring that reports are transparent, consistent, and comprehensible. This level of data transparency helps companies build trust in the market and strengthens their sense of accountability, particularly in environmentally impactful areas such as carbon emissions and resource utilization.

Walmart provides a notable example of employing data literacy to enhance the transparency and efficiency of carbon emission data management in its supply chain. By analyzing carbon emission data, Walmart improved data transparency within its supply chain, enabling employees to pinpoint critical carbon emission hotspots and optimize supplier management in terms of responsibility and transparency. This process not only extended beyond cost and efficiency optimization in Walmart's supply chain but also incorporated carbon emission control, enhancing employees' decision-making capabilities through clear data analysis (Pandey et al., 2011).

Additionally, Walmart and other companies have utilized carbon disclosure initiatives to further enhance transparency, showcasing their commitments to carbon management to stakeholders. Research indicates that Walmart's highly transparent carbon data disclosures have earned the trust of external investors and strengthened the credibility of the company's ESG reports (Lee & Han, 2008; Mahmoudian et al., 2020). By conducting in-depth analyses of supply chain carbon emission data, Walmart employees were able to identify critical carbon emission points and refine supplier selection and management strategies accordingly. This not only reduced environmental impacts but also made Walmart's ESG reports more comprehensive and transparent, elevating the company's market image in terms of social responsibility.

4.3 Mathematical Modeling

Mathematical modeling is a tool used to understand and interpret real-world phenomena by creating abstract models, playing a pivotal role in corporate ESG data analysis. It quantifies a company's environmental impact, enabling data-driven decision-making processes. For instance, mathematical modeling allows businesses to transform complex ESG data into analyzable formats, providing quantitative evidence for the development of sustainability strategies (Pandey et al., 2011).

In ESG analysis, LCA and carbon footprint calculations are among the most widely applied mathematical models. LCA aids in evaluating resource consumption and environmental emissions across various stages of a product's lifecycle, from raw material acquisition to production, transportation, and disposal. Similarly, carbon footprint calculations provide precise data on greenhouse gas emissions, helping businesses identify environmental burdens more clearly. These models not only offer scientific data for assessing environmental impacts but also provide effective methods for optimizing resource management and mitigating environmental risks (Kitamura et al., 2020).

To further illustrate the critical role of mathematical modeling in ESG practices, Table 3 provides a summary of key literature highlighting its applications, methodologies, and impacts. These studies demonstrate how mathematical models, such as LCA and carbon footprint calculations, support corporate sustainability strategies and improve ESG reporting.

Table 3. Summary of key literature on mathematical modeling in ESG practices

Author and Year	Research Topic	Key Findings	Application Example	Impact on ESG Reporting
Pandey et al. (2011)	Carbon Footprint Calculations	Highlights the importance of carbon footprint models in quantifying greenhouse gas emissions and their role in sustainability.	General corporate applications	Improves accuracy and transparency in ESG reporting.
Kitamura et al. (2020)	Lifecycle Assessment (LCA) Models	Demonstrates how LCA supports resource optimization and reduces environmental impacts across product lifecycles.	Business event sector	Enhances sustainability and reduces carbon emissions.
Sarkis & Talluri (2002)	Environmental Impact Quantification	Discusses the strategic importance of mathematical models in assessing environmental risks and optimizing supply chains.	Manufacturing sectors	Improves supplier selection and environmental responsibility.
Bø et al. (2013)	LCA in Packaging Optimization	Provides insights into using LCA for evaluating packaging materials and reducing carbon emissions.	Coca-Cola	Supports sustainable product design and resource management.

From Table 3, it is evident that mathematical modeling serves as a cornerstone in ESG practices. For example, Kitamura et al. (2020) emphasize the value of LCA models in evaluating and minimizing environmental impacts, while Sarkis & Talluri (2002) highlight their strategic application in optimizing supply chains. These findings collectively demonstrate that mathematical modeling not only enhances corporate decision-making but also strengthens transparency and accountability in ESG reporting.

Mathematical modeling is indispensable for quantifying corporate environmental impacts, particularly in areas such as carbon emissions, water resource usage, and waste management. For example, carbon footprint calculations enable companies to accurately measure their greenhouse gas emissions, identify primary emission sources, and develop targeted reduction strategies. This modeling approach provides reliable data support for ESG reporting, enhancing the transparency and credibility of reports while demonstrating corporate environmental responsibility and compliance (Sarkis & Talluri, 2002).

LCA models are also critical in managing water resources and waste. By evaluating resource use across all stages of a product lifecycle, LCA helps companies identify opportunities for optimization, such as reducing water consumption and increasing waste recycling rates (Hahn et al., 2015). These models not only support resource optimization but also raise employees' environmental awareness, encouraging a greater focus on sustainable resource utilization in ESG-related tasks.

Coca-Cola employs LCA models to analyze the resource consumption and environmental impacts associated with its products throughout their lifecycle. This approach helps Coca-Cola identify environmental burdens across production, transportation, consumption, and disposal stages. Specifically, the LCA model enables employees to understand the environmental impacts of various processes, such as the production and packaging of soft drink bottles, and their contributions to carbon emissions and resource usage. These insights allow the company to make more informed decisions in product design and supply chain management (Bø et al., 2013).

By leveraging LCA models, Coca-Cola has achieved better performance in product sustainability. For example, data provided by LCA models supports the scientific evaluation of packaging materials for bottled water and beverages, enabling the company to optimize resource consumption and reduce carbon emissions effectively. This case highlights the practical value of mathematical modeling in corporate environmental responsibility and underscores the role of LCA models in promoting environmental protection and resource management through comprehensive product lifecycle analysis.

4.4 Education for Sustainable Development

Education for Sustainable Development, a global educational initiative proposed by UNESCO, aims to raise awareness of environmental, social, and economic responsibilities through education to promote sustainable development (Bergman et al., 2018). In corporate education, ESD has significant potential, as it not only focuses on knowledge transfer but also emphasizes cultivating employees' sense of responsibility and sustainability awareness. This enables employees to understand the environmental and social impacts of their work behaviors (Bergman et al., 2018). Integrating ESD into corporate education can help employees incorporate ESG (Environmental, Social, and Governance) considerations into their daily decision-making processes, fostering a corporate culture that evolves toward greater sustainability (Cho, 2015).

Through ESD approaches, companies can enable employees not only to recognize the importance of ESG metrics but also to understand their specific roles in enhancing corporate sustainability performance. Such educational systems strengthen employees' sense of environmental and social responsibility, thereby effectively supporting the company's ESG strategies. ESD enhances employees' skills in areas such as data interpretation, risk analysis, and environmental management, enabling them to better identify and address the potential social and environmental impacts of corporate activities.

To further illustrate the role of ESD in advancing corporate ESG practices, Table 4 summarizes key literature on ESD, focusing on its objectives, findings, and applications. These studies demonstrate how ESD fosters sustainability awareness, enhances decision-making, and aligns corporate strategies with ESG goals.

Table 4. Summary of key literature on ESD and ESG practices

Author and Year	Research Topic	Key Findings	Application Example	Impact on ESG Practices
Bergman et al. (2018)	ESD and Global Sustainability	Highlights ESD's role in promoting sustainability awareness and global collaboration through education.	UNESCO Chairs Initiative	Strengthens alignment with the UN SDGs and fosters cross-sector collaboration.
Cho (2015)	Bridging Theory and Practice in ESD	Demonstrates how ESD equips individuals with practical skills and theoretical knowledge to address sustainability challenges.	Corporate waste management	Improves resource management and promotes low-emission practices.
Sarkis & Talluri (2002)	ESD in Supply Chain Management	Explores how ESD principles enhance decision-making in sustainable supplier selection.	Strategic supplier partnerships	Integrates sustainability into supply chain strategies, reducing environmental impact.

As summarized in Table 4, Education for Sustainable Development (ESD) is critical in fostering sustainability awareness and promoting responsible corporate practices. Bergman et al. (2018) emphasizes the role of ESD in aligning organizational goals with the UN SDGs, while Cho (2015) highlights its practical applications in waste management and resource optimization. Sarkis and Talluri (2002) further demonstrate how ESD principles integrate sustainability into supply chain strategies, contributing to reduced environmental impacts and improved ESG performance. Collectively, these studies underscore the transformative potential of ESD in advancing corporate sustainability.

In corporate settings, ESD serves as an educational tool to cultivate employees' environmental and social responsibility. This sense of responsibility motivates employees to focus more on achieving corporate ESG goals and to incorporate sustainability considerations into their decision-making processes. For example, research shows that ESD helps employees develop a comprehensive understanding of environmental protection and resource management, encouraging them to consider environmental impacts when selecting suppliers and materials, thereby promoting the company's sustainability objectives (Bergman et al., 2018).

Moreover, ESD bridges the gap between theory and practice, enabling employees to embody sustainability principles in their daily work. Through ESD training, employees gain not only theoretical knowledge of sustainability but also practical skills to address environmental and social impacts. For instance, in areas such as waste management and resource usage, employees trained in ESD are more likely to opt for low-emission, environmentally friendly solutions, thereby improving the company's overall performance in social and environmental domains (Cho, 2015).

IKEA has extensively applied ESD principles in its supply chain management, with a particular focus on enhancing employees' awareness of sustainability and environmentally friendly material selection. By integrating ESD into supply chain management, IKEA has improved employees' understanding of eco-friendly materials and increased their emphasis on low-carbon supply chains. Studies indicate that companies like IKEA, through ESD-focused education, enable employees to recognize the importance of environmental responsibility. This awareness is particularly evident in supplier and material selection, where employees prioritize suppliers' environmental credentials and the sustainability of materials (Sarkis & Talluri, 2002).

This practice has allowed IKEA to successfully translate ESD principles into operational guidelines within supply chain management, ensuring that employees consistently reflect the company's environmental responsibility in their daily work. This not only enhances the company's social reputation but also establishes a market-leading corporate culture centered on environmental sustainability. Ultimately, ESD has elevated employees' environmental awareness and supported IKEA in implementing low-carbon and eco-friendly strategies within its supply chain management, laying a strong foundation for the company's long-term development.

5. THE ROLE OF MATHEMATICAL EDUCATION IN ESG REPORTING: OPPORTUNITIES AND CHALLENGES

5.1 Enhancing ESG Data Interpretation

Mathematical education plays a critical role in improving employees' ability to interpret ESG data. Through mathematical education, employees acquire foundational data analysis skills, such as understanding data distributions, applying statistical models, and identifying data trends—skills essential for analyzing the complex data embedded in ESG reports. Literature highlights that mathematical education not only develops employees' logical reasoning but also enables them to identify patterns and trends within data, thereby making ESG reports more scientific and transparent (Cruz & Matos, 2023; Radovilsky et al., 2018).

Mathematical education significantly enhances employees' logical reasoning skills, enabling them to identify causal relationships between variables in ESG reports. This ability not only improves data interpretation but also equips employees to understand the driving factors behind complex ESG metrics with greater accuracy (Mumcu, 2016). Moreover, mathematical education supports employees in identifying and addressing anomalies in data, ensuring that analyses remain scientifically rigorous and consistent. This precision is particularly important in data-intensive areas such as carbon emissions and resource usage (Manteaw, 2008).

In decision-making, mathematical education further boosts employees' confidence and professionalism. Employees with strong data analysis and interpretation skills can make informed judgments on matters such as greenhouse gas reduction and social responsibility fulfillment, thereby providing robust data support for corporate ESG strategies. For instance, Walmart's carbon emission management efforts demonstrate how increased data transparency and participation in carbon disclosure projects foster stakeholder trust, highlighting the pivotal role of mathematical education in data processing and enhancing transparency (Mahmoudian et al., 2020).

5.2 Improving the Transparency and Credibility of Corporate Reports

Mathematical education is indispensable in improving the transparency and credibility of corporate ESG reports. By enabling employees to understand data sources, processing methods, and presentation techniques, mathematical education ensures that reports present clear and transparent information. This transparency not only enhances the credibility of reports but also increases stakeholder trust in corporate ESG performance, providing companies with a competitive edge in the market (Nielsen, 2023).

Accuracy and transparency in data are fundamental to building trustworthy ESG reports. Mathematical education equips employees with skills to verify data accuracy and promptly correct errors, ensuring the scientific rigor of reports (Radovilsky et al., 2018). Additionally, it teaches employees data visualization techniques, allowing them to present information in a more intuitive manner. This transparent presentation significantly contributes to the credibility of reports (Spiegeleer et al., 2020).

Walmart's supply chain carbon emission management illustrates the impact of mathematical education on data processing. Through mathematical training, Walmart employees gained precision in handling carbon footprint data, which enhanced the transparency and persuasiveness of their reports. Studies show that transparent carbon data disclosures not only built stakeholder trust but also improved the credibility of Walmart's external reporting (Lee & Han, 2008; Mahmoudian et al., 2020). Similarly, Shell's rigorous analysis of carbon footprint and lifecycle data demonstrates how mathematical education enables employees to improve data accuracy and transparency. These practices underscore the importance of mathematical education in enhancing the credibility of corporate environmental data, helping companies achieve greater market recognition in ESG reporting.

In summary, mathematical education plays a vital role in improving the transparency, accuracy, and visualization of ESG reports. These skills empower employees to present higher-quality data in reports, effectively communicating the company's genuine performance in sustainability. Mathematical education not only strengthens employees' data processing capabilities but also helps businesses gain greater recognition in long-term development and brand reputation. As sustainability demands continue to grow, data transparency will remain a core competitive advantage for companies seeking trust and support in the marketplace.

5.3 Industry-Specific Differences in Mathematical Education Needs

The need for mathematical education varies significantly across industries. Sectors such as manufacturing and energy, which heavily rely on resource usage and carbon emission data, typically require strong mathematical modeling and data analysis skills. In contrast, service industries focus more on social impact and governance data, necessitating higher data literacy and statistical analysis proficiency while relying less on mathematical modeling (Widyawati, 2020).

The energy sector depends heavily on quantitative analyses such as carbon footprint calculations and lifecycle assessments, which involve complex mathematical modeling and data processing techniques (Mashayekhi et al., 2024). These sector-specific needs suggest that mathematical education should be tailored to align with the unique ESG requirements of each industry.

To address these differences, literature recommends designing industry-specific mathematical education programs. For instance, manufacturing industries can prioritize the application of mathematical modeling and data processing tools, while service industries may focus on developing skills in data collection, processing, and visualization (Mashayekhi et al., 2024). Such customized educational content not only enhances the effectiveness of training but also equips employees to accurately interpret and apply ESG data relevant to their industries.

IKEA and Shell's ESG training practices illustrate how differing industry demands drive adjustments in mathematical education content. IKEA emphasizes sustainable material selection and low-carbon supply chain management, while Shell focuses on modeling and analyzing carbon footprints and resource consumption (Cardoni et al., 2019).

Industry-tailored educational modules can help employees acquire foundational mathematical skills integrated with sector-specific expertise. Flexible teaching methods, such as online learning, data simulations, and project-based training, can enable employees to incrementally develop mathematical skills and apply them directly to ESG data analysis in their work. This approach ensures that mathematical education is both practical and impactful, allowing employees to immediately utilize their training in real-world scenarios.

By implementing targeted, industry-specific mathematical education programs, companies can more effectively address the challenges of data complexity, resource constraints, and sector-specific needs. This approach enhances employees' performance in ESG data analysis and reporting, enabling corporations to secure a competitive edge in the increasingly complex field of sustainability.

5.4 Challenges in Implementing Mathematical Education in Corporations

As demands for corporate sustainability and compliance grow, the complexity of ESG data has significantly increased. ESG data often includes diverse types such as carbon emissions, resource usage, and social impact data, with varied sources and layered analysis requirements. Effectively interpreting this diversity and complexity necessitates a high level of mathematical literacy among employees. However, traditional ESG training often emphasizes theoretical aspects, leaving employees ill-equipped to interpret complex data (Widyawati, 2020). Additionally, the hierarchical and multi-sourced nature of ESG metrics makes it highly challenging for employees to rapidly improve their mathematical skills in a short period.

For instance, Walmart's supply chain management involves extensive supplier data and carbon emission metrics, highlighting the critical role of mathematical education in data interpretation and transparency improvement. While Walmart has demonstrated the potential of mathematical education through enhanced data transparency and carbon disclosure initiatives, the short-term enhancement of employees' mathematical literacy remains a significant hurdle for corporations (Cardoni et al., 2019). This indicates that data complexity poses a substantial challenge in promoting mathematical education.

Effective implementation of mathematical education and data training requires dedicated resource investments, including skilled trainers, data analysis tools, and employee time. Studies suggest that many small and medium-sized enterprises (SMEs) struggle to systematically adopt mathematical education due to budget constraints. Even large corporations face increased costs and coordination difficulties when implementing such programs across departments (Choi, 2022). Furthermore, the outcomes of resource investments are often challenging to quantify immediately, making it difficult for companies with limited budgets to evaluate the long-term value of mathematical education (Buallay, 2018).

While the long-term benefits of mathematical education are clear, the inability to achieve immediate returns on investment often leads management to adopt a conservative approach to resource allocation. Cost-driven companies, in particular, may find it difficult to justify the implementation of mathematical education, resulting in suboptimal progress in improving ESG data literacy.

In some corporate cultures, mathematical education may be perceived as an additional burden, especially in environments primarily focused on production and operations. Some employees and managers may view mathematical education as irrelevant to their responsibilities, leading to resistance (Cho, 2015). This lack of organizational support often limits the effectiveness of training efforts, hindering overall corporate progress in ESG data literacy.

To address this challenge, companies can foster a culture of learning and continuous improvement to increase acceptance of mathematical education. By providing examples of successful applications of mathematical education, employees can better understand its practical value in ESG data interpretation and corporate development, reducing resistance to training.

5.5 Possible Improvements for Corporate Mathematical Programs

The design of mathematical education must be guided by the specific needs of the organization and tailored to employees' skill levels. A structured approach allows employees to progressively acquire data analysis skills while translating theoretical knowledge into practical application.

Course design should begin with a need-based approach, tailoring content to the company's industry and job roles. For example, the manufacturing sector, with its complex production processes and environmental assessment needs, requires training in data modeling and predictive analysis. In contrast, the service sector focuses more on statistical analysis and data visualization to support ESG reporting on social impact and governance (Bag et al., 2020; Saxena et al., 2022). AI-driven training tools are becoming increasingly important in needs-based course design, enabling companies to dynamically adjust training content to meet employees' real-time learning requirements (Rane et al., 2024). This approach not only enhances course relevance but also addresses the disconnect between traditional training and practical scenarios.

Courses should also be stratified based on employees' mathematical backgrounds and job requirements. Basic courses might cover fundamental concepts, introductory statistics, and tools like Excel to establish preliminary data analysis capabilities (Kateryna et al., 2020). Intermediate courses could focus on data modeling, Python programming, and machine learning fundamentals to handle more complex ESG data (De Wolf et al., 2023). Advanced courses should emphasize LCA and big data analytics, incorporating tools such as Hadoop and Spark to meet high-level decision-making needs involving complex environmental data (Chaturvedi, 2024). This stratified approach not only optimizes skill development but also ensures efficient use of training resources (Tsalis et al., 2020).

Integrating real-world case studies into training is another crucial element. Case studies help employees translate abstract theories into practical skills. For instance, Shell's carbon footprint analysis courses illustrate how to interpret complex environmental data, while IKEA's green supply chain training demonstrates the application of ESG data in optimizing supplier selection (Arvidsson & Dumay, 2022). Additionally, immersive tools such as virtual reality scenarios can simulate energy usage environments, helping employees better understand the relationship between ESG data and corporate decision-making (Chaturvedi, 2024; Rouen et al., 2024).

Structured course content is key to the success of training programs. Foundational modules should focus on mathematical concepts and basic data tools, providing a strong basis for data analysis (Huang et al., 2022). Intermediate modules should introduce advanced tools such as Python, Tableau, and Power BI, equipping employees to process and visualize complex data (Bag et al., 2020; Saxena et al., 2022). Case study modules, drawing on examples from companies like Shell and IKEA, should offer employees opportunities to apply their skills in real-world scenarios, enabling them to tackle actual problems effectively (Rane et al., 2024).

The choice of tools and methods in mathematical education directly impacts training effectiveness. Basic tools like Excel and Python are the most commonly used in corporate data analysis. Excel is well-suited for preliminary data organization, while Python, with its robust data processing capabilities and integration with machine learning tools, is ideal for more complex analyses (McCarthy & Kuhlemeyer, 2024).

Advanced tools such as Tableau and Power BI excel in data visualization. These tools enable businesses to present complex trends intuitively, facilitating clearer communication of information to stakeholders (Chaturvedi, 2024). Big data analytics platforms like Hadoop and Spark are invaluable for managing large-scale ESG data, particularly in scenarios requiring real-time environmental data monitoring and prediction. Combined with AI algorithms, these tools can significantly enhance corporate ESG data management capabilities (Saxena et al., 2022).

Virtual labs and scenario simulations are essential for enhancing training outcomes. Virtual labs allow employees to simulate carbon emission scenarios and environmental data variations, testing the applicability of various analysis methods and tools (De Wolf et al., 2023). Real-time feedback mechanisms enhance the value of these labs, enabling employees to adjust their analysis strategies and improve data processing accuracy (Bag et al., 2020). AI-driven feedback systems further optimize training by identifying employees' weaknesses and providing targeted recommendations, thereby increasing efficiency (Rane et al., 2024).

Lifecycle assessment tools are particularly effective for evaluating the environmental impact of products throughout their lifecycle. For example, Shell leveraged LCA tools to optimize energy use and reduce carbon emissions, setting a valuable benchmark for other companies (Arvidsson & Dumay, 2022). Big data analytics tools also excel in handling real-time data processing needs. When combined with AI-powered analysis techniques, they further enhance corporate competitiveness in complex environmental decision-making (Rane et al., 2024; Saxena et al., 2022).

Through scientifically designed courses and advanced tools and methodologies, companies can significantly enhance employees' ESG data management skills. These strategies not only provide robust support for tackling sustainability challenges but also enhance corporate credibility and competitiveness among stakeholders. By combining industry-specific case studies and cutting-edge technologies, these recommendations offer systematic guidance for integrating mathematical education with ESG objectives effectively.

6. CONCLUSION AND IMPLICATION

6.1 Discussion

Mathematical education plays a pivotal role in enhancing the understanding of ESG metrics within corporate environments. By integrating foundational mathematical skills, data modeling capabilities, and practical applications into training programs, mathematical education provides essential support for employees to comprehend and analyze complex ESG data. This improves their professionalism and enhances corporate credibility among stakeholders. Case studies from companies like Shell and IKEA illustrate how targeted mathematical education enables employees to interpret complex data such as carbon footprints and supply chain emissions, significantly improving the transparency and reliability of ESG reporting (Arvidsson & Dumay, 2022b; Rouen et al., 2024).

The core value of mathematical education also lies in its ability to enhance the quality of corporate reporting. With tools like data visualization and lifecycle assessment, employees can present and analyze environmental, social, and governance data more precisely, establishing a robust foundation for corporate sustainability in competitive markets (Chaturvedi, 2024; Saxena et al., 2022). Furthermore, this form of education supports companies in meeting compliance requirements while enhancing brand value and market competitiveness, contributing to their long-term strategic goals (Rane et al., 2024).

This research bridges critical gaps in ESG education by emphasizing the integration of mathematical and data literacy within sustainability training programs. Unlike previous studies that narrowly focus on either theoretical ESG frameworks or isolated corporate strategies, this study introduces a practical, interdisciplinary approach designed to enhance employee competencies in handling complex ESG data. As highlighted by Yue et al. (2025), effective ESG implementation requires not only robust governance structures but also well-trained employees capable of aligning data-driven insights with sustainability goals. By proposing a measurable framework for evaluating the impact of training on reporting transparency and decision-making accuracy, this study provides actionable insights for businesses aiming to bolster their ESG credibility while addressing real-world regulatory and market demands.

This research provides a unique contribution to the field by integrating mathematical ESD to address the challenges of ESG reporting. Unlike previous studies that predominantly focus on theoretical frameworks or isolated approaches, this study develops an interdisciplinary training model tailored to enhance employees' data literacy and mathematical proficiency. This novel approach bridges the gap between theoretical knowledge and practical applications, enabling employees to interpret and manage complex ESG data effectively. Additionally, the research introduces a measurable framework to assess the impact of these training programs on improving reporting transparency and corporate decision-making accuracy. By addressing critical gaps in the existing literature, this study not only offers practical solutions for businesses but also lays a foundation for further research in interdisciplinary ESG education and training.

In conclusion, this study underscores the transformative potential of integrating mathematical education with sustainability training to address the challenges of ESG reporting. By enhancing employees' mathematical and data literacy, organizations can significantly improve the accuracy, transparency, and reliability of their ESG disclosures. This research not only provides a practical, interdisciplinary framework for corporate training programs but also contributes to advancing the broader understanding of sustainability education. Furthermore, by bridging the gap between theoretical approaches and practical applications, the findings emphasize the critical role of targeted educational strategies in meeting global sustainability goals. These contributions offer actionable insights for businesses, educators, and policymakers alike, paving the way for more robust and sustainable corporate practices in an increasingly data-driven world.

6.2 Conclusion

This study highlights the critical role of integrating mathematical education with sustainability education (ESD) in enhancing corporate employees' data literacy and analytical proficiency for improved ESG reporting. By bridging the gap between theoretical frameworks and practical applications, the research presents an interdisciplinary training model that empowers employees to interpret and manage complex ESG data effectively. The findings demonstrate that targeted mathematical education not only enhances reporting transparency and decision-making accuracy but also strengthens corporate credibility and stakeholder trust, aligning with global sustainability goals.

In comparison to previous research, this study advances the understanding of ESG reporting challenges by offering practical solutions rooted in mathematical literacy. While prior studies have emphasized the theoretical importance of data literacy in sustainability practices (Choi, 2022; Radovilsky et al., 2018), this research provides a measurable framework for assessing the real-world impact of training programs on corporate transparency and compliance. Furthermore, it extends the findings of Widyawati (2020) and Saxena et al. (2022) by incorporating interdisciplinary approaches that integrate data visualization, lifecycle assessments, and ESG metrics into actionable corporate training modules. Unlike studies that primarily focus on governance structures or regulatory frameworks (Yue et al., 2025), this research centers on employee education as a foundational component for achieving sustainability objectives.

The broader implications of these findings underscore the need for policymakers, educators, and business leaders to prioritize interdisciplinary education models. Policymakers can utilize these insights to develop industry-wide training standards, ensuring that corporations meet both regulatory demands and stakeholder expectations. For educators, this study highlights the importance of designing curricula that merge mathematical and sustainability education, preparing the next generation of professionals to address complex ESG challenges. Corporations, particularly those in resource-intensive industries, can adopt the proposed training framework to enhance workforce capabilities and mitigate sustainability-related risks.

While this study provides significant contributions to the fields of sustainability education and ESG reporting, it is not without limitations. The focus on mathematical literacy and its applications in ESG training may not fully address the unique needs of industries with distinct operational complexities. Future research should explore how these models can be tailored to meet the diverse demands of different sectors and cultural contexts. Additionally, emerging technologies such as artificial intelligence, blockchain, and virtual reality present exciting opportunities for enhancing training efficiency and scalability, warranting further investigation into their integration with mathematical education frameworks.

In conclusion, this research not only fills critical gaps in existing literature but also offers a practical and scalable model for improving ESG reporting transparency and corporate sustainability practices. By situating employee education at the center of sustainability efforts, this study provides a roadmap for achieving long-term alignment with global sustainability objectives, bridging the gap between academic discourse and practical application.

6.3 Limitations

This study primarily adopts a qualitative case study approach to explore the integration of mathematical ESD in addressing ESG reporting challenges. While this approach provides detailed insights into training frameworks and their effectiveness, it inherently limits the generalizability of the findings to a broader range of industries and corporate contexts. Additionally, the absence of comparative quantitative analyses restricts the ability to measure the direct impact of training interventions on ESG reporting outcomes. As a result, while the study highlights promising frameworks, the conclusions drawn may not fully represent all organizational settings. Future research could address this limitation by employing mixed-method designs, incorporating both qualitative and quantitative approaches to provide a more holistic evaluation of training models.

The scope of this research was constrained by the availability of case study data, which limited the sample size and diversity of industries examined. The reliance on data from specific sectors, such as manufacturing and resource-intensive industries, may overlook unique challenges faced by other fields, such as service-based industries or small and medium-sized enterprises (SMEs). Furthermore, data collection was reliant on secondary sources and self-reported insights, introducing potential biases in the interpretation of findings. These limitations suggest the need for future studies to include larger, more diverse samples and employ primary data collection methods, such as longitudinal tracking or experimental designs, to enhance the reliability and representativeness of results.

6.4 Practical Implications

This research offers valuable insights for managers, stakeholders, and policymakers to improve ESG performance and sustainability practices. For managers, the proposed integration of mathematical education with sustainability training addresses critical gaps in employees' data literacy and analytical skills. By implementing tailored training programs based on this framework, organizations can improve the accuracy and transparency of their ESG reporting, enhance compliance with regulatory standards, and strengthen their competitive advantage in sustainability-focused markets.

For stakeholders, including investors and regulators, the findings underscore the importance of fostering accountability and trust through standardized ESG education frameworks. Such initiatives can encourage corporations to align their practices with global sustainability goals while increasing the reliability of sustainability disclosures. Policymakers can also leverage this study to develop industry-wide guidelines for ESG training programs, ensuring a more consistent and transparent approach to corporate reporting. Ultimately, this research provides a pathway for organizations to embed sustainability into their operations, contributing to long-term environmental, social, and economic objectives.

6.5 Future Research Directions

Although this study has explored the multifaceted role of mathematical education in corporate settings, several areas warrant further research. The diversity of industry and regional demands presents new challenges for designing and implementing mathematical education. For example, while manufacturing industries require advanced skills in data modeling and environmental impact assessment, the service sector focuses more on data visualization and social impact analysis (Bag et al., 2020; Saxena et al., 2022). Future research could delve deeper into these inter-industry differences and develop more targeted training modules. Additionally, implementing mathematical education in cross-cultural corporations raises unique challenges, such as the impact of cultural differences on content acceptance and the need for standardized cross-regional data protocols (Tsalis et al., 2020). These challenges offer opportunities for further customization of educational modules.

Beyond exploring future research directions, this study offers immediate practical implications for real-world applications. The integration of mathematical ESD equips corporate employees with advanced data literacy skills, enabling them to interpret and utilize ESG metrics effectively. This has direct benefits for corporations, including improved ESG reporting transparency, enhanced stakeholder trust, and better compliance with regulatory standards. Furthermore, this interdisciplinary approach provides a scalable model for educational institutions to design targeted training programs, fostering the next generation of professionals adept in sustainability practices. Policymakers can also leverage insights from this study to create industry-wide guidelines for integrating data literacy and ESG education, ensuring long-term progress toward sustainable development goals. Future research should further investigate how these practical applications can be customized across industries and regions to maximize their impact.

The rapid development of emerging technologies presents exciting possibilities for the future application of mathematical education. Artificial intelligence and automation have demonstrated potential in enhancing the efficiency and accuracy of employee training through automated data analysis tools (Rane et al., 2024). Technologies such as virtual reality and augmented reality can create immersive learning experiences, enabling employees to better understand the real-world implications of ESG data in simulated environments (De Wolf et al., 2023). Additionally, blockchain technology offers promising applications for ESG reporting by ensuring data transparency and immutability, thereby increasing the credibility and transparency of corporate reports (Saxena et al., 2022).

Future research should also consider the methodological limitations identified in this study, such as the lack of longitudinal data to assess the long-term impact of mathematical education on ESG performance. Conducting longitudinal studies can provide deeper insights into how employees' analytical capabilities evolve over time and their sustained impact on corporate ESG reporting transparency. Additionally, comparative research across industries and geographic regions would help validate the interdisciplinary framework proposed in this study, ensuring its scalability and adaptability to diverse corporate environments. Further exploration of sector-specific training needs and data protocols could refine the proposed educational modules to better address the unique challenges of different industries.

Future research should focus on integrating these emerging technologies with mathematical education to deliver more efficient and practical training solutions. Quantitative studies can also evaluate the long-term impact of mathematical education on corporate ESG performance, providing empirical evidence to support policymaking and educational practices in corporate contexts.

REFERENCES

Arvidsson, S., & Dumay, J. (2022). Corporate ESG reporting quantity, quality and performance: Where to now for environmental policy and practice? *Business Strategy and the Environment*, 31(3), 1091–1110. DOI: 10.1002/bse.2937

Bag, S., Wood, L. C., Xu, L., Dhamija, P., & Kayikci, Y. (2020). Big data analytics as an operational excellence approach to enhance sustainable supply chain performance. *Resources, Conservation and Recycling*, 153, 104559. DOI: 10.1016/j.resconrec.2019.104559

Bele, A. M., Sabău-Popa, C. D., Secară, O. M. (2023). Sustainable development goals and the triangle of ESG investments. *Journal of Financial Studies, 8*(14), 11–23. DOI: 10.55654/JFS.2023.8.14.1

Bergman, Z., Bergman, M. M., Fernandes, K., Grossrieder, D., & Schneider, L. (2018). The contribution of UNESCO chairs toward achieving the UN sustainable development goals. *Sustainability (Basel)*, 10(12), 4471. DOI: 10.3390/su10124471

Bø, E., Hammervoll, T., & Tvedt, K. (2013). *Environmental impact of refillable vs. Non-refillable plastic beverage bottles in Norway.*

Boiral, O., & Heras-Saizarbitoria, I. (2019). Sustainability reporting assurance: Creating stakeholder accountability through hyperreality? *Journal of Cleaner Production*, 243, 118596. DOI: 10.1016/j.jclepro.2019.118596

Buallay, A. (2018). *Is sustainability reporting (ESG) associated with performance? Evidence from the European banking sector.*

Cardoni, A., Kiseleva, E., & Terzani, S. (2019). *Evaluating the intra-industry comparability of sustainability reports: The case of the oil and gas industry.*

Chaturvedi, A. (2024). *Modelling sustainable projects: Investigating ESG indicators through virtual reality model* [Master's thesis, Metropolia University of Applied Sciences]. Theseus. https://www.theseus.fi/handle/10024/868098

Cho, S. J. (Ed.). (2015). *The proceedings of the 12th international congress on mathematical education: Intellectual and attitudinal challenges.* Springer International Publishing. DOI: 10.1007/978-3-319-12688-3

Choi, W. (2022). Education of digital data narrative using ESG concepts. *Journal of Digital Contents Society*, 23(2), 227–235. DOI: 10.9728/dcs.2022.23.2.227

Christie, M., Rowe, P., Perry, C., & Chamard, J. (2000). Implementation of realism in case study research methodology. *International Council for Small Business, Annual Conference*, 1–21. https://www.researchgate.net/profile/Patricia-Rowe-2/publication/43095715_Implementation_of_realism_in_case_study_research_methodology/links/09e41507de130b5b6d000000/Implementation-of-realism-in-case-study-research-methodology.pdf

Cruz, C. A., & Matos, F. (2023). ESG maturity: A software framework for the challenges of ESG data in investment. *Sustainability (Basel)*, 15(3), 2610. DOI: 10.3390/su15032610

De Wolf, C., Cordella, M., Dodd, N., Byers, B., & Donatello, S. (2023). Whole life cycle environmental impact assessment of buildings: Developing software tool and database support for the EU framework level(s). *Resources, Conservation and Recycling*, 188, 106642. DOI: 10.1016/j.resconrec.2022.106642

Eisenhardt, K. M. (1989). *Building theories from case study research.*

Fekih Zguir, M., Dubis, S., & Koç, M. (2021). Embedding education for sustainable development (ESD) and SDGs values in curriculum: A comparative review on qatar, singapore and new zealand. *Journal of Cleaner Production*, 319, 128534. DOI: 10.1016/j.jclepro.2021.128534

Ferrer-Estévez, M., & Chalmeta, R. (2021). Integrating Sustainable Development Goals in educational institutions. *International Journal of Management Education*, 19(2), 100494. DOI: 10.1016/j.ijme.2021.100494

Hahn, R., Reimsbach, D., & Schiemann, F. (2015). Organizations, Climate Change, and Transparency: Reviewing the Literature on Carbon Disclosure. *Organization & Environment*, 28(1), 80–102. DOI: 10.1177/1086026615575542

Hamad, S., Lai, F. W., Shad, M. K., Khatib, S. F. A., & Ali, S. E. A. (2023). Assessing the implementation of sustainable development goals: Does integrated reporting matter? *Sustainability Accounting. Management and Policy Journal*, 14(1), 49–74. DOI: 10.1108/SAMPJ-01-2022-0029

Huang, P. B., Yang, C.-C., Inderawati, M. M. W., & Sukwadi, R. (2022). Using modified delphi study to develop instrument for ESG implementation: A case study at an indonesian higher education institution. *Sustainability (Basel)*, 14(19), 12623. DOI: 10.3390/su141912623

Jablonka, E. (2003). *Mathematical literacy.*

Kahkonen, A.-K. (2014). Conducting a case study in supply management. *Operations and Supply Chain Management: An International Journal*, 4(1), 31–41. DOI: 10.31387/oscm090054

Kateryna, A., Oleksandr, R., Mariia, T., Iryna, S., Evgen, K., & Anastasiia, L. (2020). Digital literacy development trends in the professional environment. *International Journal of Learning, Teaching and Educational Research, 19*(7), Article 7.

Keeley, A. R., Chapman, A. J., Yoshida, K., Xie, J., Imbulana, J., Takeda, S., & Managi, S. (2022). ESG metrics and social equity: Investigating commensurability. *Frontiers in Sustainability*, 3, 920955. DOI: 10.3389/frsus.2022.920955

Khasreen, M. M., Banfill, P. F. G., & Menzies, G. F. (2009). Life-cycle assessment and the environmental impact of buildings: A review. *Sustainability (Basel)*, 1(3), 674–701. DOI: 10.3390/su1030674

Khatib, S. F. A., Ismail, I. H. M., Salameh, N., Abbas, A. F., Bazhair, A. H., & Sulimany, H. G. H. (2023). Carbon emission and firm performance: The moderating role of management environmental training. *Sustainability (Basel)*, 15(13), 10485. DOI: 10.3390/su151310485

Kitamura, Y., Karkour, S., Ichisugi, Y., & Itsubo, N. (2020). Carbon footprint evaluation of the business event sector in japan. *Sustainability (Basel)*, 12(12), 5001. DOI: 10.3390/su12125001

Lambini, C. K., Goeschl, A., Wäsch, M., & Wittau, M. (2021). Achieving the sustainable development goals through company staff vocational training—The case of the federal institute for vocational education and training (BIBB) INEBB project. *Education Sciences*, 11(4), 179. DOI: 10.3390/educsci11040179

Lee, C. K., & Han, H.-J. (2008). *Analysis of skills requirement for entry-level programmer/analysts in fortune 500 corporations.*

Lui, W. (2019). *The devil is in the details.*

Mahmoudian, F., Lu, J., Yu, D., Nazari, J. A., & Herremans, I. M. (2020). *Inter- and intra-organizational stakeholder arrangements in carbon management accounting.*

Manteaw, B. O. (2008). When businesses go to school: Neoliberalism and education for sustainable development. *Journal of Education for Sustainable Development*, 2(2), 119–126. DOI: 10.1177/097340820800200209

Mashayekhi, B., Asiaei, K., Rezaee, Z., Jahangard, A., Samavat, M., & Homayoun, S. (2024). The relative importance of ESG pillars: A two-step machine learning and analytical framework. *Sustainable Development*, 32(5), 5404–5420. DOI: 10.1002/sd.2979

McCarthy, K. A., & Kuhlemeyer, G. A. (2024). Preparing analytics-enabled professionals in finance using a simultaneous team-teaching approach: A case study. *Journal of Statistics and Data Science Education : An Official Journal of the of the American Statistical Association*, 32(1), 98–107. DOI: 10.1080/26939169.2023.2197470

Mumcu, H. Y. (2016). *Using Mathematics, Mathematical Applications, Mathematical Modelling, and Mathematical Literacy: A Theoretical Study.*

Nielsen, C. (2023). ESG reporting and metrics: From double materiality to key performance indicators. *Sustainability (Basel)*, 15(24), 16844. DOI: 10.3390/su152416844

Odey, G., Adelodun, B., Kim, S.-H., & Choi, K.-S. (2021). Status of environmental life cycle assessment (LCA): A case study of south korea. *Sustainability (Basel)*, 13(11), 6234. DOI: 10.3390/su13116234

Orlikowski, Iv., & Baroudi, J. J. (1991). *Studying Information Technology In Organizations: Research Approaches And Assumptions.*

Pandey, D., Agrawal, M., & Pandey, J. S. (2011). Carbon footprint: Current methods of estimation. *Environmental Monitoring and Assessment*, 178(1–4), 135–160. DOI: 10.1007/s10661-010-1678-y PMID: 20848311

Popescu, I.-S., Gibon, T., Hitaj, C., Rubin, M., & Benetto, E. (2023). Are SRI funds financing carbon emissions? An input-output life cycle assessment of investment funds. *Ecological Economics*, 212, 107918. DOI: 10.1016/j.ecolecon.2023.107918

Radovilsky, Z., Hegde, V., & Acharya, A. (2018). *Skills Requirements of Business Data Analytics and Data Science Jobs: A Comparative Analysis. 16*(1).

Rane, N., Choudhary, S., & Rane, J. (2024). Artificial intelligence driven approaches to strengthening environmental, social, and governance (ESG) criteria in sustainable business practices: A review. SSRN *Electronic Journal*. DOI: 10.2139/ssrn.4843215

Rouen, E., Sachdeva, K., & Yoon, A. (2024). *Sustainability meets substance:* Sarkis, J., & Talluri, S. (2002). A model for strategic supplier selection. *The Journal of Supply Chain Management*, 38(4), 18–28. DOI: 10.1111/j.1745-493X.2002.tb00117.x

Saxena, A., Singh, R., Gehlot, A., Akram, S. V., Twala, B., Singh, A., Montero, E. C., & Priyadarshi, N. (2022). Technologies empowered environmental, social, and governance (ESG): An industry 4.0 landscape. *Sustainability (Basel)*, 15(1), 309. DOI: 10.3390/su15010309

Sciarelli, M., Cosimato, S., Landi, G., & Iandolo, F. (2021). Socially responsible investment strategies for the transition towards sustainable development: The importance of integrating and communicating ESG. *The TQM Journal*, 33(7), 39–56. DOI: 10.1108/TQM-08-2020-0180

Solaimani, S. (2024). From compliance to capability: On the role of data and technology in environment, social, and governance. *Sustainability (Basel)*, 16(14), 6061. DOI: 10.3390/su16146061

Spiegeleer, J. D., Hocht, S., Jakubowski, D., Reyners, S., & Schoutens, W. (2020). *ESG: A new dimension in portfolio allocation.*

Ssossé, Q., Wagner, J., & Hopper, C. (2021). Assessing the impact of ESD: Methods, challenges, results. *Sustainability (Basel)*, 13(5), 2854. DOI: 10.3390/su13052854

Tang, Q., & Luo, L. (2011). *Transparency of corporate carbon disclosure: International evidence.*

Tsalis, T. A., Malamateniou, K. E., Koulouriotis, D., & Nikolaou, I. E. (2020). New challenges for corporate sustainability reporting: United nations' 2030 agenda for sustainable development and the sustainable development goals. *Corporate Social Responsibility and Environmental Management*, 27(4), 1617–1629. DOI: 10.1002/csr.1910

Tsang, E. W. K. (2014). Generalizing from research findings: The merits of case studies. *International Journal of Management Reviews*, 16(4), 369–383. DOI: 10.1111/ijmr.12024

Widyawati, L. (2020). A systematic literature review of socially responsible investment and environmental social governance metrics. *Business Strategy and the Environment*, 29(2), 619–637. DOI: 10.1002/bse.2393

Yue, S., Bajuri, N. H. B., Khatib, S. F. A., & Alshareef, M. N. (2025). Ownership with a green twist: The role of top managers in driving environmental innovation. *China Finance Review International, ahead-of-print*(ahead-of-print). DOI: 10.1108/CFRI-03-2024-0121

Yue, S., Bajuri, N. H. B., Ye, G., & Ullah, F. (2025). Green awakening: The rising influence of minority shareholders and ESG in shaping China's sustainable future. *Sustainable Futures : An Applied Journal of Technology, Environment and Society*, 100441, 100441. Advance online publication. DOI: 10.1016/j.sftr.2025.100441

Zhang, F. (2024). Enhancing ESG learning outcomes through gamification: An experimental study. *PLoS One*, 19(5), e0303259. DOI: 10.1371/journal.pone.0303259 PMID: 38748683

Zhou, X., & Yang, Z. (2022). Research on measurement and evaluation of mathematical data analysis literacy. *Asian Journal of Education and Social Studies*, 51–61. DOI: 10.9734/ajess/2022/v30i230718

Zumente, I., & Bistrova, J. (2021). ESG importance for long-term shareholder value creation: Literature vs. Practice. *Journal of Open Innovation*, 7(2), 127. DOI: 10.3390/joitmc7020127

Chapter 10
Perceived Environmental Corporate Social Responsibility and Sustainable Innovation in the Hotel Business: The Mediating Role of Green Intrinsic Motivation

Hazem Ahmed Khairy

Hotel Management Department, Faculty of Tourism and Hotels, University of Sadat City, Sadat City, Egypt

Hanan Eid Badwy

https://orcid.org/0009-0006-0786-791X

Surveying of Natural Resources in Environmental Systems Department, Environmental Studies and Research Institute, University of Sadat City, Sadat City, Egypt

Sawsan Haider Abdullah Khreis

https://orcid.org/0000-0001-6364-8590

Department of Travel and Tourism, Faculty of Tourism and Hotels, Yarmouk University, Irbid, Jordan

ABSTRACT

This study seeks to explore the influence of perceived environmental corporate social responsibility on sustainable innovation within the hotel industry, with particular emphasis on the mediating role of green intrinsic motivation. A total of 396 responses

DOI: 10.4018/979-8-3373-0117-4.ch010

collected from full-time employees at five-star hotels in Egypt were analyzed using Partial Least Squares Structural Equation Modeling (PLS-SEM) with WarpPLS statistical software version 7.0. The findings indicate that perceived environmental corporate social responsibility has a positive impact on both sustainable innovation and green intrinsic motivation. Furthermore, green intrinsic motivation not only positively influences sustainable innovation but also serves as a mediator in the relationship between perceived environmental corporate social responsibility and sustainable innovation. Theoretically, this study provides new insights into how emerging concepts such as perceived environmental corporate social responsibility and green intrinsic motivation serve as predictors of sustainable innovation within hotel enterprises. Practically, the research highlights the importance of cultivating a more engaged and innovative workforce that is dedicated to achieving sustainability goals.

INTRODUCTION

Environmental management has historically constituted a significant area of inquiry within the domains of hospitality management (Khairy et al., 2023; Molina-Collado et al., 2022; Olya et al., 2024), primarily due to the rising ecological concerns and anticipations of consumers regarding sustainable practices, as well as the fact that the hospitality sector exerts a disproportionately adverse influence on the environment in comparison to other service-oriented industries (Al-Romeedy et al., 2024; Chen et al., 2023; Lenzen et al., 2018). Consequently, enterprises within the hospitality sector encounter increasing demands to integrate sustainable practices throughout their operational frameworks, providing "eco-conscious" offerings while simultaneously enhancing the recognition of environmental values among their workforce, who play a pivotal role in the advancement of innovative green solutions (Kalyar et al., 2021; Liu & Liu, 2023).

In light of rapidly increasing environmental consciousness within the highly competitive business landscape, hotels globally have commenced to underscore the significance of perceived environmental corporate social responsibility (PECSR) as a catalyst for sustainable innovation (Le et al., 2024; Nureen et al., 2023). PECSR represents a discretionary environmental conduct aimed at alleviating the detrimental effects of commercial activities on the natural ecosystem. This encompasses measures such as resource conservation, pollution abatement, the reduction of waste emissions, product recycling, and the adoption of environmentally sustainable production techniques (Wu & Yu, 2024), all intended to optimize production efficacy (Chuang & Huang, 2018; Salama et al., 2024), while simultaneously promoting community development and enhancing the overall quality of life for individuals

(Dhingra, 2023). To fully leverage the advantages associated with the modification of current processes and products, as well as the creation of innovative offerings aimed at environmental protection, it is imperative for organizations to incorporate PECSR into their strategies (Xie et al., 2019). Consequently, the introduction of novel eco-products and processes has the potential to enhance market valuation, elevate corporate reputation, and foster sustainable innovation (Fraj-Andrés et al., 2009; Le et al., 2024).

Stakeholders are putting significant pressure on hotels to embrace sustainable environmental practices due to the harmful nature of their services and products. Consequently, these pressures have caused corporations to actively promote and execute environmentally sustainable initiatives. Hence, CSR initiatives aimed at fostering sustainable innovation (SI) are perceived as a solution for attaining sustainable development and mitigating environmental degradation (Fosu et al., 2024). SI encompasses the integration of environmentally benign processes, products, and methodologies within manufacturing and operational activities with the objective of minimizing costs, waste, and pollution (Chang, 2011). SI aids organizations in navigating new business environments as a vital survival strategy, facilitating the execution of effective policies, and cultivating robust relationships with stakeholders (Tang et al., 2018). Furthermore, SI can be optimized through the careful selection of environmentally sustainable raw materials, minimizing waste, designing products in accordance with eco-design principles, reducing carbon emissions, and conserving water, electricity, and other resources (Bonsu et al., 2024). In light of the extensive embrace of sustainable development goals, SI is perceived as a fundamental strategy for securing a competitive edge (He et al., 2024).

The perception of CSR is posited to enhance the intrinsic motivation of employees within the workplace, as CSR embodies the ethical intentions and actions of employers aimed at contributing positively to society and the environment, thereby facilitating employees' constructive interpretation of the significance of their work (Rosso et al., 2010). Intrinsic motivation constitutes a psychological state whereby individuals are driven by an intrinsic love and passion for executing tasks, as opposed to being influenced by external rewards or incentives (Deci & Ryan, 1985). Moreover, Liu and Liu (2023) articulated that green intrinsic motivation encompasses employees' engagement in environmentally sustainable behaviors, which is driven by their intrinsic interests, identity, sense of responsibility, and achievement regarding environmental matters. Additionally, behaviors characterized by intrinsic motivation exhibit the utmost degree of self-determination and are executed based on factors such as enjoyment, interest, and inherent satisfaction (Ryan & Deci, 2000). Individuals exhibiting green intrinsic motivation tend to cultivate a more profound passion and affection for the environment (Li et al., 2020).

Despite this, there exists scarce research aimed at investigating the relationship between PECSR and emerging markets within the African context. Furthermore, there has been limited research focusing on PECSR that critically examines the sustainable innovation while considering the mediating influence of green intrinsic motivation in Africa, with particular emphasis on Egypt. Consequently, we are driven to address this significant gap and pose the below research questions:

RQ1. What are the effects of PECSR and GIM on SI?
RQ2. What is the effect of PECSR on GIM?
RQ3. To what degree does GIM mediate the relationship between PECSR and SI?

This study aims to examine the interrelationship among PECSR, GIM, and SI within the tourism and hospitality industry of Egypt. The choice of this sector is critical for a multitude of significant reasons. On a global scale, the tourism and hospitality sector exert a considerable environmental impact, characterized by its high levels of resource utilization, which consequently results in increased emissions and waste (Meng et al., 2024).

LITERATURE REVIEW AND HYPOTHESIS DEVELOPMENT

Natural Resource-Based View

The RBV theory posits that the unique resources and capabilities of an organization play a pivotal role in achieving a competitive advantage (Barney, 1991). Furthermore, the Natural Resource-Based View (NRBV) represents an extension of the RBV theory, proposing that firms can attain enduring competitive advantages by effectively addressing challenges associated with the natural environment (Hart, 1995). As per the theory, organizations can attain a competitive edge through the implementation of diverse environmental strategies, which encompass environmental safeguarding, sustainable product innovation, and ecological preservation (Hart, 1995). With respect to the emerging management paradigm, the NRBV facilitates the identification of a firm's environmental competencies, which constitute a fundamental component of the organization's core structure (Sarfraz et al., 2023).

Therefore, the perceived environmental dimensions of corporate social responsibility, green intrinsic motivation, and sustainable innovation serve as fundamental mechanisms that contribute to the preservation of ecological well-being. These competencies are instrumental in alleviating the environmental burden, which exerts a considerable influence on the organization's reputation and competitive advantage. To support this theory, we propose that sustainable innovation can be conceptualized as both an organizational resource and a dynamic capability that is in a continual state of evolution (Bonsu et al., 2024). From this perspective, enterprises may achieve a competitive edge over their counterparts by amplifying the effects of corporate social responsibility on sustainable innovation (Rehman et al., 2021).

Consequently, the examination of this model through the lens of the NRBV will empower organizations to distinguish their products and services, thereby facilitating enduring market evolution. Importantly, this approach will assist hospitality establishments in achieving ongoing enhancements in their operational efficacy through the incorporation of a stakeholder-centric viewpoint. Furthermore, it will drive these hotels to reconfigure their strategies and mitigate the risks associated with environmental challenges that impact the sustainability of innovation within enterprises. In conclusion, the integrations explored within this theoretical framework (e.g., PECSR, GIM, and SI) possess the capacity to guarantee the competitive success of firms in relation to their rivals.

Perceived Environmental Corporate Social Responsibility

CSR has emerged as a significant corporate endeavor on a global scale over recent decades. The notion of CSR was initially articulated by Sheldon in 1924; however, it did not gain substantial traction until the 1960s and subsequently thereafter. Since that time, this topic has captivated the attention of corporations, governmental bodies, societal structures, and academic institutions alike (Halkos et al., 2022). The CSR paradigm can be understood as a novel, effective, and integrated business framework that addresses the requirements of stakeholders, shareholders, societal necessities, environmental sustainability, and economic advantages ((Sánchez-Infante Hernández et al., 2020). In recent decades, enterprises have encountered escalating societal demands to adopt CSR practices as a reaction to emerging sustainability challenges (Yang & Jiang, 2023). CSR embodies the duty of organizations towards their stakeholders, the broader community, and sustainable development, materializing through corporate actions that deliberately focus on social and environmental concerns (van Marrewijk, 2003).

The principles of environmental management and CSR constitute the foundational framework for PECSR (Li et al., 2023). There exists a variety of CSR types, encompassing environmental sustainability, ethical business practices, social welfare, philanthropic endeavors, among others (Abbas, 2024). PECSR pertains to the initiatives undertaken by organizations aimed at mitigating their adverse effects on the ecosystem while promoting the integration of environmentally sustainable policies (Latif et al., 2022). The implementation of PECSR enhances an organization's public image and facilitates community acceptance (Fosu et al., 2024). PECSR is further characterized as environmentally conscientious business practices that transcend mere compliance with regulatory requirements and acknowledge accountability for any detrimental external effects stemming from their operations (Chuang & Huang, 2018). CSR represents a paradigm that encourages corporations to voluntarily integrate social and environmental considerations into their operational frameworks and stakeholder interactions (Bonsu et al., 2024). The dedication of companies to their stakeholders, society, and the environment is reflected in business strategies and conduct that influence the social and environmental standing of the enterprise (Kunnaala et al., 2013). The implementation of CSR practices is essential for the sustainability of businesses and is increasingly likely to provide a competitive advantage for diverse stakeholders (Ramzan et al., 2021).

Green Intrinsic Motivation

The perception of CSR among employees has the potential to cultivate their intrinsic motivation within the workplace (Fredrickson, 2013). Intrinsic motivation is characterized as a profound emotional state of passion and affection that drives individuals to undertake tasks, independent of external incentives or rewards (Coccia, 2019). GIM is an internally oriented motivation that emerges from participation in inherently fulfilling activities associated with environmental sustainability (W. Li et al., 2020). Furthermore, GIM, as articulated by (Amabile et al., 1994); (Deci, 1972), posits that an individual is intrinsically motivated when engaging in a task for reasons beyond extrinsic rewards, focusing instead on the inherent value of the activity and the internal drive it invokes. Consequently, individuals who are motivated by their intrinsic values, characterized by their affection, curiosity, and passionate dedication to their professional endeavors, are more inclined to experience feelings of satisfaction, engagement, and enthusiasm (Chen et al., 2023). The concept of intrinsic motivation in the workplace pertains to the phenomenon wherein employees participate in their tasks due to the intrinsic fulfillment, pleasure, self-expression, and personal interest they derive from these activities (Tang et al., 2024). Furthermore, the perception of CSR can elicit moral elevation, resulting in a favorable emotional reaction when observing ethical behaviors (Tang et al., 2024), thereby enhancing employees' enjoyment in their professional roles.

Green intrinsic motivation emerges from individual beliefs, which encourages persons to engage in responsible behaviors (Faraz et al., 2021), and due to the intrinsic nature of this motivation, employees are more inclined to exhibit pro-environmental behaviors over extended periods and in diverse contexts (Sharpe et al., 2022). In contrast to external incentives such as financial rewards, this form of motivation is derived from internal values. When motivated by an intrinsic aspiration to contribute positively to the environment, employees voluntarily embrace sustainable practices, thereby augmenting a company's CSR influence on SI. (Amabile et al., 1994) posited that individuals, driven by their passionate interest, inquisitiveness, and passion for their professions, experience a sense of excitement, engagement, and fulfillment; furthermore, she elucidated that intrinsic motivation serves as the pivotal component of innovation, fostering employee attachment to their roles, enhancing their concentration, and consequently prompting employees to engage in experimentation and exhibit heightened innovative behaviors (Le et al., 2024).

Sustainable Innovation

Environmental innovation, eco-innovation, and green innovation are often regarded as synonymous with the concept of sustainable innovation (Boons et al., 2013). SI, which represents an extension of the traditional notion of innovation, encompasses the development of novel processes and the application of technologies that actualize new and distinctive ideas aimed at reducing adverse environmental impacts, including but not limited to carbon emissions and pollution (Alketbi & Ahmad, 2024). SI is commonly characterized as the advancement of novel services, products, methodologies, and technologies that facilitate the progression and welfare of human needs and institutions while honoring the integrity of natural resources and their regenerative capacities (Tello & Yoon, 2008). More broadly, SI can be articulated as innovative or adapted processes, methodologies, practices, systems, and products that endeavor to mitigate or alleviate environmental harm, augment recycling efforts, enhance regulatory frameworks, and improve ecological, economic, and social outcomes (Rennings, 2000).

SI is intrinsically connected to CSR and sustainability, particularly with regard to its role in environmental conservation (Haldar, 2019; Wang, 2020), as corporate activities frequently exert adverse effects on ecological systems, and enterprises are perceived to have the potential to mitigate these detrimental influences through suitable interventions (Cheng, 2020). SI exhibits a greater degree of unpredictability and disruption compared to conventional innovation, as it relies on a broader spectrum of knowledge and necessitates the integration of various environmental factors (Bonsu et al., 2024). By promoting avant-garde energy-efficient technologies, harnessing renewable resources, repurposing waste and pollutants, and developing environmentally sustainable products, SI encompasses all progress in safe processes and products that benefit consumers and the environment (Chen et al., 2006). The market is shaped by issues pertaining to environmental concerns and the imperative to adhere to regulatory requirements, which may serve as catalysts for corporate behavior and market dynamics (Bekk et al., 2016). Various programs, including wastewater management and recycling initiatives, can be implemented by organizations in distinct and inventive manners to mitigate adverse ecological effects (Alketbi & Ahmad, 2024).

HYPOTHESES DEVELOPMENT

Perceived Environmental Corporate Social Responsibility and Sustainable Innovation

CSR has emerged as a critical agent of change, significantly impacting enterprises by profoundly influencing and promoting innovation within them as they strive to navigate and adopt this widespread and transformative paradigm shift. In other terms, CSR is regarded as one of the determinants that affect and enhance innovation of businesses in their efforts to adapt to contemporary market trends (Kraus et al., 2020; Li et al., 2023). Moreover, organizations can initiate SI through their involvement in CSR activities, thereby demonstrating their ecological legitimacy and enhancing their potential for superior organizational performance (Lozano, 2013). Consequently, a number of studies postulate that SI may serve as a fundamental mechanism for assessing the relationship between CSR and various outcome variables (Azam & Jamil, 2024; Feng et al., 2022). The evolution of business strategies has been shaped by a multitude of determinants, including heightened consumer environmental consciousness, regulatory frameworks pertaining to environmental issues, societal commitments to environmental stewardship, and corporate practices aimed at environmental sustainability (Badwy et al., 2025; Li et al., 2023). These advancements have prompted enterprises to develop innovative products characterized by a reduced environmental footprint and to improve overall business performance (Li et al., 2023).

According to the NRBV, organizations that strategically deploy their resources and capabilities can effectively integrate CSR with sustainable innovation (Broadstock et al., 2019). Moreover, (Shahzad et al., 2020) argue that there exists a positive correlation between CSR and the advancement of sustainable innovation. In the contemporary epoch characterized by increased awareness and social consciousness, both governmental entities and societal institutions have allocated significant attention and resources to the critical endeavor of environmental preservation, acknowledging its undeniable importance and urgent necessity (Le et al., 2024). Moreover, prior research has demonstrated that CSR positively impacts SI (Alketbi & Ahmad, 2024). In a similar vein, Hao and He (2022) established a significant correlation between CSR and SI. Furthermore, Novitasari and Tarigan (2022) indicated that organizations that prioritize environmental concerns can enhance their SI. Additionally, it has been observed that environmental CSR initiatives are positively correlated with green innovation (Fosu et al., 2024). Consequently, we posit that CSR significantly influences the SI of firms, which leads to our second hypothesis:

> ***H1:*** Perceived environmental corporate social responsibility positively correlates with sustainable innovation.

Perceived Environmental Corporate Social Responsibility and Green Intrinsic Motivation

CSR denotes the voluntary initiatives undertaken by organizations that enhance the welfare of society, the environment, and ecological systems (Aguilera et al., 2007). Research by Tang et al. (2024) and Lin (2023) indicates that enterprises exhibiting a robust dedication to PECSR are predisposed to possess elevated levels of intrinsic motivation towards environmentally sustainable practices. Their findings suggest that activities associated with PECSR may serve as a significant impetus for the cultivation of green intrinsic motivation. Leonidou and Skarmeas (2017) posited that firms involved in PECSR are more inclined to allocate resources towards training and development initiatives, which can facilitate the enhancement of green intrinsic motivation. Another research indicates that firms that emphasize environmental sustainability are more inclined to allocate resources towards research and development pertinent to eco-friendly products and methodologies, consequently fostering an enhancement in green intrinsic motivation (Li et al., 2020). The interaction of CSR and green intrinsic motivation provides a nuanced lens through which organizational strategies can engage with individual values and convictions (Shnayder et al., 2016).

Research has indicated that individuals employed in organizations that prioritize social responsibility may derive a sense of significance from their contributions to societal welfare, as employees typically possess a calling orientation aimed at enhancing the world, and perceive that CSR aligns with such aspirations (Nazir & Islam, 2020). CSR encapsulates the ethical motives and actions of employers that extend beyond mere self-interest (Bauman & Skitka, 2012), and such perceptions not only lead employees to appraise their employers favorably (Gond et al., 2017) but also influence their green intrinsic motivation towards their professional responsibilities (Leonidou & Skarmeas, 2017; Tang et al., 2024). The organizational prioritization of CSR, particularly in the realm of environmental stewardship, conveys a distinct communication to the employee base: a clear articulation of principles that resonate profoundly with the intrinsic motivation towards sustainability (Romani et al., 2016). For corporations, especially within industries such as hospitality industry where ecological footprints are significantly pronounced, this congruence is not merely advantageous but fundamentally imperative. A workforce that is both motivated and engaged, propelled by intrinsic green values, emerges as a formidable agent in the effective execution of CSR initiatives (Khamdamov et al., 2023). Moreover, Tang et al. (2024) found that Perceived CSR positively impacts intrinsic motivation. Similarly, Meng et al. (2024) revealed that Perceived CSR positively influences intrinsic motivation. So, we suggest:

H2: Perceived environmental corporate social responsibility positively correlates green intrinsic motivation.

Green Intrinsic Motivation and Sustainable Innovation

Green intrinsic motivation manifests as a formidable internal drive shaped by individual values, norms, and beliefs, driving individuals towards environmentally sustainable behaviors (Lin, 2023). This construct of green intrinsic motivation is derived from the broader notion of intrinsic motivation, which denotes a condition in which individuals are self-motivated by a genuine passion for engaging in specific activities (Deci & Ryan, 1985). Motivation constitutes a crucial determinant in an organization's determination to implement sustainable innovation practices (He et al., 2024). Typically, the foundational assumption regarding the motivation of organizations to partake in innovative endeavors is predicated on the desire to foster technological advancement and attain competitive superiority (Rennings, 2000). Furthermore, employees driven by intrinsic motivation are inclined towards the development of novel or improved products, processes, or technologies that contribute positively to both the economy and environment (Leonidou & Skarmeas, 2017; Li et al., 2020). Consequently, we propose:

H3: Green intrinsic motivation positively correlates sustainable innovation.

Green Intrinsic Motivation as a Mediator

The relationship between PECSR and SI is complex, revealing a multifaceted dynamic influenced by intrinsic motivation related to environmental sustainability. Primarily, CSR initiatives function as a manifestation of an organization's values and commitment to ecological sustainability (Spanjol et al., 2015). When employees recognize these initiatives, they may undergo an enhancement or triggering of their intrinsic motivation towards green practices (Afsar et al., 2016). Furthermore, the concept of PECSR may serve as a significant predictor of employees' environmentally innovative practices. It is characterized by the obligation to address the ecological repercussions of a company's operations, products, and associations; to mitigate waste and pollution; to optimize the utilization of accessible resources; and to curtail actions that could adversely affect the utilization of the nation's resources for future generations (Rongbin et al., 2022). The combination of the aforementioned hypotheses indicates a mediating function for green intrinsic motivation; PECSR is cultivated by internal incentives or rewards, thereby facilitating SI. Numerous studies have posited a mediating function for intrinsic motivation within the nexus of green values and green creativity (Wu et al., 2021), green mindfulness and green organizational citizenship behavior (Chen et al., 2023), as well as green inclusive leadership and green work engagement (Eladawi et al., 2024). Consequently, in the present study, we hypothesize:

> ***H4:*** Green intrinsic motivation positively mediates the relationship between perceived environmental corporate social responsibility and sustainable innovation.

The theoretical framework underpinning the study is depicted in Figure 1 presented below.

Figure 1. The conceptual model of the study

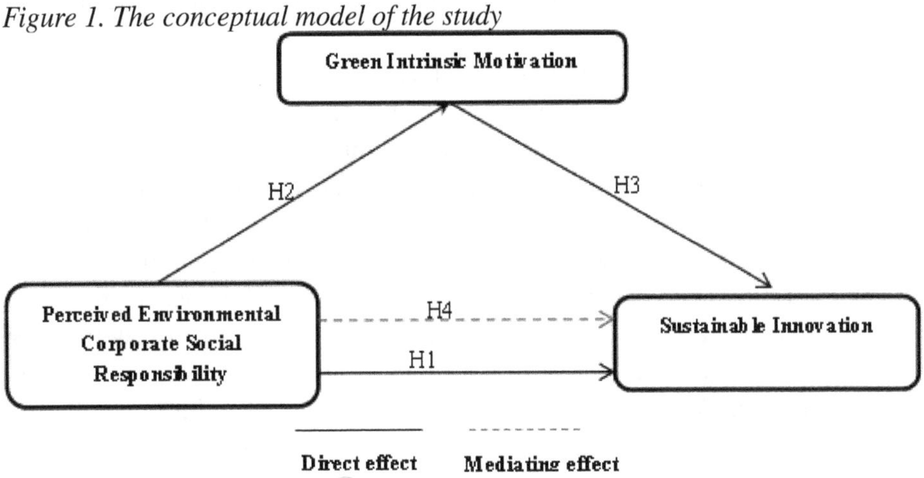

METHODOLOGY

Measures and Instrument Development

A structured survey was conducted using a quantitative research approach to collect essential data. The survey aimed to evaluate perceived environmental corporate social responsibility (PECSR) within the hospitality sector, particularly in five-star hotels, and to examine its effects on green intrinsic motivation and sustainable innovation. It consisted of two sections: the first section focused on latent variables and included 18 items, while the second section addressed the research sample's characteristics and comprised four questions.

This study employed a self-administered questionnaire method. The original questionnaire was created in English, and a back-translation technique was utilized to ensure its accuracy. Initially, a bilingual expert fluent in both English and Arabic translated the questionnaire into Arabic. A second bilingual professional then translated it back into English. To ensure consistency, the original and back-translated English versions were compared. Since the translations matched, the questionnaire was subsequently administered in Arabic to enhance clarity and maximize the response rate.

Perceived environmental corporate social responsibility (PECSR) was assessed using a six-item scale adapted from Turker (2009) and Wu et al. (2022). For example, "I can feel our hotel participates in activities which aim to protect and improve the quality of the natural environment" and "I can feel our hotel has the necessary equipment to reduce its negative environmental impact". In addition, sustainable innovation was evaluated through a separate six-item scale adapted from Delmas and Pekovic (2018). For example, "Our hotel has introduced products, processes, organizational, or marketing innovations that reduce resources and materials per unit of production" and "Our hotel has have introduced products, processes, organizational, or marketing innovations that replace materials with less polluting or hazardous substitutes". Furthermore, green intrinsic motivation was measured using a six-item scale developed by Li et al. (2020). For example, "I enjoy tackling with environmental tasks that are completely new" and "I feel excited when I have new green ideas". The complete measurement scales are detailed in the Appendix.

Sampling and Data Collection

The study model was assessed using data gathered from full-time employees at five-star hotels in Egypt, a category chosen for its significant role in the country's hospitality sector. These hotels often encounter challenges in implementing sustainability initiatives, aligning sustainability goals among stakeholders, and securing stakeholder buy-in. The fragmented nature of the hospitality industry, coupled with the financial incentives associated with sustainability initiatives, can complicate efforts to persuade stakeholders who prioritize short-term profits over long-term environmental advantages.

According to the Egyptian Ministry of Tourism and Antiquities, there were 30 five-star hotels in the Greater Cairo region as of 2022. The research employed a convenience sampling method, which is frequently utilized when randomization is impractical due to a large population and limited resources. A total of 600 questionnaires were distributed among the selected hotels, resulting in 396 valid responses, yielding a response rate of 66% from 23 five-star hotels. Hair et al. (2010) suggest determining the appropriate sample size based on the number of variables being studied, with a recommended minimum ratio of "variable = 1:10." Given the 18 items examined in this study, the minimum sample size required was 180 respondents, thus the sample size of 396 employees is deemed adequate for analysis.

Non-Response and Common Method Biases

The study found no significant differences between early and late survey responses, as indicated by t-tests ($p > 0.05$), suggesting that there were no concerns regarding non-response bias. Additionally, to evaluate common method variance (CMV), the study utilized Harman's single-factor test and principal component analysis. The results showed that no single factor explained more than 50% of the total variance, indicating that CMV is not a significant concern in this research.

Data Analysis

The study utilized partial least squares structural equation modeling (PLS-SEM), a widely accepted method for both confirmatory and exploratory research. PLS-SEM is a statistical approach that facilitates the validation and extension of theories, making it suitable for analyzing models efficiently. This technique is particularly advantageous in strategic and management studies and is frequently employed in hospitality research. The data processing was conducted using WarpPLS statistical software version 7.0.

RESULTS

Participant's Profile

Table 1 provides a demographic profile of the study participants, consisting of 396 respondents. The table breaks down the participants based on gender, age, education level, and job tenure. The majority of respondents were male (284 participants, 71.72%), while females comprised 28.28% (112 participants).in addition, most participants were between 30 and 40 years old (142 participants, 35.86%), followed by the 40 to 50 age group (104 participants, 26.26%). A smaller proportion was under 30 (62 participants, 15.66%), and 22.22% were over 50 years of age (88 participants). Moreover, the majority of respondents held a Bachelor's degree (225 participants, 56.82%). High school graduates represented 28.79% (114 participants), and 14.39% (57 participants) had obtained a Master's or PhD degree. Furthermore, most participants had 2 to less than 5 years of work experience (143 participants, 36.11%). This was followed by those with 5 to 10 years of experience (98 participants, 24.75%), less than 2 years (68 participants, 17.17%), and more than 10 years (87 participants, 21.97%). Overall, the table provides a detailed view of the demographic distribution of the respondents, helping to contextualize the research findings.

Table 1. Participant's profile (N=396)

		Frequency	Percent
Gender	Male	284	71.72
	Female	112	28.28
Age	< 30 years	62	15.66
	30: < 40 years	142	35.86
	40: 50 years	104	26.26
	>50	88	22.22
Education	High schools	114	28.79
	Bachelor	225	56.82
	Master/PhD	57	14.39
Tenure	1< 2 years	68	17.17
	2 to <5 years	143	36.11
	5 to 10 years	98	24.75
	> 10 years	87	21.97

Measurement Model

The three-factor model, encompassing perceived environmental corporate social responsibility (PECSR), sustainable innovation (SI), and green intrinsic motivation (GIM), was evaluated using confirmatory factor analysis. Kock (2017)'s fifteen fit indices were applied to assess the model's fit: APC ("P<0.05"), ARS ("P<0.05"), AARS ("P<0.05"), AVIF ("acceptable if ≤5, ideally ≤3.3"), AFVIF ("acceptable if ≤5, ideally ≤3.3"), GoF ("small ≥0.1, medium ≥0.25, large ≥0.36"), SPR ("acceptable if ≥0.7, ideally =1"), RSCR ("acceptable if ≥0.9, ideally =1"), SSR ("acceptable if ≥0.7"), NLBCDR ("acceptable if ≥0.7"), SRMR ("acceptable if ≤0.1"), SMAR ("acceptable if ≤0.1"), SChS ("P<0.05"), STDCR ("acceptable if ≥0.7, ideally =1"), and STDSR ("acceptable if ≥0.7, ideally =1"). The proposed three-factor model demonstrated a good fit, yielding the following values: APC = 0.513, P < 0.001; ARS = 0.555, P < 0.001; AARS = 0.553, P < 0.001; AVIF = 2.350; AFVIF = 2.334; GoF = 0.568; SPR = 1.000; RSCR = 1.000; SSR = 1.000; NLBCDR = 1.000; SRMR = 0.090; SMAR = 0.074; SChS = 3.112, P < 0.001; STDCR = 1.000; and STDSR = 1.000.

Table 2 provides comprehensive information on item loadings, composite reliability (CR), Cronbach's alpha (CA), average variance extracted (AVE), and variance inflation factors (VIF) for the constructs evaluated in the study. As shown in Table 2, the perceived environmental corporate social responsibility (PECSR) construct, which includes indicators PECSR.1 through PECSR.6, has item loadings ranging from 0.707 to 0.844, indicating a strong association with the construct. The composite reliability is 0.899, reflecting good internal consistency, and Cronbach's alpha is 0.864, confirming its reliability. The AVE value for PECSR is 0.598, suggesting sufficient convergent validity, while the VIF of 2.511 indicates the absence of multicollinearity issues. Additionally, for sustainable innovation (SI), which includes indicators SI.1 through SI.6, item loadings range from 0.660 to 0.833, indicating a moderate to strong association with the construct. The composite reliability is 0.871, demonstrating good internal consistency, while Cronbach's alpha is 0.822, confirming its reliability. The AVE for SI is 0.532, indicating satisfactory convergent validity, and the VIF of 2.280 suggests the absence of multicollinearity concerns. Furthermore, green intrinsic motivation (GIM), which comprises indicators GIM.1 to GIM.6, shows item loadings ranging from 0.723 to 0.839, indicating a strong relationship with the construct. The composite reliability is 0.905, reflecting excellent internal consistency, while Cronbach's alpha is 0.873, further validating its reliability. The AVE for GIM is 0.613, demonstrating good convergent validity, and the VIF of 2.212 suggests no multicollinearity concerns.

Table 2. Item loadings, Cronbach alpha, CR, AVE, and VIFs

Construct	Indicators	Loading	CR	CA	AVE	VIF
Perceived Environmental Corporate Social Responsibility (PECSR)	PECSR.1	0.756	0.899	0.864	0.598	2.511
	PECSR.2	0.823				
	PECSR.3	0.781				
	PECSR.4	0.844				
	PECSR.5	0.707				
	PECSR.6	0.717				
Sustainable Innovation (SI)	SI.1	0.660	0.871	0.822	0.532	2.280
	SI.2	0.659				
	SI.3	0.712				
	SI.4	0.833				
	SI.5	0.802				
	SI.6	0.692				
Green Intrinsic Motivation (GIM)	GIM.1	0.776	0.905	0.873	0.613	2.212
	GIM.2	0.821				
	GIM.3	0.792				
	GIM.4	0.839				
	GIM.5	0.723				
	GIM.6	0.740				

"CR: Composite reliability; CA: Cronbach's alpha; AVE: average variance extracted; VIF: variance inflation factors."

Overall, all constructs show composite reliability values above the acceptable threshold of 0.70, along with Cronbach's alpha values exceeding 0.70, indicating strong internal consistency. Moreover, the AVE values for each construct are above 0.50, validating convergent validity. The VIF values are significantly lower than 3.3, suggesting no multicollinearity concerns. Therefore, Table 2 effectively summarizes the reliability and validity of the constructs used in the study, confirming that the measures are both reliable and appropriate for the research.

Table 3 presents the discriminant validity results using the Fornell-Larcker criterion for three constructs: perceived environmental corporate social responsibility (PECSR), green intrinsic motivation (GIM), and sustainable innovation (SI). The diagonal elements represent the square roots of the average variance extracted (AVE) for each construct, while the off-diagonal elements indicate the correlations between the constructs.

Table 3. Discriminant validity results - Fornell-Larcker criterion

	PECSR	GIM	SI
Perceived Environmental Corporate Social Responsibility (PECSR)	0.773	0.702	0.713
Green Intrinsic Motivation (GIM)	0.702	0.783	0.665
Sustainable Innovation (SI)	0.713	0.665	0.729

"Off-diagonal elements are correlations and diagonal elements are square roots of AVE"

According to Table 3, PECSR has a square root of AVE value of 0.773, which is greater than its correlations with GIM (0.702) and SI (0.713). This suggests that PECSR shares more variance with its items than with other constructs, confirming discriminant validity. In addition, GIM has a square root of AVE value of 0.783, which is higher than its correlations with PECSR (0.702) and SI (0.665). This indicates that GIM is distinct from the other constructs. Furthermore, SI has a square root of AVE value of 0.729, exceeding its correlations with PECSR (0.713) and GIM (0.665), demonstrating that SI has satisfactory discriminant validity. Overall, the results show that each construct is more strongly associated with its indicators than with other constructs, thereby supporting discriminant validity based on the Fornell-Larcker criterion.

Table 4 presents the Heterotrait-Monotrait Ratio (HTMT), which is used to evaluate the validity of the constructs: perceived environmental corporate social responsibility (PECSR), green intrinsic motivation (GIM), and sustainable innovation (SI). The HTMT ratios, along with their associated p-values, provide insights into the discriminant validity of these constructs.

Table 4. HTMT for validity

HTMT ratios (good if < 0.90, best if < 0.85)	**PECSR**	**GIM**	**SI**
Perceived Environmental Corporate Social Responsibility (PECSR)			
Green Intrinsic Motivation (GIM)	0.806		
Sustainable Innovation (SI)	0.844	0.796	
P values (one-tailed) for HTMT ratios (good if < 0.05)	PECSR	GIM	SI
Perceived Environmental Corporate Social Responsibility (PECSR)			
Green Intrinsic Motivation (GIM)	<0.001		
Sustainable Innovation (SI)	<0.001	<0.001	

According to Table 4, the HTMT ratio for PECSR and GIM is 0.806, which is below the threshold of 0.90 but above 0.85, indicating a moderate correlation with some overlap between the constructs while still preserving their distinctiveness. For PECSR and SI, the HTMT ratio is 0.844, also remaining below 0.90, which suggests a moderate correlation that supports discriminant validity. The HTMT ratio between GIM and SI is 0.796, falling below both thresholds of 0.90 and 0.85, indicating good discriminant validity between these constructs. In addition, the one-tailed p-values for the HTMT ratios further reinforce these findings. For PECSR and GIM, the p-value is <0.001, signifying a statistically significant correlation while remaining acceptable for discriminant validity. Similarly, the p-value for PECSR and SI is <0.001, indicating a significant relationship that aligns with previous observations of discriminant validity. The p-value for GIM and SI is also <0.001, showing a significant correlation within acceptable limits. In conclusion, the HTMT ratios and their corresponding p-values indicate that, although the constructs exhibit significant correlations, they retain adequate discriminant validity, affirming their distinctiveness within the study's context.

Results of Testing Hypotheses

Figure 2 and Table 5 provide an overview of the direct effects among the hypothesized relationships involving perceived environmental corporate social responsibility (PECSR), green intrinsic motivation (GIM), and sustainable innovation (SI). The table presents the direct effect values (β), significance levels (p-values), t-values, and the support status of each hypothesis based on these findings.

For H1, which examines the relationship between PECSR and SI, the direct effect is 0.45, with a p-value less than 0.01 and a t-value of 9.439, indicating a strong and statistically significant positive relationship, thus supporting H1. In H2, the effect of PECSR on GIM is reported as 0.71, accompanied by a p-value under 0.01 and a t-value of 15.669, suggesting a very strong and significant positive impact, which confirms H2. Regarding H3, the direct effect of GIM on SI is 0.38, with a p-value also less than 0.01 and a t-value of 7.947, demonstrating a moderate and significant positive relationship that supports H3. In summary, the results affirm that all three proposed direct relationships are statistically significant, validating the positive effects of PECSR on both GIM and SI, as well as the influence of GIM on SI.

Figure 2. Final model of the study

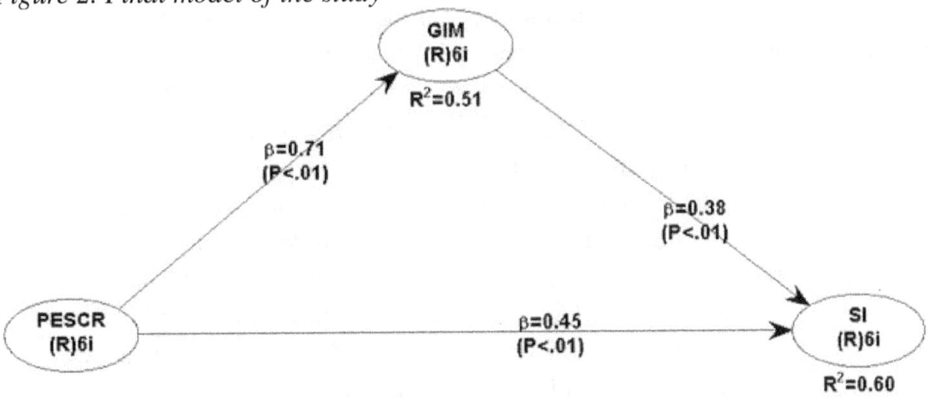

Table 5. Direct effects

Hs	Relationship	Direct effect (β)	Sig.	t-value	Decision
H1	PECSR →SI	0.45	P<0.01	9.439	Supported
H2	PECSR →GIM	0.71	P<0.01	15.669	Supported
H3	GIM→SI	0.38	P<0.01	7.947	Supported

Furthermore, the mediation effect in this study was calculated using the method developed by Preacher and Hayes (2008), which is a widely recognized statistical approach for assessing mediation. The Preacher and Hayes method provides a comprehensive framework for testing mediation effects, enabling researchers to rigorously assess the role of mediators in complex relationships among variables. In this study, this approach effectively demonstrated how GIM mediates the relationship between PECSR and SI, enhancing the understanding of these constructs in the context of sustainable innovation.

Table 6. Mediation analysis' bootstrapped confidence interval

Hypo.		Path a	Path b	Indirect Effect	SE	t-value	Bootstrapped Confidence Interval		Mediation
H4	PESCR→GIM→SI	0.710	0.380	0.270	0.034	7.935	95% LL 0.203	95% UL 0.336	Yes

Table 6 details the findings from the mediation analysis, which examines the indirect effect of perceived environmental corporate social responsibility (PECSR) on sustainable innovation (SI) via green intrinsic motivation (GIM). The table includes key metrics necessary for assessing the mediation hypothesis, such as path coefficients, the indirect effect, standard error (SE), t-value, and bootstrapped confidence intervals. Hypothesis 4 (H4) specifically looks into the mediating role of GIM between PECSR and SI. The coefficient for the path from PECSR to GIM (Path a) is 0.710, indicating a robust positive correlation. Meanwhile, the coefficient for the path from GIM to SI (Path b) is 0.380, also reflecting a positive relationship. The calculated indirect effect of PECSR on SI through GIM is 0.270, with a standard error of 0.034, illustrating the variability of this estimate. The t-value of 7.935 signifies that the indirect effect is statistically significant, far exceeding the conventional threshold of 1.96. Additionally, the 95% bootstrapped confidence interval spans from 0.203 to 0.336, reinforcing the significance of the indirect effect, as this range does not include zero in-between. Ultimately, the analysis confirms the presence of mediation, affirming that GIM plays a significant role in linking PECSR and SI. This supports the hypothesis that enhancing GIM can positively affect sustainable innovation through the framework of perceived environmental corporate social responsibility.

DISCUSSION

This study aims to examine the impact of perceived environmental corporate social responsibility (PECSR) on sustainable innovation in hotel business with a focus on the mediating role of green intrinsic motivation. The theoretical model was formulated and tested. Findings revealed that PECSR positively correlates with sustainable innovation, aligning with other research by Fosu et al. (2024) and Le et al. (2024). PECSR positively influences sustainable innovation, as it fosters a culture of creativity, experimentation, and risk-taking, crucial for promoting sustainable development (Pan et al., 2022). Environmentally responsible organizations attract and retain passionate employees who are passionate about sustainability, demonstrating a commitment to these values (Cohen et al., 2017). Organizations perceived as environmentally responsible are more likely to reduce risks through sustainable practices, avoiding potential legal or financial liabilities (Pan et al., 2022).

In addition, findings revealed that PECSR positively correlates with green intrinsic motivation, aligning with other research by Meng et al. (2024) and Tang et al. (2024). Positive perception of PECSR can inspire employees to adopt sustainable practices in their personal and professional lives, highlighting the strong relationship between PECSR and green intrinsic motivation (Zacher et al., 2023). In addition, employees who feel proud of their organization's commitment to sustainability may be more motivated to contribute to its success (Raza et al., 2021).

Lastly, findings revealed that green intrinsic motivation positively correlates with sustainable innovation and positively mediates the relationship between PECSR and sustainable innovation, aligning with other research by Leonidou & Skarmeas (2017), Li et al. (2020), and Chen et al. (2023). Green intrinsic motivation significantly influences sustainable innovation, as employees motivated by sustainable behaviors are more likely to develop and implement new ideas and practices that contribute to sustainability (Yi et al., 2019). Intrinsically motivated employees exhibit increased engagement and productivity at work, as they are more committed to their organization's goals and are more likely to be engaged in sustainable behaviors (Afsar et al., 2016). In addition, intrinsically motivated employees are more resilient, persevering despite challenges and setbacks, which is crucial for driving sustainable innovation (Steg, 2016).

This chapter primarily focused on the role of green intrinsic motivation in promoting sustainable innovation within hotel businesses, arguing that intrinsic motivation is a key driver of employees' engagement in pro-environmental practices. However, intrinsic motivation is often reinforced and complemented by external factors such as government regulations, market pressures, and societal expectations. For example, government policies that incentivize sustainable practices through tax breaks or certification programs can motivate businesses to adopt greener practices. Additionally, external market pressures, such as consumer demand for eco-friendly services, can serve as strong motivators for sustainability initiatives (Alshehri et al., 2024; Khairy et al., 2023). Organizational support also plays a crucial role in this process. Leadership commitment to sustainability, coupled with employee training, resources, and a supportive corporate culture, can enhance intrinsic motivation and further promote green innovation in hotel businesses.

Additionally, this chapter focused on how perceived environmental CSR influences sustainable innovation in the hotel industry, primarily through the lens of intrinsic motivation. However, the implementation of CSR initiatives is not without its challenges, particularly in emerging markets. In these regions, hotel businesses often face economic constraints, such as limited financial resources and a lack of access to green technologies, which can hinder the adoption of sustainable practices. Additionally, regulatory environments in emerging markets may be less developed, leading to inconsistencies in CSR standards and enforcement (Al-Romeedy & Khairy, 2024; Alqarni et al., 2023). Cultural differences and varying consumer awareness of sustainability also present challenges, as local communities may not prioritize environmental concerns in the same way as in more developed markets. To address these issues, hotel businesses in emerging markets can benefit from forming strategic partnerships with local governments, NGOs, and other businesses to share resources and knowledge. Case studies of successful CSR initiatives in emerging markets, such as those in Southeast Asia and Africa, can offer valuable lessons on overcoming these challenges and achieving sustainable innovation (Abdulrahman Al Abdulathi et al., 2024; Alhemimah et al., 2024).

Theoretical implications

This research's theoretical implications can be framed in the context of Corporate Social Responsibility (CSR) theory. *First*, the research highlights that Perceived Environmental Corporate Social Responsibility (PECSR) is not just a moral obligation but also a strategic asset that positively correlates with Sustainable Innovation (SI). The CSR theory suggests that incorporating responsible practices into core strategies can provide new opportunities for innovation within organizations. The study expands CSR theory by linking PECSR with SI, demonstrating how environmentally responsible actions can enhance a hotel's ability to develop innovative sustainability solutions. *Second*, the study reveals that green intrinsic motivation serves as a mediator between PECSR and SI, highlighting the internal mechanisms through which CSR impacts organizational outcomes. CSR theory asserts that the success of CSR initiatives is significantly influenced by stakeholder engagement, particularly among employees. The study suggests that employees motivated by environmental values are keys to sustainable innovation, enhancing the connection between CSR activities and innovation performance. *Third*, the CSR theory suggests that socially responsible practices can boost employee morale and engagement. The research demonstrates that hotels can foster a green intrinsic motivation culture by actively promoting environmental responsibility. Engaging employees in a hotel's CSR initiatives fosters a sense of alignment with sustainability goals, promoting sustainable innovation and fostering an internal innovation culture in sustainability-focused industries like hospitality. *Fourth*, this research shifts the focus from traditional CSR views to utilizing CSR as a proactive tool for innovation. The positive correlation between PECSR and SI suggests that CSR can go beyond regulatory compliance and reputation enhancement to actively promote sustainable products, service, and process development. This contribution enhances the understanding of Corporate Social Responsibility (CSR) by emphasizing the role of environmental responsibility in driving innovative practices. *Finally*, the research supports the CSR theory's belief that socially responsible practices can provide long-term benefits to organizations, potentially enhancing their competitive advantage. The study suggests that hotels with robust CSR practices can differentiate themselves in the market by continuously innovating in environmentally sustainable ways. Integrating CSR with core business practices can provide a sustained competitive advantage, particularly in industries where sustainability is increasingly valued.

This research's theoretical implications can also be framed in the context of Natural Resource-Based View (NRBV). *First*, the NRBV suggests that organizations can achieve a sustainable competitive edge by utilizing their environmental resources and capabilities. The study emphasizes the importance of Perceived Environmental Corporate Social Responsibility (PECSR) as an intangible resource that enhances a hotel's sustainable innovation capabilities. The study supports the NRBV's belief that organizations prioritizing environmental responsibility are better equipped for sustained innovation and performance. *Second*, the NRBV's focus on developing firm-specific capabilities is aligned with the introduction of green intrinsic motivation as a mediator. Green intrinsic motivation is an internal human capital resource that can significantly drive innovation and sustainability initiatives within hotels. The study suggests that motivating employees to adopt green practices is not just a cultural initiative but a crucial capability that hotels can cultivate for sustainable innovation. The NRBV framework suggests that motivation is a strategic capability that enhances a company's ability to efficiently utilize environmental resources. *Third*, the NRBV views sustainable innovation as a dynamic capability that enables organizations to adapt to environmental challenges by reconfiguring resources. The research suggests that hotels that prioritize environmental responsibility through CSR are better equipped to innovate and adapt to evolving sustainability demands. Green intrinsic motivation enhances sustainability capabilities by promoting a workforce that actively contributes to sustainability goals, providing a long-term competitive advantage. *Fourth*, the NRBV focuses on how companies integrate environmental resources into their organizational processes to achieve sustainability. The study highlights the interplay between environmental resources (PECSR) and human resources (green intrinsic motivation) in promoting sustainable innovation. The research emphasizes the role of intrinsically motivated employees in hotels' environmental goals, demonstrating how they can leverage both environmental and human capital for a sustainable competitive advantage. *Lastly*, the NRBV emphasizes resource efficiency and how businesses can minimize environmental impact while maintaining economic performance. The study suggests that hotels that engage in PECSR can enhance their reputation, innovate to reduce resource use, minimize waste, and enhance overall efficiency. Green intrinsic motivation is crucial in promoting resource-efficient practices among employees, thereby enhancing the firm's long-term competitiveness.

Practical Implications

The study indicates a positive correlation between perceived environmental corporate social responsibility and sustainable innovation in hotel businesses, suggesting that environmentally responsible organizations are more likely to adopt sustainable practices. To enhance the positive relationship between perceived environmental corporate social responsibility and sustainable innovation, hotels can adopt several effective strategies. First, they should focus on clear communication and transparency by highlighting their sustainability initiatives to employees, customers, and other stakeholders. This involves not only promoting the hotel's environmental efforts but also regularly sharing progress reports that detail advancements toward sustainability goals and achievements, thereby demonstrating commitment to these initiatives. Additionally, hotels should be transparent about any challenges or setbacks they encounter, addressing these issues openly to build trust and credibility with their stakeholders. Second, another key strategy is to focus on employee engagement and training. Hotels should actively involve their employees by encouraging participation in sustainability initiatives and providing opportunities for them to contribute ideas. To support this, offering training and education on environmental sustainability can help employees grasp the significance of these initiatives. Furthermore, recognizing and rewarding employees for their contributions to sustainability efforts can enhance motivation and foster a culture of commitment to sustainable practices within the organization. Third, investing in sustainable innovation is another crucial strategy. This involves allocating resources specifically for the research and development of sustainable technologies and practices. Furthermore, collaborating with partners such as suppliers, universities, and other organizations can foster the development of innovative solutions. Additionally, creating a culture that encourages employees to share their ideas and contribute to sustainable innovation can lead to more effective and creative approaches to sustainability within the hotel industry. Fourth, measuring and reporting progress is essential for hotels to effectively manage their sustainability efforts. This involves tracking performance to monitor progress toward achieving sustainability goals. By utilizing data-driven decision-making, hotels can identify areas for improvement and inform future sustainability initiatives. Furthermore, transparent reporting of sustainability performance to stakeholders fosters trust and credibility, reinforcing the hotel's commitment to environmental responsibility and accountability. Fifth, partnering with stakeholders is a vital strategy for hotels aiming to enhance their sustainability efforts. Engaging with customers is essential; seeking their feedback on sustainability initiatives allows hotels to address concerns and incorporate customer preferences. Additionally, collaborating with suppliers helps develop sustainable sourcing practices, reducing the environmental impact of the supply chain. Furthermore, actively participating in local sustainability initiatives and supporting community-based projects fosters strong relationships within the community, demonstrating the hotel's commitment to not only its sustainability goals but also to the well-being of the surrounding area. Finally, creating a sustainable culture within a hotel is crucial for embedding environmental responsibility into the organization's fabric. This can be achieved by fostering a workplace culture that values sustainability and encourages employees to adopt eco-friendly practices. Leadership plays a significant role in this process; leaders should demonstrate their commitment to sustainability through their actions and behaviors, setting a standard for others to follow. Additionally, recognizing and celebrating the hotel's sustainability successes can reinforce a positive culture, motivating employees to continue their efforts and contribute to the hotel's overall sustainability goals.

Green intrinsic motivation significantly influences the link between PECSR and sustainable innovation in hotel businesses, fostering a more engaged and innovative workforce committed to sustainability. To enhance green intrinsic motivation among employees, hotels can adopt several effective strategies. First, it's essential to create a meaningful connection between them and the hotel's sustainability initiatives. This can be achieved by clearly communicating the positive impact these initiatives have on the environment and the community. Sharing success stories can inspire employees and motivate them to contribute to a more sustainable future. Additionally, helping employees connect sustainability efforts to their personal values and beliefs can foster a deeper commitment to these initiatives, reinforcing their intrinsic motivation to engage in environmentally responsible practices. Second, it's important to provide opportunities for growth and development related to sustainability. This can include offering training and educational programs that equip employees with new skills and knowledge in sustainable practices. Additionally, linking participation in sustainability initiatives to career advancement opportunities can serve as a strong motivator for employees. Empowering them by granting autonomy and responsibility in contributing to sustainable initiatives can also foster a sense of ownership and commitment, encouraging deeper engagement in environmental efforts. Third, recognizing and rewarding employees for their contributions to sustainability initiatives. Publicly acknowledging their efforts can celebrate individual achievements and inspire others to participate. Offering tangible rewards, such as bonuses or time off, alongside non-monetary rewards like recognition certificates or opportunities for professional development, can motivate employees to engage more deeply in sustainability efforts. Fourth, fostering a supportive culture is equally important. Creating a positive work environment that encourages creativity and innovation helps employees feel valued and motivated. Promoting collaboration and teamwork among staff fosters a sense of community and shared purpose, reinforcing the collective commitment to sustainability. Furthermore, demonstrating strong leadership commitment to sustainability can inspire employees to align their efforts with organizational goals. Lastly, personalizing sustainability initiatives is another effective approach. Allowing employees to choose initiatives that align with their interests and skills can increase engagement and investment in these efforts. Additionally, considering flexible work arrangements, such as remote work or flexible hours, can support employees in their sustainability pursuits, making it easier for them to participate actively in initiatives that resonate with their personal values.

Limitations

This study has several limitations that should be acknowledged. First, it focuses exclusively on five-star hotels in Egypt, which may limit the generalizability of the findings to other hotel categories or geographic locations, as the unique characteristics of five-star hotels and the Egyptian hospitality sector may influence the results. Thus, the outcomes might not be fully applicable to smaller hotels or properties in other regions. Second, the use of a cross-sectional survey methodology captures perceptions and behaviors at a single point in time, making it difficult to observe dynamic changes in attitudes toward environmental corporate social responsibility (ECSR) and sustainable innovation over time, which a longitudinal approach could better address. Third, the reliance on self-reported measures may be subject to social desirability bias, as respondents might overstate their engagement in sustainability-related activities to align with perceived social norms. Finally, the use of a convenience sampling approach, although suitable given the constraints of this study, may introduce sampling bias, reducing the overall representativeness of the sample.

Avenues for Further Research

While this study makes important contributions to understanding the role of intrinsic motivation in CSR-driven sustainable innovation in the hotel industry, several avenues for future research remain open. One potential direction for future research is the exploration of external motivators. Researchers could examine the role of external incentives, such as government policies, market pressures, and certifications, in promoting sustainable practices within the hotel industry. A deeper understanding of how these external forces interact with intrinsic motivation could provide a more comprehensive view of the drivers behind CSR initiatives. Another important area for exploration is the contextualization of CSR in emerging markets. The implementation and outcomes of CSR in these markets have not been fully explored. Future studies could investigate how hotel businesses in emerging markets navigate challenges such as resource limitations, regulatory gaps, and differing cultural perceptions of CSR. Comparative studies between developed and emerging markets would be valuable in understanding the global diversity of CSR practices and their effectiveness across different contexts. In addition, longitudinal studies on sustainable innovation could provide valuable insights. To better understand the long-term effects of CSR initiatives, future research could track the evolution of sustainable innovation over time. Investigating how intrinsic motivation evolves and continues to impact green innovation in the hotel industry would offer insights that are beneficial to both academic researchers and industry practitioners. Cross-industry comparative studies also present an opportunity for further research. By comparing CSR practices in the hotel industry with those in other sectors, such as retail, manufacturing, or tourism, researchers could identify industry-specific factors that influence the adoption of sustainable innovation. Such studies could uncover broader trends in CSR and sustainability, as well as highlight best practices within individual industries. Finally, future research could examine the intersection of employee well-being and CSR. Investigating how CSR initiatives focused on environmental sustainability also contribute to employee satisfaction, retention, and overall organizational culture could provide valuable insights. Understanding the dual benefits of CSR, both for environmental outcomes and human resources, could help organizations recognize the broader impact of their sustainability efforts.

REFERENCES

Abbas, J. (2024). Does the nexus of corporate social responsibility and green dynamic capabilities drive firms toward green technological innovation? The moderating role of green transformational leadership. *Technological Forecasting and Social Change*, 208, 123698. DOI: 10.1016/j.techfore.2024.123698

Abdulrahman Al Abdulathi, M. A., Khairy, H. A., Baquero, A., Waheer Alkhaldi, D. A., Salama, W. M., & Mohamed Soliman, S. A. E. (2024). *Catalyzing green innovation in hotel and tourism businesses: leveraging green talent management, green organizational citizenship behavior, and green values.*

Afsar, B., Badir, Y., & Kiani, U. S. (2016). Linking spiritual leadership and employee pro-environmental behavior: The influence of workplace spirituality, intrinsic motivation, and environmental passion. *Journal of Environmental Psychology*, 45, 79–88. DOI: 10.1016/j.jenvp.2015.11.011

Aguilera, R. V., Rupp, D. E., Williams, C. A., & Ganapathi, J. (2007). Putting the S back in corporate social responsibility: A multilevel theory of social change in organizations. *Academy of Management Review*, 32(3), 836–863. DOI: 10.5465/amr.2007.25275678

Al-Romeedy, B. S., El-bardan, M. F., & Badwy, H. E. (2024). How is employee performance affected by employer branding in tourism businesses? Mediation analysis. *Journal of Hospitality and Tourism Insights,* (ahead-of-print). DOI: 10.1108/JHTI-05-2024-0418

Al-Romeedy, B. S., & Khairy, H. A. (2024). Eco-Innovation and Hospitality and Tourism Business Resilience: The Mediating Role of Green Dynamic Capabilities. In *Shifts in Knowledge Sharing and Creativity for Business Tourism* (17-36). IGI Global.

Alhemimah, A., Baquero, A., Al-Romeedy, B. S., & Khairy, H. A. (2024). *Green organizational learning and sustainable work behavior in tourism and hotel enterprises: leveraging green intrinsic motivation and green training.*

Alketbi, M. S., & Ahmad, S. Z. (2024). Corporate social responsibility and sustainability practices: Mediating effect of green innovation and moderating effect of knowledge management in the manufacturing sector. *The International Journal of Organizational Analysis*, 32(7), 1369–1388. DOI: 10.1108/IJOA-02-2023-3627

Alqarni, K., Agina, M. F., Khairy, H. A., Al-Romeedy, B. S., Farrag, D. A., & Abdallah, R. M. (2023). The Effect of Electronic Human Resource Management Systems on Sustainable Competitive Advantages: The Roles of Sustainable Innovation and Organizational Agility. *Sustainability (Basel)*, 15(23), 16382. DOI: 10.3390/su152316382

Alshehri, N. Z., Baquero, A., Abd-Elhady, M. H., Salama, W. M., Khairy, H. A., & Abouelenien, R. E. I. (2024). *Green HRM and green competitive advantage in hotel and tourism industry: a mediated moderation model using eco-innovation and green psychological climate.*

Amabile, T. M., Hill, K. G., Hennessey, B. A., & Tighe, E. M. (1994). The Work Preference Inventory: Assessing intrinsic and extrinsic motivational orientations. *Journal of Personality and Social Psychology*, 66(5), 950–967. DOI: 10.1037/0022-3514.66.5.950 PMID: 8014837

Azam, T., & Jamil, K. (2024). Studying the role of corporate social responsibility, green HRM and green innovation to improve green performance of SMEs. *Journal of Business & Industrial Marketing, ahead-of-print*(ahead-of-print). DOI: 10.1108/JBIM-02-2023-0087

Badwy, H. E., Qalati, S. A., & El-Bardan, M. F. (2025). Revolutionizing sustainable success: Unveiling the power of green human resource management, green innovation and green human capital. *Benchmarking*.

Barney, J. (1991). Firm Resources and Sustained Competitive Advantage. *Journal of Management*, 17(1), 99–120. DOI: 10.1177/014920639101700108

Bauman, C. W., & Skitka, L. J. (2012). Corporate social responsibility as a source of employee satisfaction. *Research in Organizational Behavior*, 32, 63–86. DOI: 10.1016/j.riob.2012.11.002

Bekk, M., Spörrle, M., Hedjasie, R., & Kerschreiter, R. (2016). Greening the competitive advantage: Antecedents and consequences of green brand equity. *Quality & Quantity*, 50(4), 1727–1746. DOI: 10.1007/s11135-015-0232-y

Bonsu, M. O.-A., Guo, Y., & Zhu, X. (2024). Does green innovation mediate corporate social responsibility and environmental performance? Empirical evidence from emerging markets. *Journal of Applied Accounting Research*, 25(2), 221–239. DOI: 10.1108/JAAR-10-2022-0271

Boons, F., Montalvo, C., Quist, J., & Wagner, M. (2013). Sustainable innovation, business models and economic performance: An overview. *Journal of Cleaner Production*, 45, 1–8. DOI: 10.1016/j.jclepro.2012.08.013

Broadstock, D. C., Managi, S., Matousek, R., & Tzeremes, N. G. (2019). Does doing "good" always translate into doing "well"? An eco-efficiency perspective. *Business Strategy and the Environment*, 28(6), 1199–1217. DOI: 10.1002/bse.2311

Chang, C.-H. (2011). The Influence of Corporate Environmental Ethics on Competitive Advantage: The Mediation Role of Green Innovation. *Journal of Business Ethics*, 104(3), 361–370. DOI: 10.1007/s10551-011-0914-x

Chen, C., Rasheed, A., & Ayub, A. (2023). Does Green Mindfulness Promote Green Organizational Citizenship Behavior: A Moderated Mediation Model. *Sustainability (Basel)*, 15(6), 5012. DOI: 10.3390/su15065012

Chen, Y.-S., Lai, S.-B., & Wen, C.-T. (2006). The Influence of Green Innovation Performance on Corporate Advantage in Taiwan. *Journal of Business Ethics*, 67(4), 331–339. DOI: 10.1007/s10551-006-9025-5

Cheng, C. C. J. (2020). Sustainability Orientation, Green Supplier Involvement, and Green Innovation Performance: Evidence from Diversifying Green Entrants. *Journal of Business Ethics*, 161(2), 393–414. DOI: 10.1007/s10551-018-3946-7

Chuang, S.-P., & Huang, S.-J. (2018). The Effect of Environmental Corporate Social Responsibility on Environmental Performance and Business Competitiveness: The Mediation of Green Information Technology Capital. *Journal of Business Ethics*, 150(4), 991–1009. DOI: 10.1007/s10551-016-3167-x

Coccia, M. (2019). Comparative incentive systems. *Global Encyclopedia of Public Administration, Public Policy, and Governance, Springer International Publishing AG, part of Springer Nature, DOI, 10*, 978-973.

Cohen, M., Cavazotte, F. S. C. N., Costa, T. M., & Ferreira, K. C. S. (2017). Corporate social-environmental responsibility as an attraction and retention factor for young professionals. *BBR.Brazilian Business Review*, 14(1), 21–41. DOI: 10.15728/bbr.2017.14.1.2

Deci, E. L. (1972). Intrinsic motivation, extrinsic reinforcement, and inequity. *Journal of Personality and Social Psychology*, 22(1), 113–120. DOI: 10.1037/h0032355

Deci, E. L., & Ryan, R. M. (1985). Conceptualizations of Intrinsic Motivation and Self-Determination. In Deci, E. L., & Ryan, R. M. (Eds.), *Intrinsic Motivation and Self-Determination in Human Behavior* (pp. 11–40). Springer US., DOI: 10.1007/978-1-4899-2271-7_2

Delmas, M. A., & Pekovic, S. (2018). Corporate Sustainable Innovation and Employee Behavior. *Journal of Business Ethics*, 150(4), 1071–1088. DOI: 10.1007/s10551-016-3163-1

Dhingra, K. (2023). Corporate Social Responsibility and Sustainability of Corporate Performance. *Jindal Journal of Business Research*, 12(1), 19–29. DOI: 10.1177/22786821231161416

Eladawi, F. M. I., Elnaggar, M. K., Hashad, M. E., Awad, A. H. I., & Abd, A. A. E.-K. G. (2024). Effect of green inclusive leadership on employees' green work engagement in hotels and travel agencies: The role of green intrinsic motivation. *Geo Journal of Tourism and Geosites*, 54(2 supplement), 885–895. DOI: 10.30892/gtg.542spl12-1263

Faraz, N. A., Ahmed, F., Ying, M., & Mehmood, S. A. (2021). The interplay of green servant leadership, self-efficacy, and intrinsic motivation in predicting employees' pro-environmental behavior. *Corporate Social Responsibility and Environmental Management*, 28(4), 1171–1184. DOI: 10.1002/csr.2115

Feng, Y., Akram, R., Hieu, V. M., & Hoang Tien, N. (2022). The impact of corporate social responsibility on the sustainable financial performance of Italian firms: Mediating role of firm reputation. *Ekonomska Istrazivanja*, 35(1), 4740–4758. DOI: 10.1080/1331677X.2021.2017318

Fosu, E., Fosu, F., Akyina, N., & Asiedu, D. (2024). Do environmental CSR practices promote corporate social performance? The mediating role of green innovation and corporate image. *Cleaner and Responsible Consumption, 12*, 100155. doi.org/10.1016/j.clrc.2023.100155

Fraj-Andrés, E., Martinez-Salinas, E., & Matute-Vallejo, J. (2009). A Multidimensional Approach to the Influence of Environmental Marketing and Orientation on the Firm's Organizational Performance. *Journal of Business Ethics*, 88(2), 263–286. DOI: 10.1007/s10551-008-9962-2

Fredrickson, B. L. (2013). Chapter One - Positive Emotions Broaden and Build. In Devine, P., & Plant, A. (Eds.), Vol. 47, pp. 1–53). Advances in Experimental Social Psychology. Academic Press., doi.org/10.1016/B978-0-12-407236-7.00001-2

Gond, J.-P., El Akremi, A., Swaen, V., & Babu, N. (2017). The psychological microfoundations of corporate social responsibility: A person-centric systematic review. *Journal of Organizational Behavior*, 38(2), 225–246. DOI: 10.1002/job.2170

Haldar, S. (2019). Towards a conceptual understanding of sustainability-driven entrepreneurship. *Corporate Social Responsibility and Environmental Management*, 26(6), 1157–1170. DOI: 10.1002/csr.1763

Halkos, G., Nomikos, S., & Tsilika, K. (2022). Evidence for Novel Structures Relating CSR Reporting and Economic Welfare: Environmental Sustainability—A Continent-Level Analysis. *Computational Economics*, 59(2), 415–444. DOI: 10.1007/s10614-020-10091-5

Hao, J., & He, F. (2022). Corporate social responsibility (CSR) performance and green innovation: Evidence from China. *Finance Research Letters*, 48, 102889. DOI: 10.1016/j.frl.2022.102889

Hart, S. L. (1995). A Natural-Resource-Based View of the Firm. *Academy of Management Review*, 20(4), 986–1014. DOI: 10.2307/258963

He, Q., Ribeiro-Navarrete, S., & Botella-Carrubi, D. (2024). A matter of motivation: The impact of enterprise digital transformation on green innovation. *Review of Managerial Science*, 18(5), 1489–1518. DOI: 10.1007/s11846-023-00665-6

Kalyar, M. N., Ali, F., & Shafique, I. (2021). Green mindfulness and green creativity nexus in hospitality industry: Examining the effects of green process engagement and CSR. *International Journal of Contemporary Hospitality Management*, 33(8), 2653–2675. DOI: 10.1108/IJCHM-09-2020-1079

Khairy, H. A., Agina, M. F., Aliane, N., & Hashad, M. E. (2023). Internal Branding in Hotels: Interaction Effects of Employee Engagement, Workplace Friendship, and Organizational Citizenship Behavior. *Sustainability (Basel)*, 15(5), 4530. DOI: 10.3390/su15054530

Khairy, H. A., Elzek, Y., Aliane, N., & Agina, M. F. (2023). Perceived Environmental Corporate Social Responsibility Effect on Green Perceived Value and Green Attitude in Hospitality and Tourism Industry: The Mediating Role of Environmental Well-Being. *Sustainability (Basel)*, 15(6), 4746. DOI: 10.3390/su15064746

Khamdamov, A., Tang, Z., & Hussain, M. A. (2023). Unpacking Parallel Mediation Processes between Green HRM Practices and Sustainable Environmental Performance: Evidence from Uzbekistan. *Sustainability (Basel)*, 15(2), 1434. DOI: 10.3390/su15021434

Kock, N. (2017). WarpPLS user manual: Version 6.0. *ScriptWarp Systems: Laredo, TX, USA, 141*, 47-60.

Kraus, S., Rehman, S. U., & García, F. J. S. (2020). Corporate social responsibility and environmental performance: The mediating role of environmental strategy and green innovation. *Technological Forecasting and Social Change*, 160, 120262. DOI: 10.1016/j.techfore.2020.120262

Kunnaala, V., Rasi, M., & Storgård, J. (2013). *Corporate social responsibility and shipping views of Baltic Sea shipping companies on the benefits of responsibility.*

Latif, B., Ong, T. S., Meero, A., Abdul Rahman, A. A., & Ali, M. (2022). Employee-Perceived Corporate Social Responsibility (CSR) and Employee Pro-Environmental Behavior (PEB): The Moderating Role of CSR Skepticism and CSR Authenticity. *Sustainability (Basel)*, 14(3), 1380. DOI: 10.3390/su14031380

Le, T. T., Tran, P. Q., Lam, N. P., Tra, M. N. L., & Uyen, P. H. P. (2024). Corporate social responsibility, green innovation, environment strategy and corporate sustainable development. *Operations Management Research : Advancing Practice Through Research*, 17(1), 114–134. DOI: 10.1007/s12063-023-00411-x

Lenzen, M., Sun, Y.-Y., Faturay, F., Ting, Y.-P., Geschke, A., & Malik, A. (2018). The carbon footprint of global tourism. *Nature Climate Change*, 8(6), 522–528. DOI: 10.1038/s41558-018-0141-x

Leonidou, C. N., & Skarmeas, D. (2017). Gray Shades of Green: Causes and Consequences of Green Skepticism. *Journal of Business Ethics*, 144(2), 401–415. DOI: 10.1007/s10551-015-2829-4

Li, W., Bhutto, M. Y., Waris, I., & Hu, T. (2023). The Nexus between Environmental Corporate Social Responsibility, Green Intellectual Capital and Green Innovation towards Business Sustainability: An Empirical Analysis of Chinese Automobile Manufacturing Firms. *International Journal of Environmental Research and Public Health*, 20(3), 1851. DOI: 10.3390/ijerph20031851 PMID: 36767217

Li, W., Bhutto, T. A., Xuhui, W., Maitlo, Q., Zafar, A. U., & Ahmed Bhutto, N. (2020). Unlocking employees' green creativity: The effects of green transformational leadership, green intrinsic, and extrinsic motivation. *Journal of Cleaner Production*, 255, 120229. DOI: 10.1016/j.jclepro.2020.120229

Li, Z., Deng, X., & Peng, L. (2020). Uncovering trajectories and impact factors of CO2 emissions: A sectoral and spatially disaggregated revisit in Beijing. *Technological Forecasting and Social Change*, 158, 120124. DOI: 10.1016/j.techfore.2020.120124

Lin, Y.-H. (2023). Determinants of Green Purchase Intention: The Roles of Green Enjoyment, Green Intrinsic Motivation, and Green Brand Love. *Sustainability (Basel)*, 15(1), 132. DOI: 10.3390/su15010132

Liu, J., & Liu, J. (2023). The greater the incentives, the better the effect? Interactive moderating effects on the relationship between green motivation and green creativity. *International Journal of Contemporary Hospitality Management*, 35(3), 919–932. DOI: 10.1108/IJCHM-03-2022-0340

Lozano, R. (2013). Are Companies Planning their Organisational Changes for Corporate Sustainability? An Analysis of Three Case Studies on Resistance to Change and their Strategies to Overcome it. *Corporate Social Responsibility and Environmental Management*, 20(5), 275–295. DOI: 10.1002/csr.1290

Meng, Z., Bhatti, S. M., Naveed, R. T., Kanwal, S., & Adnan, M. (2024). Green sustainability in the hotel sector: The role of CSR, intrinsic green motivation, and personal environmental norms. *PLoS One*, 19(6), e0295850. DOI: 10.1371/journal.pone.0295850 PMID: 38935798

Molina-Collado, A., Santos-Vijande, M. L., Gómez-Rico, M., & Madera, J. M. (2022). Sustainability in hospitality and tourism: A review of key research topics from 1994 to 2020. *International Journal of Contemporary Hospitality Management*, 34(8), 3029–3064. DOI: 10.1108/IJCHM-10-2021-1305

Nazir, O., & Islam, J. U. (2020). Effect of CSR activities on meaningfulness, compassion, and employee engagement: A sense-making theoretical approach. *International Journal of Hospitality Management*, 90, 102630. DOI: 10.1016/j.ijhm.2020.102630

Novitasari, M., & Tarigan, Z. J. H. (2022). The Role of Green Innovation in the Effect of Corporate Social Responsibility on Firm Performance. *Economies, 10*(5), 117. https://www.mdpi.com/2227-7099/10/5/117

Nureen, N., Liu, D., Irfan, M., & Işik, C. (2023). Nexus between corporate social responsibility and firm performance: A green innovation and environmental sustainability paradigm. *Environmental Science and Pollution Research International*, 30(21), 59349–59365. DOI: 10.1007/s11356-023-26675-1 PMID: 37004616

Olya, H., Ahmad, M. S., Abdulaziz, T. A., Khairy, H. A., Fayyad, S., & Lee, C.-K. (2024). Catalyzing green change: The impact of tech-savvy leaders on innovative behaviors. *Corporate Social Responsibility and Environmental Management*, 31(6), 5543–5556. DOI: 10.1002/csr.2871

Pan, C., Abbas, J., Álvarez-Otero, S., Khan, H., & Cai, C. (2022). Interplay between corporate social responsibility and organizational green culture and their role in employees' responsible behavior towards the environment and society. *Journal of Cleaner Production*, 366, 132878. DOI: 10.1016/j.jclepro.2022.132878

Preacher, K. J., & Hayes, A. F. (2008). Asymptotic and resampling strategies for assessing and comparing indirect effects in multiple mediator models. *Behavior Research Methods*, 40(3), 879–891. DOI: 10.3758/BRM.40.3.879 PMID: 18697684

Ramzan, M., Amin, M., & Abbas, M. (2021). How does corporate social responsibility affect financial performance, financial stability, and financial inclusion in the banking sector? Evidence from Pakistan. *Research in International Business and Finance*, 55, 101314. DOI: 10.1016/j.ribaf.2020.101314

Raza, A., Farrukh, M., Iqbal, M. K., Farhan, M., & Wu, Y. (2021). Corporate social responsibility and employees' voluntary pro-environmental behavior: The role of organizational pride and employee engagement. *Corporate Social Responsibility and Environmental Management*, 28(3), 1104–1116. DOI: 10.1002/csr.2109

Rehman, S. U., Kraus, S., Shah, S. A., Khanin, D., & Mahto, R. V. (2021). Analyzing the relationship between green innovation and environmental performance in large manufacturing firms. *Technological Forecasting and Social Change*, 163, 120481. DOI: 10.1016/j.techfore.2020.120481

Rennings, K. (2000). Redefining innovation — Eco-innovation research and the contribution from ecological economics. *Ecological Economics*, 32(2), 319–332. DOI: 10.1016/S0921-8009(99)00112-3

Romani, S., Grappi, S., & Bagozzi, R. P. (2016). Corporate Socially Responsible Initiatives and Their Effects on Consumption of Green Products. *Journal of Business Ethics*, 135(2), 253–264. DOI: 10.1007/s10551-014-2485-0

Rongbin, R., Wan, C., & Zuping, Z. (2022). Research on the relationship between environmental corporate social responsibility and green innovative behavior: The moderating effect of moral identity. *Environmental Science and Pollution Research International*, 29(34), 52189–52203. DOI: 10.1007/s11356-022-19541-z PMID: 35260982

Rosso, B. D., Dekas, K. H., & Wrzesniewski, A. (2010). On the meaning of work: A theoretical integration and review. *Research in Organizational Behavior*, 30, 91–127. DOI: 10.1016/j.riob.2010.09.001

Ryan, R. M., & Deci, E. L. (2000). Self-determination theory and the facilitation of intrinsic motivation, social development, and well-being. *The American Psychologist*, 55(1), 68–78. DOI: 10.1037/0003-066X.55.1.68 PMID: 11392867

Salama, W. M., Suliman, M. A., Hassanin, M., Khairy, H. A., Al Asrag, A. S. A., & Fahmy, N. S. (2024). Catalyzing green competitiveness in hotel and tourism businesses: leveraging digital dynamic capability and green creativity. *Environment and Social Psychology, 9*(9).

Sánchez-Infante Hernández, J. P., Yañez-Araque, B., & Moreno-García, J. (2020). Moderating effect of firm size on the influence of corporate social responsibility in the economic performance of micro-, small- and medium-sized enterprises. *Technological Forecasting and Social Change*, 151, 119774. DOI: 10.1016/j.techfore.2019.119774

Sarfraz, M., Ozturk, I., Yoo, S., Raza, M. A., & Han, H. (2023). Toward a new understanding of environmental and financial performance through corporate social responsibility, green innovation, and sustainable development. *Humanities & Social Sciences Communications*, 10(1), 297. DOI: 10.1057/s41599-023-01799-4

Shahzad, M., Qu, Y., Javed, S. A., Zafar, A. U., & Rehman, S. U. (2020). Relation of environment sustainability to CSR and green innovation: A case of Pakistani manufacturing industry. *Journal of Cleaner Production*, 253, 119938. DOI: 10.1016/j.jclepro.2019.119938

Sharpe, E., Ruepert, A., van der Werff, E., & Steg, L. (2022). Corporate environmental responsibility leads to more pro-environmental behavior at work by strengthening intrinsic pro-environmental motivation. *One Earth*, 5(7), 825–835. DOI: 10.1016/j.oneear.2022.06.006

Shnayder, L., van Rijnsoever, F. J., & Hekkert, M. P. (2016). Motivations for Corporate Social Responsibility in the packaged food industry: An institutional and stakeholder management perspective. *Journal of Cleaner Production*, 122, 212–227. DOI: 10.1016/j.jclepro.2016.02.030

Spanjol, J., Tam, L., & Tam, V. (2015). Employer–Employee Congruence in Environmental Values: An Exploration of Effects on Job Satisfaction and Creativity. *Journal of Business Ethics*, 130(1), 117–130. DOI: 10.1007/s10551-014-2208-6

Steg, L. (2016). Values, Norms, and Intrinsic Motivation to Act Proenvironmentally. *Annual Review of Environment and Resources, 41*(Volume 41, 2016), 277-292. doi .org/10.1146/annurev-environ-110615-085947

Tang, H., Loi, R., & Lai, S. W. (2024). Employees go green: the roles of perceived CSR and intrinsic motivation. *Evidence-based HRM: a Global Forum for Empirical Scholarship, 12*(2), 407-420. DOI: 10.1108/EBHRM-11-2022-0287

Tang, M., Walsh, G., Lerner, D., Fitza, M. A., & Li, Q. (2018). Green Innovation, Managerial Concern and Firm Performance: An Empirical Study. *Business Strategy and the Environment*, 27(1), 39–51. DOI: 10.1002/bse.1981

Tello, S. F., & Yoon, E. (2008). Examining drivers of sustainable innovation. *International Journal of Business Strategy*, 8(3), 164–169.

Turker, D. (2009). Measuring Corporate Social Responsibility: A Scale Development Study. *Journal of Business Ethics*, 85(4), 411–427. DOI: 10.1007/s10551-008-9780-6

van Marrewijk, M. (2003). Concepts and Definitions of CSR and Corporate Sustainability: Between Agency and Communion. *Journal of Business Ethics*, 44(2), 95–105. DOI: 10.1023/A:1023331212247

Wang, C. H. (2020). An environmental perspective extends market orientation: Green innovation sustainability. *Business Strategy and the Environment*, 29(8), 3123–3134. DOI: 10.1002/bse.2561

Wu, J., Chen, D., Bian, Z., Shen, T., Zhang, W., & Cai, W. (2021). How Does Green Training Boost Employee Green Creativity? A Sequential Mediation Process Model [Original Research]. *Frontiers in Psychology*, 12, 759548. Advance online publication. DOI: 10.3389/fpsyg.2021.759548 PMID: 34955979

Wu, W., & Yu, L. (2024). How Does Environmental Corporate Social Responsibility Affect Technological Innovation? The Role of Green Entrepreneurial Orientation and Green Intellectual Capital. *Journal of the Knowledge Economy*, 15(1), 3297–3328. DOI: 10.1007/s13132-023-01132-z

Wu, W., Yu, L., Li, H., & Zhang, T. (2022). Perceived Environmental Corporate Social Responsibility and Employees' Innovative Behavior: A Stimulus–Organism–Response Perspective [Original Research]. *Frontiers in Psychology*, 12, 777657. Advance online publication. DOI: 10.3389/fpsyg.2021.777657 PMID: 35173648

Xie, X., Huo, J., & Zou, H. (2019). Green process innovation, green product innovation, and corporate financial performance: A content analysis method. *Journal of Business Research*, 101, 697–706. DOI: 10.1016/j.jbusres.2019.01.010

Yang, Y., & Jiang, Y. (2023). Buyer-supplier CSR alignment and firm performance: A contingency theory perspective. *Journal of Business Research*, 154, 113340. DOI: 10.1016/j.jbusres.2022.113340

Yi, L., Uddin, M. A., Das, A. K., Mahmood, M., & Sohel, S. M. (2019). Do Transformational Leaders Engage Employees in Sustainable Innovative Work Behaviour? Perspective from a Developing Country. *Sustainability (Basel)*, 11(9), 2485. DOI: 10.3390/su11092485

Zacher, H., Rudolph, C. W., & Katz, I. M. (2023). Employee Green Behavior as the Core of Environmentally Sustainable Organizations. *Annual Review of Organizational Psychology and Organizational Behavior, 10*(Volume 10, 2023), 465-494. doi.org/10.1146/annurev-orgpsych-120920-050421

APPENDIX

Perceived Environmental Corporate Social Responsibility

PECSR1: “I can feel our hotel implements special programs to minimize its negative impact on the natural environment.”

PECSR2: “I can feel our hotel participates in activities which aim to protect and improve the quality of the natural environment.”

PECSR3: “I can feel our hotel has the necessary equipment to reduce its negative environmental impact.”

PECSR4: “I can feel our hotel makes well-planned investments to avoid environmental degradation.”

PECSR5: “I can feel our hotel targets sustainable growth which considers future generations.”

PECSR6: “I can feel our hotel makes investment to create a better life for future generations.”

Green Intrinsic Motivation (GIM)

GIM.1. “I enjoy coming up with new green ideas.”

GIM.2. “I enjoy trying to solve environmental tasks on job.”

GIM.3. “I enjoy tackling with environmental tasks that are completely new.”

GIM.4. “I enjoy improving existing green ideas at my job.”

GIM.5. “I feel excited when I have new green ideas.”

GIM.6. “I feel like becoming further engaged in the development of green ideas.”

Sustainable Innovation (SI)

SI.1. Our hotel has introduced products, processes, and organizational, or marketing innovations that reduce resources and materials per unit of production.”

SI.2. Our hotel has introduced products, processes, and organizational, or marketing innovations that reduce energy use.”

SI.3. Our hotel has introduced products, processes, and organizational, or marketing innovations that reduce carbon dioxide production.”

SI.4. Our hotel has introduced products, processes, and organizational, or marketing innovations that replace materials with less polluting or hazardous substitutes.”

SI.5. Our hotel has introduced products, processes, organizational, or marketing innovations that reduce soil, water, noise, or air pollution.”

SI.6. Our hotel has introduced products, processes, organizational, or marketing innovations to recycle waste, water, or materials."

Chapter 11
Perceptions of Retail Investors Towards Online Disclosure of Corporate Information

Manjinder Singh
Sri Guru Gobind Singh College, India

Manjit Kour
https://orcid.org/0000-0003-1043-3187
Chandigarh University, India & North-West University, Potchefstroom, South Africa

ABSTRACT

This study investigates the preferences of retail investors in India regarding the disclosure of corporate information on the internet. As corporate communication increasingly shifts from traditional hard-copy reports to electronic platforms, understanding the types of information most valued by investors is essential for enhancing transparency and building trust. A survey was conducted with 200 retail investors from major cities in Punjab and Chandigarh, gathering insights on the desirability of disclosing various types of accounting, corporate social responsibility (CSR), and corporate information online. The findings reveal that financial data, particularly financial highlights, full accounts and interim results were highly valued by investors. The study also highlighted significant interest in CSR disclosures, especially in human resources-related information. Corporate information such as a director's report and stock exchange listings were similarly rated as important.

DOI: 10.4018/979-8-3373-0117-4.ch011

1. INTRODUCTION

Globally, researchers predict that traditional hard copy annual reports will gradually become obsolete as companies increasingly adopt electronic mediums for disseminating information (e.g., Bury, 1999; Nordberg, 1999). Corporate websites have emerged as key platforms for presenting financial and non-financial information to stakeholders. The earliest use of the internet for corporate communication originated in the United States, where companies began leveraging web-based corporate disclosures as early as 1994 (Petravick and Gillett, 1996). By 1996, listed companies in regions like Hong Kong and the UK had also embraced this trend (Lymer, 1997; Fong, 1997). Over the past 29 years, extensive research (e.g., Petravick and Gillett,1996; Gray and Debreceny, 1997; Lymer, 1997; Marston and Leow, 1998; Deller et al., 1999; Pirchegger et al., 1999; Ruhaya et al., 2000; Marston and Wu, 2001; Fisher et al., 2002; Marston, 2003; Lodhia et al., 2003; Geerings et al., 2003; Vasal and Srivastava, 2003; Singh and Malhotra, 2004; Pervan, 2005; Hamid, 2005; Momany and Al-Shorman, 2006; Khan et al., 2006; Mariq, 2007; Khan et al., 2008; Bogdan and Pop, 2008; Kelton and Yang, 2008; Desoky and Mousa, 2009; Shukla and Gekara, 2010; Lamani and Cepani, 2011; Patel, 2012; Momany and Pillai, 2013; Alam and Rashid, 2014; Das and Das, 2015; Jafaru and Francis, 2016; Asogwa, 2017; Alsartawi, 2018; Keliwon et al., 2018; Pernamasari, 2019; Yassin and AI-Khatib, 2019; Boshnak, 2020; Siahaan et al., 2021; Boateng et al., 2022; Verawaty, 2022; Ahmed et al., 2023) has documented the rapid adoption of internet-based corporate information dissemination.

This widespread use can be attributed to the internet's distinctive features, including its ability to accommodate vast amounts of financial and non-financial data, integrate multimedia elements, and ensure timely updates (Koreto, 1997; Louwers et al., 1998). The cost-effectiveness of maintaining corporate websites compared to printing and distributing hard copy reports further underscores this transition. For instance, while maintaining financial data on a website costs £20,000–£30,000 annually, the expense of mailing printed annual reports averages £5 per copy (Investor Relations Society, UK, 1998).

The internet also offers unparalleled accessibility and flexibility, making it an ideal tool for investor relations. It enables private shareholders to directly access up-to-date corporate information globally, at any time (Myners, 1998; Pearce, 1998). Additionally, its adaptability allows companies to present information dynamically, catering to diverse user needs (Craven and Marston, 1999; Brennan and Hourigan, 2000). These advantages align with broader business shifts, such as the rise of consumer-driven practices and the emphasis on intellectual capital (Beattie and Pratt, 2001). Furthermore, increasing demand for transparency has spurred debates about the sufficiency of traditional historical financial reporting, advocating for greater disclosure of forward-looking, non-financial, and qualitative information (FASB, 2000).

Most empirical studies on internet financial reporting have focused on describing its nature and extent (e.g., Lymer and Tallberg, 1997; Hussey et al., 1998; Debreceny and Grey, 1999; Noor and Mohamad, 2000; Ettredge et al., 2001; Haasbroek, 2002; Marston, 2003; Friodevaux, 2004; Hamid, 2005; Sortur, 2006; Mariq, 2007; Malarvizhi and Yadav, 2008; AI-Arussi and Selamat, 2009; Garg and Verma, 2010; Khan and Ismail, 2011; Pervan and Bartulovic, 2012; Umoren and Asogwa, 2013; Keliwon et al., 2014; Gajewski and Li, 2015; Musleh Al-Sartawi, 2016; Adityawarman and Khudri, 2017; Alsartawi, 2018; Keliwon et al., 2018; Kaur & Singh,2019; Fuad et al., 2020; Siahaan et al., 2021; Verawaty, 2022; Ahmed et al., 2023) or exploring its determinants (e.g., Marston and Leow, 1998; Ashbaugh et al., 1999; Noor and Mohamad, 2000; Robrigues and Carlos, 2001; Bonson and Escobar, 2002; Joshi and Al-Modhahki, 2003; Singh and Malhotra, 2004; Prabowo and Tambotoh, 2005; Pervan, 2006; Al-shammari, 2007; Wanderley et al., 2008; Arussi et al., 2009; Khan, 2010; Bajaher and Hanifah, 2011; Oyelere and kuruppu, 2012; Jaya, 2015; Bananuka et al., 2019; Sharma & Bhardwaj, 2022). Additionally, anecdotal research has examined user attitudes and preferences toward web-based financial disclosures (e.g., Fong, 1997; AIMR, 1999; Quagli, 2001; Dulla et al., 2003; Jones and Xiao, 2004; Quagli and Riva, 2005; Kelton, 2007; Singh, 2009; Hamalainen, 2010; Khan and Ismail, 2011; Khan and Siang, 2013; Gauri, 2014; Khan and Ismail, 2014; Birt et al., 2017; Ashok & Abhishek, 2019; Harahap et al., 2021; Singh & Singh, 2022).

Despite these contributions, a critical gap exists in empirical studies exploring the perspectives of retail investors in India. Retail investors, as unsophisticated users, play a pivotal role in the financial ecosystem but are often overlooked in discussions on corporate disclosure. By understanding their preferences and concerns, companies can tailor their web-based reporting practices to better meet the needs of this key demographic.

The present study aims to address this gap by investigating the desirability of disclosing selective information online, encompassing accounting, social responsibility, and corporate data. By capturing retail investors' perspectives, this research seeks to provide actionable insights for companies looking to enhance the effectiveness and accessibility of their web-based disclosures.

The paper is organized as follows: Section 2 provides an in-depth review of existing literature on the attitudes and preferences of users toward corporate web-based disclosures of business information. Section 3 describes the research methodology employed in this study. The results are presented in Section 4, followed by an in-depth discussion of the findings in Section 5. Finally, Section 6 concludes the paper.

2. LITERATURE REVIEW

Empirical studies on corporate disclosure through the web have largely focused on descriptive statistics or explored variables influencing such disclosures. However, there is limited research exploring the attitudes and preferences of users of financial information regarding corporate web-based disclosures. A foundational effort in this field was undertaken by Marston (1996), who examined the organization of investor relations (IR) functions among large UK-listed companies using a survey of 547 firms. The study highlighted a positive correlation between the organization of IR functions and factors such as company size and overseas stock exchange listings. Ettredge et al. (1999) explored the relationship between corporate website features and users' characteristics. Their findings revealed that companies with higher analyst following provided more objective and detailed data, while those with higher retail ownership offered more subjective and concise information.

Environmental communication has also been a recurring theme in studies on corporate web usage. Jones et al. (1999) and Adam and Frost (2004) exposed the limited strategic use of websites for environmental reporting, despite growing stakeholder demand for transparency. These studies suggested that companies often fail to harness the web's potential for engaging stakeholders on environmental matters. Lodhia (2005) further demonstrated the importance of leveraging digital platforms to analyze stakeholder interaction with environmental information, offering a roadmap for improving corporate communication strategies.

Cost-benefit analyses have been another critical area of research. Hassen et al. (2000) explored CFOs' perceptions of web-based financial reporting in Malaysia, finding that the perceived benefits for both companies and users outweighed the costs. Similarly, Debreceny et al. (2001) highlighted user satisfaction with traditional financial report content presented online, advocating for clear, text- and graphic-based formats to meet user expectations. These findings stress the importance of balancing innovation with user accessibility in web-based disclosures.

Behavioral studies have provided further depth to the understanding of user interactions with online financial disclosures. Hodge (2001) and Kelton (2006) revealed that digital platforms influence decision-making processes and perceptions of reliability. For instance, users navigating hyperlinks often blend audited and unaudited information, emphasizing the need for stringent design standards to minimize such risks.

Xiao et al. (2002) and Jones and Xiao (2003) extended the discourse to future trends in online reporting, incorporating insights from experts. Their studies underscored the influence of technological and non-technological factors, such as regulatory inertia and user behavior. They predicted trends like frequent reporting and increased interactivity, some of which have materialized, highlighting the importance of such forward-looking analyses.

The auditing profession's response to internet-based reporting has been less proactive, as evidenced by Barac (2004) and Ismail and Sobhy (2009). These studies indicated a lack of established policies among audit firms and reluctance to expand auditing responsibilities in the context of web-based financial reporting. Such findings underscore a need for stronger alignment between technological advancements and professional practices.

In recent years, the adoption of eXtensible Business Reporting Language (XBRL) has garnered significant attention. Studies like Hutton et al. (2013) and Gauri (2014) explored XBRL's potential to transform financial reporting by making information more accessible and relevant. However, they also noted slow adoption rates, particularly in developing regions. This trend was corroborated by Birt et al. (2017), who demonstrated that XBRL-tagged data improved user perceptions and decision-making compared to traditional formats.

The integration of XBRL into educational and professional frameworks has been another area of focus. Wen (2019) emphasized the need to incorporate XBRL training into financial management curricula, given its growing relevance. However, the slow pace of adoption within academic institutions reflects broader challenges in embracing technological changes.

User-centric studies like Rawashdeh and Rawashdeh (2021) and Singh and Singh (2021) shed light on the behavioral and knowledge-related barriers to XBRL adoption. While users exhibited high satisfaction levels, significant knowledge deficits and low awareness among professionals underscored the need for targeted interventions to promote adoption.

The overarching trend across these studies is the recognition of the internet's transformative potential for corporate disclosure, coupled with persistent barriers to its full realization. Factors such as user characteristics, technological resistance, regulatory challenges, and educational gaps have influenced the pace and direction of adoption. While progress has been made in certain areas, such as XBRL adoption and environmental communication, much remains to be done to bridge the gaps between corporate practices and user expectations.

3. RESEARCH METHODOLOGY

This study explores the views of retail investors on the desirability of disclosing specific types of information electronically. The study's population includes educated and internet-savvy retail investors from three major cities in Punjab—Amritsar, Ludhiana, and Jalandhar—and the union territory of Chandigarh. To gather insights into the preferences of these retail investors concerning different types of information that could be made available online, a structured questionnaire was designed.

The questionnaire was developed based on prior literature addressing investors' attitudes and preferences toward internet-based reporting. It primarily employed closed-ended questions and consisted of two main sections. Section I collected demographic information about the respondents, while Section II solicited retail investors' views on the desirability of disclosing various types of information online. The questionnaire opened with a brief paragraph providing the study's background, emphasizing the importance of corporate disclosure in the digital age.

A pilot test was conducted with 10 retail investors who actively used the internet for trading securities. Based on their feedback, the content of the questionnaire was refined. To ensure proper tracking, all questionnaires were serially numbered and each was accompanied by a personally signed explanatory letter assuring the confidentiality of responses.

The questionnaire was administered to 200 respondents selected from the chosen cities. Judgment sampling was employed to target individuals who frequently used the internet for trading securities, a method deemed suitable for exploratory studies (Churchill, 1979). Reminder letters were sent after 20 days and a second request (together with another complete research package) was sent after a further 15 days. The initial mailing to all participants occurred in November 2012. The respondents represented diverse backgrounds, including variations in gender, age, education and professions. Table 1 presents the demographic distribution of the sample.

Table 1. Demographic profile of the respondents (in percent)

Gender	Age	Level of Education	Profession
Male 82.0	Up to 30 77.0	Secondary School 03.0	Professional 45.5
Female 18.0	31-45 19.5	Bachelor's Degree 34.0	Academic 23.0
	46-60 02.5	Master's Degree 33.0	Self Employed 12.5
	> 60 01.0	Doctorate Degree 06.0	Manager 11.0
		Professional Degree 24.0	Retiree 01.0
			Others 07.0
100	100	100	100

The table reveals that the majority of respondents are male (82%), with females comprising 18%. In terms of age distribution, 77% of participants are under 30 years old, 19.5% are between 31 and 45 years, and a smaller percentage falls within the older age brackets (2.5% are aged 46-60, and 1% are over 60). Regarding educational qualifications, most respondents hold a Bachelor's degree (34%), followed by a

Master's degree (33%) and a professional degree (24%), while a smaller proportion possess Doctorate degrees (6%). Professionally, 45.5% are in professional roles, 23% are academics, 12.5% are self-employed, 11% hold managerial positions, and a small percentage are retirees (1%) or belong to other professions (7%). Overall, the sample is diverse and representative across sex, age, education, and profession.

4. RESULTS

The respondents were asked to express their views on the desirability of disclosing 39 specific pieces of information using a five-point scale, ranging from 'very useful' to 'not useful at all' for each item. These 39 items were chosen based on casual empiricism, which suggested that they were commonly included in traditional printed corporate annual reports. Additionally, the selection was supported by responses from a pilot study. The 39 items were categorized into three themes: (1) accounting information disclosure (22 items), (2) corporate social responsibility disclosure (5 items), and (3) corporate information disclosure (12 items). To calculate the weighted average score (WAS) for each item, weights of 5, 4, 3, 2, and 1 were assigned to the responses 'very useful,' 'useful,' 'somewhat useful,' 'little useful,' and 'not useful at all,' respectively. The results, including simple frequencies, percentage values, and WAS, are presented in Table 2, 3, and 4.

Table 2. Desirability of disclosing selective information: Accounting information

Items of Information	Very Useful	Useful	Somewhat Useful	Little Useful	Not Useful at All	Weighted Average Score
Full set of accounts	114 (57.00%)	68 (34.00%)	8 (4.00%)	1 (0.50%)	9 (4.50%)	4.385
Interim results	89 (44.50%)	94 (47.00%)	15 (7.50%)	1 (0.50%)	1 (0.50%)	4.345
Financial highlights	96 (48.00%)	93 (46.50%)	9 (4.50%)	1 (0.50%)	1 (0.50%)	4.410
Notes to accounts	62 (31.00%)	111 (55.50%)	23 (11.50%)	3 (1.50%)	1 (0.50%)	4.150
Financial calendar	44 (22.00%)	103 (51.50%)	24 (12.00%)	28 (14.00%)	1 (0.50%)	3.805
Press releases	55 (27.50%)	93 (46.50%)	41 (20.50%)	9 (4.50%)	2 (1.00%)	3.950
Management discussion and analysis	54 (27.00%)	102 (51.00%)	23 (11.50%)	20 (10.00%)	1 (0.50%)	3.940

continued on following page

Table 2. Continued

Items of Information	Very Useful	Useful	Somewhat Useful	Little Useful	Not Useful at All	Weighted Average Score
Non-Financial information	45 (22.50%)	96 (48.00%)	34 (17.00%)	23 (11.50%)	2 (1.00%)	3.795
Financial ratios	89 (44.50%)	97 (48.50%)	10 (5.00%)	2 (1.00%)	2 (1.00%)	4.345
Shareholding pattern	71 (35.50%)	63 (31.50%)	53 (26.50%)	12 (6.00%)	1 (0.50%)	3.955
Segmental report	65 (32.50%)	64 (32.00%)	61 (30.50%)	7 (3.50%)	3 (1.50%)	3.905
Share price performance	76 (38.00%)	91 (45.50%)	27 (13.50%)	4 (2.00%)	2 (1.00%)	4.175
Inflation adjusted accounts	39 (19.50%)	61 (30.50%)	68 (34.00%)	30 (15.00%)	2 (1.00%)	3.525
Forecast information	48 (24.00%)	67 (33.50%)	69 (34.50%)	15 (7.50%)	1 (0.50%)	3.730
Value added statements	60 (30.00%)	54 (27.00%)	71 (35.50%)	14 (7.00%)	1 (0.50%)	3.790
Significant accounting policies	69 (34.50%)	74 (37.00%)	47 (23.50%)	9 (4.50%)	1 (0.50%)	4.005
Brand valuation/ equity	58 (29.00%)	88 (44.00%)	35 (17.50%)	15 (7.50%)	4 (2.00%)	3.905
Analyst report	63 (31.50%)	106 (53.00%)	22 (11.00%)	8 (4.00%)	1 (0.50%)	4.110
Consolidated accounts	79 (39.50%)	95 (47.50%)	24 (12.00%)	1 (0.50%)	1 (0.50%)	4.250
Comparative Information	77 (38.50%)	95 (47.50%)	24 (12.00%)	2 (1.00%)	2 (1.00%)	4.215
Historical data	58 (29.00%)	97 (48.50%)	35 (17.50%)	8 (4.00%)	2 (1.00%)	4.005
Auditor report	88 (44.00%)	92 (46.00%)	18 (9.00%)	1 (0.50%)	1 (0.50%)	4.325

The table indicates that among the twenty-two types of accounting information, the item 'financial highlights' received the highest weighted average score (WAS) of 4.410. This was followed by 'full set of accounts' (WAS: 4.385), 'interim results' (WAS: 4.35), 'financial ratios' (WAS: 4.345) and 'auditor's report' (WAS: 4.325). Other items included 'consolidated accounts' (WAS: 4.25), 'comparative information' (WAS: 4.215), 'share price performance' (WAS: 4.175), 'notes to accounts' (WAS: 4.15)' and 'analyst report' (WAS: 4.11). Additionally, 'significant accounting policies' had a WAS of 4.015, 'historical data' scored 4.00 and 'shareholding pattern' was rated at 3.96. 'Press releases' received a WAS of 3.95, while 'management discussions and analysis' followed with 3.94. 'Segmental report' had a WAS of 3.91 and 'brand valuation/equity' scored 3.90. 'Financial calendar' achieved a WAS of 3.81, 'non-financial information' was rated at 3.80 and 'value added statement' scored 3.79. Lastly, 'forecast information' (WAS: 3.73) and 'inflation-adjusted accounts' (WAS: 3.52) received the lowest ratings.

Table 3. Corporate social responsibility disclosure

Items of Information	Very Useful	Useful	Somewhat Useful	Little Useful	Not Useful at All	Weighted Average Score
Environmental	81 (40.50%)	68 (34.00%)	50 (25.00%)	0 (0.00%)	1 (0.50%)	4.140
Energy	67 (33.50%)	92 (46.00%)	34 (17.00%)	6 (3.00%)	1 (0.50%)	4.090
Human resources	102 (51.00%)	89 (44.50%)	7 (3.50%)	1 (0.50%)	1 (0.50%)	4.450
Community involvement	51 (25.50%)	72 (36.00%)	70 (35.00%)	4 (2.00%)	3 (1.50%)	3.820
Consumers and producers	99 (49.50%)	82 (41.00%)	15 (7.50%)	2 (1.00%)	2 (1.00%)	4.370

The table above shows that among the five types of social responsibility disclosure items, the 'human resources' item has the highest weighted average score of 4.45. It is followed by 'consumers and producers' with a weighted average score of 4.37, 'environmental information' with a score of 4.14, 'energy information' with a score of 4.09 and 'community involvement' with the lowest score of 3.82.

Table 4. Corporate information

Items of Information	Very Useful	Useful	Somewhat Useful	Little Useful	Not Useful at All	Weighted Average Score
Director's report	99 (49.50%)	78 (39.00%)	19 (9.50%)	3 (1.50%)	1 (0.50%)	4.355
Corporate profile	65 (32.50%)	92 (46.00%)	40 (20.00%)	2 (1.00%)	1 (0.50%)	4.090
Corporate objective and philosophy	62 (31.00%)	97 (48.50%)	38 (19.00%)	2 (1.00%)	1 (0.50%)	4.085
Principal activities	56 (28.00%)	127 (63.50%)	13 (6.50%)	3 (1.50%)	1 (0.50%)	4.170
Director's profile	38 (19.00%)	109 (54.50%)	38 (19.00%)	14 (7.00%)	1 (0.50%)	3.845

continued on following page

Table 4. Continued

Items of Information	Very Useful	Useful	Somewhat Useful	Little Useful	Not Useful at All	Weighted Average Score
Audit Committee	38 (19.00%)	115 (57.50%)	23 (11.50%)	10 (5.00%)	14 (7.00%)	3.765
Registered office(s)	40 (20.00%)	77 (38.50%)	53 (26.50%)	28 (14.00%)	2 (1.00%)	3.625
Auditors	55 (27.50%)	68 (34.00%)	59 (29.50%)	16 (8.00%)	2 (1.00%)	3.790
Principal bankers	50 (25.00%)	76 (38.00%)	51 (25.50%)	9 (4.50%)	14 (7.00%)	3.695
Solicitors/legal advisors	32 (16.00%)	90 (45.00%)	57 (28.50%)	17 (8.50%)	4 (2.00%)	3.645
Stock exchange listing	73 (36.50%)	108 (54.00%)	16 (8.00%)	2 (1.00%)	1 (0.50%)	4.250
Corporate governance report	69 (34.50%)	74 (37.00%)	49 (24.50%)	6 (3.00%)	2 (1.00%)	4.010

The table reveals that, among twelve types of corporate information, the director's report ranks highest with a weighted average score (WAS) of 4.35. It is followed by 'stock exchange listing' (WAS-4.25), 'principal activities' (WAS-4.17), 'corporate profile' (WAS-4.09), 'corporate objective and philosophy' (WAS-4.08), 'corporate governance report' (WAS-4.01), and 'director's profile' (WAS-3.84). Other items include 'auditors' (WAS-3.79), 'audit committee' (WAS-3.76), 'principal bankers' (WAS-3.69), 'solicitors/legal advisors' (WAS-3.64) and 'registered office(s)' (WAS-3.62).

5. DISCUSSION

The findings from this study provide valuable insights into the desirability of disclosing various types of corporate information, as viewed by the respondents. The weighted average scores (WAS) assigned to each of the 39 items shed light on which information is considered most useful by stakeholders for corporate transparency and accountability.

Among the 22 items categorized under accounting information disclosure, the results indicate a strong preference for the inclusion of financial highlights, with a WAS of 4.410, followed closely by other key financial data such as the full set of accounts, interim results, and financial ratios. These items were seen as crucial for understanding a company's financial performance and position, aligning with prior literature that suggests investors and other stakeholders rely heavily on these financial indicators to make informed decisions. The high ratings for these items suggest that stakeholders are interested in transparency regarding a company's financial status, with particular emphasis on providing an accessible overview of financial performance.

Items like shareholding pattern, press releases and management discussions and analysis received comparatively lower weighted average scores. These disclosures, while still deemed useful, appear to be less critical for stakeholders, which could reflect a perception that they provide less direct value in understanding a company's financial health or operational effectiveness. Notably, the lowest ratings were given to forecast information and inflation-adjusted accounts, which may be attributed to the speculative nature of forecasts and the complexity of inflation-adjusted reporting, which could be seen as less essential for stakeholders seeking immediate clarity on a company's present financial state.

The corporate social responsibility (CSR) disclosure items were also rated, with 'human resources' emerging as the highest-ranked item (WAS: 4.45). This suggests a growing recognition of the importance of social capital, employee welfare, and human resource management in the corporate narrative. Following this, 'consumers and producers' was also highly rated (WAS: 4.37), highlighting the importance of stakeholder engagement beyond just financial reporting. On the other hand, 'community involvement' received the lowest score within this category (WAS: 3.82), which could reflect a perception that CSR efforts related to community involvement may be more peripheral or less directly impactful on the company's immediate operations and financial outcomes.

For corporate information disclosure, the director's report received the highest WAS score (4.35), underscoring the importance of transparent governance and leadership insights into a company's strategy and performance. Other items, such as stock exchange listing and corporate profile, were also highly valued, suggesting that investors and stakeholders place importance on understanding a company's structure, activities, and market presence. Items such as auditors, audit committee and solicitors/legal advisors scored relatively lower, indicating that while these items are still relevant, they are seen as secondary to more direct financial and governance disclosures.

Overall, the study indicates a clear preference for financial disclosures that provide immediate and quantifiable information about a company's performance. Furthermore, there is also significant interest in CSR disclosures that reflect a company's human resource practices and its interactions with key stakeholders. However, less emphasis is placed on more specific or indirect disclosures, such as community involvement or legal advisors. These findings align with earlier studies by Khan and Ismail (2011, 2014), Jain (2013), Khan and Siang (2013), Khan and Omar (2013) and Singh et al. (2023).

These results carry significant implications for companies aiming to enhance transparency and fulfill stakeholder expectations. While traditional financial reporting remains a cornerstone of corporate communication, organizations should also prioritize CSR disclosures, especially in areas such as human resources and consumer relationships, to better align with stakeholder needs and expectations.

6. CONCLUSION

The transition to internet-based corporate disclosures signifies a transformative shift in corporate communication. This study underscores the growing importance of electronic platforms for disseminating financial, social, and corporate information. Through a detailed analysis of retail investors' perspectives, it provides actionable insights into their preferences and the perceived utility of various types of information shared online.

Key findings reveal that financial highlights, full sets of accounts, and interim results are the most valued components of accounting disclosures, reflecting investors' need for accessible and comprehensive financial data. Similarly, social responsibility information, particularly human resources-related disclosures, demonstrates significant appeal, underscoring the increasing focus on ethical and stakeholder-centric business practices. Among corporate information, the director's report, stock exchange listings, and principal activities rank highest, emphasizing the demand for transparency in governance and strategic direction.

The study highlights critical gaps in the alignment of corporate disclosure practices with investor expectations. While companies have increasingly adopted online platforms, the content and presentation of these disclosures often fail to cater to the diverse informational needs of retail investors. Additionally, the findings reinforce the cost-effectiveness of internet-based reporting and its ability to offer dynamic, real-time updates compared to traditional printed reports. However, the usability of these platforms and the clarity of information remain areas requiring significant improvement.

This research also emphasises the pivotal role of retail investors in shaping corporate disclosure strategies. As key stakeholders in the financial ecosystem, their preferences should guide companies in adopting more inclusive and accessible reporting practices. By tailoring disclosures to address specific needs, businesses can enhance transparency, build trust, and strengthen investor relations.

Furthermore, the study contributes to the growing body of literature on internet financial reporting, offering fresh insights into the Indian retail investor demographic—a group often overlooked in empirical research. It bridges the knowledge gap in understanding user-centric approaches to online corporate disclosures, particularly in developing markets.

The study has two notable limitations, aside from those inherent to the questionnaire-based approach. First, it focuses exclusively on Indian investors. Given that the internet serves as a global platform for information dissemination, the perspectives of domestic investors may not fully capture the broader, international viewpoint. Future research is needed to address this gap. Second, the study primarily reflects the opinions of a single user group—retail investors. Consequently, the findings may not represent the perspectives of other user groups. This limitation, however, presents an opportunity for further research to explore the views of diverse stakeholders connected to the companies (Hassen et al., 2000).

REFERENCES

Adams, C. A., & Frost, G. R. (2004). *The development of the corporate website and implications for ethical, social and environmental reporting through these media.* The Institute of Chartered Accountants of Scotland.

Adityawarman, A., & Khudri, T. Y. (2017). The impact of internet financial reporting practices on the company's market value: A study of listed manufacturing companies in Indonesia. In *6th International Accounting Conference (IAC 2017)* (48–53). Atlantis Press.

Ahmed, A. H., Elmaghrabi, M. E., Ali Alhassoon, O., & Diab, A. (2023). Perceptions of users and preparers towards corporate internet reporting: Evidence from an emerging market. *Cogent Business & Management*, 10(2), 2209976. DOI: 10.1080/23311975.2023.2209976

Al-Arussi, A. S., Selamat, H. M., & Hanefah, M. M. (2009). Determinants of financial and environmental disclosures through the internet by Malaysian companies. *Malaysian Management Journal*, 17(1), 59–76.

Al-Arussi, A. S., & Selamat, M. H. (2009). Dominant personalities in board committees, company characteristics, and internet environmental disclosure by Malaysian listed companies. *Malaysian Management Journal*, 13(1&2), 51–67.

Al-Shammari, B. (2007). *Determinants of internet financial reporting by listed companies on the Kuwait Stock Exchange*. Public Authority for Applied Education and Training.

Alam, Z., & Rashid, K. (2014). Corporate financial reporting on the internet: A survey of websites of listed companies in Pakistan. *IUP Journal of Corporate Governance*, 13(3), 17–31.

Alsartawi, A. M. (2018). Online financial disclosure and firms' performance: Evidence from the Gulf Cooperation Council countries. *World Journal of Entrepreneurship, Management and Sustainable Development*, 14(2), 178–190. DOI: 10.1108/WJEMSD-11-2017-0082

Ashbaugh, H., Johnstone, K. M., & Warfield, T. P. (1999). Corporate reporting on the internet. *Accounting Horizons*, 13(3), 241–257. DOI: 10.2308/acch.1999.13.3.241

Ashok, M. L., & Abhishek, N. D. (2019). Role of XBRL in promoting integrated reporting in Indian scenario. *IUP Journal of Accounting Research and Audit Practices*, 25(3), 25–33.

Asogwa, I. E. (2017). Impact of corporate governance on internet financial reporting in a growing economy: The case of Nigeria. *Archives of Business Research*, 5(1), 180–202. DOI: 10.14738/abr.52.2743

Association for Investment Management and Research (AIMR). (1999). Financial analysts rate conference calls best source of earnings information in AIMR study. *AIMR News Release*.

Association for Investment Management and Research (AIMR). (1999). *Using technology and the internet study: Researching corporate strategic and financial information. Survey conducted with the cooperation of Stratcom Associates*. www.aimr.com

Bajaher, M., & Hanifah, M. (2011). Internet financial reporting: The case of UAE listed companies. *Asia Pacific Business Research Conference*, Islamic Science University of Malaysia, Malaysia.

Bananuka, J., Night, S., Ngoma, M., & Najjemba, G. M. (2019). Internet financial reporting adoption: Exploring the influence of board role performance and isomorphic forces. *Journal of Economics, Finance and Administrative Science*, 24(48), 266–287. DOI: 10.1108/JEFAS-11-2018-0120

Barac, K. (2004). South African auditors' policies, practices and perceptions with regard to internet reporting. *Meditari Accountancy Research*, 12(2), 1–19. DOI: 10.1108/10222529200400013

Beattie, V., & Pratt, K. (2001). Issues concerning web-based business reporting: An analysis of the views of interested parties. *The British Accounting Review*, 35(2), 155–187. DOI: 10.1016/S0890-8389(03)00016-7

Birt, J. L., Muthusamy, K., & Bir, P. (2017). XBRL and the qualitative characteristics of useful financial information. *Accounting Research Journal*, 30(1), 107–126. DOI: 10.1108/ARJ-11-2014-0105

Boateng, R. N., Tawiah, V., & Tackie, G. (2022). Corporate governance and voluntary disclosures in annual reports: A post-International Financial Reporting Standard adoption evidence from an emerging capital market. *International Journal of Accounting & Information Management*, 30(2), 252–276. DOI: 10.1108/IJAIM-10-2021-0220

Bogdan, V., & Pop, M. C. (2008). Romanian companies' web-based disclosure choices and capital markets. *Journal of Economic Literature*, 1(10), 9–19.

Bonson, E., & Escobar, T. (2002). A survey on voluntary disclosure on the internet: Empirical evidence from 300 European Union companies. *The International Journal of Digital Accounting Research*, 2(1), 27–51. DOI: 10.4192/1577-8517-v2_2

Boshnak, H. A. (2020). Internet financial reporting practices in Saudi Arabia. *International Journal of Business and Management*, 15(9), 1–14. DOI: 10.5539/ijbm.v15n9p15

Brennan, N., & Hourigan, D. (2000). Corporate reporting on the internet by Irish companies. *The Irish Accounting Review*, 7(1), 37–68. DOI: 10.52399/001c.35353

Bury, L. (1999). Online and time. *Accounting*. 28–29.

Chander, S., & Singh, M. (2009). Perceived usefulness of corporate disclosure through web: An empirical study. *The IUP Journal of Accounting Research and Audit Practices*, 8(3–4), 61–77.

Churchill, G. A. (1979). *Marketing research: Methodological foundations* (2nd ed.). The Dryden Press.

Craven, B. M., & Marston, C. L. (1999). Financial reporting on the internet by leading UK companies. *European Accounting Review*, 8(2), 321–333. DOI: 10.1080/096381899336069

Das, S., & Das, S. (2015). Mandatory corporate reporting on the internet: An empirical study of the listed non-financial companies in Bangladesh. *International Journal of Accounting and Business Finance*, (2), 1–16. DOI: 10.4038/ijabf.v5i2.42

Debreceny, R., & Gray, G. L. (1999). Financial reporting on the internet and the external audit. *European Accounting Review*, 8(2), 335–350. DOI: 10.1080/096381899336078

Debreceny, R., Gray, G. L., & Mock, T. J. (2001). Financial reporting websites: What users want in terms of form and content? *The International Journal of Digital Accounting Research*, 1(1), 1–23. DOI: 10.4192/1577-8517-v1_1

Deller, D., Stubenrath, M., & Weber, C. (1999). Investor relations and the internet: Background, potential application and evidence from the USA, UK and Germany. *21st Annual Congress of the European Accounting Association*, Antwerp, Belgium.

Desoky, A. M., & Mousa, G. A. (2009). The impact of company characteristics and corporate governance attributes on internet investor relations: Evidence from Bahrain. *12th International Conference Organized by the American Society of Business and Behavioral Sciences*, London, UK.

Dulla, R. B., Graham, A. W., & Baldwin, A. A. (2003). Web-based financial statements: Hypertext links to footnotes and their effect on decisions. *International Journal of Accounting Information Systems*, 4(3), 185–203. DOI: 10.1016/S1467-0895(03)00009-5

Ettredge, M., Richardson, V. J., & Scholz, S. (1999). *Financial data at corporate websites: Does user sophistication matter?* [Working Paper]. University of Kansas.

Ettredge, M., Richardson, V. J., & Scholz, S. (2001). The presentation of financial information at corporate websites. *International Journal of AIS*, 2(3), 149–168.

Financial Accounting Standards Board. (2000). *Business reporting research project: Electronic distribution of business reporting information*. Steering Committee Report Series. Available at http://www.fasb.org

Fisher, R., Oyelere, P., & Laswad, F. (2002). Audit issues and content analysis of audit practices associated with corporate financial reporting on the internet. *Discussion Paper No. 96,* Commerce Division, Lincoln University, Canterbury, New Zealand.

Fong, C. C. S. (1997). *Acceptance of corporate reporting through the internet* [Working Paper]. City University, Hong Kong.

Friodevaux, A. E. (2004). *Investor relations internet disclosure and the cost of equity capital: An empiracle analysis* [Doctoral thesis, Fribourg University]. Scribd.

Fuad, K., Ariyani, N. D., & Handayani, R. T. (2020). The role of internet financial reporting (IFR) in mediating manufacturing firm value on Indonesia Stock Exchange (IDX). *Journal of Islamic Accounting and Finance Research*, 2(2), 1–12. DOI: 10.21580/jiafr.2020.2.2.5821

Gajewski, J. F., & Li, L. (2015). Can internet-based disclosure reduce information asymmetry? *Advances in Accounting*, 31(1), 115–124. DOI: 10.1016/j.adiac.2015.03.013

Garg, M. C., & Verma, D. V. (2010). Web-based corporate reporting practices in India. *IUP Journal of Accounting Research and Audit Practices*, 9(3), 7–19.

Gauri, M. (2014). XBRL in India. *Global Journal of Finance and Management*, 6(6), 517–522.

Geerings, J., Bollen, L., & Hassink, H. (2003). Investor relations on the internet: A survey of the Euronext zone. *European Accounting Review*, 12(3), 567–579. DOI: 10.1080/0963818032000083531

Gray, G., & Debreceny, R. (1997). Corporate reporting on the internet: Opportunities and challenges. *Seventh Asia-Pacific Conference on International Accounting Issues,* Bangkok, Thailand.

Haasbroek, F. (2002). *Dissemination of annual report information on the internet by South African companies* [Master's Thesis, Rand Afrikaans University].

Hamalainen, E. (2010). *Environmental marketing communication on corporate websites: Stakeholder audiences' expectations and needs* [Master's Thesis, Aalto University].

Hamid, A. Z. F. (2005). Malaysian companies' use of the Internet for investor relations. *Corporate Governance (Bradford)*, 5(1), 5–14. DOI: 10.1108/14720700510583421

Harahap, K., Rumondang, T., Putra, P. D., & Winata, J. A. (2021). Integrating XBRL technology into accounting curriculum: A survey of accounting lecturers in Medan City. *International Conference on Strategic Issues of Economics, Business and Education (ICoSIEBE 2020)* (89–97). Atlantis Press. DOI: 10.2991/aebmr.k.210220.017

Hassen, S., Jaffar, N., & Johal, S. K. (2000). *Financial reporting on the Internet by Malaysian companies: Perceptions and practices* [Working Paper]. University of Multimedia, Malaysia.

Hodge, F. (2001). Hyperlinking unaudited information to audited financial statements: Effects on investor judgments. *The Accounting Review*, 76(4), 675–691. DOI: 10.2308/accr.2001.76.4.675

Hussey, R., Guilliford, J., & Lymer, A. (1998). *Corporate communications: Financial reporting on the Internet.* Deloitte and Touche.

Hutton, E., Goldstein, J., & Piemonte, M. (2013). The adoption of XBRL reporting: Implications for industry and education. *The BRC Academy Journal of Education*, 3(1), 49–68.

Investor Relations Society. (1998, 2004). *Annual reports and the Internet.* London: Investor Relations Society.

Ismail, T. H., & Sobhy, N. M. (2009). Determinants of auditors' perceptions of the work needed in the audit of Internet-based financial reports in Egypt. *The Journal of Applied Accounting Research*, 10(2), 132–150. DOI: 10.1108/09675420910984691

Jafaru, J., & Francis, O. A. (2016). Voluntary Internet financial reporting (IFR) in the Nigerian public sector. *Journal of Accountancy*, 2.

Jain, S. K. (2013). *Corporate Internet financial reporting in international perspective: A comparative study of selected Indian and US companies* [Unpublished Ph.D. dissertation]. Dayalbagh Educational Institute, Agra, India.

Jaya, A. K., & Verawaty, V. (2015). The accessibility determinants of Internet financial reporting of Manufacture Company listed in Indonesia Stock Exchange. *Asian Economic and Financial Review*, 5(2), 229–238. DOI: 10.18488/journal.aefr/2015.5.2/102.2.229.238

Jones, K., Alabaster, T., & Hetherington, K. (1999). Internet-based environmental reporting: Current trends. *Greener Management International*, 26, 69–90.

Jones, M. J., & Xiao, J. Z. (2003). Current trends and the trends by 2010 in Internet reporting. *Accounting Forum*, 27(2), 132–165. DOI: 10.1111/1467-6303.00099

Jones, M. J., & Xiao, J. Z. (2004). Financial reporting on the Internet by 2010: A consensus view. *Accounting Forum*, 28(3), 237–263. DOI: 10.1016/j.accfor.2004.07.002

Joshi, L. P., & Al-Modhahki, J. (2003). Financial reporting on the Internet: Empirical evidence from Bahrain and Kuwait. *Asian Review of Accounting*, 11(1), 88–101. DOI: 10.1108/eb060764

Kaur, K., & Singh, K. (2019). Corporate disclosure through web: An empirical study to examine the potential benefits of corporate disclosure through web. *Journal of Commerce & Accounting Research*, 8(3), 64–74.

Keliwon, K. B., Shukor, Z. A., & Hassan, M. S. (2018). Internet financial reporting (IFR) disclosure position and firm value. *Asian Journal of Accounting and Governance*, 9, 111–122. DOI: 10.17576/AJAG-2018-09-10

Keliwon, K. B., Shukor, Z. A., Mohamed, Z. M., & Hassan, M. S. (2014). Exploring Internet financial reporting (IFR) strategies of firms in Malaysia. [MAR]. *Management Accounting Research*, 13(2), 1–21.

Kelton, S. A. (2006). *Internet financial reporting: The effect of hyperlinks and irrelevant information on investor judgments* [Ph.D. thesis, Stokely Management Center].

Kelton, S. A. (2007). *Internet financial reporting: The effect of hyperlinks and irrelevant information on investor judgments*. AAA-IS Midyear Meeting.

Kelton, S. A., & Yang, Y. (2008). The impact of corporate governance on Internet financial reporting. *Journal of Accounting and Public Policy*, 27(1), 62–87. DOI: 10.1016/j.jaccpubpol.2007.11.001

Khan, M. A. H., Muzaffar, A. T., & Mahmood, S. A. (2006). *The use of Internet for corporate reporting: A discussion of the issues and surveys of current usage in Bangladesh* [Working Paper].

Khan, M. A. H., Muzaffar, A. T., & Nazmul, A. K. (2008). *Corporate financial reporting on the Internet: Global developments and an appraisal of practices in Bangladesh* [Working Paper]. American International University, Bangladesh.

Khan, M. N. A. A. (2010). *Pelaporan kewangan menerusi Internet: Indeks, tahap pelaporan dan faktor penentunya*. [Unpublished Ph.D. dissertation]. Universiti Utara Malaysia, Sintok, Kedah.

Khan, M. N. A. A., & Ismail, N. A. (2011). The level of Internet financial reporting of Malaysian companies. *Asian Journal of Accounting and Governance*, 2(1), 27–39. DOI: 10.17576/ajag-2011-2-6539

Khan, M. N. A. A., & Ismail, N. A. (2014). An empirical investigation of preparers' and users' views on Internet financial reporting disclosure items in Malaysia. *Sains Humanika*, 2(3), 23–34.

Khan, M. N. A. A., & Omar, N. A. B. (2013). A study of important items of Internet financial reporting: A case of Malaysian auditors. *Middle East Journal of Scientific Research*, 18(3), 340–351.

Khan, M. N. A. A., & Siang, L. H. (2013). Public investor perception towards Internet financial reporting in Malaysia. *Journal of Integrated Knowledge*, 60–68.

Koreto, R. (1997). When the bottom line is online. *Journal of Accountancy*, 63–65.

Lamani, D., & Cepani, L. (2011). Internet financial reporting by banks and insurance companies in Albania. *The Romanian Economic Journal*, 42, 159–174.

Lodhia, S. (2005). *Corporate perceptions of web-based environmental communication: An exploratory study into companies in the Australian mineral industry* [Working Paper Series]. ANU School of Business and Information Management, Canberra, Australia.

Lodhia, S., Allam, A., & Lymer, A. (2003). *Corporate reporting on the Internet in Australia: An exploratory study* [Discussion Paper]. School of Business and Information Management, Australian National University, Australia.

Louwers, T. J., Pasewark, W. R., & Typpo, E. W. (1998). Silicon Valley meets Norwalk. *Journal of Accountancy*, 20–25.

Lymer, A. (1997). The use of the Internet for corporate reporting: A discussion of the issues and survey of current usage in the UK. *21st Annual Congress of the European Accounting Association*, Antwerp, Belgium.

Lymer, A., & Tallberg, A. (1997). Corporate reporting and the Internet: A survey and commentary on the use of the WWW in corporate reporting in the UK and Finland. *20th Annual Associates*, Graz, Austria.

Malarvizhi, P., & Yadav, S. (2008). Corporate environment reporting on the Internet: An insight into Indian practice. *11th Annual Convention of the Strategic Management Forum*, Indian Institute of Technology, Kanpur, India.

Mariq, M. S. (2007). Financial reporting on the Internet by Saudi joint-stock companies: Impact on the audit profession. *JPS Accountants Directory*. http://www.jps-dir.org/Forum/forum-posts.asp?TID=4664

Marston, C. (1996). The organization of the investor relations function by the large UK quoted companies. *Omega*, 24(4), 477–488. DOI: 10.1016/0305-0483(96)00015-1

Marston, C. (2003). Financial reporting on the Internet by leading Japanese companies. *Corporate Communications*, 8(1), 23–24. DOI: 10.1108/13563280310458894

Marston, C., & Leow, C. Y. (1998). Financial reporting on the Internet by leading UK companies. *21st Annual Congress of European Accounting Association*, Antwerp, Belgium.

Marston, C., & Wu, W. (2001). Financial reporting on the Internet by leading Japanese companies. *Scottish Regional Conference of the British Accounting Association*, Aberdeen.

Momany, M. T., & Pillai, R. (2013). Internet financial reporting in UAE: Analysis and implications. *Global Review of Accounting and Finance*, 4(2), 142–160.

Momany, T. M., & Al-Shorman, A. S. (2006). Web-based voluntary financial reporting of Jordanian companies. *International Review of Business Research Papers*, 2(2), 127–139.

Musleh Al-Sartawi, A. (2016). Measuring the level of online financial disclosure in the Gulf Cooperation Council Countries. *Corporate Ownership & Control Journal*, 14(1), 547–558. DOI: 10.22495/cocv14i1c4art1

Myners, P. (1998). Improving performance reporting to the market. In Carey, A., & Sancto, J. (Eds.), *Performance measurement in the digital age: Adding value to corporate reporting* (27–31). The Institute of Chartered Accountants in England & Wales.

Noor, A. I., & Mohamad, T. (2000). Financial reporting disclosure on the Internet by Malaysian public listed companies. *Akauntan Nasional*, 13(19), 28–33.

Nordberg, D. (1999). *Shareholder communication: The next wave*. Center for Business Performance, Institute of Chartered Accountants in England and Wales.

Oyelere, P., & Kuruppu, N. (2012). Voluntary IFR practices of listed companies in the United Arab Emirates. *Journal of Applied Accounting Research*, 13(3), 298–315. DOI: 10.1108/09675421211281353

Patel, N. (2012). Investor relations on the Internet: An empirical study of Indian listed companies. *IUP Journal of Corporate Governance*, 11(2), 45–59.

Pearce, C. (1998). Satisfying investor demand. In Carey, A., & Sancto, J. (Eds.), *Performance measurement in the digital age: Adding value to corporate reporting* (22–26). The Institute of Chartered Accountants in England & Wales.

Pernamasari, R. (2019). Analysis of index Internet financial reporting: Studies in banking companies in Indonesia, Malaysia, and Singapore. *International Journal of Academic Research in Accounting. Finance and Management Sciences*, 9(1), 150–159.

Pervan, I. (2005). Financial reporting on the Internet and the practice of Croatian joint stock companies quoted on the stock exchanges. *Financial Theory and Practice*, 29(2), 159–174.

Pervan, I. (2006). Voluntary financial reporting on the Internet: Analysis of the practice of stock-market listed Croatian and Slovene joint stock companies. *Financial Theory and Practice*, 30(1), 1–27.

Pervan, I., & Bartulović, M. (2012). Internet financial reporting: A comparative analysis for selected CEE countries. *Conference proceedings: International Conference of the Faculty of Economic Sarajevo (ICES)* (348–363).

Petravick, S., & Gillet, J. (1996). Financial reporting on the World Wide Web. *Management Accounting*, 26–33.

Pirchegger, B., Schader, H., & Wagenhofer, A. (1999). Financial information on the Internet: A survey of the homepages of Austrian companies. *European Accounting Review*, 8(2), 383–395. DOI: 10.1080/096381899336113

Prabowo, R., & Tambotoh, J. J. C. (2005). Internet financial reporting as a voluntary disclosure practice: An empirical analysis of Indonesian manufacturing firms using order logit regression. *Jurnal Akuntansi & Bisnis*, 5(2), 149–160.

Quagli, A. (2001). The web and corporate information to financial markets. *Economia e diritto del terziario, 1,* 177–208.

Quagli, A., & Riva, P. (2005). Do financial websites meet the users' information needs? A survey from the Italian context. http://www.ssrn.com

Rawashdeh, B., & Rawashdeh, A. (2021). Factors influencing the usage of XBRL tools. *Management Science Letters*, 11(4), 1345–1356. DOI: 10.5267/j.msl.2020.11.005

Rodrigues, L., & Carlos, M. (2001). *Financial reporting on the Internet: The Portuguese case*. Polytechnic Institute of Braganca.

Ruhaya, A., Nafsiah, M., & Normahiran, Y. (2000). *E-reporting of corporate financial information*. Universiti Teknologi Mara.

Sharma, N., & Bhardwaj, S. (2022). The influence of Internet-related aspects on financial reporting. *Poonam Shodh Rachna*, I(XII), 12–19.

Shukla, A., & Gekara, M. G. (2010). Corporate reporting in modern era: A comparative analysis of Indian and Chinese companies. *Global Journal of International Business Research*, 3(3), 42–56.

Siahaan, A. M., Waruwu, H. A., Sianipar, V. H., & Simanjuntak, O. (2021). Factors affecting financial reporting through the internet (Internet financial reporting) on the company's website: A literature study. [IJSMS]. *International Journal of Science and Management Studies*, 4(4), 1–10. DOI: 10.51386/25815946/ijsms-v4i4p101

Singh, B., & Malhotra, P. (2004). Corporate web reporting practices in India. *The Indian Journal of Commerce*, 57(3), 157–169.

Singh, H., & Singh, A. (2022). Understanding inhibitors to XBRL adoption: An empirical investigation. *Accounting Research Journal*, 35(5), 598–615. DOI: 10.1108/ARJ-05-2021-0144

Singh, M. (2009). *Corporate disclosure through web: A study of selected Indian companies* [Doctoral dissertation, Guru Nanak Dev University].

Singh, M., & Singh, N. (2021). Awareness and understanding of XBRL in India: An exploratory study of chartered accountants. *PIMT Journal of Research*, 13(3B), 22–27.

Singh, M., Singh, N., & Kaur, S. (2023). Measuring internet financial reporting: Investors' perspective. *PCMA Journal of Business*, 16(2), 26–33.

Sortur, S. (2006). Financial reporting on the Internet. *The Chartered Accountant*, 996–1006.

Umoren, A. O., & Asogwa, I. E. (2013). Internet financial reporting and company characteristics: A case of quoted companies in Nigeria. *Research Journal of Finance and Accounting*, 4(12), 72–80.

Vasul, U. K., & Srivastava, R. (2003). Internet, XBRL, and online business reporting challenges and opportunities. *Chartered Accountant*, (June), 1215–1226.

Verawaty, V. (2022). *The availability of IFR (Internet financial reporting) through e-government as public transparency, participation, and accountability means in Indonesia.*

Wanderley, O. S. L., Lucian, R., Farache, F., & Filho, S. M. J. (2008). CSR information disclosure on the web: A context-based approach analyzing the influence of country of origin and industry sector. *Journal of Business Ethics*, 82(2), 369–378. DOI: 10.1007/s10551-008-9892-z

Wen, Y. (2019, January). Construction of the curriculum system of financial management undergraduate based on XBRL. In *3rd International Seminar on Education Innovation and Economic Management (SEIEM 2018)* (204–206). Atlantis Press. DOI: 10.2991/seiem-18.2019.52

Xiao, J. Z., Jones, M. J., & Lymer, A. (2002). Immediate trends in Internet reporting. *European Accounting Review*, 11(2), 245–275. DOI: 10.1080/09638180020017087a

Yassin, M. M., & Al-Khatib, E. (2019). Internet financial reporting and expected stock return. *Journal of Accounting. Finance & Management Strategy*, 14(1), 1–28.

Chapter 12
Sustainability Assurance in Islamic Finance:
Improving Sharia Compliance and Social Responsibility

Early Ridho Kismawadi
https://orcid.org/0000-0002-9420-5212
IAIN Langsa, Indonesia

Mohammad Irfan
https://orcid.org/0000-0002-4956-1170
Christ University, India

Zakir Hossen Shaikh
https://orcid.org/0000-0003-4733-4166
Kingdom University, Bahrain

ABSTRACT

This study aims to explore the application of sustainability assurance in increasing sharia compliance and social responsibility of Islamic financial institutions. By highlighting methodologies, challenges, and best practices, this study evaluates how sustainability assurance can support sustainability reporting that is transparent, credible, and compliant with sharia principles. The results of the study show that sustainability assurance contributes significantly to sharia compliance by verifying sustainability reports involving environmental, social, and governance (ESG) aspects. The study also identified key challenges, including the lack of sustainability reporting standards specific to Islamic finance and the need to strengthen the capacity of Islamic financial institution practitioners regarding sustainability assurance. The implications of this study include practical guidance for Islamic financial institutions

DOI: 10.4018/979-8-3373-0117-4.ch012

in formulating effective and sharia-based sustainability policies.

INTRODUCTION

Amid growing global awareness of sustainability challenges, Islamic finance is emerging as a sector that has unique potential to promote ethical and responsible financial practices (Hambali & Adhariani, 2023; Jaafar & Brightman, 2022). Sharia principles, which emphasize fairness, transparency, and social responsibility, provide a robust framework for ensuring that financial transactions not only meet the criteria for profit, but also take into account social and environmental impacts. In this context, sustainability assurance serves as a key mechanism to ensure that sustainability reports prepared by Islamic financial institutions are accurate, trustworthy, and in accordance with sharia principles. Sustainability assurance, which includes the process of verifying and evaluating environmental, social, and governance (ESG) reports, serves to build trust between financial institutions, stakeholders, and the public. By validating sustainability claims made by Islamic financial institutions, these guarantees help to create the transparency necessary to maintain the integrity and reputation of the sector. This is all the more important given the increasing pressure from investors, consumers, and regulators to demonstrate a commitment to social responsibility and sustainability.

This paper explores how sustainability assurance practices can improve sharia compliance in Islamic financial institutions, as well as strengthen their social responsibility. With a focus on methodologies, challenges, and best practices in sustainability assurance, this study aims to provide in-depth insights into how Islamic financial institutions can leverage sustainability assurance to achieve their sustainability goals. Through case study analysis and an interdisciplinary approach, this paper will reveal the potential for sustainability assurance in creating long-term value, both for the financial institutions themselves and for the wider community, while maintaining compliance with the sharia principles on which their operations are based.

Although sustainability and social responsibility are increasingly becoming the main focus in the world of global finance, the literature linking sustainability assurance to Islamic finance is still limited. Most of the existing research tends to focus on sustainability practices in conventional financial institutions, without considering sharia principles and the challenges faced by Islamic financial institutions in implementing sustainability guarantees. In this context, there is a need to explore how sustainability assurance can be adapted and integrated with Islamic financial practices to ensure sharia compliance. Previous research also lacked discussions on methodologies and best practices specific to Islamic financial institutions in ensuring sustainability and transparency, as well as the challenges that may arise in the process. The lack of empirical studies investigating the impact of sustainability assurance on the reputation and performance of Islamic financial institutions makes this area a significant research gap.

With the increasing attention to the ethical and social aspects of investing, more research is needed to understand how sustainability assurance can serve as a tool to achieve sustainability goals that are in line with sharia values. The study aims to bridge this gap by providing insight into sustainability assurance practices in Islamic finance and their implications for sharia compliance and social responsibility. This research has various significant implications, both for practice in the field and for the development of theories. First, this study can provide practical guidance for Islamic financial institutions in formulating and implementing effective sustainability assurance policies, which are in accordance with sharia principles. By understanding the methodologies and best practices in sustainability assurance, institutions can improve the credibility of their sustainability reports and build trust with stakeholders.

Second, the theoretical implications of this study can enrich the existing literature on Islamic finance and sustainability. By explaining how sustainability assurance can contribute to sharia compliance and social responsibility, this research can provide a new framework for understanding the interplay between ethics, sustainability, and financial practices. This could pave the way for further research in this area, prompting a more in-depth study of the relationship between sustainability assurance, corporate reputation, and performance in the Islamic finance sector. The implications of this study also include the impact on policies and regulations. By demonstrating the importance of sustainability assurance in ensuring transparency and accountability of Islamic financial institutions, the results of this study can provide a basis for the development of a stronger regulatory framework in sustainability practices in this sector. This is important, especially given the increasing pressure from investors and the public to demand social responsibility from financial institutions. This research can contribute to a greater awareness among stakeholders about the importance of sustainability and ethics in financial practices. By promoting a better understanding of sustainability assurance, Islamic financial institutions can be a positive example for the rest of the financial sector, demonstrating how compliance with sharia principles can go hand in hand with global sustainability goals.

INTEGRATION OF SUSTAINABILITY AND SHARIA PRINCIPLES IN THE ISLAMIC FINANCE INDUSTRY

Sustainability and sharia principles can not only go hand in hand, but also reinforce each other (Hassan et al., 2022; Huda & Santoso, 2022). The integration between sustainability and sharia is unique to Islamic finance, where social, economic, and environmental aspects must be considered together. This fact could inspire a paradigm shift in the global financial industry, where conventional institutions may be able to learn from this holistic approach.

Sustainability and Sharia principles are increasingly intertwined in the global financial landscape. Green bonds have emerged as the most actively invested sustainable debt product, with 63% of global investors participating in this market. These bonds, along with sustainability bonds and sustainability-related bonds, gain traction because they align with environmental goals and Islamic finance principles.

Figure 1. Leading sustainable debt products actively invested in by global investors in 2024 (Royal Bank of Canada)

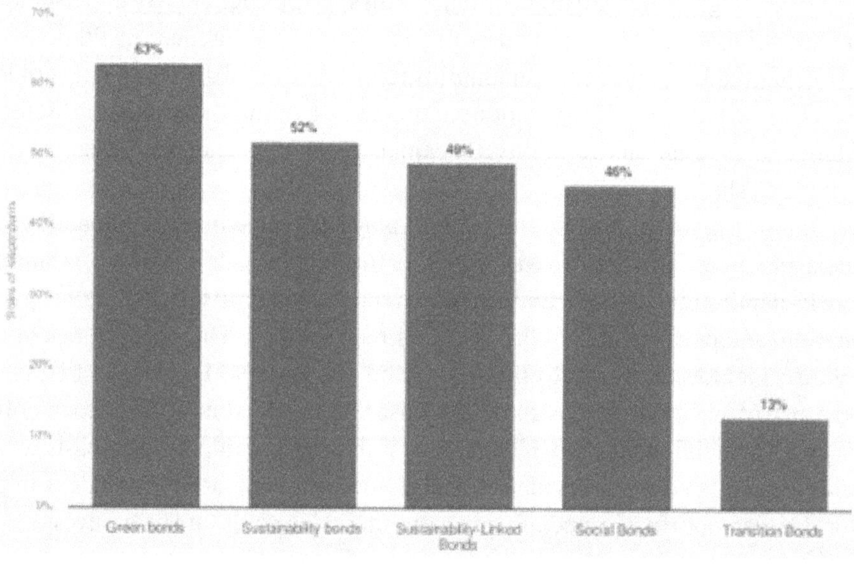

The integration of sustainability and sharia principles in the Islamic finance industry is a concept that illustrates how these two important elements can work in harmony and even reinforce each other. Both have the same goal in terms of maintaining a balance between social, economic, and environmental aspects. In the context of Islamic finance, sharia principles that emphasize ethics, justice, and social welfare provide a solid foundation for the implementation of sustainability. Sustainability, on the other hand, refers to efforts to preserve and protect natural resources and ensure that economic activities provide long-term benefits to the wider community without damaging the environment. This research highlights the importance of such integration in response to current global challenges, especially related to environmental degradation and social inequality.

Sharia principles in Islamic finance prohibit the practice of riba (interest), gharar (excessive uncertainty), and maysir (speculation), and require investment in ethical and sustainable sectors. Thus, Islamic finance inherently has a structure that supports sustainability. The transactions that are allowed in Islamic finance are those that are based on real values and provide broad socio-economic benefits. This is seen in concepts such as Mudharabah (profit-sharing) and Musharakah (cooperation), where risks and benefits are shared fairly between all parties. This principle creates transparency and avoids the inequality that often occurs in the conventional financial system. By paying attention to the sustainability aspect, Islamic finance also automatically pays attention to the environmental and social impact of every investment made.

Islamic finance also emphasizes the importance of strong corporate social responsibility (CSR), with sharia principles underlining the need to contribute to the well-being of society. In this case, sustainability is an important component. Islamic financial institutions are expected to not only maximize financial benefits but also have a positive impact on society and the environment. One clear example of this is the Green Sukuk instrument, which combines sharia principles with environmental objectives to fund environmentally friendly projects, such as renewable energy and clean water management (Abdullah & Keshminder, 2022; Alam et al., 2023; Liu & Lai, 2021). This shows how the integration of sustainability and sharia can create innovative financial products that support sustainable development.

The study also highlights that a holistic approach to Islamic finance can make a significant contribution in addressing global sustainability challenges. Islamic finance, through an integrated approach, offers an alternative model capable of combining economic growth with ethical values and social well-being. This approach differs from conventional finance which often focuses only on short-term gains and ignores the long-term impact on the environment and society. Taking into account sharia principles, Islamic finance has the potential to be a pioneer in creating a fairer and more sustainable financial system at the global level.

One of the challenges faced by the Islamic finance industry in integrating sustainability is the lack of global standards specific to the industry. Currently, many sustainability reporting standards are applied more relevant to conventional financial institutions and do not take into account the unique characteristics of Islamic finance. Therefore, reporting standards that pay attention to sharia values and social responsibility are needed. Islamic finance, with its sharia guidelines, has principles that can make a significant contribution in formulating more inclusive and equitable sustainability standards. This provides an opportunity for Islamic financial institutions to play a greater role in driving the adoption of sustainability practices around the world.

This study shows that Islamic financial institutions can take the lead in introducing innovations in sustainable finance products. As the global demand for socially and environmentally responsible investments increases, Islamic finance has an opportunity to capitalize on this trend. By promoting financial products that align with sustainability and sharia principles, such as Green Sukuk or Sustainable Waqf Funds, Islamic financial institutions can attract investors who prioritize ethics and positive impact. This also strengthens the position of the Islamic finance industry in the global market, which is increasingly aware of the importance of social and environmental responsibility.

This integrated approach also provides a competitive advantage for Islamic financial institutions. Greater trust from stakeholders, including investors, consumers, and regulators, can be earned through enhanced transparency and a clear commitment to sustainability. This is important because more and more consumers and investors are demanding financial institutions to be socially and environmentally responsible. By adopting sustainability standards that are in line with sharia principles, Islamic financial institutions can position themselves as socially and environmentally responsible institutions, as well as take the lead in promoting global sustainability.

The research also underscores the importance of collaboration between Islamic financial institutions and other stakeholders, such as governments, non-governmental organizations, and the international community. This collaboration is crucial in creating an environment conducive to the adoption of sustainability practices. Governments, for example, can provide incentives for Islamic financial institutions to invest in sustainable projects or introduce regulations that encourage more transparent and accountable sustainability reporting. On the other hand, non-governmental organizations can help monitor and evaluate the social and environmental impacts of investments made by Islamic financial institutions. With the involvement of various stakeholders, the integration between sustainability and sharia can be realized more effectively.

Furthermore, the integration of sustainability and sharia principles can also be a powerful tool to mitigate long-term financial risks. Sustainability, with a focus on resource sustainability and social well-being, can assist Islamic financial institutions in managing risks related to climate change, social instability, and global economic fluctuations. This approach, which emphasizes prudence and responsibility, can make Islamic financial institutions more resilient in the face of economic or environmental crises. By prioritizing sustainable investments, Islamic financial institutions can reduce the reputational risk and financial risks faced by many conventional financial institutions that invest in sectors that are not environmentally friendly.

This research emphasizes that the integration of sustainability and sharia principles is not only an opportunity, but also a necessity for the Islamic finance industry in the future. By maintaining a focus on ethical values, Islamic finance can continue to thrive and lead the way in promoting global sustainability. This integration is not only beneficial for Islamic financial institutions themselves, but also for society and the environment as a whole. Islamic finance, with its holistic and inclusive outlook, has great potential to play a major role in creating a more just, sustainable, and responsible global economic system.

IMPROVING SHARIA COMPLIANCE THROUGH SUSTAINABILITY ASSURANCE

Increasing sharia compliance through sustainability assurance is one of the important approaches in ensuring that Islamic financial institutions operate in accordance with sharia principles that are also in line with global sustainability goals. Sustainability assurance aims to verify and assess the accuracy of sustainability reports prepared by financial institutions, especially in relation to environmental, social, and governance (ESG) aspects (Silvola & Vinnari, 2021; Zaman et al., 2021). In the context of Islamic finance, this verification process ensures that business activities not only generate profits but also comply with sharia principles, which emphasize fairness, transparency, and social responsibility. This is becoming increasingly important given the increasing demands from investors and consumers for transparency and social responsibility in the business world.

In Islamic finance, sharia principles stipulate that all financial transactions must be in accordance with ethical values and fairness (Franzoni & Allali, 2018; Hanieh, 2020). With sustainability assurance, Islamic financial institutions can ensure that all their operational practices are in accordance with sharia rules, especially in terms of investment and risk management. This verification process includes checking ESG reports to ensure that there are no activities that violate sharia principles, such as riba (interest), gharar (excessive uncertainty), or maysir (gambling). Sustainability assurance also serves as an important tool to minimize reputational risks that can arise if Islamic financial institutions are involved in projects or investments that are contrary to sharia values.

Islamic financial institutions are under close scrutiny from stakeholders, including regulators, consumers, and investors who are concerned with business ethics. By implementing sustainability assurance, financial institutions can provide assurance to stakeholders that their operations are carried out with ethical principles and in accordance with internationally recognized sustainability standards. ESG reports that have gone through the assurance process can strengthen stakeholder trust, as assurance ensures that sustainability claims made by financial institutions can be verified and accounted for. This is important considering the increasing number of investors who demand transparency and social responsibility in business activities, including in investments made by Islamic financial institutions.

Sustainability assurance also plays a key role in increasing the accountability of Islamic financial institutions. By going through an external verification process, the resulting sustainability reports become more accurate and transparent, helping to reduce the risk of data manipulation or "greenwashing", where an institution may claim a commitment to sustainability without actually taking any concrete action. In the context of sharia, honesty and transparency are integral parts of every business transaction. Therefore, sustainability assurance helps Islamic financial institutions to adhere to not only sharia principles but also global standards in terms of sustainability and social responsibility.

Sustainability assurance also contributes to better risk management in Islamic financial institutions. Through ESG report verification, institutions can identify and evaluate risks associated with investments or projects that may not be in accordance with sharia or that have a negative impact on the environment and society. For example, if an Islamic financial institution invests in an environmentally unfriendly project, the risk to its reputation and sharia compliance may increase. With assurance, institutions can be more proactive in managing these risks and ensure that only investments that are in accordance with sharia principles are made. This process ultimately improves the long-term performance of financial institutions and provides benefits to society as a whole.

In the long term, sustainability assurance can strengthen the reputation of Islamic financial institutions in the global market. Transparent and socially responsible institutions will more easily attract investors who care about ethics and sustainability. Investor trust is an important element in the success of a financial institution, and sustainability assurance provides assurance that it operates in accordance with international standards and sharia principles. Thus, sustainability assurance not only helps Islamic financial institutions maintain sharia compliance but also improves their competitiveness in the global market, especially amid the growing demand for socially responsible investments.

The study also highlights that sustainability assurance not only focuses on verifying ESG reports but also plays a role in directing Islamic financial institutions towards achieving long-term sustainability goals. Through a continuous assurance process, financial institutions can evaluate their progress in achieving sustainability targets, such as reducing carbon emissions, improving people's welfare, and protecting the environment. This aspect is especially important in an era where sustainability is one of the main focuses in global and national policy. By implementing sustainability principles that are in line with sharia, Islamic financial institutions can play a greater role in global efforts to mitigate climate change and improve social welfare.

Pressure from regulators and government policies also plays an important role in encouraging Islamic financial institutions to adopt sustainability assurance. A number of countries, especially those with large Islamic finance industries, such as Malaysia and the Gulf states, have begun to introduce regulations that encourage or require financial institutions to adopt sustainability standards in their operations. Regulators in these countries recognize the importance of transparency and accountability in supporting the sustainable growth of the Islamic finance industry. With sustainability assurance, Islamic financial institutions can more easily comply with existing regulations and ensure that their operations are in accordance with national and international standards.

However, while sustainability assurance offers many benefits, the study also identifies some challenges in its implementation. One of the main challenges is the lack of specific standards for Islamic finance in the context of sustainability. Currently, existing sustainability assurance standards are generally developed for conventional financial institutions and may not fully meet the needs of Islamic financial institutions. Therefore, further efforts are needed to develop assurance standards that are in accordance with sharia principles, so that Islamic financial institutions can adopt best practices in terms of sustainability without neglecting sharia values. There is also a need to increase awareness and understanding among Islamic finance practitioners regarding the importance of sustainability assurance in supporting the long-term performance and social responsibility of institutions.

Sustainability assurance makes a significant contribution to improving sharia compliance in Islamic financial institutions. Through ESG report verification, Islamic financial institutions can ensure that their operations are in line with sharia principles and sustainability values. This assurance process also helps to improve transparency, accountability, and risk management in Islamic financial institutions, while strengthening their reputation in the eyes of investors and stakeholders. While challenges remain, with the development of sharia-compliant assurance standards and increased awareness among practitioners, sustainability assurance can play an important role in driving the growth of a more sustainable and responsible Islamic finance industry.

Improving Sustainability Reporting Standards

Improving the standard of sustainability reporting in Islamic financial institutions is an urgent need that is widely recognized in the literature and practice (Hamilton & Waters, 2022). While Islamic finance has foundational principles aligned with sustainability goals, sustainability reporting in Islamic financial institutions often still faces major challenges in terms of quality, transparency, and accountability. The current standards, both in terms of ESG (Environmental, Social, and Governance) reporting and sustainability assurance, are mostly developed for conventional financial institutions. These standards do not fully take into account the specific sharia challenges faced by Islamic financial institutions, thus raising the need for the development of more comprehensive and industry-specific standards.

Figure 2. Global governance, sustainability and resilience (GSR) scores in 2024, by region (Global SWF)

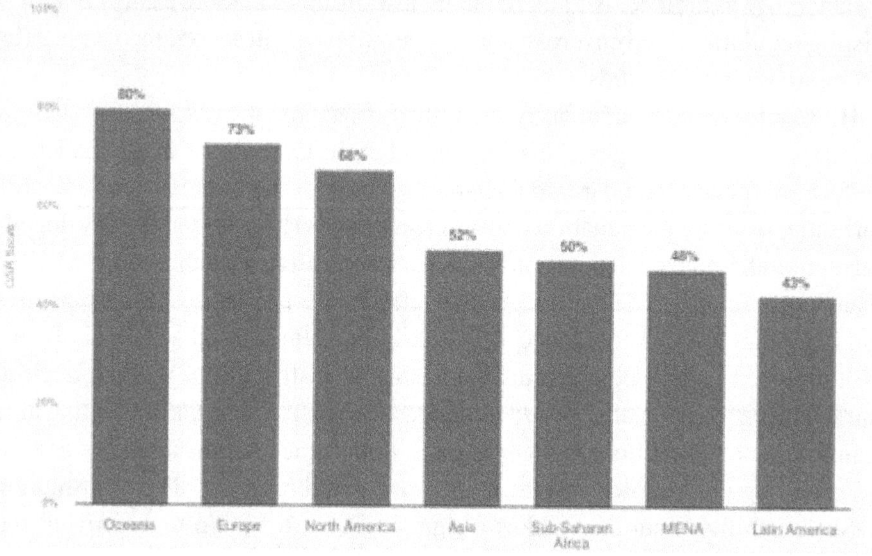

In 2024, the Oceania region recorded the highest score in governance, sustainability, and resilience (GSR) with 80 percent. Europe is in second place with a score of 73 percent, followed by North America with 68 percent. Meanwhile, the lowest GSR score was recorded in Latin America, which only reached 43 percent in the same year.

In 2023, *the Industrial and Commercial Bank of China* (ICBC) led the global green bond issuance among major banks, with a total value exceeding 31 billion US dollars. This figure includes nine overseas green bonds and five domestic bonds. In second place, Crédit Agricole issued green bonds worth nearly 10 billion US dollars. Meanwhile, the Bank of China occupies the third position with a total of 15 outstanding green bonds, with a value of slightly above 7 billion US dollars.

Current sustainability standards often fail to reflect the nuances of sharia principles, such as the prohibition against riba (interest), gharar (excessive uncertainty), and maysir (gambling). These sharia principles have profound implications for how Islamic financial institutions operate and report on their activities, including how they assess risk, build investment models, and contribute to social welfare.

For example, investments involving industries that are contrary to sharia, such as alcohol, gambling, or other non-halal sectors, are clearly not allowed. However, existing conventional sustainability standards often ignore this aspect, and do not provide sufficient guidance for Islamic financial institutions to navigate between sharia compliance and global sustainability demands.

This creates a major challenge for Islamic financial institutions, which must balance sustainability reporting demands with their obligations to sharia principles. Existing sustainability reporting standards need to be expanded to include clearer guidance on how Islamic financial institutions can integrate sharia values into their sustainability reporting. In the absence of clear guidance, there is a risk that sustainability reports issued by Islamic financial institutions may not reflect full compliance with sharia or instead miss out on the essential elements of sustainability that global stakeholders expect.

Figure 3. Value of green bond issuance of the largest banks worldwide in 2023(in million U.S. dollars) (Survey by Statista)

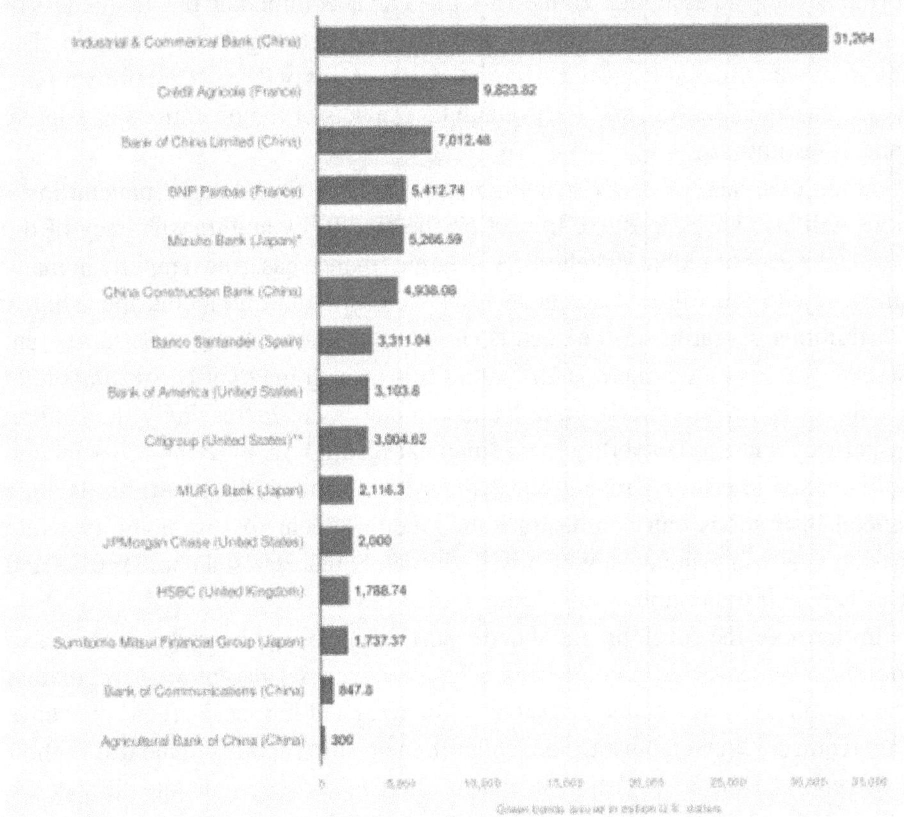

In the aspect of social responsibility, Islamic financial institutions have an obligation to support the welfare of the community, which is an integral part of sharia values. However, without clear guidance, sustainability reporting is often focused on environmental and economic issues only, while financial institutions' contributions to social well-being may be overlooked. In fact, many Islamic financial institutions invest in social initiatives, such as the development of health and education infrastructure, funding of Waqf (waqf) projects, or the provision of inclusive financial services for the underprivileged. All of this needs to be included in sustainability reporting to show the positive impact of financial institutions on society in accordance with sharia principles.

Islamic financial institutions often face challenges in compiling reports that can be easily guaranteed by external parties. Assurance or verification of sustainability reports is an important process to ensure that the information presented in sustainability reports is accurate and reliable. However, current assurance standards are not fully compatible with sharia values and practices, which require different treatment from conventional financial institutions. Therefore, there needs to be an effort to develop an assurance framework that can accommodate the uniqueness of Islamic finance, including the ethical and social aspects regulated by sharia. The framework should consider not only the financial aspects of the sustainability report, but also the social, moral, and environmental impacts of the operations of Islamic financial institutions.

The development of better sustainability standards for Islamic financial institutions will also have a positive impact on the credibility and transparency of the sector in the eyes of global stakeholders. Islamic finance has grown rapidly in many countries, with the value of assets steadily increasing and an increasing number of institutions operating in the sector. However, without strong and transparent sustainability standards, there is a risk that this growth may not be sustainable in the long term. Investors, consumers, and regulators are increasingly demanding transparency and accountability from financial institutions in terms of social and environmental impact. By raising the standard of sustainability reporting, Islamic financial institutions can demonstrate their commitment to sustainability while adhering to sharia principles, which will ultimately increase stakeholder trust and strengthen their reputation in the global market.

Furthermore, the development of better sustainability reporting standards is also important to increase the accountability of Islamic financial institutions to regulators and the public. In some countries, such as Malaysia and Indonesia, regulators have begun requiring financial institutions to implement sustainability standards in their annual reports. However, existing standards often do not accommodate the specific challenges faced by Islamic financial institutions. With more specific and sharia-compliant standards, it will be easier for regulators to evaluate whether Islamic financial institutions are truly meeting their obligations in terms of sustainability, as well as whether they are contributing to sustainable development in a tangible way.

However, while the development of these better standards is urgently needed, challenges remain. One of the main challenges is the lack of awareness and understanding among Islamic finance practitioners about the importance of sustainability reporting. Many Islamic financial institutions still view sustainability reporting as an additional burden that requires more resources and time, without providing any immediate visible benefits. Therefore, education and training in the field of sustainability need to be improved, both among Islamic finance practitioners and among regulators and other stakeholders. With this increased awareness, Islamic financial institutions will better understand the importance of sustainability in creating long-term value for businesses and society.

Another challenge is the complexity of integrating sharia principles with existing international standards. Many Islamic financial institutions operate in various jurisdictions, where each country may have different regulations and guidelines when it comes to sustainability reporting. This creates complexity in compiling reports that comply with various applicable standards, while still adhering to sharia principles. Therefore, a harmonized approach is needed in the development of sustainability reporting standards for Islamic financial institutions, which are globally acceptable but still respect the uniqueness of sharia principles in each jurisdiction.

This research confirms that the development of better sustainability reporting standards for Islamic financial institutions is key to achieving a balance between sharia compliance and sustainability. With clearer and more specific guidance, Islamic financial institutions will be able to report their contributions to sustainability in a transparent and accountable manner, while adhering to the sharia principles on which their operations are based. The standard will also help Islamic financial institutions improve their reputation in the global market, as well as strengthen their position as leaders in ethical and responsible financial practices. Although challenges in the development of these standards exist, with commitment and collaboration between regulators, practitioners, and stakeholders, Islamic financial institutions can play a key role in supporting global sustainability and equitable development.

The Role of Stakeholders in the Assurance Process

The role of stakeholders in the sustainability assurance process plays a very important role in increasing transparency, accountability, and public trust in financial institutions, especially in the context of Islamic finance. Stakeholders such as regulators, investors, the public, and activist groups have a strong influence in encouraging Islamic financial institutions to adopt higher standards in sustainability reporting. This growing pressure from stakeholders not only encourages financial institutions to be more transparent but also reinforces the importance of adopting sustainability assurance as a tool to verify sustainability claims made by these institutions. Islamic financial institutions, which operate with sharia values, have an additional obligation to ensure that their sustainability reports are in accordance with the principles of ethics and fairness mandated by sharia. Therefore, the role of stakeholders in the assurance process is not only limited to ensuring compliance with international standards but also ensuring that these institutions adhere to the sharia values they uphold.

In this context, regulators have a key role as a key stakeholder in sustainability assurance. Regulators in various jurisdictions, especially in countries with large Islamic finance industries such as Malaysia, Indonesia, and the Gulf states, have begun to introduce regulations that require or encourage financial institutions to increase their transparency through sustainability reporting. With this regulation, Islamic financial institutions are not only required to report on their sustainability performance, but also to ensure that the reports have gone through an independent and reliable verification process. Sustainability assurance provides an avenue for regulators to verify the accuracy of sustainability reports and ensure that Islamic financial institutions are actually running their operations in accordance with the set standards, both in terms of sustainability and sharia compliance.

Regulators also play a role in setting assurance standards that are in accordance with sharia principles. Current standards, which are largely developed for conventional financial institutions, often do not take into account the uniqueness of Islamic finance. Therefore, regulators must ensure that the assurance standards implemented in Islamic financial institutions reflect sharia values, such as fairness, transparency, and social responsibility. These standards should include clear guidance on how Islamic financial institutions can integrate sharia principles into their sustainability reporting and verification processes. With these guidelines in place, regulators can facilitate the wider adoption of sustainability assurance in the Islamic finance industry and ensure that these institutions comply with both global and sharia standards.

Investors are also important stakeholders in the sustainability assurance process. Investors, especially those with a focus on ethical or sustainable investments, are increasingly demanding greater transparency from financial institutions regarding their social, environmental, and governance impacts. For investors in the Islamic financial market, compliance with sharia is one of the main criteria in making investment decisions. With effective sustainability assurance, investors can feel more confident that their investments not only comply with global sustainability standards but also comply with sharia values. This provides investors with additional confidence that their funds are managed in a responsible, ethical, and sustainable manner, in accordance with Islamic teachings.

Sustainability assurance also provides assurance to investors that the financial institution they invest in is actually doing what they claim to be in terms of sustainability. In some cases, sustainability reports that are not independently verified can be vulnerable to manipulation or misrepresentation, often referred to as "greenwashing." With assurance, sustainability claims made by financial institutions can be objectively examined and verified by an independent third party. This not only provides additional confidence to investors but also prevents potential reputational risks that can arise if sustainability reports turn out to be inaccurate or misleading.

Beyond regulators and investors, the public also plays an important role in driving the adoption of sustainability assurance in Islamic financial institutions. Communities, both individually and through civil society organizations and NGOs, are increasingly voicing demands that financial institutions be responsible for the social and environmental impacts of their operations. Islamic finance, with its focus on social well-being and justice, has a moral obligation to ensure that their operations make a positive contribution to society. Independently verified sustainability reports can help the public evaluate whether Islamic financial institutions are truly committed to social responsibility and sustainability or simply meet formal obligations without any real impact.

The role of the community in sustainability assurance also extends to the aspect of accountability. The public has the right to know how financial institutions use the funds entrusted to them and how they contribute to social welfare and environmental protection. With sustainability assurance, the public can have better access to accurate and reliable information regarding the operational impact of financial institutions. This allows the public to ask questions and demand accountability from Islamic financial institutions if it turns out that their sustainability reports do not reflect the reality on the ground.

Sustainability assurance provides an opportunity for Islamic financial institutions to improve their reputation in the eyes of the public and other stakeholders. Financial institutions that are transparent and responsible in sustainability reporting tend to be more respected by the public, which in turn can strengthen their position in the market and improve their competitiveness. Islamic financial institutions that successfully meet stakeholder expectations through sustainability assurance can leverage this reputation to attract more investors and customers who care about ethics and sustainability.

However, challenges remain in effectively engaging stakeholders in the sustainability assurance process. One of the key challenges is ensuring that the assurance standards implemented are relevant to the needs of all stakeholders, including regulators, investors, and the public. Assurance standards that are too technical or focus only on financial aspects may not adequately cover the needs of society to see the wider social and environmental impacts. Therefore, an inclusive and holistic framework is needed that allows stakeholders to be actively involved in the assurance process and provide relevant input.

Another challenge is the lack of awareness and understanding among stakeholders regarding the importance of sustainability assurance. Many members of the public or investors may not fully understand what sustainability assurance is or how this process can improve transparency and accountability. Therefore, education and awareness-raising are essential to ensure that all stakeholders understand their role in encouraging financial institutions to adopt best practices in sustainability reporting and assurance.

The role of stakeholders in the sustainability assurance process is crucial in creating a more transparent, accountable, and accountable financial system. With the effective involvement of regulators, investors, and the public, Islamic financial institutions can ensure that their sustainability reports truly reflect their commitment to social and environmental responsibility, while adhering to the sharia principles on which their operations are based. Sustainability assurance, with the full support of stakeholders, can help Islamic financial institutions maintain public trust and increase their contribution to global sustainability.

THE RELATIONSHIP BETWEEN ASSURANCE AND FINANCIAL INSTITUTION PERFORMANCE

Assurance, or sustainability assurance, has an important role in providing verification of sustainability claims made by financial institutions, both related to environmental, social, and governance (ESG) aspects (Martínez-Ferrero et al., 2018; Sirilertsuwan et al., 2020; Sonnerfeldt & Pontoppidan, 2020; Zaman et al., 2021). The implementation of this assurance gives confidence to stakeholders that the reports presented by the financial institution are accurate, transparent, and trustworthy. In the context of Islamic finance, the implementation of this assurance not only serves to meet the demands of sustainability, but also complies with sharia principles that prioritize justice, transparency, and social responsibility. This not only affects the reputation of these financial institutions, but also contributes to improving their performance, both in financial and non-financial aspects.

Public trust is one of the most important elements in the financial industry. When stakeholders, including investors, customers, regulators, and the general public, have high trust in a financial institution, they tend to be more loyal and supportive of the institution. Assurance plays an important role in building and strengthening this trust, as it provides assurance that claims made by financial institutions regarding their sustainability and social responsibility can be independently verified (Goicoechea et al., 2019). In an era where transparency is increasingly valued by stakeholders, financial institutions that implement assurance effectively can more easily maintain and increase public trust. This is especially important in the context of Islamic finance, where sharia principles require financial institutions to operate in a transparent and fair manner, taking into account the social welfare as well as the environmental impact of their business activities.

The relationship between sustainability and the performance of financial institutions is increasingly important in the global banking sector. In 2024, ESG (*Environmental, Social, and Governance*) scores will be a key factor in evaluating bank performance and attracting investment. The world's major banks show variations in ESG scores from various providers, signalling the growing importance of sustainability metrics in the industry. Financial institutions are at the forefront of AI integration, which is expected to improve their sustainability efforts and overall performance. In addition, 44% of commercial real estate executives plan to invest in physical and transitional risk-related risk management capabilities, including climate-related scenario analysis, in the next 12-18 months.

The banking sector is increasingly realizing the importance of sustainability, with initiatives such as *the Net-Zero Banking Alliance* demonstrating a commitment to aligning their operations with net-zero emissions goals by 2050. This shift towards more transparent and accountable sustainability practices is expected to have a positive impact on financial performance. Investors are increasingly integrating ESG data in their decision-making processes, with ESG ratings emerging as a key factor influencing investment decisions globally. This trend shows that banks with strong sustainability practices can have a competitive advantage in attracting investments and improving their financial performance.

Figure 4. Comparison of the environmental, social and governance (ESG) scores of the 15 largest banks by market capitalization worldwide in 2024, by ESG score provider (Statista; Sustainalytics; MSCI; S&P Global)

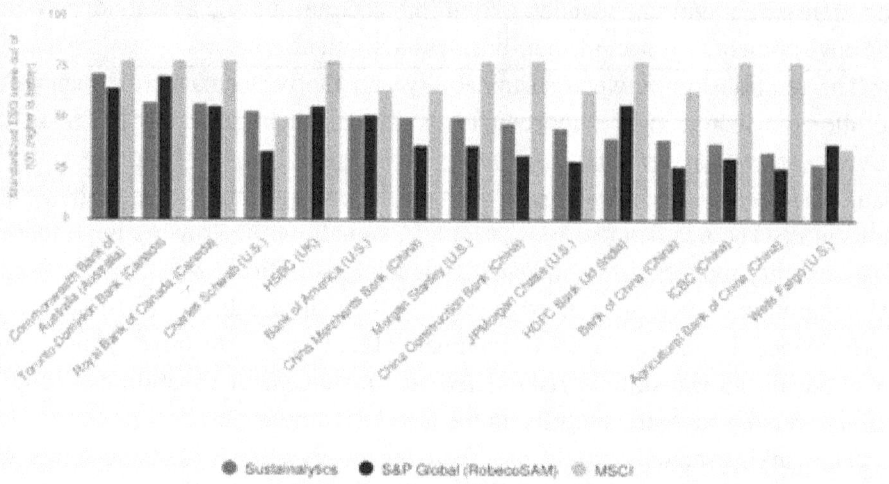

The influence of assurance on the performance of financial institutions can be seen from various aspects, both financial and non-financial (Al-Shaer & Zaman, 2019; Bui et al., 2021). From a financial perspective, the effective implementation of assurance can increase the value of the company and attract investors. Transparent and responsible financial institutions tend to be more attractive to investors who are increasingly concerned about sustainability issues. Today's investors are not only looking for financial gain but also want to ensure that the funds they invest are used for sustainable and ethical purposes. With assurance, financial institutions can provide assurance to investors that they comply with global sustainability standards and sharia, thereby increasing their investment attractiveness. This, in turn, can increase the flow of capital into these financial institutions, which will have a positive impact on long-term financial performance.

On the other hand, non-financial performance is no less important. Financial institutions that successfully implement assurance well can strengthen their reputation as responsible and ethical entities. This good reputation has a significant impact on the sustainability of their business. A positive reputation can increase customer loyalty, expand the customer base, and even attract the best talent to work at the institution. In an increasingly competitive business world, a strong reputation can be a competitive advantage that is difficult for competitors to replicate. Islamic financial institutions, in particular, that operate with sharia values that emphasize justice, honesty, and social welfare, have great potential to build a strong reputation through the effective implementation of assurance.

The implementation of assurance can also help financial institutions in managing risk better. Sustainability reports that have gone through the assurance process tend to be more accurate and reliable, providing a clearer picture of the risks faced by financial institutions, be it reputational risks, environmental risks, or social risks. With assurance, financial institutions can identify and manage these risks more proactively. This is especially important in today's business world, where risks associated with sustainability, such as climate change, social instability, and environmental damage, are increasingly becoming a major concern. Financial institutions that successfully manage these risks well through the implementation of assurance will not only improve their performance but also become more resilient in facing future challenges.

Furthermore, the implementation of assurance can provide long-term benefits for financial institutions in terms of operational efficiency. An assurance process that involves independent evaluation and verification of sustainability reports can help financial institutions to identify areas where they can improve efficiency, both in resource use and in risk management. For example, financial institutions that manage to reduce the negative environmental impact of their operations, such as reducing carbon emissions or using renewable energy, can reduce their operational costs in the long run. Financial institutions that adopt better governance practices through assurance can also improve the quality of their management, which in turn will improve the overall performance of the organization.

However, despite the many benefits that can be gained from implementing assurance, challenges remain. One of the main challenges is the costs associated with the assurance process itself. For some financial institutions, especially smaller ones, the cost of undergoing the assurance process may seem like an additional burden that is not worth the benefits. However, research shows that the long-term benefits of implementing assurance, such as improved reputation, better risk management, and greater investment attractiveness, can outweigh the costs incurred in the short term. Therefore, financial institutions must see the implementation of assurance as a strategic investment that can provide added value in the long term, not just additional operational costs.

Another challenge is the lack of understanding and awareness among some financial institutions regarding the importance of assurance in improving their performance and reputation. Some financial institutions may not fully understand how assurance can help them meet stakeholder demands and improve their overall performance. Therefore, further efforts are needed to raise awareness among financial practitioners regarding the benefits of implementing assurance, as well as provide the necessary training and guidance to implement it effectively.

The implementation of assurance is closely related to the performance of financial institutions, both in financial and non-financial aspects. Assurance plays an important role in strengthening public trust in financial institutions, improving their reputation, and assisting in risk management and operational efficiency. Although challenges remain, the long-term benefits of implementing assurance are significant, especially in the context of Islamic finance, where sharia compliance and sustainability are inseparable values. With the effective implementation of assurance, Islamic financial institutions can improve their performance, build a strong reputation, and contribute to global sustainability, while still adhering to the sharia principles they adhere to.

The Role of Technology in Sustainability Assurance

The role of technology in sustainability assurance is becoming increasingly important amid the rapid development of digital technology and the increasing demands for transparency and accuracy in sustainability reporting. Islamic financial institutions, which operate with sharia principles that prioritize ethics, justice, and social responsibility, have a great opportunity to leverage technology to improve the quality of their sustainability assurance. The two technologies that have emerged as the main catalysts in this regard are blockchain and artificial intelligence (AI). These two technologies have the potential to revolutionize the way Islamic financial institutions run and manage sustainability assurance, both in terms of efficiency, transparency, and accuracy.

Blockchain, with its decentralized, transparent, and immutable nature, offers a very powerful solution to improve integrity and accountability in sustainability assurance. Blockchain allows Islamic financial institutions to record and store their sustainability data in a secure and transparent way. Any transactions or activities related to sustainability, such as energy management, resource use, and social impact, can be recorded in the blockchain, so that the data can be verified in real-time by third parties. This provides assurance that the data presented in the sustainability report is accurate and not manipulated, as any changes made in the blockchain will be recorded and trackable by all stakeholders.

In the context of assurance, blockchain can be used to increase trust and transparency in the verification process. Traditional assurance processes often involve manual verification and take a long time and are prone to human error or data manipulation. By using blockchain, the verification process can be carried out automatically and in real-time, thereby speeding up and improving assurance accuracy. Blockchain also allows auditors or verifiers to access stored data in a more efficient way, so they can verify sustainability reports with a higher level of confidence. This is especially important in the context of Islamic finance, where transparency and fairness are core values that must be upheld in every aspect of operations, including in sustainability reporting.

Artificial intelligence (AI) also has an important role in increasing the effectiveness of sustainability assurance in Islamic financial institutions. AI can be used to analyze enormous and complex data related to sustainability, such as carbon emissions, natural resource use, and the social impact of investment projects. With advanced analytics capabilities, AI can identify patterns, trends, and anomalies in sustainability data that may not be visible to humans. This technology can be used by auditors or verifiers to identify potential risks or non-conformities in sustainability reports, thereby improving the accuracy and efficiency of the assurance process.

AI can also be used to predict the sustainability impact of various decisions or projects undertaken by Islamic financial institutions. For example, by using AI predictive models, financial institutions can estimate the long-term impact of their investments on the environment and society, as well as how this will affect compliance with sharia principles. Thus, AI not only improves assurance accuracy, but also assists financial institutions in more thoughtful and sustainable decision-making. The use of AI in sustainability assurance allows Islamic financial institutions to be more proactive in identifying and managing sustainability risks, as well as ensuring that their operations remain compliant with sharia principles.

To improving accuracy and efficiency, the use of technologies such as blockchain and AI can also strengthen public trust in Islamic financial institutions. In an era where trust is one of the key factors in the success of financial institutions, the adoption of technology that enhances transparency and accountability can provide a significant competitive advantage. Financial institutions that use this technology to improve their sustainability assurance will be more trusted by stakeholders, including investors, customers, regulators, and the general public. This trust is crucial, especially in the Islamic finance industry, where adherence to sharia values is one of the main criteria in the evaluation by stakeholders.

The use of technology in sustainability assurance can also provide benefits in terms of operational efficiency. Blockchain and AI allow financial institutions to automate many processes that previously required human intervention, such as data logging, analysis, and verification. By automating this process, financial institutions can reduce operational costs associated with reporting and assurance, as well as speed up the reporting process. In the long term, this can provide significant economic benefits for Islamic financial institutions, while still maintaining the quality and integrity of their sustainability reports.

However, the adoption of technology in sustainability assurance is not without its challenges. One of the main challenges is the costs associated with implementing technologies such as blockchain and AI. For some financial institutions, especially smaller ones, the initial cost of adopting this technology may seem high and not worth the short-term benefits that can be obtained. However, when viewed from a long-term perspective, investment in this technology can provide significant benefits, both in terms of operational efficiency, increased trust, and better risk management. Therefore, Islamic financial institutions need to see the adoption of this technology as part of their long-term strategy to improve competitiveness and sustainability.

There are other challenges related to the lack of understanding and expertise among financial practitioners regarding the use of technology in sustainability assurance. Technologies such as blockchain and AI are still relatively new to many financial institutions, and their implementation requires in-depth technical knowledge. Therefore, training and capacity building among Islamic finance practitioners are needed so that they can make effective use of this technology. Financial institutions can also work with technology providers or fintech companies to assist them in implementing this technology in their assurance process.

Technologies such as blockchain and AI have great potential to improve the effectiveness of sustainability assurance in Islamic financial institutions. The use of this technology can improve transparency, accuracy, and efficiency in the verification of sustainability reports, which in turn will strengthen public trust in these financial institutions. By utilizing this technology, Islamic financial institutions can ensure that they not only comply with global sustainability standards but also maintain compliance with sharia principles. While challenges in the adoption of these technologies remain, with the right investments and capacity building, they can be a catalyst for driving sustainable and responsible growth in the Islamic finance industry.

THE IMPACT OF ASSURANCE POLICY ON THE GLOBAL REPUTATION OF ISLAMIC FINANCIAL INSTITUTIONS

Sustainability assurance policies in the context of Islamic financial institutions (LKI) are increasingly becoming the main concern in this modern era. Amid increasing awareness of environmental, social, and governance (ESG) issues, the existence of a transparent and accountable assurance policy not only serves to meet the internal compliance of the institution but also has a significant impact on their global reputation. In this analysis, it will discuss how the implementation of sustainability assurance policies can strengthen LKI's reputation at the international level and increase the confidence of global investors looking for responsible and ethical institutions.

First, it is important to understand what sustainability assurance means. This is a verification process carried out by a third party to ensure that sustainability reports issued by financial institutions accurately reflect the environmental, social, and governance performance of the institution. By conducting assurance, LKI demonstrates their commitment to sustainability practices and transparency, which in turn can increase their credibility in the eyes of stakeholders. This policy is a strong foundation for LKI to build a good reputation, both domestically and in the international market. One of the main impacts of the implementation of the assurance policy is the increase in internal compliance of the institution. Assurance encourages financial institutions to implement better management systems in managing sustainability-related risks. With this policy in place, institutions must ensure that all their business practices are in accordance with sharia principles and meet the expected sustainability standards. This not only improves the integrity of the institution but also creates a culture of transparency that encourages innovation and continuous improvement in business processes. LKIs that have a strong commitment to sustainability will be better prepared to face challenges in an increasingly competitive market.

To improve internal compliance, the assurance policy also contributes to LKI's global reputation. In an increasingly connected world, an institution's reputation is one of its most valuable assets. LKIs that transparently report their sustainability performance through the assurance process will be easier to gain recognition in the eyes of the international community. Stakeholders, including consumers, investors, and regulators, are more likely to provide support to institutions that demonstrate a tangible commitment to social and environmental responsibility. A good reputation can serve as a magnet for investment, attracting the attention of investors who are looking for an institution that not only prioritizes profits, but also has a positive impact on society and the environment.

Furthermore, the reputation built through the assurance policy can affect the confidence of global investors. In an era where investors are increasingly paying attention to sustainability aspects in investment decision-making, LKIs that do not implement an assurance policy risk missing out on opportunities to attract capital. Many investors are now looking for financial institutions that can provide concrete evidence of how they manage environmental and social risks, as well as how they contribute to sustainable development. With an independently assured report, LKI can provide assurance to investors that they are conducting ethical and responsible business practices.

In this context, the implementation of the assurance policy also creates opportunities for LKI to differentiate itself from competitors. In a competitive market, institutions that can demonstrate superior sustainability performance through the assurance process will find it easier to stand out among other financial institutions. This not only creates a competitive advantage but also helps LKI in building stronger relationships with stakeholders. Investors and consumers are increasingly inclined to choose institutions that can prove their commitment to sustainability practices, and assurance is one way to do that.

However, despite the many benefits of implementing an assurance policy, challenges remain. Some LKIs may face obstacles in the implementation of this policy, especially those related to human resources and finance. The assurance process can require a significant investment in terms of time and cost, and not all institutions may have the capacity to do so effectively. Therefore, it is important for LKI to plan a sound strategy in implementing this policy, including training for staff and the development of adequate systems to ensure compliance with sustainability standards.

Furthermore, LKI also needs to realize that a good reputation is not only obtained from the assurance policy alone, but also from consistency in implementing sustainability principles. Investors and other stakeholders pay close attention to the real actions of the institution, not just the reports produced. Therefore, LKI must be committed to not only meeting the set standards, but also to continuously improve their sustainability performance. This includes involvement in social and environmental programs that have a positive impact on society, as well as transparent and accurate reporting on progress made.

The impact of assurance policies on the global reputation of Islamic financial institutions is significant. By implementing a transparent sustainability assurance policy, LKI not only improves their internal compliance, but also builds a strong reputation in the eyes of the international community. This good reputation contributes to the increased confidence of global investors who are increasingly looking for responsible and ethical institutions. Despite the challenges in implementation, an LKI that is committed to implementing sustainability practices through assurance policies will have an advantage in attracting investment and building positive relationships with stakeholders. Therefore, it is important for LKI to continue to develop and implement effective assurance policies as part of their strategy to face challenges and opportunities in an increasingly complex global market.

CONCLUSION

Sustainability assurance in Islamic finance has an important role in ensuring that Islamic financial institutions carry out their operations in accordance with sharia principles, as well as achieving global sustainability goals. Through a verification process that includes sustainability reports related to environmental, social, and governance (ESG) aspects, financial institutions can build trust from stakeholders, such as investors, regulators, and the public. The integration of sustainability and sharia principles, such as justice, transparency, and social responsibility, provides a solid foundation for Islamic financial institutions to meet ethical and environmental demands at the same time. The importance of improving sustainability reporting standards to better match the uniqueness of Islamic finance. Stakeholders, especially regulators, investors, and the public, play an important role in promoting transparency and accountability through sustainability assurance. This assurance process can strengthen the global reputation of Islamic financial institutions, attract investors who care about sustainability, and assist financial institutions in managing risk and improving long-term performance. Thus, sustainability assurance not only ensures sharia compliance but also becomes a strategic tool to build the reputation and sustainability of Islamic financial institutions in an increasingly competitive global market.

The implications of implementing sustainability assurance in Islamic finance are significant for various operational and strategic aspects of financial institutions. First, sustainability assurance ensures increased sharia compliance by verifying that every operation and investment is in accordance with sharia principles such as fairness, transparency, and social responsibility. This helps reduce the risk of sharia violations and increases the credibility of the institution in the eyes of regulators and other stakeholders. Sustainability assurance plays an important role in building global trust and reputation. With independently verified sustainability reports, Islamic financial institutions can convince investors and the public of the transparency and accuracy of their sustainability claims, leading to improved reputation as well as attracting investors who care about social responsibility. Sustainability assurance also encourages innovation in financial products, such as the development of green sukuk and environmentally friendly waqf funds, which allow Islamic financial institutions to further contribute to sustainable development while still adhering to sharia principles. The implementation of sustainability assurance increases the competitiveness of Islamic financial institutions in the global market, as transparency and social responsibility are increasingly the main factors sought after by investors and consumers. This process also helps institutions identify and manage sustainability-related risks, such as reputational and environmental risks, thereby supporting long-term performance improvements.

For future researchers, there are several suggestions that can be considered in developing a study on sustainability assurance in Islamic finance. First, it is important to develop sustainability assurance standards that are more specific and in accordance with sharia principles, because the current standards still focus on conventional finance. In-depth research on the integration of sharia principles, such as the prohibition of riba and gharar, in the framework of sustainability reporting and verification would be very useful. Empirical studies investigating the impact of sustainability assurance on the financial and non-financial performance of Islamic financial institutions can provide important insights into how these processes affect the profitability, reputation, and competitiveness of institutions in global markets.

Technology is also an area worth exploring further. The use of blockchain and artificial intelligence (AI) in sustainability assurance can improve the efficiency and transparency of the verification process, allowing researchers to further examine the potential of this technology in the context of Islamic finance. The analysis of the role of regulators and stakeholders in driving the adoption of sustainability assurance is also an important topic, especially how collaboration between parties can strengthen sustainability policies in the industry.

Comparative research between Islamic and conventional finance is also needed to understand the differences in approaches and challenges in both sectors, which could help identify best practices that Islamic finance can adopt. Finally, researchers can explore ways to increase awareness and capacity among Islamic finance practitioners regarding the importance of sustainability assurance, through better training and education. By focusing on these areas, further research will help enrich the literature and drive wider adoption of sustainability in the Islamic finance sector.

REFERENCES

Abdullah, M. S., & Keshminder, J. S. (2022). What drives green sukuk? A leader's perspective. *Journal of Sustainable Finance & Investment*, 12(3), 985–1005. DOI: 10.1080/20430795.2020.1821339

Al-Shaer, H., & Zaman, M. (2019). CEO Compensation and Sustainability Reporting Assurance: Evidence from the UK. *Journal of Business Ethics*, 158(1), 233–252. DOI: 10.1007/s10551-017-3735-8

Alam, A., Ratnasari, R. T., Jannah, I. L., & Ashfahany, A. E. (2023). Development and evaluation of Islamic green financing: A systematic review of green sukuk. *Environment and Ecology*, 14(1), 61–72. DOI: 10.21511/ee.14(1).2023.06

Bui, B., Houqe, M. N., & Zaman, M. (2021). Climate change mitigation: Carbon assurance and reporting integrity. *Business Strategy and the Environment*, 30(8), 3839–3853. DOI: 10.1002/bse.2843

Franzoni, S., & Allali, A. A. (2018). Principles of Islamic finance and principles of Corporate Social Responsibility: What convergence? *Sustainability (Basel)*, 10(3), 637. Advance online publication. DOI: 10.3390/su10030637

Goicoechea, E., Gómez-Bezares, F., & Ugarte, J. V. (2019). Integrated reporting assurance: Perceptions of auditors and users in Spain. *Sustainability (Basel)*, 11(3), 713. Advance online publication. DOI: 10.3390/su11030713

Hambali, A., & Adhariani, D. (2023). Sustainability performance at stake during COVID-19 pandemic? Evidence from Sharia-compliant companies in emerging markets. *Journal of Islamic Accounting and Business Research*, 14(1), 80–99. DOI: 10.1108/JIABR-01-2022-0014

Hamilton, S. N., & Waters, R. D. (2022). Mainstreaming Standardized Sustainability Reporting: Comparing Fortune 50 Corporations' and U.S. News & World Report's Top 50 Global Universities' Sustainability Reports. *Sustainability (Basel)*, 14(6), 3442. Advance online publication. DOI: 10.3390/su14063442

Hanieh, A. (2020). New geographies of financial power: Global Islamic finance and the Gulf. *Third World Quarterly*, 41(3), 525–546. DOI: 10.1080/01436597.2019.1675505

Hassan, M. K., Chiaramonte, L., Dreassi, A., Paltrinieri, A., & Piserà, S. (2022). The religious fringe of Corporate Social Responsibility. *International Review of Economics & Finance*, 80, 243–265. DOI: 10.1016/j.iref.2022.02.003

Huda, M., & Santoso, L. (2022). Implementation of Corporate Waqf Core Principles in the Development of Waqf in Indonesia. *Academic Journal of Interdisciplinary Studies*, 11(5), 114–124. DOI: 10.36941/ajis-2022-0129

Jaafar, A. Z., & Brightman, M. (2022). From Structure to Purpose: Green and Social Narratives, and the Shifting Morality of Islamic Finance in Kuala Lumpur. *Sustainability (Basel)*, 14(9), 5433. Advance online publication. DOI: 10.3390/su14095433

Liu, F. H. M., & Lai, K. P. Y. (2021). Ecologies of green finance: Green sukuk and development of green Islamic finance in Malaysia. *Environment & Planning A*, 53(8), 1896–1914. DOI: 10.1177/0308518X211038349

Martínez-Ferrero, J., García-Sánchez, I.-M., & Ruiz-Barbadillo, E. (2018). The quality of sustainability assurance reports: The expertise and experience of assurance providers as determinants. *Business Strategy and the Environment*, 27(8), 1181–1196. DOI: 10.1002/bse.2061

Silvola, H., & Vinnari, E. (2021). The limits of institutional work: A field study on auditors' efforts to promote sustainability assurance in a trust society. *Accounting, Auditing & Accountability Journal*, 34(1), 1–30. DOI: 10.1108/AAAJ-02-2019-3890

Sirilertsuwan, P., Thomassey, S., & Zeng, X. (2020). A strategic location decision-making approach for multi-tier supply chain sustainability. *Sustainability (Basel)*, 12(20), 1–37. DOI: 10.3390/su12208340

Sonnerfeldt, A. L. L., & Pontoppidan, C. A. (2020). The Challenges of Assurance on Non-financial Reporting. *Accounting, Economics, and Law : A Convivium*, 10(2), 731–757. DOI: 10.1515/ael-2018-0050

Zaman, R., Farooq, M. B., Khalid, F., & Mahmood, Z. (2021). Examining the extent of and determinants for sustainability assurance quality: The role of audit committees. *Business Strategy and the Environment*, 30(7), 2887–2906. DOI: 10.1002/bse.2777

Chapter 13
The Sustainable Practices Implemented at Mega International Events and Evaluation of Their Effectiveness in Mitigating Environmental Degradation

Vishwanathan Hariharan Iyer
https://orcid.org/0009-0007-1469-2369
Balaji Institute of International Business, Sri Balaji University, India

Pritesh Pradeep Somani
https://orcid.org/0000-0002-0039-0358
Balaji Institute of International Business, Sri Balaji University, India

Prerna Sharma
Balaji Institute of Modern Management, Sri Balaji University, India

Nilesh Gokhale
https://orcid.org/0000-0002-7354-299X
DES Pune University, India

Prachi Wani
https://orcid.org/0000-0003-1274-9660
Balaji Institute of Management and Human Resource Development, Sri Balaji University, India

Nitesh Behare
https://orcid.org/0000-0002-9338-8563
Balaji Institute of International Business, Sri Balaji University, India

Deepali Nilesh Pulekar
https://orcid.org/0009-0007-0666-9994
Balaji Institute of Management and Human Resource Management, Sri Balaji University, India

DOI: 10.4018/979-8-3373-0117-4.ch013

ABSTRACT

Mega-events like the FIFA World Cup, Olympics, international expos, and marathons, although glorified for their cultural, social, and economic significance, present considerable environmental concerns. The surge of players and spectators, along with significant infrastructure development and operating requirements, frequently leads to resource exhaustion, waste production, and environmental stress. Acknowledging the need to ease these effects, organisers have progressively implemented sustainable procedures to diminish environmental deterioration. This study examines the execution of sustainable practices at large-scale events and assesses their efficacy in promoting environmental responsibility and establishing enduring legacies. This study emphasises that despite existing hurdles, the progress achieved in incorporating sustainability provides significant insights for future initiatives. Proactive planning, stakeholder engagement, and ongoing innovation are recognised as essential facilitators of success.

INTRODUCTION:

The growth of global mega-events like the FIFA World Cup, the Olympics, international expos, and marathons has underscored their substantial socio-cultural and economic importance. Nonetheless, their environmental impact has been scrutinised due to the extensive activities necessary for their hosting. These events draw millions of participants and spectators, creating substantial demands for resources such as electricity, water, and transportation infrastructure, frequently resulting in considerable environmental degradation. Thus, the adoption of sustainable methods has emerged as a crucial priority for event organisers, politicians, and environmental proponents. Through the utilisation of creative solutions, international collaborations, and advanced technology, these events can establish standards for sustainability and impact worldwide environmental behaviour.

The core of sustainable practices in mega-events include the implementation of green building concepts, the use of renewable energy, waste management systems, and sustainable mobility techniques. Organisers are increasingly striving to incorporate sustainable practices into the planning and implementation phases to minimise carbon emissions and promote environmental stewardship. Events such as the Olympics and FIFA World Cup have made significant progress in using renewable energy sources to power venues and infrastructure, thus diminishing their reliance on fossil fuels. Likewise, programs such as employing biodegradable packaging materials and recycling waste have demonstrated efficacy in tackling waste management issues.

These initiatives highlight the dedication to reducing environmental impact while cultivating a sustainable legacy that lasts beyond the event.

Moreover, mega-events are distinctly capable of enhancing environmental consciousness and motivating extensive societal transformation. These events, with extensive audiences and international media exposure, function as venues to exhibit cutting-edge sustainable technologies and practices. Initiatives like the "green games" concept adopted at recent Olympics have attracted considerable attention, fostering environmental awareness among spectators, players, and host communities. Public engagement initiatives and sustainability seminars conducted in conjunction with these events seek to inform audiences about critical environmental challenges, therefore promoting sustainable living practices. This combined strategy—executing sustainable practices during the event and fostering change through education—significantly influences public perceptions of environmental stewardship.

Notwithstanding these developments, the efficacy of sustainability initiatives at mega-events has yielded varied results. Although several events effectively attain their environmental goals, others encounter difficulties stemming from logistical, financial, or political limitations. For example, although Qatar's 2022 FIFA World Cup featured advanced carbon-neutral venues, the substantial energy demands for air conditioning in arid conditions elicited criticism over the overall environmental advantage. Likewise, although numerous expos have prioritised sustainability in their themes, the erection of temporary infrastructure frequently leads to resource depletion. Assessing the efficacy of these activities necessitates a sophisticated comprehension of the obstacles encountered by host countries, encompassing diverse economic capabilities, regulatory structures, and public endorsement of environmental policies.

The discourse on sustainable practices in global mega-events necessitates a comprehensive examination of their long-term effects. The effectiveness of these efforts extends beyond immediate environmental advantages, since they possess the capacity to create a lasting legacy. Infrastructure constructed for events such as the Olympics or expos can facilitate urban redevelopment, yielding enduring advantages for host towns. The longevity of these developments depends on efficient post-event utilisation and upkeep. It is essential that event-related expenditures remain beneficial to communities while avoiding environmental liabilities for the overall viability of these efforts. An analytical review of historical case studies yields significant insights into optimal methods and acquired lessons.

In conclusion, the sustainable approaches adopted during global mega-events represent an amalgamation of challenges and opportunity. The magnitude of these events presents considerable environmental hazards, yet they also offer unique chances to develop novel solutions and motivate global transformation. In light of the pressing necessity to address environmental deterioration, mega-events function as significant experimental platforms for sustainable practices, providing essential insights that transcend the event's duration. Evaluating the efficacy of these activities helps to the dialogue on event management and fits with global efforts to attain sustainable development goals.

This research paper is an attempt to address the various issues related to environmental degradation caused due to the conduct of mega events at international level and the probable solutions to the same through effective implementation of sustainable practices. This implementation requires active participation of all the stake holders involved including the spectators arriving from across the world, the residents of the host nation, the political parties of the host nation, the participants (in the case of different international games), the environmentalist and every sundry person who is directly or indirectly involved in the conduct of the games.

REVIEW OF LITERATURE

(Carlsen et al., 2015) Every international event causes an economic, environmental and social issues that needs to be addressed right from the planning stage and ensured that the planning is executed at the ground level for optimising benefits with sustainability cost incurred during this process. In other words, it is the responsibility of the event planners to ensure the impacts of the event stay within acceptable limits that do not contribute to economic adversity, social disadvantage or environmental degradation.

(Talavera Abel et al., 2019) The Qatari bid to FIFA Men's World Cup, 2022 after careful analysis of previous world cups and make it first carbon neutral world cup was in alignment with the Qatar National Vision 2030, that envisions sustainable development of the country. The challenges, opportunities and progress in this scenario were evaluated accordingly exhibiting local organisers applying green technologies, and urban development concepts effectively.

(Death Carl, 2011) Numerous innovative and impactful environmental sustainability initiatives were executed in the host cities, including waste management, biodiversity conservation, public transportation, and energy efficiency. However, the 2010 FIFIA World Cup at South Africa remains the "most carbon-intensive" event recorded. The mitigation attempts were "relatively fragmented" in the broader context of the event's environmental consequences. The World Cup possessed the capacity to enhance environmental consciousness and nurture ecological modernisation; nevertheless, this opportunity was "largely overlooked" due to lack of coordination and national leadership.

(Kiani Mohammed & Nazari Leila, 2021) - Major sporting events can cause considerable harm on the environment, despite efforts taken for the preservation of the same. The Olympic Games have made efforts to emphasise environmental conservation and sustainability, as shown by the Sydney Olympics in 2000. Increased understanding and acceptance of environmental conservation initiatives by all stakeholders can reduce the ecological harm caused by athletic events.

(Sergi Cerezo-Esteve et al., 2022) Mega sporting events have more negative impact than positive impact on the environment. The giga-event (larger events) have a better management ratio than compared to mega-events or major events (small events). There is a growing concern among all the stakeholders with regard to environmental impacts of a world major event including the event promoters, host territories, politicians, residents, athletes and consumers. The organisers and promoters with varying degrees of success have begun to incorporate measures to reduce the negative effects and enhance the positive effects.

(Kellison & McCullough, 2017) In several instances, environmental objectives and assertions are aspirational and not consistently achieved without obstacles or modifications. Recent reforms by governing authorities and event organisers have been introduced to tackle concerns regarding environmental legacy; however, due to the intricate and long-term nature of effective legacy planning, it remains uncertain whether these strategies will result in significant alterations to the extent of mega sporting events' impact on the natural environment.

(Olga Parkes et al., 2016) The largest source of greenhouse gas emissions for a mega event project are from the construction materials used and transportation of people to and fro from the legacy phase, rather than the actual event itself. A novel quantitative methodology for evaluating and optimizing the environmental impacts is developed to negotiate worldwide concern.

(Lingyue Li, 2021) The ill-defined, ambiguous meaning of sustainability leaves reason for host cities to discursively strike a balance between environmental protection, social equity and economic growth but unavoidably leads to paradoxes of sustainability in actual practises. A study of 12 major mega-events conducted at Chinese metropolitans has evolved to be technocratic and inclusive, where in the focus on green technology and low carbon concepts. It has been concluded that economic sustainability and environmental sustainability emerged to work better than social sustainability.

(Polina Ermolaeva, 2024) Major sporting events can enhance environmental consciousness and raise better environmental practices and policies among the host community. Hosting major sports events can provide beneficial effects, such as increased environmental consciousness, for the host city and its inhabitants. Nonetheless, the infrastructural expansion and transformation of the host city for sports mega-events may also result in adverse environmental effects, perhaps heightening negative opinions among the local population.

(Mol, 2010) Sustainability is emerging as a worldwide central point that can be examined through the perspective of major events. Sustainability standards were redefined and shaped the 2008 Beijing Olympics, a significant worldwide mega event. The sustainability standards implemented during the Beijing Olympics have been institutionalised and integrated into the event's framework, indicating its enduring influence.

(Bashar Taha & Andrew Allan, 2024) - Efficient organisation of a mega event such as Expo 2020 necessitates the integration of event planning with the comprehensive strategic planning of the host city to establish a sustainable legacy. Organising a major event can facilitate investor attraction and accelerate infrastructure and transport enhancements in the host nation. Organising a large-scale event has difficulties, including the brief length of the event and significant financial pressures on the host nation.

(Preuss, 2013) - The mega events can contribute to the development of a green economy in the host city. The reasons for the unfulfilled environmental sustainability commitments were made during the bidding process in the context of the preparation and execution of mega events.

There are various challenges that prevent mega events from truly becoming "Green Games" and contributing to a green economy, including financial and organizational factors.

(Gaffney, 2013) The hosting of mega-events, like the Olympics, can significantly undermine long-term urban planning objectives in host cities due to the prevailing narratives of "legacy" and "sustainability," the international competition to secure events, and the accelerated timeline of event preparation. The case study of the Olympic Golf project in Rio de Janeiro illustrates how mega-event planning can compromise sustainable urban planning. Unless mega-event organizers change their bidding and selection processes, hosting these events will continue to be detrimental to the long-term sustainability of the host cities.

(Dolles & Söderman, 2010) The 2006 FIFA World Cup in Germany addressed environmental concerns and sustainability through the "Green Goal" program, which focused on four main areas: water, waste, energy, and transportation, with climate protection as a cross-sectorial task. The Green Goal measures could be applied to planning and organisation of other mega-sporting events.

(Andrea Collins & Andrew Flynn, 2024) The total ecological footprint of the 2004 FA Cup Final was 3,083 global hectares, with visitor travel being the largest contributor at 54% of the total footprint. The ecological footprint approach can be used to evaluate the environmental impact of major events and test different policy scenarios to reduce the footprint, such as encouraging more public transport use, shifting to more sustainable food options, and improving waste management. The significant environmental impacts can be generated by major events in a short period of time due to visitor consumption patterns as well.

(Roper, 2006) The 2012 London Olympics are implementing various sustainability measures, including low-emission zones, renewable energy investments, and efforts to offset carbon emissions, in order to have a low-waste, low-carbon footprint and bring long-term environmental and social benefits to the city.

(Justine Paquette et al., 2011) The concept of environmental sustainability has been defined and enacted by the International Olympic Committee (IOC). They reflected an 'Adaptive' approach during the bidding phase but shifted to a more detrimental or incremental approach during the staging of games.

(Sotiriadou & Hill, 2015) As society is becoming increasingly aware of climate change sustainability issues relating to sport facilities and events, their attitude is changing as well. Sport events have significant environmental impacts, but new efforts are emerging to encourage more environmentally responsible practices and climate change mitigation in the management of sport events and venues.

(Philjoo Moon et al., 2022) International Federations (Ifs) approach to sustainability can be understood through the lens of neo-institutional theory. A sustainability ladder model that outlines three stages of how (IFs) can integrate sustainability in their operations is developed. Five different approaches used by six cases study Ifs prove that sustainability is an important agenda for the IFs.

(Boggia et al., 2018) There exists a model called METER that can be used to measure the environmental sustainability of events. The METER index uses 9 major operational categories and sub-categories to evaluate the environmental sustainability of events across all phases of planning, organisation, implementation, and post-event as well.

(John R. Gold & Margaret M. Gold, 2013)The evolution of Olympic movements Olympic agenda showcasing how the environment emerged as an issue in the Winter Games and the various measures introduced to embed sustainability into official Olympic practice. There is also a relationship between sustainability and legacy. The effects were the outcome of the efforts taken during London 2012 Summer Olympics.

(Harris & Schlenker, 2018) Environmentally sustainable practices have become an integral part of event planning for the "best practice" public events examined. These practices target a range of environmental impact areas, including waste, energy, water, transportation, and more. The adoption of sustainable practices is primarily driven by the event organizers' own values and the expectations of attendees and the local community.

(Konstantaki, M, 2014) Sustainability is a complex issue that is not yet understood by stakeholders involved in mega-sport events in the way it must be understood. The Current sustainability policies for mega-sport events focus primarily on the physical environment, while neglecting other important social and community-related aspects of sustainability. There is a need for a more comprehensive and holistic approach to sustainability in the context of mega-sport events.

(B. Taha & A. Allan, 2022) Dubai established a structured governance system with high-level representatives from different authorities to facilitate decision-making and ensure the successful delivery of the Expo 2020 event. Dubai's plans for the Expo 2020 event were integrated with the long-term development plans for the city, with the infrastructure and buildings built for the event also serving the city's future development needs. The cooperation between local authorities and developers was crucial to maximize the benefits from the investment in hosting the Expo, by integrating the Expo site and legacy into the future urban development of the Dubai South area.

(Azzali, 2019) A framework of six factors that influence the long-term use of mega event sites and facilities, transforming these sites into open spaces are steps taken towards sustainability that helps the hosting countries to create long term legacies as well. However, there are certain common mistakes in mega event planning that include excessive cost, inability to control budgets and difficulty in aligning plans with local community needs that hamper sustainability goals to a great extent.

(Philip B. Maffetone et al., 2017) From 2005 to 2014, performance times in the World Marathon Majors enhanced by around 1% per seven years for both male and female participants. The Boston Marathon generally exhibited slower average times compared to other World Marathon Majors, although there was greater variety in performance times. Weather variables, including temperature and humidity, seemed to exert a more significant influence on performance times than the course metrics, such as the downhill characteristics of the Boston Marathon route.

(Andrew Suozzo, 2003) Since the 1990s, the Chicago Marathon has increased in importance and symbolises the social, cultural, and political challenges associated with major sporting events in large urban areas. The Chicago Marathon's success results from the collaboration of the sporting, economic, and political sectors. The Chicago Marathon enhances urban stereotypes and the city's image through its international, touristic, and cultural aspects.

(Nour El Helou et al., 2012) Air temperature is the primary environmental element affecting marathon running performance for all categories of runners. An ideal temperature range exists for peak running speed, and departures from this range, whether rises or reductions, will result in diminished running performance. Ozone pollution may affect marathon performance however its influence is probably associated with temperature effects.

(Thomas Könecke et al., 2021) The awareness of sustainability in sports is comparatively low among marathon runners in Germany; nonetheless, there is a significant willingness to invest in environmentally friendly initiatives at marathon events, particularly among German-speaking participants. There are notable disparities in environmental attitudes and payment willingness between German-speaking and English-speaking marathon runners.

(Vanos et al., 2019) The latter segment of the marathon course is anticipated to see “Hot” or “Very hot” conditions, characterised by significant heat strain and discomfort resulting from elevated humidity and minimal breeze flow. Locations with diminished sky view factors, such as those with buildings and trees, can shield observers from radiant heat; nonetheless, it is essential to manage wind flow to enhance thermal comfort. The research offers detailed spatial data on microclimate conditions and thermal comfort along the marathon route to assist in preparation and alleviation of heat stress during the Olympics.

(Iman Ibrahim & Balsam Munadhil Al-Chaderchi, 2023) The integration of biophilic and/or biomimetic design strategies in the pavilions at Dubai Expo 2020 offered visitors a distinctive experience while exemplifying sustainability principles. The research analysed the sustainability practices implemented in the pavilions, encompassing architectural design, materials, energy efficiency, and water management. The study evaluated the extent to which the pavilions embraced nature-based concepts and authentic sustainability values, intending to serve as a reference for future sustainable design initiatives.

(Shi et al., 2012) The principal elements for advancing sustainable construction at the program level encompass the establishment of a specialised department to coordinate stakeholders and the issuance of conceptual guidelines and management regulations. The research presents a system for executing sustainable building at the program management tier.

(Kanani, 2019) The Expo Milan 2015 display exemplifies the integration of sustainability principles in the planning and design of its diverse components. The study analysed multiple facets of the Expo Milan 2015 display, encompassing the public area, green areas, water features, energy production, waste management, and the project's legacy and prospective utilisation post-event. International exhibits, such as Expo Milan 2015, exert significant economic and cultural influence, drawing millions of global visitors and resulting in a legacy of architectural structures.

(Shen, 2012) - The economic factors associated with exhibitions, particularly visitor expenditure, constituted the primary contributor to the overall energy and resource consumption of large-scale exhibitions. - The selection of transportation methods for attendees, particularly international travelers arriving by air, considerably influences the environmental impact of the event. The implementation of advanced sustainable technology in display structures fails to significantly diminish their energy and resource consumption, and the brief operational lifespan of these buildings results in suboptimal performance.

(Caio Henrique Quemel Siqueira, 2021) Each host nation implemented a minimum of two standardised waste management procedures, but with variations in execution. The use of recyclable cups was a widespread initiative in all countries, with Germany choosing it as the primary strategy in 2006. Although the sustainability measures implemented by each host country had similarities, they varied in their specific strategies and execution.

(Polina Ermolaeva & Alexander Lind, 2021) The sustainability initiatives enacted for the 2018 FIFA World Cup in Russian host towns were largely superficial, failing to genuinely meet the authentic needs of the local populations. Although Kazan has made strides in sustainability initiatives, these efforts mostly aimed at fulfilling FIFA's criteria rather than to establish a lasting sustainability legacy for its residents.

(Ioannis Spanos et al., 2021) The tree nursery initiative in Qatar has the potential to realise a net reduction of 23.482 tonnes of CO2 equivalent emissions year through the utilisation of treated sewage water. The tree nursery initiative exhibits a carbon reduction potential of 21.902% relative to the maximum carbon sequestration capacity of 30.39 kg CO2 equivalent per tree annually, utilising treated sewage water and a designated fertiliser blend. The utilisation of desalinated water for the tree nursery adversely affects the carbon balance, perhaps rendering the introduction of trees in the Middle East ineffective for climate change mitigation.

STATEMENT OF THE PROBLEM:

The main goal of this paper is to look into how sustainable practices are used at global mega-events like the Olympics, the FIFA World Cup, Expos, and world's biggest races and rate how well they work at stopping environmental degradation. Even though these events are honoured for their cultural and economic value, they often cause big problems for the environment, which is why sustainability must be a part of them.

One important goal is to look at the environmentally friendly methods used in building, energy use, waste management, and transportation. The goal of this paper is to find the best practices and new ideas for planning events that cause the least amount of damage to the environment by looking at case studies from different events.

Another goal is to figure out what role mega-events play in making people more aware of the environment and encouraging them to act in environmentally friendly ways, both as players and as spectators. In order to do this, we need to look at how the public participation projects, media campaigns, and educational programs that were used during these events help to build a mind-set of environmental responsibility.

The paper also is an attempt to take a close look at the problems that come up when trying to reach green goals at mega-events. The study tries to find gaps and give useful information for making things better in the future by looking into the practical, financial, and geographical issues that might get in the way.

This paper also talks about how important legacy planning is, specifically how long-lasting sustainable practices and structures will be after an event. The goal is to figure out how investments in events can help revitalise cities and build strong communities while avoiding negative effects on the environment and money issues.

In the end, this paper aims to give a full picture of how sustainability and mega-events are connected, along with useful suggestions for better caring for the environment and making sure that the good effects last for a long time in host communities and around the world.

Figure 1. Conceptual model

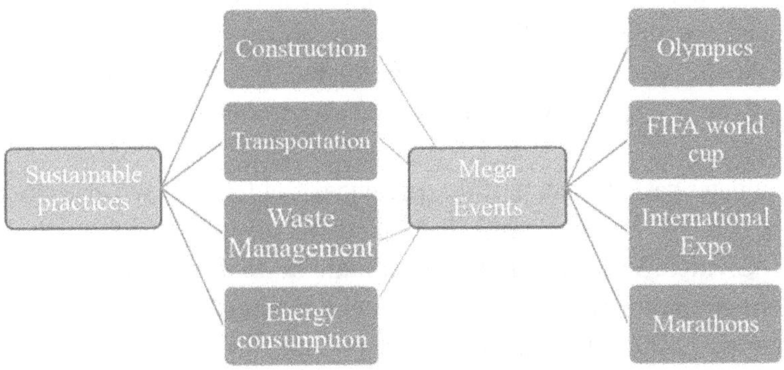

(Author's Compilation)

Mega events can be of multiple types and multiple categories spreading over different walks of life. It includes Olympic games, FIFA World Cup, International Expo, World Major Marathons and many more events that invite delegates and spectators from all over the world. There is a direct impact on three major aspects of the host country – the Economic, the Social and the Environmental. Naturally, the additional influx of people for a short period of time brings in an economic advantage to the host country. Likewise, the social bonding and local tourism of host country is boosted to a great extent. However, these advantages are derived at the cost of environmental degradation. Many researchers have confirmed this phenomenon through their studies after every event and the authorities at the helm have started taking cognizance of the impact of conducting mega events at international level. There are guidelines that are issued for ensuring sustainable practices are implemented at the ground level for environmental conservation.

From the review of literature, it has been derived that sustainable practices with reference to Construction, Transportation, Waste management and Energy Consumption need to be fixed to make any mega event environmentally viable. These are the 4 pillars that account for environmental degradation in various forms and a 'norm' related to these can bring about balance between the success and the cost incurred to earn that success in right proportion.

SUSTAINABLE PRACTICES AND OLYMPICS:

Olympics is a World stage for athletes to showcase their talent and temperament. The best athletes of the world gather to compete each other in a variety of sports to prove their supremacy. The Summer and Winer Olympics conducted by the Olympic Committee is responsible for allotting the license to become host nation. The bidding begins long before the actual time to provide enough time for the host nation to make the necessary preparation for the mega event. The planning for the conducting of the Olympics involves major stakeholders including the Government of the country.

To help athletes have the wonderful experience of a lifetime, special arrangement are required. Among various arrangement, the major capital expenditure is done in creating an "Olympic Village" for the stay of athletes. In the Olympic village, temporary constructions are made, however, enough care and diligence are followed to ensure maximum comfort for the athletes are provided. Also, enough care is taken to make commutation between the Olympic village and the Olympic stadium does not involve much complexity. The energy consumption for the conduct of Olympics is another area of concern for the organising committee. Waste management is the prime reason for environment degradation at all stages of the conduct of games. While economic benefits are huge and social benefits are innumerous, the organising committee needs to add sustainability elements to reduce the environmental degradation at these construction sites. Focus on eco-friendly materials, energy efficiency, waste management and post usage of these facilities needs to be planned out at the planning stage to make it more sustainable practically.

The following events have incorporated sustainable practices with an overview to protect the environment from degradation.

1) Beijing 2008 Olympics (China):

This Olympics concentrated on green urban development. The National Aquatics Centre utilised energy efficient materials and technologies. Large scale afforestation programs were undertaken to offset the carbon emissions and renewable energy sources like solar and geothermal power were integrated into venues. Hence, the quality of air was better and it set a precedent for green event planning. A substantial enhancement of public transit infrastructure, encompassing new tube lines and bus routes, diminished dependence on private vehicles during the games.

2) The London 2012 Olympics:

The London 2012 Olympics is considered as a benchmark for sustainable event planning. It is called as the "Green Games" as the Olympic stadium was built by using 30% recycled materials. Also, the aquatics centre's roof was constructed using 50% recycled materials. The city prioritised public transit and pedestrian-friendly routes in transportation, promoting the use of trains, buses, and bicycles among spectators. Designated "Games Lanes" enhance traffic efficiency for public transit, hence decreasing emissions. Water conservation was prioritised, with innovative water recycling technologies at venues to diminish freshwater usage and collect rainfall for landscaping. The Waste management was so efficient that it could divert 98% of the construction waste from landfills. Renewable energy sources were employed to power many facilities. These practices practically reduced carbon emissions, influencing sustainability standards for future global events.

3) Glasgow 2014 Commonwealth Games (Scotland)

This event exhibited a proper mixture of environmental benefits along with community well-being. Existing venues were refurbished to reduce resource use, and recycling of materials was extensively used while constructing Athlete's village. The public transit system was enhanced, prioritising the reduction of traffic congestion and the reduction of vehicular emissions via the expansion of bus and rail networks. Effective plumbing infrastructure and rainwater harvesting methods facilitated water conservation, guaranteeing that the games established a beneficial legacy for local populations.

4) Winter Olympics 2014 (Russia):

The Green Building Standards for construction projects were implemented to ensure sustainability during the Sochi Olympics. The waste management was done through advanced recycling technologies. The highlight of Sochi Olympics was the efforts taken to preserve biodiversity through ecological compensation projects. Transportation programs aimed at electric automobiles and enhanced public transit to reduce carbon emissions. To save water resources, the event included ecological compensatory initiatives, such as safeguarding adjacent water bodies; nonetheless, the overall effectiveness was inconsistent due to deficiencies in post-event management. There were criticisms for the Sochi Olympics for the unfulfilled promises related to event's legacy issues.

5) Rio 2016 Olympics (Brazil)

The Olympic village of this event was later converted into residential housing post-event, thereby ensuring long term utility. Renewable resources contributed 17% of the energy utilised during the games. The Rio Olympics focused on sustainable urban regeneration. The city improved public transport infrastructure, including the Bus Rapid Transit (BRT) network, to promote connectivity and decrease emissions. The need for strong post-event planning came into picture while the cleaning of the Guanabara Bay was undertaken, yielding only a partial success for avoiding environmental degradation.

6) Tokyo 2020 Olympics (Japan):

This was hailed as "Model for Sustainable Urban Development". The timber sourced from certified forests, medals crafted from metals recycled from discarded electronics were prominent examples of sustainable practice implemented by the organising committee. Solar power grids and hydrogen fueled vehicles reduced carbon footprint by transportation. The circular economy principles integrated was a classic example of showcasing sustainable practices implemented in the event planning and execution. Hydrogen-powered buses and electric vehicles (EVs) were implemented for transit, establishing a low-carbon mobility framework for the games. Bicycle-sharing schemes and improved public transit networks incentivised spectators and participants to forgo private vehicles. Rainwater harvesting systems and water-efficient fixtures at sites contributed to water conservation, minimising wastage and aligning the games with Japan's overarching sustainability objectives.

7) Paris (2024) Olympics (France):

A new benchmark was set by powering 100% venues with renewable energy. The existing infrastructures were repurposed to minimise new constructions. Public transport networks are being enhanced to promote zero-emissions mobility, integrating electric buses and bike-sharing programs. Paris intends to establish rainwater collection and reuse technologies in stadium operations, highlighting the significance of water efficiency in contemporary mega-events. The understanding of events causing environmental degradation by the past experiences, and the sustainable practices proving as the only solution, the Paris Olympics is considered as the new pathway for other mega events to follow.

SUSTAINABLE PRACTICES AND FIFA WORLD CUP:

FIFA is the apex institution that controls the conducting of Football all over the world. As this unique sport of football connects the entire world, there is a crazy fan-following for this game. Whenever the World Cups are announced, there is a mad rush for tickets and the host country needs to prepare for the event at least a year or two before the actual event kicks off. There is severe pressure on the government of the host country to accommodate the huge fans from across the world who gather to cheer for their country. Also, this adds huge pressure on the environmental factors with influx of huge human invasion for this short period of time. The implementation of sustainable practices is very important during the conduct of this event as it is vital for the host country to manage its natural resources post the event as well. The following study, with regard to the conduct of FIFA World Cups from the year 2002, reveals the importance given by the organisers on sustainable practices and the growth and development regarding the same.

1) The 2002 FIFA World Cup, South Korea and Japan:

The 2002 World Cup was one of the initial tournaments to integrate sustainability factors. The development of the stadium prioritised energy efficiency through the use of modern insulation materials and efficient lighting systems. Transportation was enhanced via upgraded public transit systems, including high-speed trains and buses, thereby diminishing dependence on private vehicles. Rainwater harvesting systems were implemented in some stadiums, enhancing water management efficiency. Although renewable energy was not a significant focus, the event signified an increasing recognition of sustainability in international athletic events.

2) The 2006 FIFA World Cup, Germany:

Germany's World Cup incorporated sustainability through energy-efficient venues, several of which had photovoltaic systems for solar energy generation. Transportation emphasises the utilisation of massive rail and bus networks, accompanied by a substantial decrease in automobile usage. Water management encompassed technologies for the collection and reutilization of rainwater for the irrigation of pitches. The event demonstrated Germany's dedication to renewable energy, featuring numerous stadiums powered by wind and solar resources, and advocated for carbon-offsetting initiatives to mitigate emissions.

3) The 2010 FIFA World Cup, South Africa:

Sustainability was central to South Africa's World Cup, encapsulated in the motto "Ke Nako – Celebrate Africa's Humanity." The construction incorporated green building certifications for new stadiums, highlighting resource efficiency and the use of locally sourced materials. Public transport services, including a new Bus Rapid Transit (BRT) network, are designed to alleviate traffic congestion and decrease emissions. Water management integrated recycling solutions for greywater, especially in arid areas. The utilisation of renewable energy was constrained; however, the event featured initiatives aimed at advancing solar energy in rural regions, thereby establishing a lasting legacy.

4) The 2014 FIFA World Cup, Brazil:

The 2014 World Cup in Brazil saw substantial investments in environmental initiatives. Stadiums such as Arena Pernambuco were constructed to meet green certification criteria, with solar panels and natural ventilation systems. Enhancements in transportation encompassed the expansion of public transit and the establishment of dedicated bus lanes. Water saving strategies included rainwater gathering and wastewater recycling at facilities. Renewable energy initiatives, including solar power systems, energised segments of the infrastructure, underscoring Brazil's commitment to integrating sustainability with large-scale events.

5) The 2018 FIFA World Cup, Russia:

The 2018 World Cup in Russia included various sustainability efforts. Stadiums were constructed to comply with FIFA's sustainable building criteria, utilising energy-efficient materials and sophisticated climate control systems. Public transport services were improved, providing complimentary transit passes to fans to promote environmentally sustainable travel. Water management focusses on recycling systems for irrigation and sanitation. The use of renewable energy was moderate, encompassing pilot projects for solar panels and wind turbines, indicative of an emerging trend towards sustainable energy solutions.

6) The FIFA World Cup, 2022, Qatar:

The FIFA World Cup 2022 emphasized on eco-friendly construction aligned with FIFA's sustainability Strategy. Stadium 974 was a brilliant example of the sustainability practices where shipping containers were utilised for construction of the stadium. This was the first fully demountable World Cup Stadium. Advanced cooling systems minimised energy and water use. Qatar constructed a sophisticated metro system fueled by renewable energy and electric buses to link stadiums, thereby diminishing dependence on private vehicles. Extensive solar energy was utilised for power consumption throughout the stadium. These efforts exhibited the sustainable practices for mega event construction.

SUSTAINABLE PRACTICES AND WORLD EXPOS: (SINCE 2000)

The dynamics of the world of business has undergone a drastic change in the 21st Century. The entire world has become a smaller market and the digital disruption has broken the geographical boundaries. However, the concept of world Expo and direct human network is a part of the growth and development of business. The World Expo ensures an assembly of sellers and buyers at a large scale from various countries and the host nation has to ensure to implement sustainable practices to survive and protect its natural resources to the best of its abilities. The various sustainable practices at the World Expos since the year 2000 have been listed for analysis purposes.

1) The Hanover Expo (2000):

The Hanover Expo highlighted sustainability with the theme "Man, Nature, and Technology." The event demonstrated sustainable construction with modular buildings that reduced resource consumption and facilitated reuse. Transportation predominantly depended on public networks and bicycles, hence diminishing carbon emissions. Water management incorporated advanced technologies like wastewater recycling and rainwater harvesting systems within the pavilions. Renewable energy sources, like as solar and wind power, provided a substantial share of the Expo's energy requirements, demonstrating Germany's dedication to sustainable technology.

2) The Aichi Expo (2005):

Expo 2005, centred on the subject "Nature's Wisdom," emphasised environmental harmony. Building materials that are sustainable, such as timber from certified forests, were utilised. The Expo utilised hydrogen-fueled vehicles and encouraged pedestrian movement on-site to reduce environmental effect. Advanced water recycling systems filtered and repurposed water on-site, diminishing reliance on external sources. Renewable energy sources, including solar panels mounted atop many pavilions, fulfilled a portion of the energy need while advancing Japan's innovation in clean technology.

3) The Shanghai Expo (2010):

The Shanghai Expo, themed "Better City, Better Life," emphasised sustainable urban life. Structures were erected using energy-efficient materials, and multiple pavilions were engineered for disassembly and recycling after the event. Electric and hydrogen-powered automobiles cut transportation emissions, bolstered by a comprehensive public transit system. Water features highlighted recycling, utilising treated wastewater for irrigation and gardening. Solar and geothermal energy were comprehensively incorporated, with Expo Boulevard being powered by one of the largest solar arrays globally at the time.

4) The Milan Expo (2015):

Expo 2015, themed "Feeding the Planet, Energy for Life," integrated sustainability into its operations. Pavilions employed recyclable and biodegradable materials, highlighting circular construction principles. Transportation aimed at minimising emissions via improved public transit connections and the encouragement of cycling. Water management systems incorporated rainwater gathering and effective irrigation for onsite vegetation. Renewable energy prominently featured, with solar panels and energy-efficient designs powering a significant portion of the Expo site while enhancing awareness of global energy issues.

5) The Dubai Expo (2020):

80% of the building construction was designed in such a way that it could be reused after the event. Buildings featured advanced energy and water saving technologies. Green Construction through technological advancement was highlighted through Dubai Expo. The renewable energy was provided through Solar trees, thereby reducing the dependence on the grid. Dubai's Expo demonstrated sustainable transport by using solar-powered autonomous vehicles and pedestrian-friendly infrastructure. To preserve water, the Expo implemented sophisticated irrigation systems, minimised water waste in landscaping, and advocated cutting-edge desalination methods for sustainable water use in a dry climate. This Expo showed the way ahead for all the future global events with respect to sustainable practices to avoid environmental degradation.

SUSTAINABLE PRACTICES AT WORLD MAJOR MARATHONS:

World Major marathons are mega events that attract large number of participants from across the world. Certain major marathons have participation that runs into lakhs. During the conduct of such events, it is observed that the economy is boosted to a great extent. Since the participants belong to the same tribe of running, the social bonding extends to a great extent. However, there is great pressure on environmental degradation that happens during the period of stay by these marathoners. Hence, it becomes an added responsibility of the organisers to ensure sustainability is practiced at all the three stages of pre, during and post conduct of the event. The following are the sustainable practices that can be summarised at the world major marathons.

1) Boston Marathon:

The Boston Marathon has consistently emphasised sustainability in its operations. Temporary buildings, like benches and tents near the finish line, are engineered for reuse to reduce material waste. Transportation is environmentally sustainable, featuring enhanced public transportation services and shuttle buses to diminish dependence on private vehicles, thereby reducing emissions. The marathon utilises energy-efficient technologies, including LED illumination and low-energy timing systems, to reduce energy consumption. Waste management is prioritised, with compostable water cups substituting plastic, and abandoned clothing from runners being donated to local organisations, so minimising landfill contributions.

2) London Marathon:

The London Marathon is renowned for its innovative sustainability efforts. Construction materials for event infrastructure are kept to a minimum, and reusable components are favoured for long-term use. Transportation is made eco-friendly through the promotion of public transit and cycling, with participants and spectators offered incentives to travel sustainably. A ground-breaking initiative replaced single-use plastic bottles with edible seaweed pods, drastically reducing waste. The marathon uses renewable energy, such as solar power, to run event zones. Comprehensive waste segregation systems ensure recyclables, compostable, and general waste are managed efficiently, with leftover food and water donated to local shelters.

3) Berlin Marathon:

The Berlin Marathon's planning is fundamentally centred on sustainability. Event infrastructure, including modular tents and stages, is engineered to be lightweight and reusable, hence reducing material use. Transportation is ecologically sustainable, with public transit collaborations offering complimentary or reduced fares for participants, while numerous attendees utilise bicycles, consistent with Berlin's cycling ethos. Energy-efficient technology, such as LED lighting, is employed to diminish energy consumption. Trash management is optimised by the implementation of reusable cups at hydration stations and the strategic placement of recycling bins along the route to facilitate appropriate trash classification.

4) New York Marathon:

The New York City Marathon, as the largest marathon globally, has implemented various sustainability initiatives. Temporary constructions, such as grandstands and banners, are constructed using recycled or recyclable materials, so assuring little environmental impact. Collaborations in public transport and ferry services facilitate efficient travel for participants and spectators while minimising emissions. Energy-efficient generators facilitate race-day operations, while timers are powered by renewable energy sources. Waste management techniques encompass extensive recycling and composting, while garments discarded by runners at the starting line are either donated to local charities or repurposed, so ensuring a substantial reduction in waste.

5) Tokyo Marathon:

The Tokyo Marathon showcases environmentally sustainable event management. Event signage and materials are produced from recyclable or biodegradable materials, reducing trash production. Sustainability in transport is achieved by promoting the use of public transport among participants and spectators, supplemented by enhanced rail services on race day. Solar panels and energy-efficient lights supply power to essential event areas, minimising energy use. garbage management activities including promoting the use of refillable water bottles and recycling plastic garbage into new products, demonstrating Tokyo's dedication to a circular economy.

6) The Chicago Marathon:

The Chicago Marathon has implemented comprehensive sustainability measures across all facets of its business. Event infrastructure, including barricades and stages, is repurposed in future races, minimising construction waste. Public transit is extensively advocated, with bike-sharing programs and carpooling incentives additionally mitigating traffic pollution. Energy-efficient technologies are utilised to operate timing systems and communications. Waste management encompasses composting and recycling, with surplus food and water bottles being donated to local organisations or repurposed, so minimising environmental impact.

7) The Paris Marathon:

The Paris Marathon prioritises sustainability in its planning. Infrastructure, encompassing signage and banners, is intended for repurposing in subsequent events, hence minimising construction waste. Transportation is environmentally sustainable, featuring subsidised metro tickets for users and advocating bike-sharing programs as alternatives to private vehicles. Renewable energy sources energise major event zones, substantially reducing greenhouse gas emissions. Compostable cups are utilised at water stops, and trash segregation systems provide effective recycling and composting, positioning the Paris Marathon as a frontrunner in environmentally responsible event management.

FINDINGS:

Mega-events like the Olympics, races, the FIFA World Cup, and Expos have made a lot of progress in using environmentally friendly methods. More and more, steps are being taken to protect the environment, such as using renewable energy, building eco-friendly materials, and using improved waste management systems. For example, the Tokyo 2020 Olympics used hydrogen-powered vehicles and materials that could be recycled, which set a new bar for planning events that are good for the environment. Also, successful resource management techniques like collecting rainwater and making buildings more energy-efficient have led to less water and energy use. For example, 98% of the building waste from the London 2012 Olympics was kept out of landfills, which is a great example of how to save resources.

Even with these improvements, there are still problems with putting sustainability steps into action. Environmental goals are often hard to reach because of problems with logistics, money, and rules. Some people didn't like how the Rio 2016 Olympics handled trash and cleaned up bodies of water, showing that there are gaps between planning and carrying out. Also, the success of sustainability efforts varies from event to event because of differences in economic capacity and regulatory frameworks between regions. This shows how important it is to use customised methods.

Getting the public involved has also become an important part of attempts to be more sustainable. Mega-events are used to bring attention to environmental issues. Campaigns and workshops teach attendees and viewers how to behave in ways that are good for the earth. Reducing the damage to the environment and increasing public awareness at the same time has a positive effect that encourages environmental responsibility beyond the events themselves.

Lastly, mega-events' lasting effects on the world depend a lot on what they leave behind. Well-planned events like the Expo 2020 in Dubai show how well-thought-out plans can help revitalise cities and build stronger communities. But some events have trouble with infrastructure that isn't being used to its full potential. This shows how important it is to plan well for legacy to make sure long-lasting benefits and avoid environmental and financial problems.

SUGGESTIONS:

A comprehensive planning strategy is needed to deal with the problems and get the most out of environmentally friendly practices at mega-events. Sustainability needs to be thought about at every stage of planning an event, from coming up with ideas to managing the event's impact afterward. Better accountability measures, like audits by a third party and clear progress reports, can help make sure that environmental goals are met and that stakeholders stay committed.

Key ways to cut down on waste and pollution are to use more renewable energy sources and adopt the concepts of the circular economy. To leave as little of an impact on the earth as possible, events should use materials that can be recycled and used again. Getting local people and other stakeholders involved in sustainability projects is another way to improve community engagement efforts. Public campaigns and educational workshops can help spread eco-friendly habits even more, making sure that most people back green actions.

For best practices and new ideas to be shared, event organisers, governments, and environmental experts must work together. Setting up a central knowledge library of successful case studies can help people plan and carry out events in the future. To make sure that solutions work and are useful, they need to be customised to fit the environmental, economic, and cultural conditions of the host areas.

To get the most out of infrastructure and new ideas in the long run, post-event legacy planning needs extra care. You can make temporary buildings more useful and less wasteful by turning them into permanent community areas or adding them to larger plans for urban development. Giving people incentives to do green things, like giving tax breaks or money to eco-friendly projects, can further push people to put sustainability first.

Mega-events can become models of environmental responsibility by taking these steps. They can balance their grandeur with real benefits to global sustainability goals. These efforts not only lessen the damage to the environment but also lead to bigger changes in society. This shows how important mega-events are for creating a healthy future.

CONCLUSION:

Global mega-events like the FIFA World Cup, Olympics, and marathons function as prominent venues for demonstrating human accomplishment and solidarity; nonetheless, they come with a significant environmental cost. As the magnitude of these events increases, so does their capacity for environmental degradation, encompassing carbon emissions, resource depletion, waste generation, and ecological disruption. The use of sustainable techniques has become essential in contemporary event management, mirroring the growing worldwide consciousness regarding climate change and environmental stewardship. The pursuit of sustainability in mega-events is characterised by notable advancements, ongoing obstacles, and important insights that extend beyond the events themselves.

The major contribution of sustainability activities at mega-events is their capacity to establish worldwide standards for ecologically acceptable behaviour. The implementation of renewable energy, sustainable design, and effective resource management has proven that large-scale events can function with diminished environmental impact. The implementation of carbon-neutral stadiums, solar-powered infrastructure, and energy-efficient architecture during events such as the FIFA World Cup and the Olympics has demonstrated the viability of incorporating green technologies into extensive operations. These approaches not only diminish the carbon footprint of events but also establish a framework for future projects, impacting industry and urban planning globally.

The influence of these occurrences on waste management and resource conservation is equally important. Mega-events frequently produce substantial trash, including packaging, promotional materials, abandoned food, and construction debris. Through the implementation of methods like recycling, composting, and utilising biodegradable materials, organisers have successfully alleviated some prominent manifestations of environmental damage. Initiatives aimed at eradicating single-use plastics or repurposing building materials for post-event projects have showcased unique solutions to the waste issue. These strategies not only mitigate immediate environmental damage but also promote stakeholders and attendees to embrace more sustainable practices in their daily lives.

Mega-events significantly contribute to nurturing environmental awareness and education. With millions of global viewers and significant media focus, these events serve as a formidable platform for promoting sustainability worldwide. Campaigns emphasising eco-friendly initiatives, workshops for attendees and participants, and public engagement programs are essential to this endeavour. Mega-events, by this means, surpass their immediate context and substitute a wider societal transition towards environmental accountability. The prominence of these projects underscores that sustainability is both essential and attainable, encouraging governments, organisations, and individuals to act.

The effectiveness of sustainability initiatives during mega-events is a complex issue. Although several programs have effectively diminished environmental impact, others have failed owing to logistical, financial, or political obstacles. Despite the global attention gained by the carbon-neutral initiatives at the Qatar FIFA World Cup 2022, critiques over the excessive reliance on air conditioning in stadiums underscored the intricacies of attaining genuine sustainability. Likewise, the momentary nature of numerous structures erected for expos and the Olympics frequently results in resource squander if post-event utilisation plans are not efficiently executed. These instances highlight the necessity for a more holistic approach to sustainability—one that takes into account not only short-term objectives but also long-term consequences and legacy considerations.

Legacy is an essential aspect of sustainability in large-scale events. The infrastructure and innovations implemented during these events must provide enduring advantages to host towns and nations. Successful instances, such as Barcelona's urban revitalisation post-1992 Olympics, demonstrate how meticulously planned initiatives may benefit local populations for decades. Conversely, inadequately managed legacies, including underused stadiums or neglected facilities, may evolve into environmental and financial liabilities. A sustainable legacy necessitates the meticulous incorporation of event-related initiatives into comprehensive urban and regional development strategies, guaranteeing that investments persist in benefiting the community while mitigating environmental impacts.

Notwithstanding the obstacles, the pursuit of sustainability at large-scale events provides significant insights for future initiatives. The significance of early and cohesive planning is paramount. Sustainability must be included in every phase of event organisation, from conception and design to execution and post-event assessment. Cooperative initiatives among governments, commercial sectors, and local communities are crucial for attaining significant results. Secondly, transparency and accountability are essential for achieving sustainability objectives. Consistent reporting, external audits, and stakeholder involvement help sustain focus and credibility. The insights gained from each event should be disseminated broadly to establish a knowledge repository that guides future initiatives.

In summary, sustainable practices adopted at global mega-events pose both a challenge and an opportunity in the international struggle against environmental degradation. Although these events naturally present environmental hazards, they also possess the capacity to catalyse sustainable innovation, motivating global action. Through the integration of renewable energy, effective resource management, and public education programs, mega-events have illustrated the feasibility of reconciling magnificence with accountability. The genuine criterion of their success is their capacity to have enduring positive effects, both on the environment and on society at large. Amidst the ongoing struggle against climate change, the sustainability initiatives of mega-events offer a crucial framework for reconciling human aspirations with environmental conservation. The path continues, although the progress achieved so far exemplifies the efficacy of collaborative efforts and innovation in adopting a sustainable future.

REFERENCES

Abel, T., Sami, A.-G., & Muammer, K. (2019). *Sustainability in Mega-Events: Beyond Qatar 2022*. https://www.mdpi.com/2071-1050/11/22/6407

Azzali, S. (2019). Challenges and key factors in planning legacies of mega sporting events: Lessons learned from London, Sochi, and Rio de Janeiro. *Archnet-IJAR: International Journal of Architectural Research*, 14(2), 203–218. DOI: 10.1108/ARCH-04-2019-0093

Boggia, A., Massei, G., Paolotti, L., Rocchi, L., & Schiavi, F. (2018). A model for measuring the environmental sustainability of events. *Journal of Environmental Management*, 206, 836–845. DOI: 10.1016/j.jenvman.2017.11.057 PMID: 29197809

Carl, D. (2011). 'Greening' the 2010 FIFA World Cup: Environmental Sustainability and the Mega-Event in South Africa. *Journal of Environmental Policy and Planning*, 13(2), https://www.tandfonline.com/doi/abs/10.1080/1523908X.2011.572656

Carlsen, J., Mair, J., Holmes, K., & Hughes, M. (2015). *Events and Sustainability* (1st ed.). Routledge.

Cerezo-Esteve, S., Inglés, E., Segui-Urbaneja, J., & Solanellas, F. (2022). *The Environmental Impact of Major Sport Events (Giga, Mega and Major): A Systematic Review from 2000 to 2021*. https://www.mdpi.com/2071-1050/14/20/13581

Collins, A., & Flynn, A. (2008). Measuring the Environmental Sustainability of a Major Sporting Event: A Case Study of the FA Cup Final. *Tourism Economics, 14*(4), 751-768. https://doi.org/10.5367/000000008786440120DOI: 10.5367/000000008786440120

Dolles, H., & Söderman, S. (2010). Addressing ecology and sustainability in mega-sporting events: The 2006 football World Cup in Germany. *Journal of Management & Organization*, 16(4), 587–600. DOI: 10.5172/jmo.2010.16.4.587

El Helou, N., Tafflet, M., Berthelot, G., Tolaini, J., Marc, A., Guillaume, M., Hausswirth, C., & Toussaint, J.F. (2012). *Impact of Environmental Parameters on Marathon Running Performance*. https://journals.plos.org/plosone/article?id=10.1371/journal.pone.0037407

Ermolaeva, P. (2024). Green? Cool. yours: The effect of sports mega-events in post-soviet Russia on citizens' environmental consumption practises (cases of 2013 Universiade in Kazan and 2014 Sochi Olympics). *ResearchGate*. https://www.researchgate.net/publication/306103267_Green_Cool_yours_The_effect_of_sports_mega-events_in_post-soviet_Russia_on_citizens'_environmental_consumption_practises_cases_of_2013_Universiade_in_Kazan_and_2014_Sochi_Olympics

Ermolaeva, P., & Lind, A. (2021). Mega-Event Simulacrum: Critical Reflections on the Sustainability Legacies of the World Cup 2018 for the Russian Host Cities. *Problems of Post-Communism*, 68(6), 498–508. DOI: 10.1080/10758216.2020.1791185

Gaffney, C. (2013). Between Discourse and Reality: The Un-Sustainability of Mega-Event Planning. *Sustainability (Basel)*, 5(9), 9. Advance online publication. DOI: 10.3390/su5093926

Harris, R., & Schlenker, K. (2018). An Exploratory Study of "Best Practice" in Environmentally Sustainable Event Management in Australian Public Events. *Event Management*, 22(6), 1057–1071. DOI: 10.3727/152599518X15346132863175

Ibrahim, I., & Al-Chaderchi, B. (2023). *Exploring sustainable approaches at Dubai Expo 2020: A blend of biophilic and biomimicry designs*. 10.22320/07190700.2023.13.02.02.

John, R. Gold & Margaret M. Gold. (2013). *"Bring It under the Legacy Umbrella": Olympic Host Cities and the Changing Fortunes of the Sustainability Agenda*. https://www.mdpi.com/2071-1050/5/8/3526

Kanani, H. (2019). Monitoring Sustainability Applications In The Planning Of International Expo Exhibitions (Case Study Expo Milan 2015). *Journal of Al-Azhar University Engineering Sector*, 14(50), 409–421. DOI: 10.21608/auej.2019.28495

Kellison, T. B., & McCullough, B. P. (2017). A pragmatic perspective on the future of sustainability in sport. In McCullough, B. P., & Kellison, T. B. (Eds.), *Routledge Handbook of Sport and the Environment* (1st ed., 445–455). Routledge., DOI: 10.4324/9781315619514-34

Kiani, M. S., & Nazari, L. (2021). *Sustainable Development and Environmental Protection at International Sporting Events*. 10.22034/JHI.2021.291241.1027. https://www.researchgate.net/publication/356290160_Sustainable_Development_and_Environmental_Protection_at_International_Sporting_Events

Könecke, T., Schunk, H., Schappel, T., Hugaerts, I., Wagner, F., & Malchrowicz-Mośko, E. (2021). *German Marathon Runners' Opinions on and Willingness to Pay for Environmental Sustainability*. https://www.mdpi.com/2071-1050/13/18/10337

. Konstantaki, M. (2014). *Environmental sustainability of mega-sport events.*

Li, L. (2021). *Contesting Sustainability of Mega-Events in Chinese Metropolises: A Narrative and Practise Review*. https://ouci.dntb.gov.ua/en/works/73gEZLQ7/

Mol, A. P. J. (2010). Sustainability as global attractor: The greening of the 2008 Beijing Olympics. *Global Networks*, 10(4), 510–528. DOI: 10.1111/j.1471-0374.2010.00289.x

Moon, P., Bayle, E., & Francois, A. (2022). *Assessing International Sport Federations' Sustainability Practices: Toward Integrating Sustainability in Their Main Sports Events*. https://www.researchgate.net/publication/357793917_Assessing_International_Sport_Federations'_Sustainability_Practices_Toward_Integrating_Sustainability_in_Their_Main_Sports_Events

Paquette, J., Stevens, J., & Mallen, C. (2011). The interpretation of environmental sustainability by the International Olympic Committee and Organizing Committees of the Olympic Games from 1994 to 2008. *Sport in Society: Vol 14, No 3*. https://www.tandfonline.com/doi/full/10.1080/17430437.2011.557272

Parkes, O., Lettieri, P., & Bogle, I.D.L. (2016). Defining a quantitative framework for evaluation and optimisation of the environmental impacts of mega-event projects. *ScienceDirect*. https://www.sciencedirect.com/science/article/pii/S0301479715303637

Philip, B. Maffetone, Rita Malcata, Ivan Rivera, & Paul B. Laursen. (2017). The Boston Marathon versus the World Marathon Majors. *PLOS ONE*. https://journals.plos.org/plosone/article?id=10.1371/journal.pone.0184024

Preuss, H. (2013). The Contribution of the FIFA World Cup and the Olympic Games to Green Economy. *Sustainability (Basel)*, 5(8), 8. Advance online publication. DOI: 10.3390/su5083581

Roper, T. (2006). *Producing environmentally sustainable olympic games and 'greening' major public events*. https://www.semanticscholar.org/paper/producing-environmentally-sustainable-olympic-games-roper/e7091ae9cd2831ff9443 6649e97a08d4afa51256

Shen, S. (2012). *The Environmental Impact of Expositions: A Study of Some Contributing Factors* [Thesis, Open Access, Te Herenga Waka-Victoria University of Wellington]. DOI: 10.26686/wgtn.16993444

Shi, Q., Zuo, J., & Zillante, G. (2012). Exploring the management of sustainable construction at the programme level: A Chinese case study. *Construction Management and Economics*, 30(6), 425–440. DOI: 10.1080/01446193.2012.683200

Siqueira, C. H. Q., de Araújo Ribeiro, A. L. (2021). Sustainable Strategies in Sports Mega-Events: An Analysis of Soccer World Cups. *Sustainable Strategies in Sports Mega-Events: An Analysis of Soccer World Cups, 11*(2), Article 2. https://app.periodikos.com.br/journal/rigd/article/doi/10.51995/2237-3373.v11i1e110012

Sotiriadou, P., & Hill, B. (2015). *Raising Environmental Responsibility And Sustainability For Sport Events: A Systematic Review. 10*(1).

Spanos, I., Kucukvar, M., Bell, T. C., Elnimah, A., Hamdan, H., Al Meer, B., Prakash, S., Lundberg, O., & Kutty, A. A. (2021). How FIFA World Cup 2022™ can meet the carbon neutral commitments and the United Nations 2030 Agenda for Sustainable Development?: Reflections from the tree nursery project in Qatar*Sustainable Development—Wiley Online Library*. https://onlinelibrary.wiley.com/doi/full/10.1002/sd.2239

Suozzo, A. (2003). *The Chicago Marathon and Urban Renaissance*. https://www.researchgate.net/publication/227564103_The_Chicago_Marathon_and_Urban_Renaissance

Taha, B., & Allan, A. (2022). *ISPRS-Annals—planning for legacy – a cost effective and sustainable approach. Case study: Dubai expo 2020*. https://isprs-annals.copernicus.org/articles/X-4-W3-2022/237/2022/

Taha, B. & Allan, A. (2024). Hosting a Mega Event, a Drive Towards Sustainable Development: Dubai's Expo 2020. In S. Geertman & Q. Zhan (Eds.), *Computational Urban Planning and Management for Smart Cities* (223-247). Springer International Publishing. DOI: 10.1007/978-3-030-19424-6_13

Vanos, J. K., Kosaka, E., Iida, A., Yokohari, M., Middel, A., Scott-Fleming, I., & Brown, R. D. (2019). Planning for spectator thermal comfort and health in the face of extreme heat: The Tokyo 2020 Olympic marathons. *The Science of the Total Environment*, 657, 904–917. DOI: 10.1016/j.scitotenv.2018.11.447 PMID: 30677956

Chapter 14
Can Music Education Foster Sustainability Awareness?
The New Perspective From Corporate Culture

Yijing Du
https://orcid.org/0009-0005-7171-1082
Universiti Teknologi Malaysia, Malaysia

Sanitah Bte Mohd Yusof
Universiti Teknologi Malaysia, Malaysia

Qiang Zhang
https://orcid.org/0009-0006-5041-6794
Universiti Teknologi Malaysia, Malaysia

Shanshan Yue
https://orcid.org/0000-0001-8783-4187
Henan Univisity of Economics and Law, China

ABSTRACT

This chapter explores the potential of music education in advancing Environmental, Social, and Governance (ESG) goals within corporate contexts. Through literature review and case analysis, it demonstrates how music education fosters ESG awareness and employee accountability via emotional engagement, team collaboration, and technological integration. Using IBM's "IBM Songbook" as a case study, the paper highlights its application in enhancing corporate culture, creativity, and

DOI: 10.4018/979-8-3373-0117-4.ch014

sustainability. Despite challenges such as resource limitations, low employee participation, and industry-specific adaptability, the study proposes modular design, technological innovation, and cultural integration as strategies to overcome these obstacles and maximize the long-term impact of music education in achieving corporate sustainability goals.

1 INTRODUCTION

The Sustainable Development Goals (SDGs) emphasize the synergistic development of environmental protection, social responsibility, and good governance (ESG). As a vital component of the global economy, corporations play a critical role in achieving these objectives (Grewal & Serafeim, 2020). Corporate actions influence global sustainability efforts not only through their direct operational impacts but also through their ability to shape societal attitudes and drive innovation. In recent years, ESG has evolved beyond a regulatory requirement, emerging as a cornerstone of corporate strategy. Substantial research confirms its positive correlation with financial performance, showcasing that companies prioritizing ESG practices often achieve higher long-term profitability and stakeholder trust (Delgado-Ceballos et al., 2023). Consequently, the integration of ESG principles has become a priority across industries. As illustrated in Fig. 1, the interplay between ESG priorities, corporate culture, and SDGs, emphasizing the dual materiality framework that links firm-level sustainability practices to societal outcomes.

Figure 1. Double materiality as the link among sustainability, ESG, and the SDGs. (Delgado-Ceballos et al., 2023)

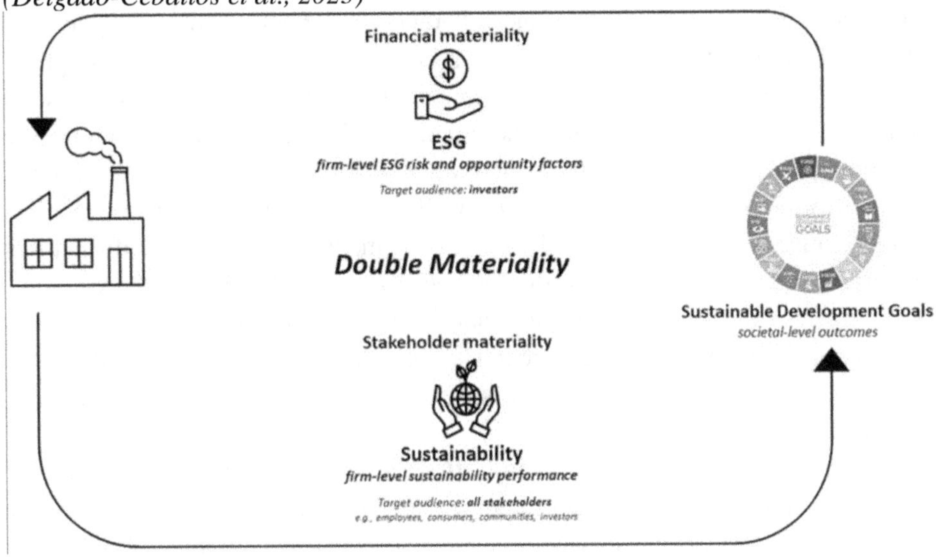

Despite this growing emphasis, a significant challenge lies in effectively enhancing employees' engagement and sense of responsibility during the implementation of ESG practices within organizations (Liou et al., 2023). Employees, as the primary executors of corporate policies, are critical in translating ESG strategies into actionable results. However, ensuring their alignment with corporate sustainability goals remains an ongoing struggle. Many employees perceive ESG initiatives as abstract or disconnected from their day-to-day responsibilities, further undermining their commitment to sustainability practices. Traditional ESG training methods, primarily lectures and online courses, have been widely adopted for their efficiency in delivering foundational knowledge. While effective in communicating policies and theoretical concepts, these methods often fall short in achieving the desired outcomes. Studies indicate that these approaches lack emotional engagement and interactivity, leading to limited awareness of ESG goals among employees and insufficient improvement in their sense of responsibility and practical capabilities (Ababneh, 2021; Agustian Zen, 2023). Furthermore, such training methods often fail to bridge the gap between theory and practice, leaving employees ill-equipped to apply the training content in real-world contexts (Xia, 2022).

Beyond the limitations of traditional approaches, there is an increasing recognition of the need for more innovative training methods that inspire genuine engagement and long-term behavioral change. Compared to conventional approaches, music education stands out as a promising and underexplored tool. With its inherent ability to evoke emotional resonance and encourage active participation, music education offers a unique means to foster deeper connections between employees and corporate ESG objectives. Musical activities are inherently collaborative, requiring coordination and teamwork, which can mirror and enhance the dynamics of workplace interactions. Research highlights that such activities not only enhance individuals' social awareness but also facilitate the connection between employees and ESG goals through creative expression and interaction (Rodriguez-Labajos, 2022; Váradi, 2022a). Moreover, music education aligns well with emerging trends in experiential learning, emphasizing hands-on and participatory methods over passive information delivery. It provides a platform for employees to explore ESG themes creatively, thereby fostering a sense of ownership and intrinsic motivation. For instance, incorporating sustainability themes into music workshops can encourage participants to reflect on environmental and social issues in innovative ways, reinforcing their commitment to corporate goals.

These characteristics make music education a novel training model worth exploring. By combining emotional engagement with practical learning experiences, it has the potential to address the shortcomings of traditional ESG training and foster a corporate culture that prioritizes sustainability and collaboration. This approach not only enhances the individual growth of employees but also contributes to broader organizational transformation, positioning music education as a valuable tool in achieving long-term corporate sustainability objectives.

1.1 Research Significance

This study explores the potential role of music education in enhancing employees' ESG awareness and fostering corporate culture, offering significant academic and practical implications. By integrating an innovative educational approach with corporate sustainability goals, this research aims to bridge existing gaps in knowledge and practice, contributing to both theoretical advancements and actionable strategies for organizations.

In the academic realm, the integration of music education into corporate training remains relatively underexplored. Current literature predominantly focuses on the role of traditional educational tools, such as online modules, workshops, and compliance-oriented training programs, in promoting ESG objectives. These tools, while effective for disseminating theoretical knowledge, often lack depth in addressing emotional and behavioral dimensions of employee engagement with ESG principles. Music education, on the other hand, introduces a unique combination of emotional resonance and participatory learning that can deeply influence employee attitudes and behaviors (Harvey et al., 2023). By incorporating music education into the corporate training framework, this study not only enriches the discourse on educational strategies for sustainability but also provides a novel perspective for research at the intersection of music and sustainable development. This research opens up new pathways for interdisciplinary exploration, connecting fields such as music pedagogy, corporate management, and environmental studies.

From a practical perspective, music education addresses one of the most pressing challenges faced by organizations: insufficient employee engagement in ESG initiatives. Traditional training often fails to generate genuine interest or a sense of ownership among employees, leading to superficial compliance rather than meaningful action. In contrast, music education leverages creative and performance-based activities to inspire a deeper sense of responsibility and teamwork among employees. These activities foster collaboration, creativity, and emotional connection, aligning employees' personal values with organizational ESG goals (Gligorijević, 2021; Rodriguez-Labajos, 2022). For example, music workshops that involve composing environmentally themed songs or participating in team performances not only enhance employees' understanding of sustainability but also strengthen interpersonal bonds, contributing to a more cohesive corporate culture.

Furthermore, the transformative impact of music education extends beyond immediate training outcomes. By embedding music education into corporate practices, organizations can drive long-term cultural change, fostering an environment where sustainability and social responsibility are integral to daily operations. Music education has the potential to cultivate a shared sense of purpose among employees, encouraging them to view ESG goals not as external mandates but as intrinsic values of the organization. This shift in perspective can lead to sustained behavioral change, greater innovation, and enhanced organizational resilience in the face of evolving global challenges.

In addition to its direct impact on employee engagement and corporate culture, music education aligns well with broader trends in corporate sustainability. As organizations increasingly recognize the importance of emotional intelligence, creativity, and collaboration in achieving long-term success, music education emerges as a versatile tool for developing these competencies. By integrating music-based activities into ESG training, companies can differentiate themselves as forward-thinking and innovative, enhancing their reputation among stakeholders and contributing to their overall sustainability strategy. Overall, this study highlights the dual significance of music education in academic and practical contexts. Academically, it introduces a fresh perspective on employee training for ESG awareness, encouraging further research into the interdisciplinary potential of music education. Practically, it offers organizations a powerful tool for fostering employee engagement, enhancing teamwork, and driving cultural transformation. These contributions underscore the value of music education as an innovative approach to achieving corporate sustainability objectives in an increasingly complex and interconnected world.

1.2 Research Questions

This study focuses on two key questions:

1. What mechanisms in music education can effectively enhance employees' ESG awareness and responsibility?
2. What are the practical pathways for implementing music education to achieve ESG objectives in corporate contexts?

To address these questions, the paper is organized into five sections. The second section analyzes the limitations of existing ESG training methods and explores the theoretical foundations of music education, specifically its alignment with ESG objectives. This addresses the first research question by identifying the unique mechanisms and potential of music education. The third section focuses on practical applications of music education, using case studies to investigate effective pathways for achieving ESG objectives, directly responding to the second research question. The fourth section examines the practical challenges of applying music education in corporate settings and offers actionable recommendations for improvement. Finally, the fifth section summarizes the study's main findings, reflects on the theoretical and practical implications, and outlines potential directions for future research to address unresolved challenges.

2 LITERATURE REVIEW

2.1 Current Status and Challenges of ESG Training

In recent years, with the growing importance of the Sustainable Development Goals (SDGs) and Environmental, Social, and Governance (ESG) standards, ESG training for employees has become a common management practice among corporations. This training aims to align employees with organizational sustainability goals, ensuring that ESG principles are not just theoretical constructs but integral to everyday corporate operations. However, the existing forms and outcomes of ESG training face numerous challenges, indicating a significant gap between intended objectives and achieved outcomes. Currently, ESG training in corporate settings primarily relies on traditional methods such as online courses, lectures, and internal workshops. These approaches focus heavily on delivering policies, frameworks, and theoretical knowledge to employees but fall short in terms of interactivity and practical application guidance (Nurillayev, 2024). For example, while lectures and online modules effectively communicate regulatory standards, they often fail to engage employees on an emotional or personal level. This creates a disconnect between the information presented and employees' ability to translate this knowledge into meaningful, actionable behaviors. Moreover, such training methods tend to emphasize compliance with external regulations rather than fostering a deeper cultural transformation within the organization. This narrow focus significantly limits their long-term impact (Kukalová et al., 2024), as employees remain disengaged from the broader goals of sustainability and social responsibility.

Although ESG-related practices are positively correlated with employee satisfaction, existing research suggests that traditional training methods have not significantly improved employees' sense of responsibility or engagement with ESG principles (Zhang et al., 2024). In many companies, ESG training is perceived as a "compliance task" rather than a strategic tool for cultural development (Lee, 2022). Recent studies have also highlighted the pivotal role of top managers in driving sustainability goals through strategic alignment with environmental objectives. Yue et al. (2025) found that managerial ownership significantly influences environmental innovation, especially when supported by mechanisms protecting minority shareholders. This emphasizes the need for organizations to not only enhance training content but also align corporate governance structures with sustainability initiatives. Furthermore, external pressures, such as regulatory frameworks or shareholder advocacy, play a crucial role in promoting sustainable practices in heavily polluting industries.

Employees often approach these programs as mandatory requirements rather than opportunities for personal or professional growth. For instance, organizations frequently lack mechanisms to follow up on training outcomes, resulting in employees quickly forgetting or neglecting the lessons learned. Without follow-up evaluation and reinforcement, the impact of training diminishes over time, leaving employees disconnected from the company's ESG objectives (Paridhi et al., 2024). This highlights a fundamental flaw in the design and implementation of ESG training, particularly in its failure to drive behavioral change. Table 1 presents regression results demonstrating the significant positive correlation between corporate ESG behavior and employee satisfaction, further supporting the need for innovative approaches to effectively engage employees with sustainability goals.

Table 1. Regression Analysis Results: Impact of ESG Behavior on Employee Satisfaction

Variable	Regression Coefficient	Standard Error	Significance Level
ESG Behavior	0.111	0.019	1%
Firm Size (Size)	1.225	0.081	1%
Financial Leverage	2.033	0.675	1%
Firm Age (Age)	1.282	0.342	1%

Source: This table is based on Zhang et al. (2024), summarizing the regression analysis results on the relationship between corporate ESG behavior and employee satisfaction.

In addition, companies face several operational and contextual challenges in implementing ESG training effectively. First, resource constraints pose a significant hurdle. Small and medium-sized enterprises (SMEs), which form a substantial portion of the global economy, often lack the financial and time resources to develop and deliver comprehensive ESG training programs. This limitation directly impacts the accessibility of high-quality training for their employees, perpetuating a gap in ESG awareness and engagement (Paridhi et al., 2024). Even in larger corporations, ESG training is often deprioritized in favor of initiatives with immediate financial returns, reflecting a short-term mindset that undermines long-term sustainability goals.

Beyond training-related challenges, the financial implications of sustainability practices also influence their implementation. Klibi et al. (2024) found that higher sustainability assurance levels, while signaling commitment to ESG principles, negatively impact market capitalization for French CAC 40 firms. This outcome is attributed to resource waste and costs exceeding perceived benefits, emphasizing the need for strategic balance in ESG investments. Such findings underline the importance of aligning sustainability initiatives not only with corporate culture but also with financial objectives, ensuring that ESG practices yield both reputational and economic benefits. Low employee engagement is another critical issue. Many employees view ESG initiatives as peripheral to their primary job responsibilities. This perception is particularly prevalent when training programs fail to align ESG principles with employees' actual work tasks and goals. Without clear connections between the training content and employees' daily roles, the programs risk being seen as irrelevant or burdensome, resulting in limited participation and minimal behavioral change (Lee, 2022). Lastly, cultural adaptability significantly affects the effectiveness of ESG training. Organizations often operate in diverse industries and regions, each with unique cultural and operational dynamics. Differences in industry priorities and regional attitudes toward ESG result in mismatches in training content and delivery methods. For example, in the financial sector, the complexity of ESG principles often leaves employees feeling overwhelmed, leading to resistance or apathy toward the training (Sarma & Sharan, 2024). Similarly, cultural insensitivity in training design can alienate employees, further reducing engagement and effectiveness.

Given these limitations, there is a growing consensus among researchers and practitioners that innovative approaches to ESG training are urgently needed. Traditional methods, while foundational, lack the dynamism and interactivity required to inspire meaningful change. Studies increasingly suggest integrating experiential learning models, gamification techniques, and art-based tools, such as music education, to enhance the emotional engagement and interactivity of training programs (Kukalová et al., 2024). These innovative methods encourage employees to actively participate in the learning process, fostering a stronger understanding and internalization of ESG goals through creative and participatory activities. For instance, music education, as a form of experiential learning, enables employees to explore sustainability themes in a collaborative and emotionally resonant way, making abstract principles more tangible and relatable. Moreover, modular training design and data-driven evaluation mechanisms are emerging as critical strategies for improving the efficiency and impact of ESG training (Nurillayev, 2024). Modular training allows organizations to customize content based on their specific needs, ensuring that employees receive targeted and relevant instruction. Meanwhile, data-driven tools enable companies to assess the effectiveness of their training programs, providing actionable insights for continuous improvement. These innovations not only address the shortcomings of traditional methods but also enhance their scalability and adaptability across different organizational contexts.

In summary, while ESG training has become an integral part of corporate development, its current forms and effectiveness remain inadequate to meet the growing demands of sustainability-driven business practices. The challenges of resource constraints, low engagement, and poor cultural adaptability highlight the need for more dynamic and emotionally engaging training methods. By introducing innovative tools such as music education and leveraging modular designs and advanced evaluation techniques, corporations have the potential to achieve significant breakthroughs in ESG practices. Such approaches promise not only to enhance employee awareness and responsibility but also to foster a deeper cultural commitment to sustainability, ensuring long-term organizational success in a rapidly evolving global landscape.

2.2 Theoretical Foundations of Music Education

Music education, as a distinctive and multifaceted form of pedagogy, holds significant potential to evoke emotional resonance, foster teamwork, and drive cultural transformation. When integrated with the principles of Education for Sustainable Development (ESD), it emerges as a powerful tool for nurturing social responsibility and environmental awareness, aligning seamlessly with corporate ESG objectives. Its ability to blend artistic expression with experiential learning makes it a versatile and innovative approach to addressing modern sustainability challenges. At its core, music education engages the emotional system directly through elements such as rhythm, melody, and harmony. This engagement has profound implications for how individuals process and internalize information, particularly in the context of sustainability and corporate values. Emotional resonance fosters a deep, intrinsic connection to abstract concepts, making them more relatable and impactful (Østergaard, 2019). For instance, the Kodály method, which emphasizes choral singing and group performance, not only enhances participants' ability to express themselves emotionally but also strengthens their sense of belonging within a group setting (Váradi, 2022b). Such emotional engagement goes beyond artistic appreciation, enabling learners to empathize with social and environmental issues on a deeper level (Jiang, 2024).

In corporate training, this emotional resonance plays a critical role in helping employees align with ESG objectives. By fostering a sense of emotional identification with sustainability goals, music education can transform ESG principles from abstract ideas into actionable commitments. Employees who experience emotional connections to these goals are more likely to internalize them and apply them in their professional and personal lives. For example, composing or performing music with themes related to environmental stewardship can deepen employees' understanding of corporate sustainability initiatives, reinforcing their alignment with organizational values. Music education also significantly enhances teamwork skills, which are critical for fostering a collaborative corporate culture. Ensemble or choral activities require participants to synchronize their efforts and coordinate with others to produce complex musical works. These activities cultivate trust, mutual understanding, and a shared sense of purpose among participants (Váradi, 2022b). Research indicates that the skills developed through musical collaboration—such as active listening, adaptability, and conflict resolution—are directly transferable to corporate management and social responsibility practices (Østergaard, 2019).

By promoting teamwork, music education offers an innovative approach to building stronger, more cohesive teams within organizations. For instance, collaborative music-making activities can simulate workplace dynamics, helping employees practice effective communication and problem-solving in a creative and low-pressure environment. This fosters a collective awareness and a sense of shared responsibility, which are essential for advancing ESG objectives. Furthermore, the inclusive nature of music education allows employees from diverse backgrounds to contribute their unique perspectives, enhancing the diversity and innovation of team projects. Beyond its impact on individuals and teams, music education serves as a catalyst for cultural transformation within organizations. Through participation in diverse musical projects, learners are exposed to a wide range of cultural values and traditions, fostering an appreciation for diversity and inclusion. This cross-cultural engagement is particularly valuable in globalized corporate environments, where cultural sensitivity and adaptability are essential for success (Jiang, 2024).

For example, designing and implementing global music festivals or cross-cultural musical activities within a corporate setting can create opportunities for employees to celebrate diversity and collaborate in meaningful ways. Such initiatives not only enhance organizational culture but also drive innovation by encouraging employees to think creatively and embrace different perspectives (Váradi, 2022b). Over time, these practices can help organizations build a more inclusive culture that values diversity as a source of strength. The integration of music education with ESD theory further broadens its applications and strengthens its relevance in achieving ESG objectives. ESD emphasizes experiential and task-based learning, both of which are central to music education. For instance, creating music projects with themes related to environmental sustainability not only enhances learners' creativity but also cultivates their sense of social responsibility and environmental consciousness (Jiang, 2024).

Moreover, specific approaches such as eco-acoustics and environmental listening deepen learners' sensitivity to the natural world, reinforcing the importance of environmental protection (Østergaard, 2019). Activities such as composing music inspired by natural soundscapes or participating in sound-based environmental awareness campaigns can effectively bridge the gap between artistic expression and ecological stewardship. These practices align with the broader goals of ESD, providing companies with innovative tools to foster employees' commitment to sustainability. The unique strengths of music education make it a compelling alternative to traditional corporate training methods. Its ability to inspire emotion, promote teamwork, and reshape organizational culture positions it as a bridge between the arts and corporate training(Li, 2024). By incorporating task-based and experiential learning theories, music education transcends conventional boundaries, helping companies cultivate socially responsible employees who are actively engaged with ESG objectives.

Another example, incorporating music-based workshops into corporate ESG training programs can enhance engagement and retention by providing employees with hands-on, creative experiences. These activities not only make learning more enjoyable but also encourage employees to explore ESG themes in depth, fostering a sense of ownership and accountability(Edgar, 2013). Over time, the integration of music education into corporate training frameworks can contribute to lasting cultural shifts, aligning organizational practices with global sustainability goals. In summary, music education, with its unique capacity to inspire emotion, foster collaboration, and drive cultural transformation, offers a robust foundation for advancing corporate ESG objectives. By leveraging the principles of ESD and integrating task-based and experiential learning approaches, it bridges the gap between theoretical understanding and practical application. As organizations seek innovative ways to engage employees and achieve sustainability goals, music education emerges as a powerful and versatile tool that combines artistic expression with meaningful learning experiences.

2.3 Integration of Music Education with ESG Objectives

Music education transcends its role as an art form to become a powerful and innovative tool for achieving Environmental, Social, and Governance (ESG) objectives within organizations. Its application demonstrates unique value in enhancing employees' sense of social responsibility, supporting the development of corporate culture, and fostering organizational innovation. By leveraging emotional engagement, creativity, and collaboration, music education creates pathways for meaningful contributions to sustainability and social impact. Music education capitalizes on the profound emotional resonance and sensory experiences it offers, making it an effective medium for advancing corporate social responsibility (CSR) goals. Transparent integrated reporting and educational activities can enhance the credibility of corporate social responsibility disclosures and build deeper trust with stakeholders(Hamad et al., 2023). For example, integrating CSR initiatives into music-based events such as festivals, charity performances, or themed concerts allows organizations to create deep emotional connections with both employees and the broader public. These initiatives help disseminate corporate values while simultaneously raising awareness about critical environmental and social issues (Green et al., 2016; Richardson, 2019a).

Recent theoretical and empirical studies have further emphasized music education's ability to connect abstract ESG principles with practical applications. Østergaard (2019) highlighted that music education strengthens social and emotional learning, fostering collaboration and empathy—two critical components of ESG practices. Similarly, Rodriguez-Labajos (2022) found that participatory musical activities, such as collective performances and creative improvisation, enable employees to internalize corporate values and sustainability goals on a personal level. These activities provide an experiential learning framework that bridges the gap between theoretical ESG principles and actionable behaviors, making sustainability concepts more relatable and impactful. Furthermore, Váradi (2022a) underscored that music education promotes a sense of ownership and intrinsic motivation among participants, both of which are essential for driving long-term commitment to ESG objectives.

One practical application is the organization of environmentally themed music festivals. These events can incorporate messages about recycling, conservation, and climate action into their design, encouraging both participants and audiences to engage with sustainability issues on a personal level. In addition, charity performances or benefit concerts can highlight specific CSR causes, such as disaster relief or education funding, fostering a sense of collective responsibility and goodwill among participants For employees, music education serves as a form of experiential learning that strengthens their identification with CSR objectives. Participating in music creation or performance activities that emphasize sustainability themes enables employees to internalize corporate values more deeply. For instance, creating music inspired by natural soundscapes or collaborating on compositions addressing global challenges fosters both personal reflection and collective action (Green et al., 2016; Østergaard, 2019). These experiences not only enhance employees' awareness of social and environmental responsibilities but also build stronger emotional connections to the company's ESG goals.

One of music education's most compelling benefits is its ability to stimulate emotional resonance and drive behavioral changes that enhance innovation within organizations. By engaging employees in creative and collaborative musical activities, companies can unlock latent creativity, encourage fresh perspectives, and foster a culture of innovation. Music's capacity to evoke emotion and spark imagination makes it uniquely suited to breaking down traditional thought patterns and encouraging out-of-the-box thinking (Schnugg & Song, 2020; Tran et al., 2018). For example, artist-in-residence programs, where musicians collaborate with employees on creative projects, have been shown to stimulate innovation by introducing new ways of thinking and problem-solving. Similarly, interdisciplinary art initiatives that combine music with other fields, such as design or technology, can encourage employees to approach challenges from diverse perspectives, ultimately driving cultural and product innovation (Schnugg & Song, 2020).

Music education also proves to be a valuable tool in product development processes. Research by Tran et al. (2018) demonstrates that applying principles of music composition during the "fuzzy front end" of product development—a phase characterized by high uncertainty and creativity—can significantly improve teams' problem-solving abilities. Environmental management training can enhance employees' ability to solve complex problems, especially in situations that require a high degree of creativity and collaboration(Khatib et al., 2023). By encouraging employees to think metaphorically and work collaboratively, music education fosters an environment where innovative ideas can flourish. In addition to fostering creativity, music education strengthens emotional connections among employees, enhancing their capacity for collaboration. This collective creativity, combined with a supportive and dynamic workplace culture, forms the foundation for sustained organizational innovation.

Music education also plays a vital role in fostering cross-cultural understanding and promoting diversity within organizations. Through improvisation, team-based composition, and collaborative performances, employees are exposed to a wide range of cultural influences, enabling them to appreciate and embrace diverse perspectives (Kagan & Kirchberg, 2016). This cultural sensitivity is increasingly important in globalized work environments, where inclusivity and adaptability are critical for success. For example, multinational companies can organize cross-cultural music workshops that encourage employees from different regions to share their musical traditions. Such activities not only enhance cultural awareness but also build stronger interpersonal connections across diverse teams. The appreciation of diversity through music contributes to organizational sustainability by promoting inclusivity and reducing cultural barriers. In practice, music festivals and educational programs have successfully integrated CSR initiatives with cross-cultural themes. Examples include events that incorporate diverse musical traditions while emphasizing sustainable practices, such as recycling programs, eco-friendly stage setups, or community engagement projects (Green et al., 2016; Richardson, 2019a). These initiatives demonstrate music education's dual capacity to celebrate diversity and advance sustainability goals, offering a template for companies seeking to integrate ESG principles into their operations.

Interdisciplinary collaboration between arts and sciences further underscores the value of music education in building and sustaining corporate culture. Music education initiatives that incorporate elements of technology, design, or environmental science offer employees new opportunities to develop leadership skills, enhance innovation capabilities, and foster deeper connections with corporate values (Schnugg & Song, 2020). For example, companies can design music-based leadership workshops that integrate principles of organizational behavior, encouraging participants to explore how collaboration and creativity intersect in both musical and professional contexts. Similarly, partnerships with educational institutions or cultural organizations can enrich music education programs by incorporating cutting-edge research or community engagement components, thereby aligning corporate training with broader social impact goals.

By embedding music education into corporate practices, organizations can create cultural traditions that reflect their commitment to sustainability, diversity, and innovation. Annual events such as songwriting contests, team performances, or music-themed hackathons can become integral to corporate identity, reinforcing values and fostering employee engagement over the long term. Music education offers a range of innovative pathways for companies to achieve their ESG objectives by supporting CSR efforts, driving innovation, and fostering diversity. By harnessing emotional resonance, teamwork, and interdisciplinary integration, music education creates a holistic framework for advancing sustainability goals. For instance, its capacity to strengthen employees' sense of responsibility while enhancing their creativity and collaboration skills positions music education as a strategic asset for organizations seeking to address complex global challenges.

The practical applications of music education in promoting sustainability are supported by both theoretical and empirical evidence. For example, Østergaard (2019) highlights how music education can heighten employees' awareness of environmental issues, while Richardson (2019) underscores the role of music festivals in promoting recycling and eco-conscious behaviors. These findings suggest that integrating music education into corporate training can yield tangible benefits, ranging from increased employee engagement to improved organizational performance. In conclusion, music education provides companies with a distinctive and versatile tool for implementing more efficient, inclusive, and sustainable development strategies. Its unique ability to blend emotional engagement with practical learning makes it an invaluable resource for organizations striving to align their operations with ESG principles while fostering a vibrant and innovative corporate culture.

3 CORPORATE APPLICATIONS OF MUSIC EDUCATION AND CASE ANALYSIS

Music education, as an innovative corporate training method, offers unique possibilities for advancing Environmental, Social, and Governance (ESG) objectives through diverse practical applications and technological support. By leveraging musical activities, companies can enhance employees' sense of social responsibility, foster teamwork, and promote cultural identity, leading to meaningful behavioral change. This section combines IBM's classic case study with insights from relevant literature to explore the applications and outcomes of music education in corporate contexts, highlighting its role in achieving ESG objectives.

3.1 Practical Forms of Music Education

Music education in corporate settings can be implemented through various formats, including composition, performance, and thematic workshops tailored to align with organizational goals. One notable example is IBM's "IBM Songbook" project, a groundbreaking initiative that successfully integrated music education into corporate culture. By encouraging employees to create and perform company songs, the project conveyed corporate values in a deeply engaging manner, enhancing employees' emotional and cultural connection to organizational goals (El-Sawad & Korczynski, 2007). The participatory nature of the project empowered employees to internalize corporate messages, making abstract values more accessible and relatable.

Beyond IBM, the broader application of music education has been extensively validated. Studies show that musical activities, such as choral singing, improve communication and collaboration skills through collective performance, fostering teamwork and unity among employees (Giaver et al., 2017). Additionally, music creation and performance are particularly valuable in advancing sustainability awareness. For instance, community-focused music festivals often integrate workshops and educational events addressing environmental themes. These events provide an engaging platform for disseminating ideas about sustainable development, bridging the gap between corporate initiatives and public understanding (Gabeiras Vázquez & Barahona Arroyo, 2020; Richardson, 2019b). Thematic workshops provide another avenue for integrating music education into corporate training. Workshops centered on creating environmentally themed compositions or performing music inspired by cultural diversity not only engage participants creatively but also align their efforts with ESG objectives. These workshops offer a dual benefit: enhancing individual employee engagement and fostering a collective sense of responsibility toward organizational goals.

3.2 Technological Support and Innovation

Advancements in technology have significantly enhanced the impact and scalability of music education in corporate contexts. The integration of artificial intelligence (AI) and virtual reality (VR) into music education has opened up new possibilities for creating immersive, interactive, and personalized learning experiences. For instance, AI-powered platforms can analyze learners' musical performances and provide real-time feedback, tailoring suggestions to optimize individual progress (Yu et al., 2023). This level of customization not only improves the learning efficiency of employees but also deepens their engagement with the training process.

Virtual reality further enriches the music education experience by simulating complex musical performance scenarios in immersive environments. Xiao (2022) demonstrated that VR-enabled settings allow participants to experience the challenges and rewards of teamwork and creativity in ways that are both realistic and transformative. Such technologies enable employees to rehearse collaborative dynamics and problem-solving skills in a controlled, yet emotionally impactful, virtual space.

In addition to enhancing individual engagement, data-driven tools have revolutionized the evaluation of music education activities. Companies now use data analytics to quantify the impact of their initiatives, such as assessing behavioral changes among participants or measuring the effectiveness of sustainability campaigns integrated into music festivals (Brennan et al., 2019; Gabeiras Vázquez & Barahona Arroyo, 2020). These insights provide companies with actionable evidence to refine their strategies and better align their efforts with ESG objectives. For example, in organizing music festivals or charity concerts, data analysis tools can track metrics such as audience participation, employee feedback, and the environmental footprint of the event. These evaluations allow companies to demonstrate their commitment to ESG principles while identifying areas for improvement, ensuring the long-term success and sustainability of their initiatives.

3.3 Case Analysis: IBM's Music Education Practices

IBM's "IBM Songbook" project remains a quintessential example of music education's transformative potential in corporate settings. The initiative encouraged employees to collaborate on the creation and performance of corporate songs, effectively bridging the gap between abstract organizational values and day-to-day employee experiences. These songs were regularly featured in corporate events, fostering cross-departmental collaboration and strengthening employees' emotional connection to corporate goals (El-Sawad & Korczynski, 2007). The project's success underscores the ability of music education to enhance cultural cohesion within organizations. By involving employees in creative processes, the initiative not only reinforced corporate values but also provided a platform for employees to express their individuality and contribute to a shared identity. Furthermore, the regular performance of these songs created opportunities for employees to celebrate collective achievements, boosting morale and fostering a sense of unity.

Despite its success, the IBM Songbook project also highlights areas for future improvement. While the initiative effectively utilized music as a cultural tool, it did not fully capitalize on modern technological advancements. For example, incorporating AI-generated lyrics or using VR to simulate large-scale performances could have further amplified employee engagement and extended the project's reach (Xiao, 2022; Yu et al., 2023). These technologies offer exciting possibilities for creating more immersive and scalable applications of music education, suggesting potential avenues for extending this model to other industries. Additionally, robust governance mechanisms, such as minority shareholder protection (MSP) and high ESG ratings, could further enhance the scalability and impact of similar initiatives. Yue et al. (2025) emphasized that MSP frameworks, when combined with high ESG ratings, significantly drive environmental and social innovation by aligning stakeholder interests with corporate sustainability goals. For a project like IBM Songbook, integrating MSP-driven governance structures could foster greater accountability and investment in technological advancements, ensuring such initiatives not only align with corporate objectives but also resonate with broader societal expectations for sustainability.

3.4 Outcomes and Lessons Learned

Music education has demonstrated substantial potential in corporate applications, particularly in enhancing employees' sense of responsibility, teamwork skills, and alignment with ESG objectives. By leveraging emotional resonance and interactive learning methods, music education creates an environment where employees can more readily embrace and practice corporate values (Giaver et al., 2017; Publicover et al., 2019). This alignment is critical for advancing sustainability goals and fostering a cohesive corporate culture. The integration of technology further elevates the effectiveness of music education. For instance, AI and VR tools enhance the immersive and evaluative capacities of music-based training activities, allowing companies to achieve measurable outcomes in areas such as creativity, collaboration, and sustainability awareness (Gabeiras Vázquez & Barahona Arroyo, 2020; Yu et al., 2023). These innovations ensure that music education remains relevant and impactful in an increasingly digital and interconnected world.

However, challenges persist in the broader adoption of music education within corporate settings. Resource limitations, including the cost of technology and the time required for implementation, remain significant barriers (Creech et al., 2022; Richardson, 2019b). Additionally, employee acceptance poses a challenge, particularly in industries where music education may be perceived as unrelated to professional objectives(Hu, 2024). Addressing these barriers requires a balanced approach that combines traditional educational methods with technological innovations and emphasizes the practical benefits of music education for achieving ESG objectives.

In conclusion, IBM's "IBM Songbook" project exemplifies the transformative potential of music education in corporate culture building. By incorporating modern technologies and addressing existing challenges, companies can expand upon this model to create innovative and scalable solutions for advancing ESG objectives. With careful design and strategic implementation, music education offers a powerful tool for fostering creativity, collaboration, and sustainability within organizational contexts.

4 CHALLENGES AND RECOMMENDATIONS FOR MUSIC EDUCATION IN ESG

Music education presents significant potential as an innovative training method for advancing Environmental, Social, and Governance (ESG) objectives. Its capacity to foster emotional engagement, teamwork, and cultural transformation positions it as a valuable tool for corporate training. However, its application in corporate contexts faces substantial challenges, including resource constraints, employee acceptance, and industry-specific adaptability. To enhance music education's contribution to ESG goals, a critical examination of these implementation challenges and the formulation of practical strategies are crucial.

4.1 Key Challenges in Implementation

Implementing music education within corporate settings often demands significant time, budget, and specialized resources, posing a considerable challenge for organizations. Small and medium-sized enterprises (SMEs), which typically operate under tighter financial constraints, find it particularly difficult to invest in long-term initiatives like music education. Liou et al. (2023) emphasize that SMEs often prioritize projects with immediate, measurable returns, sidelining initiatives such as music education that yield more intangible and long-term benefits. This short-term perspective neglects the potential of music education to build employees' innovation capabilities and strengthen their alignment with ESG objectives. Even in resource-rich large corporations, music education programs are frequently undervalued. Overland (2017) highlights the lack of comprehensive cost-benefit analyses for these programs, leading to their underfunding or outright dismissal. Without clear evidence of immediate returns, organizations may fail to recognize the broader impact of music education on employee engagement, corporate culture, and long-term sustainability goals. This resource challenge highlights the need for frameworks that effectively communicate the long-term value of music education to organizational stakeholders.

While music education is recognized for its potential to engage employees emotionally, a lack of interest or willingness to participate often limits its effectiveness. Viterouli et al. (2022) found that many employees perceive musical activities as irrelevant to their professional development, regarding them as "entertainment" rather than meaningful training. This perception undermines the potential impact of music education, reducing participation rates and limiting its ability to drive meaningful change. Furthermore, Yong (2017) identifies a critical flaw in the design of many music education initiatives: a lack of personalization and diversity in activity formats. Programs that fail to resonate emotionally with participants or that are perceived as generic often struggle to capture employees' attention. This disconnect underscores a broader challenge in aligning educational activities with employees' professional goals and personal interests. Without tailored designs that connect music education to workplace realities, employees may view such initiatives as peripheral to their responsibilities.

The adaptability of music education varies significantly across industries. Creative sectors, such as media and entertainment, often embrace music education as a natural extension of their cultural ethos, using it to promote teamwork, innovation, and social responsibility (Rodriguez-Labajos, 2022). In contrast, more traditional industries, such as manufacturing, tend to exhibit lower acceptance. These industries often lack the historical or cultural foundations to integrate music education seamlessly into their operations, making implementation more challenging. Additionally, distinct ESG priorities across industries pose another barrier to the adoption of music education. For example, financial and healthcare sectors may prioritize highly technical ESG objectives, such as regulatory compliance or operational efficiency, over cultural initiatives. Tailoring music education to address these specific industry needs requires careful planning and customization, which can increase costs and complicate program design. These challenges highlight the necessity of sector-specific strategies for the effective integration of music education.

4.2 Proper Ways to Improve the Dilemma

A modular approach to music education offers a practical solution to resource and adaptability challenges. (Springborg, 2012) introduced the concept of micro-course modularization, which breaks down educational initiatives into short, flexible units that can be adapted to fit different corporate contexts. These modules enable companies to implement music education incrementally, reducing financial and time-related barriers. For example, instead of launching comprehensive music programs, organizations could begin with short-term workshops or team-building exercises focused on specific ESG themes, such as environmental awareness or diversity inclusion. These smaller-scale initiatives allow companies to demonstrate the value of music education, gradually building support for more extensive programs. Modular designs also facilitate customization, enabling companies to tailor content to align with their unique industry priorities and employee needs.

Technological advancements provide effective solutions to many challenges associated with music education. AI and VR technologies, in particular, offer new possibilities for creating engaging and scalable educational experiences. Oğul (2024) highlights how AI-powered platforms can analyze employees' musical performance in real-time, offering personalized feedback that enhances learning outcomes. This level of customization ensures that music education remains relevant and impactful for diverse employee groups. Similarly, VR technology creates immersive environments where participants can explore complex musical scenarios. Xiao (2022) demonstrated that VR simulations, such as virtual team ensembles or environmentally themed concerts, allow employees to practice teamwork and creativity in a controlled yet emotionally impactful setting. These experiences foster a deeper connection to ESG principles while enhancing employees' collaboration and problem-solving skills.

Additionally, data-driven tools offer significant benefits for evaluating the outcomes of music education initiatives. For instance, analytics can be used to measure employee engagement, track behavioral changes, and assess the long-term impact of training programs. These insights provide companies with evidence to justify investments in music education and refine their strategies for future implementations. Embedding music education into corporate culture is essential for maximizing its long-term impact. Yong (2017) emphasizes that annual music events, such as songwriting contests or team performances, can create traditions that reinforce corporate values and foster employee engagement. These events not only evoke emotional resonance but also serve as platforms for employees to collaborate and connect with organizational goals. Schmidt & Robbins (2011) further argue that aligning music education with career development frameworks strengthens employees' sense of belonging and responsibility. For example, incorporating music-based activities into leadership training programs can help employees develop essential skills, such as empathy, active listening, and creative problem-solving. By linking music education to professional growth, companies can enhance its perceived relevance, ensuring higher levels of participation and engagement.

To achieve these outcomes, the design of music education activities must closely reflect corporate core values. For instance, a company focused on sustainability could organize workshops where employees compose and perform music inspired by natural soundscapes(Overland, 2017). This alignment ensures that music education is not only meaningful but also integral to the company's broader ESG strategy. While music education holds significant promise for achieving corporate ESG goals, addressing its limitations requires a balanced and strategic approach. Resource constraints are not limited to financial challenges but often reflect a lack of long-term vision in corporate planning. Institutional support, such as cross-departmental collaborations and external partnerships, can help mitigate these barriers. For example, partnering with educational institutions or cultural organizations can provide companies with access to resources and expertise that enhance the quality and scalability of music education initiatives.

Low employee acceptance highlights the need for more employee-centered designs that align with workplace realities and professional goals. Personalization, gamification, and participatory methods can help make music education more engaging and relevant. Industry-specific adaptability also requires tailored solutions, with programs designed to address the unique ESG priorities and cultural contexts of different sectors. Finally, while technological innovations improve the effectiveness of music education, their high costs and complexity may limit adoption, particularly among SMEs. Policy incentives, such as government subsidies or grants, could help smaller companies integrate these technologies into their training programs, ensuring broader access to the benefits of music education. Music education faces several challenges, including resource constraints, low employee engagement, and industry-specific barriers. However, these obstacles can be effectively addressed through modular design, technological innovation, and cultural integration. By balancing short-term priorities with long-term goals, companies can unlock the full potential of music education as a tool for advancing ESG objectives. Future efforts should focus on developing targeted, scalable educational models that cater to diverse corporate contexts, ensuring that music education continues to drive cultural transformation and social responsibility in the workplace.

5 CONCLUSION AND DISCUSSION

This study validates the significant potential of music education in advancing Environmental, Social, and Governance (ESG) objectives. By integrating emotional resonance, technological support, and cultural alignment, music education offers innovative pathways to enhance employees' ESG awareness and foster a stronger sense of corporate responsibility. However, its practical implementation faces notable challenges, including resource constraints, low employee engagement, and industry-specific adaptability. To effectively achieve ESG goals, organizations must adopt flexible design strategies, leverage technological innovations, and embed music education into their long-term cultural frameworks. This section summarizes the main findings, addresses challenges, and discusses the theoretical and practical implications, concluding with directions for future research.

The findings of this study highlight several key contributions of music education to ESG practices. First, music activities driven by emotional engagement allow employees to connect with corporate sustainability objectives on a deeper, more personal level. Activities such as environmentally themed music creation help transform abstract concepts into tangible, relatable goals, fostering a stronger alignment between employees and organizational values (Gabeiras Vázquez & Barahona Arroyo, 2020; Richardson, 2019b). Second, collaborative music-making strengthens teamwork and shared responsibility among employees. For example, IBM's "IBM Songbook" project demonstrated how group composition and performance could enhance cross-departmental collaboration while reinforcing corporate values (El-Sawad & Korczynski, 2007). Third, three primary pathways—modular design, technological support, and cultural integration—emerge as effective strategies for implementing music education in corporate contexts. Modular design allows organizations to break training into flexible, scalable units, making it particularly accessible for SMEs with limited resources (Springborg, 2012). Technological support, including tools like AI and VR, further enhances engagement and efficiency by personalizing learning experiences and creating immersive environments (Xiao, 2022; Yu et al., 2023).

Lastly, integrating music education into long-term corporate strategies, such as annual events or songwriting competitions, fosters sustained emotional connections to organizational goals (Schmidt & Robbins, 2011).

Despite its advantages, the application of music education in corporate settings is not without challenges. Resource constraints remain a primary obstacle, particularly for SMEs, where limited budgets and time often favor short-term, results-oriented training programs over long-term initiatives like music education (Liou et al., 2023). Even in resource-rich corporations, music education may be undervalued due to the perceived lack of immediate economic returns, as highlighted by Overland (2017). Furthermore, low employee acceptance poses another challenge. Many employees view music education as irrelevant to their career advancement, particularly when its connection to professional objectives is not explicitly demonstrated (Viterouli et al., 2022). This disconnect limits participation and undermines the effectiveness of music education programs. Finally, industry-specific adaptability presents a significant barrier, as acceptance and application vary widely across sectors. Creative industries, with their natural alignment to artistic endeavors, readily adopt music education, while traditional sectors like manufacturing struggle to integrate such initiatives into their existing frameworks (Rodriguez-Labajos, 2022).

This study makes significant theoretical contributions by expanding the research framework of corporate training and ESG practices. By validating music education as an innovative tool for employee engagement, it bridges the gap between emotional resonance and organizational objectives. This interdisciplinary perspective offers new insights into the integration of artistic and experiential learning methods within sustainability strategies, an area often overlooked in traditional corporate training research. Additionally, the findings provide practical implications for organizations seeking to overcome implementation challenges. Modular design and technological support offer scalable solutions to resource and engagement barriers, while cultural integration strategies ensure that music education becomes a meaningful and enduring part of corporate identity. However, balancing cost and effectiveness remains a critical challenge, particularly for SMEs and resource-constrained sectors. Policymakers and industry leaders must work collaboratively to address these challenges, potentially through grants, subsidies, or public-private partnerships.

Future research should explore several areas to build upon the findings of this study. Industry-specific customization is essential, as different sectors exhibit varying levels of acceptance and demand for music education. For example, traditional industries may require tailored programs to address their unique cultural gaps and operational priorities (Rodriguez-Labajos, 2022). Additionally, the synergy between technology and music education warrants further investigation. Emerging technologies, such as blockchain, could facilitate transparent evaluation of training outcomes, while cost-effective AI tools could help reduce financial barriers for SMEs (Oğul,

2024; Yu et al., 2023). Finally, the long-term impact of music education on corporate culture and ESG objectives should be validated through longitudinal studies. Future research could employ both quantitative and qualitative methods to assess how music education influences employee behavior, organizational innovation, and sustainability practices over time.

In conclusion, music education, by leveraging emotional resonance, technological innovation, and cultural integration, provides an innovative and effective pathway for achieving ESG objectives. Its capacity to enhance employee engagement, foster collaboration, and drive cultural transformation positions it as a valuable tool for corporate sustainability. While challenges such as resource constraints, low employee acceptance, and industry-specific barriers persist, these obstacles can be addressed through modular design, advanced technologies, and tailored approaches. Moving forward, music education must be more closely aligned with long-term corporate strategies to unlock its full potential. By adopting targeted and scalable models, organizations can harness music education as a powerful driver of sustainability, innovation, and cultural cohesion. With continued research and practical refinement, music education has the potential to become a cornerstone of corporate training and a key contributor to global sustainability goals.

6. IMPLICATIONS AND FUTURE RESEARCH DIRECTIONS

This study underscores the potential of music education as an innovative tool for achieving ESG objectives. By fostering emotional engagement, teamwork, and sustainability-oriented behavior, music education addresses gaps in traditional ESG training methods. The findings highlight its capacity to enhance employee alignment with organizational values and promote cultural cohesion, making it a valuable addition to corporate training frameworks(Østergaard, 2019). Practically, organizations can integrate music education into ESG initiatives through activities like sustainability-themed music workshops or collaborative performances. These approaches not only foster creativity but also build stronger connections between employees and corporate sustainability goals (Rodriguez-Labajos, 2022).

By embedding music education within ESG initiatives, organizations can leverage its unique capacity to foster emotional resonance, which goes beyond traditional training methods. For instance, sustainability-themed music workshops do not merely educate employees about environmental goals; they create an emotional connection that motivates individuals to act. This emotional engagement is essential in bridging the gap between knowledge acquisition and behavior transformation, as employees are more likely to internalize and sustain ESG principles when they feel a personal stake in these initiatives. Furthermore, music education's emphasis on collaboration mirrors the interdependence required for achieving corporate sustainability goals. Activities such as group performances or collaborative composition exercises encourage employees to experience teamwork in a dynamic and creative setting, promoting skills like empathy, adaptability, and collective problem-solving. These competencies align with the interpersonal demands of implementing ESG strategies, particularly in complex organizational environments. Through such innovative approaches, music education not only enhances individual engagement but also cultivates a cohesive corporate culture that prioritizes sustainability.

Future research could explore several promising directions. One key area is the cross-cultural adaptability of music-based ESG initiatives, particularly in multinational corporations operating across diverse regions. Understanding how regional cultural norms influence the design and implementation of these programs could provide valuable insights into their scalability and global applicability. Additionally, emerging technologies, such as artificial intelligence (AI), offer opportunities to enhance the effectiveness of music-based training. For example, AI-powered tools could personalize music education experiences, while creating immersive environments that deepen employee engagement with ESG principles (Xiao, 2022). Longitudinal studies are also needed to evaluate the sustained impact of music education on organizational innovation, employee behavior, and ESG performance.

Another avenue for future exploration is the role of hybrid learning models that combine in-person and virtual music education. Such models could bridge resource gaps in geographically dispersed organizations while maintaining the personal engagement of traditional music training. Additionally, researchers could investigate the psychological mechanisms underpinning the effectiveness of music education in ESG contexts, such as how it fosters intrinsic motivation and emotional connection to sustainability principles. Future studies should also assess the scalability of music-based ESG initiatives in resource-constrained settings, such as small and medium-sized enterprises, to ensure wider accessibility. Furthermore, examining how music education can be integrated into corporate governance structures, such as sustainability reporting or leadership training, could unlock new strategies for embedding ESG principles into organizational culture. Finally, interdisciplinary collaborations between music educators, environmental scientists, and organizational psychologists could lead to innovative methodologies for integrating music into corporate training. These studies would not only broaden theoretical frameworks but also offer actionable insights for organizations aiming to leverage music education for transformative ESG outcomes.

REFERENCES

Ababneh, O. M. A. (2021). How do green HRM practices affect employees' green behaviors? The role of employee engagement and personality attributes. *Journal of Environmental Planning and Management*, 64(7), 1204–1226. DOI: 10.1080/09640568.2020.1814708

Brennan, M., Scott, J. C., Connelly, A., & Lawrence, G. (2019). Do music festival communities address environmental sustainability and how? A Scottish case study. *Popular Music*, 38(2), 252–275. DOI: 10.1017/S0261143019000035

Creech, A., Zhukov, K., & Barrett, M. S. (2022). Signature pedagogies in collaborative creative learning in advanced music training, education and professional development: A meta-synthesis. *Frontiers in Education*, 7, 929421. Advance online publication. DOI: 10.3389/feduc.2022.929421

Delgado-Ceballos, J., Ortiz-De-Mandojana, N., Antolín-López, R., & Montiel, I. (2023). Connecting the sustainable development goals to firm-level sustainability and ESG factors: The need for double materiality. *Business Research Quarterly*, 26(1), 2–10. DOI: 10.1177/23409444221140919

Edgar, S. N. (2013). Introducing Social Emotional Learning to Music Education Professional Development. *Update - University of South Carolina. Dept. of Music*, 31(2), 28–36. DOI: 10.1177/8755123313480508

El-Sawad, A., & Korczynski, M. (2007). Management and music: The exceptional case of the IBM songbook. *Group & Organization Management*, 32(1), 79–108. DOI: 10.1177/1059601106294488

Gabeiras Vázquez, P., & Barahona Arroyo, M. (2020). Plan de acción para la adaptación de los festivales de música a la agenda 2030. *Periferica*, 21(21), 234–237. DOI: 10.25267/Periferica.2020.i21.21

Giaver, F., Vaag, J. R., & Wennes, G. (2017). Choral singing as an arts-based organisational intervention: A qualitative study of employees' experiences. *Arts & Health*, 9(1), 26–41. DOI: 10.1080/17533015.2016.1182564 PMID: 31038036

Gligorijević, J. (2021). Micronational spaces: Rethinking politics in contemporary music festivals. In J. Williams & S. Horlor (Eds.), *Musical Spaces* (1st ed., 375–399). Jenny Stanford Publishing. DOI: 10.1201/9781003180418-26

Green, T., Sinclair, G., & Tinson, J. (2016). Do they know it's CSR at all? An exploration of socially responsible music consumption. *Journal of Business Ethics*, 138(2), 231–246. DOI: 10.1007/s10551-015-2582-8

Grewal, J., & Serafeim, G. (2020). Research on corporate sustainability: Review and directions for future research. *Foundations and Trends® in Accounting, 14*(2), 73–127. DOI: 10.1561/1400000061

Hamad, S., Lai, F. W., Shad, M. K., Khatib, S. F. A., & Ali, S. E. A. (2023). Assessing the implementation of sustainable development goals: Does integrated reporting matter? *Sustainability Accounting. Management and Policy Journal*, 14(1), 49–74. DOI: 10.1108/SAMPJ-01-2022-0029

Harvey, J.-F., Cromwell, J. R., Johnson, K. J., & Edmondson, A. C. (2023). The dynamics of team learning: Harmony and rhythm in teamwork arrangements for innovation. *Administrative Science Quarterly*, 68(3), 601–647. DOI: 10.1177/00018392231166635 PMID: 37560020

Hu, W. (2024). Exploration of music teaching reform program in colleges and universities oriented on the development of corporate culture industry. *International Journal of Science and Engineering Applications*. DOI: 10.7753/IJSEA1305.1003

Jiang, M. (2024). The role of experiential learning in transforming music appreciation education and pedagogical practices. *Pacific International Journal*, 7(5), 157–162. DOI: 10.55014/pij.v7i5.715

Kagan, S., & Kirchberg, V. (2016). Music and sustainability: Organizational cultures towards creative resilience – a review. *Journal of Cleaner Production*, 135, 1487–1502. DOI: 10.1016/j.jclepro.2016.05.044

Khatib, S. F. A., Ismail, I. H. M., Salameh, N., Abbas, A. F., Bazhair, A. H., & Sulimany, H. G. H. (2023). Carbon emission and firm performance: The moderating role of management environmental training. *Sustainability (Basel)*, 15(13), 10485. DOI: 10.3390/su151310485

Klibi, E., Damak, S., & Elwafi, O. (2024). The impact of sustainability assurance levels on market capitalization: The case of French firms. *Journal of Financial Reporting and Accounting*. https://www.emerald.com/insight/content/doi/10.1108/jfra-03-2024-0162/full/html

Kukalová, G., Ibragimova, R., Fayzullayev, D., Narmanov, O., & Nazarova, L. (2024). Axiological approach in ESG education. *E3S Web of Conferences, 538*, 05005. DOI: 10.1051/e3sconf/202453805005

Lee, J. J. (2022). *Engaging employees through ESG Lee Janice Report v1.*

Li, Y. (2024). The impact of music education on the quality of talent cultivation. *Transactions on Comparative Education*, 6(1). Advance online publication. DOI: 10.23977/trance.2024.060110

Liou, J. J. H., Liu, P. Y. L., & Huang, S.-W. (2023). Exploring the key barriers to ESG adoption in enterprises. *Systems and Soft Computing*, 5, 200066. DOI: 10.1016/j.sasc.2023.200066

Nurillayev, E. (2024). *Embedding ESG in finance education: The impact of ESG education within graduate finance programs on ESG-related problems. SSRN*. DOI: 10.1108/IJSHE-06-2024-0388

Oğul, S. (2024). In tune with ethics: Responsible artificial intelligence and music industry. *Istanbul Bilgi University*, 1. DOI: 10.47613/reflektif.2024.150

Østergaard, E. (2019). Music and sustainability education – a contradiction? *Acta Didactica Norge*, 13(2), 2. DOI: 10.5617/adno.6452

Overland, C. T. (2017). Music education, inc. *Music Educators Journal*, 104(1), 55–61. DOI: 10.1177/0027432117719462

Paridhi, R., Ritika, , Arora, H., Arora, P., & Saini, N. (2024). Unlocking the path to sustainability: A hierarchical model for understanding corporate barriers to ESG reporting adoption. *Journal of Risk and Financial Management*, 17(12), 527. DOI: 10.3390/jrfm17120527

Publicover, J. L., Wright, T. S., Baur, S., & Duinker, P. N. (2019). Engaging with environmental issues as a musician: Career perspectives from the musicians of the *playlist for the planet.Popular Music and Society*, 42(2), 167–187. DOI: 10.1080/03007766.2018.1426367

Richardson, N. (2019). Corporate social responsibility or sustainability in music festivals. *The International Journal of Organizational Analysis*, 27(5), 1257–1273. DOI: 10.1108/IJOA-03-2018-1368

Rodriguez-Labajos, B. (2022). Artistic activism promotes three major forms of sustainability transformation. *Current Opinion in Environmental Sustainability*, 57, 101199. DOI: 10.1016/j.cosust.2022.101199

Sarma, A., & Sharan, D. S. (2024). *Enhancing educational efficiency: Integrating esg criteria into administrative model.*

Schmidt, P., & Robbins, J. (2011). Looking backwards to reach forward: A strategic architecture for professional development in music education. *Arts Education Policy Review*, 112(2), 95–103. DOI: 10.1080/10632913.2011.546702

Schnugg, C., & Song, B. (2020). An organizational perspective on ArtScience collaboration: Opportunities and challenges of platforms to collaborate with artists. *Journal of Open Innovation*, 6(1), 6. DOI: 10.3390/joitmc6010006

Springborg, C. (2012). *Perceptual refinement: Art-based methods in managerial education.*

Tran, M. K., Goulding, C., & Shiu, E. (2018). The orchestra of ideas: Using music to enhance the 'fuzzy front end' phase of product innovation. *Journal of Business Research*, 85, 504–513. DOI: 10.1016/j.jbusres.2017.10.029

Váradi, J. (2022). A review of the literature on the relationship of music education to the development of socio-emotional learning. *SAGE Open*, 12(1), 21582440211068501. DOI: 10.1177/21582440211068501

Viterouli, M., Belias, D., Koustelios, A., & Tsigilis, N. (2022). Refining employees' engagement by incorporating self-directedness in training and work environments. *European Conference on Management Leadership and Governance, 18*(1), 414–422. DOI: 10.34190/ecmlg.18.1.870

Xia, J. (2022). A systematic review: How does organisational learning enable ESG performance (from 2001 to 2021)? *Sustainability (Basel)*, 14(24), 16962. DOI: 10.3390/su142416962

Xiao, H. (2022). Innovation of digital multimedia VR technology in music education curriculum in colleges and universities. *Scientific Programming*, 2022(1), 6566144. DOI: 10.1155/2022/6566144

Yong, Z. (2017). The relationship between corporate music and corporate image building. *Proceedings of the 2017 7th International Conference on Social Network, Communication and Education (SNCE 2017)*. 2017 7th International Conference on Social Network, Communication and Education (SNCE 2017), Shenyang, China. DOI: 10.2991/snce-17.2017.102

Yu, X., Ma, N., Zheng, L., Wang, L., & Wang, K. (2023). Developments and applications of artificial intelligence in music education. *Technologies*, 11(2), 42. DOI: 10.3390/technologies11020042

Yue, S., Bajuri, N. H. B., Khatib, S. F., & Alshareef, M. N. (2025). Ownership with a green twist: The role of top managers in driving environmental innovation. China Finance Review International. https://www.emerald.com/insight/content/doi/10.1108/CFRI-03-2024-0121/full/html

Yue, S., Bajuri, N. H. B., Ye, G., & Ullah, F. (2025). Green awakening: The rising influence of minority shareholders and ESG in shaping China's sustainable future. *Sustainable Futures : An Applied Journal of Technology, Environment and Society*, 100441. Advance online publication. DOI: 10.1016/j.sftr.2025.100441

Zen, A. (2023). Determinants of employee engagement and productivity: An analysis of work motivation, competence, compensation and transactional leadership. *East Asian Journal of Multidisciplinary Research*, 2(2), 863–892. DOI: 10.55927/eajmr.v2i2.2981

Zhang, T., Zhang, J., & Tu, S. (2024). An empirical study on corporate ESG behavior and employee satisfaction: A moderating mediation model. *Behavioral Sciences (Basel, Switzerland)*, 14(4), 274. DOI: 10.3390/bs14040274 PMID: 38667070

Compilation of References

Ababneh, O. M. A. (2021). How do green HRM practices affect employees' green behaviors? The role of employee engagement and personality attributes. *Journal of Environmental Planning and Management*, 64(7), 1204–1226. DOI: 10.1080/09640568.2020.1814708

Abbas, J. (2024). Does the nexus of corporate social responsibility and green dynamic capabilities drive firms toward green technological innovation? The moderating role of green transformational leadership. *Technological Forecasting and Social Change*, 208, 123698. DOI: 10.1016/j.techfore.2024.123698

Abdulla, A., Wang, B., Qian, F., Kee, T., Blasiak, A., Ong, Y. H., Hooi, L., Parekh, F., Soriano, R., Olinger, G. G., Keppo, J., Hardesty, C. L., Chow, E. K., Do, D., & Ding, X. (2020). Project IDentif. AI: Harnessing artificial intelligence to rapidly optimize combination therapy development for infectious disease intervention. *Advanced Therapeutics*, 3(7), 2000034. DOI: 10.1002/adtp.202000034 PMID: 32838027

Abdullah, M. S., & Keshminder, J. S. (2022). What drives green sukuk? A leader's perspective. *Journal of Sustainable Finance & Investment*, 12(3), 985–1005. DOI: 10.1080/20430795.2020.1821339

Abdulrahman Al Abdulathi, M. A., Khairy, H. A., Baquero, A., Waheer Alkhaldi, D. A., Salama, W. M., & Mohamed Soliman, S. A. E. (2024). *Catalyzing green innovation in hotel and tourism businesses: leveraging green talent management, green organizational citizenship behavior, and green values.*

Abel, T., Sami, A.-G., & Muammer, K. (2019). *Sustainability in Mega-Events: Beyond Qatar 2022*. https://www.mdpi.com/2071-1050/11/22/6407

Abeysek.era, I. (2022). A framework for sustainability reporting. *Sustainability Accounting, Management and Policy Journal*, 1386-1409.

Abhayawansa, S., Adams, C., & Neesham, C. (2021). Accountability And Governance In Pursuit Of Sustainable Development Goals: Conceptualising How Governments Create Value. *Accounting, Auditing & Accountability Journal*, 34(4), 923–945. DOI: 10.1108/AAAJ-07-2020-4667

Accountancy Europe. (2024). *CSRD readiness: Limited assurance approach to transition plans*. Accountancy Europe.

Adams, & Whelan. (2009). Conceptualising future change in corporate sustainability reporting. *Accounting, Auditing & Accountability Journal*, 118-143.

Adams, C. A., & Frost, G. R. (2004). *The development of the corporate website and implications for ethical, social and environmental reporting through these media*. The Institute of Chartered Accountants of Scotland.

Adams, C., & Evans, R. (2004). Accountability, Completeness, Credibility and the Audit Expectation Gap. *Journal of Corporate Citizenship*, 2004(14), 97–115. DOI: 10.9774/GLEAF.4700.2004.su.00010

Adebayo, A. (2023). Synthesizing State-Owned Enterprises and Public Entrepreneurship. *International Journal of Interdisciplinary Organizational Studies*, 18(2), 37–64. DOI: 10.18848/2324-7649/CGP/v18i02/37-64

Adityawarman, A., & Khudri, T. Y. (2017). The impact of internet financial reporting practices on the company's market value: A study of listed manufacturing companies in Indonesia. In *6th International Accounting Conference (IAC 2017)* (48–53). Atlantis Press.

Afsar, B., Badir, Y., & Kiani, U. S. (2016). Linking spiritual leadership and employee pro-environmental behavior: The influence of workplace spirituality, intrinsic motivation, and environmental passion. *Journal of Environmental Psychology*, 45, 79–88. DOI: 10.1016/j.jenvp.2015.11.011

Aguado-Correa, F., de la Vega-Jiménez, J. J., López-Jiménez, J. M., Padilla-Garrido, N., & Rabadán-Martín, I. (2023). Evaluation of non-financial information and its contribution to advancing the sustainable development goals within the Spanish banking sector. *European Research on Management and Business Economics*, 29(1), 100211.

Aguilera, R. V., Rupp, D. E., Williams, C. A., & Ganapathi, J. (2007). Putting the S back in corporate social responsibility: A multilevel theory of social change in organizations. *Academy of Management Review*, 32(3), 836–863. DOI: 10.5465/amr.2007.25275678

Ahmad, H., Yaqub, M., & Lee, S. H. (2024). Environmental-, social-, and governance-related factors for business investment and sustainability: A scientometric review of global trends. *Environment, Development and Sustainability*, 26(2), 2965–2987. DOI: 10.1007/s10668-023-02921-x PMID: 36714213

Ahmad, M., & Solms, R. V. (2023). Information Security Assurance and the Impact of ISO 27001 in Cyber Risk Management. *Journal of Information Security and Applications*, 72, 102919.

Ahmed, A. H., Elmaghrabi, M. E., Ali Alhassoon, O., & Diab, A. (2023). Perceptions of users and preparers towards corporate internet reporting: Evidence from an emerging market. *Cogent Business & Management*, 10(2), 2209976. DOI: 10.1080/23311975.2023.2209976

Ain, Q. U., Yuan, X., & Javaid, H. M. (2021). The impact of board gender diversity and foreign institutional investors on firm innovation: Evidence from China. *European Journal of Innovation Management*, 25(3), 813–837. DOI: 10.1108/EJIM-10-2020-0439

Akhter, F., Hossain, M. R., Elrehail, H., Rehman, S. U., & Almansour, B. (2023). Environmental disclosures and corporate attributes, from the lens of legitimacy theory: A longitudinal analysis on a developing country. *European Journal of Management and Business Economics*, 32(3), 342–369.

Akhter, W., & Hassan, A. (2024). Does corporate social responsibility mediate the relationship between corporate governance and firm performance? Empirical evidence from BRICS countries. *Corporate Social Responsibility and Environmental Management*, 31(1), 566–578. DOI: 10.1002/csr.2586

Al Amosh, H. A. M., & Mansor, N. (2018). *Sustainability and corporate reporting: A review on environmental and social accounting disclosure.*

Alam, A., Ratnasari, R. T., Jannah, I. L., & Ashfahany, A. E. (2023). Development and evaluation of Islamic green financing: A systematic review of green sukuk. *Environment and Ecology*, 14(1), 61–72. DOI: 10.21511/ee.14(1).2023.06

Alam, Z., & Rashid, K. (2014). Corporate financial reporting on the internet: A survey of websites of listed companies in Pakistan. *IUP Journal of Corporate Governance*, 13(3), 17–31.

Al-Arussi, A. S., Selamat, H. M., & Hanefah, M. M. (2009). Determinants of financial and environmental disclosures through the internet by Malaysian companies. *Malaysian Management Journal*, 17(1), 59–76.

Al-Arussi, A. S., & Selamat, M. H. (2009). Dominant personalities in board committees, company characteristics, and internet environmental disclosure by Malaysian listed companies. *Malaysian Management Journal*, 13(1&2), 51–67.

Alexander, S. (2020). A Study On Effectiveness Of Reward System On Employee Motivation In BPO Sector. *IJRAR*, 523-530.

Alhemimah, A., Baquero, A., Al-Romeedy, B. S., & Khairy, H. A. (2024). *Green organizational learning and sustainable work behavior in tourism and hotel enterprises: leveraging green intrinsic motivation and green training*.

Aliyu, S. (2024). Issues in sustainability reporting assurance: Evidence from interviews. *Sustainability Accounting. Management and Policy Journal*, 15(3), 628–653. DOI: 10.1108/SAMPJ-07-2023-0457

Alketbi, M. S., & Ahmad, S. Z. (2024). Corporate social responsibility and sustainability practices: Mediating effect of green innovation and moderating effect of knowledge management in the manufacturing sector. *The International Journal of Organizational Analysis*, 32(7), 1369–1388. DOI: 10.1108/IJOA-02-2023-3627

Almadadha, R. (2024). Blockchain technology in financial accounting: Enhancing transparency, security, and ESG reporting. *Blockchains*, 2(3), 312–333. DOI: 10.3390/blockchains2030015

AlMalki, H. A., & Durugbo, C. M. (2023). Systematic review of institutional innovation literature: Towards a multi-level management model. *Management Review Quarterly*, 73(2), 731–785. DOI: 10.1007/s11301-022-00259-8

Alqarni, K., Agina, M. F., Khairy, H. A., Al-Romeedy, B. S., Farrag, D. A., & Abdallah, R. M. (2023). The Effect of Electronic Human Resource Management Systems on Sustainable Competitive Advantages: The Roles of Sustainable Innovation and Organizational Agility. *Sustainability (Basel)*, 15(23), 16382. DOI: 10.3390/su152316382

Al-Romeedy, B. S., & Khairy, H. A. (2024). Eco-Innovation and Hospitality and Tourism Business Resilience: The Mediating Role of Green Dynamic Capabilities. In *Shifts in Knowledge Sharing and Creativity for Business Tourism* (17-36). IGI Global.

Al-Romeedy, B. S., El-bardan, M. F., & Badwy, H. E. (2024). How is employee performance affected by employer branding in tourism businesses? Mediation analysis. *Journal of Hospitality and Tourism Insights,* (ahead-of-print). DOI: 10.1108/JHTI-05-2024-0418

Alsahali, K. F., & Malagueño, R. (2022). *An empirical study of sustainability reporting assurance: current trends and new insights. Journal of accounting & organizational change, 18*(5), 617-642.

Alsahali, K. F., & Malagueño, R. (2022). An empirical study of sustainability reporting assurance: current trends and new insights. *Journal of accounting & organizational change*, 18(5), 617-642. DOI: 10.1108/JAOC-05-2020-0060

Alsartawi, A. M. (2018). Online financial disclosure and firms' performance: Evidence from the Gulf Cooperation Council countries. *World Journal of Entrepreneurship, Management and Sustainable Development*, 14(2), 178–190. DOI: 10.1108/WJEMSD-11-2017-0082

Al-Shaer, H. (2020). Sustainability reporting quality and post-audit financial reporting quality: Empirical evidence from the UK. *Business Strategy and the Environment*, 2355-2373.

Al-Shaer, H., & Zaman, M. (2018). Credibility of sustainability reports: The contribution of audit committees. *Business Strategy and the Environment*, 27(7), 973–986. DOI: 10.1002/bse.2046

Al-Shaer, H., & Zaman, M. (2019). CEO Compensation and Sustainability Reporting Assurance: Evidence from the UK. *Journal of Business Ethics*, 158(1), 233–252. DOI: 10.1007/s10551-017-3735-8

Al-Shammari, B. (2007). *Determinants of internet financial reporting by listed companies on the Kuwait Stock Exchange*. Public Authority for Applied Education and Training.

Alshehri, N. Z., Baquero, A., Abd-Elhady, M. H., Salama, W. M., Khairy, H. A., & Abouelenien, R. E. I. (2024). *Green HRM and green competitive advantage in hotel and tourism industry: a mediated moderation model using eco-innovation and green psychological climate*.

Aluchna, M., Roszkowska-Menkes, M., Jastrzębska, E., & Bohdanowicz, L. (2023). Sustainability reporting as a social construct: The systematic literature review within socio-political view. *Social Responsibility Journal*, 19(8), 1535–1554. DOI: 10.1108/SRJ-06-2022-0231

Alves, S. (2021). CEO duality, earnings quality and board independence. *Journal of Financial Reporting and Accounting*, 21(2), 217–231. DOI: 10.1108/JFRA-07-2020-0191

Amabile, T. M., Hill, K. G., Hennessey, B. A., & Tighe, E. M. (1994). The Work Preference Inventory: Assessing intrinsic and extrinsic motivational orientations. *Journal of Personality and Social Psychology*, 66(5), 950–967. DOI: 10.1037/0022-3514.66.5.950 PMID: 8014837

Amel-Zadeh, A., & Serafeim, G. (2018). Why and how investors use ESG information: Evidence from a global survey. *Financial Analysts Journal*, 74(3), 87–103. DOI: 10.2469/faj.v74.n3.2

Antonini, C., & Conde, J. (2024). Environmental Management Control Systems and Environmental Innovation: Unintended Consequences of the EU Non-financial Reporting Directive. *Management Accounting Research*, 65, 2015–2045. DOI: 10.1016/j.mar.2024.100903

Ardiana, P. (2023). Stakeholder engagement in sustainability reporting by Fortune Global 500 companies: A call for embeddedness. *Meditari Accountancy Research*, 31(2), 344–365. DOI: 10.1108/MEDAR-12-2019-0666

Arvidsson, S., & Dumay, J. (2022). Corporate ESG reporting quantity, quality and performance: Where to now for environmental policy and practice? *Business Strategy and the Environment*, 31(3), 1091–1110. DOI: 10.1002/bse.2937

Asante-Appiah, B., & Lambert, T. A. (2022). The role of the external auditor in managing environmental, social, and governance (ESG) reputation risk. *Review of Accounting Studies*, 28(4), 2589–2641. DOI: 10.1007/s11142-022-09706-z

Ashbaugh, H., Johnstone, K. M., & Warfield, T. P. (1999). Corporate reporting on the internet. *Accounting Horizons*, 13(3), 241–257. DOI: 10.2308/acch.1999.13.3.241

Ashok, M. L., & Abhishek, N. D. (2019). Role of XBRL in promoting integrated reporting in Indian scenario. *IUP Journal of Accounting Research and Audit Practices*, 25(3), 25–33.

Asogwa, I. E. (2017). Impact of corporate governance on internet financial reporting in a growing economy: The case of Nigeria. *Archives of Business Research*, 5(1), 180–202. DOI: 10.14738/abr.52.2743

Association for Investment Management and Research (AIMR). (1999). Financial analysts rate conference calls best source of earnings information in AIMR study. *AIMR News Release*.

Association for Investment Management and Research (AIMR). (1999). *Using technology and the internet study: Researching corporate strategic and financial information. Survey conducted with the cooperation of Stratcom Associates*. www .aimr.com

Atta, N., Sharifi, A., & Ying Lee, C. (2024). The relationship between the rule of law and environmental sustainability: Empirical evidence from the analysis of global indices. *International Journal of Sustainable Development and World Ecology*, 31(8), 1–17. DOI: 10.1080/13504509.2024.2371159

Avrampou, A., Skouloudis, A., Iliopoulos, G., & Khan, N. (2019). Advancing the sustainable development goals: Evidence from leading European banks. *Sustainable Development*, 27(4), 743–757. DOI: 10.1002/sd.1938

Awa, H. O., Ojiabo, O. U., & Orokor, L. E. (2017). Integrated technology-organization-environment (TOE) taxonomies for technology adoption. *Journal of Enterprise Information Management*, 30(6), 893–921. DOI: 10.1108/JEIM-03-2016-0079

Azam, T., & Jamil, K. (2024). Studying the role of corporate social responsibility, green HRM and green innovation to improve green performance of SMEs. *Journal of Business & Industrial Marketing, ahead-of-print*(ahead-of-print). DOI: 10.1108/JBIM-02-2023-0087

Azzali, S. (2019). Challenges and key factors in planning legacies of mega sporting events: Lessons learned from London, Sochi, and Rio de Janeiro. *Archnet-IJAR: International Journal of Architectural Research*, 14(2), 203–218. DOI: 10.1108/ARCH-04-2019-0093

Baalouch, F., Ayadi, S., & Hussainey, K. (2019). A study of the determinants of environmental disclosure quality: Evidence from French listed companies. *The Journal of Management and Governance*, 23(4), 939–971. DOI: 10.1007/s10997-019-09474-0

Baddache, F. (2023). *Impact, inclusion, stakeholders, sustainable development goals (SDG): 9 principles for effective stakeholder collaboration.*

Badwy, H. E., Qalati, S. A., & El-Bardan, M. F. (2025). Revolutionizing sustainable success: Unveiling the power of green human resource management, green innovation and green human capital. *Benchmarking*.

Bag, S., Srivastava, G., Gupta, S., Sivarajah, U., & Wilmot, N. (2024). The effect of corporate ethical responsibility on social and environmental performance: An empirical study. *Industrial Marketing Management*, 117, 356–370. DOI: 10.1016/j.indmarman.2024.01.016

Bag, S., Wood, L. C., Xu, L., Dhamija, P., & Kayikci, Y. (2020). Big data analytics as an operational excellence approach to enhance sustainable supply chain performance. *Resources, Conservation and Recycling*, 153, 104559. DOI: 10.1016/j.resconrec.2019.104559

Bai, C., & Sarkis, J. (2010). Green supplier development: Analytical evaluation using. *Journal of Cleaner Production*, 18(12), 1200–1210. DOI: 10.1016/j.jclepro.2010.01.016

Bai, C., Sarkis, J., & Dou, Y. (2021). Blockchain technology for enhancing sustainable supply chains. *International Journal of Production Research*, 59(5), 1450–1465. DOI: 10.1080/00207543.2020.1871594

Baier, C., Göttsche, M., Hellmann, A., & Schiemann, F. (2022). Too good to be true: Influencing credibility perceptions with signaling reference explicitness and assurance depth. *Journal of Business Ethics*, 178(3), 695–714. DOI: 10.1007/s10551-020-04719-7

Bai, G. V., Frank, D., & Prabhu, K. S. (2024). Does ESG disclosure enhance firm performance during COVID-19? Evidence from Nifty 500 firms. *Investment Management and Financial Innovations*, 21(3), 74–83. DOI: 10.21511/imfi.21(3).2024.07

Bajaher, M., & Hanifah, M. (2011). Internet financial reporting: The case of UAE listed companies. *Asia Pacific Business Research Conference*, Islamic Science University of Malaysia, Malaysia.

Balaji, K. (2024) Artificial Intelligence for Enhanced Anti-Money Laundering and Asset Recovery: A New Frontier in Financial Crime Prevention. In *2024 Second International Conference on Intelligent Cyber Physical Systems and Internet of Things (ICoICI)*. Coimbatore, India. 1010-1016, DOI: 10.1109/ICoICI62503.2024.10696100

Balaji, K. (2024). Harnessing AI for Financial Innovations: Pioneering the Future of Financial Services. In Jermsittiparsert, K., Phongkraphan, N., & Lekhavichit, N. (Eds.), *Modern Management Science Practices in the Age of AI* (91–122). IGI Global., DOI: 10.4018/979-8-3693-6720-9.ch004

Balaji, K. (2024). The Nexus of Smart Contracts and Digital Twins Transforming Green Finance With Automated Transactions in Investment Agreements: Leveraging Smart Contracts for Green Investment Agreements and Automated Transactions. In Jafar, S., Rodriguez, R., Kannan, H., Akhtar, S., & Plugmann, P. (Eds.), *Harnessing Blockchain-Digital Twin Fusion for Sustainable Investments* (287–315). IGI Global., DOI: 10.4018/979-8-3693-1878-2.ch012

Balaji, K. (2025). AI as a Game Changer: How Digital Entrepreneurs Are Redefining Business Practices. In Tunio, M. (Ed.), *Improving Entrepreneurial Processes Through Advanced AI* (21–48). IGI Global., DOI: 10.4018/979-8-3693-1495-1.ch002

Bananuka, J., Night, S., Ngoma, M., & Najjemba, G. M. (2019). Internet financial reporting adoption: Exploring the influence of board role performance and isomorphic forces. *Journal of Economics, Finance and Administrative Science*, 24(48), 266–287. DOI: 10.1108/JEFAS-11-2018-0120

Bansal, R. (2023). *Corporate Social Responsibility and Business Sustainability.* Issue 2 Indian JL & Legal Rsch., 5, 1.

Barac, K. (2004). South African auditors' policies, practices and perceptions with regard to internet reporting. *Meditari Accountancy Research*, 12(2), 1–19. DOI: 10.1108/10222529200400013

Barker, R., & Eccles, R. G. (2018). Should corporations have a purpose? *Harvard Business Review*, 96(3), 1–7.

Barney, J. (1991). Firm resources and sustained competitive advantage. *Journal of Management*, 17(1), 99–120. DOI: 10.1177/014920639101700108

Bauman, C. W., & Skitka, L. J. (2012). Corporate social responsibility as a source of employee satisfaction. *Research in Organizational Behavior*, 32, 63–86. DOI: 10.1016/j.riob.2012.11.002

Beattie, V., & Pratt, K. (2001). Issues concerning web-based business reporting: An analysis of the views of interested parties. *The British Accounting Review*, 35(2), 155–187. DOI: 10.1016/S0890-8389(03)00016-7

Bebbington, U. J., & Eds, O. (2014). *Sustainability Accounting and Accountability.* Routledge.

Bebbington, J., Larrinaga, C., & Moneva, J. (2008). Corporate Social Reporting and Reputation Risk Management. *Accounting, Auditing & Accountability Journal*, 21(3), 337–361. DOI: 10.1108/09513570810863932

Bekk, M., Spörrle, M., Hedjasie, R., & Kerschreiter, R. (2016). Greening the competitive advantage: Antecedents and consequences of green brand equity. *Quality & Quantity*, 50(4), 1727–1746. DOI: 10.1007/s11135-015-0232-y

Bele, A. M., Sabău-Popa, C. D., Secară, O. M. (2023). Sustainable development goals and the triangle of ESG investments. *Journal of Financial Studies, 8*(14), 11–23. DOI: 10.55654/JFS.2023.8.14.1

Bellagarda, J. S., & Abu-Mahfouz, A. M. (2022). An updated survey on the convergence of distributed ledger technology and artificial intelligence: Current state, major challenges and future direction. *IEEE Access : Practical Innovations, Open Solutions*, 10, 50774–50793. DOI: 10.1109/ACCESS.2022.3173297

Benabou, R., & Tirole, J. (2010). Individual and corporate social responsibility. *Economica*, 77(305), 1–19. DOI: 10.1111/j.1468-0335.2009.00843.x

Bena, J., Ferreira, M. A., Matos, P., & Pires, P. (2017). Are foreign investors locusts? The long-term effects of foreign institutional ownership. *Journal of Financial Economics*, 126(1), 122–146. DOI: 10.1016/j.jfineco.2017.07.005

Benoit, D. F., & Gilson, C. (2017). Institutional investors, corporate governance, and firm performance. *Corporate Governance*, 25(3), 206–217.

Bergman, Z., Bergman, M. M., Fernandes, K., Grossrieder, D., & Schneider, L. (2018). The contribution of UNESCO chairs toward achieving the UN sustainable development goals. *Sustainability (Basel)*, 10(12), 4471. DOI: 10.3390/su10124471

Berrone, P., Cruz, C., Gomez-Mejia, L. R., & Larraza-Kintana, M. (2021). Socioemotional wealth and corporate responses to institutional pressures: Do family-controlled firms pollute less? *Administrative Science Quarterly*, 55(1), 82–113. DOI: 10.2189/asqu.2010.55.1.82

Bessire, D., & Onnée, S. (2010). Assessing corporate social performance: Strategies of legitimation and conflicting ideologies. *Critical Perspectives on Accounting*, 21(6), 445–467. DOI: 10.1016/j.cpa.2010.01.015

Bian, H., Kuo, J.-M., Pan, H., & Zhang, Z. (2023). The role of managerial ownership in dividend tunneling: Evidence from China. *Corporate Governance*, 31(2), 307–333. DOI: 10.1111/corg.12478

Bick, R., Halsey, E., & Eknega, C. (2018). The Global Environmental Injustice of Fast Fashion. *Environmental Health : A Global Access Science Source*, 17(1), 1–4. DOI: 10.1186/s12940-018-0433-7 PMID: 30591057

Birindelli, G., Dell'Atti, S., & Patrizia Iannuzzi, A. (2022). ESG ratings and corporate sustainability: Evidence from European banks. *Journal of Cleaner Production*, 364, 132526. DOI: 10.1016/j.jclepro.2022.132526

Birt, J. L., Muthusamy, K., & Bir, P. (2017). XBRL and the qualitative characteristics of useful financial information. *Accounting Research Journal*, 30(1), 107–126. DOI: 10.1108/ARJ-11-2014-0105

Bjarnason, E., Runeson, P., Borg, M., Unterkalmsteiner, M., Engström, E., Regnell, B., Sabaliauskaite, G., Loconsole, A., Gorschek, T., & Feldt, R. (2014). Challenges and practices in aligning requirements with verification and validation: A case study of six companies. *Empirical Software Engineering*, 19(6), 1809–1855. DOI: 10.1007/s10664-013-9263-y

Bø, E., Hammervoll, T., & Tvedt, K. (2013). *Environmental impact of refillable vs. Non-refillable plastic beverage bottles in Norway.*

Boateng, R. N., Tawiah, V., & Tackie, G. (2022). Corporate governance and voluntary disclosures in annual reports: A post-International Financial Reporting Standard adoption evidence from an emerging capital market. *International Journal of Accounting & Information Management*, 30(2), 252–276. DOI: 10.1108/IJAIM-10-2021-0220

Bodhanwala, S., & Bodhanwala, R. (2023). Environmental, social and governance performance: Influence on market value in the COVID-19 crisis. *Management Decision*, 61(10), 2442–2466. DOI: 10.1108/MD-08-2022-1084

Boffo, R., & Patalano, R. (2020). ESG investing: Practices, progress and challenges. *OECD Paris Working Papers on Finance, Insurance, and Private Pensions.*

Bogdan, V., & Pop, M. C. (2008). Romanian companies' web-based disclosure choices and capital markets. *Journal of Economic Literature*, 1(10), 9–19.

Boggia, A., Massei, G., Paolotti, L., Rocchi, L., & Schiavi, F. (2018). A model for measuring the environmental sustainability of events. *Journal of Environmental Management*, 206, 836–845. DOI: 10.1016/j.jenvman.2017.11.057 PMID: 29197809

Boiral, O. (2007). *Corporate greening through ISO 14001: a rational myth?. organization science, 18*(1), 127-146.

Boiral, O. (2012). ISO certificates as organizational degrees? Beyond the rational myths of the certification process. *Organization Studies*, 33(5-6), 633–654. DOI: 10.1177/0170840612443622

Boiral, O. (2013). Sustainability Reports as Simulacra? A Counter-account of A and A+ GRI Reports. *Accounting, Auditing & Accountability Journal*, 26(7), 1036–1071. DOI: 10.1108/AAAJ-04-2012-00998

Boiral, O., & Henri, J. F. (2017). Is sustainability performance comparable? A study of GRI reports of mining organizations. *Business & Society*, 56(2), 283–317. DOI: 10.1177/0007650315576134

Boiral, O., & Heras-Saizarbitoria, I. (2019). Sustainability reporting assurance: Creating stakeholder accountability through hyperreality? *Journal of Cleaner Production*, 243, 118596. DOI: 10.1016/j.jclepro.2019.118596

Boiral, O., Heras-Saizarbitoria, I., & Brotherton, M. C. (2019). Assessing and improving the quality of sustainability reports: The auditors' perspective. *Journal of Business Ethics*, 155(3), 703–721. DOI: 10.1007/s10551-017-3516-4

Boiral, O., Heras-Saizarbitoria, I., & Brotherton, M. C. (2020). Professionalizing the assurance of sustainability reports: The auditors' perspective. *Accounting, Auditing & Accountability Journal*, 33(2), 309–334. DOI: 10.1108/AAAJ-03-2019-3918

Boiral, O., Heras-Saizarbitoria, I., Brotherton, M., & Bernard, J. (2019). Ethical Issues in the Assurance of Sustainability Reports: Perspectives from Assurance Providers. *Journal of Business Ethics*, 159(4), 1–15. DOI: 10.1007/s10551-018-3840-3

Boiral, O., Talbot, D., & Brotherton, M. C. (2020). Measuring sustainability risks: A rational myth? *Business Strategy and the Environment*, 29(6), 2557–2571. DOI: 10.1002/bse.2520

Bolton, P., & Kacperczyk, M. (2021). Do investors care about carbon risk? *Journal of Financial Economics*, 142(2), 517–549. DOI: 10.1016/j.jfineco.2021.05.008

Bonson, E., & Escobar, T. (2002). A survey on voluntary disclosure on the internet: Empirical evidence from 300 European Union companies. *The International Journal of Digital Accounting Research*, 2(1), 27–51. DOI: 10.4192/1577-8517-v2_2

Bonsu, M. O.-A., Guo, Y., & Zhu, X. (2024). Does green innovation mediate corporate social responsibility and environmental performance? Empirical evidence from emerging markets. *Journal of Applied Accounting Research*, 25(2), 221–239. DOI: 10.1108/JAAR-10-2022-0271

Boons, F., Montalvo, C., Quist, J., & Wagner, M. (2013). Sustainable innovation, business models and economic performance: An overview. *Journal of Cleaner Production*, 45, 1–8. DOI: 10.1016/j.jclepro.2012.08.013

Boshnak, H. A. (2020). Internet financial reporting practices in Saudi Arabia. *International Journal of Business and Management*, 15(9), 1–14. DOI: 10.5539/ijbm.v15n9p15

Bowen, F., & Aragon-Correa, J. A. (2014). Greenwashing in corporate environmentalism research and practice:The importance of what we say and do. *Organization & Environment*, 27(2), 107–112. DOI: 10.1177/1086026614537078

Branco, M. C., & Rodrigues, L. L. (2008). Social responsibility disclosure: A study of proxies for the public visibility of Portuguese banks. *The British Accounting Review*, 40(2), 161–181.

Brendan LeBlanc, CPA, C. I. A., & Kislevitz, J. (2016). Integrating sustainability into enterprise risk management. *The CPA Journal*, 86(6), 12.

Brennan, M., Scott, J. C., Connelly, A., & Lawrence, G. (2019). Do music festival communities address environmental sustainability and how? A Scottish case study. *Popular Music*, 38(2), 252–275. DOI: 10.1017/S0261143019000035

Brennan, N., & Hourigan, D. (2000). Corporate reporting on the internet by Irish companies. *The Irish Accounting Review*, 7(1), 37–68. DOI: 10.52399/001c.35353

Broadstock, D. C., Managi, S., Matousek, R., & Tzeremes, N. G. (2019). Does doing "good" always translate into doing "well"? An eco-efficiency perspective. *Business Strategy and the Environment*, 28(6), 1199–1217. DOI: 10.1002/bse.2311

Buallay, A. (2018). *Is sustainability reporting (ESG) associated with performance? Evidence from the European banking sector.*

Bui, B., Houqe, M. N., & Zaman, M. (2021). Climate change mitigation: Carbon assurance and reporting integrity. *Business Strategy and the Environment*, 30(8), 3839–3853. DOI: 10.1002/bse.2843

Bureau Veritas. (n.d.). *Verification of sustainability data.*

Bury, L. (1999). Online and time. *Accounting*. 28–29.

Busch, T., Bauer, R., & Orlitzky, M. (2016). Sustainable development and financial markets: Old paths and new avenues. *Business & Society*, 55(3), 303–329. DOI: 10.1177/0007650315570701

Cahaya, F. R., Nursalim, N., & Dhirathiti, N. (2023). Expectations on Labour-Related CSR Reporting: Voices from Labour Unions in Indonesia and Thailand. *Social and Environmental Accountability Journal*, 43(3), 235–258. DOI: 10.1080/0969160X.2023.2167847

Cahyono, S., Harymawan, I., & Kamarudin, K. A. (2023). The impacts of tenure diversity on boardroom and corporate carbon emission performance: Exploring from the moderating role of corporate innovation. *Corporate Social Responsibility and Environmental Management*, 30(5), 2507–2535. DOI: 10.1002/csr.2500

Camilleri, M. (2014). Advancing the sustainable tourism agenda through strategic CSR perspectives. *Tourism Planning & Development*, 11(1), 42–56. DOI: 10.1080/21568316.2013.839470

Campana, P. E., Mainardis, M., Moretti, A., & Cottes, M. (2021). Corrigendum to "100% renewable wastewater treatment plants: Techno-economic assessment using a modelling and optimization approach.". *Energy Conversion and Management*, 244, 114531. DOI: 10.1016/j.enconman.2021.114214

Capelle-Blancard, G., & Petit, A. (2017). The weighting of CSR dimensions: One size does not fit all. *Business & Society*, 56(6), 919–943. DOI: 10.1177/0007650315620118

Cardoni, A., Kiseleva, E., & Terzani, S. (2019). *Evaluating the intra-industry comparability of sustainability reports: The case of the oil and gas industry.*

Carl, D. (2011). 'Greening' the 2010 FIFA World Cup: Environmental Sustainability and the Mega-Event in South Africa. *Journal of Environmental Policy and Planning*, 13(2), https://www.tandfonline.com/doi/abs/10.1080/1523908X.2011.572656

Carlsen, J., Mair, J., Holmes, K., & Hughes, M. (2015). *Events and Sustainability* (1st ed.). Routledge.

Carol, A. (2014). The Ethical, Social and Environmental Reporting-performance Portrayal Gap. *Accounting, Auditing & Accountability Journal*, 731–757.

Carter, C., & Spence, C. (2014). Being a successful professional: An exploration of who makes partner in the Big 4. *Contemporary Accounting Research*, 31(4), 949–981. DOI: 10.1111/1911-3846.12059

Castka, P., Searcy, C., & Fischer, S. (2020). Technology-enhanced auditing in voluntary sustainability standards: The impact of COVID-19. *Sustainability (Basel)*, 12(11), 4740. DOI: 10.3390/su12114740

Cerezo-Esteve, S., Inglés, E., Segui-Urbaneja, J., & Solanellas, F. (2022). *The Environmental Impact of Major Sport Events (Giga, Mega and Major): A Systematic Review from 2000 to 2021.* https://www.mdpi.com/2071-1050/14/20/13581

Cescon, F. (2002). Short-term perceptions, corporate governance and the management of R & D in Italian companies. *The Journal of Management and Governance*, 6(3), 255–270. DOI: 10.1023/A:1019631730439

Chagas, E. J. M. D., Albuquerque, J. D. L., Maia Filho, L. F. A., & Ceolin, A. C. (2022). Sustainable development, disclosure to stakeholders and the Sustainable Development Goals: Evidence from Brazilian banks' non-financial reports. *Sustainable Development*, 30(6), 1975–1986.

Chander, S., & Singh, M. (2009). Perceived usefulness of corporate disclosure through web: An empirical study. *The IUP Journal of Accounting Research and Audit Practices*, 8(3–4), 61–77.

Chang, C.-H. (2011). The Influence of Corporate Environmental Ethics on Competitive Advantage: The Mediation Role of Green Innovation. *Journal of Business Ethics*, 104(3), 361–370. DOI: 10.1007/s10551-011-0914-x

Channuntapipat, C., Samsonova-Taddei, A., & Turley, S. (2019). Exploring diversity in sustainability assurance practice: Evidence from assurance providers in the UK. *Accounting, Auditing & Accountability Journal*, 32(2), 556–580. DOI: 10.1108/AAAJ-05-2017-2940

Channuntapipat, C., Samsonova-Taddei, A., & Turley, S. (2020). Variation in sustainability assurance practice: An analysis of accounting versus non-accounting providers. *The British Accounting Review*, 52(2), 100843. DOI: 10.1016/j.bar.2019.100843

Chatterji, A. K., Durand, R., Levine, D. I., & Touboul, S. (2016). Do ratings of firms converge? Implications for managers, investors and strategy researchers. *Strategic Management Journal*, 37(8), 1597–1614. DOI: 10.1002/smj.2407

Chaturvedi, A. (2024). *Modelling sustainable projects: Investigating ESG indicators through virtual reality model* [Master's thesis, Metropolia University of Applied Sciences]. Theseus. https://www.theseus.fi/handle/10024/868098

Chatzitheodorou, K., Tsalis, T. A., Tsagarakis, K. P., Evangelos, G., & Ioannis, N. (2021). A new practical methodology for the banking sector to assess corporate sustainability risks with an application in the energy sector. *Sustainable Production and Consumption*, 27, 1473–1487. DOI: 10.1016/j.spc.2021.03.005

Chauvey, J. N., Giordano-Spring, S., Cho, C. H., & Patten, D. M. (2015). The normativity and legitimacy of CSR disclosure: Evidence from France. *Journal of Business Ethics*, 130(4), 789–803.

Chebbi, K. (2024). Examining the interplay of sustainable development, corporate governance, and stock Price crash risk: Insights from ESG practices. *Sustainable Development (Bradford)*, 32(1), 1291–1309. DOI: 10.1002/sd.2733

Chelli, M., & Gendron, Y. (2013). Sustainability ratings and the disciplinary power of the ideology of numbers. *Journal of Business Ethics*, 112(2), 187–203. DOI: 10.1007/s10551-012-1252-3

Chen, S., Farooq, U., Aldawsari, S. H., Waked, S. S., & Badawi, M. (2024). Impact of environmental, social, and governance performance on cash holdings in BRICS: Mediating role of cost of capital. *Corporate Social Responsibility and Environmental Management*, n/a(n/a). DOI: 10.1002/csr.3012

Chen, C., Rasheed, A., & Ayub, A. (2023). Does Green Mindfulness Promote Green Organizational Citizenship Behavior: A Moderated Mediation Model. *Sustainability (Basel)*, 15(6), 5012. DOI: 10.3390/su15065012

Cheng, B., Ioannou, I., & Serafeim, G. (2018). Corporate social responsibility and access to finance. *Strategic Management Journal*, 35(1), 1–23. DOI: 10.1002/smj.2131

Cheng, C. C. J. (2020). Sustainability Orientation, Green Supplier Involvement, and Green Innovation Performance: Evidence from Diversifying Green Entrants. *Journal of Business Ethics*, 161(2), 393–414. DOI: 10.1007/s10551-018-3946-7

Chen, S., Song, Y., & Gao, P. (2023). Environmental, social, and governance (ESG) performance and financial outcomes: Analyzing the impact of ESG on financial performance. *Journal of Environmental Management*, 345, 118829. DOI: 10.1016/j.jenvman.2023.118829

Chen, Y., & Chag, S. (2013). Greenwash and Green Trust: The Mediation Effects of Green Consumer Confusion and Green Perceived Risk. *Journal of Business Ethics*, 114(3), 489–500. DOI: 10.1007/s10551-012-1360-0

Chen, Y.-S., Lai, S.-B., & Wen, C.-T. (2006). The Influence of Green Innovation Performance on Corporate Advantage in Taiwan. *Journal of Business Ethics*, 67(4), 331–339. DOI: 10.1007/s10551-006-9025-5

Cho, S. J. (Ed.). (2015). *The proceedings of the 12th international congress on mathematical education: Intellectual and attitudinal challenges*. Springer International Publishing. DOI: 10.1007/978-3-319-12688-3

Cho, H., C., Michelon, G., M. Patten, D., & W. Roberts, R. (2014). CSR report assurance in the USA: An empirical investigation of determinants and effects. Sustainability Accounting. *Management and Policy Journal*, 5(2), 130–148.

Choi, W. (2022). Education of digital data narrative using ESG concepts. *Journal of Digital Contents Society*, 23(2), 227–235. DOI: 10.9728/dcs.2022.23.2.227

Cho, M., Michelon, G., Patten, D. M., & Roberts, R. W. (2015). CSR disclosure: The more things change…? *Accounting, Auditing & Accountability Journal*, 28(1), 14–35. DOI: 10.1108/AAAJ-12-2013-1549

Chowdhury, M. A. A., Dey, M., & Abedin, M. T. (2020). Firms' attributes and environmental disclosure: Evidence from listed firms in Bangladesh. *Asian Journal of Accounting Perspectives*, 13(2), 57–77. DOI: 10.22452/AJAP.vol13no2.4

Christie, M., Rowe, P., Perry, C., & Chamard, J. (2000). Implementation of realism in case study research methodology. *International Council for Small Business, Annual Conference*, 1–21. https://www.researchgate.net/profile/Patricia-Rowe-2/publication/43095715_Implementation_of_realism_in_case_study_research_methodology/links/09e41507de130b5b6d000000/Implementation-of-realism-in-case-study-research-methodology.pdf

Chuang, S.-P., & Huang, S.-J. (2018). The Effect of Environmental Corporate Social Responsibility on Environmental Performance and Business Competitiveness: The Mediation of Green Information Technology Capital. *Journal of Business Ethics*, 150(4), 991–1009. DOI: 10.1007/s10551-016-3167-x

Chung, C. Y., & Song, J. M. (2024). Institutional investors by nationality and long-term investor value appropriation. *Research in International Business and Finance*, 67, 102153. DOI: 10.1016/j.ribaf.2023.102153

Churchill, G. A. (1979). *Marketing research: Methodological foundations* (2nd ed.). The Dryden Press.

Clauß, T., Kraus, S., & Jones, P. (2022). Sustainability in family business: Mechanisms, technologies and business models for achieving economic prosperity, environmental quality and social equity. *Technological Forecasting and Social Change*, 176, 121450. DOI: 10.1016/j.techfore.2021.121450

Coca-Cola Company. (2023). *2023 environmental update*. The Coca-Cola Company.

Coccia, M. (2019). Comparative incentive systems. *Global Encyclopedia of Public Administration, Public Policy, and Governance, Springer International Publishing AG, part of Springer Nature, DOI, 10*, 978-973.

Cohen, M., Cavazotte, F. S. C. N., Costa, T. M., & Ferreira, K. C. S. (2017). Corporate social-environmental responsibility as an attraction and retention factor for young professionals. *BBR.Brazilian Business Review*, 14(1), 21–41. DOI: 10.15728/bbr.2017.14.1.2

Collins, A., & Flynn, A. (2008). Measuring the Environmental Sustainability of a Major Sporting Event: A Case Study of the FA Cup Final. *Tourism Economics, 14*(4), 751-768. https://doi.org/10.5367/000000008786440120DOI: 10.5367/000000008786440120

Connaker, A., & Madsbjerg, S. (2019). The state of socially responsible investing. *Harvard Business Review*, 17.

Cooray, T., Gunarathne, A. D., & Senaratne, S. (2020). Does Corporate Governance Affect the Quality of Integrated Reporting? *Sustainability (Basel)*, 12(10), 4262. DOI: 10.3390/su12104262

Cosma, S., Venturelli, A., Schwizer, P., & Boscia, V. (2020). Sustainable development and European banks: A non-financial disclosure analysis. *Sustainability*, 12(15), 6146.

Craven, B. M., & Marston, C. L. (1999). Financial reporting on the internet by leading UK companies. *European Accounting Review*, 8(2), 321–333. DOI: 10.1080/096381899336069

Creech, A., Zhukov, K., & Barrett, M. S. (2022). Signature pedagogies in collaborative creative learning in advanced music training, education and professional development: A meta-synthesis. *Frontiers in Education*, 7, 929421. Advance online publication. DOI: 10.3389/feduc.2022.929421

Cruz, C. A., & Matos, F. (2023). ESG maturity: A software framework for the challenges of ESG data in investment. *Sustainability (Basel)*, 15(3), 2610. DOI: 10.3390/su15032610

Curado, C., & Mota, A. (2021). A systematic literature review on sustainability in family firms. *Sustainability (Basel)*, 13(7), 3824. DOI: 10.3390/su13073824

Dahlsrud, A. (2008). How corporate social responsibility is defined: An analysis of 37 definitions. *Corporate Social Responsibility and Environmental Management*, 15(1), 1–13. DOI: 10.1002/csr.132

Dalal, K. K., Thaker, N., & IUP. (2019). ESG and corporate financial performance: A panel study of Indian companies. *The IUP Journal of Corporate Governance, XVIII*(1). Retrieved from https://www.researchgate.net/publication/371177996

Dando, N., & Swift, T. (2003). Transparency and assurance: Minding the credibility gap. *Journal of Business Ethics*, 44(2), 195–200. DOI: 10.1023/A:1023351816790

Dasinapa, M. B., & Ermawati, Y. (2024). Insights into Emerging Trends Shaping the Future of Audit and Assurance. *Advances in Managerial Auditing Research*, 2(2), 75–86. DOI: 10.60079/amar.v2i2.292

Das, S., & Das, S. (2015). Mandatory corporate reporting on the internet: An empirical study of the listed non-financial companies in Bangladesh. *International Journal of Accounting and Business Finance*, (2), 1–16. DOI: 10.4038/ijabf.v5i2.42

Dawkins, C. E. (2018). Elevating the role of divestment in socially responsi- ble investing. *Journal of Business Ethics*, 153(2), 465–478. DOI: 10.1007/s10551-016-3356-7

De Silva, P., Gunarathne, N., & Kumar, S. (2024). *Exploring the impact of digital knowledge, integration and performance on sustainable accounting, reporting and assurance*. Meditari Accountancy Research. https://doi.org/10.1108/MEDAR-02-2024-2383

De Wolf, C., Cordella, M., Dodd, N., Byers, B., & Donatello, S. (2023). Whole life cycle environmental impact assessment of buildings: Developing software tool and database support for the EU framework level(s). *Resources, Conservation and Recycling*, 188, 106642. DOI: 10.1016/j.resconrec.2022.106642

Debreceny, R., & Gray, G. L. (1999). Financial reporting on the internet and the external audit. *European Accounting Review*, 8(2), 335–350. DOI: 10.1080/096381899336078

Debreceny, R., Gray, G. L., & Mock, T. J. (2001). Financial reporting websites: What users want in terms of form and content? *The International Journal of Digital Accounting Research*, 1(1), 1–23. DOI: 10.4192/1577-8517-v1_1

Deci, E. L. (1972). Intrinsic motivation, extrinsic reinforcement, and inequity. *Journal of Personality and Social Psychology*, 22(1), 113–120. DOI: 10.1037/h0032355

Deci, E. L., & Ryan, R. M. (1985). Conceptualizations of Intrinsic Motivation and Self-Determination. In Deci, E. L., & Ryan, R. M. (Eds.), *Intrinsic Motivation and Self-Determination in Human Behavior* (pp. 11–40). Springer US., DOI: 10.1007/978-1-4899-2271-7_2

Deegan, C. (2002). Introduction: The Legitimising Effect of Social and Environmental Disclosures – A Theoretical Foundation. *Accounting, Auditing & Accountability Journal*, 15(3), 282–311. DOI: 10.1108/09513570210435852

Deegan, C. M. (2019). Legitimacy theory: Despite its enduring popularity and contribution, time is right for a necessary makeover. *Accounting, Auditing & Accountability Journal*, 32(8), 2307–2329. DOI: 10.1108/AAAJ-08-2018-3638

Deegan, C., & Rankin, M. (1996). Explaining Corporate Annual Report Disclosures: A Legitimacy Theory Perspective. *Accounting, Auditing & Accountability Journal*, 9(2), 18–38.

Delgado-Ceballos, J., Ortiz-De-Mandojana, N., Antolín-López, R., & Montiel, I. (2023). Connecting the sustainable development goals to firm-level sustainability and ESG factors: The need for double materiality. *Business Research Quarterly*, 26(1), 2–10. DOI: 10.1177/23409444221140919

Deller, D., Stubenrath, M., & Weber, C. (1999). Investor relations and the internet: Background, potential application and evidence from the USA, UK and Germany. *21st Annual Congress of the European Accounting Association*, Antwerp, Belgium.

Delmas, A., & Burbano, V. (2011). The Drivers of Greenwashing. *California Management Review*, 54(1), 64–87. DOI: 10.1525/cmr.2011.54.1.64

Delmas, M. A., & Pekovic, S. (2018). Corporate Sustainable Innovation and Employee Behavior. *Journal of Business Ethics*, 150(4), 1071–1088. DOI: 10.1007/s10551-016-3163-1

Deloitte. (n.d.). *Globally consistent ESG reporting*. Deloitte.

Demjanovičová, M., & Varmus, M. (2021). Changing the perception of business values in the perspective of environmental sustainability. *Sustainability (Basel)*, 13(9), 5226. DOI: 10.3390/su13095226

Deng, S., & He, J. (2024). Managerial inclusiveness and corporate innovation in China. *Accounting and Finance*, 64(1), 381–410. DOI: 10.1111/acfi.13149

Desoky, A. M., & Mousa, G. A. (2009). The impact of company characteristics and corporate governance attributes on internet investor relations: Evidence from Bahrain. *12th International Conference Organized by the American Society of Business and Behavioral Sciences*, London, UK.

Dhingra, K. (2023). Corporate Social Responsibility and Sustainability of Corporate Performance. *Jindal Journal of Business Research*, 12(1), 19–29. DOI: 10.1177/22786821231161416

Dhuri, M., Sinha, R., Shukla, S., & CRISIL. (2024). ESG ratings in India: Assessing their reliability for investment decisions. *European Economic Letters, 10*(1), 27–31. Retrieved from http://eelet.org.uk

Dienes, D., Sassen, R., & Fischer, J. (2016). *Sustainability accounting, management and policy journal, 7*(2), 154–189

Diouf, D., & Boiral, O. (2017). The quality of sustainability reports and impression management: A stakeholder perspective. *Accounting, Auditing & Accountability Journal*, 30(3), 643–667. DOI: 10.1108/AAAJ-04-2015-2044

Dolles, H., & Söderman, S. (2010). Addressing ecology and sustainability in mega-sporting events: The 2006 football World Cup in Germany. *Journal of Management & Organization*, 16(4), 587–600. DOI: 10.5172/jmo.2010.16.4.587

Dora, M., Kumar, A., Mangla, S. K., Pant, A., & Kamal, M. M. (2022). Critical success factors influencing artificial intelligence adoption in food supply chains. *International Journal of Production Research*, 60(14), 4621–4640. DOI: 10.1080/00207543.2021.1959665

Do, T., & Vo, X. (2023). Is Mandatory Sustainability Disclosure Associated With Default Risk? Evidence From Emerging Markets. *Finance Research Letters*, 55, 1038–1056. DOI: 10.1016/j.frl.2023.103818

Doyle, T. M. (2018). Ratings that don't rate: the subjective world of ESG ratings agencies. American Council for Capital Formation, 65-71.

Dulla, R. B., Graham, A. W., & Baldwin, A. A. (2003). Web-based financial statements: Hypertext links to footnotes and their effect on decisions. *International Journal of Accounting Information Systems*, 4(3), 185–203. DOI: 10.1016/S1467-0895(03)00009-5

Dyck, A., Lins, K. V., Roth, L., & Wagner, H. F. (2019). Do institutional investors drive corporate social responsibility? International evidence. *Journal of Financial Economics*, 131(3), 693–714. DOI: 10.1016/j.jfineco.2018.08.013

Eccles, R. G., Ioannou, I., & Serafeim, G. (2014). The impact of corporate sustainability on organizational processes and performance. *Management Science*, 60(11), 2835–2857. DOI: 10.1287/mnsc.2014.1984

Eccles, R. G., & Klimenko, S. (2019). The investor revolution. *Harvard Business Review*, 97(3), 106–116.

Eccles, R. G., Lee, L., & Stroehle, J. C. (2020). The social origins of ESG: Analyzing the ESG rating industry through a multiple lens approach. *Organization & Environment*, 33(4), 566–591.

Eccles, R., & Serafeim, G. (2013). A tale of two stories: Sustainability and the quarterly earnings call. *The Bank of America Journal of Applied Corporate Finance*, 25(3), 8–19. DOI: 10.1111/jacf.12023

Edgar, S. N. (2013). Introducing Social Emotional Learning to Music Education Professional Development. *Update - University of South Carolina. Dept. of Music*, 31(2), 28–36. DOI: 10.1177/8755123313480508

Edgley, C., Jones, M. J., & Atkins, J. (2015). The adoption of the materiality concept in social and environmental reporting assurance: A field study approach. *The British Accounting Review*, 47(1), 1–18. DOI: 10.1016/j.bar.2014.11.001

Eisenhardt, K. M. (1989). *Building theories from case study research.*

El Helou, N., Tafflet, M., Berthelot, G., Tolaini, J., Marc, A., Guillaume, M., Hausswirth, C., & Toussaint, J.F. (2012). *Impact of Environmental Parameters on Marathon Running Performance.* https://journals.plos.org/plosone/article?id=10.1371/journal.pone.0037407

Eladawi, F. M. I., Elnaggar, M. K., Hashad, M. E., Awad, A. H. I., & Abd, A. A. E.-K. G. (2024). Effect of green inclusive leadership on employees'green work engagement in hotels and travel agencies: The role of green intrinsic motivation. *Geo Journal of Tourism and Geosites*, 54(2 supplement), 885–895. DOI: 10.30892/gtg.542spl12-1263

El-Sawad, A., & Korczynski, M. (2007). Management and music: The exceptional case of the IBM songbook. *Group & Organization Management*, 32(1), 79–108. DOI: 10.1177/1059601106294488

Ermolaeva, P. (2024). Green? Cool. yours: The effect of sports mega-events in post-soviet Russia on citizens' environmental consumption practises (cases of 2013 Universiade in Kazan and 2014 Sochi Olympics). *ResearchGate*. https://www.researchgate.net/publication/306103267_Green_Cool_yours_The_effect_of_sports_mega-events_in_post-soviet_Russia_on_citizens'_environmental_consumption_practises_cases_of_2013_Universiade_in_Kazan_and_2014_Sochi_Olympics

Ermolaeva, P., & Lind, A. (2021). Mega-Event Simulacrum: Critical Reflections on the Sustainability Legacies of the World Cup 2018 for the Russian Host Cities. *Problems of Post-Communism*, 68(6), 498–508. DOI: 10.1080/10758216.2020.1791185

Escrig-Olmedo, E., Fernández-Izquierdo, M. Á., Ferrero-Ferrero, I., Rivera-Lirio, J. M., & Muñoz-Torres, M. J. (2019). Rating the raters: Evaluating how ESG rating agencies integrate sustainability principles. *Sustainability (Basel)*, 11(3), 915. DOI: 10.3390/su11030915

Escrig-Olmedo, E., Muñoz-Torres, M. J., Fernández-Izquierdo, M. Á., & Rivera-Lirio, J. M. (2017). Measuring corporate environmental performance: A methodology for sustainable development. *Business Strategy and the Environment*, 26(2), 142–162. DOI: 10.1002/bse.1904

Ettredge, M., Richardson, V. J., & Scholz, S. (1999). *Financial data at corporate websites: Does user sophistication matter?* [Working Paper]. University of Kansas.

Ettredge, M., Richardson, V. J., & Scholz, S. (2001). The presentation of financial information at corporate websites. *International Journal of AIS*, 2(3), 149–168.

Faraz, N. A., Ahmed, F., Ying, M., & Mehmood, S. A. (2021). The interplay of green servant leadership, self-efficacy, and intrinsic motivation in predicting employees' pro-environmental behavior. *Corporate Social Responsibility and Environmental Management*, 28(4), 1171–1184. DOI: 10.1002/csr.2115

Farooq, M. B., Azantouti, A. S. A., & Zaman, R. (2023). Non-financial information assurance: a review of the literature and directions for future research. Sustainability accounting, management and policy journal, (ahead-of-print).

Farooq, M. B., Azantouti, A. S. A., & Zaman, R. (2024). Non-financial information assurance: A review of the literature and directions for future research. *Sustainability Accounting. Management and Policy Journal*, 15(1), 48–84. DOI: 10.1108/SAMPJ-03-2023-0166

Farooq, M. B., & De Villiers, C. (2017). The market for sustainability assurance services: A comprehensive literature review and future avenues for research. *Pacific Accounting Review*, 29(1), 79–106. DOI: 10.1108/PAR-10-2016-0093

Farooq, M. B., & De Villiers, C. (2019). How sustainability assurance engagement scopes are determined, and its impact on capture and credibility enhancement. *Accounting, Auditing & Accountability Journal*, 33(2), 417–445. DOI: 10.1108/AAAJ-11-2018-3727

Fekih Zguir, M., Dubis, S., & Koç, M. (2021). Embedding education for sustainable development (ESD) and SDGs values in curriculum: A comparative review on qatar, singapore and new zealand. *Journal of Cleaner Production*, 319, 128534. DOI: 10.1016/j.jclepro.2021.128534

Feng, Y., Akram, R., Hieu, V. M., & Hoang Tien, N. (2022). The impact of corporate social responsibility on the sustainable financial performance of Italian firms: Mediating role of firm reputation. *Ekonomska Istrazivanja*, 35(1), 4740–4758. DOI: 10.1080/1331677X.2021.2017318

Ferrell, A., Liang, H., & Renneboog, L. (2016). Socially responsible firms. *Journal of Financial Economics*, 122(3), 585–606. DOI: 10.1016/j.jfineco.2015.12.003

Ferrer-Estévez, M., & Chalmeta, R. (2021). Integrating Sustainable Development Goals in educational institutions. *International Journal of Management Education*, 19(2), 100494. DOI: 10.1016/j.ijme.2021.100494

Financial Accounting Standards Board. (2000). *Business reporting research project: Electronic distribution of business reporting information*. Steering Committee Report Series. Available at http://www.fasb.org

Fisher, R., Oyelere, P., & Laswad, F. (2002). Audit issues and content analysis of audit practices associated with corporate financial reporting on the internet. *Discussion Paper No. 96,* Commerce Division, Lincoln University, Canterbury, New Zealand.

Flammer, C. (2013). Corporate social responsibility and shareholder reaction: The environmental awareness of investors. *Academy of Management Journal*, 56(3), 758–781. DOI: 10.5465/amj.2011.0744

Flammer, C. (2018). Green bonds: Effectiveness and implications for public policy. *Environmental and Energy Policy and the Economy*, 1(1), 1–31.

Florini, A., & Pauli, M. (2018). *Collaborative governance for the Sustainable Development Goals.*

Fong, C. C. S. (1997). *Acceptance of corporate reporting through the internet* [Working Paper]. City University, Hong Kong.

Fosu, E., Fosu, F., Akyina, N., & Asiedu, D. (2024). Do environmental CSR practices promote corporate social performance? The mediating role of green innovation and corporate image. *Cleaner and Responsible Consumption, 12*, 100155. doi.org/10.1016/j.clrc.2023.100155

Fraj-Andrés, E., Martinez-Salinas, E., & Matute-Vallejo, J. (2009). A Multidimensional Approach to the Influence of Environmental Marketing and Orientation on the Firm's Organizational Performance. *Journal of Business Ethics*, 88(2), 263–286. DOI: 10.1007/s10551-008-9962-2

Franzoni, S., & Allali, A. A. (2018). Principles of Islamic finance and principles of Corporate Social Responsibility: What convergence? *Sustainability (Basel)*, 10(3), 637. Advance online publication. DOI: 10.3390/su10030637

Fredrickson, B. L. (2013). Chapter One - Positive Emotions Broaden and Build. In Devine, P., & Plant, A. (Eds.), Vol. 47, pp. 1–53). Advances in Experimental Social Psychology. Academic Press., doi.org/10.1016/B978-0-12-407236-7.00001-2

Free, C., Jones, S., & Tremblay, S. (2024). Greenwashing and sustainability assurance: A review and call for future research. *Journal of Accounting Literature*, 256–291. DOI: 10.1108/JAL-11-2023-0201

Freeman, R. E. (1984). *Strategic management: A stakeholder approach.* Pitman.

Freeman, R. E., & Reed, D. L. (1983). Stockholders and Stakeholders: A New Perspective on Corporate Governance. *California Management Review*, 25(3), 88–106. DOI: 10.2307/41165018

Friede, G., Busch, T., & Bassen, A. (2015). ESG and financial performance: Aggregated evidence from more than 2000 empirical studies. *Journal of Sustainable Finance & Investment*, 5(4), 210–233. DOI: 10.1080/20430795.2015.1118917

Friodevaux, A. E. (2004). *Investor relations internet disclosure and the cost of equity capital: An empiracle analysis* [Doctoral thesis, Fribourg University]. Scribd.

Fuad, K., Ariyani, N. D., & Handayani, R. T. (2020). The role of internet financial reporting (IFR) in mediating manufacturing firm value on Indonesia Stock Exchange (IDX). *Journal of Islamic Accounting and Finance Research*, 2(2), 1–12. DOI: 10.21580/jiafr.2020.2.2.5821

Fuhrmann, S., Ott, C., Looks, E., & Guenther, T. W. (2017). The contents of assurance statements for sustainability reports and information asymmetry. *Accounting and Business Research*, 47(4), 369–400. DOI: 10.1080/00014788.2016.1263550

Furrer, B., Hamprecht, J., & Hoffmann, V. H. (2012). Much ado about nothing? How banks respond to climate change. *Business & Society*, 51(1), 62–88.

Gabeiras Vázquez, P., & Barahona Arroyo, M. (2020). Plan de acción para la adaptación de los festivales de música a la agenda 2030. *Periferica*, 21(21), 234–237. DOI: 10.25267/Periferica.2020.i21.21

Gaffney, C. (2013). Between Discourse and Reality: The Un-Sustainability of Mega-Event Planning. *Sustainability (Basel)*, 5(9), 9. Advance online publication. DOI: 10.3390/su5093926

Gajewski, J. F., & Li, L. (2015). Can internet-based disclosure reduce information asymmetry? *Advances in Accounting*, 31(1), 115–124. DOI: 10.1016/j.adiac.2015.03.013

Gálvez-Rodríguez, M. D. M., Ovelar-Fernández, W. D., & Caba-Pérez, C. (2024). Information Disclosure on the Integration of SDGs into Banking Management: The MERCOSUR Countries Case. In *Environmentally Sustainable Production: Research for Sustainable Development* (pp. 37–56). Springer Nature Switzerland.

Gao, S., & Zhang, J. (2019). Internal audit involvement in sustainability assurance. *Journal of Corporate Governance*, 434-449.

Gao, F., Dong, Y., Ni, C., & Fu, R. (2016). Determinants and economic consequences of non-financial disclosure quality. *European Accounting Review*, 25(2), 287–317.

García-Meca, E., & Martínez-Ferrero, J. (2021). Is SDG reporting substantial or symbolic? An examination of controversial and environmentally sensitive industries. *Journal of Cleaner Production*, 298, 126781.

García-Meca, E., & Pucheta-Martínez, M. C. (2018). How Institutional Investors on Boards Impact on Stakeholder Engagement and Corporate Social Responsibility Reporting. *Corporate Social Responsibility and Environmental Management*, 25(3), 237–249. DOI: 10.1002/csr.1451

García-Sánchez, I.-M., Aibar-Guzmán, B., Raimo, N., & Vitolla, F. (2024). Embracing tomorrow: Global insights on corporate commitment to the 2030 Agenda. *Measuring Business Excellence*, ahead-of-print(ahead-of-print). DOI: 10.1108/MBE-04-2024-0044

García-Sánchez, I. M. (2021). Corporate social reporting and assurance: The state of the art: Información social corporativa y aseguramiento: El estado de la cuestión. *Revista de Contabilidad-Spanish Accounting Review*, 24(2), 241–269.

García-Sánchez, I. M., Aibar-Guzmán, B., & Aibar-Guzmán, C. (2022). What sustainability assurance services do institutional investors demand and what value do they give them? Sustainability Accounting. *Management and Policy Journal*, 13(1), 152–194.

García-Sánchez, I. M., Raimo, N., Amor-Esteban, V., & Vitolla, F. (2023). Board committees and non-financial information assurance services. *The Journal of Management and Governance*, 27(1), 1–42. DOI: 10.1007/s10997-021-09613-6

García-Sánchez, I.-M., Aibar-Guzmán, C., & Aibar-Guzmán, B. (2020). The effect of institutional ownership and ownership dispersion on eco-innovation. *Technological Forecasting and Social Change*, 158, 120173. DOI: 10.1016/j.techfore.2020.120173

García-Sánchez, I.-M., Aibar-Guzmán, C., Núñez-Torrado, M., & Aibar-Guzmán, B. (2022). Are institutional investors "in love" with the sustainable development goals? Understanding the idyll in the case of governments and pension funds. *Sustainable Development (Bradford)*, 30(5), 1099–1116. DOI: 10.1002/sd.2305

Garg, M. C., & Verma, D. V. (2010). Web-based corporate reporting practices in India. *IUP Journal of Accounting Research and Audit Practices*, 9(3), 7–19.

Gauri, M. (2014). XBRL in India. *Global Journal of Finance and Management*, 6(6), 517–522.

Geerings, J., Bollen, L., & Hassink, H. (2003). Investor relations on the internet: A survey of the Euronext zone. *European Accounting Review*, 12(3), 567–579. DOI: 10.1080/0963818032000083531

George, G., Haas, M. R., & Pentland, A. (2021). Big data and management. *Academy of Management Journal*, 57(2), 321–326. DOI: 10.5465/amj.2014.4002

Ghani, E. K., Jamal, J., Puspitasari, E., & Gunardi, A. (2018). Factors influencing integrated reporting practices among Malaysian public listed real property companies: A sustainable development effort. *International Journal of Managerial and Financial Accounting*, 10(2), 144–162. DOI: 10.1504/IJMFA.2018.091662

Giaver, F., Vaag, J. R., & Wennes, G. (2017). Choral singing as an arts-based organisational intervention: A qualitative study of employees' experiences. *Arts & Health*, 9(1), 26–41. DOI: 10.1080/17533015.2016.1182564 PMID: 31038036

Gibson, R., & Krueger, P. (2018). The sustainability footprint of institutional investors. *Journal of Business Ethics*, 149(1), 53–72. DOI: 10.1023/B:BUSI.0000004367.60776.b3

Giese, G., Lee, L., Melas, D., Nagy, Z. I., & Nishikawa, L. (2019). Foundations of ESG Investing: How ESG Affects Equity Valuation, Risk, and Performance. *Journal of Portfolio Management*, 45(5), 69–83. DOI: 10.3905/jpm.2019.45.5.069

Gillet-Monjarret, C., & Rivière-Giordano, G. (2017). *Sustainability assurance: A literature review.*

Gligorijević, J. (2021). Micronational spaces: Rethinking politics in contemporary music festivals. In J. Williams & S. Horlor (Eds.), *Musical Spaces* (1st ed., 375–399). Jenny Stanford Publishing. DOI: 10.1201/9781003180418-26

Global Reporting Initiative. (n.d.). *Global Reporting Initiative.*

Goicoechea, E., Gómez-Bezares, F., & Ugarte, J. V. (2019). Integrated reporting assurance: Perceptions of auditors and users in Spain. *Sustainability (Basel)*, 11(3), 713. Advance online publication. DOI: 10.3390/su11030713

Gond, J. P., Patriotta, G., & Schultz, F. (2021). How do companies embed corporate social responsibility across organizational functions? *The Academy of Management Annals*, 15(1), 229–287.

Gond, J.-P., El Akremi, A., Swaen, V., & Babu, N. (2017). The psychological microfoundations of corporate social responsibility: A person-centric systematic review. *Journal of Organizational Behavior*, 38(2), 225–246. DOI: 10.1002/job.2170

González-Benito, Ó., Muñoz-Gallego, P. A., & García-Zamora, E. (2016). Role of collaboration in innovation success: Differences for large and small businesses. *Journal of Business Economics and Management*, 17(4), 645–662. DOI: 10.3846/16111699.2013.823103

Gray, G., & Debreceny, R. (1997). Corporate reporting on the internet: Opportunities and challenges. *Seventh Asia-Pacific Conference on International Accounting Issues,* Bangkok, Thailand.

Green, T., Sinclair, G., & Tinson, J. (2016). Do they know it's CSR at all? An exploration of socially responsible music consumption. *Journal of Business Ethics,* 138(2), 231–246. DOI: 10.1007/s10551-015-2582-8

Grewal, J., & Serafeim, G. (2020). Research on corporate sustainability: Review and directions for future research. *Foundations and Trends® in Accounting, 14*(2), 73–127. DOI: 10.1561/1400000061

Groww. (n.d.). *Explore stocks*. Retrieved January 5, 2025, from https://groww.in/stocks/user/explore

Guidara, A., Ammari, A. E., & Khlif, H. (2022). Strength of auditing and reporting standards, ethical behavior of firms and sustainability: A cross-country investigation. *EuroMed Journal of Business*, 17(1), 105–116. DOI: 10.1108/EMJB-10-2020-0107

Gunawan, J., Permatasari, P., & Sharma, U. (2022). Exploring sustainability and green banking disclosures: A study of banking sector. *Environment, Development and Sustainability*, 24(9), 11153–11194. DOI: 10.1007/s10668-021-01901-3

Guthrie, J., Cuganesan, B., & Ward, B. (2006). Legitimacy Theory and Corporate Social Disclosure. *Accounting, Auditing & Accountability Journal*, 19(1), 1–29.

H.P., H., & Rishad, A. (2020). An empirical examination of investor sentiment and stock market volatility: Evidence from India. *Financial Innovation, 6*(1), Article 26. DOI: 10.1186/s40854-020-00198-x

Haasbroek, F. (2002). *Dissemination of annual report information on the internet by South African companies* [Master's Thesis, Rand Afrikaans University].

Hahn, R., Reimsbach, D., & Schiemann, F. (2015). Organizations, Climate Change, and Transparency: Reviewing the Literature on Carbon Disclosure. *Organization & Environment*, 28(1), 80–102. DOI: 10.1177/1086026615575542

Haimberg, Y. (2021). *Can an Agency Role-Reversal Lead to an Organizational Collapse? A Study Proposal.*

Haldar, S. (2019). Towards a conceptual understanding of sustainability-driven entrepreneurship. *Corporate Social Responsibility and Environmental Management*, 26(6), 1157–1170. DOI: 10.1002/csr.1763

Halkos, G., Nomikos, S., & Tsilika, K. (2022). Evidence for Novel Structures Relating CSR Reporting and Economic Welfare: Environmental Sustainability—A Continent-Level Analysis. *Computational Economics*, 59(2), 415–444. DOI: 10.1007/s10614-020-10091-5

Haller, A., Van Staden, C. J., & Landis, C. (2018). Value added as part of sustainability reporting: Reporting on distributional fairness or obfuscation? *Journal of Business Ethics*, 152(3), 763–781. DOI: 10.1007/s10551-016-3338-9

Hamad, S., Lai, F. W., Shad, M. K., Khatib, S. F. A., & Ali, S. E. A. (2023). Assessing the implementation of sustainable development goals: Does integrated reporting matter? *Sustainability Accounting. Management and Policy Journal*, 14(1), 49–74. DOI: 10.1108/SAMPJ-01-2022-0029

Hamalainen, E. (2010). *Environmental marketing communication on corporate websites: Stakeholder audiences' expectations and needs* [Master's Thesis, Aalto University].

Hambali, A., & Adhariani, D. (2023). Sustainability performance at stake during COVID-19 pandemic? Evidence from Sharia-compliant companies in emerging markets. *Journal of Islamic Accounting and Business Research*, 14(1), 80–99. DOI: 10.1108/JIABR-01-2022-0014

Hamid, A. Z. F. (2005). Malaysian companies' use of the Internet for investor relations. *Corporate Governance (Bradford)*, 5(1), 5–14. DOI: 10.1108/14720700510583421

Hamilton, S. N., & Waters, R. D. (2022). Mainstreaming Standardized Sustainability Reporting: Comparing Fortune 50 Corporations' and U.S. News & World Report's Top 50 Global Universities' Sustainability Reports. *Sustainability (Basel)*, 14(6), 3442. Advance online publication. DOI: 10.3390/su14063442

Hanieh, A. (2020). New geographies of financial power: Global Islamic finance and the Gulf. *Third World Quarterly*, 41(3), 525–546. DOI: 10.1080/01436597.2019.1675505

Hao, J., & He, F. (2022). Corporate social responsibility (CSR) performance and green innovation: Evidence from China. *Finance Research Letters*, 48, 102889. DOI: 10.1016/j.frl.2022.102889

Harahap, K., Rumondang, T., Putra, P. D., & Winata, J. A. (2021). Integrating XBRL technology into accounting curriculum: A survey of accounting lecturers in Medan City. *International Conference on Strategic Issues of Economics, Business and Education (ICoSIEBE 2020)* (89–97). Atlantis Press. DOI: 10.2991/aebmr.k.210220.017

Harindahyani, S., & Agustia, D. (2023). The assurance providers' role in improving the independent assurance statement quality on sustainability reporting. *Accounting Research Journal*, 36(1), 37–54. DOI: 10.1108/ARJ-01-2021-0024

Harjoto, M. A., Jo, H., & Kim, Y. (2015). Corporate governance and CSR nexus. *Journal of Business Ethics*, 132(3), 453–469.

Harris, R., & Schlenker, K. (2018). An Exploratory Study of "Best Practice" in Environmentally Sustainable Event Management in Australian Public Events. *Event Management*, 22(6), 1057–1071. DOI: 10.3727/152599518X15346132863175

Hart, S. L. (1995). A Natural-Resource-Based View of the Firm. *Academy of Management Review*, 20(4), 986–1014. DOI: 10.2307/258963

Harvey, J.-F., Cromwell, J. R., Johnson, K. J., & Edmondson, A. C. (2023). The dynamics of team learning: Harmony and rhythm in teamwork arrangements for innovation. *Administrative Science Quarterly*, 68(3), 601–647. DOI: 10.1177/00018392231166635 PMID: 37560020

Hasan, H. R., Musamih, A., Salah, K., Jayaraman, R., Omar, M., Arshad, J., & Boscovic, D. (2024). Smart agriculture assurance: IoT and blockchain for trusted sustainable produce. *Computers and Electronics in Agriculture*, 224, 109184. DOI: 10.1016/j.compag.2024.109184

Hassan, M. K., Chiaramonte, L., Dreassi, A., Paltrinieri, A., & Piserà, S. (2022). The religious fringe of Corporate Social Responsibility. *International Review of Economics & Finance*, 80, 243–265. DOI: 10.1016/j.iref.2022.02.003

Hassen, S., Jaffar, N., & Johal, S. K. (2000). *Financial reporting on the Internet by Malaysian companies: Perceptions and practices* [Working Paper]. University of Multimedia, Malaysia.

Hausman, J. A. (1978). Specification tests in econometrics. *Econometrica*, 46(6), 1251–1271. DOI: 10.2307/1913827

Hawn, O., Chatterji, A. K., & Mitchell, W. (2017). *Do investors actually value sustainability? New evidence from investor reactions to the Dow Jones Sustainability Index (DJSI).*

Hayatun N. Burhan, A., & Rahmanti, W. (2022). *The impact of sustainability reporting on company performance.*

Hazaea, S. A., Zhu, J., Khatib, S. F., Bazhair, A. H., & Elamer, A. A. (2022). Sustainability assurance practices: A systematic review and future research agenda. *Environmental Science and Pollution Research International*, 29(4), 4843–4864. DOI: 10.1007/s11356-021-17359-9 PMID: 34787810

He, Y., Gao, X., & Wang, Y. (2022). *Sustainable financial development: Does it matter for greenhouse gas emissions?*

Helfaya, A., Whittington, M., & Alawattage, C. (2019). Exploring the quality of corporate environmental reporting. *Accounting, Auditing & Accountability Journal*, 32(1), 63–193.

He, Q., Ribeiro-Navarrete, S., & Botella-Carrubi, D. (2024). A matter of motivation: The impact of enterprise digital transformation on green innovation. *Review of Managerial Science*, 18(5), 1489–1518. DOI: 10.1007/s11846-023-00665-6

He, Y., Zhao, X., & Zheng, H. (2023). How does the environmental protection tax law affect firm ESG? Evidence from the Chinese stock markets. *Energy Economics*, 127, 107067. DOI: 10.1016/j.eneco.2023.107067

Hill, D. C., & Seabrook, K. A. (2013). Safety& Sustainability: Understanding the Business Value. *Professional Safety*, 58(06), 81–92.

Hillman, A. J., & Keim, G. D. (2001). Shareholder value, stakeholder management, and social issues: What's the bottom line? *Strategic Management Journal*, 22(2), 125–139. DOI: 10.1002/1097-0266(200101)22:2<125::AID-SMJ150>3.0.CO;2-H

Hilson, G., & Maconachie, R. (2017). Formalizing Artisanal and Small-Scale Mining: Insights, Contestations and Clarifications. *Area*, 49(4), 443–451. DOI: 10.1111/area.12328

Hoang, T. D., Ky, N. M., Thuong, N. T. N., Nhan, H. Q., & Ngan, N. V. C. (2022). Artificial intelligence in pollution control and management: Status and future prospects. In Ong, H. L., Doong, R., Naguib, R., Lim, C. P., & Nagar, A. K. (Eds.), *Artificial intelligence and environmental sustainability: Challenges and solutions in the era of Industry 4.0* (23–43). Springer., DOI: 10.1007/978-981-19-1434-8_2

Hodge, K., Subramaniam, N., & Stewart, J. (2009). *Assurance of sustainability reports: Impact on report users' confidence and perceptions of information credibility.*

Hodge, F. (2001). Hyperlinking unaudited information to audited financial statements: Effects on investor judgments. *The Accounting Review*, 76(4), 675–691. DOI: 10.2308/accr.2001.76.4.675

Hong, Z., & Xiao, K. (2024). Digital economy structuring for sustainable development: The role of blockchain and artificial intelligence in improving supply chain and reducing negative environmental impacts. *Scientific Reports*, 14(1), 3912. Advance online publication. DOI: 10.1038/s41598-024-53760-3 PMID: 38365912

Hooker, J., & Kim, T. W. (2019). Ethical Implications of the Fourth Industrial Revolution for Business and Society. *Business & Society*, •••, 360.

Hossain, M. I., Ong, T. S., Teh, B. H., Said, R. M., & Siow, M. L. (2022). Nexus of Stakeholder Integration, Green Investment, Green Technology Adoption and Environmental Sustainability Practices: Evidence from Bangladesh Textile SMEs. *Pertanika Journal of Social Science & Humanities*, 30(1). Advance online publication. DOI: 10.47836/pjssh.30.1.14

Hu, W. (2024). Exploration of music teaching reform program in colleges and universities oriented on the development of corporate culture industry. *International Journal of Science and Engineering Applications*. DOI: 10.7753/IJSEA1305.1003

Huang, P. B., Yang, C.-C., Inderawati, M. M. W., & Sukwadi, R. (2022). Using modified delphi study to develop instrument for ESG implementation: A case study at an indonesian higher education institution. *Sustainability (Basel)*, 14(19), 12623. DOI: 10.3390/su141912623

Huang, R., & Kisgen, D. J. (2019). Corporate governance, managerial ownership, and the impact of institutional investors on ESG ratings. *Journal of Financial Intermediation*, 40, 36–57.

Huda, M., & Santoso, L. (2022). Implementation of Corporate Waqf Core Principles in the Development of Waqf in Indonesia. *Academic Journal of Interdisciplinary Studies*, 11(5), 114–124. DOI: 10.36941/ajis-2022-0129

Hummel, C., & Schilck, C. (2016). The Relationship between Sustainability Performance and Sustainability Disclosure-Reconciling Voluntary Disclosure Theory and Legitimacy. *Theory.Journal of Accounting and Public Policy*, 35(5), 455–476. DOI: 10.1016/j.jaccpubpol.2016.06.001

Hummel, K., Schlick, C., & Fifka, M. (2019). The role of sustainability performance and accounting assurors in sustainability assurance engagements. *Journal of Business Ethics*, 154(3), 733–757. DOI: 10.1007/s10551-016-3410-5

Humphrey, C., O'Dwyer, B., & Unerman, J. (2017). Re-theorizing the configuration of organizational fields: The IIRC and the pursuit of 'Enlightened' corporate reporting. *Accounting and Business Research*, 47(1), 30–63. DOI: 10.1080/00014788.2016.1198683

Hussey, R., Guilliford, J., & Lymer, A. (1998). *Corporate communications: Financial reporting on the Internet*. Deloitte and Touche.

Hutton, E., Goldstein, J., & Piemonte, M. (2013). The adoption of XBRL reporting: Implications for industry and education. *The BRC Academy Journal of Education*, 3(1), 49–68.

Iatridis, K., & Kesidou, E. (2018). What drives substantive versus symbolic implementation of ISO 14001 in a time of economic crisis? Insights from Greek manufacturing companies. *Journal of Business Ethics*, 148(4), 859–877.

Ibrahim, I., & Al-Chaderchi, B. (2023). *Exploring sustainable approaches at Dubai Expo 2020: A blend of biophilic and biomimicry designs*. 10.22320/07190700.2023.13.02.02.

IFAC. (2023). *International Standards on Assurance Engagements (ISAE) 3000: Assurance on Non-Financial Information*. IFAC Official Website.

Ijaz, A., Siddiqui, S. H., & Rasheed, R. (2020). SDGs implementation and future recommendations: A case of banking sector in Pakistan. *Pakistan Journal of Social Sciences*, 40(4), 1687–1699.

Indrasari, M., Syamsudin, N., & Tampubolon, L. R. R. U. (2024). Enhancing SME product brand equity in the digital age as strategic approaches in the era of artificial intelligence. *International Journal of Business, Law, and Education*, 5(1), 1139–1152. DOI: 10.56442/ijble.v5i1.512

Institute of Internal Auditors. (2022). *Internal audit's role in integrated reporting assurance*. Institute of Internal Auditors.

International Auditing and Assurance Standards Board (IAASB). (2013). ISAE 3000 (revised), assurance engagements other than audits or reviews of historical financial information. *International Auditing and Assurance Standards Board*. www.iaasb.org/publications-resources/international-standard-assurance-engagements-isae-3000-revised-2

Investor Relations Society. (1998, 2004). *Annual reports and the Internet*. London: Investor Relations Society.

Ioannou, I., & Serafeim, G. (2021). Corporate sustainability: A strategy? *California Management Review*, 64(1), 1–23.

Iqbal, R., Shahzad, K., & Chaudhary, R. (2023). Green human resource management practices as a strategic choice for enhancing employees' environmental outcomes: An affective events theory perspective. *International Journal of Manpower*.

Isack, M., & Aschauer, E. (2024). The Role of CSR Report Assurance and ESG Rating in Bank Manager's Judgement on ESG Lending Decisions. *International Journal of Auditing*. Advance online publication. DOI: 10.1111/ijau.12369

Ismail, T. H., & Sobhy, N. M. (2009). Determinants of auditors' perceptions of the work needed in the audit of Internet-based financial reports in Egypt. *The Journal of Applied Accounting Research*, 10(2), 132–150. DOI: 10.1108/09675420910984691

Jaafar, A. Z., & Brightman, M. (2022). From Structure to Purpose: Green and Social Narratives, and the Shifting Morality of Islamic Finance in Kuala Lumpur. *Sustainability (Basel)*, 14(9), 5433. Advance online publication. DOI: 10.3390/su14095433

Jabeur, S. B., Ballouk, H., Mefteh-Wali, S., & Omri, A. (2022). Forecasting the macrolevel determinants of entrepreneurial opportunities using artificial intelligence models. *Technological Forecasting and Social Change*, 175. *Article*, 121353, 121353. DOI: 10.1016/j.techfore.2021

Jablonka, E. (2003). *Mathematical literacy.*

Jafaru, J., & Francis, O. A. (2016). Voluntary Internet financial reporting (IFR) in the Nigerian public sector. *Journal of Accountancy*, 2.

Jagatheesaperumal, S. K., Rahouti, M., Ahmad, K., Al-Fuqaha, A., & Guizani, M. (2021). The duo of artificial intelligence and big data for industry 4.0: Applications, techniques, challenges, and future research directions. *IEEE Internet of Things Journal*, 9(15), 12861–12885. DOI: 10.1109/JIOT.2021.3139827

Jain, S. K. (2013). *Corporate Internet financial reporting in international perspective: A comparative study of selected Indian and US companies* [Unpublished Ph.D. dissertation]. Dayalbagh Educational Institute, Agra, India.

Jaya, A. K., & Verawaty, V. (2015). The accessibility determinants of Internet financial reporting of Manufacture Company listed in Indonesia Stock Exchange. *Asian Economic and Financial Review*, 5(2), 229–238. DOI: 10.18488/journal.aefr/2015.5.2/102.2.229.238

Jeanine, K.-K., Benedikt, M., Nevena, S., & Nannan, X., lHarald, K., & Juho, H. (2024). Challenges In The Adoption Of Sustainability Information Systems: A Study On Green IS In Organizations. *International Journal of Information Management*, 1027–1054.

Jeffrey, R., Cohen, J., & Simnett, R. (2015). CSR and Assurance Services: A Research Agenda. *Auditing*, 59–74.

Jeriji, M., & Nasfi, A. (2023). The value relevance of mandatory sustainability reporting assurance. *South African Journal of Accounting Research, 37*(2), 122-138.

Jia, F., Yin, S., Chen, L., & Chen, X. (2020). The circular economy in the textile and apparel industry: A systematic literature review. *Journal of Cleaner Production*, 259, 120728. DOI: 10.1016/j.jclepro.2020.120728

Jiang, M. (2024). The role of experiential learning in transforming music appreciation education and pedagogical practices. *Pacific International Journal*, 7(5), 157–162. DOI: 10.55014/pij.v7i5.715

Jiraporn, P., Jiraporn, N., Boeprasert, A., & Chang, K. (2018). Does corporate social responsibility (CSR) improve credit ratings? Evidence from geographic identification. *Journal of Banking & Finance*, 79, 115–135.

John, R. Gold & Margaret M. Gold. (2013). *"Bring It under the Legacy Umbrella": Olympic Host Cities and the Changing Fortunes of the Sustainability Agenda.* https://www.mdpi.com/2071-1050/5/8/3526

Jones, S., & Tremblay, M.-S. (2024). *Greenwashing and sustainability assurance: A review and call for future research.*

Jones, K., Alabaster, T., & Hetherington, K. (1999). Internet-based environmental reporting: Current trends. *Greener Management International*, 26, 69–90.

Jones, M. J., & Xiao, J. Z. (2003). Current trends and the trends by 2010 in Internet reporting. *Accounting Forum*, 27(2), 132–165. DOI: 10.1111/1467-6303.00099

Jones, M. J., & Xiao, J. Z. (2004). Financial reporting on the Internet by 2010: A consensus view. *Accounting Forum*, 28(3), 237–263. DOI: 10.1016/j.accfor.2004.07.002

Joseph, J. (2020). Exploring the Agency-Structure Dynamics in State–Society Relations in Contemporary China: The Case of Securitization of the Environmental Sector. *China Report (New Delhi, India)*, 56(2), 182–203. DOI: 10.1177/0009445520916873

Joshi, L. P., & Al-Modhahki, J. (2003). Financial reporting on the Internet: Empirical evidence from Bahrain and Kuwait. *Asian Review of Accounting*, 11(1), 88–101. DOI: 10.1108/eb060764

Junior, R. M., Best, P. J., & Cotter, J. (2014). Sustainability reporting and assurance: A historical analysis on a world-wide phenomenon. *Journal of Business Ethics*, 120(1), 1–11. DOI: 10.1007/s10551-013-1637-y

Kagan, S., & Kirchberg, V. (2016). Music and sustainability: Organizational cultures towards creative resilience – a review. *Journal of Cleaner Production*, 135, 1487–1502. DOI: 10.1016/j.jclepro.2016.05.044

Kahkonen, A.-K. (2014). Conducting a case study in supply management. *Operations and Supply Chain Management: An International Journal*, 4(1), 31–41. DOI: 10.31387/oscm090054

Kallia, M., van Borkulo, S. P., Drijvers, P., Barendsen, E., & Tolboom, J. (2021). Characterising computational thinking in mathematics education: A literature-informed Delphi study. *Research in Mathematics Education*, 23(2), 159–187. DOI: 10.1080/14794802.2020.1852104

Kalyar, M. N., Ali, F., & Shafique, I. (2021). Green mindfulness and green creativity nexus in hospitality industry: Examining the effects of green process engagement and CSR. *International Journal of Contemporary Hospitality Management*, 33(8), 2653–2675. DOI: 10.1108/IJCHM-09-2020-1079

Kanani, H. (2019). Monitoring Sustainability Applications In The Planning Of International Expo Exhibitions (Case Study Expo Milan 2015). *Journal of Al-Azhar University Engineering Sector*, 14(50), 409–421. DOI: 10.21608/auej.2019.28495

Kaptein, M. (2011). Developing and testing a measure for the ethical culture of organizations: The Ethical Culture Index. *Journal of Business Ethics*, 617–634.

Karaali, G. (2023). Artificial intelligence, basic skills, and quantitative literacy. *Numeracy*, 16(1), 9. DOI: 10.5038/1936-4660.16.1.1438

Karaman, A. S., Orazalin, N., Uyar, A., & Shahbaz, M. (2021). CSR achievement, reporting, and assurance in the energy sector: Does economic development matter? *Energy Policy*, 149, 112007. DOI: 10.1016/j.enpol.2020.112007

Kateryna, A., Oleksandr, R., Mariia, T., Iryna, S., Evgen, K., & Anastasiia, L. (2020). Digital literacy development trends in the professional environment. *International Journal of Learning, Teaching and Educational Research, 19*(7), Article 7.

Kaur, A., & Lodhia, S. K. (2014). The state of disclosures on stakeholder engagement in sustainability reporting in Australian local councils. *Pacific Accounting Review*, 26(1/2), 54–74. DOI: 10.1108/PAR-07-2013-0064

Kaur, K., & Singh, K. (2019). Corporate disclosure through web: An empirical study to examine the potential benefits of corporate disclosure through web. *Journal of Commerce & Accounting Research*, 8(3), 64–74.

Kay, I., Brindisi, C., & Martin, B. (2020). *The stakeholder model and ESG*. Pay Governance LLC.

Kaya, H. D., & Tuncer, G. (2021). Sustainability reporting practices of global companies: Trends and challenges. *Sustainable Development*, 29(4), 664–680. DOI: 10.1002/sd.2174

Kazeem, K. O., Olawumi, T. O., & Osunsanmi, T. (2023). Roles of artificial intelligence and machine learning in enhancing construction processes and sustainable communities. *Buildings (Basel, Switzerland)*, 13(8), 2061. Advance online publication. DOI: 10.3390/buildings13082061

Keeley, A. R., Chapman, A. J., Yoshida, K., Xie, J., Imbulana, J., Takeda, S., & Managi, S. (2022). ESG metrics and social equity: Investigating commensurability. *Frontiers in Sustainability*, 3, 920955. DOI: 10.3389/frsus.2022.920955

Keliwon, K. B., Shukor, Z. A., & Hassan, M. S. (2018). Internet financial reporting (IFR) disclosure position and firm value. *Asian Journal of Accounting and Governance*, 9, 111–122. DOI: 10.17576/AJAG-2018-09-10

Keliwon, K. B., Shukor, Z. A., Mohamed, Z. M., & Hassan, M. S. (2014). Exploring Internet financial reporting (IFR) strategies of firms in Malaysia. [MAR]. *Management Accounting Research*, 13(2), 1–21.

Kellison, T. B., & McCullough, B. P. (2017). A pragmatic perspective on the future of sustainability in sport. In McCullough, B. P., & Kellison, T. B. (Eds.), *Routledge Handbook of Sport and the Environment* (1st ed., 445–455). Routledge., DOI: 10.4324/9781315619514-34

Kelton, S. A. (2006). *Internet financial reporting: The effect of hyperlinks and irrelevant information on investor judgments* [Ph.D. thesis, Stokely Management Center].

Kelton, S. A. (2007). *Internet financial reporting: The effect of hyperlinks and irrelevant information on investor judgments*. AAA-IS Midyear Meeting.

Kelton, S. A., & Yang, Y. (2008). The impact of corporate governance on Internet financial reporting. *Journal of Accounting and Public Policy*, 27(1), 62–87. DOI: 10.1016/j.jaccpubpol.2007.11.001

Kennedy, H., & Hill, R. L. (2018). The feeling of numbers: Emotions in everyday engagements with data and their visualisation. *Sociology*, 52(4), 830–848. DOI: 10.1177/0038038516674675

Khairy, H. A., Agina, M. F., Aliane, N., & Hashad, M. E. (2023). Internal Branding in Hotels: Interaction Effects of Employee Engagement, Workplace Friendship, and Organizational Citizenship Behavior. *Sustainability (Basel)*, 15(5), 4530. DOI: 10.3390/su15054530

Khairy, H. A., Elzek, Y., Aliane, N., & Agina, M. F. (2023). Perceived Environmental Corporate Social Responsibility Effect on Green Perceived Value and Green Attitude in Hospitality and Tourism Industry: The Mediating Role of Environmental Well-Being. *Sustainability (Basel)*, 15(6), 4746. DOI: 10.3390/su15064746

Khamdamov, A., Tang, Z., & Hussain, M. A. (2023). Unpacking Parallel Mediation Processes between Green HRM Practices and Sustainable Environmental Performance: Evidence from Uzbekistan. *Sustainability (Basel)*, 15(2), 1434. DOI: 10.3390/su15021434

Khamis, N. I., & Wan Ismail, W. K. (2021). The impact of corporate social responsibility on corporate image in the construction industry: A case of SMEs in Egypt. *Journal of Sustainable Finance & Investment*, 12(1), 128–146. DOI: 10.1080/20430795.2021.1930992

Khan, M. A. H., Muzaffar, A. T., & Mahmood, S. A. (2006). *The use of Internet for corporate reporting: A discussion of the issues and surveys of current usage in Bangladesh* [Working Paper].

Khan, M. A. H., Muzaffar, A. T., & Nazmul, A. K. (2008). *Corporate financial reporting on the Internet: Global developments and an appraisal of practices in Bangladesh* [Working Paper]. American International University, Bangladesh.

Khan, M. N. A. A. (2010). *Pelaporan kewangan menerusi Internet: Indeks, tahap pelaporan dan faktor penentunya.* [Unpublished Ph.D. dissertation]. Universiti Utara Malaysia, Sintok, Kedah.

Khan, M. N. A. A., & Siang, L. H. (2013). Public investor perception towards Internet financial reporting in Malaysia. *Journal of Integrated Knowledge*, 60–68.

Khan, H. Z., Bose, S., Mollik, A. T., & Harun, H. (2021). "Green washing" or "authentic effort"? An empirical investigation of the quality of sustainability reporting by banks. *Accounting, Auditing & Accountability Journal*, 34(2), 338–369. https://doi.org/10.1108/AAAJ-01-2018-3330

Khan, M. N. A. A., & Ismail, N. A. (2011). The level of Internet financial reporting of Malaysian companies. *Asian Journal of Accounting and Governance*, 2(1), 27–39. DOI: 10.17576/ajag-2011-2-6539

Khan, M. N. A. A., & Ismail, N. A. (2014). An empirical investigation of preparers' and users' views on Internet financial reporting disclosure items in Malaysia. *Sains Humanika*, 2(3), 23–34.

Khan, M. N. A. A., & Omar, N. A. B. (2013). A study of important items of Internet financial reporting: A case of Malaysian auditors. *Middle East Journal of Scientific Research*, 18(3), 340–351.

Khan, M., Serafeim, G., & Yoon, A. (2016). Corporate sustainability: First evidence on materiality. *The Accounting Review*, 91(6), 1697–1724. DOI: 10.2308/accr-51383

Khasreen, M. M., Banfill, P. F. G., & Menzies, G. F. (2009). Life-cycle assessment and the environmental impact of buildings: A review. *Sustainability (Basel)*, 1(3), 674–701. DOI: 10.3390/su1030674

Khatib Khatri, I., & Kjærland, F. (2023). Sustainability reporting practices and environmental performance amongst nordic listed firms. *Journal of Cleaner Production*, 418, 138172. DOI: 10.1016/j.jclepro.2023.138172

Khatib, S. F., & Nour, A. (2021). The impact of corporate governance on firm performance during the COVID-19 pandemic: Evidence from Malaysia. *Journal of Asian Finance, Economics and Business, 8*(2), 0943-0952.

Khatib, S. F. A. (2024). Sustainability Assurance and Corporate Environmental Accountability. *Social and Environmental Accountability Journal*, 44(2), 176–177. DOI: 10.1080/0969160X.2024.2336721

Khatib, S. F. A., Ismail, I. H. M., Salameh, N., Abbas, A. F., Bazhair, A. H., & Sulimany, H. G. H. (2023). Carbon emission and firm performance: The moderating role of management environmental training. *Sustainability (Basel)*, 15(13), 10485. DOI: 10.3390/su151310485

Kiani, M. S., & Nazari, L. (2021). *Sustainable Development and Environmental Protection at International Sporting Events*. 10.22034/JHI.2021.291241.1027. https://www.researchgate.net/publication/356290160_Sustainable_Development_and_Environmental_Protection_at_International_Sporting_Events

Kitamura, Y., Karkour, S., Ichisugi, Y., & Itsubo, N. (2020). Carbon footprint evaluation of the business event sector in japan. *Sustainability (Basel)*, 12(12), 5001. DOI: 10.3390/su12125001

Kitchen, J. (2020). A stakeholder theory perspective on business models: value creation for sustainability: Freudenreich, B., Lüdeke-Freund, F. and Schaltegger, S. (2019). *Journal of Business Ethics*. In press: DOI: . *Social and Environmental Accountability Journal*, 40(1), 98.DOI: 10.1007/s10551-019-04112-z

Klibi, E., Damak, S., & Elwafi, O. (2024). The impact of sustainability assurance levels on market capitalization: The case of French firms. *Journal of Financial Reporting and Accounting*. https://www.emerald.com/insight/content/doi/10.1108/jfra-03-2024-0162/full/html

Knechel, W. R., & Salterio, S. E. (2022). *Auditing: Assurance and Risk*. Routledge.

Kock, N. (2017). WarpPLS user manual: Version 6.0. *ScriptWarp Systems: Laredo, TX, USA, 141*, 47-60.

Kolk, A. (2008). Sustainability, Accountability, and Corporate Governance: Exploring Multinationals' Reporting Practices. *Business Strategy and the Environment*, 17(1), 1–15. DOI: 10.1002/bse.511

Könecke, T., Schunk, H., Schappel, T., Hugaerts, I., Wagner, F., & Malchrowicz-Mośko, E. (2021). *German Marathon Runners' Opinions on and Willingness to Pay for Environmental Sustainability*. https://www.mdpi.com/2071-1050/13/18/10337

Koreto, R. (1997). When the bottom line is online. *Journal of Accountancy*, 63–65.

Kotsantonis, S., Pinney, C., & Serafeim, G. (2016). ESG integration in investment management: Myths and realities. *The Bank of America Journal of Applied Corporate Finance*, 28(2), 10–16. DOI: 10.1111/jacf.12169

Kotsantonis, S., & Serafeim, G. (2019). Four things no one will tell you about ESG data. *The Bank of America Journal of Applied Corporate Finance*, 31(2), 50–58. DOI: 10.1111/jacf.12346

Kouloukoui, D., Sant'Anna, Â. M. O., Gomes, S. M. d. S., Marinho, M. M. d. O., de Jong, P., Kiperstok, A., & Torres, E. A. (2019). *Factors influencing the level of environmental disclosures in sustainability reports: Case of climate risk disclosure by Brazilian companies.*

KPMG. (2005). *KPMG international survey of corporate responsibility reporting 2005.*

KPMG. (2008). *KPMG international survey of corporate responsibility reporting 2008.*

KPMG. (2011). *KPMG international survey of corporate responsibility reporting 2011.*

KPMG. (2013). *The KPMG survey of corporate responsibility reporting 2013.*

KPMG. (2015). *The KPMG survey of corporate responsibility reporting 2015.*

KPMG. (2017). *The road ahead: The KPMG survey of corporate responsibility reporting 2017*.

KPMG. (2020). The time has come the KPMG survey of sustainability reporting 2020. *KPMG's Global Center of Excellence for Climate Change and Sustainability*. https://assets.kpmg/content/dam/kpmg/xx/pdf/2020/11/the-time-has-come.pdf

KPMG. (2022). Sustainability Report Big shifts, small steps. *KPMG's Global Center of Excellence for Climate Change and Sustainability*.https://assets.kpmg.com/content/dam/kpmg/xx/pdf/2023/04/big-shifts-small-steps.pdf

KPMG. (2023). *Guía práctica de ESG: Medio ambiente, sociedad y gobernanza*. https://assets.kpmg.com/content/dam/kpmg/co/sac/pdf/2023/03/bc-ESG-esp.pdf

KPMG. (2024). *European Commission FAQs: CSRD & ESRS*. KPMG.

Kraus, S., Rehman, S. U., & García, F. J. S. (2020). Corporate social responsibility and environmental performance: The mediating role of environmental strategy and green innovation. *Technological Forecasting and Social Change*, 160, 120262. DOI: 10.1016/j.techfore.2020.120262

Krippendorff, K. (2018). *Content analysis: An introduction to its methodology*. Sage publications.

Kukalová, G., Ibragimova, R., Fayzullayev, D., Narmanov, O., & Nazarova, L. (2024). Axiological approach in ESG education. *E3S Web of Conferences, 538*, 05005. DOI: 10.1051/e3sconf/202453805005

Kulkarni, A. V., Joseph, S., & Patil, K. (2023). *Role of artificial intelligence in sustainability reporting by leveraging ESG theory into action*. https://www.researchgate.net/publication/371434141

Kunnaala, V., Rasi, M., & Storgård, J. (2013). *Corporate social responsibility and shipping views of Baltic Sea shipping companies on the benefits of responsibility*.

Kuzmina, J., Maditinos, D., Norena-Chavez, D., Grima, S., & Kadłubek, M. (2023). ESG integration as a risk management tool within the financial decision-making process. In *Contemporary Studies in Economic and Financial Analysis* (pp. 105–113). DOI: 10.1108/S1569-37592023000111A007

La Torre, M., Mango, F., Cafaro, A., & Leo, S. (2020). Does the ESG index affect stock return? Evidence from the Eurostoxx50. *Sustainability (Basel)*, 12(16), 6387. DOI: 10.3390/su12166387

Lamani, D., & Cepani, L. (2011). Internet financial reporting by banks and insurance companies in Albania. *The Romanian Economic Journal*, 42, 159–174.

Lambini, C. K., Goeschl, A., Wäsch, M., & Wittau, M. (2021). Achieving the sustainable development goals through company staff vocational training—The case of the federal institute for vocational education and training (BIBB) INEBB project. *Education Sciences*, 11(4), 179. DOI: 10.3390/educsci11040179

Larrinaga, C., Rossi, A., Luque-Vilchez, M., & Núñez-Nickel, M. (2020). Institutionalization of the contents of sustainability assurance services: A comparison between Italy and United States. *Journal of Business Ethics*, 163, 67–83.

Latif, B., Ong, T. S., Meero, A., Abdul Rahman, A. A., & Ali, M. (2022). Employee-Perceived Corporate Social Responsibility (CSR) and Employee Pro-Environmental Behavior (PEB): The Moderating Role of CSR Skepticism and CSR Authenticity. *Sustainability (Basel)*, 14(3), 1380. DOI: 10.3390/su14031380

Lau, A. K. W., Lee, P. K. C., & Cheng, T. C. E. (2024). The relationships between ethical codes of conduct, ethical supplier risks, and financial performance: A buyer-supplier perspective. *Production Planning and Control*, •••, 1–20. DOI: 10.1080/09537287.2024.2359547

Laufer, W. (2003). Social Accountability and Corporate Greenwashing. *Jouranl of Business Ethics*, 253-261.

Leal, G. d. S. S., Guédria, W., & Panetto, H. (2019). *Interoperability assessment: A systematic literature review.*

Lee, C. K., & Han, H.-J. (2008). *Analysis of skills requirement for entry-level programmer/analysts in fortune 500 corporations.*

Lee, J. J. (2022). *Engaging employees through ESG Lee Janice Report v1.*

Lee, C. C., & Brahmasrene, T. (2020). Emerging trends in integrating artificial intelligence into sustainability reporting. *Environmental Research Letters*, 15(2), 024011. DOI: 10.1088/1748-9326/ab719f

Lee, S. P., & Isa, M. M. (2020). Environmental, Social and Governance (ESG) Practices and Performance in Shariah Firms: Agency or Stakeholder Theory? *Asian Academy of Management Journal of Accounting and Finance*, 16(1), 1–34. DOI: 10.21315/aamjaf2020.16.1.1

Lemma, T. T., Negash, M., Lulseged, A., & Maroun, W. (2024). Sustainability assurance and corporate environmental accountability. *Business Strategy and the Environment*, 33(4), 3167–3183. DOI: 10.1002/bse.3643

Lenton, T.M., Benson, S., Smith, T., Ewer, T., Lanel, V., Petykowski, E., Powell, T., Abrams, J.F., Blomsma, F., & Sharpe, S. (2022). Operationalising positive tipping points towards global sustainability. *Global Sustainability*, 5.

Lenzen, M., Sun, Y.-Y., Faturay, F., Ting, Y.-P., Geschke, A., & Malik, A. (2018). The carbon footprint of global tourism. *Nature Climate Change*, 8(6), 522–528. DOI: 10.1038/s41558-018-0141-x

Leonidou, C. N., & Skarmeas, D. (2017). Gray Shades of Green: Causes and Consequences of Green Skepticism. *Journal of Business Ethics*, 144(2), 401–415. DOI: 10.1007/s10551-015-2829-4

Lepore, M. (2024). A holistic framework to model students' cognitive processes in mathematics education through fuzzy cognitive maps. *Heliyon*, 10(16). Advance online publication. DOI: 10.1016/j.heliyon.2024.e35863

Le, T. T., Tran, P. Q., Lam, N. P., Tra, M. N. L., & Uyen, P. H. P. (2024). Corporate social responsibility, green innovation, environment strategy and corporate sustainable development. *Operations Management Research : Advancing Practice Through Research*, 17(1), 114–134. DOI: 10.1007/s12063-023-00411-x

Li, L. (2021). *Contesting Sustainability of Mega-Events in Chinese Metropolises: A Narrative and Practise Review*. https://ouci.dntb.gov.ua/en/works/73gEZLQ7/

Liang, H., & Renneboog, L. (2017). On the foundations of corporate social responsibility. *The Journal of Finance*, 72(2), 853–910. DOI: 10.1111/jofi.12487

Li, L., Saat, M. M., Khatib, S. F. A., Chu, P., & Sulimany, H. G. H. (2024). Navigating the impact: A comprehensive analysis of ESG disclosure consequences through systematic review. *Business Strategy & Development*, 7(2), e382. DOI: 10.1002/bsd2.382

Lilhore, U. K., Poongodi, M., Kaur, A., Simaiya, S., Algarni, A. D., Elmannai, H., & Hamdi, M. (2022). Hybrid model for detection of cervical cancer using causal analysis and machine learning techniques. *Computational and Mathematical Methods in Medicine*, 2022(1), 4688327. DOI: 10.1155/2022/4688327

Lin, Y.-H. (2023). Determinants of Green Purchase Intention: The Roles of Green Enjoyment, Green Intrinsic Motivation, and Green Brand Love. *Sustainability (Basel)*, 15(1), 132. DOI: 10.3390/su15010132

Liou, J. J. H., Liu, P. Y. L., & Huang, S.-W. (2023). Exploring the key barriers to ESG adoption in enterprises. *Systems and Soft Computing*, 5, 200066. DOI: 10.1016/j.sasc.2023.200066

Liu, F. H. M., & Lai, K. P. Y. (2021). Ecologies of green finance: Green sukuk and development of green Islamic finance in Malaysia. *Environment & Planning A*, 53(8), 1896–1914. DOI: 10.1177/0308518X211038349

Liu, J., & Liu, J. (2023). The greater the incentives, the better the effect? Interactive moderating effects on the relationship between green motivation and green creativity. *International Journal of Contemporary Hospitality Management*, 35(3), 919–932. DOI: 10.1108/IJCHM-03-2022-0340

Liu, M., Ling, Y., & Lee, C. (2024). Does ESG performance and investor attention affect stock volatility? An empirical study based on panel data and mixed-frequency data. *Applied Economics*, 1–15. Advance online publication. DOI: 10.1080/00036846.2024.2423068

Liu, Z., Jubb, C., & Abhayawansa, S. (2024). Choice of financial audit firm and ESG assurance firm: The role of board of director characteristics. *The British Accounting Review*, 101505, 101505. Advance online publication. DOI: 10.1016/j.bar.2024.101505

Li, W., Bhutto, M. Y., Waris, I., & Hu, T. (2023). The Nexus between Environmental Corporate Social Responsibility, Green Intellectual Capital and Green Innovation towards Business Sustainability: An Empirical Analysis of Chinese Automobile Manufacturing Firms. *International Journal of Environmental Research and Public Health*, 20(3), 1851. DOI: 10.3390/ijerph20031851 PMID: 36767217

Li, W., Bhutto, T. A., Xuhui, W., Maitlo, Q., Zafar, A. U., & Ahmed Bhutto, N. (2020). Unlocking employees' green creativity: The effects of green transformational leadership, green intrinsic, and extrinsic motivation. *Journal of Cleaner Production*, 255, 120229. DOI: 10.1016/j.jclepro.2020.120229

Li, W., & Zhang, R. (2019). Corporate social responsibility, institutional investors, and firm value: Evidence from China. *Sustainability*, 11(12), 1–19.

Li, Y. (2024). The impact of music education on the quality of talent cultivation. *Transactions on Comparative Education*, 6(1). Advance online publication. DOI: 10.23977/trance.2024.060110

Li, Z., Deng, X., & Peng, L. (2020). Uncovering trajectories and impact factors of CO2 emissions: A sectoral and spatially disaggregated revisit in Beijing. *Technological Forecasting and Social Change*, 158, 120124. DOI: 10.1016/j.techfore.2020.120124

Lock, I., & Seele, P. (2016). Deliberative Lobbying? Toward a Noncontradiction of Corporate Political Activities and Corporate Social Responsibility? *Journal of Management Inquiry*, 25(4), 415–430. DOI: 10.1177/1056492616640379

Loconto, A. M. (2017). Models of assurance: Diversity and standardization of modes of intermediation. *The Annals of the American Academy of Political and Social Science*, 670(1), 112–132. DOI: 10.1177/0002716217692517

Lodhia, S. (2005). *Corporate perceptions of web-based environmental communication: An exploratory study into companies in the Australian mineral industry* [Working Paper Series]. ANU School of Business and Information Management, Canberra, Australia.

Lodhia, S., Allam, A., & Lymer, A. (2003). *Corporate reporting on the Internet in Australia: An exploratory study* [Discussion Paper]. School of Business and Information Management, Australian National University, Australia.

Lodhia, S., Kaur, A., & Kuruppu, S. C. (2022). The disclosure of sustainable development goals (SDGs) by the top 50 Australian companies: Substantive or symbolic legitimation? *Meditari Accountancy Research*, 31(6), 1578–1605.

Lopez-de-Silanes, F., McCahery, J. A., & Pudschedl, P. C. (2024). Institutional Investors and ESG Preferences. *Corporate Governance: An International Review*, n/a(n/a). DOI: 10.1111/corg.12583

Louwers, T. J., Pasewark, W. R., & Typpo, E. W. (1998). Silicon Valley meets Norwalk. *Journal of Accountancy*, 20–25.

Low, K. Y., & Boo, E. F. (2012). Do contrasting statements improve users' understanding of different assurance levels conveyed in assurance reports? *International Journal of Auditing*, 16(1), 19–34. DOI: 10.1111/j.1099-1123.2011.00439.x

Lozano, R. (2013). Are Companies Planning their Organisational Changes for Corporate Sustainability? An Analysis of Three Case Studies on Resistance to Change and their Strategies to Overcome it. *Corporate Social Responsibility and Environmental Management*, 20(5), 275–295. DOI: 10.1002/csr.1290

Lozano, R., Lukman, R., Lozano, F. J., Huisingh, D., & Lambrechts, W. (2013). Declarations for Sustainability in Higher Education: Becoming Better Leaders, through Addressing the University System. *Journal of Cleaner Production*, 48, 10–19. DOI: 10.1016/j.jclepro.2011.10.006

Lui, W. (2019). *The devil is in the details.*

Lui, T. K., & Zainuldin, M. H. (2024). From boardroom to sustainability reporting: stakeholder-RBV insights into ESG disclosures among Malaysian banks. *The Bottom Line (New York, N.Y.)*. Advance online publication. DOI: 10.1108/BL-04-2024-0046

Luo, Y., Wang, Y., Hong, C., He, P., & Zheng, X. (2023). The shattered "Iron Rice Bowl": Effects of Chinese state-owned enterprise reform on depressive symptoms in later life. *Social Psychiatry and Psychiatric Epidemiology*, 58(8), 1193–1200. DOI: 10.1007/s00127-023-02437-9 PMID: 36973356

Lymer, A. (1997). The use of the Internet for corporate reporting: A discussion of the issues and survey of current usage in the UK. *21st Annual Congress of the European Accounting Association*, Antwerp, Belgium.

Lymer, A., & Tallberg, A. (1997). Corporate reporting and the Internet: A survey and commentary on the use of the WWW in corporate reporting in the UK and Finland. *20th Annual Associates*, Graz, Austria.

Lyu, F., Zhang, Z., Fu, G., Liu, Z., & Treepongkaruna, S. (2024). Multiple shareholding institutional investors and green governance of heavy-polluting industries. *Business Strategy and the Environment*, 33(4), 3569–3587. DOI: 10.1002/bse.3667

Maas, K., Schaltegger, S., & Crutzen, N. (2016). Integrating corporate sustainability assessment, management accounting, control, and reporting. *Journal of Cleaner Production*, 136, 237–248. DOI: 10.1016/j.jclepro.2016.05.008

Maclean, K., Greenaway, A., & Grünbühel, C. M. (2022). Developing methods of knowledge co-production across varying contexts to shape Sustainability Science theory and practice. *Sustainability Science*, 17(2), 325–332. DOI: 10.1007/s11625-022-01103-4 PMID: 35194465

Mahdi Sahi, A., Mahdi Sahi, A., Abbas, A. F., & Khatib, FA, S. (2022). Financial reporting quality of financial institutions: Literature review. *Cogent Business & Management*, 9(1), 2135210. DOI: 10.1080/23311975.2022.2135210

Mahmoudian, F., Lu, J., Yu, D., Nazari, J. A., & Herremans, I. M. (2020). *Inter- and intra-organizational stakeholder arrangements in carbon management accounting.*

Mahran, K., & Elamer, A. A. (2024). Shaping ESG commitment through organizational psychological capital: The role of CEO power. *Business Strategy and the Environment*, n/a(n/a). DOI: 10.1002/bse.4007

Majeed, A. H., Abbas, A. F., Kadhim, K. G., & Kzar, M. F. (2024). Poverty reduction and the sustainable development goals: A bibliometric study focused on the Global South. *Development in Practice*, 1–25. DOI: 10.1080/09614524.2024.2428801

Makarenko, I., Sukhonos, V., Zhuravlyova, I., Legenchuk, S., & Szołno, O. (2020). Sustainability reporting assessment for quality and compliance: The case of Ukrainian banks' management reports. *Banks and Bank Systems*, 15(2), 117–129. DOI: 10.21511/bbs.15(2).2020.11

Malarvizhi, P., & Yadav, S. (2008). Corporate environment reporting on the Internet: An insight into Indian practice. *11th Annual Convention of the Strategic Management Forum*, Indian Institute of Technology, Kanpur, India.

Manetti, G., & Becatti, L. (2008). *Assurance services for sustainability reports: Standards and empirical evidence.*

Manetti, G., & Becatti, L. (2009). Assurance services for sustainability reports: Standards and empirical evidence. *Journal of Business Ethics*, 87(S1), 289–298. DOI: 10.1007/s10551-008-9809-x

Manetti, G., & Toccafondi, S. (2012). The role of stakeholders in sustainability reporting assurance. *Journal of Business Ethics*, 107(3), 363–377. DOI: 10.1007/s10551-011-1044-1

Manokaran, K. R., Ramakrishnan, S. A., Hishan, S. S., & Soehod, K. (2018). The Impact Of Corporate Social Responsibility On Financial Performance: Evidence from Insurance firms. *Management Science Letters*, 8, 913–932. DOI: 10.5267/j.msl.2018.6.016

Manokaran, K. R., Ramakrishnan, S., & Shanker, H. S. (2023). Sectoral Analysis of Malaysian Companies' CSR Initiatives for Organizational Risk Management. *International Journal of Academic Research in Business & Social Sciences*, 13(9). Advance online publication. DOI: 10.6007/IJARBSS/v13-i9/18583

Manteaw, B. O. (2008). When businesses go to school: Neoliberalism and education for sustainable development. *Journal of Education for Sustainable Development*, 2(2), 119–126. DOI: 10.1177/097340820800200209

Mariq, M. S. (2007). Financial reporting on the Internet by Saudi joint-stock companies: Impact on the audit profession. *JPS Accountants Directory*. http://www.jps-dir.org/Forum/forum-posts.asp?TID=4664

Maroun, W. (2019). Does external assurance contribute to higher quality integrated reports? *Journal of Accounting and Public Policy*, 38(4), 106670.

Maroun, W. (2020). A conceptual model for understanding corporate social responsibility assurance practice. *Journal of Business Ethics*, 161(1), 187–209. DOI: 10.1007/s10551-018-3909-z

Marquis, C., Toffel, M. W., & Zhou, Y. (2016). Scrutiny, norms, and selective disclosure: A global study of greenwashing. *Organization Science*, 27(2), 483–504. DOI: 10.1287/orsc.2015.1039

Marston, C. (1996). The organization of the investor relations function by the large UK quoted companies. *Omega*, 24(4), 477–488. DOI: 10.1016/0305-0483(96)00015-1

Marston, C. (2003). Financial reporting on the Internet by leading Japanese companies. *Corporate Communications*, 8(1), 23–24. DOI: 10.1108/13563280310458894

Marston, C., & Leow, C. Y. (1998). Financial reporting on the Internet by leading UK companies. *21st Annual Congress of European Accounting Association*, Antwerp, Belgium.

Marston, C., & Wu, W. (2001). Financial reporting on the Internet by leading Japanese companies. *Scottish Regional Conference of the British Accounting Association*, Aberdeen.

Martínez-Ferrero, J., & García-Sánchez, I. (2017). Coercive, normative and mimetic isomorphism as determinants of the voluntary assurance of sustainability reports. *International Business Review*, 26(1), 102–118.

Martínez-Ferrero, J., & García-Sánchez, I. M. (2018). The level of sustainability assurance: The effects of brand reputation and industry specialisation of assurance providers. *Journal of Business Ethics*, 150(4), 971–990. DOI: 10.1007/s10551-016-3159-x

Martínez-Ferrero, J., García-Sánchez, I.-M., & Ruiz-Barbadillo, E. (2018). The quality of sustainability assurance reports: The expertise and experience of assurance providers as determinants. *Business Strategy and the Environment*, 27(8), 1181–1196. DOI: 10.1002/bse.2061

Marx, B., & van Dyk, V. (2011). Sustainability reporting and assurance: An analysis of assurance practices in South Africa. *Meditari Accountancy Research*, 19(1/2), 39–55. DOI: 10.1108/10222521111178628

Mashayekhi, B., Asiaei, K., Rezaee, Z., Jahangard, A., Samavat, M., & Homayoun, S. (2024). The relative importance of ESG pillars: A two-step machine learning and analytical framework. *Sustainable Development*, 32(5), 5404–5420. DOI: 10.1002/sd.2979

Mathur, V. N., Price, A. D. F., & Austin, S. (2008). *Conceptualizing stakeholder engagement in the context of sustainability and its assessment.*

McCarthy, K. A., & Kuhlemeyer, G. A. (2024). Preparing analytics-enabled professionals in finance using a simultaneous team-teaching approach: A case study. *Journal of Statistics and Data Science Education : An Official Journal of the of the American Statistical Association*, 32(1), 98–107. DOI: 10.1080/26939169.2023.2197470

Meher, B. K., Hawaldar, I. T., Mohapatra, L., Spulbar, C., & Birau, R. (2020). The effects of environment, society, and governance scores on investment returns and stock market volatility. *International Journal of Energy Economics and Policy*, 10(4), 234–239. DOI: 10.32479/ijeep.9311

Menassa, E. (2010). Corporate social responsibility: An exploratory study of the quality and extent of social disclosures by Lebanese commercial banks. *Journal of applied accounting research*, *11*(1), 4-23.

Meng, Z., Bhatti, S. M., Naveed, R. T., Kanwal, S., & Adnan, M. (2024). Green sustainability in the hotel sector: The role of CSR, intrinsic green motivation, and personal environmental norms. *PLoS One*, 19(6), e0295850. DOI: 10.1371/journal.pone.0295850 PMID: 38935798

Mercer. (2019). *The ABC of ESG*. Canada: https://www.mercer.ca/content/ dam/mercer/attachments/north-america/canada/ca-2019-the-abc-of- esg-environmental-social-governance.pdf

Meseguer-Sánchez, V., Gálvez-Sánchez, F. J., López-Martínez, G., & Molina-Moreno, V. (2021). Corporate social responsibility and sustainability. A bibliometric analysis of their interrelations. *Sustainability (Basel)*, 13(4), 1636. DOI: 10.3390/su13041636

Michelon, G., Patten, D. M., & Romi, A. M. (2019). Creating legitimacy for sustainability assurance practices: Evidence from sustainability restatements. *European Accounting Review*, 28(2), 395–422.

Michelon, G., Pilonato, S., & Ricceri, F. (2015). CSR reporting practices and the quality of disclosure: An empirical analysis. *Critical Perspectives on Accounting*, 33, 59–78. DOI: 10.1016/j.cpa.2014.10.003

Miller, K. C., Fink, L., & Proctor, T. Y. (2017). Current trends and future expectations in external assurance for integrated corporate sustainability reporting. *J. Legal Ethical & Regul. Isses*, 20, 1.

Mio, C. (2010). Corporate social reporting in Italian multiutility companies: An empirical analysis. *Corporate Social Responsibility and Environmental Management*, 17(5), 247–271. DOI: 10.1002/csr.213

Mnif Sellami, Y., Dammak Ben Hlima, N., & Jarboui, A. (2019). An empirical investigation of determinants of sustainability report assurance in France. *Journal of Financial Reporting and Accounting*, 17(2), 320–342.

Mock, T. J., Strohm, C., & Swartz, K. M. (2007). An examination of worldwide assured sustainability reporting. *Australian Accounting Review*, 17(41), 67–77. DOI: 10.1111/j.1835-2561.2007.tb00455.x

Modise, P. (2024). *A collaborative journey towards the Sustainable Development Goal 7.*

Mol, A. P. J. (2010). Sustainability as global attractor: The greening of the 2008 Beijing Olympics. *Global Networks*, 10(4), 510–528. DOI: 10.1111/j.1471-0374.2010.00289.x

Molina-Collado, A., Santos-Vijande, M. L., Gómez-Rico, M., & Madera, J. M. (2022). Sustainability in hospitality and tourism: A review of key research topics from 1994 to 2020. *International Journal of Contemporary Hospitality Management*, 34(8), 3029–3064. DOI: 10.1108/IJCHM-10-2021-1305

Momany, M. T., & Pillai, R. (2013). Internet financial reporting in UAE: Analysis and implications. *Global Review of Accounting and Finance*, 4(2), 142–160.

Momany, T. M., & Al-Shorman, A. S. (2006). Web-based voluntary financial reporting of Jordanian companies. *International Review of Business Research Papers*, 2(2), 127–139.

Moodaley, W., & Telukdarie, A. (2023). Greenwashing, Sustainability Reporting, and Artificial Intelligence: A Systematic Literature Review. *Sustainability (Basel)*, 15(2), 1481–1502. DOI: 10.3390/su15021481

Mooij, S. (2017). *The ESG rating and ranking industry; Vice or virtue in the adoption of responsible investment?* https://dx.doi.org/10.2139/ssrn.2960869

Moon, P., Bayle, E., & Francois, A. (2022). *Assessing International Sport Federations' Sustainability Practices: Toward Integrating Sustainability in Their Main Sports Events.* https://www.researchgate.net/publication/357793917_Assessing_International_Sport_Federations'_Sustainability_Practices_Toward_Integrating_Sustainability_in_Their_Main_Sports_Events

Moratis, L., & Brandt, S. (2017). Corporate stakeholder responsiveness? Exploring the state and quality of GRIbased stakeholder engagement disclosure of European firms. *Corporate Social Responsibility and Environmental Management*, 24(4), 312–325. DOI: 10.1002/ csr.1408

Morioka, S. N., & de Carvalho, M. M. (2016). A Systematic Literature Review Towards A Conceptual Framework For Integrating Sustainability Performance Into Business. *Journal of Cleaner Production*, 136, 134–146. DOI: 10.1016/j.jclepro.2016.01.104

MSCI. (2010). MSCI Inc. to Acquire RiskMetrics Group, Inc. [Press release]. http://ir.msci.com/static-files/15e6a432-4c0a-424a-ae5c-e79490273e90

Mulligan, C., Morsfield, S., & Cheikosman, E. (2024). Blockchain for sustainability: A systematic literature review for policy impact. *Telecommunications Policy*, 48(102676). Advance online publication. DOI: 10.1016/j.telpol.2023.102676

Mumcu, H. Y. (2016). *Using Mathematics, Mathematical Applications, Mathematical Modelling, and Mathematical Literacy: A Theoretical Study.*

Musleh Al-Sartawi, A. (2016). Measuring the level of online financial disclosure in the Gulf Cooperation Council Countries. *Corporate Ownership & Control Journal*, 14(1), 547–558. DOI: 10.22495/cocv14i1c4art1

Myners, P. (1998). Improving performance reporting to the market. In Carey, A., & Sancto, J. (Eds.), *Performance measurement in the digital age: Adding value to corporate reporting* (27–31). The Institute of Chartered Accountants in England & Wales.

Nazir, O., & Islam, J. U. (2020). Effect of CSR activities on meaningfulness, compassion, and employee engagement: A sense-making theoretical approach. *International Journal of Hospitality Management*, 90, 102630. DOI: 10.1016/j.ijhm.2020.102630

Nestlé. (n.d.). *Approach to sustainability: Nature & environment.*

Nielsen, C. (2023). ESG reporting and metrics: From double materiality to key performance indicators. *Sustainability (Basel)*, 15(24), 16844. DOI: 10.3390/su152416844

Noor, A. I., & Mohamad, T. (2000). Financial reporting disclosure on the Internet by Malaysian public listed companies. *Akauntan Nasional*, 13(19), 28–33.

Nordberg, D. (1999). *Shareholder communication: The next wave.* Center for Business Performance, Institute of Chartered Accountants in England and Wales.

Novitasari, M., & Tarigan, Z. J. H. (2022). The Role of Green Innovation in the Effect of Corporate Social Responsibility on Firm Performance. *Economies, 10*(5), 117. https://www.mdpi.com/2227-7099/10/5/117

Nureen, N., Liu, D., Irfan, M., & Işik, C. (2023). Nexus between corporate social responsibility and firm performance: A green innovation and environmental sustainability paradigm. *Environmental Science and Pollution Research International*, 30(21), 59349–59365. DOI: 10.1007/s11356-023-26675-1 PMID: 37004616

Nurillayev, E. (2024). *Embedding ESG in finance education: The impact of ESG education within graduate finance programs on ESG-related problems. SSRN.* DOI: 10.1108/IJSHE-06-2024-0388

Nuseir, M., Basheer, M. F., & Aljumah, A. (2020). Antecedents of entrepreneurial intentions in smart city of Neom Saudi Arabia: Does the entrepreneurial education on artificial intelligence matter? *Cogent Business & Management*, 7(1). *Article*, 1825041, 1825041. DOI: 10.1080/23311975.2020

O'Dwyer, B. (2011). The case of sustainability assurance: Constructing a new assurance service. *Contemporary Accounting Research*, 28(4), 1230–1266. DOI: 10.1111/j.1911-3846.2011.01108.x

O'Dwyer, B., & Owen, D. L. (2005). Assurance statement practice in environmental, social and sustainability reporting: A critical evaluation. *The British Accounting Review*, 37(2), 205–229. DOI: 10.1016/j.bar.2005.01.005

O'Dwyer, B., Owen, D., & Unerman, J. (2011). Seeking legitimacy for new assurance forms: The case of assurance on sustainability reporting. *Accounting, Organizations and Society*, 36(1), 31–52. DOI: 10.1016/j.aos.2011.01.002

O'Dwyer, B., & Unerman, J. (2023). The Role of Assurance in Sustainability and ESG Reporting. *Accounting, Auditing & Accountability Journal*, 36(4), 861–888.

Obaideen, K., Abdelkareem, M. A., Wilberforce, T., Elsaid, K., Sayed, E. T., Maghrabie, H. M., & Olabi, A. G. (2022). Biogas role in achievement of the sustainable development goals: Evaluation, challenges, and guidelines. *Journal of the Taiwan Institute of Chemical Engineers*, 131, 104207. Advance online publication. DOI: 10.1016/j.jtice.2022.104207

Odey, G., Adelodun, B., Kim, S.-H., & Choi, K.-S. (2021). Status of environmental life cycle assessment (LCA): A case study of south korea. *Sustainability (Basel)*, 13(11), 6234. DOI: 10.3390/su13116234

Odintsova, T. (2024). Updating the Informational and Control Practices in the Sustainability Agenda. *Economics and Culture*, 21(1), 133–148. DOI: 10.2478/jec-2024-0010

Oğul, S. (2024). In tune with ethics: Responsible artificial intelligence and music industry. *Istanbul Bilgi University*, 1. DOI: 10.47613/reflektif.2024.150

Ohalete, N. C., Aderibigbe, A. O., Ani, E. C., Ohenhen, P. E., Daraojimba, D. O., & Odulaja, B. A.Nzubechukwu Chukwudum OhaleteAdebayo Olusegun AderibigbeEmmanuel Chigozie AniPeter Efosa OhenhenDonald Obinna DaraojimbaBukola A. Odulaja. (2023). AI-driven solutions in renewable energy: A review of data science applications in solar and wind energy optimization. *World Journal of Advanced Research and Reviews*, 20(3), 401–417. DOI: 10.30574/wjarr.2023.20.3.2433

Olya, H., Ahmad, M. S., Abdulaziz, T. A., Khairy, H. A., Fayyad, S., & Lee, C.-K. (2024). Catalyzing green change: The impact of tech-savvy leaders on innovative behaviors. *Corporate Social Responsibility and Environmental Management*, 31(6), 5543–5556. DOI: 10.1002/csr.2871

Oncioiu, I. D-M, P., AE, A., A, ., F, R., M, P., & Marin-Pantelescu. (2020). The Role of Environmental, Social, and Governance Disclosure in Financial Transparency. *Sustainability*.

Orlikowski, Iv., & Baroudi, J. J. (1991). *Studying Information Technology In Organizations: Research Approaches And Assumptions*.

Østergaard, E. (2019). Music and sustainability education – a contradiction? *Acta Didactica Norge*, 13(2), 2. DOI: 10.5617/adno.6452

Overland, C. T. (2017). Music education, inc. *Music Educators Journal*, 104(1), 55–61. DOI: 10.1177/0027432117719462

Oware, K. M., & Moulya, V. H. (2023). The outlook of sustainability assurance in global trends: A bibliometric review and research agenda. *South Asian Journal of Marketing*, 4(2), 110–127. DOI: 10.1108/SAJM-06-2022-0039

Oyelere, P., & Kuruppu, N. (2012). Voluntary IFR practices of listed companies in the United Arab Emirates. *Journal of Applied Accounting Research*, 13(3), 298–315. DOI: 10.1108/09675421211281353

P., P., & A., K. (2012). Multinationals' Accountability on Sustainability: The Evolution of Third-party Assurance of Sustainability Reports. *Journal of Business Ethics*, 173-190.

Palgrave Macmillan, Cham. (2018). *Sustainability assurance: Who are the assurance providers and what do they do?* Palgrave Macmillan.

Panarello, D., Gatto, A., Sadik-Zada, E. R., & Aldieri, L. (2024). Energy sustainability, vulnerability and resilience. *Discover Sustainability*, 5(1), 326. DOI: 10.1007/s43621-024-00534-6

Pan, C., Abbas, J., Álvarez-Otero, S., Khan, H., & Cai, C. (2022). Interplay between corporate social responsibility and organizational green culture and their role in employees' responsible behavior towards the environment and society. *Journal of Cleaner Production*, 366, 132878. DOI: 10.1016/j.jclepro.2022.132878

Pandey, D., Agrawal, M., & Pandey, J. S. (2011). Carbon footprint: Current methods of estimation. *Environmental Monitoring and Assessment*, 178(1–4), 135–160. DOI: 10.1007/s10661-010-1678-y PMID: 20848311

Paquette, J., Stevens, J., & Mallen, C. (2011). The interpretation of environmental sustainability by the International Olympic Committee and Organizing Committees of the Olympic Games from 1994 to 2008. *Sport in Society: Vol 14, No 3.* https://www.tandfonline.com/doi/full/10.1080/17430437.2011.557272

Paridhi, R., Ritika, , Arora, H., Arora, P., & Saini, N. (2024). Unlocking the path to sustainability: A hierarchical model for understanding corporate barriers to ESG reporting adoption. *Journal of Risk and Financial Management*, 17(12), 527. DOI: 10.3390/jrfm17120527

Park, S.R., & Jang, J.Y. (2021). The Impact of ESG Management on Investment Decision: Institutional Investors'. Perceptions of Country-Specific ESG Criteria. *International Journal of Financial Studies.*

Parkes, O., Lettieri, P., & Bogle, I.D.L. (2016). Defining a quantitative framework for evaluation and optimisation of the environmental impacts of mega-event projects. *ScienceDirect.* https://www.sciencedirect.com/science/article/pii/S0301479715303637

Patel, N. (2012). Investor relations on the Internet: An empirical study of Indian listed companies. *IUP Journal of Corporate Governance*, 11(2), 45–59.

Pathirana, S. M., Zhang, J., & Cheung, R. (2022). Blockchain and artificial intelligence for ESG verification: A comprehensive review. *Journal of Environmental Management*, 320, 115803. DOI: 10.1016/j.jenvman.2022.115803

Perego, P., & Kolk, A. (2012). Multinationals' accountability on sustainability: The evolution of third-party assurance of sustainability reports. *Journal of Business Ethics*, 110(2), 173–190. DOI: 10.1007/s10551-012-1420-5

Perez-Batres, L. A., Miller, V. V., Pisani, M. J., Henriques, I., & Renau-Sepulveda, J. A. (2012). Why do firms engage in national sustainability programs and transparent sustainability reporting? Evidence from Mexico's clean industry program. *Management International Review*, 52, 107–136. DOI: 10.1007/s10551-012-1419-y

Performance Review Of ESG Investing In India. (2023). Rabindra Bharati University. *Journal of Economics*, XXVII(10), 121–122.

Pernamasari, R. (2019). Analysis of index Internet financial reporting: Studies in banking companies in Indonesia, Malaysia, and Singapore. *International Journal of Academic Research in Accounting. Finance and Management Sciences*, 9(1), 150–159.

Pervan, I. (2005). Financial reporting on the Internet and the practice of Croatian joint stock companies quoted on the stock exchanges. *Financial Theory and Practice*, 29(2), 159–174.

Pervan, I. (2006). Voluntary financial reporting on the Internet: Analysis of the practice of stock-market listed Croatian and Slovene joint stock companies. *Financial Theory and Practice*, 30(1), 1–27.

Pervan, I., & Bartulović, M. (2012). Internet financial reporting: A comparative analysis for selected CEE countries. *Conference proceedings: International Conference of the Faculty of Economic Sarajevo (ICES)* (348–363).

Petravick, S., & Gillet, J. (1996). Financial reporting on the World Wide Web. *Management Accounting*, 26–33.

Pflugrath, G., Roebuck, P., & Simnett, R. (2011). Impact of assurance and assurer's professional affiliation on financial analysts' assessment of credibility of corporate social responsibility information. *Auditing*, 30(3), 239–254. DOI: 10.2308/ajpt-10047

Philip, B. Maffetone, Rita Malcata, Ivan Rivera, & Paul B. Laursen. (2017). The Boston Marathon versus the World Marathon Majors. *PLOS ONE*. https://journals.plos.org/plosone/article?id=10.1371/journal.pone.0184024

Pirchegger, B., Schader, H., & Wagenhofer, A. (1999). Financial information on the Internet: A survey of the homepages of Austrian companies. *European Accounting Review*, 8(2), 383–395. DOI: 10.1080/096381899336113

Pizzi, S., Venturelli, A., & Caputo, F. (2024). Restoring trust in sustainability reporting: The enabling role of the external assurance. *Current Opinion in Environmental Sustainability*, 68, 101437. DOI: 10.1016/j.cosust.2024.101437

Popescu, I.-S., Gibon, T., Hitaj, C., Rubin, M., & Benetto, E. (2023). Are SRI funds financing carbon emissions? An input-output life cycle assessment of investment funds. *Ecological Economics*, 212, 107918. DOI: 10.1016/j.ecolecon.2023.107918

Porter, M. E., & Kramer, M. R. (2006). *Strategy & society. The link between competitive advantage and corporate.*

Prabowo, R., & Tambotoh, J. J. C. (2005). Internet financial reporting as a voluntary disclosure practice: An empirical analysis of Indonesian manufacturing firms using order logit regression. *Jurnal Akuntansi & Bisnis*, 5(2), 149–160.

Preacher, K. J., & Hayes, A. F. (2008). Asymptotic and resampling strategies for assessing and comparing indirect effects in multiple mediator models. *Behavior Research Methods*, 40(3), 879–891. DOI: 10.3758/BRM.40.3.879 PMID: 18697684

Preuss, H. (2013). The Contribution of the FIFA World Cup and the Olympic Games to Green Economy. *Sustainability (Basel)*, 5(8), 8. Advance online publication. DOI: 10.3390/su5083581

Publicover, J. L., Wright, T. S., Baur, S., & Duinker, P. N. (2019). Engaging with environmental issues as a musician: Career perspectives from the musicians of the *playlist for the planet.Popular Music and Society*, 42(2), 167–187. DOI: 10.1080/03007766.2018.1426367

PwC (2023). *Our anti-greenwashing framework: A preventive approach.*

Quagli, A. (2001). The web and corporate information to financial markets. *Economia e diritto del terziario, 1,* 177–208.

Quagli, A., & Riva, P. (2005). Do financial websites meet the users' information needs? A survey from the Italian context. http://www.ssrn.com

Quick, R., & Inwinkl, P. (2020). Assurance on CSR reports: Impact on the credibility perceptions of non-financial information by bank directors. *Meditari Accountancy Research*, 28(5), 833–862.

Radovilsky, Z., Hegde, V., & Acharya, A. (2018). *Skills Requirements of Business Data Analytics and Data Science Jobs: A Comparative Analysis. 16*(1).

Rahdari, A. H., & Rostamy, A. A. A. (2015). Designing a general set of sustainability indicators at the corporate level. *Journal of Cleaner Production*, 108, 757–771. DOI: 10.1016/j.jclepro.2015.05.108

Rajak, S., & Vinodh, S. (2015). Application of fuzzy logic for social sustainability performance evaluation: A case study of an Indian automotive component manufacturing organization. *Journal of Cleaner Production*, 108, 1184–1192. DOI: 10.1016/j.jclepro.2015.05.070

Ramzan, M., Amin, M., & Abbas, M. (2021). How does corporate social responsibility affect financial performance, financial stability, and financial inclusion in the banking sector? Evidence from Pakistan. *Research in International Business and Finance*, 55, 101314. DOI: 10.1016/j.ribaf.2020.101314

Rane, N., Choudhary, S., & Rane, J. (2024). Artificial intelligence driven approaches to strengthening environmental, social, and governance (ESG) criteria in sustainable business practices: A review. SSRN *Electronic Journal*. DOI: 10.2139/ssrn.4843215

Rane, N., Choudhary, S., & Rane, J. (2023). Sustainable tourism development using leading-edge artificial intelligence (AI), blockchain, internet of things (IoT), augmented reality (AR) and virtual reality (VR) technologies. *SSRN*. DOI: 10.2139/ssrn.4642605

Raut, R. K., Shastri, N., Mishra, A. K., & Tiwari, A. K. (2023). Investor's values and investment decision towards ESG stocks. *Review of Accounting and Finance*, 22(4), 449–465. DOI: 10.1108/RAF-12-2022-0353

Rawashdeh, B., & Rawashdeh, A. (2021). Factors influencing the usage of XBRL tools. *Management Science Letters*, 11(4), 1345–1356. DOI: 10.5267/j.msl.2020.11.005

Raza, A., Farrukh, M., Iqbal, M. K., Farhan, M., & Wu, Y. (2021). Corporate social responsibility and employees' voluntary pro-environmental behavior: The role of organizational pride and employee engagement. *Corporate Social Responsibility and Environmental Management*, 28(3), 1104–1116. DOI: 10.1002/csr.2109

Rehman, S. U., Kraus, S., Shah, S. A., Khanin, D., & Mahto, R. V. (2021). Analyzing the relationship between green innovation and environmental performance in large manufacturing firms. *Technological Forecasting and Social Change*, 163, 120481. DOI: 10.1016/j.techfore.2020.120481

Reimsbach, Hahn, & Gürtürk, A. (. (2018). Integrated reporting and assurance of sustainability information: An experimental study on professional investors' information processing., 27(3), 559-581. *European Accounting Review*, 559–581. DOI: 10.1080/09638180.2016.1273787

Rennings, K. (2000). Redefining innovation — Eco-innovation research and the contribution from ecological economics. *Ecological Economics*, 32(2), 319–332. DOI: 10.1016/S0921-8009(99)00112-3

RepRisk. (2019). *About Us*. https://www.reprisk.com/about-reprisk

Rhodes, C. (2016). Democratic Business Ethics: Volkswagen's Emissions Scandal and the Disruption of Corporate Sovereignty. *Jouranl of Busienss Ethics*, 1501-1518.

Richardson, N. (2019). Corporate social responsibility or sustainability in music festivals. *The International Journal of Organizational Analysis*, 27(5), 1257–1273. DOI: 10.1108/IJOA-03-2018-1368

Rimmel, G. (2020). Sustainability audit and assurance. In *Accounting for Sustainability* (pp. 180–192). Routledge. DOI: 10.4324/9781003037200-17

Robert, E., Michael, K., & Sydney, R. (2014). *The Integrated Reporting Movement: Meaning, Momentum, Motives, and Materiality*. Wiley.

Rob, G., Dave, O., & Keith, M. (1987). *Corporate Social Reporting: Accounting and Accountability*. Prentice Hall.

Rodrigues, L., & Carlos, M. (2001). *Financial reporting on the Internet: The Portuguese case*. Polytechnic Institute of Braganca.

Rodriguez-Labajos, B. (2022). Artistic activism promotes three major forms of sustainability transformation. *Current Opinion in Environmental Sustainability*, 57, 101199. DOI: 10.1016/j.cosust.2022.101199

Rodriguez, S., & Cruz, R. (2023). Integrating AI and blockchain for improved ESG reporting: A case study approach. *Sustainable Business Review*, 8(2), 45–62. DOI: 10.1016/sbr20234562

Romani, S., Grappi, S., & Bagozzi, R. P. (2016). Corporate Socially Responsible Initiatives and Their Effects on Consumption of Green Products. *Journal of Business Ethics*, 135(2), 253–264. DOI: 10.1007/s10551-014-2485-0

Romero Ariza, M., Quesada Armenteros, A., & Estepa Castro, A. (2024). Promoting critical thinking through mathematics and science teacher education: The case of argumentation and graphs interpretation about climate change. *European Journal of Teacher Education*, 47(1), 41–59. DOI: 10.1080/02619768.2021.1961736

Rongbin, R., Wan, C., & Zuping, Z. (2022). Research on the relationship between environmental corporate social responsibility and green innovative behavior: The moderating effect of moral identity. *Environmental Science and Pollution Research International*, 29(34), 52189–52203. DOI: 10.1007/s11356-022-19541-z PMID: 35260982

Roopa, S., & Rani, M. S. (2012). Questionnaire designing for a survey. *The Journal of Indian Orthodontic Society*, 46(4, suppl1), 273–277. DOI: 10.1177/0974909820120509S

Roper, T. (2006). *Producing environmentally sustainable olympic games and 'greening' major public events.* https://www.semanticscholar.org/paper/producing-environmentally-sustainable-olympic-games-roper/e7091ae9cd2831ff9443 6649e97a08d4afa51256

Rosso, B. D., Dekas, K. H., & Wrzesniewski, A. (2010). On the meaning of work: A theoretical integration and review. *Research in Organizational Behavior*, 30, 91–127. DOI: 10.1016/j.riob.2010.09.001

Rouen, E., Sachdeva, K., & Yoon, A. (2024). *Sustainability meets substance:* Sarkis, J., & Talluri, S. (2002). A model for strategic supplier selection. *The Journal of Supply Chain Management*, 38(4), 18–28. DOI: 10.1111/j.1745-493X.2002.tb00117.x

Rubino, F. E., & Napoli, F. (2020). What Impact Does Corporate Governance Have on Corporate Environmental Performances? An Empirical Study of Italian Listed Firms. *Sustainability (Basel)*, 12(14), 5742. DOI: 10.3390/su12145742

Ruhaya, A., Nafsiah, M., & Normahiran, Y. (2000). *E-reporting of corporate financial information*. Universiti Teknologi Mara.

Ruiz-Barbadillo, E., & Martínez-Ferrero, J. (2020). Empirical analysis of the effect of the joint provision of audit and sustainability assurance services on assurance quality. *Journal of Cleaner Production*, 266, 121943. DOI: 10.1016/j.jclepro.2020.121943

Ryan, R. M., & Deci, E. L. (2000). Self-determination theory and the facilitation of intrinsic motivation, social development, and well-being. *The American Psychologist*, 55(1), 68–78. DOI: 10.1037/0003-066X.55.1.68 PMID: 11392867

Şahin, Z., & Çankaya, F. (2020). The importance of sustainability and sustainability reporting. New Approaches to CSR. *Sustainability and Accountability*, I, 45–59.

Saini, M., Aggarwal, V., Dhingra, B., Kumar, P., & Yadav, M. (2023). ESG and financial variables: A systematic review. *International Journal of Law and Management*, 65(6), 663–682. DOI: 10.1108/IJLMA-02-2023-0033

Salama, W. M., Suliman, M. A., Hassanin, M., Khairy, H. A., Al Asrag, A. S. A., & Fahmy, N. S. (2024). Catalyzing green competitiveness in hotel and tourism businesses: leveraging digital dynamic capability and green creativity. *Environment and Social Psychology, 9*(9).

Salgado, F. P., Abbott, D., & Wilson, G. (2017). *Dimensions of professional competences for interventions towards sustainability*.

Sánchez-Infante Hernández, J. P., Yañez-Araque, B., & Moreno-García, J. (2020). Moderating effect of firm size on the influence of corporate social responsibility in the economic performance of micro-, small- and medium-sized enterprises. *Technological Forecasting and Social Change*, 151, 119774. DOI: 10.1016/j.techfore.2019.119774

Saraswati, E., Rachmawati, Y., & Anjani, A. (2023). Quality of Banking Sustainability Reports: Symbolic or Substantive? *European Journal of Applied Sciences, Vol*, 11(6), 157–171.

Sardianou, E., Stauropoulou, A., Evangelinos, K., & Nikolaou, I. (2021). A materiality analysis framework to assess sustainable development goals of banking sector through sustainability reports. *Sustainable Production and Consumption*, 27, 1775–1793. DOI: 10.1016/j.spc.2021.04.020

Sarfraz, M., Ozturk, I., Yoo, S., Raza, M. A., & Han, H. (2023). Toward a new understanding of environmental and financial performance through corporate social responsibility, green innovation, and sustainable development. *Humanities & Social Sciences Communications*, 10(1), 297. DOI: 10.1057/s41599-023-01799-4

Sari, R. (2024). Assurance Practices for Ethical and Sustainable Business Practices. *Advances in Managerial Auditing Research*, 2(2), 97–108. DOI: 10.60079/amar.v2i2.342

Sarma, A., & Sharan, D. S. (2024). *Enhancing educational efficiency: Integrating esg criteria into administrative model.*

Saruchera, F. (2025). *Sustainability: A concept in flux? The role of multidisciplinary insights in shaping sustainable futures.*

Saxena, A., Singh, R., Gehlot, A., Akram, S. V., Twala, B., Singh, A., Montero, E. C., & Priyadarshi, N. (2022). Technologies empowered environmental, social, and governance (ESG): An industry 4.0 landscape. *Sustainability (Basel)*, 15(1), 309. DOI: 10.3390/su15010309

Schmidt, P., & Robbins, J. (2011). Looking backwards to reach forward: A strategic architecture for professional development in music education. *Arts Education Policy Review*, 112(2), 95–103. DOI: 10.1080/10632913.2011.546702

Schnugg, C., & Song, B. (2020). An organizational perspective on ArtScience collaboration: Opportunities and challenges of platforms to collaborate with artists. *Journal of Open Innovation*, 6(1), 6. DOI: 10.3390/joitmc6010006

Sciarelli, M., Cosimato, S., Landi, G., & Iandolo, F. (2021). Socially responsible investment strategies for the transition towards sustainable development: The importance of integrating and communicating ESG. *The TQM Journal*, 33(7), 39–56. DOI: 10.1108/TQM-08-2020-0180

Sebastião, A. M., Tavares, M. C., & Azevedo, G. (2024). Evolution and Challenges of Sustainability Reporting in the Banking Sector: A Systematic Literature Review. *Administrative Sciences*, 14(12), 333. DOI: 10.3390/admsci14120333

Securities and Exchange Board of India. (2021). *Business responsibility and sustainability reporting by listed entities: Annexure 2.*

Seguí-Mas, E., Bollas-Araya, H. M., & Polo-Garrido, F. (2018). Assurance on corporate governance reports in Spain: Towards an enhanced accountability or a new form of public relations? *Administrative Sciences*, 8(3), 32. DOI: 10.3390/admsci8030032

Sethi, S. P., Martell, T. F., & Demir, M. (2017). An evaluation of the quality of corporate social responsibility reports by some of the world's largest financial institutions. *Journal of Business Ethics*, 140, 787–805.

Shahzad, M., Qu, Y., Javed, S. A., Zafar, A. U., & Rehman, S. U. (2020). Relation of environment sustainability to CSR and green innovation: A case of Pakistani manufacturing industry. *Journal of Cleaner Production*, 253, 119938. DOI: 10.1016/j.jclepro.2019.119938

Shahzad, M., Qu, Y., Ur Rehman, S., Ding, X., & Razzaq, A. (2022). Impact of stakeholders' pressure on green management practices of manufacturing organizations under the mediation of organizational motives. *Journal of Environmental Planning and Management*, 66(10), 2171–2194. DOI: 10.1080/09640568.2022.2062567

Sharma, N., & Bhardwaj, S. (2022). The influence of Internet-related aspects on financial reporting. *Poonam Shodh Rachna*, I(XII), 12–19.

Sharma, S., Singh, G., Sharma, C. S., & Kapoor, S. (2024). Artificial intelligence in Indian higher education institutions: A quantitative study on adoption and perceptions. *International Journal of System Assurance Engineering and Management*. Advance online publication. DOI: 10.1007/s13198-023-02193-8

Sharpe, E., Ruepert, A., van der Werff, E., & Steg, L. (2022). Corporate environmental responsibility leads to more pro-environmental behavior at work by strengthening intrinsic pro-environmental motivation. *One Earth*, 5(7), 825–835. DOI: 10.1016/j.oneear.2022.06.006

Shen, S. (2012). *The Environmental Impact of Expositions: A Study of Some Contributing Factors* [Thesis, Open Access, Te Herenga Waka-Victoria University of Wellington]. DOI: 10.26686/wgtn.16993444

Sheskin, D. J. (2011). *Handbook of Parametric and Nonparametric Statistical Procedures* (5th ed.). Chapman and Hall/CRC.

Shi, Q., Zuo, J., & Zillante, G. (2012). Exploring the management of sustainable construction at the programme level: A Chinese case study. *Construction Management and Economics*, 30(6), 425–440. DOI: 10.1080/01446193.2012.683200

Shnayder, L., van Rijnsoever, F. J., & Hekkert, M. P. (2016). Motivations for Corporate Social Responsibility in the packaged food industry: An institutional and stakeholder management perspective. *Journal of Cleaner Production*, 122, 212–227. DOI: 10.1016/j.jclepro.2016.02.030

Shrivastava, P., & Berger, S. (2010). *Sustainability principles: A review and directions*. Concordia University.

Shukla, A., & Gekara, M. G. (2010). Corporate reporting in modern era: A comparative analysis of Indian and Chinese companies. *Global Journal of International Business Research*, 3(3), 42–56.

Siahaan, A. M., Waruwu, H. A., Sianipar, V. H., & Simanjuntak, O. (2021). Factors affecting financial reporting through the internet (Internet financial reporting) on the company's website: A literature study. [IJSMS]. *International Journal of Science and Management Studies*, 4(4), 1–10. DOI: 10.51386/25815946/ijsms-v4i4p101

Sierra, L., Zorio, A., & García-Benau, M. A. (2013). Sustainable Development and Assurance of Corporate Social Responsibility Reports Published by Ibex-35 Companies. *Corporate Social Responsibility and Environmental Management*, *20*(6), 359-370. .1303DOI: 10.1002/csr

Silva, S. (2021). Corporate contributions to the Sustainable Development Goals: An empirical analysis informed by legitimacy theory. *Journal of Cleaner Production*, 292, 125962.

Silvola, H., & Vinnari, E. (2021). The limits of institutional work: A field study on auditors' efforts to promote sustainability assurance in a trust society. *Accounting, Auditing & Accountability Journal*, 34(1), 1–30. DOI: 10.1108/AAAJ-02-2019-3890

Simnett, R., Vanstraelen, A., & Chua, W. F. (2009). Assurance on sustainability reports: An international comparison. *The Accounting Review*, 84(3), 937–967. DOI: 10.2308/accr.2009.84.3.937

Simnett, R., Vanstraelen, A., & Chua, W. F. (2020). Assurance on sustainability reports: Revisiting the influence of auditor and firm characteristics. *Accounting, Organizations and Society*, 47, 16–26.

Singh, A. P. (2021). *Integrating corporate sustainability and sustainable development goals: Towards a multi-stakeholder framework.*

Singh, M. (2009). *Corporate disclosure through web: A study of selected Indian companies* [Doctoral dissertation, Guru Nanak Dev University].

Singhania, M., & Saini, N. (2022). Systems approach to environment, social and governance (ESG): Case of Reliance Industries. *Sustainable Operations and Computers*, 3, 103–117. DOI: 10.1016/j.susoc.2021.11.003

Singh, B., & Malhotra, P. (2004). Corporate web reporting practices in India. *The Indian Journal of Commerce*, 57(3), 157–169.

Singh, H., & Singh, A. (2022). Understanding inhibitors to XBRL adoption: An empirical investigation. *Accounting Research Journal*, 35(5), 598–615. DOI: 10.1108/ARJ-05-2021-0144

Singh, J., de los Salmones Sanchez, M. D. M. G., & del Bosque, I. R. (2008). Understanding corporate social responsibility and product perceptions in consumer markets: A cross-cultural evaluation. *Journal of Business Ethics*, 80(3), 597–611. DOI: 10.1007/s10551-007-9457-6

Singh, M., & Singh, N. (2021). Awareness and understanding of XBRL in India: An exploratory study of chartered accountants. *PIMT Journal of Research*, 13(3B), 22–27.

Singh, M., Singh, N., & Kaur, S. (2023). Measuring internet financial reporting: Investors' perspective. *PCMA Journal of Business*, 16(2), 26–33.

Siqueira, C. H. Q., de Araújo Ribeiro, A. L. (2021). Sustainable Strategies in Sports Mega-Events: An Analysis of Soccer World Cups. *Sustainable Strategies in Sports Mega-Events: An Analysis of Soccer World Cups, 11*(2), Article 2. https://app.periodikos.com.br/journal/rigd/article/doi/10.51995/2237-3373.v11i1e110012

Sirilertsuwan, P., Thomassey, S., & Zeng, X. (2020). A strategic location decision-making approach for multi-tier supply chain sustainability. *Sustainability (Basel)*, 12(20), 1–37. DOI: 10.3390/su12208340

Smith, J., Haniffa, R., & Fairbrass, J. (2011). A conceptual framework for investigating 'capture' in corporate sustainability reporting assurance. *Journal of Business Ethics*, 99(3), 425–439.

Solaimani, S. (2024). From compliance to capability: On the role of data and technology in environment, social, and governance. *Sustainability (Basel)*, 16(14), 6061. DOI: 10.3390/su16146061

Sonnerfeldt, A. L. L., & Pontoppidan, C. A. (2020). The challenges of assurance on non-financial reporting. *Accounting, Economics, and Law : A Convivium*, 10(2), 20180050. DOI: 10.1515/ael-2018-0050

Sortur, S. (2006). Financial reporting on the Internet. *The Chartered Accountant*, 996–1006.

Sotiriadou, P., & Hill, B. (2015). *Raising Environmental Responsibility And Sustainability For Sport Events: A Systematic Review. 10*(1).

Spanjol, J., Tam, L., & Tam, V. (2015). Employer–Employee Congruence in Environmental Values: An Exploration of Effects on Job Satisfaction and Creativity. *Journal of Business Ethics*, 130(1), 117–130. DOI: 10.1007/s10551-014-2208-6

Spanos, I., Kucukvar, M., Bell, T. C., Elnimah, A., Hamdan, H., Al Meer, B., Prakash, S., Lundberg, O., & Kutty, A. A. (2021). How FIFA World Cup 2022™ can meet the carbon neutral commitments and the United Nations 2030 Agenda for Sustainable Development?: Reflections from the tree nursery project in Qatar*Sustainable Development—Wiley Online Library*. https://onlinelibrary.wiley.com/doi/full/10.1002/sd.2239

Spence, M. (1973). Job market signaling. *The Quarterly Journal of Economics*, 87(3), 355–374. DOI: 10.2307/1882010

Spiegeleer, J. D., Hocht, S., Jakubowski, D., Reyners, S., & Schoutens, W. (2020). *ESG: A new dimension in portfolio allocation.*

Springborg, C. (2012). *Perceptual refinement: Art-based methods in managerial education.*

Springer, Cham. (2017). *Sustainability in a digital world needs trust.* Springer, Cham.

Srivastava, A., & Maity, R. (2023). Assessing the potential of AI–ML in urban climate change adaptation and sustainable development. *Sustainability (Basel)*, 15(23), 16461. Advance online publication. DOI: 10.3390/su152316461

Ssossé, Q., Wagner, J., & Hopper, C. (2021). Assessing the impact of ESD: Methods, challenges, results. *Sustainability (Basel)*, 13(5), 2854. DOI: 10.3390/su13052854

Stedman, C., & Paul, L. G. (2024, August 22). *10 top ESG reporting frameworks explained and compared.*

Steg, L. (2016). Values, Norms, and Intrinsic Motivation to Act Proenvironmentally. *Annual Review of Environment and Resources, 41*(Volume 41, 2016), 277-292. doi .org/10.1146/annurev-environ-110615-085947

Steinmeier, M., & Stich, M. (2017). *Does sustainability assurance improve managerial investment decisions?*

Stotz, O. (2021). Expected and realized returns on stocks with high- and low-ESG exposure. *Journal of Asset Management*, 22(2), 133–150. DOI: 10.1057/s41260-020-00203-z

Suchman, M. (1995). Managing legitimacy: Strategic and institutional approaches. *Academy of Management Review*, 20(3), 571–610.

Sulaiman, M., & Alhaji Zakari, M. (2019). Financial sustainability of state waqf institutions (SWIs) in Malaysia. *Journal of Islamic Accounting and Business Research*, 10(2), 236–258. DOI: 10.1108/JIABR-05-2016-0054

Sult, A., Wobst, J., & Lueg, R. (2023). The role of training in implementing corporate sustainability: A systematic literature review. *Corporate Social Responsibility and Environmental Management*, •••, 1–30.

Suozzo, A. (2003). *The Chicago Marathon and Urban Renaissance*. https://www.researchgate.net/publication/227564103_The_Chicago_Marathon_and_Urban_Renaissance

SustainAbility (2018). Rate the raters 2018: Ratings revisited. London: New York, San Francisco. https://sustainability.com/wp-content/ uploads/2017/12/SA-RateTheRaters_Ratings-Revisited_March18.pdf

Taghikhah, F., Erfani, E., Bakhshayeshi, I., Tayari, S., Karatopouzis, A., & Hanna, B. (2022). Artificial intelligence and sustainability: Solutions to social and environmental challenges. In Asadnia, M., Razmjou, A., & Beheshti, A. (Eds.), *Artificial intelligence and data science in environmental sensing* (93–108). Academic Press. DOI: 10.1016/B978-0-323-90508-4.00006-X

Taha, B. & Allan, A. (2024). Hosting a Mega Event, a Drive Towards Sustainable Development: Dubai's Expo 2020. In S. Geertman & Q. Zhan (Eds.), *Computational Urban Planning and Management for Smart Cities* (223-247). Springer International Publishing. DOI: 10.1007/978-3-030-19424-6_13

Taha, B., & Allan, A. (2022). *ISPRS-Annals—planning for legacy – a cost effective and sustainable approach. Case study: Dubai expo 2020*. https://isprs-annals.copernicus.org/articles/X-4-W3-2022/237/2022/

Tahinakis, P. D., & Samarinas, M. P. (2017). Attributes of audit quality and weak fiscal sustainability countries. International Journal of Banking. *Accounting and Finance*, 8(1), 20–51.

Tang, H., Loi, R., & Lai, S. W. (2024). Employees go green: the roles of perceived CSR and intrinsic motivation. *Evidence-based HRM: a Global Forum for Empirical Scholarship, 12*(2), 407-420. DOI: 10.1108/EBHRM-11-2022-0287

Tang, Q., & Luo, L. (2011). *Transparency of corporate carbon disclosure: International evidence*.

Tang, H. (2022). The Effect of ESG Performance on Corporate Innovation in China: The Mediating Role of Financial Constraints and Agency Cost. *Sustainability (Basel)*, 14(7), 3769. DOI: 10.3390/su14073769

Tang, M., Walsh, G., Lerner, D., Fitza, M. A., & Li, Q. (2018). Green Innovation, Managerial Concern and Firm Performance: An Empirical Study. *Business Strategy and the Environment*, 27(1), 39–51. DOI: 10.1002/bse.1981

Tang, Y. M., Chau, K. Y., Fatima, A., & Waqas, M. (2022). Industry 4.0 technology and circular economy practices: Business management strategies for environmental sustainability. *Environmental Science and Pollution Research International*, 29(33), 49752–49769. DOI: 10.1007/s11356-022-19081-6 PMID: 35218493

Tao, M., Lin, B., & Poletti, S. (2024). From policy to practice: How China's emissions trading scheme shapes ESG greenwashing at the firm level? *Journal of Environmental Management*, 370, 122681. DOI: 10.1016/j.jenvman.2024.122681 PMID: 39366221

Task Force on Climate-related Financial Disclosures. (n.d.). *About the Task Force on Climate-related Financial Disclosures.*

Tello, S. F., & Yoon, E. (2008). Examining drivers of sustainable innovation. *International Journal of Business Strategy*, 8(3), 164–169.

Teoh, S. H., & Francis, J. R. (2023). Assurance and Professional Judgment in the Digital Age. *Auditing*, 42(2), 27–54.

Tercan, H., & Meisen, T. (2022). Machine learning and deep learning-based predictive quality in manufacturing: A systematic review. *Journal of Intelligent Manufacturing*, 33(7), 1879–1905. DOI: 10.1007/s10845-022-01963-8

The European Business Review. (2025). *From risks to rewards: How collaboration fuels sustainability success.* The European Business Review.

The Forum for Sustainable and Responsible Investment. (2018). Sustain- able investing assets reach $12 trillion as reported by the US SIF Foundation's biennial Report on US Sustainable, Responsible and Impact Investing Trends [Press release]. Retrieved from https://www. ussif.org/files/US%20SIF%20Trends%20Report%20 2018% 20Release.pdf

Tobias, H., Jonatan, P. L. P., & Frank, F. (2015). Tensions in Corporate Sustainability: Towards an Integrative Framework. *Journal of Business Ethics*, 297–316.

Torreli, R., Balluchi, F., & Lazzini, A. (2020). Greenwashing and Environmental Communication: Effects on Stakeholders' Perceptions. *Business Strategy and the Environment*, 29(2), 407–421. DOI: 10.1002/bse.2373

Tran, M. K., Goulding, C., & Shiu, E. (2018). The orchestra of ideas: Using music to enhance the 'fuzzy front end' phase of product innovation. *Journal of Business Research*, 85, 504–513. DOI: 10.1016/j.jbusres.2017.10.029

Traxler, A. A., Schrack, D., & Greiling, D. (2020). Sustainability reporting and management control–A systematic exploratory literature review. *Journal of Cleaner Production*, 276, 122725. DOI: 10.1016/j.jclepro.2020.122725

Truong, T. H. D. (2024). Environmental, social and governance performance and firm value: Does ownership concentration matter? *Management Decision*, ahead-of-print(ahead-of-print). DOI: 10.1108/MD-10-2023-1993

Truong, Y., Mazloomi, H., & Berrone, P. (2021). Understanding the impact of symbolic and substantive environmental actions on organizational reputation. *Industrial Marketing Management*, 92, 307–320.

Tsalis, T. A., Malamateniou, K. E., Koulouriotis, D., & Nikolaou, I. E. (2020). New challenges for corporate sustainability reporting: United nations' 2030 agenda for sustainable development and the sustainable development goals. *Corporate Social Responsibility and Environmental Management*, 27(4), 1617–1629. DOI: 10.1002/csr.1910

Tsang, E. W. K. (2014). Generalizing from research findings: The merits of case studies. *International Journal of Management Reviews*, 16(4), 369–383. DOI: 10.1111/ijmr.12024

Turker, D. (2009). Measuring Corporate Social Responsibility: A Scale Development Study. *Journal of Business Ethics*, 85(4), 411–427. DOI: 10.1007/s10551-008-9780-6

Tur-Porcar, A., Roig-Tierno, N., & Llorca Mestre, A. (2018). Factors affecting entrepreneurship and business sustainability. *Sustainability (Basel)*, 10(2), 452. DOI: 10.3390/su10020452

Tyler, B. B., Lahneman, B., Cerrato, D., Cruz, A. D., Beukel, K., Spielmann, N., & Minciullo, M. (2023). Environmental practice adoption in SMEs: The effects of firm proactive orientation and regulatory pressure. *Journal of Small Business Management*, 62(5), 2211–2246. DOI: 10.1080/00472778.2023.2218435

Umoren, A. O., & Asogwa, I. E. (2013). Internet financial reporting and company characteristics: A case of quoted companies in Nigeria. *Research Journal of Finance and Accounting*, 4(12), 72–80.

Unilever. (2024). *Utilising AI to redefine the future of customer connectivity.*

Upadhyaya, C., Khan, S., & Sandanshive, V., Awasthi, G. (2023). A study of the impact of behavioral factors on ESG investment. *Journal of Contemporary Issues in Business and Government*, 29(1), 546–548. DOI: 10.47750/cibg.2023.29.01.039

Valentinov, V. (2023). Stakeholder Theory: Toward a Classical Institutional Economics Perspective. *Journal of Business Ethics*, 188(1), 75–88. DOI: 10.1007/s10551-022-05304-w

van Marrewijk, M. (2003). Concepts and Definitions of CSR and Corporate Sustainability: Between Agency and Communion. *Journal of Business Ethics*, 44(2), 95–105. DOI: 10.1023/A:1023331212247

Van Mourik, C., & Walton, P. J. (Eds.). (2014). *The Routledge companion to accounting, reporting and regulation*. Routledge.

Vander Bauwhede, H., & Van Cauwenberge, P. (2022). Determinants and value relevance of voluntary assurance of sustainability reports in a mandatory reporting context: Evidence from Europe. *Sustainability (Basel)*, 14(15), 9795. DOI: 10.3390/su14159795

Vanos, J. K., Kosaka, E., Iida, A., Yokohari, M., Middel, A., Scott-Fleming, I., & Brown, R. D. (2019). Planning for spectator thermal comfort and health in the face of extreme heat: The Tokyo 2020 Olympic marathons. *The Science of the Total Environment*, 657, 904–917. DOI: 10.1016/j.scitotenv.2018.11.447 PMID: 30677956

Vanstraelen, A. (2022). Harmonization of Assurance Standards: Challenges and Opportunities. *European Accounting Review*, 31(3), 453–478.

Váradi, J. (2022). A review of the literature on the relationship of music education to the development of socio-emotional learning. *SAGE Open*, 12(1), 21582440211068501. DOI: 10.1177/21582440211068501

Vasul, U. K., & Srivastava, R. (2003). Internet, XBRL, and online business reporting challenges and opportunities. *Chartered Accountant*, (June), 1215–1226.

Vaverková, M. D., Polak, J., Kurcjusz, M., Jena, M. K., Murali, A. P., Nair, S. S., Aktaş, H., Hadinata, M. E., Ghezelayagh, P., Andik, S. D. S., Rahmana, A., & Franc-Dąbrowska, J. (2024). *Enhancing sustainable development through interdisciplinary collaboration: Insights from diverse fields*.

Vaz Ogando, N., Ruiz Blanco, S., & Fernandez-Feijoo, B. (2018). A provider's approach to the assurance market of sustainability reports in Spain. *Administrative Sciences*, 8(3), 28. DOI: 10.3390/admsci8030028

Velte, P. (2024). Climate board governance and carbon assurance – European evidence. *Journal of Global Responsibility*, ahead-of-print(ahead-of-print). DOI: 10.1108/JGR-02-2024-0034

Venturelli, A., & Pizzi, S. (2024). SDG reporting in social and environmental accounting research. In *The Routledge Handbook of Accounting for the Sustainable Development Goals*. Routledge. DOI: 10.4324/9781003404118-27

Verawaty, V. (2022). *The availability of IFR (Internet financial reporting) through e-government as public transparency, participation, and accountability means in Indonesia.*

Verdantix. (2013). *Global sustainability leaders survey: Brands.*

Viterouli, M., Belias, D., Koustelios, A., & Tsigilis, N. (2022). Refining employees' engagement by incorporating self-directedness in training and work environments. *European Conference on Management Leadership and Governance, 18*(1), 414–422. DOI: 10.34190/ecmlg.18.1.870

Wallage, P. (2000). Assurance on sustainability reporting: An auditor's view. *Auditing*, 19(s-1), 53–65. DOI: 10.2308/aud.2000.19.s-1.53

Wanderley, O. S. L., Lucian, R., Farache, F., & Filho, S. M. J. (2008). CSR information disclosure on the web: A context-based approach analyzing the influence of country of origin and industry sector. *Journal of Business Ethics*, 82(2), 369–378. DOI: 10.1007/s10551-008-9892-z

Wang, C. H. (2020). An environmental perspective extends market orientation: Green innovation sustainability. *Business Strategy and the Environment*, 29(8), 3123–3134. DOI: 10.1002/bse.2561

Wang, L., & Yung, K. (2011). Do State Enterprises Manage Earnings More than Privately Owned Firms? The Case of China. *Journal of Business Finance & Accounting*, 38(7–8), 794–812. DOI: 10.1111/j.1468-5957.2011.02254.x

Wang, Z., & Sarkis, J. (2017). Corporate Social Responsibility Governance, Outcomes, and Financial Performance. *Journal of Cleaner Production*, 162, 1607–1616. DOI: 10.1016/j.jclepro.2017.06.142

WatchWire. (n.d.). *Sustainability reporting deadlines & timelines*. WatchWire.

Wen, Y. (2019, January). Construction of the curriculum system of financial management undergraduate based on XBRL. In *3rd International Seminar on Education Innovation and Economic Management (SEIEM 2018)* (204–206). Atlantis Press. DOI: 10.2991/seiem-18.2019.52

Wicks, A.C., & Harrison, J.S. (2020). *Towards a More Productive Dialogue Between Stakeholder Theory and Strategic Management.*

Widyawati, L. (2020). A systematic literature review of socially responsible investment and environmental social governance metrics. *Business Strategy and the Environment*, 29(2), 619–637. DOI: 10.1002/bse.2393

Wong, J., Wong, N., Li, W. Y., & Chen, L. (2016). Sustainability assurance: An emerging market for the accounting profession. *Pacific Accounting Review*, 28(3), 238–259. DOI: 10.1108/PAR-11-2014-0038

World Economic Forum. (2024). *How multi-stakeholder partnerships drive sustainable development*. World Economic Forum.

World Economic Forum. (2025). *Unlocking green growth: Sustainability as a key driver of corporate innovation*. World Economic Forum.

Wu, J., Chen, D., Bian, Z., Shen, T., Zhang, W., & Cai, W. (2021). How Does Green Training Boost Employee Green Creativity? A Sequential Mediation Process Model [Original Research]. *Frontiers in Psychology*, 12, 759548. Advance online publication. DOI: 10.3389/fpsyg.2021.759548 PMID: 34955979

Wu, W., & Yu, L. (2024). How Does Environmental Corporate Social Responsibility Affect Technological Innovation? The Role of Green Entrepreneurial Orientation and Green Intellectual Capital. *Journal of the Knowledge Economy*, 15(1), 3297–3328. DOI: 10.1007/s13132-023-01132-z

Wu, W., Yu, L., Li, H., & Zhang, T. (2022). Perceived Environmental Corporate Social Responsibility and Employees' Innovative Behavior: A Stimulus–Organism–Response Perspective [Original Research]. *Frontiers in Psychology*, 12, 777657. Advance online publication. DOI: 10.3389/fpsyg.2021.777657 PMID: 35173648

Wu, Y., Zhang, K., & Xie, J. (2020). Bad greenwashing, good greenwashing: Corporate social responsibility and information transparency. *Management Science*, 66(7), 3095–3112. DOI: 10.1287/mnsc.2019.3340

Xia, J. (2022). A systematic review: How does organisational learning enable ESG performance (from 2001 to 2021)? *Sustainability (Basel)*, 14(24), 16962. DOI: 10.3390/su142416962

Xiao, H. (2022). Innovation of digital multimedia VR technology in music education curriculum in colleges and universities. *Scientific Programming*, 2022(1), 6566144. DOI: 10.1155/2022/6566144

Xiao, J. Z., Jones, M. J., & Lymer, A. (2002). Immediate trends in Internet reporting. *European Accounting Review*, 11(2), 245–275. DOI: 10.1080/09638180020017087a

Xie, X., Huo, J., & Zou, H. (2019). Green process innovation, green product innovation, and corporate financial performance: A content analysis method. *Journal of Business Research*, 101, 697–706. DOI: 10.1016/j.jbusres.2019.01.010

Yadav, S. (2024). *Beyond materiality: Materiality in ESG disclosures under securities regulations in India.*

Yan, M., Jia, F., Chen, L. & Yan, F. (2022). *Assurance process for sustainability*

Yang, C., Zhu, C., & Albitar, K. (2024). ESG ratings and green innovation: A U-shaped journey towards sustainable development. *Business Strategy and the Environment*, n/a(n/a). DOI: 10.1002/bse.3692

Yang, C., Lai, H., & Leing Tan, B. (2008). Managerial Ownership Structure and Earnings Management. *Journal of Financial Reporting and Accounting*, 6(1), 35–53. DOI: 10.1108/19852510880000634

Yang, Y., & Jiang, Y. (2023). Buyer-supplier CSR alignment and firm performance: A contingency theory perspective. *Journal of Business Research*, 154, 113340. DOI: 10.1016/j.jbusres.2022.113340

Yang, Z., Su, D., Xu, S., & Han, X. (2024). Institutional investors and corporate green innovation: Evidence from China. *Pacific Economic Review*, 29(2), 230–266. DOI: 10.1111/1468-0106.12440

Yan, M., Jia, F., Chen, L., & Yan, F. (2022). Assurance process for sustainability reporting: Towards a conceptual framework. *Journal of Cleaner Production*, 377, 134156. DOI: 10.1016/j.jclepro.2022.134156

Yassin, M. M., & Al-Khatib, E. (2019). Internet financial reporting and expected stock return. *Journal of Accounting. Finance & Management Strategy*, 14(1), 1–28.

Yekini, K., Omoteso, K., & Adegbite, E. (2021). CSR communication research: A theoretical-cummethodological perspective from semiotics. *Business & Society*, 60(4), 876–908.

Yi, L., Uddin, M. A., Das, A. K., Mahmood, M., & Sohel, S. M. (2019). Do Transformational Leaders Engage Employees in Sustainable Innovative Work Behaviour? Perspective from a Developing Country. *Sustainability (Basel)*, 11(9), 2485. DOI: 10.3390/su11092485

Yin, X., Li, J., & Su, C. (2023). How does ESG performance affect stock returns? Empirical evidence from listed companies in China. *Heliyon*, 9(5), e16320. DOI: 10.1016/j.heliyon.2023.e16320 PMID: 37305472

Yong, Z. (2017). The relationship between corporate music and corporate image building. *Proceedings of the 2017 7th International Conference on Social Network, Communication and Education (SNCE 2017)*. 2017 7th International Conference on Social Network, Communication and Education (SNCE 2017), Shenyang, China. DOI: 10.2991/snce-17.2017.102

Yue, S., Bajuri, N. H. B., Khatib, S. F. A., & Alshareef, M. N. (2025). Ownership with a green twist: The role of top managers in driving environmental innovation. *China Finance Review International, ahead-of-print*(ahead-of-print). DOI: 10.1108/CFRI-03-2024-0121

Yue, S., Bajuri, N. H. B., Khatib, S. F., & Alshareef, M. N. (2025). Ownership with a green twist: The role of top managers in driving environmental innovation. China Finance Review International. https://www.emerald.com/insight/content/doi/10.1108/CFRI-03-2024-0121/full/html

Yue, S., Norkhairul, B. H., Khatib, S. F. A., & Lee, Y. (2024). Financing creativity: How state-owned and foreign ownership shape innovation engagement in China. *Kybernetes*, ahead-of-print(ahead-of-print). DOI: 10.1108/K-03-2024-0797

Yue, S., Bajuri, N. H. B., Ye, G., & Ullah, F. (2025). Green Awakening: The Rising Influence of Minority Shareholders and ESG in Shaping China's Sustainable Future. *Sustainable Futures : An Applied Journal of Technology, Environment and Society*, 100441, 100441. Advance online publication. DOI: 10.1016/j.sftr.2025.100441

Yue, S., Bajuri, N. H., Khatib, S. F. A., & Lee, Y. (2024). New quality productivity and environmental innovation: The hostile moderating roles of managerial empowerment and board centralization. *Journal of Environmental Management*, 370, 122423. DOI: 10.1016/j.jenvman.2024.122423 PMID: 39243639

Yu, X., Ma, N., Zheng, L., Wang, L., & Wang, K. (2023). Developments and applications of artificial intelligence in music education. *Technologies*, 11(2), 42. DOI: 10.3390/technologies11020042

Zacher, H., Rudolph, C. W., & Katz, I. M. (2023). Employee Green Behavior as the Core of Environmentally Sustainable Organizations. *Annual Review of Organizational Psychology and Organizational Behavior, 10*(Volume 10, 2023), 465-494. doi.org/10.1146/annurev-orgpsych-120920-050421

Zadek, S., Raynard, P., Forstater, M., & Oelschlaegel, J. (2004). The future of sustainability assurance. *ACCA Research Report*.

Zaman, R., Farooq, M. B., Khalid, F., & Mahmood, Z. (2021). Examining the extent of and determinants for sustainability assurance quality: The role of audit committees. *Business Strategy and the Environment*, 30(7), 2887–2906. DOI: 10.1002/bse.2777

Zeff, S. A., & Nobes, C. W. (2023). *International Financial Reporting: A Comparative Approach*. Wiley.

Zeidan, S. (2020). *An effective framework for bridging the gap between industry and academia*.

Zen, A. (2023). Determinants of employee engagement and productivity: An analysis of work motivation, competence, compensation and transactional leadership. *East Asian Journal of Multidisciplinary Research*, 2(2), 863–892. DOI: 10.55927/eajmr.v2i2.2981

Zhang, F. (2024). Enhancing ESG learning outcomes through gamification: An experimental study. *PLoS One*, 19(5), e0303259. DOI: 10.1371/journal.pone.0303259 PMID: 38748683

Zhang, J., Li, Y., Xu, H., & Ding, Y. (2023). Can ESG ratings mitigate managerial myopia? Evidence from Chinese listed companies. *International Review of Financial Analysis*, 90, 102878. DOI: 10.1016/j.irfa.2023.102878

Zhang, T., Zhang, J., & Tu, S. (2024). An empirical study on corporate ESG behavior and employee satisfaction: A moderating mediation model. *Behavioral Sciences (Basel, Switzerland)*, 14(4), 274. DOI: 10.3390/bs14040274 PMID: 38667070

Zhang, Y., Tian, H., & Lee, S. (2023). Transparency and innovation in ESG disclosures: The role of technology in shaping stakeholder trust. *Business Strategy and the Environment*, 32(1), 45–58. DOI: 10.1002/bse.3502

Zheng, C., & Kouwenberg, R. (2019). A Bibliometric Review of Global Research on Corporate Governance and Board Attributes. *Sustainability (Basel)*, 11(12), 3428. DOI: 10.3390/su11123428

Zhou, X., & Yang, Z. (2022). Research on measurement and evaluation of mathematical data analysis literacy. *Asian Journal of Education and Social Studies*, 51–61. DOI: 10.9734/ajess/2022/v30i230718

Zhou, K. Z., Gao, G. Y., & Zhao, H. (2017). State Ownership and Firm Innovation in China: An Integrated View of Institutional and Efficiency Logics. *Administrative Science Quarterly*, 62(2), 375–404. DOI: 10.1177/0001839216674457

Zhou, P., Song, F. M., & Huang, X. (2023). Environmental regulations and firms' green innovations: Transforming pressure into incentives. *International Review of Financial Analysis*, 86, 102504. DOI: 10.1016/j.irfa.2023.102504

Zieni, B., Chitchyan, R., & Heckel, R. (2017). *Trust as a sustainability requirement. CEUR-WS. org. Abbott, A. (2014). The system of professions: An essay on the division of expert labor*. University of Chicago press.

Zimon, G., Arianpoor, A., & Salehi, M. (2022). Zimon G, Arianpoor A, Salehi M. Sustainability Reporting and Corporate Reputation: The Moderating Effect of CEO Opportunistic Behavior. Sustainability. 2022; 14(3):1257. *Sustainability*, 1257–1275. DOI: 10.3390/su14031257

Zorio, A., García-Benau, M. A., & Sierra, L. (2013). Sustainability development and the quality of assurance reports: Empirical evidence. *Business Strategy and the Environment*, 22(7), 484–500. https://doi.org/10.1002/bse.1764

Zrnic, A., Pekanov, D., & Borozan, D. (2024). Assessing the Sustainability Reporting Transparency and Engagement of European Energy Companies. *Energies*, 17(19), 19. Advance online publication. DOI: 10.3390/en17194934

Zumente, I., & Bistrova, J. (2021). ESG importance for long-term shareholder value creation: Literature vs. Practice. *Journal of Open Innovation*, 7(2), 127. DOI: 10.3390/joitmc7020127

About the Contributors

Saleh F. A. Khatib is an assistant professor in Accounting and Finance at the Faculty of Business, Sohar University, Oman. He has been awarded a Ph.D. in Finance from Universiti Teknologi Malaysia (UTM) in 2022. His exceptional work and dedication to the field also earned him the Chancellor Award and Best Postgraduate Student Award. Throughout his academic career, Dr. Khatib has conducted extensive research on various functional domains, including Corporate Governance, Auditing, Corporate Finance, Corporate Social Responsibility, and Sustainability Disclosure. Dr. Khatib's articles are published in top-tier academic journals, including the Business Strategy and The Environment, Management Review Quarterly, Journal of Financial Reporting and Accounting, Global Business Review, Corporate Governance, Meditari Accountancy Research, and Environmental Science and Pollution Research, among others.

Alhamzah F. Abbas is an Iraqi senior lecturer currently based at Universiti Teknologi Malaysia (UTM) in Johor Bahru. He holds a PhD in Management (Marketing) from UTM, focusing on the impact of intrinsic and extrinsic motivations on cyber-market mavens' information sharing behavior. Alhamzah's academic journey includes a Master of Business Administration (Marketing) With a strong background in marketing and business management, he has worked in Iraq universities before transitioning into UTM. His specialty research areas include Digital Marketing, Marketing Analytics, Tourism Marketing, Entrepreneurship, and Sustainability. He has contributed to various indexed journals with his research findings. His publications delve into consumer behavior, strategic marketing, and innovative technology applications within diverse industries.

***

Olayiwola Alfa Abdullahi has a PhD in Information systems from the prestigious Universiti Teknologi Malaysia. Master's in Information Technology and a Bsc. in computer science. He is a Senior Lecturer at the school of Computing and the Department of Artificial intelligence (AI) at the Federal Polytechnic Offa Kwara state Nigeria.

Najua Syuhada is a senior lecturer in Faculty of Educational Sciences and Technology at Universiti Teknologi Malaysia. Her teaching focus is on argumentation in mathematics, mathematical thinking, primary and secondary teaching and learning, motivation in learning mathematics, and other psychological aspect in mathematics education. She focuses on quantitative research.

K. Balaji is an Assistant Professor in Business and Management, Christ University, Bangalore. He did Ph.D. from KLU Business School, KL University,Vijayawada. He is having 12 years of teaching experience. He has to his credit 23 Research Articles published in reputed National and International Journals. He has participated and presented more than 12 papers in both National and International Seminars/Conferences and also attended more than 50 workshops/ FDPS organized by various reputed organizations. He has also participated in more than 50 seminars / webinars organized by various reputed organizations. He has also attended in 6 Short Term Training programs.He has successfully conducted 3 webinars, one 5 day FDP and one International Conference on Reimaging marketing in New Normal. He is a ratified as Assistant Professor by both JNTUH, JNTU Anantapur and Sri Venkateswara University,Tirupati. His specialized areas include, Accounting and Financial management, Marketing Management, Retailing Management, Consume

Nitesh Behare is an accomplished author with a wealth of knowledge and 16 years of experience in the academic field. He currently holds the position of Associate Professor at the Balaji Institute of International Business (BIIB), Sri Balaji University Pune (SBUP). Throughout his career, Dr. Behare has made significant contributions to the academic world through the publication of numerous research papers and book chapters, establishing himself as a recognized authority in his field.

Carmen Caba-Perez is a Full Professor in the Public Management Sector at the University of Almeria. Her research is concerning to online transparency of public administration; business companies and nonprofit organizations. She is author of several articles published in JCR publications including *The American Review of Public Administration, International Review of Administrative Science, Online Information Review, Government Information Quarterly, Voluntas, Latin American Research Review* or *Public Administration and Development, Public*

Relations Review, *Information Development*, etc. Also, she has written more than 20 book chapters.l

Maria del Mar Gálvez-Rodríguez is an Associate Professor in Management at the University of Almeria. Her research is concerning to online transparency and sustainability companies and nonprofit organizations. She is the author of several articles published in JCR publications including *Online Information Review*, *Voluntas*, *Public Relations Review*, *Information Development*, etc. Also, she has written more than 15 book chapters.

Maria García-González is a PhD Student in Finance and Accounting at colaborator reserarcher at the Department of Economics & Business Administration from the University of Almería (Spain)

Nilesh Gokhale is an academic with more than 22 years of experience in teaching, research and academic leadership. He is currently a Professor and Deputy Head Academics at Sri Balaji University Pune. His research areas include Consumer behaviour and AI, Brand Management and Social Media influencers. He is a Ph.D. guide and a member of the Board of studies of reputed universities. He has published widely referred textbooks, book chapters and research papers in ABDC, SCOPUS and Web of Science indexed Journals. Dr. Gokhale is also a reviewer for journals of international repute.

Chinmoy Goswami is a seasoned educator and researcher with extensive experience in teaching Digital Marketing, E-commerce, Artificial Intelligence and Project Management. He is committed to enhancing professional and personal development through innovative teaching methods and comprehensive research. Prof. Chinmoy Goswami is an Assistant Professor at the Balaji Institute of Technology and Management, Sri Balaji University, Pune. He is currently pursuing a PhD in Management from Ajeenkya D Y Patil University, holds an MBA in Systems (IT) from Symbiosis International University(SIU), and a B.E. in Computer Science and Engineering from Visveswaraiah Technological University(VTU).

Mohammad Irfan is presently working as an Associate Professor at School of Business and Management, Christ University, Bengaluru, India. Dr. Irfan has done his Ph.D. from the Central University of Haryana. He is MBA (Finance), M.Com (Account and Law), and MA (Economics). He has qualified UGC-JRF/SRF/NET in Management and Commerce. Dr. Irfan certified NSEs (NCFM) and BSEs certification. He has more than sixteen years' experience in the area of SAPM, Artificial Intelligence, Machine Learning, Blockchain, Cryptocurrency, Financial Engineering, Fintech, Green Finance, and Alternative Finance. He has to his credit more than 63+ Scopus Indexed articles, includes *The Journal of Economic Cooperation and Development* (Q2), *International Journal of Business Excellence* (IJBEX), *International Journal of Economics and Management* (IJEM), *Montenegrin Journal of Economics* (Q2), *Cogent Business & Management* (Taylor & Francis) (Q2), *Indian Journal of Finance* (IJF) and *Journal of Islamic Monetary Economics and Finance* (JIMF). His citations reached 494+ along with 13 H-index. Dr. Irfan has published 10 books with Springer and IGI Global Scientific Publishing (Scopus indexed).

Vishwanathan Iyer is a research enthusiast who is exploring finance, accounting, marketing, HR, and every other field of academics to the best of his abilities. His research is based on primary data as well as secondary data. Being consistent at research and providing quality research work is the ultimate aim of Dr Iyer. Collaborating with authors across spectrum is one of his strengths. Publishing articles and writing chapters are motivating factors for Dr Iyer to pursue his dream of becoming a Researcher to be reckoned with.

Hazem Ahmed Khairy is an associate professor at the Faculty of Tourism and Hotels, University of Sadat City - Egypt. He is a former visiting scholar at Auburn University in the USA. He has a career certification in human resource management from the American University in Cairo (AUC). His research interests are organizational behavior, human resources management and development, consumer behavior, hospitality and tourism management, and sustainability in tourism and hospitality, in addition to hospitality marketing and leadership.

Early Ridho Kismawadi, S.E.I, MA is a lecturer at the Department of Islamic Banking, Faculty of Islamic Economics and Business IAIN Langsa, Aceh, Indonesia, he has been a lecturer since 2013, he has completed a doctoral program in 2018 majoring in Sharia economics at the State Islamic University of North Sumatra. He was appointed head of the Islamic economics Law study program (2023) Islamic banking study program (2020) and Islamic financial management study program (2019) at Langsa State Islamic Institute (IAIN Langsa), Aceh, Indonesia. His research interests include financial economics, applied econometrics, Islamic economics, banking, and finance. He has published articles in national and international journals. In addition, he is also a reviewer of several reputable international journals such as Finance Research Letters, Financial Innovation, Cogent Business & Management, Journal of Islamic Accounting and Business Research. He has also presented his papers at various local and international seminars.

Manjit Kour is working as Professor at University Business School at Chandigarh University. She holds a PhD in Business Management from IK Gujral

Punjab Technical University, India. She has a good research record with several research papers published in reputed journals. She is an editorial board member and reviewer of many reputed journals including Scopus and ABDC-indexed journals. Her areas of interest include sustainability, green practices, Fintech, online marketing trends and business ethics.

Dantong Li is currently pursuing a PhD in Mathematics Education at Universiti Teknologi Malaysia. Her research interests include K-12 mathematics education, integration of AI and education, mathematical argumentation and proof, aiming to develop students' higher-order thinking skills and problem-solving abilities to promote sustainable development.

Ninglin Li is currently a Ph.D. candidate at the Faculty of Management, Universiti Teknologi Malaysia, where his academic and professional achievements continue to accumulate. Ninglin's deep passion for knowledge is evident in his active engagement in research related to supply chain and digital transformation. He demonstrates his commitment and enthusiasm for the field through authoring journal articles, contributing chapters to books, and presenting his research findings at various academic conferences. His academic journey highlights his expertise, leadership, and steadfast dedication to both industry and academia.

Khartic Rao Manokaran completed his Ph.D. at the Faculty of Management, Universiti Teknologi Malaysia, capping a journey marked by academic and professional achievements. Khartic's commitment to knowledge extends beyond teaching; he has authored journals, contributed a book chapter, and presented papers at conferences, demonstrating his passion for advancing scholarship in his field. His academic and professional journey underscores his expertise, leadership, and unwavering dedication to both industry and academia.

Sharifah Osman received her B.Sc. (Hons) in Chemistry from Universiti Kebangsaan Malaysia, DipEd in Chemistry Studies from Maktab Perguruan Batu Pahat, Malaysia and obtained her Ph.D. in Engineering Education from Universiti Teknologi Malaysia. She is currently a associated professor at the Faculty of Educational Sciences and Technology, Universiti Teknologi Malaysia. Her research interests focus on qualitative research, grounded theory, critical thinking, mathematical thinking, engineering education, and mathematics education.

Walter Daniel Ovelar-Fernández is an Associate Professor in Management at the Autonomus University of Asunción, Paraguay. Her research is concerning to online transparency and sustainability companies. His the author of several articles published in JCR publications including Plos One and has written some book chapters.

Deepali Pulekar is on a mission to help leaders and early-stage entrepreneurs by offering services for getting industry-ready offering a signature module of Leadership on Transformational Leadership of Chhatrapati Shivaji Maharaj- Ageless Inspiration for Corporates and students. She also offers an online skill enhancement workshop on industry readiness for students and leadership for early-stage entrepreneurs to improve skill sets on doing effective and efficient leadership the right way. Her expertise is in Chhatrapati Shivaji Leadership, learning and development, and design and delivery. She is interested in collaboration on Student readiness training and Leadership Programmes & POSH sensitization and awareness programs. Industry Readiness Trainer, Leadership Coach, and Consultant, Author, Speaker & ISO Certified POSH Practitioner are a variety of roles that she has been able to integrate into her career which has allowed her to have a satisfactory and committed professional career.

Amresh K. Ray is an expert in ESG and Sustainability with over 10 years of cross-functional and diverse experience. He holds an MBA from FMS-Delhi, an MA in Economics from KIIT, a Post Graduate Diploma in Environmental Law and Policy from WWF-India in collaboration with the National Law University, and a B. Tech in Electrical and Electronics Engineering from Guru Gobind Singh Indraprastha University, Delhi. Currently, he serves as Manager - ESG & Sustainability at Forvis Mazars India.

Zakir Shaikh, Assistant Professor, in the Department of Accounting and Finance, College of Business Administration, Kingdom University, Bahrain. He has 12 years of industry and 16 years of academic experience. He is an Editorial Board member in five Journals, published numerous articles in Scopus, ABDC, Web of Science, and other referred journals, participated and presented in a variety of seminars, forums, workshops in the areas of specialization, including Islamic Accounting, Banking, and Finance. He obtained his Ph.D. (Accounting and Finance), master's in commerce, Business Administration, Finance, and Control. He is a member of the American Accounting Association (AAA), The Chartered Institute of Islamic Finance Professionals (CIIF), Malaysia, The Indian Accounting Association; The Orissa Commerce Association, and associated with the Accounting & Auditing Organization for Islamic Financial Institutions (AAOIFI), Bahrain.

Akansha Sharma is a sustainability professional with post-graduation in Environmental Studies and Resources Management from TERI School of Advanced

Studies and 3 years of experience in Sustainability and related fields, currently working as a consultant: ESG & Sustainability Practices.

Prerna Sharma is working as Sr. Assistant Professor at Balaji Institute of Modern management. Sri Balaji University, Pune. She has an experience of 6 years in teaching accounting and management related subjects to UG and PG courses including Hospital Administration and mass journalism. She is versed with accounting subjects and few from marketing as well. She has presented papers at national and international conferences along with published paper at Scopus indexed journals as well. She aims to go further a deeper in research for better understanding and contribution to the stream She is related to.

Pritesh Somani is working as an Assistant professor at Balaji Institute of International Business, Sri Balaji University, Pune with a widespread teaching experience of more than 11 years teaching subjects spread across General Management and Research. He specialises in Research Methodology with good experience in operating SPSS. He has conducted sessions through Faculty Development Programs on Statistical analysis as an integral part of Research Methodology. He has published chapters across different disciples which are Scopus Indexed. He has contributed a few chapters in a few international publications. Also, a few papers are published in ABDC journal (Q2). Many research articles are published in UGC care and peer reviewed journals. He has a grant of 2 International patents from Republic of South Africa. Keeping in pace with the upcoming trends in the field of research, Dr Pritesh hopes to find a place in the top researchers of the institute.

Abhijeet Thakur is an accomplished Assistant Professor in Business Analytics with vast experience in academia, research, and industry. Specializing in data-driven decision-making, predictive analytics, and operations management, Dr Abhijeet Thakur has a proven track record of integrating theoretical insights with practical applications to solve complex business problems.

Prachi Wani comes with a total experience of over 17 years in the hospitality industry and education sector. She holds a PhD in Marketing. She believes in inspiring, empowering, and mentoring the next generation of leaders and managers in the industry. Dr Wani is an entrepreneur herself who has experience running two F & B outlets. Dr Prachi has presented and published multiple papers and has a patent on her name.

Shanshan Yue is an Associate Professor at Henan University of Economics and Law. She completed her PhD at Universiti Teknologi Malaysia, specializing in corporate governance, environmental innovation and SDGs. Her research bridges theoretical depth with practical relevance, leveraging advanced quantitative methods to address global challenges. Her recent works have been published in esteemed journals like Journal of Environmental Management, Corporate Social Responsibility and Environmental Management, China Finance Review International and so on.

Mohamad Ikram Zakaria earned his Ph.D. in mathematics education from Universiti Kebangsaan Malaysia, Bangi, Selangor. With over one year of experience, he serves as a Senior Lecturer in the School of Education, Faculty of Social Sciences and Humanities at Universiti Teknologi Malaysia (UTM). His current focus in research revolves around students' learning and development across various educational levels and domains. His published works encompass topics such as problem-solving, problem-based learning, mobile learning (m-learning), and the heutagogical approach within the field of mathematics education. For inquiries, he can be reached via email at mohamad.ikram@utm.my.

Zhang Qiang is a PhD candidate in Mathematics Education at the School of Education, Universiti Teknologi Malaysia. His research focuses on integrating technology into the teaching and learning of mathematics, particularly quadratic functions, to enhance students' academic performance and motivation. With a strong interest in educational innovation, he is dedicated to developing interactive and practical solutions for improving mathematics education.

Index

A

B

C

D

E

G

H

I

M

T

www.ingramcontent.com/pod-product-compliance
Lightning Source LLC
LaVergne TN
LVHW080614300926
849162LV00005B/1159
* 9 7 9 8 3 3 7 3 0 1 1 7 4 *